Dell Tate
Fall '80

/6.20

I mut
4/80

MODERN
ELEMENTARY
CURRICULUM

MODERN ELEMENTARY CURRICULUM

fifth edition

William B. Ragan
Gene D. Shepherd

University of Oklahoma

Holt, Rinehart and Winston
New York Chicago San Francisco Atlanta Dallas Montreal Toronto London Sydney

Photo Credits: pages 249, 295, and 322 courtesy Educational Materials Center, University of Oklahoma, Norman, Oklahoma; pages 60, 70, 110, 128, 221, 223, 224, 329, 342, 344, 365, 385, 448, and 495 courtesy Moore Public Schools, Moore, Oklahoma; pages 219, 253, and 395 courtesy Oklahoma City Public Schools, Oklahoma City, Oklahoma.

Library of Congress Cataloging in Publication Data
Ragan, William Burk, 1896-1971
    Modern elementary curriculum.

    Includes bibliographies and index.
    1. Education, Elementary—Curricula.
I. Shepherd, Gene D., joint author, II. Title.
LB1570.R3   1977   372.1′9   76-56225

ISBN 0-03-089934-6

To Bill Ragan, the knower, doer,
and teacher whose life and beliefs
have continuity because he cared.

PREFACE

The basic beliefs about education that have influenced the writing of this fifth edition of *Modern Elementary Curriculum* are essentially the same as those of the previous editions: (1) the elementary school curriculum consists of all the experiences of children for which the school accepts responsibility; (2) the ultimate purpose of education is learning how to learn for purposes of improving individual and group living; (3) the realities of the times, culture, and society determine the curriculum to a large extent; (4) effective teaching strategies are predicated upon the knowledges of the growth, learning, and development of children, the nature of content vehicles, and the interactions of individual and group behaviors.

Developments in schools, curricula, relevant knowledges, and society have made a new edition appropriate. The style, flavor, and emphasis of previous editions have been maintained in this significant revision.

Part 3 of the book contains six chapters on the major curriculum areas of the modern elementary school. Each chapter now includes an interdisciplinary section, which relates that chapter to major movements uniting all curriculum areas, such as career education, values clarification, and a potential strategy. Each chapter has been reorganized, enriched, and made current. In Part 1, the chapter on children has been expanded to stress the theories of growth, learning, and development. For example, the section on Piaget as a developmentalist now provides a more specific application to the decisions of curriculum makers. In

Part 2, the new chapter added to provide a potential strategy for teaching is abstracted from the knowledges presented throughout the book. In Part 4, the chapter on "futurism" has been organized around the themes of stabilities, instabilities, and challenges. All other chapters of the book have been reorganized and rewritten.

The organization of the book has been changed. For example, considerable attention has been devoted to the order of headings in an effort to increase the functionality of the book as a text. The index has been expanded to include both name and subject indexes in order to provide a superior reference source. The "Situations" and "Problems and Projects," which enrich and extend the potential involvement of the student, have been completely rewritten. The annotated reading lists at the end of chapters have been revised.

This major revision has been done in an effort to both update and increase the functionality of the book. The author is appreciative of the special support provided for this revision by Rena Waddelow, Carol Snow, and Cecilia Faulconer. The author also wishes to thank Richard Owen and Jeanette Ninas Johnson of Holt, Rinehart and Winston for their support and faith in this large endeavor.

Each person is to some degree the reflection of others; to Bill Ragan, and all others who have lifted, pushed, and rested me, I thank you.

Norman, Oklahoma   Gene D. Shepherd
December 1976

CONTENTS

MODERN
ELEMENTARY
CURRICULUM

prologue

The Meaning of
CURRICULUM

Curriculum development, though relatively young as a science, has nevertheless shown much vitality in schools and schooling since our founding.

Delmo Della-Dora, *Perspectives on Curriculum Development, 1776–1976*, Foreword. Yearbook of Association for Supervision and Curriculum Development, O. L. Davis, Jr., Chairperson and Editor. (Washington, D.C.: ASCD, 1976), p. iii.

THE SETTING FOR CURRICULUM

The past several years and the immediate future can be characterized as a time of disequilibrium. It is a time characterized by the impact of instability in the economy, the policies, the politics, and the spirit of our nation. It is a period when inflation and recession, integration and resegregation, violence of war, and violence for peace have coexisted. The solidarity of the past is being challenged.

Each disequilibrium and its companion accommodation by society has had its impact upon the school as an institution of that society. Therefore the schools and their curriculum vehicles have also experienced a testing of mission and purpose, of program, and of product as well as a critical appraisal of service and spirit. The tensions of the school and its curriculum vehicles seem to originate from three sources: the potential displacement of the family through the school as an agency of a nation-state; the movement from an industrial culture to a yet unrealized future culture; and the accommodations to the constitutional conditions of independence and dependence, individuality and conformity, and inclusion and exclusion. In general, the functioning of the curriculum in the socialization of individuals is the prime source of the powerful tensions being experienced by the schools.

During this period of tension and disequilibrium, the number and variety of curriculum alternatives available have rapidly multiplied. The alternatives range from "back to the basics" to "forward to the future." In unsettled times, alterna-

1

tives are apt to be presented as dichotomies. Although it is most unlikely that movement can go backward and forward in the same instant, it is just as likely that the continuity involved in the development of an individual and an institution can be maintained and furthered.

CURRICULUM CONCEPTS

The author of this text does not regard it as necessary, or even advisable, to quote at this point a long list of definitions of the curriculum stated by various writers in the field. What follows is an attempt to identify three broad categories of the curriculum and to explain how the concept presented in this text differs from others. It should be obvious that a single-sentence definition is not an adequate explanation of anything as complex as the life and program of an elementary school. Although most authors of elementary curriculum texts state their own concepts of the curriculum near the beginning of the text, it is unlikely that students will fully understand the implications of the concepts until they have read the entire book. It should be recognized also that there are many legitimate uses of the word *curriculum*, depending upon the situation in which it is used; the concern in this text is with the curriculum of the modern elementary school.

Curriculum: Courses Offered

A dictionary definition of the curriculum states simply that it is the whole body of courses offered by an educational institution, or by a department thereof. This, in terms of the space limitations of a dictionary, is sufficient. However, the elementary school curriculum as a field of study or as a concern of the staff of a school system includes more than the courses offered.

Curriculum: Documents

The reader of this text will discover that some writers view the curriculum as a document, a course of study, or a design developed by one group to be used by another group involved in the education of children. This concept separates curriculum development from teaching, implies that the curriculum has been developed before a teacher meets a group of pupils, and views the role of the teacher as one of implementing the curriculum. It is only fair to state that authors who present this concept of the curriculum may frequently devote the remainder of their texts to a description of learning experiences for children which is similar to that found in texts written by authors who hold a broader view of the curriculum.

Curriculum: Experience

The author of this text views the elementary school curriculum as including *all the experiences of children for which the school accepts responsibility*. This has been called the *broad* concept of the curriculum; it may also be called the *dynamic* concept—the curriculum consists of the ongoing experiences of children under the guidance of the school. The experiences can never be completely anticipated in advance. The course of study (the document prepared in advance of teaching and learning) has the same relationship to the curriculum as a road map has to the actual experiences involved in taking a trip. Curriculum documents provide general directions and help guide the teacher's organization of appropriate happenings which are directed by the nature of the individuals and group. These documents keep teachers from becoming lost in the mazes of potential experiences, subject matter, and individual variances. Yet, these documents do not prescribe the events and happenings that may occur along the way.

A course of study or curriculum guide suggests activities in which children may engage in order to achieve certain objectives; other objectives as well as other activities actually emerge as the teacher and the pupils work together from day to day. Indeed, the most important phase of curriculum planning is that which takes place when teacher and pupils plan together.

The last part of the definition above indicates that this author does not advocate a planless curriculum nor a rigidly planned curriculum; what is needed is continuous planning, both before the teacher meets the pupils and during the teaching-learning processes. The curriculum should not be as broad as life itself; it should represent a special environment that has been systematized, edited, and simplified. It is concerned with helping children achieve self-realization through active participation in life through school, community, nation, and world.

The school, as an institution which reflects and serves society, is created to induct the young into educational experiences and thereby perpetuate the structure of society. Although at present the school is the primary vehicle for the institutionalization of education, it may very well not be the only vehicle for achieving this purpose in the future.

Curriculum serves as the operational medium through which the school displays and coordinates the patterns of transmission, translation, and transposition of the educative experiences for which it assumes responsibility. Curriculum includes the planned and unplanned, the situational and institutional, the dynamic actualities and the documented intentions, and the incidents and accidents. Curriculum parameters are made flexible by selected interactions in schools.

Part 1

History

Society

Children

PERSPECTIVES
for CURRICULUM

Curriculum is rooted in the dynamics and demands of time, place, and culture; in the conditionings and continuities of history; and in the awarenesses of and attitudes toward children. The dynamics among these forces are not always in balance. Part 1 explores the impact of—and the balances among—the forces of society, history, and knowledge about children upon curriculum development.

chapter 1

Influencing
HISTORY

While a history of education does not provide the prospective teacher with a blueprint for classroom processes, it may serve to recall previous practices with which others have had success or failure. Its main significance, however, lies in building a foundation from which to appreciate and understand the forces which made our schools and the critics who wish to alter them.

John D. Pulliam, *History of Education in America,* 2d ed.
(Columbus, Ohio: Charles E. Merrill Publishing Co., 1976), p. 2.

The establishment of a free public elementary school system for all children by all state legislatures was the action that began a unique social experiment. Free public elementary school education for all quickly became associated with our most cherished ideals. Although continuously challenged by critics, the elementary schools in this country have significantly contributed to the actualization of the "American dream."

Elementary schools in the United States have been responsive to the needs of an expanding and diversified society. This responsiveness of the schools has resulted in emphasis of one or more of the following purposes of education at different times:

1. Maintenance of the present society and its present needs
2. Changing the existing society and its structures, orders, and dynamics in predetermined directions
3. Preparation of individuals who will define and implement the social changes appropriate to their lives and future

The remainder of this chapter groups by factors and influences the evolution of curriculum development from 1647 to the present. Each grouping is discussed in terms of the dominant motives of the times, the curriculum content, organization, typical schools, methods, and status of teacher education. A careful reading of the chapter and its summary will enable the reader to consider both the historical development of curriculum and its responsiveness to the needs of society.

DEPENDENCE TO INDEPENDENCE: 1647–1776

The pressures within the Puritan community in New England necessitated the creation of schools to maintain the existing society and its current needs. The Puritans believed that the Bible was the guide to salvation, that children should learn to read the Bible, and that schools should be established for this purpose. It cannot be said, however, that they intended to establish a great system of state schools to support a democratic society. Rather, the missionary zeal in this period was directed more toward benefiting the church than for humanity.[1] Yet, the idea that the education of children should be a public rather than a private responsibility originated with our Puritan ancestors in New England. In his famous document addressed to the mayors and aldermen of German cities, Martin Luther urged in 1524 that the task of educating the young should immediately be assumed by the city officials lest they "be obliged to feel in vain the pangs of remorse forever."[2]

The language used in the preamble of the "Old Deluder Satan" Act, passed by the General Court of the Massachusetts Bay Colony in 1647, indicated the religious motive for education in the New England colonies. "One chief project of the Old Deluder Satan, to keep men from a knowledge of the Scriptures" was listed as the primary reason for requiring towns to establish common schools and grammar schools. This Act was not only the first piece of legislation in America requiring that schools be established, but was also the first example in the history of the world of a *law* requiring that children be provided with schooling at the expense of the community. This was truly a revolutionary idea, and one that foreshadowed the development on this continent of a unique plan of public education. The date, therefore, provides a convenient starting point for a discussion of more than three centuries of curriculum development in the United States. It should be remembered, however, that schools existed in Massachusetts before this law was passed and that more than two hundred years elapsed before a system of free, universal, public education was established in the United States as a whole.

The details of erecting buildings, levying school taxes, and hiring teachers were left to the people of the various towns. Legislation passed in 1693 gave selectmen authority to levy school taxes with the consent of a majority of the people of a town, and later legislation provided that common-school teachers should be examined and certified by the selectmen. As the people moved from the compact communities to more remote areas, it became necessary to organize district schools rather than town schools. Thus, Massachusetts and other New

---

[1] William E. Drake, *The American School in Transition.* (Englewood Cliffs, N.J.: Prentice-Hall, Inc., 1955), p. 64.

[2] J. D. Russell and C. H. Judd, *The American Educational System.* (Boston: Houghton Mifflin Company, 1940). pp. 19–21.

England colonies provided precedents for taxation for school purposes, certification of teachers, the district school, and the local board of education.

Various types of schools existed in the colonies—charity schools, dame schools, apprenticeship schools, and parochial schools. The curriculum consisted of reading, writing, spelling, arithmetic, the catechism, prayers, and the singing of hymns. Pupils were taught by the memorizing method, and the schools were expected merely to add a veneer of literacy to the education the child received at home and at church.

The famous *New England Primer*, which was the most-used book in colonial schools and which continued to be used for more than a hundred years, gave additional evidence of the religious motive for education. It has been estimated that more than three million copies of this book were sold. It contained an illustrated alphabetical rhyme, beginning with "In Adam's fall we sinned all," and ending with "Zacheas he did climb a tree his Lord to see." It also contained a list of the books in the Old and the New Testaments, the Lord's Prayer, the Apostles' Creed, the Ten Commandments, and the Shorter Catechism. Reisner suggested that it was not only a religious book, but one that was religious in "the strict and narrow sense of Calvinistic orthodoxy."[3]

The discipline in colonial schools was in harmony with the theological belief of that time—that children were conceived in iniquity and born in sin. It was believed that they could be regenerated only by the severest type of discipline. The expression, "beat the devil out of them," which is sometimes heard today, was taken literally in colonial schools. The whipping post and the dunce stool were familiar objects in classrooms, and continual flogging, wailing, and fear made the school resemble a prison more than a place for busy, happy children. These practices reflected the harshness and brutality of a time when young people were sometimes put to death for disobedience of parents.

In Virginia and other southern colonies generally, where the class distinctions of the old country were retained, the apprenticeship system prevailed. The upper classes employed tutors or sent their children to England to be educated. But these people believed that it was the business of the poor to work rather than to think. "To make society happy," they said, "it is requisite that great numbers should be ignorant as well as poor." Governor Berkeley of Virginia wrote in 1671, "I thank God there are no free schools or printing presses, and I hope we shall not have them these hundred years." His hope was more than realized, for Virginia did not develop a system of free schools until the middle of the nineteenth century.

The Massachusetts type of school was adopted in all the New England colonies except Rhode Island, where the devotion to religious freedom was too strong to permit the establishment of schools dominated by one religious sect. Outside New England, colonial legislatures showed little interest in education, and schools developed more or less at random through church and private effort.

---

[3] Edward H. Reisner, *The Evolution of the Common School.* (New York: Crowell Collier and Macmillan, Inc., 1930), p. 40.

The law of 1647 was followed by a period of decline in education in Massachusetts and in other New England colonies. School districts were not able to maintain schools as good as towns had provided before they were divided into districts. When the Revolution began, New England had poorer schools than those that had existed a century earlier.

SITUATION 1.1   During the colonial period, various school forms were in existence: charity schools; dame schools; apprentice schools; parochial schools; etc. Contrast and compare these schools as the following questions are examined:

a. What requirements needed to be met before one was qualified to teach?
b. By whom were the schools supported?
c. What was the nature of the curriculum?
d. What were the characteristic methods of instruction?

This brief account of developments in elementary education during colonial times illustrates the idea that schools tend to reflect the conditions and beliefs of the social group that supports them. It also reveals that only small beginnings were made toward the development of a truly American elementary school.

INDEPENDENCE TO NATIONALISM: 1776–1876

A less restrictive purpose for education began to emerge during the revolutionary and early nationalistic developments. Many of the leaders during these times saw clearly that free public schools were necessary to the support of a popular government. Madison wrote, "A popular government without popular information, or the means of acquiring it, is but a prologue to a farce or a tragedy or perhaps both." Jefferson expressed the belief of many of the leaders when he said, "If a nation expects to be ignorant and free in a state of civilization, it expects what never was and never will be."

Other prominent men of the time were calling attention to backwardness of American education and were formulating plans for a system of education that would be free, state controlled, nonsectarian, tax supported, and open to all children and youth. The liberal views of these forward-looking men were illustrated by the statement of Robert Coram, "Education should not be left to the caprice or neglect of parents, to chance, or confined to the children of wealthy parents. If education is necessary for one man, my religion tells me that it is equally necessary for another." The emphasis on liberty, equality, and the rights of the individual—found in great documents such as the Declaration of Independence, the Bill of Rights, and the Northwest Ordinance—stimulated many to see the need for a system of education in harmony with these ideals.

The ideas of these liberal leaders, however, were not shared by the governing authorities of the time. The Constitution of the United States made no mention of education. Few of the liberal leaders of the period were present at the convention; Jefferson was in Paris, Samuel Adams was not chosen, and Patrick Henry refused to attend. The framers of the Constitution wanted a stable government, one that would be capable of protecting property and one that would not be too responsive to the wishes of the masses. Washington certainly had no illusions about the capacity of people generally to participate in determining policies. He wrote, "Mankind, when left to themselves, are unfit for their own government." Alexander Hamilton's views on the subject are well known; he said, "Your people sir—your people is a great beast." Gouverneur Morris stated the same view: "Give the votes to the people who have no property and they will sell them to the rich." John Adams described democracy as "the most ignoble, detestable and unjust form of government," and added, "There never was a democracy that did not commit suicide." During this period a dominant society emerged which, as with the Puritans, necessitated the creation of elementary schools for the maintenance and expansion of itself. This time, rather than establishing schools for maintenance of a society by inculcating religious doctrine, the elementary schools were intended to maintain a society by inculcating political doctrines.

The Public School Revival

In 1823 the first private normal school was established at Concord, Vermont, for the preparation of teachers. Previously, private schools and church schools in many states offered the only facilities for the education of children. The practice of granting public funds to private schools was common, and some states passed laws to permit certain localities to establish "pauper" schools for children of poor parents. The idea of establishing public schools in the various states met strong opposition from private schools, from religious sects, and from those who believed that it was unjust to tax people who had no children to support schools.

Yet, by 1876, the principle of free public schools had been accepted in all the states, state systems of education had been established everywhere except in some southern states, public normal schools had been generally established, and the system had been extended to include four years of high school. How was so much accomplished in a period of fifty years? To answer this question, it is necessary to examine the movement called "the public school revival," and to identify the forces that contributed to its success. The "public school revival" is a collective term used to describe a series of events and movements that resulted in the establishment and improvement of public schools. It involved changing long-established attitudes of those who influenced school legislation, persuading voters to cast their ballots for increased school appropriations, getting schools established where none had existed, establishing state departments of education, making provision for teacher education, and enriching the curriculum. It represented a tremendous awakening of the American conscience with respect to the education of children. Its contribution to the strength of the nation in the years that have followed can scarcely be overestimated. An examination of some of the significant developments that contributed to the success of the movement is therefore a must for those who would understand the changing curriculum of the American elementary school.

The Influence of the Frontier

Thomas Jefferson drafted a plan in 1779 for a complete system of public education for Virginia. The only part of his plan that he lived to see established was the University of Virginia. It was not until the influence of the frontier began to bring about significant changes in American life that legislatures began to enact legislation providing for public schools. By 1803, four new states had been admitted to the Union from the territory west of the Appalachians; by 1810, this region had a population of one million. It was here that the characteristics commonly regarded as typically American were developed; it was here that the ideas and traditions of the older settlements were abandoned; and it was here that new ideas, customs, and institutions emerged. "For the frontier," says Agar, "democracy was not an ideal; it was an inescapable condition, like the weather."[4] The property qualification for voting and holding office was omitted from the constitutions of all the states west of the Appalachians except Mississippi; there was an increase in the number of offices to be filled by popular vote; and representation in state legislatures was changed from the basis of wealth to the basis of population. Other reforms that indicated increasing confidence in the people followed, and although some of the older states delayed until the middle of the nineteenth century, eventually they followed suit. As the right to vote was extended to all white male citizens, agitation for free public schools increased; citizens who were to have a part in determining the policies of the government must be qualified to vote intelligently.

SITUATION 1.2   Examine Thomas Jefferson's 1779 plan for a complete system of public education in Virginia for possible influence by Martin's Luther's document addressed to mayors and aldermen of German cities in 1524.

The Influence of Pestalozzi

During the period of the public school revival, educational reforms in this country were greatly influenced by European examples. The influence of the reformer Johann Heinrich Pestalozzi (1746–1827), was particularly important. In fact, Knight has said, "Pestalozzi, probably more than any other educational reformer, laid the basis for the modern elementary school and helped to reform elementary-school practice."[5] The first pedagogical book published in the United States, Sam-

---

[4] Herbert Agar, *The People's Choice.* (Boston: Houghton Mifflin Company, 1933), p. 109.
[5] Edgar W. Knight, *Education in the United States,* 3d rev. ed. (Boston: Ginn and Company, 1951).

uel R. Hall's *Lectures on School Keeping* (1829), reflected the influence of Pestalozzi; the first state normal school, established at Lexington, Massachusetts, in 1839, clearly bore his stamp; and the educational philosophy of Horace Mann, Henry Bernard, and other leaders of the public school revival was basically that of Pestalozzi. Reisner says, "Clearly the most influential source of educational ideas during the 'Common School Revival' were the examples and theories of Pestalozzi and the systems of public education in Prussia and other German states."[6]

Pestalozzi's concept of child growth and development was an organismic rather than a mechanistic one; he recognized that the narrow, mechanical exercises in reading that were used in his time were inadequate to prepare children for intelligent citizenship; and he taught that the chief function of the teacher was to provide a good learning environment and to lead pupils into vital experiences. He set forth his educational ideas in a book called *How Gertrude Teaches Her Children* and experimented with a teacher education program at Burgdorf, Switzerland.

SITUATION 1.3   List ten educational ideas set forth by Pestalozzi in *How Gertrude Teaches Her Children*, and draw parallels from these ideas to specific practices incorporated as the teacher education programs and modern elementary school developed in the United States.

The Influence of the Prussian Example

After their defeat by Napoleon in 1806, the Prussians were determined to establish a national system of education as a means of building a stronger nation. Young men were sent to observe the work of Pestalozzi in Switzerland and return to Prussia to work out instructional procedures in harmony with those they had seen him using. When Calvin E. Stowe, Horace Mann, and other leaders of the public school revival visited Prussia, they found the Prussian-Pestalozzian systems in operation and returned to the United States to publish reports containing elaborate descriptions of the system. Edward A. Sheldon established a normal school in Oswego, New York, which became famous for the use of Pestalozzian procedures.

It seems ironical that suggestions for so many features of the public schools developed in this country came from a state whose political institutions were so different from those of the United States. However, the American leaders had no place to go except Prussia to study the features of an effective program of public education. The system they studied and later imitated in this country included an effective state agency for education, special institutions for the education of teachers, grading pupils on the basis of ability, effective methods of instruction, and more intelligent methods of discipline than had prevailed previ-

6 Reisner, p. 349.

ously. How these features were gradually modified to develop a distinctively American system provides much of the content of the history of American education.

The Influence of Great Britain

Three educational movements originating in Great Britain influenced developments in the United States. In 1815 Robert Owen established an infant school in Scotland for children whose parents were working in factories. This school taught cleanliness, plays and games, and the art of working together. Samuel Writherspin organized the Infant School Society in England in 1824, and reading, writing, arithmetic, geography, and natural history were added to the curriculum. Infant schools were established in Boston in 1818, in New York and Philadelphia in 1827, and in Providence, Rhode Island, in 1828. The infant school, which at first was distinct from the elementary school, became the primary department of the elementary school when both were taken over by public school authorities.

Robert Raikes organized the first Sunday school in England in 1780 for the purpose of providing instruction in reading and the catechism to children who were working in factories. Sunday schools were introduced in this country about 1790, and existed as secular institutions for nearly a half-century. After the churches took them over, the secular instruction was dropped. They made a contribution to the success of the public school revival by getting people accustomed to the idea of secular instruction for children.

The monitorial system, which also originated in England, played an important role in getting public schools established in the United States. Andrew Bell used the monitorial system in an orphan asylum in India, and later Joseph Lancaster used a similar plan with industrial classes in England. A Lancasterian school was opened in New York City in 1806, and soon Philadelphia, Pittsburgh, Baltimore, Washington, and Louisville had schools operating on the Lancasterian plan. Lancaster himself came to the United States in 1818 to help promote the movement.

Lancaster published manuals giving minute directions for the conduct of recitations and for classroom management. By using pupils as monitors and by reducing classroom routine to military precision, it was possible for one teacher to direct the instruction of several hundred pupils. The plan was received with great enthusiasm by proponents of public education in the United States. In 1809 Governor Clinton said, "when I perceive one great assembly of a thousand children under the eye of a single teacher, marching with unexampled rapidity and with perfect discipline to a goal of knowledge, I confess that I recognize in Lancaster the benefactor of the human race." In order to get any system of public education established at that time, it was essential that the expense be very small. As late as 1834, Philadelphia had an average of 218 pupils per teacher, and the annual per-pupil cost was only $5.00. The monitorial system was mechanical, it gave little attention to individual differences in pupils, and it consisted primarily of using those who knew little to teach those who knew less. By the middle of the nineteenth century the people were looking for something better, and enthusiasm for the monitorial system began to wane. It had, however, served a useful purpose by getting people accustomed to having tax-supported schools for their children to attend.

Educational Leadership

The success of the public school revival depended to a large extent upon the work of intelligent, persistent educational leaders. Some say that it was merely the lengthened shadow of Horace Mann. Although he was its most outstanding leader, other men prepared the way for him, and significant developments in America and elsewhere contributed to the success of the movement to which he gave intelligent, effective, and courageous leadership.

James G. Carter was instrumental in getting the legislature to establish the first state board of education in Massachusetts in 1837, and Horace Mann became its first secretary. Mann had been an attorney, had worked for social reforms, and, as president of the senate, had signed the Act creating the position that he later accepted. He said, "I have abandoned jurisprudence and betaken myself to the larger sphere of mind and morals." He served twelve years in this position, collecting and publishing information about the condition of the schools, traveling up and down the state addressing conventions and public meetings, and visiting Prussia and other European states to study school systems. His annual reports were models of readability, directness, and simplicity. While he occupied this position, three normal schools were established, a full month was added to the average school term, public high schools were gradually substituted for private academies, appropriations for schools were doubled, school libraries were developed, and methods of instruction based on the ideas of Pestalozzi were adopted. During these twelve years the attitude of the people of Massachusetts toward public schools changed from one of apathy to one of active enthusiasm.

Leadership in the cause of free public education was not limited to any one profession or group. Literary men, statesmen, and representatives of industry and labor helped to build a climate favorable to public education. One of these was Samuel Gompers, an intelligent leader in the labor movement for more than sixty years. He insisted that every individual, regardless of the circumstances into which he was born, was entitled to the greatest possible opportunity for self-achievement and that an education which developed the creative abilities of the individual brought into the life of the nation a force which made for a larger measure of freedom. He expressed the central American belief in the worth of the individual as follows: "You cannot weigh a human soul on the same scales with a piece of pork."

Thus, these many forces, together with other favorable developments, combined to make the public school revival a success. The first breakthrough came in Pennsylvania when Thaddeus Stevens won the historic battle in the legislature in 1835. His address to the members of the legislature in favor of public tax-supported schools for every child was perhaps the most effective presentation of the cause that had been made up to that time. In 1849 the Massachusetts State Supreme Court ruled in the Roberts' case that separate but equal facilities were legal when a Negro attempted to enroll in a Caucasian school. By 1876, the principle of public elementary education had been accepted in all the states, and schools had been established everywhere except in the states of the Deep South, where economic conditions following the Civil War left the states too poor to support schools. It remained for future generations of Americans to expand and improve the schools.

SITUATION 1.4   The public school revival (1826–1876) was concerned with persuading legislatures to increase appropriations for public schools, awakening the American conscience in respect to the education of children, establishing effective state departments of education, improving teacher preparation, and enriching the curriculum. Present evidence shows that these are still basic concerns among educators. Explain how our aspirations relating to these problems have been extended.

AGRICULTURE TO INDUSTRY: 1876–1929

The years from 1876 to 1929 witnessed the expansion of the United States in business and industry, in territory, and in influence on world affairs. The history of these fifty-three years is the story of the efforts of a free people to adjust government machinery to rapidly changing economic and social circumstances. The growth of cities, of factories, and of monopolies produced a complex, industrialized economy in place of the simple, agricultural one of former years. Social and economic forces and the energy and initiative of individuals were building a powerful nation, but progress was not always measured in terms of human welfare. The exploitation of human and natural resources, the slums and sweatshops, child labor, and the unwholesome influence of money in politics brought with them the demand for reform. The continuing struggle to meet these problems accounts for a large portion of the historical subject matter of that period.

An examination of the political history of this period reveals a continuous emphasis on reform. Grover Cleveland fought continually for tariff reform. Theodore Roosevelt was energetic in his efforts to reduce the power of "big business" over government. Woodrow Wilson was keenly concerned with the progress of these reforms and with extending what he called "the new freedom." These reforms represented more than the desires of official leaders—to no small degree they expressed the spirit of the times.

As leaders began to agree upon desired changes within the orders, structures, and dynamics of society, schools became instrumental in preparation of individuals who could implement these adjustments within the existing society. Again the American elementary schools were called upon and utilized to contribute to the revitalization of the American ideals.

Expansion and Reform in Elementary Education

The period from 1876 to 1929 was one of expansion and reform for the public elementary school. Quantitatively, the elementary school of 1929 had little resemblance to that of 1876. The enrollment had more than doubled, many new subjects had been added to the curriculum, the length of the school term had been increased by more than 30 percent, and per-pupil expenditures had been enormously increased.

Teacher education, always a major influence in determining the quality of the curriculum, expanded rapidly during this period. The first private normal school was established at Concord, Vermont, in 1823, and the first state normal school at Lexington, Massachusetts, in 1839; by 1861 normal schools existed in all except the newer states. The first permanent, exclusively professional chair in education was established at the University of Michigan in 1879. The amount of professional training possessed by most teachers at the close of the nineteenth century, however, was pitifully small. As late as 1914 it was possible to obtain a teaching certificate by passing an examination on the common branches and answering a few simple questions dealing with a subject called "pedagogy." Not even a high school education was required.

By 1929 many normal schools had become four-year teachers' colleges, and schools of education had been established in virtually all universities. The curriculum in teacher education had been expanded to include educational psychology, child psychology, educational measurement, special methods, history and philosophy of education, curriculum development, and practice teaching.

At the beginning of this period, pupil progress was evaluated by means of oral quizzes, written examinations prepared by teachers, ciphering matches, and spelling bees. By the end of the period, schools were using standardized achievement tests in the school subjects, individual and group intelligence tests, adjustment inventories, and aptitude tests. Supervisors of instruction and directors of research had been added to the school staff to make the teaching of the several subjects more uniform and more efficient.

SITUATION 1.5   Investigate current accountability legislation of the state for implications related to the utilization and incorporation of standardized tests.

Much progress was made during this period in providing for individual differences among pupils—differences revealed by the use of objective tests developed by psychologists and measurement experts. The curriculum was, in the main, still regarded as a number of subjects to be mastered, but efforts were being made to allow the slow child, the average child, and the bright child to master the subjects at different rates of speed.

Factors Operating To Entrench the Formal, Regimented Type of Program

During this period several factors operated to entrench the formal, regimented, undemocratic program of elementary education that had been imported from Europe during the mid-nineteenth century. One factor was the rapid growth of high schools, which by various means managed to impress upon the elementary schools the necessity for pupils to master a standardized list of facts and skills as preparation for entrance to high school. A second factor was the mechanistic, stimulus-response psychology that emphasized repetition as the means of learning and the reproduction of the material learned as the proof of learning. A third factor was the influence of the factory ideal on school practice (see Fig. 1.1). In the report of their survey, *Middletown*, the Lynds stated that the typical school of 1925 was "like the factory—a thoroughly regimented affair."[7]

Reform Movements in Education

The theme of reform, which provided much of the content for political discussions of the time, was also prominent in the field of education. The limitations of the typical school of this era were recognized by educational leaders in Europe and America, and many of the features that are now firmly established in educational theory and practice can be traced to the ideas of men and women who were ahead of their time. Space is not available here for a detailed exposition of the views of educational reformers of this period, but the influence of a few on education in this country was so profound that they need to be mentioned.

Johann Friedrich Herbart, a German psychologist and educator, lived from 1776 to 1841. His most productive years covered the first third of the nineteenth century, but fifty years were to elapse after his death before the impact of his ideas on education in this country was to become pronounced. After his death, his educational views were carried on at the University of Jena by many of his followers, among whom was Wilhelm Rein, Professor of Pedagogics. Charles de Garmo, Charles A. McMurry, and his brother Frank M. McMurry were among the Americans who studied with Rein in the 1880s, before graduate instruction had been provided in American universities to any great extent. These young men became crusaders for Herbartian ideas and practices in the United States. The Herbart Club was formed in 1892; it became the National Herbart Society for the Scientific Study of Education in 1895 and the National Society for the Study of Education in 1902. The National Herbart Society published a yearbook and a supplement each year between 1895 and 1899. The general pattern of the National Society for the Study of Education has been to publish two yearbooks (Part I and Part II) each year since 1902.

Herbart taught that the chief purpose of education was to develop personal character and to prepare for social usefulness, that instruction should be adapted to the past experiences and present interests of pupils, that school subjects should be correlated, and that it was the function of the teacher to provide new and real experiences for pupils.

Herbart's influence was exerted against assignments from a single textbook to be memorized and recited; he provided examples of a more enlightened form of instruction, which depended more on the interests of children, which emphasized meaning rather than memorization, and which was directed toward the

<hr>

[7] Robert S. and Helen M. Lynd, *Middletown*. (New York: Harcourt Brace Jovanovich, Inc., 1929), p. 188.

ADOPTED BY THE

Pottawatomie Co. Teachers' Association, Dec. 1894.

OUTLINE OF THE GRADES.

FIRST GRADE:—McGuffey's First, supplemented by blackboard and primer. NUMBERS—Teach the combination to ten, orally and with objects, teach the value of units and tens order, also one-half, one-fourth, two-fourths, one-sixth and similar fractions. Language in connection with reading.

SECOND GRADE:—Reading—McGuffey's Second. Give plenty of supplementary reading in all reading classes. Numbers,—oral and written work, combination to eighteen, teach the value of periods to thousands, give practical examples for slate work, continue simple fractions. Language,—in connection with reading, also a few short stories about pictures might be introduced. Geography,—first and second grade combined, develop the idea of hill, valley, direction, etc., teach the geography of their county, two or three lessons per week. Writing—read paper on writing. Spelling—in reading lesson. Bear in mind, that phonetic spelling should begin in the first grade and be continued until learned.

THIRD GRADE:—Reading—McGuffey's Third. Arithmetic—Rays Practical. Language—oral and written work, develop the idea of sentence, statement, question, etc., teach how to write names, the use of capitals and letter writing. Geography—Barnes Elementary. Spelling —McGuffey's.

FOURTH GRADE:—Reading—McGuffey's Fourth. Arithmetic— Rays Practical. Language—Lessons in English, begun and completed. Geography—Barnes Elementary (completed.) Spelling—McGuffey's, two lessons per day, oral and one written.

FIFTH GRADE:—Reading—Barnes Elementary history. Arithmetic—Rays Practical. Grammar—Harveys English. Geography— Barnes Complete. Spelling—McGuffey's, written.

SIXTH GRADE:—Reading — Fifth Reader. Arithmetic — Rays Practical. Grammar—Harveys English. Geography—Barnes Complete (completed.) Spelling—McGuffey's, written.

Curricula from *Course of Study for the Public Schools of Pottawatomie County* (Pottawatomie County, Oklahoma: Pottawatomie County Teachers' Association, December 1894).

development of intelligent behavior. Herbart's pedagogy, in spite of the new direction that it gave to teaching, was based on an inadequate psychology. A more modern theory of instruction could not be developed until psychologists provided more insight into the nature of the learning process. The "five formal steps" of the recitation—preparation, presentation, comparison and abstraction, generalization or definition, and application—could, of course, be carried to an extreme. In normal schools under Herbartian influence, it was the practice to formalize these steps, showing where each step began and ended, and what was to be done within each step. The fact remains, however, that the Herbartian movement directed attention to a method of instruction that was centered on the acquisition of meanings, raised questions about the traditional practice of teaching each subject without reference to other subjects, introduced the idea of correlation of subjects, and advanced the idea of adapting psychological principles to instructional practices. Moreover, the current emphasis on "unit teaching" can easily be traced to the Herbartian influence of the 1890s. Educational reforms, like inventions, stand on each other's shoulders.

Friedrich Wilhelm August Froebel (1782–1852) had a very important influence on education in America. The idea of self-realization through social participation and the principle of learning to do by doing can be traced to Froebel. His emphasis on the social aspects of education provided a precedent for Francis W. Parker, who conducted the Cook County Normal School to prepare teachers "in the methods of democracy . . . that which will set the souls of children free." His most concrete contribution to American schools was the kindergarten, which was developed more widely here than in any European country. The first kindergarten connected with a public school system in this country was established at St. Louis, Missouri, in 1873, by Superintendent William T. Harris. Modern psychologists have generally rejected the mystic symbolism of Froebel's theories, and kindergarten practices have been modified in more recent years.

Maria Montessori (1870–1952) was a remarkable Italian physician who became interested in the education of young children, and who founded the world-famous *Case dei Bambini*. These were preschools in the slum quarters of Rome and Milan, run on revolutionary principles. Basic to her concept of education was the notion that the child should have freedom to proceed at his own pace in learning, choosing and directing his own activities within the limits of a prepared environment. The equipment in this prepared environment consisted of highly imaginative teaching materials designed for specific purposes. Some emphasized sensory training. For example, materials were prepared to teach children to recognize various Euclidean shapes—square, rectangle, polygon, and so on—by inserting each form into the appropriately shaped hole in a large frame, or by tracing it. Children traced sandpaper letters with their fingertips before attempting to reproduce the letters. Some equipment was designed to provide exercises in practical living. There were button charts, which the child could use in practicing buttoning and unbuttoning, equipment for learning how to tie shoelaces, pour from a pitcher, and carry out other tasks. The teacher gave a child individual instruction in each task, for Montessori deemed it important that the child learn the right way of carrying out the task; errors are learned through cluttered experiences. Didactic materials for teaching language and arithmetic were also available to the child. Through tactile and muscular sensations the child learned to differentiate first the vowels and next the consonants. The next step consisted of combining letters to form simple words; and the final step was to put words together to form sentences that could then be read back.

Running throughout all of Montessori's writings is the theme that preschool children are ready to learn, and that they can and do teach themselves many things, if given the opportunities. Moreover, they have a zest for learning; every reader of Montessori comes away from her books impressed with the spontaneous interest of the child in tackling what might seem very routine tasks and spending long periods of time with them. Today's psychologist refers to such spontaneous interest as "intrinsic motivation." No adult keeps the child at a given task; having intellectual curiosity satisfied as the child discovers how things work may be the motivating force at work here.

Today Montessori's theories are having a revival. Schools patterned after those that she founded are increasing rapidly in the United States. Some enthusiastic followers tend to be doctrinaire; they abide strictly by the letter of the law laid down in the doctoressa's books, and would have the curriculum follow along the exact same lines as that of the *Case dei Bambini*. Others argue for an updating of materials and activities because the exercises in practical living suited to slum children in Rome at the turn of the century hardly seem appropriate for the middle-class children who make up the greatest part of the population in today's Montessori schools (though the exercises might be more easily adjusted for disadvantaged children). Nevertheless, the contribution of self-chosen and self-directed activities to intrinsic motivation, the use of self-correcting equipment, and the need to match activities to deficiencies in background are the rewarding ideas from Montessori that can be put to good use today.

John Dewey (1859–1952) exerted a wide influence on educational theory and practice through his writing, through his teaching, and through the experimental school that he established at the University of Chicago in 1896. The school was important, not only because it was the first experimental laboratory school in America, but also because it provided an opportunity to demonstrate a new type of teaching.

In 1897 Dewey published a compact statement called *My Pedagogical Creed*. The statement, which seems almost inspired in its simplicity, has been called the "emancipation proclamation of childhood." It expresses the philosophy that children should live and learn happily and well according to their needs and interests today as the best possible preparation for worthy living tomorrow. Joy Elmer Morgan, who for many years was editor of the journal of the National Education Association, said that this statement was as important for the revolution that was taking place in education as Thomas Paine's *Common Sense* was for the political revolution of 1776.

Dewey explored five significant issues in the field of educational theory: what education is, what the school is, the subject matter of education, the nature of method, and the relationship of the school to social progress. These issues, of course, existed before Dewey's time; they are at the center of the controversies about education which are raging today; and they will continue to be live issues as long as men cherish the ideal of free society nourished by a dynamic program of public education.

Dewey regarded education as a social process—a process of bringing children to share in the inherited resources of the race, and to use their powers for social ends. Although he believed that education must begin with psychological insight into children's capacities, interests, and habits, he did not neglect the social side of the process. He said, "This educational process has two sides— one psychological and the other sociological—and neither can be neglected or subordinated to the other without evil results following."

He regarded the school as a form of community life. He said, "The school must represent present life, life as real and vital to the child as that which he carries on in the home, in the neighborhood, or on the playground." He believed that the school should take up and continue the activities with which each child was already familiar in the home, and that the influence of the school should flow into the life of the community. Dewey said, "Save as the efforts of the educator connect with some activity which the child is carrying on of his own initiative independent of the educator, education becomes reduced to pressure from without. It may, indeed, give certain external results, but it cannot truly be called educative."

Dewey believed that the subjects taught in school were frequently too far removed from the day-to-day experiences of children. He became so strongly convinced of this that he established an experimental school in which none of the conventional school subjects was taught. He and his followers, Meriam and Collings, conducted elementary schools in which "normal child activities" (that is, artistic activities, construction activities, story activities, excursion activities, and play activities) replaced conventional school subjects. In connection with a project on Holland, for example, the children learned a great deal about the geography and history of that country because they were interested in finding out these things. They used books and other resources to find answers to problems. They employed a wide range of artistic activities and had occasion to discover and make applications of certain laws of science. In fact, there was hardly an area of human interest that was not stimulated in connection with the study.

"The result, to my mind," he said, "justifies completely the conviction that children in a year of such work . . . get infinitely more acquaintance with the facts of science, geography, and anthropology than they get when information is the professed end and object, when they are simply set to learning facts in fixed lessons." Dewey regarded subject matter as anything that helped a pupil solve a problem; subject matter, according to his view, was a means rather than an end.

The best known of Dewey's ideas about method is his principle of learning to do by doing. He taught that the active side of the child's development preceded the passive side, that movement came before conscious sensations, and that muscular development came before sensory development. He believed that neglect of these principles caused a great deal of friction in school work. He said, "Symbols are a necessity in mental development, but they have their place as tools for economizing effort; presented by themselves they are a mass of meaningless and arbitrary ideas imposed from without."

The idea that teachers should begin where the children are was certainly implicit in Dewey's teaching. He said, "I believe that the question of method is ultimately reducible to the question of the order of development of the child's powers and interests. The law for presenting and treating material is the law implicit within the child's own nature." The modern version of this part of his pedagogical creed is, of course, the philosophy of continuous growth, which holds that each child should be assisted in growing according to his or her natural design, without depriving the bright child of the opportunity of accomplishing as much as ability and effort will permit or forcing the slow child to live up to standards that were never meant for him. This philosophy is inherent in many practices in modern education: the continuous progress school; the open school; contract and competency-based instruction; inquiry; and others.

Like Herbart and others who preceded him, Dewey maintained that interest was an important factor in learning. He did not, as some suppose, teach that the interests of the child should be the sole criterion of method. He said, "Interests are the signs and symptoms of growing power. . . . Accordingly, the constant and careful observation of interests is of the utmost importance for the educator." He stated, however, that children's interests were neither to be humored nor repressed. "To repress interest," he said, "is to substitute the adult for the child, and so to weaken intellectual curiosity and alertness, to suppress initiative, and to deaden interest. To humor the interests is to substitute the transient for the permanent." The idea that children should never be told what to do was not a part of Dewey's creed. He said, "Since the teacher has presumably a greater background of experience, there is the same presumption of the right of the teacher to make suggestions as to what to do as there is on the part of the head carpenter to suggest to apprentices something of what they are to do."

Dewey regarded education as the fundamental method of social progress and reform; he believed that reforms which rested simply on the enactment of laws were transitory and futile. He said, "Education is a regulation of the process of coming to share in the social consciousness; and . . . the adjustment of individual activity on the basis of this social consciousness is the only sure method of social reconstruction." He believed that, through education, society could formulate its own purposes, organize its own means, and propel itself in the direction in which it wished to move. He said that everyone interested in education should insist that society endow the educator with sufficient equipment to perform his task. Publications such as *Self-Renewal: The Individual and the Innovative Society,* "The Central Purposes of American Education," and *Guiding Learning in the Elementary Schools* are, in a sense, echoes of Dewey's ideas about education as a regulative agency. Dewey would have probably supported the third statement of purpose given in the introduction to this chapter—the preparation of individuals who will define and implement the social changes appropriate to their lives and future.[8]

8 See John Gardner, *Self-Renewal: The Individual and the Innovative Society.* (New York: Harper & Row, Publishers, 1963); John Renner, Gene Shepherd, and Robert Bibens, *Guiding Learning in the Elementary School.* (New York: Harper & Row, Publishers, 1973); Educational Policies Commission, "The Central Purpose of American Education," *NEA Journal* (September 1961), pp. 13–16.

The work of John Dewey is one of the principal sources of twentieth century progressive educational theory and practice. It is an error, however, to equate all the doctrines and practices growing out of the influence of the Progressive Education Association with the educational theory of John Dewey. A careful reading of his *Experience and Education* reveals that he was one of the most incisive critics of the excesses growing out of a misinterpretation of progressive education theory.[9]

SITUATION 1.6   *Modern Versions of Dewey's Creed*

1. Dewey wrote in 1897 that *education* was *a social process*—a process of bringing children to use their powers for social ends. Find evidences in the Selected Readings at the end of this chapter that this idea persists.
2. Dewey wrote in 1897 that *children learn by doing*. Find evidence that the "new" curricula expect pupils to become actively involved in their own education.
3. Dewey *regarded subject matter as a means rather than an end* of education. Read the summary on page 35 of the Renner and Ragan reference.
4. Dewey believed that *education was the only sure method of social reform*. See the first chapter in the book by Haan for a recurrence of this idea.

Although Dewey was one of the principal sources of the twentieth-century progressive education theory and practices, what were the misinterpretations he strongly criticized in *Experience and Education?*

The Progressive Education Movement

Few terms are as little understood today as the term "progressive education." Some critics of modern education use the term with the intention of damning any practice in the public schools which they happen to dislike. Lloyd Williams gave a plausible explanation of this tendency when he said, "Frustrated by the seemingly insoluble problems of the twentieth century, and thereby needing something or someone to blame, some of us abuse progressive education and unorthodox educational thinkers."[10]

The progressive education movement in this country was not the creature of John Dewey or the Progressive Education Association, although both played a part in it. Far from beginning with either of these, it dates back to Comenius and Locke, to Rousseau and Pestalozzi, to Herbart and Froebel. The long list

---

[9] John Dewey, *Experience and Education.* (New York: Crowell Collier and Macmillan, Inc. 1938).
[10] Lloyd Williams, "The Illegible Contours of Progressive Education—An Effort at Clarification," *The Educational Forum* (January 1963), p. 224.

of names of those who contributed to the movement in this country would include Horace Mann and Francis W. Parker, John Dewey and William H. Kilpatrick, Boyd Bode and George S. Counts, to mention only a few. Progressive educators believe that children learn best when the material meets some recognized need, not when they are forced to memorize meaningless material; that children should have many contacts with concrete objects, places, and people, as well as with books and other printed materials; that the school should be concerned with children's physical, emotional, and social development, as well as with their mental development. They believe that the school should foster freedom, not license; that subject matter should be a means rather than an end in the educative process; that understanding rather than fear should be used to motivate acceptable behavior; and that purposeful activity is more productive than imposed routine.

The Progressive Education Association was founded in 1919 and disbanded in 1955. Its official journal, *Progressive Education,* ceased publication in 1957. Although it had the support of some of the most capable leaders in American education, it never had a large following. The idea that the public schools were ever taken over by the Progressive Education Association is indeed naive. Referring to the announced principles of the Association, Hartford said, "Progressive education, on that basis, is far from being in control of American schools. Studies of the views of teachers show that they are neither progressive nor traditional but partly both."[11]

The Progressive Education Association, like the broader movement of which it was a part, has been subjected to much criticism and misinterpretation. The subject is freely discussed by many who have never consulted a single source that spells out the principles of the Progressive Education Association or recites the research findings concerning the achievements of children attending schools in which these principles were followed. Many of the misconceptions can be clarified by reading two articles in *Progressive Education.*[12]

The first article sets forth the philosophy of the Progressive Education Association in great detail. Where can we find a basic direction for American education? The Association held that the dominant ideals of our democratic culture, continuously reinterpreted and refined, provided this central direction; that children should have the fullest opportunity for achieving their potential: that education should make people aware of social changes that force breaks with traditional ways of living, thereby opening new possibilities for the future; that it is only in the process of living and working together that optimal development of personality can be achieved; that the school should see the child as a unity— a unique, dynamic living organism; that the physical and mental health of children should be a major concern of the school; that children should be provided

---

[11] Ellis F. Hartford, *Education in These United States.* (New York: Crowell Collier and Macmillan, Inc., 1964), p. 525.

[12] The Progressive Education Association, "Progressive Education: Its Philosophy and Challenge," and "New Methods vs. Old in American Education," *Progressive Education* (May 1941).

with opportunities for self-expression at all stages of their development and in many diverse areas of experience; and that children should have increasing freedom to direct their own behaviors as their knowledge and experiences increase.

The second article is an abstract of the report of a committee appointed by the Progressive Education Association to evaluate the achievement of children who were attending schools in which the newer practices were used. Studies are reported from Lincoln School at Teachers College, Columbia University; from Winnetka, Illinois; from Roslyn, New York; and from Santa Monica, Pasadena, and Los Angeles, California. In general, these studies reported superior results for pupils in schools where the newer procedures were used. It was reported also that the newer procedures were introduced into the schools to attain broad individual and social goals, in addition to raising the standards of achievement in learning, in initiative, in self-direction, and in social understandings and in responsibilities on the part of pupils.

During this period, the abilities to make money and obtain possessions for each individual were established as part of the American ideal. This necessitated and resulted in the changing of the existing orders, structures, and dynamics of society.

DEPRESSION TO HIROSHIMA: 1929–1945

Two great upheavals, international in scope, overshadowed everything else that happened between 1929 and 1945: the Great Depression and World War II. These two periods of national emergency stimulated new developments in science and technology, brought about changes in policies of the national government, and placed increased responsibilities on the public schools.

The stock market crash of 1929 marked the end of the period of prosperity which followed World War I and ushered in a period of economic depression, business failures, and unemployment. These conditions centered attention on all our institutions and gave rise to a new way of looking at the relationship between the government and the economic system which had vast importance for the American future. This was the period of the "New Deal," of the "technocrats"—those who advocated production for use rather than for profit—of the Townsend movement, and of many other proposals for remaking our economic machine so that it would meet our needs. These innovative philosophies represented the efforts of a free people to provide a maximum of economic security for all while preserving the features that gave the economic system its motive power. As Frederick Lewis Allen has suggested, "when the ship of state was not behaving as it should, one did not need to scrap it and build another, but by a series of adjustments and improvements, repair it while keeping it running— provided the ship's crew were forever alert, forever inspecting it and tinkering with it."[13]

---

[13] Frederick Lewis Allen, *The Big Change.* (New York: Harper & Row, Publishers, 1952), p. 105.

The fears and anxieties that were present in the American culture during this period were reflected in demands for reform in the school program. It was suggested that school programs were not geared to social realities, that the schools should build a new social order, that conventional school subjects should be eliminated, and that radical changes should be made in curriculum organization. Although many of the proposals for curriculum change were not implemented, they did serve to focus attention on the need for a school program more in harmony with the demands of society.

World War II placed heavy demands on the American social and economic institutions and increased the responsibilities of the schools. Selective Service records revealed that an amazing number of young men were physically or mentally unfit to serve in the armed forces. However, United States troops fought in practically every quarter of the globe, we developed a two-ocean fleet, the airplane came into its own as a major weapon, and our country became the arsenal as well as the breadbasket of the Free World. Teachers left classrooms to take their places in the armed forces and in war industries, while food rationing and other war-related services were added to the duties of those who remained in classrooms, and the armed services developed new methods of teaching and new instructional media. At the close of the war, teaching had risen to a new position of importance and recognition in our culture.

Curriculum Changes

An effort to assign certain developments to a specific time runs the risk of engaging in oversimplification. Some of the trends that will be mentioned had their origin long before 1929, and many of them continued beyond 1945. Nonetheless, it can be said that the following changes were clearly evident during the period under discussion.

1. Progress was made in developing a more unified elementary school curriculum. Instead of nearly twenty separate subjects taught in isolation from one another, schools began to combine these subjects into broad fields such as language arts and social studies.
2. The emphasis on democratic living in the classroom increased. Experimental evidence concerning the effects of democratic and autocratic control of groups accumulated. Teachers became more expert in working with groups, and descriptions of ways in which teachers helped pupils identify goals, make plans, and evaluate progress became available in greater quantity.
3. The community school idea received a great deal of emphasis during this period. What was taught in school was more directly related to life outside the school. This was accomplished through class visits to places in the community, through bringing resource persons from the community into the classroom, through building the curriculum around life in the community, and through using the school as a community service center.
4. Progress was made in breaking the lockstep system of regulating pupil

progress through elementary school. Rigid promotion schedules, grade standards, and minimum essentials were being modified. More attention was given to individual differences among pupils in rates of learning. The two-division elementary school (the primary school consisting of first-, second-, and third-year pupils and the intermediate school consisting of fourth-, fifth-, and sixth-year pupils), with no annual promotions within these divisions, gained considerable acceptance. Frequently, the same teacher remained with a group of pupils for two or three years, making it possible for the teacher to understand the abilities, interests, and needs of individuals better.

5. Progress had been made toward requiring specialized preparation for elementary school teachers and principals; it was becoming less common for individuals whose preparation had been for high school work to be assigned to elementary schools. Single salary schedules and higher certification requirements had increased the prestige of the elementary school principal and teacher.

6. The traditional recitation based on a single textbook gave way to unit teaching in which emphasis was placed on pupil participation in planning and carrying out learning activities, and in which content was drawn from many sources.

7. Classroom teachers were participating more actively in determining the purposes, content, and scope of the curriculum. Committees of teachers, assisted by specialists in content and methods, were developing curriculum guides and resource units in the various curriculum areas, and in some school systems, the teachers were actually writing textual materials for pupils to use.

8. The child-centered school movement continued to influence practice during this period. It emphasized the selection of learning activities in terms of the interests and needs of pupils instead of in terms of conventional subjects. Although practices within this movement were open to much debate, the movement did much to free elementary classrooms from the tedium of memorization and abstract drill, exclusive dependence upon textbooks, and autocratic practices on the part of the teacher.

9. The social-centered, or life-centered, school movement (see Chapter 6) received a great deal of attention in the 1930s. It replaced school subjects with significant aspects of living in organizing learning activities of pupils. This movement tended to narrow the gap between school and community, and gave the elementary school program social orientation.

PEACE TO SPUTNIK: 1945–1957

Soon after the first atomic bomb fell on Hiroshima in August 1945, humans began to realize that a new age had been born, an age in which many of the existing methods and products would soon become obsolete. This explosive splitting of the atom was the forerunner of the tremendous power that would be available for constructive or destructive purposes. It was a dramatic illustration of the fact that technology had become too dominant and the earth had become so small that society would have to restrain the unwise use of power.

The time span between the first atomic bomb and the first artificial earth satellite consisted of a scant twelve years, but more spectacular changes were packed into these twelve years than during any previous period in history. The impact of this age of miracles on our institutions and on our daily lives has not yet been fully realized. Yet, one conclusion soon became apparent: It would be necessary for humans to learn faster than they had ever learned before if civilization was to remain intact.

After World War II, the United States reversed its policy of isolationism and embarked on a new and strange course as the leader of the Free World. The effort to develop a program of joint action with other free nations has occupied the center of attention in national affairs and has supplied the prime motive for many of the changes in school programs.

The population of the the United States increased rapidly during this period, and significant shifts from rural to urban and suburban living took place. Overcrowded classrooms, shortages of well-qualified teachers, and half-day sessions became common. There was a large-scale migration of Blacks from the South to the North and West and from rural to urban areas. The Supreme Court decision that racial segregation in public schools was illegal imposed a new obligation on the schools, that of integrating a disadvantaged segment of the population into the life and program of the school.

The productivity of American industry increased rapidly; by 1957 the United States, with one-twentieth of the world's population, was producing half the world's manufactured goods. Human skills released by a program of universal education played a major role in this unprecedented production. The advent of automation made it possible to do many jobs with machines instead of with human hands. The production of air-conditioning, radio and television sets, and time-saving appliances for home, farm, and factory increased rapidly during this period. New types of elementary school buildings and automated instructional media also became common.

Changes in Elementary Schools

Events during this period increased the role of the United States in world affairs, reduced the size of the world in terms of hours of travel and communication, and provided dramatic evidence of the interdependence of the people of the whole world. These developments broadened the scope of educational objects. Learning a second language, using air-age maps or polar projections, and studying problems of the world community are cases in point.

Elementary school buildings constructed between 1945 and 1957 differed in important respects from those built earlier. Greater consideration was given to the type of program to be carried on inside the buildings. Two- and three-story buildings were giving way to one-story buildings; 74 percent of those constructed in 1951 were one-story buildings. School sites were larger, the average size being between 10 and 15 acres. Classrooms also were larger; the typical classroom of 1950 contained nearly 400 more square feet of floor space than did the typical classroom of 1930.

The single textbook, once the principal resource for learning, had been supplemented by a great variety of learning resources. By 1954, centralized libraries were maintained in 57 percent of the elementary schools in cities with a population of 100,000 or more, 49.61 percent of those in cities with a population between 9,999 and 25,000, and 41.93 percent of those in cities with a population between 500 and 9,999. The use of radio and television, motion pictures, and resource persons grew rapidly during this period.

Much progress was made in providing special educational programs for exceptional children—the physically handicapped, the mentally retarded, the gifted, and the social deviates. There was an 83 percent increase in the number of schools offering special education services between 1948 and 1953. The number of pupils in kindergarten through the sixth grade receiving foreign language instruction grew from 5,000 in 1941 to 300,000 in 1957.

One of most pronounced developments during this period was the rapid increase in kindergartens. Enrollments in kindergartens in public schools increased from 595,000 in 1939–1940 to 1,474,000 in 1953–1954. Almost all states had authorized local school systems to provide kindergartens, and in two-thirds of the states local funds for kindergartens were supplemented by state funds.

Criticisms of schools, which date back at least to the year 500 B.C., established new records during the postwar period. One of the most frequent charges was that elementary schools were neglecting the fundamentals. Critics who were lambasting the schools on this issue had seldom visited classrooms in various sections of the country, studied reports of school surveys, or examined the evidence from dozens of careful studies of children's achievements.[14]

Much of the difficulties that school systems encountered during this period of "the new and marvelous" might be attributed to the lack of attention to a national purpose. Prosperity, growth, technological advances, and the beginning ripples of what is now called "future shock" resulted in a lack of attention to our ecology and national purpose.

ASSERTION TO APOLLO II: 1957–1969

The beginning of the age of space travel witnessed mounting criticisms of schools and of teacher-training practices. Criticisms of schools are nothing new, but critics reached new heights of disapproval during the post-Sputnik period. There were several factors contributing to the public debate. The tremendous increase in public monies for education made necessary by increased enrollments following the postwar baby boom caused many taxpayers to protest their resultant

[14] See Harold D. Shane, "We Can Be Proud of the Facts," *Nation's Schools* (September 1957), p. 44.

higher taxes. The flight of the middle class to the suburbs brought about a concentration of parents who sought status for their children through education and who demanded better schools. Articulate spokesmen like Admiral Rickover and Arthur Bestor publicly defined what was wrong: schools were too soft and had too many frills; teachers did not stress fundamentals like phonics and turned out many Johnnies who couldn't read. Such criticisms were salt to the wounds of Americans whose national pride had been dealt a severe blow by Sputnik. There was increased concern particularly for bright children who might conceivably correct the imbalance in cold-war technology if they had the proper training. As a result, new programs in foreign languages, science, and mathematics were introduced into the elementary school. New and old systems of teaching phonics flourished. Varieties of ability grouping that had been in vogue in the 1920s made a comeback, usually under a different name, and special classes for "gifted" children became commonplace in many schools. The use of standardized tests spread rapidly, and more attention was paid to student evaluation.

Although the critics offered little in the way of "hard" evidence about educational deficiencies, although their concern was chiefly for the upper-middle-class suburban child, and although their solutions were nineteenth century ("Let's go back to the good, old days and give children the kind of education that *we* got and that European children continue to get"), there were positive results. The American public became more concerned about the schools and more aware of the importance of education than ever before. And professional educators whose energies had been concentrated on providing the buildings and the personnel for the baby boom came to take a hard, critical look at programs, as well as facilities. An exciting period of curricular experimentation, innovation, and evaluation got under way.

Curriculum Reform

Reform had its birth in 1952 with the establishment of the University of Illinois Committee on School Mathematics, called, in this day of the alphabet, UICSM for short. The Committee, composed of mathematicians and educators, was interested in constructing a four-year curriculum that would move the teaching of high school mathematics out of the eighteenth century and into the twentieth. With the support of special foundation grants, the Committee developed and tested text materials and retrained high school teachers in special institutes to teach the "new math." Additional reform groups sponsored by the National Science Foundation (a federal agency) came into being and extended curriculum revision into the junior high.

Before Sputnik the reform in the sciences had already begun. In 1956 the National Science Foundation established the Physical Science Study Committee (PSSC) to construct a new curriculum in high school physics based upon the concepts used in modern physics. Preliminary editions of a revised textbook were tried out, and today the course is widely used in high school classes. Again, physics teachers were retrained in special institutes in the subject matter and teaching of the new course.

Curriculum revisionists in the biological sciences and in chemistry swiftly followed the mathematicians and physicists. The Modern Language Association began a critical examination of the teaching of foreign languages, and began to reappraise that curriculum area also, with emphasis upon speaking the language and upon training the student through an aural-oral (hearing-speaking) approach rather than a purely visual one. Finally a reform movement began among teachers of English, perhaps the part of the curriculum most difficult to revise. All these reform approaches followed the pattern set by the sciences: trial materials and testing them in the schools, revising and publishing final versions, and setting up summer institutes to teach instructors how to use the new materials.

Two things are interesting to note at this point: One is that all new curricula were the result of the cooperative efforts of academicians and professional educators who for the first time worked together to build a curriculum. The second is that the curriculum groups were nonofficial in that they were not local or state educational authorities. Nevertheless, they met with a warm reception in many schools, partly because the group had academic respectability and partly because the schools, stung by the critics, wanted to offer "harder" courses to students.

Actually, it was not the intent of the curriculum study groups to provide curricula that were simply more difficult; they were interested in curricula that would be better. "Better" in this case meant that the students would study those concepts that make up the *structure* of a subject and are essential to an understanding of that subject. Descartes, the noted French philosopher and mathematician, articulated the principle of selection in this way: The facts to know about any discipline are the facts that can be used over and over again. Such facts have mileage and are key concepts, unlocking the door to a great storehouse of knowledge. That for any action in one direction there is an equal and opposite reaction is an example of a key concept. It can be used to explain why the broad jumper pushes backward in order to spring forward; it also explains why an inflated balloon released into the air will push forward rapidly as the air jets out behind, employing exactly the same principle as that of the jet airplane. Curriculum reform, in fact, has succeeded in large measure because academicians have analyzed their disciplines to find what is important to learn.

Curriculum study groups were interested not only in content; they were also interested in method. Almost without exception, the "inquiry" method was incorporated into the new materials. The essence of the inquiry method is that the teacher provides materials or designs a situation so that the pupil can discover a basic concept. Thus, for example, a teacher of science might organize a series of lessons so that the class would arrive at the generalization that the form of a plant or animal is related to function.

Curriculum reform began at the secondary school level, but it was not long in emerging in the elementary schools as well. Math, science, and social studies projects flourished, as well as new approaches to teaching reading (and old ones under a new guise). Many of these projects will be reviewed in subsequent chapters.

During the early years of this development period, the major concern of educators was the education of the gifted. As the movement for human and civil rights gained momentum, the focus of the curriculum reform movements was increasingly upon what was termed as the "culturally different," "culturally deprived," or "culturally disadvantaged child." The gap between our American ideal and the social injustice imposed by society and its schools upon these children became evident in clear detail.

SITUATION 1.7　　The past ten years has witnessed the involvement of the federal legislature in making monies available for special education. Review legislation that allocates monies to one of the following areas:

1. Gifted
2. Minority or ethnic groups
3. Mentally retarded
4. Physically handicapped
5. Learning disabled
6. Preschool

After years of neglecting to pursue our national purposes, we were compelled by judicial decisions, violent and nonviolent protests by students, minority groups, and others to reconsider our national dynamics, orders, and structures. For example, the federal government responded with significant financial aid to change the schools to better serve a regrouped society. Spurred by new monies and the increased attention of society, schools attempted to respond to the disequilibrium in social needs.

EXPLORATION TO MAN: 1969–PRESENT

Physically and technologically the Earth's dominion has been expanded to include the moon and the planets beyond. Environmental resources have received increasingly tender attention from federal and state legislatures, and from concerned groups of citizens and ecologists. The economy has been studied in an effort to establish a rational basis of growth. The courts have made significant rulings concerning the protection of the constitutional rights of individuals. The resignation of a president and vice-president under a cloud of suspicion as well as the transgression and conviction of high federal and state governmental officials have served to feed citizens' growing pessimism concerning the strength, integrity, and value of political-social institutions.

The elementary schools have not escaped this period of disillusion and unrest. Elementary school buildings and buses have been bombed and burned. Violent and nonviolent protests have occurred concerning the nature and use of textbooks and literature in schools. School-bond propositions to raise monies to build school buildings have been defeated at a rate equal to the rate of disapproval existent during the 1920 depression period. Professional groups of educa-

	DEPENDENCE TO INDEPENDENCE 1647-1776	INDEPENDENCE TO NATIONALISM 1776-1876	AGRICULTURE TO INDUSTRY 1876-1929
Dominant Motive	Religion	Popular Government	Labor/Management
CURRICULUM CONTENT	Reading, writing, spelling, arithmetic, prayers, hymns, catechism	Reading, writing, spelling, arithmetic, physiology, hygiene, grammar, composition, history, geography, drawing, music, agriculture, good behavior	Same as previous period plus art, civics, drama, domestic science, manual training, and nature study
ORGANIZATION	Ungraded, separate subjects	Ungraded rural school, graded city schools, separate subjects	Graded, platoon correlation, fusion, self-contained classroom
TYPICAL SCHOOLS	Dame schools, apprentice schools, reading and writing schools, ciphering schools	Kindergartens, eight-year elementary schools	Nursery, kindergartens, six-year elementary schools
METHODS	Memorization, drill, individual instruction	Monitorial system, group instruction, single textbook	Recitation, supervised study, project method
TEACHER EDUCATION	None	Normal schools	Teachers' colleges, schools of education, in-service education
MATERIALS	Hornbook, *New England Primer*	Ungraded textbooks	State-adopted textbooks for each subject, supplementary texts

DEPRESSION TO HIROSHIMA 1929-1945	PEACE TO SPUTNIK 1945-1957	ASSERTION TO APOLLO 1957-1969	EXPLORATION TO MAN 1969-Present
Economic Recovery	Spectacular Change	Fear and Survival	Disequilibrium
Language arts, social studies, arithmetic, science, fine arts, health and physical education, foreign language	Same as previous period. Increased emphasis on a second language, air-age education, and world affairs. Some national curriculum improvement projects initiated	New content developed by national projects, more difficult content introduced, emphasis on the structure of disciplines	Emphasis on the affective and psychomotor domains, emphasis on self-concept and actualization, emphasis on learning how to learn through content
Beginning of nongraded organization, separate subjects, broadfields organization	Graded school, experimentation with new types of organization, special teachers for some subjects, unified programs increasing	Nongraded dual progress, team teaching, unified social studies program	Open facilities, open curriculum, modula-scheduling, contract-competency based instruction, learning centers, mainstreaming
Primary schools, intermediate schools, segregated schools, child-centered schools, social-centered schools, community schools	Early childhood schools, later childhood schools, segregated schools	Increase in kindergartens, integrated schools, and experimental schools. Revival of Montessori schools	Modular schools, preprimary schools, alternative schools, specialized schools, private schools
Recitation project method, unit teaching	Recitation, unit teaching, group work	New teaching strategies, concept learning, learning by discovery, individualized instruction, teacher as a guide, more effective evaluation	Strategies of humanism, value processing, and of the affective domain. Learning by inquiry, peer group instruction
Increased specialization, the workshop an important means of teacher education	Standards of accrediting teacher, education programs developed by national councils and associations, increase in research on factors influencing teacher effectiveness	Five-year programs of college preparation, experimentation with new types of teacher education programs, selective admission to teacher education programs emphasized	Field-based programs, clinical professionalships, competency-based peer-group instruction, internships, community of professionals
Textbooks, libraries, audio-visual materials.	Same as previous period plus radio and television	Many new electronic aids, learning resources center, teacher-made materials, self-instruction devices, language laboratories, programmed textbooks	Simulation activities, alternative materials, ethnic cultural materials, less stereotyped sexism and racism, newspapers, magazines

tors have split apart and negotiated with each other in antagonistic relationships; classroom teachers have been denied membership to some administrative groups, and administrators have similarly denied membership to some classroom teacher groups. Accountability systems for schools have been vigorously created by various state legislatures, and many of these are regarded by some educators as a threat to their professional status.

"Future shock" has been actualized within institutions and people as they strive to survive, to adjust, and readjust to the forces supporting disequilibrium during this period.

Curriculum Reform

The nature of the curriculum reform for the elementary schools has shifted its emphasis from better content, or even more content, to the development of better functioning and self-actualizing individuals. Curriculum projects have been designed to stress humaneness, the development of a positive self-concept, a process for the clarification of values, a reemphasis on the affective domain, and early childhood education.

School buildings have been redesigned from the type of egg-crate facilities to open, flexible arrangements which reinforce more positively the interaction between facilities and programs (that is, space for individual, small group, and large group activities). Furthermore, the modern elementary school has experimented with the fundamental resource of time. The nature of the activities and the needs of the learner have influenced the division and allocation of periods during the school day. The length of time spent with one teacher or team of teachers has been varied, and the proportions distributed in one curriculum area or within an organizational unit (that is, open education) have become flexible.

The nature of the instructional materials for the modern elementary school has been diversified. Kits, simulations, competency-based packages, and highly individualized systems of materials have become easily available.

Serious efforts have been made to eliminate the stereotypes of sexism and racism contained in early editions of textbooks. Materials developed especially for various minority culture groups have been prepared and utilized. The days of the old Mother Hubbard, cut-and-paste, tear-and-color workbooks seem to be gone.

The changes which have occurred in the modern elementary school will be discussed further in subsequent chapters. Now it is sufficient to identify the great strides made within the modern elementary school to accommodate and respond to a society attempting to correct disequilibrium.

EPILOGUE

This chapter has presented a brief review of the evolution of the modern elementary school and its interdependence with the dynamics of its time and social climate. Schools do change—too fast for some, too slow for others. The forces impelling changes in the school seem to originate more often from outside the

institution and within the needs of the dominant society, rather than from vision-
ary professionals.

Parable

Man first stood as a toolmaker. He patterned tools from the models he found
within himself. His first implements were fashioned to magnify the strength of
his muscles: spears, hammers, bows and arrows, guns, tomahawks, levers, and
others. He became a user and victim of these muscle-expanding tools. Man then
fashioned tools to extend his senses: telegraph, telephone, television, micro-
scope, telescopes, and others. He became a user and victim of these sensory-
expanded tools. Now man is fashioning tools to supplement the energy of his
brain: computers. He is both a user and victim of the brain-extending tools.
Man has been and will continue to be a tool builder, user, and victim. What
within himself will be his model for the next phase of tool building? Why not
his spirit and essence? Can he not take the early preliminary tools of psychology,
psychiatry, sensitivity training, value processing, human relation, and individualized instruction, and raise those to the level of perfection of his previous
tools? If not, will he become only a victim of his tool creations? A victim to be
destroyed in body by the power to overkill, in mind by the power of medically
and chemically induced adjustments? If his next tools are not projections of his
spirit, then he may very well find himself reverting to a search for more destructive tools of muscle-power.

SIGNIFICANT DATES

1524 Martin Luther's letter to the mayors and aldermen of German cities
1636 Harvard University established
1647 The "Old Deluder Satan" Act passed by the Colonial Court in Massa-
      chusetts
1785 The Northwest Ordinance required that land be set aside for schools
1806 First Lancasterian school established in the United States
1823 First private normal school in Concord, Vermont
1829 First pedagogical books published in the United States (Samuel R. Hall,
      Lectures on School Keeping)
1835 First state to provide for free public elementary school (Pennsylvania)
1837 Horace Mann became Secretary of the Massachusetts State Board of
      Education
1839 First public normal school established in Lexington, Massachusetts
1848 First graded elementary school in the United States (Quincy, Massa-
      chusetts)
1867 First United States commissioner of education (Henry Barnard)
1873 First kindergarten in connection with a public school system (St. Louis,
      Missouri)
1879 First professional chair in education at the University of Michigan
1890 First full-time compulsory attendance law (Connecticut)

1893   The six-six plan of organization recommended by the Committee of Ten

1896   John Dewey established an experimental school at the University of Chicago

1917   World War I

1919   The Progressive Education Association was founded

1941   World War II

1948   *Education for All American Children* was published by the Educational Policies Commission of the National Education Association

1950   Korean War

1954   The Supreme Court ruled that public school segregation according to race was unconstitutional

1957   Sputnik launched by USSR

1958   Congress passed the National Defense Education Act designed chiefly to promote science, mathematics, and foreign-language instruction

1958   First of many court rulings at all levels influencing the school's role and function concerning desegregation

1962   U.S. military advisors began accompanying Vietnamese soldiers into combat

1963   Supreme Court ruling banned required Bible reading and/or prayer as a mandatory exercise in public schools

1964   *Central Purpose of American Education* published by the Educational Policies Commission of the National Education Association

1964   Supreme Court ruled that neither teacher nor students left their constitutional rights at the schoolhouse gate

1965   Congress appropriated more than a billion dollars primarily to provide better educational opportunities for culturally deprived children; the "Head Start" program was inaugurated

1969   Apollo II landed on the moon

1970   Four Kent State University students killed in war protest demonstration

1972   Supreme Court decision exempted Amish children (religious sect) from state compulsory attendance laws

1973   United States Supreme Court ruled unconstitutional the crossing of school district boundaries for desegregation purposes

1973   United States Supreme Court in Rodriguez case from Texas upheld the financing of education as dependent upon local rather than state wealth

1974   United States Supreme Court in New York and Pennsylvania cases ruled unconstitutional the use of state monies for maintenance and repair to nonpublic schools and for reimbursement of parents for private school expenses

1974   Family Educational Rights and Privacy Act required school records to be opened upon request to inspection and review by parents

1974   Richard Nixon resigned as President of the United States

1975   Supreme Court ruling concerning the application of due-process procedures to suspension from school

1976   Viking I landed on Mars

SUMMARY

1. When elementary schools were established in this country by state legislatures, the action represented a unique social experiment.

2. An examination of the historical development of the American elementary school illustrates the idea that a changing society demands reforms in education.

3. The "Old Deluder Satan" Act, passed by the General Court of the Massachusetts Bay Colony in 1647, was the first legislation in America that required that schools be established.

4. The language of the "Old Deluder Satan" Act, the contents of the *New England Primer*, and the disciplinary practices in colonial schools revealed the religious motive for education.

5. The "public school revival" was successful in making elementary schools available for all children, except in a few southern states, by 1876.

6. Several factors combined during the period between 1876 and 1929 to make the elementary school a thoroughly regimented affair—like a factory.

7. Critics and criticisms of the public schools became a matter for large-scale public debate, beginning during the 1950s.

8. The judicial and legislative branches of federal government began to utilize the school to accomplish national purposes: compensatory programs, desegregation, and so on.

9. A new visibility and vulnerability was created for the public school through both state legislation and the accountability movement.

Problems and Projects

NOTE: Lest the instructor, the student, or the in-service teacher become disturbed by the lack of definitive answers to the questions about to be raised, let us explain that in many cases there are no "right" answers. The problems and projects are intended to stimulate thinking and to help the reader see the relationship between the content of the chapter and actual classroom practice. Readers will find that their answers will be based upon their own value systems—that is, upon what they conceive to be right and good and true. This, in turn, depends upon their grasp of the concept of democratic education and their knowledge of how children grow and develop. It is hoped that this text will aid the teacher in building a sound value system so that "answers" will result in better education for American children.

1. What is a teacher? Who is a teacher? What are the governing factors determining who will teach? From these questions has evolved what is now commonly referred to as "certification."

   a. Trace the history of teacher-preparation requirements and programs from the colonial period to the present. Is there a pattern or similarity in the triggering factors which necessitated increased sophistication of teacher-preparation programs?

   b. Increasingly more students are being granted diplomas from schools and colleges of education throughout the nation. If the student has been given proper advisement, certification is merely a procedural formality to be completed. However, upon observation and conversation, these "certified" new teachers are often frustrated in that they do not feel qualified to teach in all grades for which they have received certification. Interview three to five recent elementary education graduates or beginning teachers. List the areas in which they feel weak. As the interviews are reviewed, decide whether the problem is a result of the curriculum structure or a result of certification policies. Are we approaching the point where certification procedures must be reevaluated? List the adjustments you would propose, either in the curriculum structure or certification policies, to rectify or alleviate somewhat the anxiety related to the training of new teachers.

c. Examine and evaluate the certification requirements in five states. How do they differ? How are they alike? Where do the states fall in teacher-pay scale surveys? How are the states rated in quality of education surveys? What current movements exist to bridge certification differences and align certification requirements among states?

2. The "Old Deluder Satan" Act passed by the General Court of Massachusetts Bay Colony in 1647 was a landmark in the history of education. Its passage marked the first law in the history of the world which required that schools be provided at community expense. Today, schools are struggling to survive under the fire of critics and the impact of repeated defeats of school-bond propositions designed to raise monies to build schools.

a. Discuss the significant legislation in the history of education related to the taxation of the people for schools. Who were the leaders? How were the taxes distributed among the type of schools in existence (that is, public, private, and so on)?

b. Research the history of bond elections specific to the school system in your community since 1955. How does your community compare with the current national trend?

c. Investigate results of school-bond propositions within the last five years for towns
   (1) below 5000 population.
   (2) between 5,000 and 15,000.
   (3) between 15,000 and 50,000.
   (4) between 50,000 and 100,000.
   (5) over 100,000 population.

d. Discuss with the individuals listed below their reasons for support or lack of support for school-bond propositions.
   (1) Private businessman
   (2) Lawyer
   (3) Teacher
   (4) Salesperson
   (5) Doctor
   (6) Parent

What adjustments would the schools need to create a more favorable relationship with the community?

3. "Spare the rod and spoil the child!" "Conceived in iniquity and born in sin." "Beat the devil out of them." At times, such phrases in the past have characterized and justified the practice of severe discipline within the walls of the schoolhouse.

Discipline! It is a recurring theme in teacher-preparation institutions. Once, teachers were concerned with which method of discipline to incorporate; now, under the shadow of court decisions, teachers are seeking an understanding of exactly which rights and responsibilities are those of the teacher and which are those of the student.

    a. Examine recent court rulings (within the past five years) related to the constitutional rights of the student and the rights of the school. What questions and issues prompted these rulings? What individuals or groups of individuals have been most active in pressing for court decisions?

    b. Visit a total of five classrooms in different elementary schools. Discuss with the teacher(s) the philosophy of discipline incorporated. What methods of disciplining were incorporated? Does the type of discipline vary with age of student? Did the classroom observation coincide with the philosophy of the teacher? Based upon the observations made, what relationships appeared between classroom discipline nad classroom atmosphere?

    c. Interview two college instructors in elementary education concerning their philosophies of classroom discipline within the elementary school and within institutions of higher learning. Do their disciplining philosophies support research studies related to the impact of disciplining techniques upon classroom environments?

    4. For a period of time (for example, four weeks) collect current articles on education from newspapers and news magazines. What are the major headings under which these articles can be grouped? Now refer back to issues of these same sources five years ago. Will the major headings you developed for the current articles coincide with the content of the five-year-old articles?

Selected Readings

Dewey, John, *Experience and Education*. New York: Crowell Collier and Macmillan, Inc., 1938. Makes it clear that John Dewey did not advocate the doctrines that have been attributed to extremes of Progressive Education.

Good, Harry G., and James D. Teller, *A History of American Education*. New York: Crowell Collier and Macmillan, Inc., 1973. A review of the trends, issues, people, and developments significant to the establishment of the American systems of education.

Goodlad, John L., and Harold G. Shane (Eds.), *The Elementary School in the United States*. National Society for the Study of Education, 72nd Yearbook, Part II. Chicago: University of Chicago Press, 1973. A collection of essays discussing the history, status, and projected changes needed.

Grambs, Jean Dresden, John C. Carr, and E. G. Campbell (Eds.), *Education in the World Today*. Reading, Mass.: Addison-Wesley Publishing Company, Inc., 1972. Section B contains a series of articles on the areas of conflict in education.

Haan, Aubrey, *Education for the Open Society*. Boston: Allyn and Bacon, Inc., 1962. Chapter 1 explains the responsibility of the schools in maintaining a free society.

Hillson, Maurie, *Elementary Education: Current Issues and Research*. New York: The Free Press, 1967. The prologue and chapter 19 deal with the nature and sources of the current reform movement in elementary education.

Knight, Edgar W., *Education in the United States*, 3d rev. ed. Boston: Ginn and Company, 1951. Traces the development of public education from the colonial times through the 1940s.

Pulliam, John D., *History of Education in America*, 2d ed. Columbus, Ohio: Charles E. Merrill Publishing Co., 1976. An expanding discussion of the history of the development of education in America.

Renner, John W., and William B. Ragan, *Teaching Science in the Elementary School*. New York: Harper & Row, Publishers, 1968. Presents a discovery-centered approach to teaching science in the elementary school.

Russell, J. D., and C. H. Judd, *The American Educational System*. Boston: Houghton Mifflin Company, 1940. Pages 19–21 contain an excerpt from Martin Luther's letter to the mayors and aldermen of the cities of Germany.

Seguel, Mary Louise, *The Curriculum Field: Its Formative Years*. New York: Teachers College Press, Columbia University, 1966. A review of the trends and developments in curriculum.

Squire, James R. (Ed.), *A New Look at Progressive Education*. Yearbook of the Association for Supervision and Curriculum Development. Washington, D.C.: Association for Supervision and Curriculum Development, 1972. A review of the major ideas of progressive education and the relationship of these ideas to current practices.

chapter 2

Influencing SOCIETY

The history of American schools has been replete with criticism. It is an undocumented but accepted premise that in no other previous or contemporary society has so much been hoped for, asked from, given to, or taken on by schools. Under such an assumption it is not difficult to understand why schools in America have been a focal point for criticism.

James B. Macdonald and Esther Zaret (eds.), *Schools in Search of Meaning.* (Washington, D.C.: Association for Supervision and Curriculum Development, 1975), p. 12.

Schools are both tools *of* society and tools *for* the society. The dominant society—whether ethnic, religious, political, or nationalistic—establishes dynamics to gain the school's contributions—contributions either to maintain the present social order or to prepare citizens for previously agreed upon changes within the society. The programs of the schools have characteristically moved with the purposes established by the dominant society.

Historically, the elementary school has been both responsive to and dependent upon the goodwill of its community. In today's pluralistic community, where one group advocates what another group opposes, the elementary schools have been very vulnerable. For example, the judicial system has utilized the schools as a tool for implementing its judgments in cases concerning racial and sexual discrimination. The courts have also made recent rulings affecting almost all areas of the school operation: transportation and attendance areas; pupil records; disciplining procedures; employment and dismissal procedures; and so on. The legislative branch of our federal government has adopted legislation establishing numerous programs which require the use of public schools as a tool for effecting the intent of the federal legislature.

Within our pluralistic society, these federal court rulings and laws have not always had wide support within local school communities. These schools are often faced with the dilemma of interpretation and application, with no clearly defined, dominant, local society available to define the issue, solve the dilemma, and alleviate the pressures. School communities experience much less disequilibrium and criticism when they function only as tools of a clearly defined, dominant society.

Schools are both tools *of* and tools *for* society's maintenance, growth, and change. During previous times, schools might have been able to avoid and hide from conflicts within the society. Apparently this luxurious avoidance will no longer be tolerated by our pluralistic society. Schools were once referred to theoretically as the "melting pot" of our society, implying that schools helped establish one unified, dominant society. Today, schools may very well be the substantive melting pot itself, the pot in which and through which alternative resolutions are stirred, mixed, and boiled down to a resolution.

Our society is changing so rapidly that anyone who is responsible in any way for influencing the elementary school curriculum must constantly reexamine the social scene. There can be no such thing as a "completed" education for the school administrator, the supervisor, the director of curriculum, or the teacher. Children who are now attending elementary schools will spend many years in the twenty-first century: this means that intelligent planning of instructional programs must take into consideration the significant social trends of the recently past decade which are likely to be projected into the future. There is little to be gained from wishing that circumstances were different or from longing for a return to the "good old days." The broad outlines of an elementary school curriculum suited to the demands of today and adaptable to those of tomorrow are determined to a large extent by the stern realities of the age in which we are living.

SITUATION 2.1   Read five journal articles written in the past five years which are related to the interaction between changes in society and educational reform. What appears to be the consensus concerning the most urgent areas of educational reform?

It cannot be assumed that this chapter will give the student a comprehensive view of social changes which have implication for curriculum planning. The most it can do is to encourage the student to critically examine the idea that a rapidly changing society demands reforms in school programs, using a few aspects of American life as examples of the constantly accelerated rate of social change. It should be recognized also that data used to illustrate the "quickening pace" of social change soon become out of date. The student, however, can supplement the information contained in this chapter by examining books, educational journals, and popular magazines, which are devoting an increasing amount of space to the spectacular changes in our society.

EDUCATION IN AN ERA OF CHANGE

Among the outstanding characteristics of the times in which we are now living are both the constantly accelerated rate of change and the resulting disequilibrium (future shock) upon individuals and institutions. Writers frequently use the words "revolution" or "explosion" to identify the nature of new developments taking place: the technological revolution, the space revolution, the biological revolution, the communication revolution, the population explosion, and the knowledge explosion are examples. These and other developments have transformed patterns of living for individuals, modified the functions of the family, erased community boundaries, increased the functions of government and education, and introduced a wide range of recreation and leisure time activities. The result has been the obsolesence of the structures and operations of many of our social institutions and a need for the application of human intelligence to the solution of problems of living on a scale never before realized. Many adults in our country can remember the horse-and-buggy era, yet they have seen the development of automobiles and jet airplanes, watched the growth of radios and television, seen electricity replace steam as the principal source of power, witnessed the use of atomic energy, watched men set foot on the moon, and accepted as commonplace machines which can do jobs that only persons could do in the past.

Each age in the history of civilization has been shorter than the preceding one. The stone age covered hundreds of thousands of years; the bronze age lasted for several thousand years; the iron age lasted about half as long; and the steel age is a little more than a hundred years old. When the first atomic bomb fell on Hiroshima in August 1945, Norman Cousins wrote that it marked "the violent death of one stage in man's history and the beginning of another."[1] Only twelve years later, when Russia launched Sputnik I, Peter Drucker wrote that we had entered the "post-modern" era.[2] Again, it was only twelve years after Sputnik that two Americans set foot on the moon and ushered in another, as yet unnamed, era in history.

The idea that a rapidly changing society calls for reforms in educational programs has been the central theme of much that has been written about education during the past three decades. No clearer statement of this principle has ever been written than that contained in Harold Benjamin's *Saber-Tooth Curriculum*, published in 1939.[3] According to Benjamin, the first school was established in paleolithic times to teach fish-grabbing, tiger-scaring, and horse-clubbing—the means by which people at that time met their basic needs: food, protection, and clothing. When a glacial drift changed circumstances so that these activities were no longer relevant to problems of living, the paleolithic schools went right on teaching the same "basic" subjects. George S. Counts wrote in 1958, "The task of bringing our old minds into accord with the facts of the new world is a gigantic and urgent educational undertaking."[4] George B. Leonard wrote in

[1] Norman Cousins, *Modern Man Is Obsolete*. (New York: The Viking Press, Inc., 1946), p. 8.
[2] Peter F. Drucker, *Landmarks of Tomorrow*. (New York: Harper & Row, Publishers, Inc., 1959), p. ix.
[3] Harold Benjamin, *The Saber-Tooth Curriculum*. (New York: McGraw-Hill, Inc., 1939).
[4] George S. Counts, "Education and the Technological Revolution," *Teachers College Record* (March 1959), p. 318.

1968, "But now Civilization as it has existed for 15,000 years is ending and a new kind of order, a new kind of education are upon us."[5]

Although changes in schools generally lag behind changes in other aspects of American life, there exists an era of change in education. As the subsequent chapters indicate, a massive curriculum reform movement is occurring; deeper insights into how children learn and develop are being gained; innovations in school organization are providing opportunities for pupils to progress at their own rates of learning; teachers are being deployed in order to make better use of their strengths; exciting new materials and electronic devices are making it possible for pupils to learn more in a given length of time; and pupils are being taught to think for themselves rather than merely memorize ready-made solutions to problems. Curriculum planning has become a continuous process, with more intimate relationships between what is learned in school and what occurs in life inside and outside the classroom.

ECONOMIC TRENDS

Throughout history, Americans have been more concerned with production and consumption than with distribution and conservation. The assumption was that sufficient growth in production and consumption would create an economic flow that would provide for distribution. Production would create both supply and jobs, while jobs would provide the monies for demand. A naiveté existed concerning the impact of uncontrolled production and consumption upon ecology and the conservation of our natural resources. The United States, with approximately one-twentieth of the world's population, consumes approximately one-third of the world's resources. Accustomed to a system of production for abundance, Americans can barely accept and realize a scarcity of resources: energy, for example. Although the United States has freely given of its abundance to the world, Americans are not prepared for the questions now being asked by the peoples of the world: "Why should you (United States) consume one-third of the world resources?"; or, "By what rights do you have two loaves of bread when I have only a crust?"

SITUATION 2.2   Ecologic conservation —the respectful utilization of our natural resources. In a few years, ecological decisions will be made by youth currently attending educational institutions. Educators are responsible for providing experiences which will be related to the life of the individual as it is affected by ecology. Briefly describe one project for each level within the elementary school to increase students' experiences with and awarenesses of ecological relationships and the conservation movement.

Wealth has traditionally been controlled by those who controlled the pro-

[5] George B. Leonard, *Education and Ecstasy.* (New York: Dell Publishing Co., Inc.; Delacorte Press, 1969), p. 81.

duction systems. Now, with an increasing scarcity of raw materials, wealth may become controlled by the owners of the raw materials, rather than by the producer. An illustration is the shift of the world's economic income toward the Arab Block through its control of the raw material, oil. Formerly, a country's ownership of the production systems gave control of wealth; now the wealth is flowing to those who control the raw material, not the refinery. This shifting of wealth from control of production systems to control of raw materials may eventually be balanced by recognizing that children are the most important raw material and that their education represents basic wealth.

Unemployment, inflation, lack of control of basic raw materials to support production, the interdependence between production and the ecological balance, all are problems plaguing the economic system. Unemployment during the mid-1970s approached the levels of the 1929 depression era. If inflation continues at the rate it has advanced in the past decade, a family unit will need approximately 3.4 times as much income in 1984 to purchase what it did in 1974. Countries other than the United States own and control the majority of the raw materials essential to both our production capacities and standards of living. These countries are now asking full value for the utilization of their resources.

This is the setting of the schools of the mid-1970s. More importantly, the present students attending the modern elementary school are the citizens who are affected by these problems and who must effect their resolutions. Theodore Schultz commented:

> It became clear to me that in the United States many people are investing heavily in themselves as human agents, that these investments in man are having a pervasive influence upon economic growth, and that the key investment in human capital is education.[6]

POVERTY IN AN AFFLUENT SOCIETY

Gunnar Myrdal, the distinguished Swedish economist, wrote: "There is an ugly smell rising from the basement of the stately American mansion."[7] Myrdal was referring to the millions of Americans who were undereducated, underemployed, or unemployed. For every two students who graduate from high school, there is one who drops out or is pushed out before graduation. While 75 percent of the upper-middle and upper economic class youth who rank in the upper quarter in intellectual ability finish four years of college, only 25 percent of less advantaged youth with comparable mental ability do so.

Although whites make up the greater number of those classified within the lower economic class, the chances percentage wise of a minority group member being within this economic classification is almost double that of a white. The percentage of undereducated, underemployed, or unemployed members of

---

6 Theodore W. Schultz, *The Economic Value of Education*. (New York: Columbia University Press, 1963), p. viii.

7 Gunnar Myrdal, "It's Time To Face the Future," *Look* (Nov. 19, 1963), p. 105.

minority culture groups is so high that it supports the conclusion that the disparity reflects a racist problem.[8]

Schools may be perpetuating the economic cycle of children from economically disadvantaged families who become parents of economically disadvantaged families. The federal government began in the early 1960s to fund what was called "compensatory" education programs. These compensatory programs and funds were to be used to support, extend, and enrich the schooling of children from economically disabled groups. The evaluation of the impact of these programs as a catalyst in the release of children from this self-defeating economic cycle presents conflicting conclusions. Hard, empirical evidence has not yet been produced to show that schools adequately serve those citizens locked into poverty.

THE CHALLENGE OF NONWORKING TIME

Work—is it something done, not because of joy, but because of necessity? Work for the sake of work—not because it is joyful, meaningful, and productive, but because it is moral and right? Must difficult and unpleasant tasks, usually called "work," be experienced in order to develop good character and discipline? The work ethic, "Do your work, children, and then we can have fun," serves as conditioning for becoming a replaceable part within an industry. Harvey Cox, writing from a religious point of view, and John Holt shared and presented the idea that the future holds a radical change in ideas about work.[9]

With the steadily decreasing amount of time an individual spends as an employee, should only employed time be called work? Should the assumption that work is valuable only in economic terms be dominant? Should we accept the separation between enjoyment and work, and between self-fulfillment and work? Perhaps when the future of an elementary school-child was one that required 66 hours as a laborer in the 1850s or even the 40-plus hours of the 1960s, the school could rightly or carelessly perpetuate this work ethic.

Silberman, in his *Crisis in the Classroom*, stressed the idea that "poetry, music, painting, dance and the other arts are not fields to be indulged in if time is left over from the real business of education; they are the real business of education."[10] The work of education is the development of the intellectual, emotional, spiritual, and ethical character of the human. Therefore, the modern elementary school cannot afford the luxury of the present definitions of those activities labeled "the work of pupils" and "the fun for pupils." Worthy use of leisure time has long been accepted as a goal; perhaps the goal for worthy use of work will become a guide for curriculum of today.

---

[8] John Holt, *Freedom and Beyond*. (New York: E. P. Dutton & Co., Inc., 1972).
[9] Harvey Cox, *The Secular City*. (New York: Crowell Collier and Macmillan, Inc., 1965), chap. 9.
[10] Charles E. Silberman, *Crisis in the Classroom: The Remaking of American Education*. (New York: Random House, Inc., 1970).

THE FAMILY IN TRANSITION

The family and the school are this country's major institutions for educating the young. The family is the first socializing influence in the child's life. It is from mother that the child learns about living with other people, then from father, then from brothers and sisters, then from other relatives, and then from an ever-widening circle of people. Although changes in American life have tended to limit the educational opportunities provided by the home, it is still a major factor in determining what the child will become as an adolescent and later as an adult.

Anthropologists from other countries who have studied the American people have been impressed with the great prestige of mothers in American society. They call the United States *motherland*; they say that in this country a person's conscience may be defined by the expectations of the individual's mother. Psychiatrists have provided a great deal of evidence that adequately mothered infants have been relatively free from emotional and physiological upsets, while inadequately mothered infants have reacted by excessive crying and by physiological upsets. Studies of orphanage children have provided some evidence that, even with the best of physical care but with no opportunity to relate themselves to anyone who could give them affection, they displayed aggressive behavior throughout adolescence, were unable to form genuine attachments to people, were deficient in language usage, and had difficulty in developing concepts.[11]

During the nineteenth century the family was a self-contained unit for economic production. The father, the mother, and the children worked together to produce food, clothing, shelter, and other economic goods and services. The urban family of today is an economic unit for consumption, but not for production. Recreation, which formerly centered in the home, has been taken over by the movies, sports, and other forms of commercialized recreation. The girl once learned social skills at her mother's knee; the boy received preparation for his life of work by working with his father. Today the social skills and work preparation are often acquired by both sexes through organizations and institutions such as nursery schools, kindergartens, scouts, trade or professional schools. The stability of the family has been reduced by the continuing increase in divorce; divorce rates have increased by 3 percent each year since the Civil War. The number of households rose to an estimated 70 million in 1974, some 6.5 million more than in 1964. Of the 70 million, 67 percent were husband-wife households, while 12 percent were families in which no legal spouse was present. In 1974, 16 million households were headed by women. With an increase of 25 percent during the 1970s, households headed by women became the fastest growing type. Households headed by singles under age 34 jumped 55 percent between 1970 and 1974 to a total of 2,700,000 units. The married, two-partner households increased by 6 percent during the same period. The increasing proportion of mothers who are gainfully employed, the greater mobility of

11 See Louis Kaplan, *Mental Health and Human Relations in Education* (New York: Harper & Row, Publishers, 1959), pp. 105–134.

population, urbanization, the decrease in the proportion of one-family houses, the increased diversity of family structures, and other factors have tended to lessen the educational opportunities offered children in the home.

The school was established (in the United States) not to provide an education in the sense that the term is used today, but to add a little book learning to the education that the child was getting in the home. Changes in American life have caused many of the educational functions of the home to be transferred to the school. The modern school is still expected to teach the conventional subjects; it is expected also to develop stable personalities, foster physical and mental health, prepare for home and family living, develop economic competence, teach citizenship, and contribute to world understanding.

There are those who propose a very simple solution to the problem of an overloaded school curriculum; they would allocate certain functions to the school, others to the home, and still others to various community agencies. Aside from the very practical problem of finding an individual or group with the authority to make such an allocation of functions, the proposal overlooks the fact that children are not divisible. Suppose, for example, that all responsibility for the health of the child were to be allocated to the home and the family physician. It is easy to see that living conditions and procedures used in the school would continue to influence the health of the child. The home, the school, and the community must work in close harmony if the needs of the child are to be met in the area of health as well as in other important areas.

Elementary schools alone cannot provide adequate educational opportunities for children; it requires the home, the school, and the community. In many elementary schools, parents take part in study groups, share information with teachers about the characteristics and needs of children, help teachers feel at home in the community, and try to provide better living conditions for children in homes and in the community. The elementary school supplements the work of parents in providing the best opportunities possible for children to learn and grow. Good elementary schools provide guidance service, home visitors, nursery schools and kindergartens, parent-teacher conferences, special classes for exceptional children, and in many other ways try to adapt the school program to educational needs arising from the changed status of the home.

POPULATION CHANGES

The educational implications of population phenomena have been given a great deal of attention in recent years. The Project on Instruction of the National Education Association stated, "More and more, plans and decisions in education should be based upon sound demographic information and understanding as our population continues to increase, as age distribution continues to shift, as population centers shift, and as teaching becomes more complex."[12]

[12] Project on the Instructional Program in the Public Schools, *Education in a Changing Society.* (Washington, D.C.: National Education Association, 1963), p. 97.

The population of the United States was about 100 million in 1917, 144 million in 1947, 175 million in 1959, 192 million in 1964, 201 million in 1968, and 215 million in 1975.

Enrollment in public and private elementary schools reflected the changes in population growth and possibly a change in the dominant society's attitude. Enrollments in public and private elementary and secondary schools increased from 28.6 million in 1949–1950 to 42.4 million in 1959–1960 to 50 million in 1969–1970 to 51.9 million in the 1973–1974 school year; there were 31.3 million pupils in public elementary schools (K-8) and 3.8 million in private elementary schools. During 1974–1975, there were 30.7 million pupils in public elementary schools. The figures indicate a decrease of approximately 700,000 pupils from 1973–1974, with a loss of 600,000 in public schools and 100,000 in private schools. College and university enrollments grew from 1.3 million in 1946 to 3.5 million in 1957 to 7.5 million in 1968 and to 8.6 million in 1975.

In 1975, the birthrate was 1.9 per family; for the second year in a row, this was below the replacement rate of 2.0. However, the 1975 birthrate had an increase of 0.1 per family over the 1974 birthrate, suggesting the beginnings of a possible increase in birthrate. A birthrate below the replacement rate and the increasing life expectancy to more than 70 years result in a higher average age of the population.

The impact of the changes in our population has had tremendous influence upon schools, hospitals, housing, and other public services. In schools, for example, financial support has often been granted on a per-pupil basis. So, fewer pupils will mean less money for a budget already weakened by inflation. Fewer pupils will mean fewer teaching positions available and a potential oversupply of individuals qualified to teach. When supply outstrips demand, the increase of competition tends to hold salaries and fringe benefits down. Therefore, even the teacher presently employed may experience a loss of actual purchasing power because of both the supply-demand relationship and inflation. Some teacher groups are combating these tendencies by forming strong organizations to negotiate for salaries, benefits, and working conditions. One residual effect of this movement is the tendency to establish a labor-management relationship between administrators and teachers. Even if the school-age population begins to increase again, and there are some signs in this direction, it is likely that the actions partially stimulated by a declining birthrate will strongly affect the future of the school.

The Urban Crisis

The rapid growth of American cities is an aspect of the population problem which deserves special attention. The big city is a relatively new development in American society. It was not until 1820 that any city in the United States had a population of 100,000; we now have one city with a population of 8 million (16 million in the metropolitan area, including suburbs) and four others with more than 3 million each. Only 51 percent of our people were living in urban communities in 1920; by 1965, two-thirds of our people lived in metropolitan areas.

The 1970 census indicated a migration to metropolitan areas of 1.2 million. There were 7.7 million moves from one metropolitan area to another.[13] This migration was not to the central city but to the surrounding suburbs; thus, in many cases, leaving the central city school districts to become the schools for the poor. In 1910, only 27 percent of Blacks lived in urban communities. Today 93 percent of the elementary school pupils in Washington, D.C., are Blacks; in Detroit, St. Louis, Baltimore, and Philadelphia, the figure is almost 70 percent.

A recent development generating the urban crisis has been the financial trouble arising in the urban centers. For example, New York City has been within hours of defaulting in payment of its obligations—salaries, bonds, interest, and so on. The New York City teacher groups loaned more than a million dollars to the city government in an effort to ward off a default and the resulting loss of jobs by teachers and other city government employees. The incidence of aggressive acts of students toward teachers in urban schools has mushroomed to the extent that some teacher negotiation groups are demanding hazardous duty pay for those teachers assigned to central city schools. During the 1974–1975 school year, the schools of Chicago spent approximately $10 million on security measures. Of this, $3 million was spent for security personnel. The December 1975 report of the National School Public Relations Association stated that vandalism and violence are rapidly becoming major problems.

CRITICS

A generation of new critics of the schools has been fostered by the dynamics of the change, trends, and disequilibriums reviewed briefly in previous sections. Critics have always drawn their authority from their perceptions of both social ills and the adequacy of the school's contributions toward resolving these ills—usually, the critic's solution. A fundamental aspect of democracy is the evolving, shifting, adjusting nature of society. This essential nature of democracy has supported the existence of critics from the beginning of the United States. Critics of schools, therefore, have been, are, and will always be present; for example, Ben Franklin's Academy was a reaction to his criticism of existing schools. Critics —whether of schools, government, or religion—serve valuable functions. They often provide perspectives and insights not readily available to those busily engaged in operating society's institutions. Yet, objectivity and insight are not the sole possession of critics, nor are subjectivity and tunnel vision the sole faults of those who operate within society's institutions. New directions and progress are forced from the heat of the friction generated by the interfacing of alternatives and evaluations.

Recent critics of the schools of the 1970s have drawn their authority from the information concerning the contributions of the schools to those citizens labeled "disadvantaged" for reasons of economic, cultural, or ethnic group membership. Most of these recent critics have then extended their fault finding to include the schools' contributions toward resolution of selected problems in

[13] "Urban Zero Population Growth," *Daedalus*, 102:191–206, Fall 1973.

today's or tomorrow's society. Their findings are provided substance by the fact that children from low socioeconomic families are two or three years below achievement norms. These families are identified as segregated ethnic groups, specifically of Indian and Spanish origin. Black children appear to lag even further behind.

In the mid-70s the major focus of criticism is the failure of schools to correct the plight of the "disadvantaged." The criticisms dwell on, or are concerned with, so-called cognitive qualities, an outgrowth of the criticisms of the 50s and the input of the cognitive psychologists such as Piaget and Bruner. They can be traced in lineage from attacks against the "life adjustment" concept of schooling (Arthur Bestor, James Koerner, etc.); through the structure of the disciplines (Jerome Bruner, etc.); into the mastery syndrome (Benjamin Bloom, etc.); down to behavioral objectives (Robert Mager and James Popham, etc.); and back again to proponents of intellectual growth (Jean Piaget, Lawrence Kohlberg, etc.).[14]

Other critics coming from somewhat the same energy source are called "geneticists" or "environmentalists." The geneticist assumes that capacity (IQ) is spread differently among ethnic and social groups. The environmentalist assumes that if the schools fulfill the basic needs; give a "head start," provide mental health, and remove environmental conditions, then each person will achieve his full potential within the present system.[15]

The scholarly, cognitive labels attached to the current critics of schools seem appropriate, although current and past reformers might be given affective labels such as "uncritical lovers," "unloving critics," or "critical lovers." The uncritical lovers, usually called "defenders" or "protagonists" rather than critics, are so deeply committed to the spirit of schooling that they can see nothing faulty. They utilize their public platforms to remind us of the great contributions of schools throughout our history, of our dependency upon schools, and of the promising innovations appearing in schools. The unloving critics, either overtly or covertly, would "de-school" society, and they utilize their platforms to shout about the schools' failures, the oppression of the institution and its inflexible nature, and the value of education rather than schooling. The critical lovers provide the "most unkindest cuts of all." They utilize the public stages to speak of faith and belief, of failures and successes, of inflexibility and the need for flexibility, of the blindness of hindsight and the fragility of prophesy. The protagonist loves schools because of their tradition. The unloving critic dislikes schools because they are. The critical lover cares for what schools are and may become.

A brief listing of some of the books from critics within the past two decades includes:

1953   Bestor, *Educational Wastelands*
1956   Lynn, *Quackery in the Public Schools*

[14] James B. Macdonald and Esther Zaret (Eds.), *Schools in Search of Meaning*, 1975 Yearbook of the Association for Supervision and Curriculum Development. (Washington, D.C.: Association for Supervision and Curriculum Development, 1975), p. 18.
[15] Macdonald and Zaret, *Schools in Search of Meaning*, p. 19.

1959   Smith, *Diminished Mind*
1959   Smith, *And Madly Teach*
1962   Goodman, *Compulsory Miseducation*
1964   Holt, *How Children Fail*
1967   Kozol, *Death at an Early Age*
1969   Kohl, *The Open Classroom*
1969   Postman, *Teaching as a Subversive Activity*
1970   Goodlad, *Behind the Classroom Doors*
1970   Silberman, *Crisis in the Classroom*
1972   Illich, *De-Schooling Society*
1973   Reimer, *School Is Dead*

This is not a complete listing of published critiques nor is it a listing of critics from any one category—critical lovers, uncritical lovers, or unloving critics. A student of education should be familiar with the perspectives and concerns of all leading writers on the subject, since they often provide viewpoints which become viable, functioning contributions to the development of schools.

SITUATION 2.3   Read a recent publication by a critical lover. What are the alternatives proposed by the author? Defend your classification of the author as a "critical lover."

NATIONAL GOALS

A monolithic society ruled by a dictator or a ruling class has clearly defined goals toward which the energies of the entire nation are directed, and the school program is designed to contribute to the realization of these goals. During Stalin's regime in the U.S.S.R., for example, all important decisions concerning education were made by the party in control of the national government, and teachers were essentially technicians who translated into practice the directions of this group.[16] The United States, on the other hand, is a pluralistic society; there is no one official agency charged with the responsibility of formulating national goals. According to our concept of democracy, goals evolve gradually from the interaction of individuals and groups; they represent the combined judgments of a majority of citizens at any given time; and they are subject to continuous redefinition and interpretation in terms of rapid changes in American life.

Many groups have made goal statements for the schools. Samplings of the summaries of their goal statements follow.

Commission on Reorganization of Secondary Education

In 1918, the Commission of the National Educational Association issued a report containing the Seven Cardinal Principles of Education. Crucial excerpts

---

[16] George S. Counts and Nucia P. Lodge, *I Want To Be Like Stalin*. (New York: The John Day Company, Inc., 1974), pp. 15–16.

from this report were reprinted and circulated by the millions. The seven cardinal principles were health, command of fundamental process, worthy home membership, vocational competence, citizenship, worthy use of leisure, and ethical character. The inclusion of the areas of health, home, vocation, and avocation helped to legitimate these as appropriate areas of concern for schools. The report also made curriculum recommendations. As a result of this commission's report, the "expanding horizons" organization for the elementary social studies curricula was developed.

The Bobbitt Classification, and the Counts and Chapman Classification

In 1924, John Franklin Bobbitt developed the following classification of human activities for curriculum building purposes: language, health, citizenship, general social activities, spare-time activities, mental fitness, religion, parental activities, and vocational activities. Also in 1924, George S. Counts, the social reconstructionist, and James C. Chapman identified six great interests around which human life revolves. Humans must always care for their bodies, rear their children, secure economic necessities, organize for civic actions, engage in recreation, and satisfy their religious needs. Bobbitt, along with Counts and Chapman, again legitimated the broadening of the schools' concerns to include most aspects of the learner's being.

The Department of Superintendence Classification

In 1928, the Department of Superintendence of the National Education Association identified four general areas of education by listing the relation of individuals: (1) to their own growth and development; (2) to the world of nature; (3) to the systems of organized society and (4) to the Power that in some way orders the development of the individual and the universe. "The individual self, nature, society, and God"—these four, and in particular the adjustments the individual self must make—constitute the objectives of education.

The Educational Policies Commission Classification

"The Purposes of Education in American Democracy," a document issued in 1938 by the Educational Policies Commission of the National Education Association ranks among the influential documents published during the past century concerning schools in America. The Commission stated:

> The general end of education in America at the present time is the fullest possible development of the individual within the framework of our present industrialized democratic society. The attainment of this end is to be observed in individual behavior or conduct.[17]

The report of the Commission identified four aspects of educational objectives. The first area provides a description of the educated person; the second, a de-

---

[17] Educational Policies Commission, "The Purposes of Education in American Democracy." (Washington, D.C.: National Education Association, 1938), p. 41.

scription of the educated member of the family and community group; the third, a description of the educated producer or consumer; and the fourth, a description of the educated citizen.

This statement of educational objectives recognized two functions of education: to produce better, informed citizens, and to change their behavior in relation to important individual and social problems. It is significant that the "fundamental processes" are included under the objectives of self-realization. This reflects the modern concept that these subjects are not ends in themselves but are means to the complete development of the child. If the values implied in this statement of objectives can be implemented in school programs all over the nation, the public school will take its place as the bulwark of a democratic society.

The Mid-Century Committee on Outcomes in Elementary Education

One of the most comprehensive studies of the objectives of elementary education was made by the Mid-Century Committee on Outcomes in Elementary Education, published in 1953.[18] The Committee received suggestions from subject-matter specialists and from specialists on personal development and social maturation. The following curriculum areas were identified: physical development, health, body care; individual social and emotional development; ethical behavior, standards, values; social relations; the social world; the physical world; esthetic development; communications; and quantitative relationships. Outcomes appropriate for children at the third-, sixth-, and ninth-grade levels in each of the nine curriculum areas were listed in terms of knowledge and understanding; skills and competencies; attitudes and interests; and action patterns. This report assumed that education is for the purpose of bringing about desirable changes in behavior, that growth and learning are continuous, and that outcomes are to be considered in terms of the range of abilities found within a group of children at any of the three levels.

The President's Commission on National Goals

President Eisenhower appointed a Commission on National Goals in 1959. The report of this Commission was published in book form in 1960.[19] It presented a platform of basic American goals, including respect for the worth of the individual, equality of opportunity, preserving and perfecting the democratic process, adequate educational opportunities for all Americans, and removal of barriers to full opportunities based on prejudice. The report, however, went far beyond the mere listing of basic American goals; it identified actions which must be taken if these goals are to be achieved.

[18] Nolan C. Kearney, *Elementary School Objectives*. (New York: Russell Sage Foundation, 1953).
[19] *President's Commission on National Goals, Goals for Americans*. (Englewood Cliffs, N.J.: Prentice-Hall, Inc., 1960).

The Educational Policies Commission

In 1962 the Educational Policies Commission published "The Central Purpose of American Education." This statement of purposes was the forerunner of the increasing concern with the intellectual development of children. The EPC proclaimed: "The purpose which runs through and strengthens all other purposes—the common thread of education—is the development of the ability to think."[20] The following statements are excerpts from, "The Central Purposes of American Education."

1. *Whenever an objecive has been judged desirable for the individual or the society, it has tended to be accepted as a valid concern of the school.*

2. *The basic American value, respect for the individual, has led to one of the major charges which the American people have placed on their schools: to foster that development of the individual capacities which will enable each human being to become the best person he is capable of becoming.*

3. *The schools have been designed to serve society's needs.*

4. *No school fully achieves any pupil's goals in the relatively short time he spends in the classroom. The school seeks rather to equip the pupil to achieve them for himself.*

5. *Freedom of the mind is a condition which each individual must develop for himself. In this sense, no man is born free. A free society has the obligation to create circumstances in which all individuals may have opportunity and encouragement to attain freedom of the mind. If this goal is to be achieved, its requirements must be specified.*

6. *The free man, in short, has a rational grasp of himself, his surroundings and the relationship between them.*

7. *The cultivated powers of the free mind have always been basic in achieving freedom. The powers involve the processes for recalling and imagining, classifying and generalizing, comparing and evaluating, analyzing and synthesizing, and deducing and inferring. These processes enable one to apply logic and the available evidence to his ideas, attitudes and actions, and to pursue better whatever goals he may have. This is not to say that the rational powers are all of the life or all of the mind, but they are the essence of the ability to think.*

8. *Thus the rational powers are central to all the other qualities of the human spirit. These powers flourish in a humane and morally responsible context and contribute to the entire personality. The rational powers are to the entire human spirit as the hub is to the wheel.*

9. *The person in whom—for whatever reason—they (rational powers) are not well developed is increasingly handicapped in modern society. Only [to] the extent that an individual can realize his potentials, especially the development of his ability to think, can he fully achieve for himself the dignity that goes with freedom.*

10. *Many profound changes are occurring in the world today, but there is a fundamental force contributing to all of them. That force is the expanding*

---

[20] Educational Policies Commission, "The Central Purpose of American Education." (Washington, D.C.: National Education Association, 1962), p. 12.

role accorded in modern life to the rational powers of man. While man is using the powers of his mind to solve old riddles, which have long intrigued him, he is creating new ones. Basic assumptions upon which mankind has long operated are being challenged or demolished.

11. The rational powers of the human mind have always been basic in establishing and preserving freedom. In furthering personal and social effectiveness they are becoming more important than ever. They are central to dignity, human progress and national survival.

12. The purpose which runs through and strengthens all other educational purposes—the common thread of education—is the ability to think. This is the central purpose to which the school must be oriented if it is to accomplish either its traditional tasks or those newly accentuated by recent changes in the world. To say that it is central is not to say only, but that it must be a pervasive concern in the work of the school. Many agencies contribute to achieving educational objectives, but this particular objective will not be generally attained unless the school focuses on it. In this context, therefore, the development of every student's rational powers must be recognized as centrally important.[21]

President's Science Advisory Committee

In 1964, the President's Science Advisory Committee continued the emphasis started by the Educational Policies Committee in 1962. The Science Advisory Committee report emphasized (1) stimulation of the will to learn—giving students a sense of the pleasure of intellectual work; and (2) creation of general intellectual skills—skills that transcend any particular subject matter. The report stated:

Good education fosters disinterested curiosity and love of understanding, but it also fosters the desire to connect—theory and practice, intelligence and conduct. The Panel believes that today's children must be prepared to cope with new patterns of life, that they must be equipped with good information and trained in viable modes of thinking to create new solutions.[22]

Center for the Study of Education

In 1971 the National Education Association published *Schools for the 70s and Beyond: A Call to Action.*[23] This publication set forth a number of ideas as the basis for a proposed nationwide dialogue concerning the crucial questions of education. The report concluded that the school should promote humane ends:

A school that draws its energy from humanistic values is one that celebrates personal differences and also emphasizes human commonalities; helps the student to understand his antecedents, to grow from them, and finally, to not be restricted by them; encourages superior scholarship which allows the inquirer to contribute to his society and to strengthen his own personality; and provides

[21] Educational Policies Commission, "The Central Purpose of American Education."
[22] President's Science Advisory Committee, *Innovation and Experiment in Education.* (Washington, D.C.; U.S. Government Printing Office, 1964).
[23] *Schools for the 70s and Beyond: A Call to Action.* (Washington, D.C.: National Education Association, Center for the Study of Instruction, 1971).

the resources for the individual to examine his own life so that he can enlarge his maturity and help cause growth in others.[24]

Twilight of the Goals

Harold Shane stated that during the 1970s more than a few Americans speculated that the society was moving into a "Twilight of Goals"[25] which foreshadowed a social and political Armageddon likely to occur in the next decade. Two occurrences may reinforce that speculation: first, no recent statement of goals or purposes has captured the national scene; and secondly, goals are being set through a judicial and legislative process. Several national commissions have issued reports (that is, National Commission on Secondary Education, President's Science Advisory Committee, and the Coleman reports), but none, in the author's judgment, has served to counterbalance the impact of the increased influence of judicially and legislatively established goals.

Goal Development in a Democracy

That democracy is the highest social ideal of United States citizens has been amply demonstrated. The theme of human freedom runs like a bright-colored thread through their literature, art, and music. Although it has been frequently violated in practice, it remains a vital force in education and in government. The idea that the school is the chief formal agency for preserving and improving the democratic way of life is not new. For almost 200 years, wise leaders have been proclaiming that the youth, in order to grow into citizens capable of fostering democracy, must be exposed to an educational program that is suited to a democracy.

Democracy has been repudiated in practice by teachers and school administrators because they have not fully understood its meaning. It has been variously defined as a form of government, as a spirit, and as the right to do as one pleases. It is not surprising that those who hold such limited views of democracy find it difficult to make it work in schools. *Democracy is a process, a quality of human relationships, that has the welfare of the individual as its paramount objective.* In this sense, democracy can operate in any group of individuals, whether it be a nation, a family, a classroom, a factory, or a civic organization. Furthermore, it can be seen in operation, provided one knows what to look for. Some of the essential characteristics of the democratic process are listed in the following sections as yardsticks for school practices. It is the conviction of the author that the success or failure of curriculum improvement programs will be determined by the extent to which these principles are understood and practiced.

The Method of Experimentation

In a democracy, individuals and groups are free to experiment, to work out unique solutions to their problems. This is one of the innate strengths of democ-

[24] National Education Association, *Schools for the 70s and Beyond,* p. 20.
[25] Harold G. Shane, "The Rediscovery of Purpose in Education," in Glen Hass, et al., *Curriculum Planning: A New Approach.* (Boston: Allyn and Bacon, Inc., 1974), pp. 217–221.

Citizens of a democracy need to experience the planning of a social system.

racy. Things are true only if they work out in practice and not merely because someone in authority said they were true. Democratic educational practices give each teacher and each child a chance to experiment, to individual expression, to work out the solution to individual problems under wise guidance. Authoritarian systems, whether in nations or in schools, dig their own graves by suppressing all ideas except those of individuals who are in positions of authority. How much authoritarian teaching can be found in today's classrooms? How free are pupils to experiment? How much authoritarian school administration can be found? How free are teachers to experiment with new methods, new materials, and new ideas? Classrooms and school systems need to be evaluated in terms of these questions if democracy is to be promoted in education.

Equality of Opportunity

Equality of opportunity does not mean equality of possessions or equality of achievement. It simply means that individuals will have an *opportunity to achieve* as much as their individual abilities and efforts permit; that the school will provide opportunities for all children rather than for a selected few. It means that grade standards, promotion policies, or a narrow book-centered curriculum will not stand in the way of helping children develop to the fullest extent whatever talents they have. The school curriculum that provides opportunities for only the intellectual elite is out of harmony with democratic principles. The curriculum that does not offer any challenge to the more capable pupils is likewise undemocratic.

Participation by All Persons Involved in a Given Action

The democratic process broadens the base of judgments on which policies rest. School policies resulting from the combined judgments of all persons involved are more stable than those resulting from the decision of one person. Furthermore, the success of a democracy is strengthened as teachers and children grow in the qualities which result from sharing in the choice of activities to be undertaken and from accepting responsibility for subsequent results. Teachers who recognize their obligation to develop responsible, self-directing citizens will deliberately organize their teaching so that every pupil contributes to the work of the class. Principals who understand and appreciate democratic values organize their work so that every teacher shares in the process of making decisions. It is only through meaningful participation that pupils and teachers grow in the ability to function effectively in democratic group activities.

Faith in People

The great leaders of the past have had faith in the ability of the people to make the right decisions when given adequate information. Democracy in education requires faith in the ability of children to become increasingly self-directing if given enough encouragement and guidance. It also requires faith in the ability of teachers to make intelligent plans for the school program when they are given sound leadership and sufficient time to do the job.

Respect for Personality and Human Worth

In a democracy, human beings are ends rather than means. School practices must be judged according to their effect on the children involved. A school may be very efficient and still be ineffective when evaluated for democratic values. The schools of Nazi Germany were very efficient, but from the standpoint of democratic values they were very ineffective schools. Schools must be evaluated in terms of the quality of living which they foster.

The teachers who wish to evaluate their teaching in the light of the democratic principle of respect for personality should ask themselves the following questions:

1. Do I expect all pupils to measure up to the same standard of conduct and achievement?
2. Am I tolerant of a pupil with an undesirable personality?
3. Is it ever possible for the slower pupils to experience success?
4. Are bright pupils challenged to achieve as much as their abilities permit, rather than merely reaching grade standards?
5. Can a pupil admit lack of information without fear of criticism?

Principals who wish to evaluate their leadership in the light of the democratic principle of respect for personality should ask themselves the following questions:

1. Do I expect all teachers to use the same methods in teaching arithmetic, spelling, and other subjects?
2. Am I patient with a teacher who has difficulty in adjusting to newer procedures but is trying to improve?
3. Do I take time to try to discover the special talents of teachers and compliment them for outstanding achievements?
4. Are important responsibilities distributed among the teachers, or do the most capable ones get all of the interesting and challenging assignments?
5. Do teachers feel free to admit mistakes without fear of criticism?
6. Do I make deliberate efforts to build teacher morale?

Opportunities for the Individual To Learn To Be Free

Discovering and using the methods of democracy involves clear understanding of the nature of freedom and how individuals obtain it. Teachers in the public schools have a particular responsibility for understanding this problem, for they must not only teach the tricks of numbers and the shapes of letters, but they must also help our future citizens learn the ways of democracy.

Freedom is not a gift; it is an achievement. The problem of the teacher is not how to give children freedom but how to help them learn to be free. Children do not learn freedom simply by being released from adult control; neither do they learn it by being held under the complete domination of the teacher from year to year. Freedom is achieved as individuals learn self-control, which frees them from the necessity of social control. In the democratic school there is a decreasing amount of teacher control as children grow older and are able to take more responsibility for their own behavior.

Freedom involves the mastery of skills and techniques. Individuals who cannot spell have little freedom of self-expression in writing; if they have not mastered certain techniques related to form and color, they have little freedom of self-expression in art. Even if we were to regard freedom as the right of children to do as they please, they would still have to learn *how* to do as they please. A school curriculum is democratic to the extent that it helps children learn the skills, attitudes, and information necessary to exist as free persons.

Cooperation for the Common Good

Democracy cannot survive in a group composed of selfish individuals. A school curriculum that stresses competition alone cannot develop citizens capable of sustaining democratic values. The teacher who cannot work effectively as a member of a team, who has not developed the skills of democratic cooperation, has no place in an elementary school. Principals who are interested primarily in promoting themselves, who have not developed the techniques of democratic leadership, are also unfit for their position.

This does not mean, of course, that all competition must be eliminated from the life of the elementary school; some competition is inevitable in school as well as in life outside the school. It simply means that children must learn the skills involved in cooperation as well as those involved in competition if they are to be prepared for effective living in a society that involves both.

The argument is frequently heard that pupils must be trained for competition because they live in a competitive society. The answer is that they also live in a society in which it is necessary for individuals to cooperate with others if they are to accomplish anything worthwhile. Furthermore, the school should help to develop those traits and abilities needed for building a better society, rather than merely perpetuating the undesirable features of the society we now have.

Trends in the Development of Goals

Accountability

Beginning in the 1950s the U.S. Department of Defense began to use a "systems management" approach. This approach called for drawing up specifications of the program product, establishing a timetable for the sequence of subobjectives appropriate for the product, and conducting a cost analysis for every phase of each system sequence. This interrelated systems approach provided for effort coordination, cost control, and management effectiveness. In spite of some tremendous cost overruns within the Department of Defense, the approach became a model for industries and was gradually accepted in school administrations. The apparent inherent efficiency and effectiveness of systems management attracted the attention of legislators who were providing larger and larger appropriations for schools. Taxpayer groups saw in this kind of management a way of increasing the service returns for those tax dollars allocated to public institutions as well as a method for controlling the increasing tax rates.

Complimenting this trend toward systems management was a move to make public institutions more open to public scrutiny. The holding of secret meetings by the governing boards of public institutions and the barring of press representatives from such meetings were ruled inappropriate by many court judgments. The "right of the public to know" became a viable, determined movement (Ralph Nader's work in consumer affairs is an example).

A concomitant effect of the court rulings concerning desegregation of schools was to involve the general public more directly in both the management and programs of schools. The provision for an increasing amount of federal monies for categorical aid to specific curriculum areas or designated groups of pupils served to call the public's attention to the "claimed" inadequacies within these segments of the school program. The energies and directions of the new critics were transmitted to the public through the news media, slick magazines, and popular trade books. Education and schools became news: first *from fear*—the Russians are ahead of us in education (see the discussion of Sputnik in Chapter 1); and then *from concern*—the role of schools in desegregating society. The schools became public business.

In many states these forces and trends culminated in legislative acts establishing "accountability" programs. The application of the concept of accountability to schools received its impetus during the late 1960s, according to Leon Lessinger, an official in the U.S. Office of Education. Accountability programs were intended to directly involve the public with the professional in the determination of the goals and priorities for schools. They were to filter empirical data back to the public, reporting the relationship between the schools' performances and these goals and priorities. The nature of the legislative acts varied from those that prescribed a standardized testing program to others that provided the machinery for involving the professional with the public in the determination of needs, goals, and performances.

Just as legislative acts providing for accountability programs vary, so do the present definitions of accountability. The range of definitions can be represented by the following samples:

A. *The requirement of the occupant of a role by those who authorize that role, to answer for the results of work expected from him in the role.*[26]

B. *Accountability . . . may be defined as an assignable, measurable responsibility to be fulfilled under certain conditions and with certain constraints.*[27]

C. 1. *Accountability is a process that occurs in a relationship between those entrusted with the accomplishment of specific tasks (stewards) and those having power of review (reviewers).*

2. *The heart of the processes for the party standing to account (the steward) to explain as rationally as possible the results of the efforts to achieve the specific task objectives of his stewardship.*

3. *Of major concern to the parties reviewing the stewardship of the tasks performed in the matching of performance and attainment levels against their expectations as expressed in the task specifications and determining their level of confidence in the steward and his efforts.*

4. *Of major concern to the steward standing to account in his ability to accomplish the specified tasks as well as his ability to explain attainment levels in a manner that maintains or builds the reviewer's confidence in his stewardship.*[28]

The trend to legislate accountability programs may be diminishing. Yet, the majority of states either have enacted legislation or have legislation pending which establishes accountability programs. Whatever, the legislative enactment of accountability programs is creating a dichotomous grouping within both the community and educators. For one group, accountability systems represent a powerful value tool; for the other group, accountability systems represent a dangerous or threatening weapon. Accountability systems are so varied that both groups are partially correct and perhaps differ only in which part of the elephant they are seeing.

For example, those people who view accountability systems as a valuable

26 A. D. Newman and R. W. Rowbottom, *Organization Analysis.* (Carbondale, Ill.: Southern Illinois University Press, 1968), p. 26.

27 Russell B. Valranderen and Arthur P. Ludka, "Evaluating Education in a Changing Society, An Emerging State's Responsibilities for Education," in E. L. Morphet and D. L. Jessen (Eds.), *Improving State Leaderships in Education.* (Denver, Colo.: Colorado State Department of Education, 1970), p. 145.

28 Lesley H. Brosder, Jr., William A. Atkins, Jr., and Esin Kaya, *Developing an Educationally Accountable Program.* (Berkeley, Calif.: McCutchan Publishing Corp., 1973), p. 6.

tool may be perceiving a saw for cutting off unproductive appendages of schooling, while those who view it as a weapon may be perceiving a saw used willfully and arbitrarily to cut off preselected appendages of schooling.

Accountability and its related programs, systems management programs, behavioral objectives, performance-based contracting, and others are realities. Those aspects of accountability programs that enable the professional and the public to cooperatively plan goals and priorities seem desirable. The need for schools to become more explanatory to the student and the public concerning its intended outcomes seems reasonable. However, what may be threatening is an imposed set of goals, a limited set of intended outcomes, the negotiation with a pluralistic society for a common set of goals, or simply a visible accountability system for the powers and responsibilities of schools. Chapter 13 includes a discussion of accountability as part of an evaluation program.

SITUATION 2.4   After investigating several current methodologies practiced and disciplining techniques being utilized within the elementary schools, discuss those you believe will increase the likelihood of goal development in a democracy.

Federal Control

Goals for United States elementary schools are currently being established through the actions of the federal government. The federal government, especially through judicial rulings and legislation, has established the desegregation of our society as a goal. The enactment of federal legislation which provides funds for the establishment of special curriculum programs for selected ethnic groups, economic classifications, or disabled learners results in the establishment of these programs as goal priorities. Judicial rulings, legislative programs, and the regulatory provisions of congressional acts all result in the shaping and establishing of goals for the public schools.

It is appropriate for the courts and legislatures to utilize the school as the agent to implement selected goals which effect desirable changes within our society. The school is our government's creation, and within our representative democracy the government should represent all the people, but a disequilibrium results from dispersal of control among federal, state, and local authorities. Essentially, schools are agencies of state governments, but states have traditionally established only minimal regulatory requirements within which local units must operate. Compounding this lack of coordination are the recent activities of the federal government, which have introduced a new level of control by formulating and imposing regulatory requirements. Thus, federal intervention conflicts with the traditional concept of local control. Moreover, it tends to demand and require, leaving local school authorities to impose compliance upon its local community and to negotiate community adaptations with a distant, but distinct, level of control.

Those who argue for acceptance of this new federal level of control see a need for a powerful intervention to counterbalance the inertia, lack of perspective, and vested interests which characterize local control. Would local control, for example, have eventually provided a compensatory program for children from economically disadvantaged family units? Would local control have perpetuated the more traditional pattern of distributing monies in a manner which may not have reflected the educational needs of its community? Would the vested interests of a community have prevented a local response to the potential role(s) of schools in the desegregation of society?

Those who argue against the intervention of federal goal determination and regulation argue from one of two positions. First, rather than counterbalance the weaknesses which may exist within a system of local control, federal intervention has served to unbalance the dynamics of control. Such a position maintains that a creeping federalism is becoming the dominant controlling agency. The position calls for federal participation with less control. The second position argues that local control was working and would have continued to work; therefore, federal intervention is unwise, unnecessary, and inappropriate. This position calls for the federal government to supply additional resources to be used at the discretion of the local agency.

SUMMARY

1. The broad outlines of an elementary curriculum for the second half of the twentieth century will be determined to a large extent by the realities of the age in which we live.

2. Curriculum workers must be students of contemporary United States society; they must look for clues to its nature in the conditions, trends, practices, and aspirations of its citizens.

3. The anthropologist, the sociologist, the political scientist, and specialists in other disciplines can supply information that will help shape an effective educational program.

4. Curriculum making must be a continuous process if schools are to keep pace with rapidly changing conditions in our society.

5. Curriculum planning must take into account the interdependence of contemporary life and the changes that are taking place in the family.

6. Curriculum decisions must be based on sound information about the population explosion, the shifts in age distribution, and the shifts in population centers.

7. Curriculum planning must take into account the fact that the United States is a prosperous nation, in an era of broadening opportunity and in an age in which many of the world's people do not share the same general prosperity.

8. New adventures in international affairs place a heavy obligation on the schools to prepare children for intelligent world citizenship.

9. Curriculum planning needs to take into account the forces working in this era to increase the responsibilities of the federal government and the extent to which education is a factor in the economic strength of the nation.

10. National goals are subject to continuous redefinition and refinement.

Problems and Projects

1. In 1939, Harold Benjamin candidly brought to the attention of educators the needs for educational reform in a changing society. Thirty years later, George Leonard wrote, "Civilization as it has existed for 15,000 years is ending, and a new kind of order, a new kind of education are upon us."[29] Read *The Saber-Tooth Curriculum* by Harold Benjamin and *Education and Ecstasy* by George B. Leonard. List the philosophical agreements and disagreements between these authors regarding the position of education amid a changing society.

2. As a "future shocked" society struggles to redefine and restructure the concept of work, so must educators—not only for themselves, but also for the relevancy of those tasks which will invade the time of students. Interview ten elementary school children. Inquire as to what activities they consider work and what activities they consider fun. Have the students classify the named activities into two categories:

    a. Those activities participated in at school.

    b. Those activities participated in away from school.

Ask the children what work activities they would like to do at school, and what fun activities they would prefer. What are your conclusions? What recommendations would you make to elementary teachers as they search to restructure the concept of work, both themselves and within their classrooms?

3. This chapter has attempted to provide the reader with a classification system which should enable the reader to interpret and evaluate more objectively the messages of the critics. Read recent literature by critics of the schools, such as those identified within the chapter. What alternatives do they propose? Classify these individuals as

    a. uncritical lover.

    b. unloving critic.

    c. critical lover.

Support the justification of your classifications.

Selected Readings

Benjamin, Harold, *The Saber-Tooth Curriculum*. New York: McGraw-Hill, Inc., 1939. Remains a classic among the efforts to explain the impact of environmental changes on the curriculum.

Coleman, James Samuel, et al., *Equality of Educational Opportunity*. Washington, D.C.: U.S. Department of Health, Education and Welfare, Office of Education, U.S. Printing Office, 1966. The Coleman report dominated the programs of the late 1960s and early 1970s, which were designed to educate disadvantaged youths.

Committee on Educational Finance, *Financial Status of Public Schools*. Washington, D.C.: National Education Association, published annually. Includes data on population trends, enrollments and employment in schools, and expenditures and sources of revenue for schools.

Counts, George S., *Dare the Schools Build a New Social Order?* New York: Random House & Crown Publishers (Arno Press, Inc.), 1969. A classic statement of the school's role in building a society.

[29] Leonard, p. 81.

Della-Dora, Delmo, and James House (Eds.), *Education for an Open Society*. Yearbook of the Association for Supervision and Curriculum Development. Washington, D.C.: Association for Supervision and Curriculum Development, 1974. A thoughtful series of statements relating how schools may contribute to the self-realization of individuals and society.

Dennison, George, *The Lives of Children*. New York: Random House, Inc., 1970. An account of the author's work in an inner-city school and his efforts to develop a "free school."

Myrdal, Gunnar, "American Values and American Behavior: A Dilemma," in James P. Shaver and Harold Berlak, *Democracy, Pluralism, and the Social Studies*. Boston: Houghton Mifflin Company, 1968, pp. 86–97. Contains an excellent discussion of American ideals.

Ragan, William B., and George Henderson, *Foundations of American Education*. New York: Harper & Row, Publishers, 1970. Part IV deals with environmental influences on children who grow up in poverty.

Toffler, Alvin, *Future Shock*. New York: Random House, Inc., 1970. A penetrating discussion of projected changes and the psychological impact of these changes.

chapter 3

Influencing CHILDREN

The person, insofar as he is a real person, is his own main determinant.
Every person is, in part, "his own project" and makes himself. The process
of growth (development) is the process of becoming *a person. Being a person*
is different.

From A. H. Maslow, "Perceiving, Behaving, Becoming: A New Focus
for Education," *Yearbook, 1962.* (Washington, D.C.: Association
for Supervision and Curriculum Department, 1962), p. 234.

This chapter is concerned with three aspects of children's potential: growth,
learning, and development. The contributions of the biological sciences that are
relevant to growth, the contributions of psychology that are relevant to learning, and the contributions of curriculum study that are relevant to development
will be reviewed. To present information about growth, learning, and development, a separation of these aspects has been contrived. This is not to imply that
there is an actual separation. To the contrary, a child is a total, whole being who
always acts and interacts among and within these aspects of growth, learning,
and development. The idea that those who plan school programs for children
should seek guidance from a study of children themselves has been the central
theme of much that has been written about education in the past. Rousseau
complained in 1780, "The wisest writers devote themselves to what a man ought
to know, without asking what a child is capable of learning."[1] The theme was
prominent in the writings of John Dewey both before and after 1900 and more
recently in the writings of Robert Gagné, Carl Rogers, Lawrence Kohlberg,
A. H. Maslow, Jean Piaget, and others.

GROWTH—LEARNING—DEVELOPMENT

The terms growth, learning, and development are found again and again as
one examines the literature relating to child study. An understanding of the

[1] Jean-Jacques Rousseau, *Emile*, trans. by Barbara Foxley. (New York: E. P. Dutton & Co.
Inc., 1950), p. 3.

Three aspects of children—growth, learning, and development.

meaning of each and of the relationships among them is therefore central to the task of curriculum planning.

Growth is a characteristic that is shared by all living things. It is generally used to denote increases in the amount of something, such as height, weight, and the size of muscles. It is influenced to a large extent, although not entirely, by factors within the learner.

Learning, on the other hand, refers to changes in the behavior of an individual which occur as the result of the interaction between the individual and the environment. Gagné stated, "Learning is a change in human disposition or capability, which can be retrained, and which is not simply ascribable to the process of growth.[2] He explains that the kind of change called *learning* is exhibited in a change in behavior. What is learned is deduced and inferred from existing or changing behavioral patterns.

Development is a general term used to denote changes which result from the combined influence of growth and learning. Child development is such a broad field that special segments of it are sometimes selected for intensive study. Thus, we have volumes dealing with intellectual development, social development, and emotional development. This should not be taken to mean that these phases are independent phenomena. More specifically, it should not be taken to mean that learning is confined to the accumulation of information and skills relating to school subjects. Gagné, whose writing illustrates the current emphasis on intellectual development, has explained, "The reader needs to be made aware [also] that there are some problems of great importance to education which cannot be solved by applying a knowledge of the principles of learning as they

[2] Robert M. Gagné, *The Conditions of Learning,* 2d ed. (New York: Holt, Rinehart and Winston, 1970), p. 3.

are described here."[3] He mentions particularly attitudes and values as aspects which are developmental.

Growth

The increase in size, weight, height, coordination, strength, and other male and female characteristics is primarily a function of the child's heredity. Yet, environment makes a significant contribution to maximizing or minimizing of the potential imparted through heredity. Nutrition and physical utilization have long been recognized as influences complementary to heredity. Undernourished, inactive children tend to experience less growth than well-nourished active children. Typically, a learner's potential is underestimated, while the range of experience is overestimated.

Leonard has presented a summary of an impressive array of experiments in which electric shock and chemicals have been used to stimulate the functioning (growth) of the brain, change behavior, and increase the individual's ability to give long and intense attention to a problem. He concluded that anything that can be done by these artificial devices can be done better by the activity defined as education. He said:

> Now, for the first time, mankind has gained the physical, technological ability to create almost any kind of environment he can imagine. . . . We are now capable—without brain machines, without drugs, without eugenics—of educating people so that, not the few, but the many would appear to our present perceptions as geniuses of thinking, perceiving, feeling and being.[4]

David Krech reported findings of research in brain biochemistry and behavior which he believed have favorable consequences for education, provided educators supply learning experiences which prepare the individual for the work of the biochemist. He said, "Educators probably change brain structure and chemistry to a greater degree than any biochemist in the business."[5]

Learning

No one theory of learning provides an adequate basis for structuring the curriculum to foster the fullest development of human potential. Two approaches to the nature of learning have been influential in the development of new curricula for the modern elementary school. Curriculum organization and teaching procedures may be based upon S-R (stimulus-response) association and field theories. Teaching and curriculum practices often include concepts from each of these. Both provide an understanding of how learning occurs in human beings.

S-R Association Approach

The S-R approach includes conditioning theories of learning. The statements which follow are among the general assumptions of the S-R association approach

[3] Gagné, p. 25.

[4] George B. Leonard, *Education and Ecstasy*. (New York: Delacorte Press, 1968), p. 40.

[5] David Krech, "Psychoneurobiochemeducation," *Phi Delta Kappan*, March 1969, p. 373.

and explanations of learning known as conditioning, stimulus-response, behaviorism, associationism, and connectionism. The S-R approach holds that a person acquires new responses through a conditioning process. This conditioning process is called "learning." The urge to act (motivation or drive) results from a stimulus. Behavior (response) is directed by a stimulus, usually from the environment. The learner's selection of one response over another results from a particular combination of conditioning and psychological drives operating at that moment. Within the S-R theories, the basic learning unit is a rewarded response. A reward may be different from moment to moment, and from learner to learner. To be a reward, it must be important, pleasant, and satisfying to the learner. The S-R theories are cause-and-effect oriented.

Behavior modification means to increase the frequency of a desired behavior (response) through reward while decreasing or extinguishing the frequency of an undesired behavior (response) through punishment or lack of recognition. The learner must first experience a situation in which the desired behavior occurs; then, he must recognize the two behaviors (desired and undesired); and finally, he must pair the reward with the desired behavior. Initially, the teacher identifies the kind of behavior to be increased, decreased, or extinguished. Secondly, the teacher must identify the situation in which the target behavior occurs, as well as the present frequency of occurrence. Thirdly, the teacher must establish a pattern of rewarding, disapproving, or ignoring the target behavior. Finally, the teacher must evaluate the increase or decrease in the target behavior to determine if the system is complete. Behavior modification is the conscious management of the environment of the learner.

B. F. Skinner is usually credited with having developed the behavior modification system. In *Beyond Freedom and Dignity*, he presented both the system and its rationale.[6] Prior to Skinner's development of the system of behavior modification, he was recognized as one of the major contributors to the development of teaching machines, that is, devices that presented programmed instructions.

In 1954, Skinner and his associates developed a number of systematic programs based on the premise that immediate positive reinforcement was more effective than delayed reinforcement or punishment in influencing learning. They maintained that pupils learn in gradual steps and that positive reinforcement occurs when a learner gets the right answer and immediately finds that it is right.

The teaching machines and programmed instructions were regarded by advocates as vehicles for helping pupils learn more, helping pupils to become more actively involved in their learning, and helping teachers to free their time for the more creative aspects of teaching and learning. Opponents of the system maintained that these vehicles dehumanized education, limited the creativity of teachers, and subjected pupils to a form of academic force-feeding.[7] The debate concerning the efficiency, effectiveness, and impact of teaching machines, pro-

---

[6] B. F. Skinner, *Beyond Freedom and Dignity*. (New York: Alfred A. Knopf, Inc., 1971).

[7] William C. Kvaraceus, in Maurie Hillson, *Elementary Education: Current Issues and Research*. (New York: The Free Press, 1967), chap. 20.

grammed instruction, and educational technology is a vigorous and continuing one.

The S-R association approach to learning theory is a mechanistic, cause-and-effect explanation which emphasizes parts, subparts, and gradual steps in a controlled sequencing. It has had tremendous influence upon education.

Field Theory Approach *accepted theory*

The field theory approach includes the explanations of learning known as perceptual psychology; gestalt field, cognitive field, third-force psychology; and humanistic psychology. Abraham Maslow, Carl R. Rogers, Earl C. Kelly, and Arthur W. Combs have made contributions to the field theory approach.[8] These psychologists and others who have contributed to the theory state that "wholeness" is primary. Learning moves from the total aspects of a situation to the particulars and back to the whole. Another premise is that the whole is greater than the sum of its parts (gestalt). For example, seeing a motion picture is perceiving more than the thousands of still frames of pictures that make up the movie.

Particularly important to perceptual psychology is the idea that behavior and learning are functions of perception. The individual's perceptions result in meanings which most effect the possible learnings. Self-concept is central and functions as a dominant influence over the nature of an individual's perceptions and resulting meanings. Within the cognitive/perceptual/gestalt field explanations, the basic units of learning are the meaningfulness of the whole, the importance of generalizations, the principles and organizations in learning, personal meanings, and the significance of the self-concept.

In the perceptual-cognitive field of learning position, man acts, originates, and thinks, and this is the most important source of his learning. In the S-R conditioning theory, man learns by reaction to forces outside himself.[9]

From the field theory approach, the focus of education would be upon the development of an adequate, fully functioning person—one who has a positive self-concept, is open to experiences, can relate to a wide range of individuals, and has available a broad perceptual field. The concept of a self-actualizing person is fundamental to the field theory approaches.

SITUATION 3.1   What are the most efficient, effective means of instruction? View educational programs geared to children in your locale (that is, "Sesame Street," "The Electric Company," "Mister Rogers," and so on). To what theories of learning (field theory or S-R association) would you link the programs or aspects of the programs? Identify specific examples of learning activities to support your decisions.

---

[8] Association for Supervision and Curriculum Development, NEA, "Perceiving, Behaving, Becoming: A New Focus for Education," *Yearbook, 1962.* (Washington, D.C.: Association for Supervision and Curriculum Development, 1962).

[9] Glen Hass, Joseph Bondi, and Jon Wiles, *Curriculum Planning: A New Approach.* (Boston: Allyn and Bacon, Inc., 1974), p. 113.

Principles of Learning

A wide gap exists between current knowledge of the nature of the learning process and actual practice in most elementary school classrooms. Principles of learning accepted for decades are still often violated in many classrooms. The principles discussed here are among those commonly disregarded.

RELATIONSHIP OF ACTIVITIES TO PUPIL PURPOSES

The activities in which children engage in classrooms take on unity and meaning when they are closely related to purposes that are real to children. Such activities call forth greater effort on the part of pupils and foster the development of initiative, originality, and self-direction—qualities that are recognized as essential in a democratic society.

Pupil purposes serve the functions of organizing, vitalizing, and relating the activities in which children engage. It is the responsibility of the teacher, therefore, to utilize purposes that children already have and to reveal to them purposes they can understand and accept. This does not mean that the teacher is helpless when confronted by a group of children who do not have clearly defined purposes. The teacher can create situations that cause children to realize the need for certain abilities. Such a situation exists, for example, in a unit of work when a child wants to paint an object a certain color. Instead of beginning with a lesson on the blending of color, the teacher helps the children experiment with the blending of various colors in response to their needs for a certain color.

It is a misconception of modern education to assume that pupil purposes constitute both the means and ends of education. Many things must be learned, simply because of the demands of living in the world as it is. In addition to utilizing purposes that children already have, the teacher has the responsibility of helping pupils develop worthwhile purposes. Pupil purposes must come from somewhere, and since teachers have a broader background of experience, they have the same obligation to make suggestions for worthwhile undertakings that the master carpenter has for making suggestions to the apprentice. Pupil purposes are the means rather than the ends of education. They cannot tell us where we should go; they can only help us to get there.

THE CONTINUITY OF GROWTH AND LEARNING

Children have been growing and learning for several years before they enter school. Teachers are giving more attention to what children already know when they enter school and are making greater efforts to relate school learning to what has already taken place. After children enter school, they continue to learn during the hours spent out of school. More consideration is being given to what they learn out of school, and school experiences are being related more closely to that knowledge. The problem of providing continuity in these learning experiences will be treated in detail in Chapters 5 and 6.

THE UNIQUENESS OF RATE OF LEARNING

Individual differences among children have been recognized for several decades. In a physical contest, no one would think of pitting a child who weighs only 80 pounds against another who weighs 150 pounds. Yet, in spite of the findings of research relating to individual differences, school practices are still largely geared to the class-as-a-whole procedure.

Elementary schools which have advanced beyond the talk stage in meeting individual differences are eliminating the competitive marking system; adopting newer practices with regard to grouping, promoting, and reporting on the progress of pupils; substituting developmental tasks for minimum grade standards; providing each teacher with a supply of reading materials of varying levels of difficulty; and modifying teaching procedures to permit students to find the group and the activity that is best suited to their individual interests and abilities.

In their attempts to cope with individual differences, elementary schools in the past have, by and large, concentrated on slow and average learners and have neglected the gifted child. Since Sputnik, however, there has been increasing concern about children with high intellectual ability, and a number of plans have been advanced for these children. Unfortunately, misconceptions have also developed; one of these lies in the definition of "gifted." In our present efforts to provide for the brightest, many children are being mistakenly labeled as "gifted." In some school systems, classrooms bearing the label "gifted class" are being set up, with an intelligence quotient of 120 as the floor for entrance to the special class. Yet, in the present generation of test-wise children, an intelligence quotient of 120 is hardly remarkable. Since the minimum IQ for successful completion of a good college is estimated to be about 120, some children mistakenly labeled as gifted may be terribly disillusioned later in their school careers when they find themselves in the bottom half of their college graduating class. A more realistic floor for intellectual excellence would be an intelligence quotient of 150.

It is not an impossible task for teachers to accommodate children with intelligence quotients of 120, 130, or even 140 within the self-contained classroom of the elementary school. Translated into grade scores, this means that a third-grade teacher must plan for some children who can do beginning fourth- or fifth-grade work, and—at the most—an occasional individual who can do sixth-grade work. Grouping for instruction in some subjects, which most teachers do anyway, and providing advanced learning materials for fast learners are relatively simple adjustments in any grade.

Whether special classes or schools for gifted children (IQ of 150 or above) should be set up depends upon many factors. Where these classes do exist, whether a child should be placed in one depends upon the maturity of the child, distance to the special class, and adjustment of the child, as well as intellectual ability. However, since these children are rare (150 IQ occurs once in 1,000 cases; 180 IQ once in one million), only very large communities or communities with unusual populations (for example, a university community) have enough gifted pupils at any one grade level to make special classes feasible. Most school systems must attempt to meet the needs of these children in other ways.

LEARNING SEVERAL THINGS AT ONCE

Children do not learn only one thing in a given situation. This is the familiar principle of concomitant learning. The learning that is supposed to be incidental to the main task is frequently as important as the material to be learned. The personality effects that flow from the learning experience are of major importance. If the process of learning to read is so unpleasant that the child never wants to read again, there is a need to reexamine the teaching procedure.

ADJUSTING THE TASK TO THE CHILD'S LEVEL OF MATURITY

All children who are six years of age are not equally ready for a formal program of reading instruction. The rush to see that every child has acquired a vocabulary of a specified number of words by Thanksgiving and that every child has completed a given number of readers by the end of the first year in school results in overlooking completely the differences in maturity levels existing among children of the same chronological age. To expect more of children than they are mature enough to accomplish is harmful; to fail to challenge children to work up to the limit of their capacities is equally harmful. If kindergartners are ready to read, they should be taught to do so.

Experiments in the teaching of arithmetic have shown that it is a waste of time and effort to try to teach concepts and processes before the child is mature enough to profit from the experience. These experiments have resulted in the postponement of certain topics and processes to later in the school program. Why pay a high price for strawberries in February when they will be much cheaper in June? On the other hand, there is evidence that bright children become bored with too slow a pace and form habits that waste their time. These children also need tasks that are adjusted to their maturity.

LIFELIKE EXPERIENCES

The best learning situation is the one in which children participate, under the guidance of the teacher, in the solution of problems. Children formerly learned most of the things they needed to know by actual participation in the work that parents were doing. As this situation changed and children had to learn in school most of the things they needed to know, it became difficult to retain this type of learning by doing. Schools came to depend more and more on learning from books, and less and less on learning through participation in real-life experiences. Someone once said, "A curse came upon learning with the invention of printing."

SITUATION 3.2   Interview a kindergarten or first-grade teacher who has been teaching for the past ten or more years. Questions should be related to the changes observed by the teacher in the nature of learners upon entry into school, the degree of readiness experiences the learners bring, and the teacher's personal viewpoints related to factors influencing change. What accommodations in curricula has the teacher observed? Were these accommodations an outgrowth of the changes in the nature of the learners, parental pressures, school personnel, or other influences?

There has been a trend in recent years to introduce more of this "home" type of learning into the school program. By the use of audio-visual resources, excursions, school gardens, care of pets in school, school clubs, and various types of problem-solving activities, modern elementary schools are bringing more real-life activities into the curriculum.

Development

Changes which result from the combined influences of growth and learning are called "developmental changes," or changes in development. The development of a child includes such a broad field that the classical subareas of development (intellectual, psychological, and social) will be utilized. The utilization of these subareas to discuss development is for convenience since the traditional position of their independent functioning is no longer accepted. Also, reference to opinions of a current authority within any one of these subareas may slightly distort that authority's viewpoint because current writers tend to express their views in terms of the gestalt in moral, affective, or basic needs development. The classical area of social development seems to have evolved into a framework more acceptable to today's authorities. This author elects to categorize the current theories because he believes that they emphasize specific aspects of human development. Therefore, placing these authorities in classical subareas reminds the reader of the difficulties of explaining human development as a gestalt or as parts. For the reader, however, these parts may form the elements of a self-directing gestalt.

Intellectual Development

Recent innovations in elementary school instructional programs have been stimulated by the many inquiries into the nature of the intellectual development of children. Can many children begin the learning of "difficult" subjects much earlier than has been supposed? Is there a critical period in the life of children when what they will achieve in school and what kind of person they will become are determined to a large degree? What is the role of intelligence? How is the structure of knowledge related to learning? What conditions influence learning by inquiry? To what extent can the school foster critical thinking? Curriculum workers are becoming increasingly dependent upon research in the area of intellectual development in dealing with problems raised by these questions. It is appropriate, therefore, to call attention to some of the significant contributions of research in this area.

THE CRUCIAL PERIOD

Early childhood is the crucial period in the intellectual development of individuals. The quality of the perceptual and verbal experiences of children in their early years determines to a great extent their achievements in later years. Worth pointed out that the "critical-years hypothesis" is not new, but that there is a great deal of new evidence to support it.[10] He cited studies which revealed that

---

[10] W. H. Worth, "The Critical Years," in *The Canadian Administrator*. (Edmonton, Canada: University of Alberta, January 1965).

(1) approximately 50 percent of general school achievement attained at grade 12 has been reached by the end of the third grade; (2) in terms of intelligence measured at age 17, about 50 percent of the development takes place between conception and age 4, about 30 percent between ages 4 and 8, and about 20 percent between ages 8 and 17; (3) language structures and speaking habits of many children are almost completely set in the early years; (4) for boys particularly, the period between the ages of six and ten is the crucial time for the crystallization of the desire for task mastery and intellectual competence; and (5) the qualifications and salaries of elementary teachers correlate more highly with retention rate than do those of secondary teachers. Worth's data strongly supported the following measures: extending school services for children under six years of age; providing more adequate guidance services at the elementary school level; permitting pupils to progress through the school program according to their own rates of learning; and improving the quality of instruction in the kindergarten and primary grades.

Robert J. Havighurst supplied a definition of a "developmental task" as:

> . . . a task which arises at or about a certain period in the life of an individual, successful achievement of which leads to happiness and to success with later tasks, while failure leads to unhappiness in the individual, disapproval by the society, and difficulty with later tasks.[11]

Havighurst identified developmental tasks from biological, psychological, and cultural basis in a sequence from infancy to old age. From his listing, examples of tasks necessary for intellectual development are: infancy—learning to talk, forming simple concepts of social and physical reality; middle childhood—developing fundamental skills in reading, writing, and calculating; adolescence—selecting and preparing for an occupation, developing intellectual skills and concepts necessary for social competence. Havighurst's listing of developmental tasks served to identify the school's purposes, along with the society's, in helping the individual achieve certain developmental tasks.

An additional value of the concept of developmental tasks and the three crucial periods was stated by Havighurst in terms of "teachable moments": "When the body is ripe, and society requires, and self is ready to achieve a certain task, the teachable moment has come."[12] According to Havighurst, efforts at premature teaching of a developmental task are largely wasted. If, however, teaching coincides with the teachable moment for a developmental task, efficient and effective outcomes will occur.

David P. Ausbel said that it is difficult to cite specific instances in which developmental principles have provided definitive answers to curriculum problems.[13] Yet these principles are powerful tools for the generalized planning of curriculum. Ausbel used the term "optimal age" in a fashion similar to Havig-

---

[11] Robert J. Havighurst, *Developmental Tasks and Education.* (New York: David McKay Co., Inc., 1972), p. 2.
[12] Havighurst, p. 5.
[13] David P. Ausbel, "Viewpoints from Related Disciplines: Human Growth and Development," *Teachers College Record,* LX, No. 5 (February 1959), pp. 245–254.

hurst's "teachable moment." In Ausbel's discussion of optimal age, he agreed with Havighurst that to postpone learning beyond the optimal age, or to prematurely expose a learning task before the optimal age, wastes time; furthermore, postponement may develop emotional attitudes not conducive to later learning.

CHANGING VIEWS ABOUT INTELLIGENCE

Not long ago most teachers assumed that a score on an intelligence test represented "native intelligence"; that intellectual capacity was inherited and could not be altered by changing the learning environment. These notions about the nature of intelligence are now regarded as sheer nonsense.[14] Piaget takes the position that intelligence grows as the individual interacts with his environment.[15] Hunt expressed the belief that ". . . we might raise the average level of intelligence during the next generation or two by about 30 points of IQ—provided we reach children early enough."[16] It is difficult for us to imagine what this could mean in terms of developing a truly educated society.

Our new knowledge about children is illustrated by what is called the "self-fulfilling prophecy." When teachers assume, even before they have seen the pupils, that they have a "slow learning" group, the pupils tend to perform according to the teachers' expectations.[17] Many minority-group children may therefore be deprived of the opportunity of developing their full potential because of the low expectations of teachers.

SITUATION 3.3   How do we learn? Some men have devoted major portions of their life to the observation, experimentation, and behavioral analyzation of learners. Read articles written by B. F. Skinner or about B. F. Skinner's behavioral reinforcement, stimulus-response theory. Contrast or compare Skinner's theory of learning to the theories of Piaget.

PIAGET'S THEORY OF HOW INTELLECT DEVELOPS

A section on the intellectual development of children would not be complete today without the inclusion of a discussion of the contribution of Jean Piaget. Piaget, a Swiss psychologist who had been working in Geneva for over fifty years, attempted to trace the development of intelligence from birth to adolescence. He and his colleague, Mlle. Inhelder, devised a series of ingenious techniques to get at the thinking processes of children. They presented the child with a task demanding a logical solution and analyzed the child's answers. From

14 William B. Ragan and George Henderson, *Foundations of American Education.* (New York: Harper & Row, Publishers, 1970), chap. 6.

15 Jean Piaget, *The Psychology of Intelligence.* (New York: Harcourt Brace Jovanovich, Inc., 1950).

16 John K. Lagemann, "Can We Make Human Beings More Intelligent?" *The Reader's Digest* (May 1966), p. 77.

17 Robert Rosenthal and Lenore Jacobson, *Pygmalion in the Classroom.* (New York: Holt, Rinehart and Winston, 1968).

their research, they put together a picture of how logical intelligence (cognition) develops.

A graduate class of elementary school teachers observed a six-year-old boy perform on one of Piaget's tasks. The boy was shown a box of wooden beads, most of which were red, but two of which were yellow. It was established by questioning that all of the beads were made of wood, that some of the beads were both red and wooden, and two were yellow and wooden. All of this the child understood. Then the experimenter said, "Are there more red beads or more wooden beads?" The boy answered, "More red beads because there are only two yellow ones." The experimenter reviewed the facts so far, and the boy asserted that, yes, all beads were made of wood. Then the question was rephrased in terms of the comparative length of a necklace made of wood and one made of red beads. Again the subject insisted that the red one would be longer because there were only two yellow ones.

In the discussion that followed the teachers expressed dismay that a six-year-old could give answers so obviously wrong. They insisted that the boy really had the ability to solve the task and that he was merely confused by the language. "He didn't listen carefully enough," was the usual explanation. According to Piaget's theory, if the task were to be repeated, perhaps in a different format but one where the distinction between "all" and "some" was still crucial, the boy would fail again.

The boy understood the facts in the problem, but when he was asked to compare the whole with a part, he lost sight of the whole and compared a part with a part.

SITUATION 3.4   Piaget's studies should not be taken to mean that logical thinking appears suddenly at age 12, without any effort on the part of the teacher. A class of sixth-year pupils in a low-income area of a large city was planning a model city. The pupils had a central committee and separate committees for each of the services the city would need to provide. The tentative plan called for locating the industrial area on the west side and the residential area on the east side of the city. One pupil pointed out that the prevailing winds were from the west. He said, "Last night after I went to bed I kept imagining that I could smell packing town. We have to do something about that." What light does this situation throw on the problem of logical thinking? What does it indicate about getting pupils involved in the solution of problems?

Another common reaction of teachers when they hear a pupil giving a wrong answer is that there is something peculiar to the apparatus that induces such a response. A ten-year-old girl was given two metal cylinders to hold, identical in size, but one weighing twice as much as the other. She was asked to predict what would happen when each was immersed in a separate beaker of water. She predicted that the heavier one would make the water level go up higher. "It pushes harder on the water and pushes more up," she said. She was then asked to insert each cylinder in its beaker, and was astounded to see that the water in each container moved upward to exactly the same level. Again the observer found it hard to accept the lack of logic in the child, and in this case argued that the pupil was thinking wrongly about the problem because she was accustomed to associating metal cylinders with the weights used in two-plan balances.

To the mature adult, the illogic of the child in incomprehensible. Despite teachers' professional sophistication, they *expect* children to give the right answers to seemingly simple problems. It is disconcerting, to say the least, to have a child so steadfastly adhere to what is logically not possible, and when the child does give "wrong" answers, the adult is even more at a loss as to what to do next than the teacher is in the classroom. At least in teaching a class one can always call on other pupils and hope that their answers are "right." Rare is the teacher who knows the cognitive processes appropriate to the developmental levels of children and does not expect them to be somewhat adult in their cognitive processes. If we accept as a goal of education the improvement of cognition, then teachers must be able to diagnose thought processes. Piaget's great contribution has been precisely on this point. His theory is helpful in understanding the nature of the mental operations children engage in when they answer a question, and how these mental operations change at different stages in the course of development. The stages identified by Piaget occur in a constant, invariant sequence, but the ages of these occurrences have no specified delineations.

Piaget's developmental theory begins in the cradle. The first stage, covering approximately the first eighteen months of infant life, is that of sensory-motor intelligence. From their own motor actions and from what they see, hear, touch, or otherwise sense, infants assimilate sensations about the physical world. Such sensations are stored away in developing mental structures. With each fresh sensation, the mental structure changes to accommodate the new information, and behavior is changed accordingly. From many experiences in grasping objects, for example, infants come to pattern the position of their fingers to the shape of objects to be grasped, adapting them in one way for a rattle and another for a bottle. At the same time there are developing mental structures containing information about how an object relates to space, and so the infant may, for example, in trying to get a long narrow object between the slats of a playpen, turn the object sidewise, accommodating behavior to the shape of the object. During the first two years of life, mental structures continue to develop and change. Through sensory perceptions and motor experiences, new information about objects and the space they occupy, about time and causality, is assimilated, and structures are accordingly modified. The infant acts and perceives the consequences of actions. If the consequences conflict with what is already structured mentally, the mental structure is modified to restore equilibrium to the system. Intelligence, however, is preverbal; it is the intelligence of action. With the advent of language, thinking processes develop and knowledge accumulates fast.

By the time of entrance into first grade, the child has built a structure of knowledge of the four great cornerstones of the physical world—space, time, matter, and causality. If asked to give an explanation of a phenomenon or to predict what may happen under certain circumstances, a child is never at a loss for an answer. The only difficulty is that the answer is frequently "wrong." Children can tell you that the caterpillar develops into a butterfly, but they think that the caterpillar must die first, and furthermore that the caterpillar knows it. They think that the amount of liquid changes with a change in shape of a container, or that the amount increases when it is poured from a flat, wide-mouthed container into one that is tall and thin.

To the adult, young children frequently appear to operate illogically because, just as with the adult, they operate in terms of personal perceptions of how things look. The developmental level of a learner determines what perceptions are available and which cognitive processes may operate upon them. To children, the amount of liquid in the tall, thin container looks as if it were more, and the visual image is so overpowering that they apparently do not perceive other relationships that might affect the amount of liquid. To cognitively operate at a higher developmental level about the problem requires that the learner give up arriving at conclusions on the basis of sensory data alone. A higher developmental level requires the reordering of data in the mind and the performance of cognitive operations upon additional perceptions. Until approximately seven and one-half years of age, children are in what Piaget calls the "preoperational stage," where judgments are made in terms of whatever factor or variable stands out. A child believes that a ball made into a hot dog contains more "stuff" after the transformation. It is the length of the hot-dog-shaped object that is misleading; the child does not yet know how to coordinate the length of the object with its diameter.

Teachers in the first two grades can expect to find many children who are preoperational in their thinking. We can summarize the characteristics of the cognitive processes at this level as follows: Preoperational children

1. *Are perceptually oriented*. They make judgments in terms of how things *look* to them. They may, for example, be confused in thinking about space by the objects placed in that space. When given a problem where ten blue counters are laid in a row and they are asked to form a new row of red counters underneath the blue with exactly the same number of counters, these children can perform the task. But, then, if the blue counters are bunched together while the red are still spread out, these same children will deny that there are still the same number. Even when they count, they deny equality because they do not understand that there is a logical necessity by which ten must equal ten. Piaget has shown that this same type of perceptual judgment enters into their thinking about space, time, number, and causality. It is only as they go beyond their perceptions to perform displacements upon the data in their mind (for example, visualizing the second row of counters straightened out again) that conservation appears.

2. *Center on one variable only*. Usually, it is the variable that stands out

visually. Children lack the ability to coordinate variables. For example, a kindergarten child is pouring juice into paper cups. The standard size cups are used up and the teacher substitutes some that are much taller but are also smaller in diameter. As the children drink their juice, several comment on the fact that Jimmy, Eddie, and Danny have more juice. And why? Their cups are taller. The dimension of height stands out, not that of width, in this case. Children's thinking is rigid. They do not perform operations on what they see. Later, they will reason that "higher than" is compensated for by "skinnier than," and that both kinds of cups may hold the same amount of juice. This ability to see reciprocal changes in two sets of data is an important logical tool available to older children but not to the preoperational child.

3. *Have difficulty in realizing that an object can possess more than one property and that multiplicative classifications are possible.* It is hard for the child to see that one can live in Champaign and in Illinois at the same time; that a bird is also an animal; and that an Impala is also a Chevrolet. The operation of combining elements to form a whole and then seeing a part in relationship to the whole has not as yet developed, and so hierarchical relationships cannot be mastered.

Children's cognitive processes continue to change as they assimilate information from fresh experiences and accommodate mental structures to the new information. Gradually, it becomes possible for them to transform what they are perceiving by mentally manipulating the data. They perform mental operations upon data by putting two and two together, figuratively speaking, to arrive at a logical result by making analogies between the present problem and others they know, by making comparisons between a whole idea and its parts, and by retracing their thinking and returning to the starting point. Present these children with the problem of the two rows of counters, and they will no longer be misled by the appearance of the long line of red. They will say, "The rows are still the same because you haven't added anything or taken anything away," or, "You can put the blue ones back the way they were, so they've got to be the same." They have some mental operations available to them by means of which they can arrive at logical conclusions. These operations at this stage involve concrete data rather than abstract; mental activity is oriented toward concrete objects and events.

For Piaget, the cognitive actions of the child during the stage of concrete operations are really *systems* of action with definite structural properties. He uses a logico-mathematical model to describe these properties. They are four in number:

1. *Additive composition.* It is possible for concrete operational children to think of a whole as being made up of the sum of its parts, and to put parts together to form a class. They can build a concept, for example, of animals as composed not just of mammals (their earlier, perceptual notion), but also of all living things other than plants, including insects, snakes, birds, and so on. They come to see that Cleveland is in Ohio and that Ohio is but one of fifty states.

They can form classes and superclasses in a hierarchical arrangement and see that the whole is greater than any one of the parts—that the set of animals is larger than the set of ducks because ducks are animals.

2. *Reversibility*. A second property of logical thought is that it is reversible. In fact, every cognitive action can be reversed. Concrete operational children can combine subclasses of animals into a supraclass and they can reverse the process, separating them into the original groups. If they are asked, "Suppose all the animals in the world were dead, would there be any birds left?," they can quickly put mammals, birds, insects, fishes together to form the supraclass of animals (additive composition) and then reverse the combining process to see that all subclasses of animals would have to be dead if all animals were.

3. *Associativity*. Thought is flexible at this stage of cognitive development. Concrete operational children can put data together in various ways to solve a problem. When shown a long stick and a series of segments that add up to the same length, they are sure that the segments together will equal the long stick, regardless of whether they are arranged in zigzag fashion. There are different ways of putting parts together or of thinking about the same problem, and a result obtained in two different ways remains the same in both cases.

4. *Identity*. When comparing two classes of objects or events, concrete operational children can establish identity by making a one-to-one correspondence between the elements in each class. Suppose the teacher asks sixth-grade pupils, "Would you say that the bat is a bird?" To answer the question, pupils must think of the characteristics of bats and those of birds, and then do a one-to-one correspondence between the two. If the elements can be said to be identical and all the elements are used, then the two sets are identical. Whenever pupils are asked to compare or contrast, they make use of such an identity operation.

Note, however, that cognitive actions *are* really systems of action. In the example above, children may first use additive composition, putting together the properties of birds to arrive at the concept of "bird-ness." They do the same thing with the properties of the bat before performing the identity operation. And they may reverse their thoughts at any one point, reminding themselves of the question with which they started and checking to make sure they are still on the right track. Thought has a group-like structure, possessing the properties described above, and in the course of logical reasoning, thought in reference to a particular problem may have one or more of these properties.

Children's thinking during the stage of concrete operations *is* concrete; that is, they tend to solve problems with reference to the concrete problem at hand, rather than abstractly. When they enter what Piaget calls the "stage of formal operations," they tend to do "propositional" thinking. When faced with a problem, they can identify the variables and state them in terms of propositions: "It's got to be this or this that's making the toy truck stand still on an inclined plane," they say, and then they proceed to test each variable systematically, one at a time, holding the others constant. Often they state the result abstractly, in terms of a generalization.

Suppose pupils are studying the pendulum in sixth-grade science class. They are presented with a pendulum in the form of an object suspended from a string and are asked to figure out what determines how frequently the pendulum will complete a full swing. The factors that vary are the length of the string, the weight of the suspended object, and the strength of the initial push given the object. Pupils in the concrete stage think about the problem in terms of specific, concrete factors. They will say (erroneously): "This little weight goes more slowly because it isn't as heavy." Pupils in the stage of formal operations tend to think in abstract terms: "It's the length of string that makes it go faster or slower; the weight doesn't make any difference. *The shorter the string, the faster the swing.*" At this stage they are coordinating variables and are able to state an inverse correspondence. That is, they are able to see in some problem solving that as one variable increases in size, the other decreases proportionally. Manipulating data so as to establish an inverse correspondence is a mental skill pupils use to solve many problems. The skill, along with others, becomes possible when they can deal not solely with the data, but also with the combinations of data they make mentally.

What does this developmental picture mean for teachers? What can they do to foster logical thinking in pupils? Piaget lists four factors contributing to development:

1. *Maturation.* The modern view of the maturation process is that it can be affected by environmental variables. We used to regard maturation as a neural ripening, occurring regardless of experience. Today, it is clear that stimulation is essential to the development of the nervous system; thus, the age at which a certain stage appears is not the same for all human beings. Maturation independent of experience cannot explain why logical development is advanced or retarded.

2. *Experience.* While experience is essential for concept development, alone it is not enough. Children may participate in an experiment or demonstration, but unless their minds are actively engaged in operating upon the data, there will be no learning. As Piaget points out, knowledge is not drawn from the objects; it is acquired from actions effected upon objects.

3. *Social transmission.* The third factor that Piaget lists is that of social transmission. Passing on information to the child by speech or by texts is a fundamental factor, but again it is not enough. If children *only* read or listen, they may arrive at a false concept or, as Piaget puts it, deform the knowledge in some way. Each child must *operate* upon the information, mentally digesting it and changing previous mental structures.

4. *Equilibration.* The act of operating upon information involves equilibration, which for Piaget is the most fundamental of all the factors. If children are presented with a situation producing a cognitive conflict, they will react in order to compensate for the disturbance and consequently tend toward equilibrium. The reactions take the form of the logical operations. Momentary incompatibilities are overcome by means of operations, making possible a higher level of equilibrium.

Teaching offers innumerable possibilities to foster the development of logical operations. Throughout this text and in the Problems and Projects, readers will find examples of specific ways in which they can help pupils become more logical in their thinking.

Following are some brief samples of the application of Piaget's developmental stages to curriculum:

A. Preoperational
  1. Most kindergarten and first-grade pupils are in the preoperational stage. The author's use of the Piagetian tasks have shown that approximately 75 percent of the first graders are nonconservers in two or more areas (preoperational).
  2. Preoperational children are limited in their thinking to the data resulting from their own perceptions. They cannot accommodate the perceptions of others in their thinking processes. Because the teacher's perceptions are not available to the child, the teacher must establish what the child perceives and augment it with additional data. When teachers describe their perceptions to preoperational children, the children are hearing about an object, action, or event that is distinctly separate from what they perceived.
  3. Preoperational children will parallel their physical manipulations of an object with their cognitive processes. They cannot cognitively create an object and cannot cognitively manipulate the object. For example, for these children to think about an object in a space, the object must be in that space. The concrete operational learner can cognitively visualize a chair, for example, in several locations within a room and anticipate the effects of these various locations. The preoperational child, however, must physically locate the chair in the various positions. Also, if the objects of the learning situation are rearranged. the preoperational child cannot cognitively translate the new order back to the previous order. For example, $3+2=5$ and $5-3=2$ are two separate and distinct problems. The learning of one does not seem to reduce the number of trials needed to learn the other.
  4. The preoperational child explains an object, action, or event in relation to one variable. For example, a teacher says, "Give me a word that sounds like 'hat' begins." Several children may respond with "bat," "rat," "cat," and so on. The variable "sounds like" may have caused the pupils to center upon sound, and therefore to have supplied rhyming words. A more functional question for the teacher to ask might be, "Give me a word that starts with the same letter as the word 'hat.'" The author has observed that, through conditioning, children can learn to respond to the question, "Give me a word that sounds like 'hat' begins," with something other than rhyming words. When learners are asked to perform cognitive operations above their developmental level, stimulus-response mechanisms must be used. The

result is a learning environment characterized by drill, repetition, review, forgetting, and punishment and reward.

B. Concrete operational

1. Most third- through sixth-grade pupils are in the concrete operational stage. Research done on 588 students in Oklahoma suggested that not even 66 percent of the high school seniors are formal operational.[18]

2. A concrete operational learner cannot cognitively control several variables simultaneously so as to develop a "controlled" experiment. For example, given a problem to determine the effect of weight, thickness, length, and material as factors in the bending of metal rods, the concrete operational learner will likely determine through a controlled experiment the function of one variable, but will be unable to cognitively design experiments to determine the functioning and inter-relationships of all.

3. Although concrete operational learners can think about their thinking and perform cognitive operations on objects not being physically manipulated, they still need the support of concrete or vicarious objects. They cannot think about the consequences of their thinking. Reading as the only information input system tends to leave concrete operational learners without an object, so they revert to the low-energy cognitive acts of recognition and recall.

4. Models are helpful to learners, but they will learn the model rather than what the model represents if the model represents an abstraction. For example, given a model of an engine, the concrete learner can translate from model to object, if the object is present and the relationship is between the model and object are experienced. Given a model of an atom, the concrete learner learns the model and does not seem to translate to the abstraction called "atom."

Psychological Development

This section briefly presents the theories of Robert J. Havighurst and Abraham H. Maslow. Havighurst's identification of developmental tasks included those tasks with a psychological basis. Maslow's identification is of human motivation classified as what he considers to be the basic needs of humans. Maslow's hierarchy is discussed under the classical area of psychological development because Maslow stated, after presenting his theory of human needs, "So far, we have mentioned the cognitive needs only in passing."[19] Maslow also discussed the cognitive capacities (perceptual, intellectual, learning): ". . . as a set of adjustive tools which have, among other functions, that of satisfaction of our basic needs. . . ."[20] These two points seem to exclude Mas-

18 John W. Renner, Don G. Stafford, and William B. Ragan, *Teaching Science in the Elementary Schools,* 2d ed. (New York: Harper & Row, Publishers, 1973), p. 342.

19 A. H. Maslow, "Personality Development and The Self," in Don E. Hamachek (Ed.), *The Self in Growth, Teaching and Learning: Selected Readings.* (Englewood Cliffs, N.J.: Prentice-Hall, Inc., 1965), p. 258.

20 Maslow, p. 259.

low's hierarchy from a cognitive one; furthermore, since Maslow's theory is based upon human motivation, it has been placed within the psychological development section for discussion purposes.

The following developmental tasks defined by Havighurst were selected as examples of psychological development: infancy and early childhood—learning to relate oneself emotionally to parents, siblings and other people; middle childhood—building wholesome attitudes toward oneself as a growing organism; adolescence—achieving emotional independence of parents and other adults.[21] These examples were selected to introduce Havighurst's theory and to encourage the reader to review the total list of developmental tasks.

A summary outline of Maslow's hierarchy of human needs follows:

Hierarchy of Human Needs (Goals)
A Taxonomy or Prepotent Hierarchy

I. Physiological—a need to survive
  A. Homeostasis—balance of internal bodily functions
  B. Appetites—need for nurturance—food, air, sleep, elimination
  C. Sex, physiological only—not needed for survival, may not belong here!
II. Safety—freedom from damage and threat
  A. Routines and rules (know and accept)
  B. Consistency and security
  C. Unmet need observable in all kids and neurotic adults
III. Belongingness—need for love and affection. Identify.
  A. Intimate relations with other people
  B. To be accepted, wanted and cherished
  C. Most common locus of adult failure
IV. Esteem—status, recognition, competence, importance, independence
  A. Personal—need for strength, mastery
  B. Group—reputation, status, dominance, appreciation
  C. Status symbols most common failure
V. Self-Actualization
  A. To satisfy potential—you must *be what you can be*
  B. Very rare
  C. Cognitive—to know and understand
  D. Aesthetic—perceive and appreciate beauty, elegance, and splendor

Note: *The self-actualizing person:*

  A. Perceives reality accurately and [is] compatible with it.
  B. Accepts himself and others and the realities of human nature.
  C. Evidences spontaneous reactions.
  D. Problem-centers outside of self. Not self-conscious. Can devote attention and competencies to task, duty, and mission.
  E. Needs privacy.
  F. Maintains a degree of autonomy.
  G. Displays a continued freshness of appreciation of the basic "goods" of

[21] Havighurst, pp. 25–41, 11–202.

life. Does not lump experiences together and dismiss them as "nothing
but"; Does not demand "something more".[22]

A prepotent hierarchy is an ordering in which the energy of one level of
the ordering may monopolize the available energy until its demands are satisfied. Also, when the energy demands of a level are satisfied, the energy then
becomes available to the demands of another level. This assumes humans are
perpetually wanting beings; therefore, the satisfaction of one level of need does
not satisfy all needs, but rather releases energy for a higher level of need satisfaction.

According to Maslow, the blocking of these basic goals (needs), or a
danger to the defenses which protect them or to the conditions which support
them, is considered to be a psychological threat. "With few exceptions all psy-
chopathology may be partially traced to such threats."[23]

Maslow, Havighurst, and others have defined a hierarchy for the development of goals or tasks in the psychological area. Maslow's formulations prescribe a sequencing of the human needs emphasis for the modern elementary
school. A modern elementary school would first establish that the physiological
needs are satisfied; then the safety needs of freedom from threat and danger;
then the "new needs center" of love, affection, and "belongingness"; then the
needs of self-esteem, self-respect, and the esteem of others; and finally, the goals
of self-actualization become available to both the learner and the school.

Social Development

Social development is a phase of growing from immaturity toward maturity.
Because children must live in a "sea of human relationships," they must learn
gradually to engage wisely and constructively in the activities of ever-enlarging
groups of people. Although their lives outside the school provide many opportunities for social learning, the school is perhaps the most effective social laboratory because it is possible to structure the school environment so that social
development is more systematic.

The expression "social needs" refers to those needs which cannot be satisfied by any means other than membership in a group. These needs are as real as
the need for food, exercise, and sleep. Moreover, they are closely associated
with achievement in school subjects, as every parent knows who has observed
what happens when children are excluded by their peer group at school. Children need to gain acceptance by a group near their own age level; merely being
with other children does not satisfy their need for belonging. They can achieve
self-fulfillment within the group only as they are accepted and respected by
other members of the group; only as they work with others toward the achievement of mutual goals; only as they make useful contributions to group enter-

---

[22] Supplied by Gerald Kowitz, Professor of Education (Guidance and Counseling), University
of Oklahoma, and referenced to A. H. Maslow, *Motivation and Personality*. (New York: Harper
& Row, Publishers, 1954).
[23] Maslow, p. 267.

prises; and only as they learn that both initiative and conformity are essential to group life.

The teacher must understand the stages of social development of children in order to work effectively with them. Norms for social development have been formulated. The Vineland Social Maturity Scale, for example, indicates what normal children can be expected to do on their own at various ages from six to eighteen years of age.[24] Several books are available from which students and teachers can gain information concerning social characteristics of elementary school children.[25]

Lawrence Kohlberg, Erik H. Erikson, and Robert J. Havighurst are among the leading professionals who have made contributions to the understanding of social development. Each has provided a hierarchical sequence for the social development of the child. Havighurst has been included in the area of social development because he identified those developmental tasks with a cultural basis. Erikson has been included because his hierarchy is of psychosocial development emphasizing the human, social environment and the ways in which culture shapes the individual. Kohlberg's stages of moral development has been included because the stages illustrate a process of learning based upon interaction with the environment.

The following developmental tasks from Havighurst were selected as examples of the tasks of social development: infancy to early childhood—forming simple concepts of social and physical reality, learning to distinguish right and wrong, and developing a moral conscience; middle childhood—learning to get along with age-mates, learning an appropriate masculine or feminine social role, developing conscience, morality and a scale of values, developing attitudes toward social groups and institutions; adolescence—achieving more mature relationships with age-mates of both sexes, acquiring a set of values and an ethical system as a guide to behavior. The reader should review Havighurst's total listing of developmental tasks from infancy to old age.[26]

Kohlberg investigated the development of moral thought. He formulated a theory of stages of moral development. There is some evidence that the sequence of Kohlberg's stages, ". . . cannot be altered and occurs in a step by step fashion with no skipping."[27] Turiel also said that the moral stage at which a child is functioning sets significant levels upon what can be comprehended or changed. For example, judgments or ideas directly above a child's stage may have some influence, while ideas more than one stage of moral development

---

[24] Edgar A. Doll, *The Vineland Social Maturity Scale.* (Vineland, N.J.: The Training School, 1936).

[25] Celia Stendler Lavatelli and Faith Stendler, *Readings in Child Development and Behavior,* 3d ed. (New York: Harcourt Brace Jovanovich, Inc., 1972, Part V.)

[26] Havighurst, pp. 9–17, 25–41, 111–202.

[27] Elliot Turiel, "Stage Transition in Moral Development," in R. M. Travers (Ed.), *Second Handbook on Research on Teaching.* (Skokie, Ill.: Rand McNally & Company, 1973), pp. 732–758.

above the child's stage seem to have no influence in the moral thinking of the child.[28] *stages sequential + hierarchical facts*

3 levels Kohlberg presented three levels of moral thought. Each level included two *2 stage* stages of moral development. The first level is the preconventional level in *in each* which the child responds primarily to the pain-pleasure effects of action and *level* the physical power of the authorities, and in which the first stage of moral development is punishment-obedience orientation. Here, the child avoids punishment and responds to authority because it is perceived as powerful. The second stage of the first level is the instrumental-relativist orientation. This is a pragmatic, moral position in which whatever satisfies one's needs, or at times the needs of others, is right.

Kohlberg's second level of moral thought is the conventional level, which involves loyalty to and support of the perceived social order as well as the expectations of family and group memberships. In this second level the first stage is interpersonal-concordance orientation. Here, the child considers good behavior to be that behavior which pleases or helps others and conforms to "appropriate" behavior. The second stage is authority and social-order maintenance orientation. In this stage, right behavior comprises doing one's duty, respecting authority, and maintaining a given social order for its own sake.

The third level of Kohlberg's definition concerns postconventional, autonomous, or principled behavior. At this level of moral thought, the individual attempts to define valid, moral principles as concepts separated from the authority of individuals or group membership. The first stage within this level is the social-contract, legalistic orientation, in which the individual critically and rationally examines the utility of laws and rights. Personal values are relative, while societally accepted standards are important. The second stage relates to universal, ethical, principle orientation, in which the individual respects the dignity of individuals and utilizes conscious, self-chosen, logical procedures to arrive at ethical principles. "Rights are abstract and ethical (for example, the Golden Rule), not concrete and moral (for example, the Ten Commandments)."[29]

Kohlberg's stages of moral development and Piaget's stages of intellectual development are beautiful examples of a developmental hierarchy stressing one dimension of human development (moral or cognitive) with far-reaching applications to most, if not all, aspects of human development. Both theories stress the influences of interaction with the environment to form structures or organizations (moral or cognitive). Both Kohlberg and Piaget have researched and written about cognitive and affective development.[30] When writing about the

[28] Turiel, p. 744.
[29] N. L. Gage and David Berliner, *Educational Psychology*. (Skokie, Ill.: Rand McNally & Company, 1975), p. 394.
[30] Piaget's stages of moral development are presented and related to Kohlberg's stages in an article by Ronald E. Galbraith and Thomas M. Jones, entitled "Teaching Strategies for Moral Dilemmas: An Application of Kohlberg's Theory of Moral Development to the Social Studies Classroom," *Social Education*, Vol. XXXIX, No. 1 (January 1975), pp. 16–22; Jean Piaget, in *The Moral Judgment of the Child* (New York: Humanities Press, Inc., 1952); and Lawrence Kohlberg, "Early Education: A Cognitive Developmental View," in Lavatelli, p. 500.

development of moral conceptions, Piaget stated that adults judge naughtiness or wickedness on the basis of intentions, while a preoperational child judges naughtiness in terms of perceived damage. Young children, according to Piaget, say that a lie consists of naughty words, whereas older children believe that a lie is a statement not consistent with fact; still older children say that a lie is an untruth told with the purpose to deceive. Piaget and Kohlberg emphasize the sequencing from stage to stage, rather than the age or time in which a stage occurs. Neither Piaget nor Kohlberg seemed concerned with the acceleration of development, although their disciples emphasize this. Their concern lies rather with the appropriateness of experiences to the child's present stage.

Erik H. Erikson formulated a hierarchy for the eight ages of man, and the psychosocial adaptions and crises which are normative for each of the eight ages.[31] These relationships perceived by Erikson can be illustrated by a square matrix (see Fig. 3.1). The eight ages of man are: (1) oral-sensory; (2) muscular anal; (3) locomotor-genital; (4) latency; (5) puberty and adolescence; (6) young adulthood; (7) adulthood; (8) maturity. These ages form the vertical axis of the matrix. The diagonal axis is formed by the psychosocial adaptions normative for an age and are: (1) basic trust versus mistrust; (2) autonomy versus shame and doubt; (3) initiative versus guilt; (4) industry versus inferiority; (5) identity versus role confusion; (6) intimacy versus isolation; (7) generativity versus stagnation; (8) ego integrity versus despair. For example, basic trust versus mistrust are the psychosocial adaptions and crises normative for the oral-sensory age; autonomy versus shame and doubt are normative for the muscular anal age. This pattern continues on the diagonal axis until the pairing progresses to ego integrity versus despair and the age of maturity.

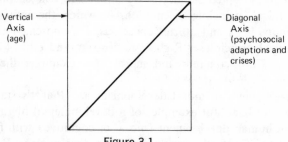

Figure 3.1

Erikson selected a matrix which positioned the eight psychosocial adaptions and crises on the diagonal axis to illustrate that each adaption and crises existed in some form at all preceding and following ages. Proper psychosocial development, according to Erikson, depends upon a systematic progression and a positive resolution of each adaption and crisis at its normative age. The tolerance and variations for the positive resolution of each is provided for but not defined.

Erikson deserves, as do the other authorities included in this social develop-

[31] Erik H. Erikson, "Eight Ages of Man," in Lavatelli, pp. 19–30.

ment section, a more thorough discussion and reading than given here. His contribution of a hierarchy, ordering, and definitions of "ages," "adaptions," and "crises" provide a significant developmental frame.

The Role of Social Development in Learning

A great deal has been written in recent years about the importance of a positive image of self. How children feel about themselves and others determines to a large extent how well they learn school subjects.[32] As Kelley has indicated, "Subject matter and feeling are so closely intertwined that they can no longer be considered a duality. Everyone who learns something has some feeling about it, and so, as in so many other areas, they are inseparable."[33] The role of the emotions in the educative process has been discussed under many different titles, including affective learning, personality development, and mental-health aspects of instructional practices.

Information about the development of social behavior provides significant clues for curriculum workers. Studies in this area of child development indicate that the social behavior that can be expected of a twelve-year-old cannot be expected of a six-year-old; that the social behavior which is normal for a child from a middle-class home may be foreign to a child from a disadvantaged home. The summaries which preceded and which follow are merely introductions to this fascinating phase of child development. The readings listed at the end of the chapter will provide an opportunity to explore it in greater depth.

1. Preschool, kindergarten, and some first-year children are essentially egocentric. Their friendships are casual, unstable, and transient, their contacts are limited primarily to members of their own family and a few other children who are near their own ages; and they have not yet learned to play group games which involve taking turns and making choices.

2. When they enter school, they may encounter their first large group experiences, and their classmates soon become their most important socialization agents. They also meet many new demands for conformity, such as "take your seat," "stay in line," and "put your books away."

3. During middle childhood, "gang" activities predominate and children learn to play appropriate sex roles—boys are not expected to be "sissies" and girls are not expected to be "tomboys." The children's choices of games, dress, speech, and food are heavily influenced by their peer group.

4. Factors which influence the choice of friends during the elementary school period include social class, chronological age, physical maturity, and race.

5. The early years of a child's life, as noted previously, are crucial in terms

---

[32] See especially *Perceiving—Behaving—Becoming.* (Washington, D.C.: Association for Supervision and Curriculum Development, 1962).

[33] Earl C. Kelley, "The Place of Affective Learning," *Educational Leadership* (April 1965), pp. 455–457.

of achievement in school subjects; they are also crucial in terms of the development of social attitudes and behavior. Positive and negative attitudes toward race and religion are developed both within and outside the classroom, but the classroom influence is extremely important.[34]

Social development is an important phase of growing into the culture—of becoming fully human. The essence of our democratic beliefs is respect for individual worth, and the opportunity for individuals to achieve self-realization and find a place in society according to their personal abilities and efforts. The school cannot be held responsible for all the prejudices which children develop, but it can continue the socialization process which began in the home, provide a favorable environment for the development of positive attitudes towards others, and eliminate materials and practices which tend to develop prejudices.

THE SCHOOL'S RESPONSIBILITY

The mental-health emphasis in instructional practices is concerned primarily with understanding the basic personality needs of children and with helping to meet these needs. The following discussions of basic needs of children are by no means inclusive. Almost every reader will have a few items to add to it. The points discussed here merely illustrate the needs approach to mental health.

Biological Needs

Biological factors of growth and development have important implications for the mental health of the child. As children grow from infancy to adolescence, they are confronted with the need for adjusting to adult expectations with regard to eating, cleanliness, and muscular activity. They need help in accepting the reality of their personal appearances, in developing muscular coordination, and in making an adequate adjustment to the development of sex drives.

Most teachers are aware of the necessity for regular physical examinations of pupils, for cleanliness, light, heat, and play space. They are aware also of the importance of good nutrition, the need for a proper rhythm of rest and activity, the influence of good health on the child's ability to learn, and the effects of physical deformities on the personality. Biological factors that have implications for mental health but are not so well understood include differences among children in energy output, differences in body build, and differences in rates of physical growth.[35]

The curriculum of the modern elementary school provides for meeting the biological needs of children through the programs of physical education and health instruction, and through planning activities which accommodate physical abilities of children at various age levels.

---

[34] See Ragan and Henderson, chap. 6.

[35] For a more detailed discussion of the relation of biological factors to the problem of mental health, see Bernice Neugarten, "Body Processes Help to Determine Behavior and Development," in *Fostering Mental Health in our Schools*. (Washington, D.C.: Association for Supervision and Curriculum Development, 1950), chap. 4.

Achieving Status in Changing Social Groups

In the early years of their lives children are highly self-centered. The process of growing up involves identifying themselves with peer groups, gaining group acceptance, and contributing to group enterprises. Before they start going to school, children's groups are relatively stable, consisting of the members of their own family and a few neighborhood playmates. When they begin schooling, one of the most difficult tasks they face is adjusting to a much larger group, a group consisting primarily of strangers. As they continue in the elementary school, they are confronted with the need for adjusting to a shifting peer code of behavior, for resolving conflicts between the code of their parents and that of the peer group to which they belong, and for adjusting more and more to adult standards of behavior.

The curriculum of the elementary school is the instrumentality through which the child grows into our democratic culture. The elementary school is both a product of the culture and the workshop in which the growing child learns the ways of democratic living. In modern elementary schools, education is recognized as a social process, and the curriculum is developed in terms of the social needs of growing children.

Children are not to be regarded as candidates for membership in the culture; they already are members and are entitled to their share of the happiness that comes from participation in the life of the group. Teachers must recognize their responsibility for helping children acquire the social skills needed for getting along with others and for becoming effective group members. These skills, like others, are learned through meaningful experiences. The practice of democratic skills in the classroom provides the basis for effective citizenship in the wider groups of the community, state, and nation.

But care must be taken that social skills are not learned at the expense of individualism. One of the criticisms of modern schools is that they concern themselves too much with group adjustment and provide no antidote to the pressures for conformity in our society. Sometimes this is done unwittingly in classrooms where children have too many opportunities to criticize one another's reports, pictures, and performances. For example, a child gives an oral report and then must wait for comments from the class. The class has been taught that they must be polite and considerate, so the first critic's remarks are prefaced with, "That was a good report, but . . ." and then lets fly with the criticism. Some children learn from experiences such as these that the way to avoid caustic comment is to confine oneself to a rather narrow range of behaviors, that it is dangerous to be different (that is, original and creative), and that it is safer to go along with what the group thinks is acceptable. Occasionally, parents report that their child has refused to include an interesting object or piece of information in a report because "The other kids won't like it," "The other kids will think it's funny if I bring in extra things," or "We didn't vote to do that." If criticism is needed, the teacher should give it in a kindly, constructive way. When the group is used continually to approve or disapprove the actions of other children, too much concern for group opinion may develop and overconformity may result. Group work must be planned so that the individual is not lost in the group.

Too many group projects also kill individualism. It is true that children learn social skills by practicing them, but group projects should be limited to such activities as plays and necessary committee work, which, because of their nature, call for this kind of activity. Designing a map, constructing a story, working on an experiment may occasionally be done with no loss to creativity by two or three close friends who stimulate one another intellectually, but too often in a group project the incentive to be creative is killed. Furthermore, since everyone in the group, even the slacker, will receive the same credit for the job, there is little incentive to put forth one's best effort, and a desirable achievement drive may be weakened.

Yet, it is within a group that individuals learn to define major aspects of their individuality. Therefore, the teacher interacts with both the groups and the individual on key factors. Haim Ginott[36] and William Glasser[37] have provided some practical methods of fostering groups and individual self-concepts.

Growing Gradually from Dependence to Independence

Perhaps the most significant single change in the behavior pattern of individuals as they mature is the growth and transition from excessive dependence upon adults to independence. Parents and teachers who are sensitive to the biological and academic needs of children frequently overlook almost completely their social needs. The child needs considerable adult guidance in learning to bridge the gap between dependence upon others, which is characteristic of young children, and independence, which is expected more and more as the child grows up. One cannot develop self-direction in children merely by "taking the lid off" and leaving them to do as they please.

The process of growing up, of becoming increasingly independent of adult control, is a long and gradual one; it requires years of growing, experimenting, and guidance. For the five-year-old it is a matter primarily of learning to make decisions, under wise adult guidance, concerning immediate problems, such as sharing possessions, observing safety rules, and taking responsibility for caring for toys and articles of clothing. As children grow older, they are expected to develop increasing ability to do long-range planning.

Teaching that takes into account the child's need for becoming increasingly independent and self-directing provides experiences in identifying problems, planning to solve problems, gathering information, making decisions, acting upon decisions, and evaluating outcomes. The function of the teacher in this process is that of a guide and a resource person. As the child's ability to make decisions grows, direction by the teacher gradually decreases. The teacher always provides enough guidance to give pupils a sense of security, but not enough to discourage initiative.

[36] Haim Ginott, *Teacher and Child.* (New York: (Crowell Collier and Macmillan, Inc., 1972).
[37] William Glasser, *Schools without Failure.* (New York: Harper & Row, Publishers, 1968).

Security and Satisfaction

Many children lack security in life outside the school. The increasing number of broken homes and the tendency of families to move from one place to another result in a large number of children who have nothing that can give them a feeling of security. The school has a particular responsibility to children from such families. Children need to feel that they are surrounded by adults upon whom they can depend, that they have a reasonable chance to succeed at least a part of the time, and that they can predict fairly well what will be expected of them.

One of the fundamental human needs is a feeling of confidence in oneself, a recognition of personal worth, and a knowledge that one is recognized by others as a worthwhile person. Children who grow up without the opportunity to develop self-confidence, who are continually criticized for inability to meet adult standards, who are not allowed to develop skills in line with their abilities and special talents, lose confidence in themselves and soon develop antisocial behavior traits. Negativism, attention-getting devices, and bullying are frequently the result of failure to find ways of obtaining security and satisfaction through acceptable types of behavior. The adults who are boastful, who are always promoting themselves, are usually those who lack personal security and therefore feel they must call attention to their own abilities and achievements if they are not to go unnoticed by others.

The need for security and satisfaction is met in modern elementary schools through helping children develop efficiency in the use of such important skills as reading, writing, using numbers, and speaking in accordance with their individual abilities; through discovering special needs and interests; through providing opportunities for the development of social skills in group situations; through supplying understanding and assistance to atypical children; through using praise and criticism discriminatingly; and through developing a classroom environment for happy, cooperative living.

Getting and Giving Affection

Children need to develop in home and school in an environment of sincere affection. They need to be loved and appreciated by those who are most important to them. Overdoses of affection, overprotection, and a possessive parental attitude are hazards to the mental health of children, but children need at least one adult who has an interest in them, who understands their problems, and who loves them, not because they are good or beautiful or bright, but because they are themselves. As children develop, they also need to learn to give affection, to form friendships, and later to build a strong bond of affection with a possible marriage partner.

The elementary school should be staffed with teachers who understand the need that children have for getting and giving affection, who are genuinely fond of children, and who can accept children emotionally, not only for what they are but for what they may become under wise guidance.

Developing Appropriate Communication Skills

The needs of children cannot be understood apart from the environment in which they develop. Success and recognition in school life depend upon the development of skills and concepts in reading, listening, oral expression, and written expression. If the child fails to make satisfactory progress in these skills, social and emotional maladjustments soon follow. The relationship of these skills to the mental health of the school child is discussed in detail in Chapter 7. Here, it is sufficient to point out that emphasis on the mental health of a child is as integral a part of instruction practices in the language arts as it is in all areas of the curriculum. Failure to understand normal growth patterns of children and failure to develop language arts programs in terms of developmental tasks have caused language to become a hazard to the mental health of children rather than a means to their wholesome development.

Learning To Face Reality

Children need to learn to face reality, to understand their own strengths and weaknesses, to build on their innate strengths, and to accept situations that cannot be changed. The well-adjusted person is not the one who always succeeds at everything but the one who is content to see others excel in some things while he excels in others. One of the leading causes of frustration and nervous tension in adults as well as children is failure to adjust one's aspirations to one's talents. Children who are upset whenever the least thing goes wrong, who cannot bear to see others succeed where they have failed, are as much in need of guidance as the child who is having difficulty in learning to add or subtract.

One phase of development is learning to face reality. The program of the modern elementary school provides many opportunities for the teacher and the pupil to work together in learning to understand and accept the facts of different abilities, different physical features, and different achievements. It provides opportunities to learn that failure in little things provides an opportunity to learn from mistakes and to correct errors.

The work of the teacher is frequently hindered by parents who have ambitions for their children which do not correspond to abilities or interests. This situation points up the need for a closer working relationship between teachers and parents in helping children learn to face reality. Parents and teachers need to understand that they must work in harmony with each child's developmental needs rather than formulate a plan for the child and then try to force the child to conform to their wishes. An acceptance of the democratic philosophy of education will result in the practice of helping children develop their own unique potentialities, rather than the practice of expecting children to attain some arbitrary standards.

Principals and teachers can examine the practices in their schools in the light of the basic personality needs of children by using the following questions as guides:

1. Does the school program take into consideration the biological, social, emotional, and intellectual needs of pupils?
2. Are teachers and principals patient and tolerant with pupils who are having difficulty in adjusting to adult standards of behavior?
3. Do school policies make it possible for all children, despite differences in abilities, to meet their needs?
4. Do teachers help children set goals consistent with their own unique abilities?
5. Are parents helped and encouraged to face reality in the expectations they have for their children?
6. Are failures of children in school subjects studied to find the causes, and are efforts made to prevent wholesale failure by adjusting the work to developmental needs?
7. Are adequate opportunities provided for exceptional children to succeed to the extent of their abilities?
8. Are opportunities provided for children to learn to work as members of a group and to learn to become increasingly self-directing?
9. Do teachers look upon skills in communication, use of numbers, and other areas as a means of helping children meet their developmental needs rather than ends in themselves?
10. Does the social climate of the school encourage children to discuss freely their problems and needs with teachers?

SITUATION 3.5   Investigate programs for the gifted which are currently in operation in your geographical vicinity. What is the IQ floor for entrance? What has research revealed about the grouping of superior students? What are the advancement results for the superior students when grouped together? What are the advancement results for those students isolated from the superior students?

As trustees of the cultural heritage, it is natural for teachers to attempt to help children conform, as far as possible, to the standards accepted by the culture. But often a lack of understanding of the developmental patterns of children causes our demands to bear too heavily upon children before they are ready for it. To help children learn gradually to conform to the world as it is and at the same time take into consideration the relentless urges of their own nature is no easy task. If we can learn to be less rigid in our demands, if we can take more of our cues from children themselves as they pursue their developmental course, if we can urge conformity upon them at the times when they are ready to accept, we will be collaborating with the demands of their developmental patterns, and their adjustments will be accomplished with less friction and more satisfaction. These factors signify the importance of teachers' and parents' understandings of the facts related to human growth and learning development.

SUMMARY

1. Growth is an increase in amount (that is, height, weight, etc.).

2. Learning is a change in human behavior resulting from the interactions between individuals and their environments. Learning is deduced and implied from behavior.

3. Development refers to those changes in human behavior resulting from the interaction of learning and growth.

4. Environment influences growth, learning, and development in significant ways.

5. The two families of learning theories are the S-R association approach and the field theory approach.

6. Behavior modification is one the S-R association theories, and as such utilizes conditioning to establish behaviors called "learning."

7. A developmental task is one that arises at or about a certain period in the life of an individual, and the successful achievement of the task contributes to satisfaction.

8. Piaget, Havighurst, Maslow, Kohlberg, and Erikson have each contributed theories of development.

9. The school is responsible for creating an environment conducive to the interaction of learning and growth for the appropriate developmental tasks.

Problems and Projects

---

1. As educators seek to teach the "whole" child, not just the child's mind, and as research has revealed more and more information related to the dynamic impact of affective transfers and blocks upon cognitive activities, there has arisen a growing emphasis within educational institutions upon affective education (value education, values-clarification, and so on). Write brief statements which depict your opinions concerning teachers' involvement in the following areas:

   a. movement of the learner from dependence to independence
   b. the security present within the child's environment outside the school-house walls
   c. the learner's experiences with the giving and receiving of affection
   d. the learner's emotional maturity to face life
   e. the learner's evaluation and assessment of personal strengths and weaknesses

Review the literature on affective education. From the literature reviewed (publications, doctoral dissertations, psychological studies, etc.) record supportive statements for your viewpoints.

2. Administer the following Piagetian tasks (procedures for administering follow):

   a. Conservation of Number
   b. Conservation of Liquid Amount
   c. Conservation of Solid Amount

d. Conservation of Area
e. Conservation of Length
f. Conservation of Weight

The Piagetian tasks are designed to differentiate among preoperational and concrete operational learners. These are tasks, not tests; therefore, relax, observe, and listen to the child. The materials can be easily gathered (that is, pill vials for the conservation of volume; plastic drinking straws for length; houses or hotels from the game of Monopoly for barns).

Early during the administering of each task, the child must agree to "sameness" (that is, same number of red and black checkers; same amounts of clay). If the child will not agree to sameness and if the objects cannot be equalized to the satisfaction of the child that sameness does exist, the task must be aborted.

After the child agrees to sameness, the administrator performs some action on the objects. Following the action, the child must then be asked the questions related to conservation: more than, less than, or the same as. If the child can perceive sameness, the cognitive operation of conservation exists. Conservation is a characteristic of concrete operational learners.

a. *Task:* Conservation of Number
   Objects Required: 1. six identical black checkers
                             2. six identical red checkers
   Setting: Have the child line six black checkers in one row and six red checkers in another row.
   Agreement to Sameness: Ask the child: :"Do you agree that there are the same number of red checkers as there are black checkers?" If the child does not perceive sameness, and objects cannot be manipulated to the child's satisfaction, the task must be aborted at this point.
   Action: After agreement to sameness, stack the red checkers, one on top of the other, leaving the black checkers in their original row placement.
   Questions Related to Conservation: Ask the child: "Are there more red checkers, less red checkers, or the same number of red checkers as there are black checkers?"
   Interpretation: If the child's answer indicates that the same number of red and black checkers is perceived, then the child is able to conserve number. If the answer indicates a perceived difference in number, then the child is unable to conserve number.

b. *Task:* Conservation of Liquid Amount
   Objects Required: 1. two transparent containers of equal size
                             2. one transparent container which is taller and more slender than the two containers first chosen
                             3. enough liquid to fill the two containers about one-half full
                             4. eyedropper
   Setting: Pour the same amount of liquid into two containers of equal size.
   Agreement to Sameness: Ask the child: "Do you agree that the containers are the same size and that they contain the same amount of liquid?" If the child does not perceive sameness and objects cannot be manipulated (that is, use of eyedropper to increase or partially remove liquid present in containers) to the child's satisfaction, the task must be aborted at this point.

Action: After agreement to sameness, pour the liquid into a taller, thinner container. If the administrator is willing to risk a spill, let the child do it; personal involvement by the child is advantageous.

Questions Related to Conservation: Ask the child: "Is there more liquid, less liquid, or the same amount of liquid in the tall container as there is in the other container?"

Interpretation: If the child's answer indicates that the same amount of liquid is perceived in the two containers, then the child is able to conserve liquid amount. If the answer indicates a perceived difference in the amount of liquid, then the child is unable to conserve liquid amount.

c. *Task:* Conservation of Solid Amount

Objects Required: Two amounts of clay which may differ in color.

Setting: Roll two equal amounts of clay into balls of equal size. For discussion purposes, two colors of clay (that is, blue and red) may be used.

Agreement to Sameness: Ask the child: "Do you agree that there is the same amount of blue clay as there is red clay?" If the child does not perceive sameness and objects cannot be manipulated (that is, portions of clay removed from one of the balls) to the child's satisfaction, the task must be aborted at this point.

Action: After agreement to sameness, deform the piece of red clay by rolling it into a "snake" form.

Questions Related to Conservation: Ask the child: "Is there more red clay, less red clay, or the same amount of red clay as there is blue clay?"

Interpretation: If the child's answer indicates that the same amount of clay is perceived, then the child is able to conserve solid amount. If the answer indicates that a difference is perceived in the amount of clay between the two shapes, the child is unable to conserve solid amount.

d. *Task:* Conservation of Area

Objects Required: 1. two identical fields of grass (that is, green construction-paper squares and rectangles)
2. eight identical barns (that is, hotels from the game of Monopoly)
3. scissors (possibly required for trimming fields)

Setting: Show the child two fields of grass of equal size. Explain that Mr. McCoy, a farmer, owns one field of grass and Mr. Brown, another farmer, owns the other field of grass.

Agreement to Sameness: Ask the child: "Do you agree that there is just as much grass in Mr. McCoy's field as there is in Mr. Brown's field?" If the child does not perceive sameness and objects cannot be manipulated (that is, allow the child to trim either field as required) to the child's satisfaction, the task must be aborted at this point.

Action: After agreement to sameness, place an identical barn in an identical position on each field, explaining to the child that both Mr. McCoy and Mr. Brown have built a barn on their fields.

Agreement to Sameness: Ask the child: "Are the barns identical in size?" Agreement to sameness must be reached or the task must be aborted. It is permissible for the child to examine the barns to determine their sameness.

Questions Related to Conservation: After the child has agreed to the sameness of the field sizes and barns, ask: "Is there more grass, less grass, or the same amount of grass in Mr. McCoy's field as there is in Mr. Brown's field?"

Interpretation: At this point, the administrator should merely record the child's response.

Action: After the child has responded, place another barn next to the existing barn in Mr. Brown's field, and then place a second barn in Mr. McCoy's field in a corner diagonal to the existing barn. Explain to the child that Mr. Brown built a second barn next to his first barn, and that Mr. McCoy built a second barn across the field from his first barn.

Questions Related to Conservation: Ask the child: "Is there more grass, less grass or the same amount of grass in Mr. McCoy's field as there is in Mr. Brown's field?"

Interpretation: At this point, as before, the recording of the child's response is all that is required.

Action: After the child has responded, place another barn next to the existing two barns in Mr. Brown's field, and then place a third barn in the center of Mr. McCoy's field. Explain that both Mr. Brown and Mr. McCoy built a third barn in each of their fields. Show that Mr. Brown built his third barn next to the other two barns and that Mr. McCoy built a third barn in the center of his field.

Questions Related to Conservation: Ask the child: "Is there more grass, less grass or the same amount of grass in Mr. McCoy's field as there is in Mr. Brown's field?"

Interpretation: If the child's answer indicates that the same area is perceived in the two fields, then the child is able to conserve area. If the answer indicates that a difference is perceived, then the child is unable to conserve area.

Note: If the child continually counts the barns, it is possible that the child is conserving number rather than area. To verify conservation of area, place a fourth barn in Mr. Brown's field next to the three existing barns, and then place a fourth barn in Mr. McCoy's field on top of an existing barn, making a two-story structure. Repeat the question: "Is there more grass, less grass, or the same amount of grass in Mr. McCoy's field as there is in Mr. Brown's field?" If the answer is that there is more grass in Mr. McCoy's field or that there is less grass in Mr. Brown's field, the child conserves area. If the answer is inconsistent with either of these two statements, the child is unable to conserve area.

e. *Task:* Conservation of Length

 Objects Required: 1. two identical rods (that is, dowel rods, plastic drinking straws)

 2. two toy cars which are identical except for color

Setting: Place two rods of equal length side by side. These two rods represent two roads.

Agreement to Sameness: Ask the child: "Do you agree that both roads are the same length?" If the child does not perceive sameness and objects cannot be manipulated (that is, the rods cut or moved) to the child's satisfaction, the task must be aborted at this point.

Action: After agreement to sameness, place an identical toy car at the beginning of each road, explaining that both cars are going to start at the same time and travel at the same speed until each car reaches the end of its road. For discussion purposes, the cars may be two different colors (that is, yellow and green).

Questions Related to Conservation: Ask the child: "If both cars start at the same speed, will the yellow car reach the end of its road before, after, or at the same time as the green car reaches the end of its road?"

Interpretation: At this point, merely record the child's answer.

Action: Move one of the rods so that it extends beyond the other rod. Place the cars at the beginning of the roads once more. Place the yellow car (or equivalent) at the beginning of the extended rod.

Questions Related to Conservation: Ask the child: "If both cars start at the same time and travel at the same speed, will the yellow car reach the end of its road before, after, or at the same time as the green car reaches the end of its road?"

Interpretation: If the child's answer indicates that the cars will reach the end of the road at the same time, then the child is able to conserve length. If the answer indicates that a difference is perceived, then the child is unable to conserve length.

f. *Task:* Conservation of Weight

Objects Required: two equal amounts of clay which may differ in color

Setting: Form two proportionally equal balls of clay containing the same amount. For discussion purposes, two colors of clay (that is, red and blue) may be used.

Agreement to Sameness: Ask the child: "Do you agree that there is the same amount of blue clay as red clay?" If the child does not perceive sameness and objects cannot be manipulated (that is, portions of clay removed from one ball) to the child's satisfaction, the task must be aborted at this point. If the child does agree to sameness, the child should not be allowed to touch the clay again during the administering of this task.

Action: Flatten the blue clay into a "pancake" shape.

Questions Related to Conservation: Ask the child: "Is there more blue clay, less blue clay, or the same amount of blue clay as there is red clay?"

Interpretation: If the child's answer indicates that the same weight of the clay is perceived, then the child is able to conserve weight. If the answer indicates that a difference is perceived, then the child is unable to conserve weight.

Selected Readings

ASCD, *Perceiving—Behaving—Becoming.* Washington, D.C.: Association for Supervision and Curriculum Development, 1962. Explains the characteristics of the adequate, fully functioning person; chapter 14 presents some implications for education.

Ausubel, David, *Educational Psychology: A Cognitive View.* New York: Holt, Rinehart and Winston, 1968. Contains reports of investigations relating cognitive structure, concept development, thinking, and problem solving.

Gage, N. L., and David C. Berliner, *Educational Psychology.* Chicago: Rand McNally & Company, 1974. Unit 18 provides a description of Piaget's and Jerome Bruner's theories.

Gagné, Robert M., *The Conditions of Learning,* 2d ed. New York: Holt, Rinehart and Winston, 1970. Explains how learning takes place, reviews some leading theories of learning, and relates conditions of learning to teaching procedures.

Hass, Glen, Joseph Bondi, and Jon Wiles (Eds.), *Curriculum Planning: A New Approach.* Boston: Allyn & Bacon, Inc., 1974. Sections 2 and 3 contain readings of human development and the nature of learning.

Inhelder, Bärbel, and Jean Piaget, *The Growth of Logical Thinking from Child-hood to Adolescence*. New York: Basic Books, Inc., Publishers, 1958. Presents the theory and supporting observations of Piaget.

Leonard, George B., *Education and Ecstasy*. New York: Dell Publishing Co., Inc. (The Delacorte Press), 1968. Chapter 2 summarizes artificial devices for altering the functioning of the brain, and points to positive reinforcement and humanistic psychology as promising efforts to expand human potentials.

Ragan, William B., and George Henderson, *Foundations of American Education*. New York: Harper & Row, Publishers, 1970. Chapter 6 gives a summary of the social characteristics of elementary school children; explains changing views of intelligence tests.

Rosenthal, Robert, and Leonore Jacobson, *Pygmalion in the Classroom*. New York: Holt, Rinehart and Winston, 1968. Reports experimental evidence that teacher expectations influence student performance.

Skinner, B. F., *Beyond Freedom and Dignity*. New York: Alfred A. Knopf, Inc., 1971. A challenging and logical application of behavior modification.

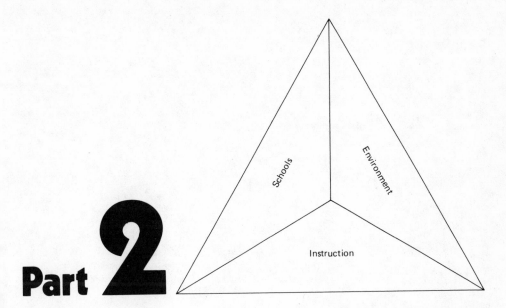

Part **2**

PATTERNS
for CURRICULUM

The organization of the institution, the environment of classrooms and schools, and the processes of instruction interact to shape the curriculum. Part 2 explores the patterns of these facets of curriculum.

Organizing
SCHOOLS

I fervently hope that diversity will replace the remarkable similarity of our schools, and I believe that a more interesting world will result.

Bruce R. Joyce, *Alternative Models of Elementary Education.*
(Waltham, Mass.: Blaisdell Publishing Company, 1970), Foreword.

A student on one end of a log and Mark Hopkins on the other is a pattern of bringing a teacher and a pupil together for instructional purposes. But what about the forming of groups for instructional purposes whenever there are 200 pupils and 6 teachers, or 500 pupils and 20 teachers, or 1,200 pupils and 28 teachers? What about a teacher at Everyman's School? A teacher of classes or a class, a member of a department or a team, in one building of many in a district or the only building in a district? How can the patterns for forming instructional groups be described in these settings? What are self-contained classrooms, departmentalized classes, heterogeneous groups, homogeneous groups, teacher teams, gradedness, nongradedness, and so on?

Within the elementary school, the movement of pupils occurs in two major directions, vertically and horizontally. Utilizing these two major directions as axes, the existing patterns for the forming of instructional groups will be identified, described, and analyzed. A pattern will be identified as either vertical or horizontal, depending upon its function.

VERTICAL ORGANIZATION

The first major direction of pupil movement within the elementary school is vertical. Beginning the elementary school at the age of five or six, in first grade or in level one, pupils complete elementary school at the chronological age of eleven or twelve, in sixth grade or level fifteen. Vertical organization is the plan of the school for identifying when and who is ready to enter, as well as the procedures for regulating pupil progress through the elementary school to a completion point. The NEA Project of Instruction stated, "Vertical organization

The facilitating of learning requires organization.

provides a system for classifying students and moving them upward from entry to departure from the school unit."[1]

States have adopted legislation that defines the entry point of children into the elementary schools, usually in terms of chronological age. The majority of children enter school at six years of age. If kindergarten is a legally recognized part of the elementary school program in a state, then children will enter at five years of age. The statutes of the various states do not define the completion point for the elementary school, but they do define the upper limit of compulsory attendance as fourteen, fifteen, sixteen, seventeen, or eighteen years of age. A plan for the vertical organization of the elementary school must accommodate the entry point as defined by the legislation of that particular state. There is considerable need for legislation that will recognize additional aspects of child growth and development as significant for entry into the elementary school.

Two plans have evolved to facilitate the vertical movement of pupils through the elementary school. The oldest of the plans is called the "graded school." The newer plan is called "the nongraded school."

The Graded School

The graded elementary school grew out of conditions that existed in the nineteenth century when public school systems were being established. The necessity of dividing children into groups for instructional purposes, the relative simplicity of giving a single assignment to an entire class, the scarcity of instructional materials, the economic necessity of maintaining large classes, the low level of

---

[1] Project on the Instructional Program of the Public Schools, *Planning and Organizing for Teaching.* (Washington, D.C.: National Education Association, 1963), p. 70.

teacher preparation, the apparent factory-like precision present in the industrial era—these were some of the factors that contributed to the establishment of the graded school.

Horace Mann's visit to and evaluation of the Prussian graded school suggested to him that the graded pattern was a solution to these conditions. In his "Seventh Annual Report" Mann reviewed the graded system and urged its adoption.

SITUATION 4.1   What is our heritage in the graded vertical organizational pattern? Review Horace Mann's *Seventh Annual Report*, and then compare his recommendations with *Schools for the 70's*, a report from the National Education Association Project on Instruction (see Selected Readings).

The first graded school established in the United States was the Quincy School in Boston in 1848. By 1860 the graded school had become the model for the elementary schools. A nationwide survey of more than 2,300 elementary principals, conducted in 1968, suggested that the graded pattern dominates the vertical organization of elementary schools. Approximately 84 percent of these principals reported that the primary units under their supervison were graded and that 91 percent of the intermediate units were also graded.[2] The author has been unable to locate a national survey of the organizational patterns of elementary schools since 1968. The tentative plan of the Department of Elementary Principals, NEA, is to replicate the 1968 study during 1978.

The term "graded school" has become such an inclusive term that definition is best done through illustration. However, it is possible to identify some basic features which characterize most, but not all, graded schools.

Basic Features of the Graded-School Pattern

1. The graded school recognizes chronological age as the primary, if not the only, determiner of entry. Chronological age and years in school are the major ingredients of the decisions that locate the child within the vertical sequence.

2. The graded school has identified a body of skills, knowledges, and appreciations, and has placed them in a sequence of six or seven positions called "grades." Each position equals one school term, or approximately nine months.

3. As a result of these positions and their sequence, graded textbooks were developed. Textbooks are typically assigned to a position within the sequence, and pupils at that position study the assigned text.

4. The decisions governing the vertical movement of pupils through the sequence are made at the end of the school term. Some variations have been introduced to provide for quarterly or semester promotions.

5. Promotion from one position to the next higher position within the

---

[2] Department of Elementary School Principals, NEA, *The Elementary School Principalship in 1968*. (Washington, D.C.: National Education Association, 1968), p. 65.

sequence is dependent upon the pupil's having completed, with average or below success, all the work of the preceding position.

6. Graded schools may utilize the horizontal organizations of the self-contained classroom, departmentalization, platoon, or team.

7. The symbols expressing a graded organization are 1–6, or K–3 and 4–6, as applied to a building. For a school district the symbols, elementary through secondary, might be: K–5, 6–8, 9–10, and 11–12, or K–8 and 9–12. These symbols represent the vertical organization and the commitments of the district to kindergarten, middle school, mid-high, and high school.

8. At its lowest level, gradedness is essentially a lockstep system. Tewksbury has characterized this level as follows:

> *The total work of the elementary school is divided into six levels, more commonly referred to as grades. The work to be accomplished in each grade is clearly designated. It usually consists of specific skills, topics and textbooks to be covered. All boys and girls in a given grade are expected to do only that work reserved for that grade and complete it in a year's time. If they cannot complete it, they are retained for a year to repeat all of the work.*[3]

Fortunately, not all graded schools operate at this low level. Many have found ways to eliminate some of the weaknesses that are generally associated with gradedness.

Protests against this lockstep system began before the beginning of this century; as early as 1892 President Charles W. Eliot of Harvard University advocated instruction addressed to the individual. Three developments since the turn of the century have been particularly influential in creating dissatisfaction with the graded system. One of these has been the increasing amount of information about the wide differences that exist among children in any given grade in school. Pupils entering the first grade generally differ in mental age by approximately four years; by the time children reach the sixth grade, the spread amounts to five or six years. This means that the first-grade teacher must work with some pupils who are not ready for the work laid out for the first grade, and that the sixth-grade teacher must work with pupils who differ even more widely in ability to perform school tasks. A rule of thumb is that the range of instructional and achievement differences within a group is normally greater than one-half the chronological age. The second development has been the increasing acceptance by school people of the philosophy of continuous growth, which holds that children should be assisted in growing according to their natural patterns without depriving bright students of the opportunity to learn as much as their abilities and efforts permit, and without trying to force slow-learning children to live up to standards that were never intended for them. The third development may be called the "quest for quality, equality, and personalization"—the emphasis on efforts to identify the gifts of children and to help them maximize these gifts.

---

[3] J. L. Tewksbury, *Nongrading in the Elementary School.* (Columbus, Ohio: Charles E. Merrill Publishing Co., 1967), p. 2.

Between Gradedness and Nongradedness

Increasing numbers of nonpromotions, brighter children who were not challenged by the standardized curriculum, and the increasing number of dropouts in the upper grades motivated schools to modify the graded pattern. The schools in St. Louis adopted a quarterly promotion plan in 1862, hoping to break the lock-step. The Pueblo plan was adopted in 1888 to permit the formation of instructional groups based on ability.

During the first three decades of the twentieth century, the Dalton Plan, the Winnetka Plan, the Cambridge Plan, the Elizabeth Plan, the Portland Plan, the North Denver Plan, and the Santa Barbara Plan appeared as innovations intended to correct the faults and increase the flexibility of the graded plan. Descriptions of these plans are available from many sources. They are mentioned here only to indicate that dissatisfaction with the graded system has existed for many years.

SITUATION 4.2   Research two of the following innovative vertical organizational plans: Dalton; Winnetka; Cambridge; Elizabeth; Portland; North Denver, Santa Barbara. What characterized the attempts of these plans to correct the faults and increase the flexibility of the graded vertical organizational pattern?

The history of education is replete with the names of famous plans to move pupils through a standardized body of content. Greatly altered versions of these plans can be found in the literature describing the grouping practices of the elementary schools of the present era. The patterns of the present era carry different labels, operate in different settings, and are designed, to some extent, to serve purposes other than escorting pupils through a standard body of content at different rates. It is an error, for example, to equate the modern nongraded school with the one-room rural school of the 1900s.

A new arrangement of the vertical organization sequence within the graded pattern is symbolized as 5–8, or 6–8. This organization expresses the creation of the "middle school," consisting of grades 5 or 6 through 8. The rapid growth of the middle-school pattern may be explained by the following factors: (1) today's youngsters are more mature, so that sixth-graders are apparently more like seventh- or eighth-graders than like fifth-graders, and so that ninth-graders are more like tenth-graders than seventh- and eighth-graders; (2) the creation of a junior high that includes fifth and sixth graders from several feeder elementary schools furthers the experience of pupils at an earlier age in a more cosmopolitan population; (3) the counting of credits earned in ninth grade for both high school graduation and college entrance imposes a structure on the ninth grade unlike grades 7 or 8 and like grades 10 through 12. The release of staff and the increased flexibility of time scheduling resulting from the moving of ninth-graders has fostered some creative innovations in several middle-schools in their horizontal organization patterns.

The advocates of the middle school have revised and modified the premises fundamental to what was called a "junior high." This is not to imply that the middle-school movement does not have a new integrity and quality. The transition from a junior high to a middle school is a sound movement. The advocates of the middle-school movement represent a philosophy of instruction more than a plan of organization. Many former teachers in elementary schools are now teaching in middle schools. One of the strengths of the movement is the integration of the elementary school approach and the senior high approach. Some of the brightest innovations in schools are occurring within the middle school. It seems to have quickly established itself as a movement and plan with quality and promise.

The Nongraded School (Continuous Program Plan)

A new plan to govern the vertical movement of pupils through the elementary school began to penetrate the organizational patterns of schools during the 1950s. This pattern probably started in 1934 in Western Springs, Illinois; in Milwaukee, Wisconsin, in 1942; and in Park Forest, Illinois, in 1948. But it was not until the 1950s that the plan began to spread.

Information concerning the actual utilization of this pattern is meager and somewhat confusing. For example, one 1962 study of 600 elementary schools across the nation found that 6 percent of these schools were nongraded during 1956, 12 percent by 1961, with 26 percent of this group expecting to be nongraded by 1966.[4] Robert Anderson said in 1967 that "about one school out of four is attempting to develop nongradedness."[5] However, a 1968 survey of 2,318 elementary principals suggested that a little more than 10 percent of the schools under their supervision were nongraded in the primary years, with less than 4 percent of the intermediate units being nongraded.[6] This same survey also reported that of the 2,318 elementary principals, 27.5 percent had used the nongraded plan at the primary level and 17.1 percent had used it at the upper levels. Apparently the prediction that one of four schools would attempt the nongraded plan was correct. However, a significant number of the users have discontinued the nongraded plan.[7]

Whatever the degree of penetration and utilization this new pattern had, it was the first significant break in the domination of the vertical axis by the graded pattern. It is not a necessarily happy comment on the United States elementary school system that, during this period of great change in other aspects of the scene, the schools made little if any modification in their vertical organization patterns.

Basic Features of the Nongraded Plan

An analysis of the descriptive materials developed by districts to explain their nongraded organization tends to support Shea's definition:

---

[4] Project on the Instructional Program of the Public Schools, *The Principal Looks at the School.* (Washington, D.C.: National Education Association, 1962), Preface and pp. 39–40.
[5] Robert H. Anderson, "The Nongraded Elementary School: An Overview," *National Elementary Principal* (November 1967), pp. 5–10.
[6] Department of Elementary School Principals, NEA, p. 65.
[7] Department of Elementary School Principals, NEA, p. 65.

The nongraded primary or primary cycle is simply a plan in which children beyond kindergarten but not yet classified as first graders can be grouped together on the basis of age and achievement in reading. Children move forward through a series of designated levels of attainment in reading.[8]

However, the two writers who are usually given credit for bringing the attention of the nation's educators to the nongraded pattern, John I. Goodlad and Robert H. Anderson, seem uneasy with this kind of definition. Goodlad and Anderson wrote,

While we are heartened by the lively interest that has been shown, we confess to a deep concern over the superficiality and inadequacy of much of what is done in the name of nongrading. Many of the so-called nongraded plans are little different from the graded plans they replace, and except for the levels scheme in reading there are few changes of real significance to children.[9]

Although programs and definitions vary, the following features are common to most of them.

1. Continuous progress, vertical and horizontal movement, of pupils is provided for throughout the school year.

2. Curriculum articulation is provided by means of the identification of skills, knowledges, and appreciations to be developed within a content area or areas over a wide span of years without a specific length of time being assigned to any portion of this span.

3. The pupil is positioned in the sequence based on his ability in and achievement of these skills, knowledges, and appreciations without regard for the number of years in school.

4. Extensive reporting and record-keeping systems are developed between teachers and between teachers and parents.

5. A successful experience is provided for each pupil at his position with no failure or retention.

Advantages Claimed for the Nongraded Plan

1. Children are positioned, accepted, and supported at their maturity levels and progress at their own rates of development.

2. The plan requires teachers to be more specific about objectives, materials, and procedures.

3. A child who experiences success is more motivated and challenged to continue to develop than one who experiences failure.

4. The use of individualized instruction models and materials are facilitated.

5. The plan involves more cooperation and communication between and among teachers.

6. There is more continuity in the child's learning experiences.

7. The plan requires more cooperation and communication between and among teachers and parents.

[8] Joe L. Frost and S. Thomas Rowland (Eds.), *The Elementary School: Principles and Problems.* (Boston: Houghton Mifflin Company, 1969), p. 333.

[9] John I. Goodlad and Robert H. Anderson, *The Nongraded Elementary School.* (New York: Harcourt Brace Jovanovich, Inc., 1963), introduction, p. vii.

8. Several studies have indicated that the academic achievement and positive attitudes of children are as good or better for students in the nongraded plan when compared to the graded plan.[10]

Limitations Claimed for the Nongraded Plan

1. The plan is an organizational pattern with implications for the vertical movement of pupils. It does not provide a class or horizontal group that is alike in all aspects. The teacher has a great burden to study the individual pupil, and to provide instruction and guidance that is geared to individual needs and abilities.

2. The plan could, and has in some cases resulted in an imbalance in the curriculum. For example, a sequence and clustering of skills in reading is a more common practice for the plan than a sequence of skills, knowledges, and appreciations for several or all curriculum areas.

3. The identification of a sequence can result in limiting each child's experiences to the same sequence. Or a teacher could become overly concerned about pupil positioning in the sequence and teach only for the sequence, thereby limiting the range of materials used and denying pupils opportunities for participating in the selection and planning of learning experiences.

4. Parents and teachers are conditioned to the graded plan and the reporting practices based upon the graded-school pattern. A great amount of time and effort is required to help them understand the nongraded plan and its reporting practices.

HORIZONTAL ORGANIZATION

The influence of state government upon the selection of a horizontal pattern by a school district is not imposed by statute. The state may recommend a specific pattern, but its real control is through its establishment and approval of preparation programs in the institutions that prepare teachers for state certification.

The certification, or licensing, of teachers is a responsibility of the state. As one of its functions under this responsibility, the state inspects, evaluates, and approves or disapproves the teacher preparation programs of the colleges and universities. Many times the programs are designed to supply teachers especially prepared, or at least better prepared, to work within one of the possible patterns on the horizontal and vertical axes. So, a local school district may choose any pattern from these axes, yet its choice may be such that it would create a need for an in-service education program for its staff.

Horizontal patterns determine and govern the distribution and division of pupils into instructional groups or classes as well as the allocation of teachers at the various levels, grades, or positions on the vertical axis. The following patterns of organization—self-contained, departmentalized, platoon or dual progress, and

[10] Lyn S. Martin and Barbara N. Pavan, "Current Research on Open Space Nongrading, Vertical Grouping and Team Teaching," *Phi Delta Kappan*, Vol. 57 (January 1976), pp. 310–16.

team—are the most frequently chosen plans for the horizontal axis of elementary schools.

Self-Contained Classroom

The proponents of the self-contained classroom emphasize the need for planning for individual differences. A pamphlet devoted entirely to a discussion of the advantages of this plan stated that the self-contained classroom "develops a climate of learning which encourages, stimulates and guides boys and girls according to their individual abilities and interests."[11] This plan, however, is unique among the plans discussed in this section in that it represents prevailing practice, whereas the others represent proposals for change. The nationwide survey of 2,318 elementary principals cited earlier reported that more than 95 percent of schools utilized the self-contained classroom pattern during the primary years. At the intermediate level these principals reported that 88 percent of fourth grades, 80 percent of fifth grades and 71 percent of sixth grades were self-contained.[12] Proponents of the self-contained classroom plan, therefore, urge that those who are considering reorganization should examine the plan carefully in order to be fully aware of what they are changing.

Critics of the self-contained classroom have been increasing in numbers for several years. They generally describe it at its worst—an organization in which special teachers cannot be used; a classroom in which the teacher and a group of pupils are cut off from association with other teachers and pupils; a classroom in which instruction is addressed to the class as a whole; and a classroom in which little consideration is shown for pupils with high or low ability, since instruction is aimed at pupils with "average" ability. Proponents of the plan, on the other hand, tend to describe the self-contained classroom at its best. It may be well to repeat in this connection the statement that no plan of organization can, of itself, improve instruction; the most that it can accomplish is to provide a framework in which the imaginative teachers can instruct as well as they are capable of doing.

Advantages Claimed for the Self-Contained Classroom

1. The self-contained classroom calls for placing a group of pupils with a teacher for the major portion of a school day. This enables the teacher to learn a great deal about individual pupils through long association and observation of them in a wide variety of learning situations.

2. The teacher in the self-contained classroom is in a good position to help pupils understand the interrelatedness of subject-matter fields.

3. Pupils in a self-contained classroom have more opportunities for learning to participate effectively in group enterprises; they stay with the same group, under the guidance of the same teacher, for a major portion of the school day.

4. The self-contained classroom permits a more flexible use of time; sig-

---

11 *The Self-Contained Classroom.* (Washington, D.C.: Association for Supervision and Curriculum Development, 1960), p. 1.
12 Department of Elementary School Principals, NEA, p. 66.

nificant learning experiences are not brought to an abrupt end because pupils must go to another class. It is easier to schedule fields trips and other experiences that involve more than one period in the daily schedule.

5. Although sound subject-matter knowledge is important for elementary teachers, other competencies, such as understanding of child growth and development and ability to organize learning experiences, are also important. The scope and depth of subjects taught in elementary schools are not so great that they cannot be acquired by regular classroom teachers.

6. The self-contained classroom plan can be modified to permit teachers who are weak in certain fields to exchange classes with other teachers.

Limitations Claimed for the Self-Contained Classroom

1. The need for greater achievement in basic subjects calls for greater depth of preparation on the part of the teacher than teachers in self-contained classrooms generally have.

2. Critics of the self-contained classroom maintain that pupils need experiences with many teachers.

3. Teachers who are not well prepared in all areas may neglect the areas in which they lack competence; this leads to imbalance in the school program.

4. Teachers in self-contained classrooms tend to become isolated from other teachers, rather than working as members of a team.

Departmentalization

Departmentalization may be viewed as allocating an area of specialization to each teacher and then scheduling pupil groups between and among the specialized teachers. The area of specialization allocated to a teacher may be one curriculum area or a combination of curriculum areas. Departmentalization may also be viewed as a plan for grouping pupils which permits the teacher to specialize in the teaching of one or a few subjects, as contrasted to the self-contained classroom, which requires that the teacher be a generalist who teaches all or nearly all subjects to the pupils in her classroom.

The self-contained classroom plan prevailed throughout the second half of the nineteenth century; departmentalization spread rapidly after the turn of the century—by 1929 some form of departmentalization existed in 35 percent of the elementary schools surveyed, and by 1949 it existed in 51 percent. By mid-century, however, it was losing favor. A national survey conducted in 1959 indicated that only 9.9 percent of the schools were completely departmentalized.[13] A study reported three years later (1962) indicated a slight trend toward more departmentalization: some departmentalization, 36 percent; all departmentalization, 3 percent.[14] The survey of 2,318 principals conducted by the Department of Elementary School Principals during the 1967–1968 school year found that approximately 1 percent of the primary classrooms were depart-

[13] Henry J. Otto and David C. Sanders, *Elementary School Organization and Administration,* 4th ed. (New York: Appleton-Century-Crofts, 1964), p. 75.
[14] Project on the Instructional Program of the Public Schools, p. 13.

mentalized, with 8.5 percent, 16.4 percent, and 23 percent of departmentalization being reported for the intermediate grades. Of the 2,318 principals, 19
percent had used departmentalization in the primary years. Of this group, 21.9
percent rated it as being very valuable, and 39.4 percent rated it as "not worth
the cost." At the intermediate level, 54.8 percent of the 2,318 principals had
utilized the departmentalization pattern. Of this group, 65 percent rated it as
very valuable and 7.4 percent rated it as "not worth the cost."[15] Departmentalization, with pupils or teachers moving from classroom to classroom at the end of
each period, is practiced more frequently in the fourth, fifth, and sixth grades
than it is in the lower grades. It remains to be seen whether departmentalization
will again take over in elementary schools as more and more critics favor the
need to teach more content and skills.

Advantages Claimed for Departmentalization

1. The new programs, particularly in mathematics and science, emphasize
teaching each subject according to the structure of the discipline; only the teacher
who has specalized in the discipline can do this.

2. It is a rare teacher who has high-level competence in the teaching of more
than one or two subjects.

3. Departmentalization makes it easier for the teacher to keep up with new
developments in methods, materials, and equipment in one or two fields.

4. More young men may be attracted to teaching in the elementary school
if they are not required to teach all subjects and can specialize.

5. It is easier to provide special equipment for one or two rooms in a building than it is to provide special equipment for all classrooms.

Limitations Claimed for Departmentalization

1. It is difficult for a teacher who has a different group of pupils each period
of the school day to learn to know every pupil well.

2. There is little opportunity to help pupils see the interrelationships among
school subjects.

3. There is little opportunity for unit teaching, which cuts across subject-
matter lines and usually requres more than one period in the school day.

4. The plan encourages teachers to regard themselves as subject-matter
specialists rather than as specialists working with children.

5. Routine matters such as record keeping, evaluation, guidance, and reporting to parents are difficult to handle under this plan.

The Platoon School and Dual Progress ⇒

An effort to integrate the strengths of the self-contained classroom with the
strength of the departmentalized classes has resulted in what is called the "platoon school." Half of a pupil's day is spent in a homeroom, and the other half
with specialized, departmentalized teachers. The homeroom teacher usually
teaches language arts and reading plus one or two other subjects. Specialized

---

15 Department of Elementary School Principals, NEA, p. 104.

teachers are assigned to mathematics, science, art, physical education, music, and so on.

The Gary plan, initiated in 1908 by William A. Wirt, was one of the most highly publicized as well as one of the most frequently imitated. A pamphlet has been preserved which gives in Wirt's own words his reasons for establishing the Work-Study-Play School.[16] This record reveals that his objectives included a great deal more than the installation of the platoon type of elementary school organization; his stated objective was "making the city a good place for rearing children." Accordingly, he wanted the Gary School to be a child's world and a people's clubhouse; he wanted a longer school week; and he wanted all child welfare facilities merged with the school program. Schools throughout the country, however, adopted the platoon type of elementary school organization without including the other features of the original Gary plan. Pupils were divided into two groups, or platoons. While one group met in regular classrooms to study the fundamental subjects, the other group met in the auditorium, the gymnasium, and other special rooms to engage in various activities. One reason for the popularity of the plan was that it provided for a more economical use of the school plant.

A popular application of the platoon organization is the "dual progress plan" developed by Stoddard. The plan, as presented by Stoddard and tried out in selected school systems, divided the subjects taught in the elementary school into two groups called "cultural imperatives" and "cultural electives." Pupils above the third grade spend a half-day with a homeroom teacher studying the cultural imperatives—language arts, social studies, health, and physical education. They spend the other half of the school day with special teachers studying the cultural electives—mathematics, science, art, music, and foreign language. As the name of the plan implies, a dual system of regulating pupil progress is employed; pupils progress through a graded sequence in the cultural imperatives and through a nongraded sequence in the cultural electives. Thus, pupils who have exceptional talents in science may move rapidly through the sequential levels in that subject while staying in their particular homeroom in which grouping is based on "all-around maturity."

Like the original Gary plan, this plan goes far beyond presenting a procedure for assigning pupils to groups for instructional purposes. This is implied by the subtitle of Stoddard's book[17] which explores new approaches to subject matter, teaching methods, and the education of teachers.

Advantages Claimed for the Dual Progress Plan

1. The dual progress plan extends downward into the elementary school a modified form of the grouping practices used in junior high and middle schools.

2. Responsibility for counseling is assigned to the homeroom teacher, who has an opportunity to know individual pupils, their families, and their neighborhoods well.

[16] William A. Wirt, *The Great Lockout in America's Citizenship Plants.* (printed by students of Horace Mann School, 1937).
[17] George D. Stoddard, *The Dual Progress Plan: A New Philosophy and Program in Elementary Education.* (New York: Harper & Row, Publishers, 1961).

3. The pupil spends enough time with one teacher to develop a feeling of belonging to a group; the individual is not lost in the shuffle of classes as may be the case in a departmentalized system.

4. The homeroom teacher has an opportunity to help pupils see the interrelationship between the language arts and the social studies.

5. There is a closer relationship between teacher competence and teacher assignment. Teachers who hate mathematics are not called upon to teach it; those who are interested and well prepared in the subject can provide a higher quality of instruction.

6. Pupils have an opportunity to become acquainted with several teachers, each of whom differs in method and personality.

7. The opportunity to specialize in the teaching of one area may attract more capable teachers to the elementary school.

8. Pupils who possess special interests and talents in one area may progress more rapidly in that area than they could do in a graded school.

9. Special teachers offer work on a longitudinal basis throughout the elementary school; they are in a good position to identify pupils with exceptional talents and to guide their development over a period of years.

Limitations Claimed for the Dual Progress Plan

1. The rationale for designating certain school subjects as cultural imperatives and others as cultural electives is confusing. It is not difficult to make a case for language arts, social studies, and health as cultural imperatives; it is more difficult to understand why mathematics and science are not also cultural imperatives.

2. The plan does not provide for continuous progress, since pupils who do not meet the grade standards in the graded portion of the plan may be required to repeat the work of the entire grade.

3. It is difficult for the special teachers in the nongraded portion of the plan to come to know each pupil well; parents must consult several teachers to learn about pupil progress; and pupils must move from one class to another about every 40 minutes.

4. Teacher specialists in the nongraded portion of the plan must devote a great deal of time to planning content and activities to be included in each sequential level and to constructing tests to determine when a pupil is ready to move from one level to the next.

5. The preplanning of content for each level may deprive pupils of the experience of discovering useful materials and of exercising initiative in planning learning activities.

SITUATION 4.3   Examine George D. Stoddard's *The Dual Progress Plan: A New Philosophy and Program in Elementary Education* for new approaches and methodologies you would contemplate adopting as an elementary teacher.

Team Teaching

Those who like to find historical precedents for current innovations in educational practices frequently point out that the cooperative group plan, developed by James F. Hosic and his associates in the early 1930s, was a forerunner of the team-teaching technique that is receiving a great deal of attention today.[18] The two plans do have certain common characteristics: Each teacher works as a member of a group of teachers; one teacher serves as the chairman or leader; each teacher bears certain special responsibilities; and space specifically designed for particular types of activity is essential. The fact that the two plans have common characteristics, however, does not justify an assumption that team teaching is nothing more than a revival of the cooperative group plan of the 1930s.

Team teaching began to receive a great deal of attention in 1957 when the Harvard Graduate School of Education sponsored a program in Franklin School at Lexington, Massachusetts. The experiment was financed by a grant from the Fund for the Advancement of Education. Robert H. Anderson, director of the project, and Francis Keppel, Dean of the Harvard Graduate School of Education, were primarily responsible for getting the program under way. Other programs were soon started at Concord and Newton, Massachusetts, "to narrow the gap between research and practice by linking the university with public school systems to make teaching more attractive and effective and to extend the influence of gifted teachers." "The time has come," said Dean Keppel, "to recognize the difference between those who make a lifetime career in education and those who stay only a few years, or who teach part-time. . . . At present organizational patterns treat all alike."[19]

From this beginning, team teaching has become one of the most widely discussed and frequently adopted educational innovations in recent years. Programs vary from the cooperative efforts of two teachers to programs involving several staff members, several classes, and a variety of grouping patterns. The principal characteristics of the plan have been stated as follows:

Basically, team teaching is an arrangement that provides for having two or more teachers, with abilities and skills that complement each other, assume joint responsibility for directing the learning activities of a group of students. Together, the members of the team take charge of planning lessons, developing appropriate methods and materials, and teaching and evaluating a program of studies for their student group.[20]

A study mentioned earlier in the chapter reported that in 1955–1956, 5 percent of the schools surveyed used the team-teaching pattern and in 1960–1961,

[18] J. F. Hosic et al., *The Cooperative Group Plan for the Organization of Elementary Schools.* (New York: Teachers College Press, 1931).
[19] Arthur D. Morse, *Schools of Tomorrow—Today.* (New York: Doubleday & Company, Inc., 1960), pp. 21–22.
[20] National Elementary Principal, *Elementary School Organization: Purposes, Patterns, Perspectives.* (Washington, D.C.: National Education Association, December 1961), p. 115.

15 percent of these schools used team teaching, and predicted that in 1965–1966, 30 percent of these schools would be utilizing team teaching.[21] During the 1967–1968 school year, another study, also mentioned earlier in this chapter, found that 2.5 percent of the primary units utilized team teaching, with 3.3 percent of the fourth grades, 4.7 percent of the fifth grades, and 5.7 percent of the sixth grades attempting to adopt it. At the primary level, 22 percent of the principals included in this study had used the team-teaching pattern. Of this group, 50 percent felt that it was very valuable, while 8 percent felt that it was not worth the time and cost. At the intermediate level, 29 percent of the principals had used this teaching pattern, with 61 percent reporting that it was very valuable and 3 percent that it was not worth the time and cost.[22]

As schools have become involved in the establishment of the team pattern, many plans of organization and operation have emerged. Most of the plans provide for large-group learning situations, as well as opportunity for pupils to work alone on individual projects. One plan uses three teachers and a clerical aide for seventy-five pupils at one grade level. One teacher is designated as team leader and is paid an additional sum for this responsibility; the other two are cooperating teachers. Another version, used in a university campus school, has an experienced teacher who serves as team leader, an inexperienced teacher, two student teachers, and a teacher aid for fifty-five pupils at the second- and third-grade levels. The team leader calls the members together frequently to plan and evaluate the program. The inexperienced member teaches those phases of the program for which he is best prepared. The student teachers have an opportunity to observe more than one teacher, to teach certain topics for which they have made special preparation, to join in the planning and evaluation of learning activities, and to have their performance evaluated by more than one teacher. The teacher aide performs many routine tasks and makes it possible for the professional members of the team to concentrate on more important aspects of teaching. The team leader closed an account of the experiment with the statement: "We have a learner-centered organization where our activities are not hampered as in an egg crate organization."[23]

Advantages Claimed for Team Teaching

1. Team teaching provides for a better utilization of the competencies of superior teachers, and more can profit from their teaching. Their influence is reflected in the planning of better programs of instruction.

2. Teaching teams can utilize any of the horizontal organizations: a self-contained team, a departmentalized team, two teams (one self-contained and one departmentalized) for platooning.

3. Superior teachers receive increases in salary without leaving the classroom to take administrative positions.

[21] Project on the Instructional Program of the Public Schools, p. 18.
[22] Department of Elementary School Principals, NEA, p. 66.
[23] Hattie Orr, "UTTO: Ungraded Team Teaching Organization," *Oklahoma Teacher* (December 1963), pp. 6–9.

4. The plan facilitates the orientation of new teachers to the school system and to the community.

5. Student teachers gain valuable experience by observing the teaching of more than one teacher and by participating in cooperative planning.

6. The use of clerical aides and noncertificated personnel relieves teachers of many nonteaching chores.

7. Pupils gain valuable experience by being able to work in large-group learning situations, in small-group learning situations, and as individuals.

8. The plan facilitates a more effective use of space, materials, and equipment.

9. The work of the pupils can go on more effectively when one member of the team is absent because of illness than it does when one teacher is responsible for the entire program.

10. Beginning teachers have a better opportunity for in-service growth than they do when they are isolated in one room.

Limitations Claimed for Team Teaching

1. The success of team teaching depends to a great extent on the ability of members of the team to work together harmoniously; if friction develops in interpersonal relations, the program suffers.

2. Members of the team must spend a great deal of time working on plans for scheduling, for group activities, and for individual projects.

3. The problem of selecting superior teachers to serve as group leaders is a complex one; teachers who are very successful at working with a group of pupils may experience frustration when they are faced with the semiadministrative tasks involved in serving as team leaders.

4. Unless the team leader is particularly adept at encouraging new teacher-members to suggest new materials and procedures, pupils may be deprived of experiences that these teachers could provide.

5. Instruction in the large-group situations tends to be the formal lecture type of instruction; pupils have little opportunity to ask questions or make contributions.

6. Superior teachers who serve as team leaders have little contact with pupils; the actual instruction that pupils receive comes primarily from teachers with less experience and competence.

7. Team teaching can operate at its highest level of effectiveness only in a building that has been planned and constructed for this purpose.

SITUATION 4.4   Select one vertical organizational pattern and one horizontal organizational pattern in which you are interested. Review the publications available for research related to these organizational patterns singularly or combined.

INTERCLASS GROUPING *Know adv + disadv*

The horizontal organization previously identified may be viewed as primarily a means of allocating teachers. Instructional groups or classes of pupils must then be formed to be distributed to, between, or among teachers according to the aspects of the selected horizontal pattern. This is called "interclass" grouping. For example, the selection of a vertical pattern (gradedness) and a horizontal pattern (self-contained) does not automatically determine which factors will be considered in the forming of instructional groups or classes. This selection identifies a set of pupils, fifth-graders, at a specific position on the vertical sequence to be distributed among teachers who are assigned as self-contained classroom teachers. The labels identifying the two predominate patterns of grouping pupils are "heterogeneous" and "homogeneous."

Heterogeneous Grouping

Heterogeneous instructional groups or classes are formed whenever no single factor governs the assignment of pupils to groups and classes. Heterogeneous classes are viewed as containing the same ranges of instructional and individual differences as the total group at that position on the vertical sequence.

Advantages Claimed for Heterogeneous Grouping

1. The interaction of the various ability levels contributes to development and achievement.
2. Heterogeneous groups are more like the relationships in life.
3. The models and alternatives available to pupils and teachers are more numerous.
4. Some research studies generally favor social, affective, and maturational advantages for children in heterogeneous groups.[24]

Disadvantages Claimed for Heterogeneous Grouping

1. The research evidence concerning achievement generally suggests that there is no difference between the two grouping plans.[25]
2. The wider range of variations in achievement needs and capacities makes it difficult for the teacher to provide for the individualization of instruction.
3. The pupils who learn more slowly are less likely to have opportunities for leadership and success because of the presence of quicker pupils.

Homogeneous Grouping

Homogeneous instructional groups or classes are formed whenever a single factor or a combination of factors is used to assign pupils to subgroups. This is called "ability" grouping when the single factor or controlling factor in the assignment of pupils is mental maturity, usually as measured by a group test yielding an

[24] Martin and Pavan, p. 312.
[25] Martin and Pavan, p. 312.

intelligence quotient or mental age score. It is called "achievement" grouping when the single or controlling factor is the achievement of the pupil in one or more content areas, usually as measured by a standardized group test yielding a grade placement score, a percentile score, or a standard score.

Homogeneous grouping is an attempt to form instructional groups composed of pupils who are nearly enough alike in one or more traits to justify teaching them as a group and to reduce the task of adapting instruction to individual differences. The plan has been used in large schools, with several teachers at each grade level, for the purpose of assigning pupils to the various teachers on the basis of ability to learn; it has also been used for the purpose of grouping pupils within a single classroom according to their ability to learn. Measures of intelligence (mental age and IQ) have been used by many schools as the basis for forming homogeneous groups; other schools have based grouping on chronological age, achievement (chiefly in reading), social maturity, and special abilities and disabilities.[26]

Discussions of homogeneous grouping generally mention the Detroit, Michigan, schools, where the famous X-Y-Z grouping plan was introduced about 1920. The 10,000 pupils entering the first grade were apportioned in each school into the X group (containing the upper 20 percent), the Y group (containing the middle 60 percent), and the Z group (containing the lower 20 percent). The number of schools using ability grouping increased noticeably until the late 1950s. A national survey indicated, however, that by 1959 only 28 percent of the schools reporting were using the plan.[27] Studies conducted by Otto, Goodlad, and others, revealed, some significant information regarding the extent to which so-called ability grouping provided a teacher with a homogeneous group of pupils: When two sections are created, variability is reduced by 7 percent; when three sections are created, variability is reduced by 17 percent.[28]

Advantages Claimed for Homogeneous Grouping

1. The teacher who has a group of abler pupils can challenge these pupils to work up to their capacity by using more difficult materials, expecting them to progress more rapidly from one level of difficulty to another, and requiring a higher quality of performance.

2. The teacher who has a group of less capable pupils can gear the instruction to their level of ability by using easier materials, giving them more time to progress from one level of difficulty to another, and setting more realistic standards for performance.

3. Differentiated instruction in terms of ability and effort enhance equality of opportunity for pupils with wide variations in ability.

[26] See Robert Hill Lane, *The Teacher in the Modern Elementary School.* (Boston: Houghton Mifflin Company, 1941), chap. 3.

[27] Stuart E. Dean, *Elementary School Administration and Organization,* Bulletin No. 11. (Washington, D.C.: U.S. Government Printing Office, 1960), chap. 10.

[28] Otto and Sanders, p. 104.

4. Parents, especially those whose children are in the upper ability group, generally favor the plan.

5. Teachers, who are inclined to hope that some plan will be found to give them a group of pupils who are somewhat alike in ability, generally favor the plan.

6. It is more true to life to have pupils compete with those who are somewhere near their own level of ability; slow pupils particularly have better opportunities to become leaders in their own groups.

7. Teachers have an opportunity to do a better job of teaching the skill subjects when the pupils in their classes do not vary so widely in ability.

8. The teacher has a better opportunity to work with individuals when the range of ability in the class is reduced somewhat.

Limitations Claimed for Homogeneous Grouping

1. Grouping pupils into high, average, and low groups does not significantly reduce variations among the pupils in these groups: teachers must still provide differentiated instruction within these groups.

2. The plan will not accomplish the purpose of providing instruction for each pupil according to his ability unless the materials provided or each group are suitable for pupils of that general level of ability; this is not always done.

3. The plan violates the pupils' right to be different; when they are labeled slow, average, or bright, they began to think of themselves in these terms and begin to try to be like others in their group.

4. The plan pays little attention to any characteristic of a pupil other than the trait used as the basis for grouping; there is evidence that pupils with similar scores on intelligence tests may differ widely with respect to other characteristics.

5. It is difficult to find teachers who are willing to work only with slow groups.

6. Ability grouping is a form of segregation; the pupils in the high ability group generally come from families at the higher socioeconomic level.

7. Parents frequently object to having their children assigned to the slow group.

8. There is no evidence to support the contention that higher achievement occurs as a result of homogeneous grouping.

SITUATION 4.5   Upon reexamination of the studies on homogeneous grouping conducted by Otto and Goodlad, briefly state your personal opinions concerning the implications for the modern elementary school.

DEVELOPING PATTERNS   *New trend*

The organizational patterns used in school are relatively few in number. The vertical organizational pattern of gradedness almost completely dominates. Although the dominance of the horizontal organizational pattern of self-contained classroom is lessening, it is still the most commonly adopted pattern. Alterna-

The forming of instructional groups requires planning.

tive organizational patterns are needed to provide the flexibility that human and community variabilities seem to demand.

The following section will briefly review the plans, programs, and approaches that show promise of becoming alternative patterns on the horizontal or vertical axis. Although the several patterns offer strong plans, programs, or approaches to curriculum, instruction, use of facilities, and so on, none has yet developed into an organizational plan with unique characteristics.

Open Education

The British primary school movement, which began in Great Britain during World War II and was introduced in the United States through the writings of Joseph Featherstone, has shown promise as a potent combination of organizational patterns and a philosophy of instruction. The terms "open education" or "opening education" are now used to label this movement, especially within the United States.

As conceived and as it operates in Great Britain, open education is a highly sophisticated, nongraded, self-contained, team pattern.[29] It is nongraded because of the intensity of the effort to provide successful experiences for each learner within a curriculum growing out of the learner's needs and because of the recognition that time is a resource which is ultimately controlled by the energies of the learner. Within the British primary schools, each classroom is different from another because each teacher observes and responds to the children, and evolves beliefs about children's learning. Continuous progress, success, individualization, and freedom in the use of the fundamental resources of

[29] Vincent R. Rogers, "English and American Primary Schools," in Glen Hass, Joseph Bondi, and Jon Wiles (Eds.), *Curriculum Planning: A New Approach*. (Boston: Allyn & Bacon, Inc., 1974), pp. 296–303.

time, space, materials, peers, and staff are characteristic of the nongraded British primary school. These schools would be labeled, on the horizontal axis, as self-contained team systems—self-contained in that a group of children tend to spend the major portion of a day together with a teacher; a team in that a variety of other professionals and paraprofessionals also work intimately with the groups of children. Family grouping (children of various ages in one class) and reception classes for young migrant pupils are commonly included within the organizational pattern.

Approximately 30 percent of the British primary schools are characterized by the following:

1. A strong commitment in philosophy and practice to the combined influences of John Dewey and Jean Piaget. For example, education is not the preparation for life, but *is* life. Life in these classrooms is rich in interactions with the environment to facilitate growth, learning, and development.

2. Subject matter is perceived as a vehicle to facilitate interactions. There are few "basics" or "essentials" of subject matter. The curriculum evolves from an interaction, a question, an observation, an experience, and so on. Little attention is apparently given to what is called in the United States school "continuity of curriculum."

3. The approach to a topic of study that may evolve in British classrooms is almost totally interdisciplinary. For example, the integration and role of the aesthetics (art, music, movement, poetry) is extremely important in the approach to a topic of study.

4. Learning is considered more important than teaching, and evaluation is focused on the child's processes rather than the child's product. The teacher is a facilitator who inquires about the child's learning with the questions "how" and "why" rather than the question "what."

5. There is more concern with independence, responsibility, informality, and joy than with togetherness, control, formality, and work.

The impact of the British primary school and the movement called "open education" upon the elementary schools of the United States seems to have been primarily upon the design of facilities. Many if not most of the facilities built for elementary schools since the late 1960s have been "open," that is, open in the sense that the traditional egg-crate pattern was broken. These "open" facilities provide fewer interior walls, and have large open areas and places for individual or small groups. Carpeting, air conditioning, and easy access to material and learning centers also characterize these newer facilities.

The impact of open education upon curriculum revision and organizational patterns have been less dramatic. Within these "open" facilities there has been a more gradual adjustment toward nongradedness and team patterns. A common pattern is a self-contained team in which teachers of several different subject areas work with a group of pupils. Programs for the individualization of instruction are also increasing within these open-facility schools.

The movement has not yet gained the integrity within the United States that it has in Great Britain. For example, when a particular school in the United States is called "open," it may mean:

1. The facilities have few interior walls, thereby providing large open spaces.

2. The school invites volunteer, noncertified personnel to participate in the instructional program.

3. Aspects of the instructional experiences provided for the pupils occur away from the school building.

4. The individual pupil is presented with some alternative curriculum models from which he may select.

5. The school is either graded or nongraded.

6. The school is self-contained, departmentalized, platoon, or team.

7. The school has one or more of the preceding six features.

Lyn S. Martin and Barbara N. Pavan have gathered the research related to open-space classrooms. A brief summary of their report follows:

1. Open-space classrooms and open education have been mistakenly equated in the United States.

2. The differences in organizational climate between open-space and conventional schools are not discerned by several studies.

3. The differences found in individualization, self-concept, attitude, and personality were slight. Generally favored in the open space were: risk-taking behaviors of children, creativity, more small group and after-school activities, affective factors, self-esteem, and positive attitudes toward school.

4. The findings concerning cognitive achievement did not clearly favor either the open space or the conventional classroom.

Martin and Pavan concluded that the research is scanty and more studies are needed before we can accept the findings with confidence. "Innovative programs of all types can exist within old buildings originally intended for traditional classrooms, and it seems evident that changes in architecture do not, in and of themselves, make a great difference."[30]

We Americans seem to value our innovativeness so much that we may not use other models well. Or more positively, as American ingenuity interacts with the British model, a more powerful model with its own integrity may develop within the United States. The British primary school is proving to be a successful adventure for the children of Britain and a model of British education. Among the lighthouse schools within the movement in the United States are: Open Corridor Project, New York; Tucson Early Education Project, Tucson, Arizona; and Education Development Center Open Educational Model, Newton, Massachusetts.

SITUATION 4.6   Examine Lillian S. Stephens' *The Teacher's Guide to Open Education* for new approaches and methodologies you would contemplate adopting as an elementary teacher.

---

[30] Martin and Pavan, p. 311.

Joplin Plan

The Joplin plan, usually accredited to the schools of Joplin, Missouri, is a variation of any existing combination from the vertical or horizontal axis The variation is planned to strengthen instruction in reading. At a scheduled time, a homogeneous group of pupils, in terms of reading achievement, move to meet with an assigned teacher.

Individually Prescribed Instruction

diagnose where each child + plan instruction for that child

Individually Prescribed Instruction (IPI) was originally developed at the Learning Research and Development Center at the University of Pittsburgh.[31] Dissemination and testing of IPI is now done in Philadelphia by Research for Better Schools, Inc. (RBS). IPI was used in over 300 elementary schools during the 1971–1972 school year. It is a very systematic approach to learning based upon sets of specific behavioral objectives correlated with diagnostic instruments, materials, teaching techniques, and management capabilities. The emphasis is upon pupil mastery (85 percent) of the prescribed program. The individualization of instruction results from the variations in rates of pupils as they move through the system. Branching and many alternative approaches are incorporated to provide for individual differences.

IPI can be utilized in any combination of the plans now existing on the horizontal and vertical axes. Probably a nongraded plan from the vertical axis would be more consistent with the intention of IPI.

Alternative Schools '60

The term "alternative schools" is utilized to describe a wide range of programs. Some of the more predominant programs are briefly described below:

1. *The Voucher Plan.* In 1971 the Office of Economic Opportunity (OEO) granted funds for a feasibility study of the voucher plan to the public schools of Gary, Indiana; Seattle, Washington; and Alum Rock, California. This plan financed schools through a direct payment to parents of a voucher of a predetermined value. The parents would then select a school and present the voucher or payment for their child's schooling.

accommodate people who learn differently

2. *The Choice Model.* Within this plan, a school district establishes an open enrollment policy and provides a choice to the parents in terms of the kind of school programs offered. For example, one school unit might be traditional in organization, curriculum, control, and so on; another might be nontraditional and open; another might be emphasizing learning through vocational applications; or another might be patterned after Montessori. In 1974, Philadelphia had 110 alternative program schools serving 7,500 children from ages 10–18.[32]

trad - Open School Choice

3. *Storefront and Boulevard Schools.* Usually, these schools are nonpublic, schools financed by grant monies from the federal government or from business.

Not traditional

[31] "Experiment Remaking the Face of Education," *Education U.S.A.* (Dec. 11, 1967).
[32] "Alternative Programs Network: September 1973–June 1974." (Philadelphia: The School District of Philadelphia, July 1974), Foreword.

The label "storefront" was adopted because several schools rented vacant buildings in business districts. Programs of the schools varied from traditional academics to highly negotiable curriculum patterns to community resource development.

Mainstreaming

Mainstreaming is a plan for integrating exceptional children into the regular school program. Exceptional children are allowed to leave their special classes and join a heterogeneous group of pupils in selected curriculum areas. For example, a child diagnosed as a learning-disabled student might attend learning disability classes for half of the school day, and then attend regular classes in social studies, physical education, or music for the remainder of the day. Some states (Georgia, for example) have passed legislation requiring the mainstreaming of exceptional children. The rationale for this movement and the implementing legislation is that special classes have a detrimental labeling and isolation impact upon children who do need special services.

UNDERSTANDING ORGANIZATIONAL PATTERNS

A classroom teacher will become a member of a building faculty that has created or inherited some combination of the previously described patterns. The odds are that the teacher will be a self-contained classroom teacher within a graded school. Whatever the organization structure of such a group, it is important that the teacher understand and help implement the organizational pattern without assuming or overextending its implications.

For example, none of these patterns totally determines the kind of relationships that teachers will establish with their pupils. Each claims in its own way to recognize and provide for individual differences. However, each plan is completely dependent upon a teacher who will recognize and provide for the personalization of instruction. No organizational pattern makes a teacher good, or for that matter, bad. A good or bad teacher makes an organizational pattern functional or nonfunctional.

Organizational patterns do not totally prescribe the methods that a teacher may create, select, and adapt. Certain plans may emphasize the interrelationships of subjects, while others may deemphasize them. Yet the teacher's selection of methods will ultimately determine the extent to which interrelationships will occur. Organizational patterns do not determine the reward and punishment patterns that a teacher develops and utilizes. Nor do they set the motivational climate of the classroom. Teachers do these things.

Another point for a teacher to consider is that hard data do not exist which will absolutely support one pattern or combination of patterns over another. Numerous research studies have been done concerning pupil achievement in the various different organizational plans. Some studies support one, others support another, but most suggest that there are no significant differences between patterns. Other studies have concentrated on pupil attitude, self-concept methods, and so on; again the results have been directional and far from conclusive.

That the findings of educational research cannot conclusively support any one organizational pattern may be interpreted in two ways. First, it may be that each pattern contains a set of strengths and weaknesses that balance out its potential advantage over another pattern. Second, it may be that the research designs and measurement tools available for educational research are not adequately sensitive to reflect the differences that exist. While better designs, tools of measurement, and new organizational systems are being developed, teachers must maximize the opportunities available.

Since hard data are not available to direct and support the selection or creation of organizational patterns, then what criteria are the bases for their formulation?

A FACILITATING ORGANIZATION

The decisions that are made concerning the selection and creation of an organizational pattern to govern the vertical and horizontal movement of pupils within the elementary school should be made in light of the established purposes of the school. In Chapter 2 the various national lists of purposes were identified. Each building unit and district should develop its own specific purposes from which an organizational plan can be developed to orchestrate the resources of the school, pupils, facilities, materials, time, and personnel (see Fig. 4.1).

Schools utilize organizational patterns to achieve quality, equality, and personalization. Quality is the establishment of an education program which fosters pupil development in the basic areas of growth, learning, and development. Equality is the inclusion of quality experience in the education program for the full range of pupil variation in these areas. Personalization is the assignment and allocation of these educational programs to the three basic areas and to the needs of each pupil.

Other purposes of the school and its organization are accountability, flexibility, and dynamics. Accountability involves establishing and communicating the criteria for each aspect and role within the organization. Flexibility means that pupils, teachers, and principals have a variety of alternatives available to them to achieve their purposes. Dynamics suggest that the organization is always in a fluid state of adjusting and readjusting to feedback from those who are working within the organization.

ORGANIZING ROLES

The term "role" is used here to mean the set of expectations applied to a person who occupies a particular position within a social system or in an organization. The person constructs a "role" from perceptions of system expectations balanced against personal needs and goals. Institutions do not employ on the basis of the individual's need for a position. Institutions employ people because the institution has a need for a function, service, or task to be performed. Individuals accept positions to satisfy first their fundamental needs for food, clothing, shelter. The paycheck provides the means to satisfy those needs for security.

Know

Paper

2

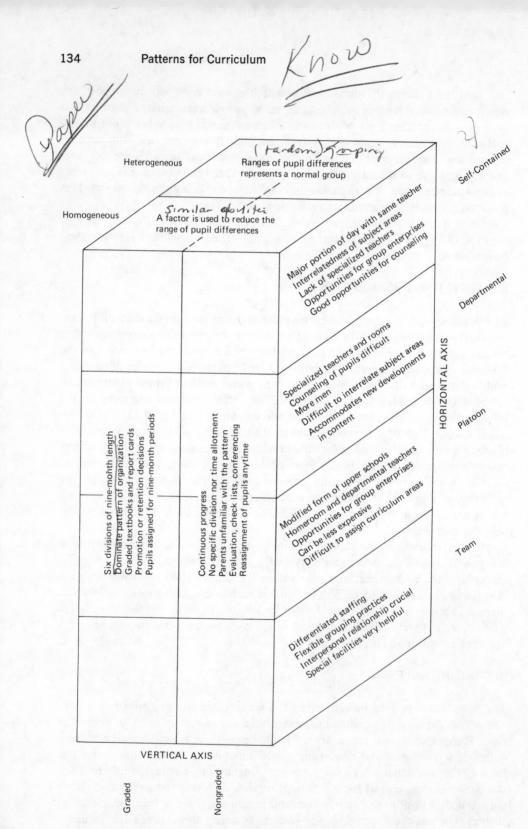

Heterogeneous

(random) grouping

Ranges of pupil differences represents a normal group

Self-Contained

Homogeneous

Similar abilities

A factor is used to reduce the range of pupil differences

Major portion of day with same teacher
Interrelatedness of subject areas
Lack of specialized teachers
Opportunities for group enterprises
Good opportunities for counseling

Departmental

Specialized teachers and rooms
Counseling of pupils difficult
More men
Difficult to interrelate subject areas
Accommodates new developments in content

Platoon

HORIZONTAL AXIS

Six divisions of nine-month length
Dominate pattern of organization
Graded textbooks and report cards
Promotion or retention decisions
Pupils assigned for nine-month periods

Continuous progress
No specific division nor time allotment
Parents unfamiliar with the pattern
Evaluation, check lists, conferencing
Reassignment of pupils anytime

Modified form of upper schools
Homeroom and departmental teachers
Opportunities for group enterprises
Can be less expensive
Difficult to assign curriculum areas

Team

Differentiated staffing
Flexible grouping practices
Interpersonal relationship crucial
Special facilities very helpful

VERTICAL AXIS

Graded

Nongraded

Figure 4.1   Grouping for instruction.

When the security needs are satisfied, the individual begins to expect that the accepted position satisfies the personal needs of belonging, fulfillment, status, and recognition. Usually, there is a fundamental conflict between the needs of the institution and those of the second but very strong personal needs of the individual. Life within an institution is in a constant equilibration between these two needs. To say that there is conflict and a constant equilibration is not to say that institutional life is necessarily an unhappy one; it's just that "doing your own thing" and the "institution's thing" need to be reconciled.

The Role of the Teacher

The teacher is both servant and master—a servant as degrees are accumulated to qualify for employment, and as the institution demands assistance with the maintenance of a secure institution through the supervision of playgrounds, lunchrooms, bus loading, and so on; a master in that fundamental data required to service individual pupil needs are more readily available to the teacher through proximity with the pupil. The wise diagnosis of the individual needs which the institution has made available to the teacher will provide the authority needed to mediate the institution's more generalized expertise for teaching. Don't do it their way or your way, but the learner's way! Seek the ultimate expression of personal needs in the judicious service of the learners, and the institution will accommodate a wider range of variations from institutional practice and policy. Form a kinship with the personal needs of the learner, which at times may conflict with those of the institution. Certainly, the negotiation of those personal needs of the teacher which align with those needs of the learners is not an antagonistic one.

This is not to imply that the role of the teacher is to sublimate personal needs not aligned with learner's needs. The teacher also lives in the modern elementary school, and therefore has a right to exert influence to increase the institution's accommodation of personal needs. An adversary relationship need not occur in the negotiating of the teacher's needs and role expectations not aligned with those of the learners. Attempts should be made to negotiate within a model where the needs and expectations of all are met.

The Role of the Principal

The problems of leadership in the interactions involved in the improvement of instruction are similar to the problems of teachers in developing a learning environment in the classroom. Both enterprises involve mutual understanding, shared purposes, respect for the uniqueness of each human being, and feedback procedures for effective ways of working together.

The principals are both servants and masters—servants as they perform to maintain the favor of subordinates and superordinates; masters as they have easy access to the insights that reflect the means through which a unit may best serve its pupils, staff, and community.

The principalship is truly a middle position. On one side are the efforts of superordinates to establish a school system rather than a system of schools.

On the other side are the needs of the staff and community to have a school serving the particular needs of its clientele. The role is neither that of "master teacher" nor "top boss." The principal's actions and decisions are visible both vertically and horizontally within the institution. This position, more nearly than any other, is directly in the middle of the conflicts between institutional and personal needs, including the principal's.

As negotiation agreements with their grievance and arbitration procedures appear in the schools, principals often find themselves in an adversary relationship with teachers. Many principals are having to reconsider their identifications. They are no longer permitted to participate in teacher groups and are being aggressively recruited by superintendents. The stress being experienced in the role of the principalship is probably greater than it has ever been.

The principles that mold an individual's thoughts and guide an educator's actions when entrusted with the responsibilities of instructional leadership are discussed in the following paragraphs.

SITUATION 4.7   Discuss with one or more principals and/or superintendents the procedures for the selection of horizontal organizational patterns within their particular school.

Basis of Instructional Leadership

In a profession that emphasizes the application of intelligence to the solution of problems of living, leadership is entrusted to the one who knows. The magnetic personality, the common touch, and the imposing physical stature no longer suffice. Leaders need a thorough grasp of the entire school program in its social setting—historical background, objectives, the relationship among parts, methods, and procedures. In addition, leaders need to be well grounded in the techniques of evaluating the effectiveness of the school program. They cannot rely entirely on their preservice education for these abilities; they must serve as students and as practitioners long enough to gain the intimate understanding of teaching that comes only through an integration of theory and practice.

There is a special burden placed upon the supervising principal in an elementary school to become acquainted with educational methods at all grade levels and in all curriculum areas. To be truly a leader, the principal must understand the teaching of primary reading and language development; must understand recent developments in the teaching of foreign languages in the elementary school; must be prepared to assist in the development of a program for science teaching in the elementary grades; must know the field of child growth and development. The principal whose training has been inadequate must make up for its inadequacy through a program of formal course work, through reading, attendance at professional conferences, and classroom visitation. And even the best-prepared educational leaders must continue to be students of education if they are to furnish intelligent leadership for the programs of the modern elementary school.

PERSONAL INTEGRITY

Since we teach better by example than by precept, the leaders' behaviors are more important than what they know or what they say. Instructional leadership is based on a high degree of personal integrity. The term "personal integrity," as used here, means that the leader really stands for certain principles and can be depended upon to see that these principles are observed in staff relationships. If they believe in the principle of group planning, they should in practice try to carry out the policies agreed upon by the staff. Unless leaders have this kind of personal integrity, group processes become a form of busywork, and the morale of the staff steadily declines.

The subject of national morality has been given a great deal of attention in recent years. National morality is nothing more than the sum of the characters of the individuals comprising the nation. The public schools have a part in building character. It is not surprising, therefore, that the behavior of educational leaders should be the subject of the closest examination and that personal integrity should be regarded as an essential qualification for leadership.

PROMOTING AN ATMOSPHERE OF INFORMALITY

Intelligence and informality are by no means mutually exclusive. Intelligence and knowledge are no substitute for friendliness, nonpossessive warmth, empathy, and genuineness. By showing an interest in the hobbies, interests, and skills of each staff member, by inviting the staff to social meetings, and by encouraging the use of first names instead of formal titles, the leader can help to create an atmosphere of friendliness that contributes to smoother human relations in the school, provided such informality comes from a genuine interest in people. Informality that is a pose is easily recognized as such and frequently resented.

BUILDING MORALE

The success of an organization depends to a large degree upon staff morale. Morale is the factor that enables individuals to live up to their highest possibilities. When the morale of the group is low, each member contributes only a small fraction of what they have to give; when morale is high, members of the group work together in good will and with enthusiasm.

Effective staff relationships are impossible unless the leader demonstrates that group morale is a major concern. Morale grows slowly in an atmosphere of mutual respect and confidence. It can be severely stunted by one false action that shows that the leader has no respect for decisions reached by the group. This situation cannot be remedied merely by developing a new type of organization on paper. It can be remedied only by the slow process of rebuilding staff morale.

Effective staff relationships are also made more difficult when the leader fails to take into account the fact that many teachers identify with their groups.

That is, teachers come to feel that the successes and failures of the group are really their successes and failures. When a group does well in a school assembly and is commended by the principal, it is just as if each teacher had been on the stage; feelings about oneself are bolstered. Adverse criticism of an individual child or a group to the teacher in charge, and particularly before peers, can destroy a wholesome psychological climate. If it is customary for a principal or supervisor to do this, group morale will suffer.

Educational leadership has no greater responsibility than that of developing in the members of the staff an *esprit de corps*, a sense of participation in the total life of the school, a feeling that all are engaged in a work whose contributions to mankind are unquestioned, and that all bring their unique talents to the accomplishment of a common goal. By giving attention to the health needs of teachers, by reducing the teaching load, by helping to improve the social status of teachers in the community, by recognizing outstanding accomplishments, by giving each teacher a feeling of being wanted and appreciated by the school system, by working for good salaries and working conditions for the staff, by keeping the staff informed concerning actions taken in their behalf, by providing attractive classrooms and teachers' lounges, by promoting from within the ranks when possible, by consulting teachers before taking actions which will affect them, and by showing a willingness to work with a teacher in solving a problem created by the teacher's own mistake—by these and countless other methods the leader can help to build better staff morale.

FORESIGHT OF AN INSTRUCTIONAL LEADER

Teachers who have no visions of the results of their work in the form of richer and more successful lives for the children they teach are enmeshed in a sorry round of details. Similarly, the instructional leader who does not visualize the school as an agency for helping children achieve full measure of their capabilities is unfit for the position. Genuine leaders must work and strive for educational opportunities that far surpass those provided for children at the present time; they must have a vivid concept of what constitutes adequate educational opportunities; they must rest their faith on a long-range program rather than on immediate ends; they must not let the drudgery of current details obscure a vision for a better tomorrow for the children in elementary schools. They must be gap-seekers who are totally aware of the realities of the immediate, but who never lose the awareness of the differences between what is and what ought to be.

THE COURAGE TO FACE DIFFICULT TASKS

There can be no easy route to success for an individual who aspires to instructional leadership in these times. They must continuously study educational theory and practice; they must keep abreast of the ever-changing social structure in which the school exists; they must utilize opportunities for study and travel; and they must welcome tasks that are difficult. Growth comes through continuous striving, not necessarily through attaining leadership. Great leaders are not developed by the performance of easy tasks. Competency as an instructional leader comes only with the courage to face difficult tasks. Ben M. Harris expresses this with the phrase "tolerance for turbulence."[33]

HOW THE METHODS OF DEMOCRACY HELP

Respect for the individual is the essence of democracy. Without respect for the individual, instructional leaders cannot measure up to their responsibilities. Leaders reflect this respect in their dealings with pupils, teachers, parents, and other citizens. Intelligence, personal integrity, modesty, the common touch, the ability to build morale and vision and courage are all included in the principle of respect for human worth. Without faith in the ability of individuals to work out their own problems if given the opportunity to work on them cooperatively, all other qualifications for instructional leadership are ineffective.

Rationale for Change

Several agents work in reversible action to effect change: teachers to pupils; teachers to teachers; principals to teachers; supervisory personnel to principals and teachers. A fundamental basis for the interactions within group and between individuals is to promote change or, more suitably, to encourage development which will incorporate changes.

Yet, the processes of change are often sorely misunderstood, leaving the potential change agent fussing about the unwillingness of some to change. There are fundamental and rational reasons why individuals should and will resent an upset of their *status quo*. Perhaps a recognition and acceptance of these reasons are prerequisites to the functioning of a change agent.

To argue for change only upon the objective, cognitive bases of right, fact, research, and so on, deals with only one dimension of the dilemma of those who would make changes. How many of us know what we should do but fail to do it?

Change is often viewed as a learning process. This position, applied to the teacher or administrator especially, is an incomplete statement of the process or processes involved. These individuals have already learned procedures for interacting with problems or situations, and therefore realize that change means not only learning, but also unlearning and then relearning. First, one must learn of the new or different procedures, then unlearn the habits of the procedures one has been practicing, and finally relearn the application and substitution of the new or different procedures as responses to old situations.

The change agent is often excited by the initial reactions during the first learning phase of change. There may even be a temporary spurt of the learners to put the new procedures into practice. But suddenly, to the change agent's dismay, there is a tremendous dropoff in application. The individuals are reverting to former practices and developing resistance to what they once endorsed.

[33] Ben M. Harris, *Supervisory Behavior in Education.* (Englewood Cliffs, N.J.: Prentice-Hall, Inc., 1963), p. 61.

This characterizes the behaviors of individuals when unlearning becomes a prerequisite to implementing new procedures.

Unlearning involves the temporary loss of power and stability, control, and predictability. The experienced professional has a procedure for dealing with a situation, and its very existence extends to the user a measure of power, control, and predictability so that whatever problems the individual perceives within the situation are familiar ones and therefore tend to be nonthreatening.

During the initial learning phase the intended practitioner may have focused upon the new procedure as a problem-solving means. Yet, a more realistic view is that each procedure carries its own set of problems. Figuratively, changing procedures only changes the nature of the problems. It is reasonable to change simply because the new set of problems are more manageable, although new problems are much more threatening than the old familiar ones.

Also, through experience with the existing procedures the practitioners have gained skills and competencies. Any new procedure means that they will experience a significant, even though temporary, drop in these capabilities. Loss of skill and competency in what was a familar setting is an upsetting experience.

Another factor is that the rewards for changing or the penalties for not changing are often confused. The rewards to an alcoholic in becoming a nondrinking alcoholic are visible, real, and reinforced by a large segment of his society. The rewards to a teacher are not so real. Even the teacher's peers may be divided in the nature of reinforcemnt given: some supportive, some nonsupportive. Also, the teacher's practices often occur in the isolation of the classroom, and are not always readily visible. In a very real way, the dynamics of change for a teacher must be internal and strong within the teacher because the external dynamics may be remote, conflicting, and mixed.

None of the above discussion is to even imply that change is impossible. Rather, it is intended to remind us that, at various times, each person reaches a plateau in most behaviors—a plateau with growth-arresting, feedback cycles operating to make our responses habitual. To break these cycles and start growth again is a difficult task, a task that requires patience, proximity, risk, and ingenuity.

Organizing for Cooperative Action

An important responsibility of the offiical leader in any school is that of helping the staff develop and improve the organization for cooperative action. It should be understood, of course, that organizing for curriculum improvement is a continuous process rather than a single act of setting up a finished structure. Since curriculum improvement involves changes in the behavior of individuals, any plan of organization must take into account the experiences and abilities of the personnel involved and the problems existing in the community the school serves.

Our system of public education places a great deal of responsibility for planning in the hands of the local administrative unit. The principal of an elementary school can, of course, develop an organization without consulting any members of the staff. Development of an organization in this manner will hinder the accomplishment of the real objectives accepted by the members of the staff, and will consume valuable time that might otherwise be used for constructive purposes. The principle of the consent of the governed is deeply embedded in our culture. The democratic process, although slower and more difficult to manage, seems to produce better results in the long run.

The skills required for working cooperatively with a group of teachers are as challenging and difficult to learn as those required in any other profession. Teachers who have been accustomed to authoritarian administrative practices over a long period of years find it difficult to unlearn habits of conformity or irresponsibility and to acquire the abilities demanded in cooperative work. Only gradually can they be led to examine and help improve the machinery for cooperative action, for resolving differences of opinion, and for distinguishing between the executive function, which belongs to the administration, and the policy-making function, which belongs to the staff. Teachers, no less than children, learn by doing, and it is the responsibility of those who are in positions of leadership to assist in providing the machinery for participation in group enterprises.

The progress that is being made in defining more clearly the purposes of the elementary school and in developing an organization that coordinates the efforts of teachers in the accomplishment of these purposes has been given a great deal of attention in educational publications. Detailed descriptions of county, city, and state programs in current use are available.[34] It is sufficient, therefore, to present at this point some basic principles that should be followed in setting up an organization for curriculum improvement in an elementary school.

1. The organization should serve to utilize the potential abilities of individuals. In almost any school there are some teachers with much experience, others with little; some with one type of preparation, some with another. All have talents they can share, all have limitations, and all need to develop unused capabilities. The organization in which they work may stimulate development, encourage initiative, and release potential abilities. On the other hand, it may stifle development, discourage initiative, and reduce individual effort to a mere routine of conforming to imposed patterns. The leader who has a broad understanding of human relationships and skill in working with people can encourage each teacher to make unique contributions and still work as a member of the team.

2. The organization should be flexible enough to permit groups of teachers to work on problems of real concern to themselves. The organization should facilitate the achievement of purposes, and when it gets in the way of teachers who have important work to do, it should be examined critically. For example, teachers of young children may want to come together to discuss the characteristics of children at that stage of development, instructional materials that

34 Ross L. Neagley and N. Dean Evans, *Handbook for Effective Curriculum Development.* (Englewood Cliffs, N.J.: Prentice-Hall, Inc., 1967), chaps. 3 and 6.

have proved to be useful, or ways of working with parents. Teachers of older children may want to work on an entirely different set of problems. The organization should serve the real needs of individuals rather than stand in the way of getting work done.

3. The success of any type of organization depends upon the climate in which it exists. A democracy, no less than a dictatorship, requires organization. The organization in a dictatorship exists in a climate of fear and distrust, of arbitrary authority and enforced conformity. In a democracy, the organization must facilitate a climate of mutual respect and confidence in the authority derived from the consent of the group, and of willingness to work for the success of plans agreed upon by the group.

The Individual School as the Center for Curriculum Study and Improvement

The individual school is the functional unit for curriculum improvement. This is true because curriculum improvement must always be done in terms of a specific group of children. There can be no such thing as the best arithmetic program for all children; there can only be a program that is best for a given group of children experiencing a given environment. The experiences children have in an elementary school improve only as the teachers in that school gain a better understanding of child growth, learning, and development; define more clearly the objectives of elementary education; and increase their skills in guiding child growth, learning, and development toward behaviors defined by their objectives.

How can the staff of an individual elementary school organize for curriculum improvement? What problems are studied and how are problems selected? How can the resources of the local community and the school district best be brought into the program? These problems are being solved in a variety of ways by good elementary schools throughout the country.

One of the newer and more exciting means is the application of the concept of differentiated staffing within the organizational pattern of team teaching. The team is composed of individuals who have a variety of special talents and skills. The opportunities for cooperative planning to result in significant curriculum improvement activities are tremendous.

The identification of master teachers, the employment of teacher aides, the establishment of media centers with special personnel, all have brought competencies valuable for curriculum improvement activities to the individual school. The increasing use of grade-level planning committees, of departmental planning committees, and of task-oriented *ad hoc* committees has been part of the solution. The aggressive search for, and use of, specialists within the district to help with the study of a staff has been successful and is therefore increasing.

The possibilities of organizing for curriculum improvement at the building level are numerous. The key is the awareness of a leader that autonomy in curriculum improvement activities comes from developing services for the unique set of individuals, pupils and teachers, within the building unit and school community.

System-Wide Organization for Curriculum Improvement Purposes

A school system organizes to facilitate curriculum development and improvement activities in two ways. First, a district provides a supervisory and curriculum department. The staff of specialists in the department is provided the time, freedom of access, and support necessary for system and individual building curriculum activities.

> A consistent relationship is revealed between the size of school district and the extent of curriculum development efforts. The larger the pupil enrollment, the greater the degree of large-scope revision.[35]

The supervisory and curriculum staff includes personnel with titles such as supervisor, consultant, helping teacher, director of curriculum, assistant superintendent for instruction, and coordinator. This staff and department are administered by an official leader who is usually directly responsible to the superintendent. Other members of the department do not usually have administrative authority. The authority of members of a curriculum department is derived from their knowledges and skills in a specialized area; their abilities to provide assistance and service to others as they strive to achieve individual and system goals; and their skills in human relations, group processes, and persuasion.

The second way a school district organizes to facilitate curriculum development and improvement activities is through a committee and in-service structure. Standing and *ad hoc* curriculum committees are established to recommend, select, revise, and evaluate the many aspects of the curriculum. These committees usually prove to be the very heart of the curriculum improvement program. Committees are usually more successful when they are relatively small, when they represent a cross section of the school system, when the members of the committee understand clearly the relationship between their work and the overall program, and when committee work is considered a part of the teachers' regular duties.

In many school systems, each school is represented by a teacher and the principal in a system-wide curriculum council or council on instruction. In some systems there is an intermediate group, called a regional council, between the individual school staff and the system-wide council. It is the responsibility of the system-wide curriculum council to maintain a program, from the kindergarten through to senior high school, which is unified but flexible enough to allow for special needs and problems of communities served by the several building units. Although these system-wide councils allow for initiative on the part of the facul-

---

[35] Morton Alpren, "What Curriculum Developments Are Finding Their Way into Practice?" *The Bulletin of the National Association of Secondary School Principals* (March 1962), pp. 16–17.

ties of local building units, they provide guidance, stimulation, and an overall view of the school program for the staff of the individual school. The system-wide curriculum council is a policy-making group on such matters as obtaining financial support for the instructional program, developing bulletins needed by teachers, releasing teachers for curriculum work, and receiving accurate impressions of the reactions of the public to the programs of the schools.

Providing for Participation by the Community

The idea that the school alone cannot provide an adequate education for the modern child—that this requires the whole community—is emphasized throughout this book. Elementary school principals and teachers are realizing increasingly the importance of working closely with parents and other interested citizens in improving the school program. Many elementary schools, however, fail to utilize fully the contributions of the community to the improvement of the school program, either because they do not fully understand the importance of doing this or because they have failed to organize properly for it.

Participation at the individual-classroom level is relatively simple to arrange. Many teachers make use of the special knowledge, hobbies, and talents of lay persons in the community in relation to many aspects of the curriculum, such as science, storytelling, local history, information about foreign countries visited, art work, and excursions. There are relatively few schools, however, in which every teacher is making full use of consultant lay persons.

Participation at the individual school level is also common. The improvement of the health program, education for family living, the development of a better system of reporting pupil progress, work with committees in the preparation of a list of objectives for the school, improvement of the school library, and more effective use of audiovisual materials are some of the ways in which lay persons are helping to improve the school program. In the better elementary schools, the staff would not think of making any important change in the school program without first discussing it with interested lay persons in the community.

Participation in the formulation of policies and plans for curriculum improvement at the system-wide level is also important. In some systems, provision is made for this by adding community representatives to the curriculum council; in other systems, separate advisory committees have been formed to work with the curriculum council.

Plans used for involving the community in curriculum improvement programs vary greatly from one situation to another. Although these plans contain valuable suggestions, it is the responsibility of the leadership in each school system to develop the plans best suited to local needs and circumstances.

Using Outside Consultants

The practice of inviting outside consultants to help with the program of curriculum improvement, either at the individual school level or at the system-wide level, is becoming rather common. These consultants usually come from a teacher-education institution, from the state department of education, or from another public school system. The use of outside consultants is based on valid assumptions—that an outsider can frequently arouse more interest in curriculum improvement, can help the local staff look at the program more objectively, and can bring special knowledges and skills to bear on the solution of problems. These values can be achieved only when the consultant selected brings to the task the competencies needed, knows well in advance what will be expected, and possesses excellent group-process and human relations skills.

Few school systems have on the professional staff enough individuals sufficiently trained in research procedures and the techniques required in curriculum improvement to be able to carry on the program without consultant services from the outside. The job of the consultant is to help the local staff learn how to solve problems themselves rather than to provide the answers. The consultant is concerned with helping the professional staff and the community involved define their problems, and find the resources and procedures by which the problems can be solved. The services of the consultant should be such that the local professional staff becomes less dependent and more independent as the program progresses.

Providing Time for Curriculum Work

The curriculum improvement program that involves adding 2 hours once a week or twice a month to the heavy schedule of work that teachers are already carrying defeats some, if not all, of the purposes for which the program exists. Unless curriculum work is regarded as an integral part of the teacher's load rather than as something extra that is added at the expense of the time the teacher has left for relaxation and for looking after personal problems; unless at least most of the work can be done on regular school time for which the teacher is paid; unless a better time can be found for it than the hour or so immediately after school, when teachers are worn out by the duties of the regular school day; unless some solution can be found for the problem of finding time for curriculum work, the improvement program is almost certain to result in failure.

Fortunately, several ways have been found to deal with the problems of time for curriculum work. Included within the school calendar, and therefore in the salaries of teachers, are up to ten days for professional activities. Summer workshops are jointly sponsored by local school systems and teacher-education institutions where teachers can work on curriculum programs while earning credit toward degrees, certification, or salary. Committees of teachers are employed during the summer to write a final draft of work started during the school year. By providing substitutes, schools are releasing teachers to attend professional meetings or to prepare and edit curriculum materials.[36]

Techniques of Working Together

Leadership in the modern elementary school is an enterprise in human relationships. It involves the use of techniques of group management that have been

[36] Neagley and Evans, *Handbook for Effective Curriculum Development*, chap. 5.

proven successful as practices in the elementary school have moved away from autocracy toward democracy. Democracy, no less than despotism, requires the mastery of techniques. If groups of teachers are to formulate their own purposes rather than accept those of the official leader, if they are to make their own plans for achieving those purposes, then it is the function of the leader to help them master the techniques for setting these objectives and getting the jobs done. This section deals with some of the promising techniques that have been developed for helping teachers learn to work together effectively.

TEACHERS' MEETINGS

On the basis of the generally accepted principle that education should help individuals to do better the worthwhile things they will do anyway, teachers should certainly be interested in the improvement of teachers' meetings. Most teachers spend a great deal of time attending staff meetings of various types, and few would deny that these meetings could be improved. Unless teachers' meetings exemplify the principles of good teaching, the time is largely if not entirely wasted. In the old type of meeting, which was formal and stilted, teachers were called together for routine business, announcements, or to listen to a lecture by the principal or a visiting college professor. The teachers expected little in the form of ideas for better teaching; they felt that the meetings belonged to the principal and were a waste of valuable time.

If teachers can be made to feel that the meetings belong to them, if the agenda is prepared by a committee of teachers, if a pleasant meeting place is provided and an informal atmosphere is maintained, teachers' meetings can result in professional growth for the entire staff.

If teachers' meetings are to promote professional growth, they must be organized around problems that teachers consider important in their work with children. This is not likely to be accomplished if the principal always prepares the agenda and presides at all the meetings. The agenda should be prepared by a committee of teachers elected by the entire faculty for the purpose of planning and conducting meetings. The agenda containing the items to be discussed should be made available to all members of the staff before the meeting so that each member can be prepared to discuss the items listed. Opportunity should be provided for any member of the staff to hand to the chairman of the committee any item he wants placed on the agenda. Opportunity should also be provided for items to be added to the agenda at the beginning of each meeting. Membership of the committee should be changed frequently in order to make it possible for more teachers to participate in planning the meetings and in assuming responsibility for their success. The chairman of the planning committee should ordinarily preside, although another member may be requested to preside if the problem for discussion happens to be one in which the chairman is particularly interested. The planning committee may also be responsible for selecting a meeting place, arranging the furniture, providing refreshments, and securing consultants for the meeting.

The room selected for the teachers' meeting is a very important factor; the worst possible place is a classroom with rows of screwed-down desks. If at all possible, the regular meetings should be held in a room in which the seats can be arranged in a circle or a semicircle. If meetings are held after school, it is desirable to devote the first part of the session to social activities and to serving refreshments; this helps to bridge the gap between regular classroom activities and participation in the meeting, and it allows the members of the staff to arrive at different times without the embarrassment of breaking into on-going discussion.

The time when meetings are held must be determined by the staff after all factors have been considered objectively and after experimenting with various times. In some schools the hour before school starts in the morning has been found satisfactory; some have met at the noon hour, at dinnertime in the evening, after dinner, or on Saturdays. The most common practice, of course, is to meet after school hours in the afternoon. The length of time needed for the meeting is a determining factor in deciding when it should be held. Some schools have one short session each week for routine business and a longer meeting once a month for discussion of policies and long-range planning.

THE CURRICULUM WORKSHOP

Workshops have been conducted on university and college campuses and in public school systems for many purposes and by a variety of procedures for many years. Some have been well staffed with competent consultants capable of giving expert guidance to teachers seeking help in many aspects of the public school program, such as the uses of television and newspapers; conservation, outdoor and environmental education; guidance; selecting and preparing behavioral objectives, evaluation instruments, and programmed learning materials; or the education of various groups of exceptional children. Others have had a single staff member available to assist in working out plans for the improvement of one area in the curriculum, such as social studies.

Some workshops have been organized primarily for the purpose of providing professional growth for the participants. An example of this type was the annual Association for Childhood Education (ACE) workshop, sponsored jointly by the Oklahoma branch of the Association for Childhood Education International, the College of Education, and the Extension Division of the University of Oklahoma. From 60 to 160 elementary school teachers and principals from Oklahoma and nearby states attended these two-week workshops. The staff consisted of a full-time director, two lecturers (one for each of the two weeks) who were always selected from the outstanding authorities in various phases of elementary education, and ten or more leaders for the study and discussion groups in teacher-pupil interaction, children's speech, children's literature, the use of audiovisual materials, mental hygiene, creative arts, elementary school science, and child development.

The participants in this workshop and many of the staff members lived in the building in which the workshop was held, had their meals together, and participated in various social and recreational activities. Membership in this workshop was not limited to any particular type of teacher and no patterns were imported from workshops carried on at other places. Rather, it represented an indigenous movement developed to meet conditions existing in the elementary schools of Oklahoma. The fact that it was called a workshop could no doubt be traced to the fact that someone on the original planning committee had heard of workshops being held elsewhere, but neither those who were in charge nor the participants were concerned about how far the practices were out of line with the aims and ideals of the workshop concept. At any rate, the writer has found teachers in remote sections of the state who give much of the credit for their increased competence to the ACE workshop.

Another type of workship is the one that is established to produce instructional materials to be used with adaptations by the participants and by other teachers. For this type of workshop the participants are carefully selected in terms of their ability to produce outstanding materials rather than their need for help from the workshop. Of course it is expected that participants in any workshop will benefit from the experience in the form of professional growth, but the participants in the production type of workshop are selected primarily on the basis of the competence they have already attained rather than on the competencies they need to develop through the workshop experiences.

The production type of workshop usually has a director, a secretary and librarian, and several consultants, selected because of their competence in the various curriculum areas for which instructional materials are to be prepared. This type of workshop requires a meeting place large enough to accommodate the entire group of participants and a number of smaller seminar or conference rooms as meeting places for the various committees. Materials relating to the various curriculum areas should be at hand, and adequate secretarial help should be available.

These brief sketches of types of workshops illustrate the principle that there need be no rigid pattern of workshop procedure. It is true that the early workshops sponsored by the Progressive Education Association for the staff members of the thirty schools involved in the eight-year study exhibited certain common characteristics and that many workshops sponsored by colleges and universities without financial support from an outside agency tried to follow as closely as possible the procedures used in these early workshops. It is also true that some summer sessions have tried to attract students by attaching the name "workshop" to regular summer-session courses. It should be obvious, however, that a workshop, like any other device used in public education, must be adapted to time, place, and circumstance.

Downes called attention to the fact that workshop procedures, when used in teacher education, are based on the same principles of learning as those utilized in the modern classroom.

The chief virtue of the workshop is in its emphasis on learning by doing—perhaps another way of saying that twenty-five years after John Dewey's idea began to be applied in the education of children, someone realized that it might be valid also for those persons who were already practicing it on children. If purposing, planning, executing and evaluating are desirable learning activities for children, they are also important for adults. The corollary to this assumption as applied to a workshop—and essential to it—is the workshop's emphasis on informality, social experience, individual initiative and responsibility, and personality development.[37]

The workshop movement has grown rapidly since the Progressive Education Association provided the idea and the General Education Board of the Rockefeller Foundation furnished the funds for the first workshop at Ohio State University in the summer of 1936. The Progressive Education Association sponsored three workshops the following summer—at Columbus, Ohio; Bronxville, New York; and Denver, Colorado—and by 1939 was sponsoring ten. By that time the workshop was installed as a regular feature of the summer-session program in almost every college and university participating in the preparation of teachers.

PRESCHOOL CONFERENCES

The fact that most school calendars now include several professional days makes it possible for the staff to have a planning session before school opens. These conferences vary in length from two days to two weeks. The agenda is usually prepared cooperatively by the curriculum staff and the teachers in order to insure that the problems discussed are the ones that are considered important.

Time is usually provided for both general sessions and meetings of special-interest groups. Consultants are usually selected cooperatively by the staff and paid by the board of education. It is not unusual for a public school system to bring in specialists in several areas of the school program from outside the state.

The objectives of the preschool conference include the following:

1. To plan for the program of curriculum improvement for the coming year
2. To assist new teachers in becoming acquainted with members of the staff, the philosophy and practices of the school, and the nature of the community
3. To plan for a more effective use of instructional resources
4. To develop a friendly working atmosphere among school personnel, parents, and other interested citizens
5. To foster democratic group processes in the school system

RETREATS

The practice of removing the staff from the site of their school or system to a place that is somewhat isolated, or at least offers privacy, is becoming popular. The retreat may be located at a lodge, resort, farm, or even in the few facilities built especially for such endeavors. The value rests in the opportunities for both work and socialization to occur over a period of time, reinforced by proximity

[37] James E. Downes, "An Evaluation of Workshops," *Elementary School Journal* (April 1947), p. 446.

and privacy. The agenda is usually developed ahead of time and then modified during the retreat. The use of this type of conference—away from the pressures of phone, community, and shop—seems to be a particularly promising practice.

SITUATION 4.8   From your experience as a teacher or your interactions with other teachers, list the types of teacher preparation program experiences needed to enlighten teachers in the interactions with and functions of principals, supervisors, and faculty meetings.

Moving from Discussion to Action

One complaint frequently heard from teachers with regard to curriculum-improvement programs is, "We talk ,talk, talk, but we never do anything about it." Curriculum improvement is, of course, a long-range program, but we cannot sit around and wait until all the facts are in. If the official leader takes too seriously the advice, "You must not go too fast," the participants are likely to conclude that they didn't get anywhere. To agree on a working philosophy, which can be revised later, if necessary, is better than taking a whole year to work on a statement of objectives that is assumed to be the last word. Working up some resource units which contain materials and activities that can be tried out immediately in the classrooms is better than holding everything up until the "new" curriculum can be "installed." School leaders who are always absorbed in building a background through study and discussion without ever putting any of the ideas into practice are like the person who took a 2-mile run to get up momentum for jumping a fence: When he got to the fence, he was too exhausted to jump.

Closely related to the problem of moving from discussion to action is the responsibility of the administration to act upon the decisions of the group. To have committees at work for months on projects that are ultimately shelved by the administration is destructive of staff morale as well as a waste of human energy. The concept of readiness for change also applies to teachers. All teachers are not ready at the same time to make the same movements in curriculum improvement. Therefore, curriculum projects should not be delayed until all teachers are ready, nor should administrative authority be used in an effort to force all teachers to move in identical directions with equal speed. Growth in curriculum improvement does not occur along a regular, consistent, straight-line front, but along a circumscribed front. By capitalizing upon readiness where it is and using this readiness to foster growth, an imbalance will be created which will motivate growth in other aspects of the institution. The impetus of this growth encourages the balanced interaction necessary among the organizational patterns of the school, the role definitions and assignments, and the group processes utilized to develop, affirm, and modify the organization, roles, and curriculum.

SUMMARY

1. Every generation of United States educators has struggled with the problems of forming instructional groups. Objective data are not available to prove conclusively that one organizational pattern is superior. Therefore, organizational patterns should be selected and evaluated in terms of how well a pattern facilitates the organization's purposes.

2. Organizational patterns guide, control, and govern the movement of pupils in vertical and horizontal directions.

3. The graded and the nongraded patterns are organizational plans for the vertical axis of the elementary school.

4. Self-contained, departmentalized, platoon, and team are patterns for the horizontal axis of the elementary school.

5. The nongraded pattern represents an effort to remedy the weaknesses of the graded pattern by making better provisions for individual differences and establishing a philosophy of continuous progress.

6. The dual progress plan permits pupils to progress through a graded sequence in certain subjects, called "cultural imperatives," and through an ungraded sequence in other subjects, called "cultural electives." The plan also provides for the use of specialists to teach the cultural electives.

7. The self-contained classroom calls for placing a group of pupils with one teacher for the major portion of the school day; it is designed to enable the teacher to learn a great deal about each pupil by observing him in a wide variety of learning situations.

8. Team teaching is an arrangement that provides for having two or more teachers, with abilities and skills that complement each other, assume joint responsibility for directing the learning activities of a group of pupils. The plan provides for large-group situations, small-group learning situations, and individual learning situations.

9. Departmentalization may be viewed as a plan for grouping pupils which permits the teacher to specialize in the teaching of one or two subjects. The plan is used more in grades 4, 5, and 6 than it is in the lower grades.

10. Homogeneous grouping refers to the practice of forming instructional groups composed of pupils who are nearly enough alike in some aspect to justify teaching them as a group and to reduce the task of adapting instruction to differences of ability.

11. Grouping pupils for instructional purposes is only one facet of the problem of elementary school organization. Organizing learning experiences, developing an effective classroom organization, and organizing the staff for curriculum improvement are other important facets.

12. Schools use organizational plans to orchestrate the resources of the school to facilitate the purposes of quality, equality, and personalization.

13. It is the responsibility of instructional leadership to help the staff develop an organization through which members can participate in the manner best suited to their talents in the improvement of the elementary school curriculum.

14. Instructional leadership in a democracy is based on principles that mold the leaders' thoughts and guide their actions when entrusted with the success of others. Instructional leadership is based on intelligence, personal integrity, and

facile communicativeness. Good leadership promotes an atmosphere of mutual respect and trust, is inconspicuous, builds morale, and requires foresight and courage.

15. The individual school is the operational center for curriculum study and improvement.

Problems and Projects

1. Who determines when the child will enter schools? Investigate the particular laws in your state which regulate vertical movement into and through the public schools. What individuals or groups of individuals are influential factors in deciding this issue?

2. Consult an elementary teacher and/or principal who is or has been intimately involved with both the graded and nongraded vertical organizational patterns. List this educator's concerns with each vertical organization.

3. Education majors often may find their teacher preparation programs have been slanted toward one horizontal organization with only minor attention to other alternatives. What courses or activities are presently available in your institution of higher learning to acquaint you with the various horizontal organizational patterns? Propose a curriculum and indicate the area, time sequencing, and activities during which such exposure should occur.

4. During the past several years, much attention has been given to "open education," "open classrooms," "open schools," and other systems. Yet, the term "open" still may often remain vague and general for the education major. Review ten journal articles bearing the term "open education" in the title. List the articles reviewed; below each article listed make reference to the article's definition (given or implied) of "open" (that is, methodology, physical structure, and so on). What are your conclusions? Do your findings account for the vagueness and generalities often heard from those attempting to define "open" as it relates to education?

5. Examine the curriculum programs for one grade. Is the program used system wide or is it an outgrowth of the individual teacher's constructs for that particular level? If designed by an individual teacher or small group of teachers, what are the provisions for curriculum articulation between and among levels? If designed by a system-wide council, what is the communication network between the classroom and the council?

Selected Readings

Crary, Ryland W., *Humanizing the School: Curriculum Development and Theory.* New York: Alfred A. Knopf, Inc., 1969. Chapter 11 presents a discussion of the construction and arrangements for the elementary school.

Cook, Ruth C., and Ronald C. Doll, *The Elementary School Curriculum.* Boston: Allyn & Bacon, Inc., 1973. Presents a chapter on grouping and organization.

Dean, Stuart E., *Elementary School Administration and Organization.* Washington, D.C.: U.S. Government Printing Office, 1969. Chapter 10 of this national survey of practices and policies of elementary schools deals with trends in grouping practices.

Goodlad, John I., and Robert H. Anderson, *The Nongraded Elementary School.* New York: Harcourt Brace Jovanovich, Inc., 1963. This book was a prime factor in the growth of the nongraded movement.

Goodlad, John I., and Harold G. Shane (Eds.), "The Elementary School in the United States," in the Seventy-second Yearbook of the National Society for the Study of Education. Chicago: The University of Chicago Press, 1973. Contains chapters on organizing and staffing the schools.

Hatch, James, et al., *A Catalog of Educational Alternatives.* Trenton, N.J.: New Jersey State Department of Education, August 1974. A listing and description of alternative schools and programs.

Hillson, Maurie, *Change and Innovation in the Elementary School Organization.* New York: Holt, Rinehart and Winston, 1965. Contains readings and analyses which deal with the major organizational innovations at the elementary level.

Joyce, Bruce R., *Alternative Patterns of Elementary Education.* Waltham, Mass.: Blaisdell Publishing Company, 1969. Chapter 1 presents a discussion of the decisions that create schools.

Mann, Horace, *Life and Works of Horace Mann Vol. III: Annual Reports of the Secretary of the Board of Education for the Years, 1839–1844,* Mary Mann (Ed.). Boston: Lee and Shepard, 1891. Compilation of Mann's annual reports.

Otto, Henry J., and David C. Sanders, *Elementary School Organization and Administration,* 4th ed. New York: Appleton-Century-Crofts, 1964. A basic book on the organization of the elementary schools; includes chapter on grouping.

Saylor, J. Galen (Ed.), *The School of the Future Now.* Washington, D.C.: Association for the Supervision and Curriculum Development, 1972. Proposals for early childhood, elementary, middle, and high school levels.

Schools for the 70's and Beyond: A Call to Action. Washington, D.C.: National Education Association, Center for the Study of Instruction, 1971. A guide for planning modern schools.

Stephens, Lillian S., *The Teacher's Guide to Open Education.* New York: Holt, Rinehart and Winston, 1974. A practical discussion of open education with suggested activities and procedures.

Van Til, William (Ed.), *Curriculum: Quest for Relevance.* Boston: Houghton Mifflin Company, 1974. Selection of readings on alternative schools and open education.

Wolcott, Harry F., *The Man in the Principal's Office: An Ethnography.* New York: Holt, Rinehart and Winston, 1973. A case study of the activities of an elementary principal.

chapter 5

Organizing
INSTRUCTION

*O, it's comf'rtable and kind in the prison of my mind, where every
day is like the day before, but I sometimes wish that I could free myself to
try, with eyes and ears accepting more and more . . .*

Bill Martin, Jr., *Freedom Series: I Reach Out to the Morning.*
(Glendale, Calif.: Bowmar Press, 1970), pp. 6–7.

Organizing for learning involves assuming a position in relationship to several
issues. These fundamental issues seem to nest in the following areas: content,
learner, method, communication environment, objectives, and goals. These areas
are so fundamental in guiding the behavior of a teacher that the author has yet
to meet one who does not have a position within each issue area. Yet, some
teachers seem unaware of their position(s) or even engage in behaviors that
contradict their stated positions, but their assumed positions, either covertly or
overtly, guide their teaching behaviors.

THE SUBSTANCE OF CONTENT

A critical curriculum decision area involves what is selected as content from a
subject field. Traditionally, the principle of complete coverage was dominant.
If a subject was to be taught, then it was to be thoroughly covered. The technique of selection functioned only to assign topics in a curriculum sequence.
Typically, the assignment of sequential topics was ordered from the simple to
the complex content. Coverage meant that the topics in each segment of the
total sequence would be studied and that when all had been completed, the subject field would have been covered. In a sense, each learner was led toward
"expertise" by completing the sequence and covering the content. As knowledge
within a subject field expanded, the new topics were inserted into the sequence.
Gradually, the number, weight, and bulk of content topics became such that
the achievement of coverage became difficult, if not impossible. For example,
the amount of information available doubled between the year A.D. 1 and A.D.
1750. Another doubling occurred between A.D. 1750 and A.D. 1900; this time

doubling occurred in a period of 150 years as compared with a period of 1,750 years needed for the first doubling. The third doubling came in 50 years, 1900 to 1950; the fourth doubling occurred between 1950 and 1960; the fifth doubling occurred during the period of 1960 to 1967; and it is estimated that the information available now doubles on three- or four-year cycles.

As a result of this periodic explosion of knowledge, the principle of coverage was modified by selecting representative content topics from subject fields. Curricula are now constructed in that way. However, the basis upon which representative content topics are to be selected remains unsettled. The oldest guideline for the selection is "classical." Classical content topics are those which society regards as the hallmark of an educated person (for example, knowledge of Latin). Another guideline for the selection of representative content topics is "practicality." Practical content topics are those which enable an individual to become initially employable. This guideline has become unstable as a result of the constantly changing nature of the vocational world (for instance, one of the impacts of technology has been the creation of new employment opportunities and the elimination of existing employment opportunites).

More recent literature suggests three additional guidelines for the selection of representative content topics from a subject field: relevancy, humaneness, and structure. As with the criteria of classical and practical, the newer criteria of relevancy and humaneness are not necessarily related to the fundamental nature of the subject matter field from which representative content topics are to be selected. Relevancy relates to the selection of those representative content topics which are functional in terms of the "realities" of the present and future. Humaneness is concerned with the selection of those representative content topics which nurture, depict, and enrich the essence of "the good man living the good life." Structure, as a criterion for the selection of representative content topics, is specifically and intimately related to the nature of the subject matter field. Those topics which unify a subject matter field, serving as tools both to manage existing data and to generate new data within the field, are topics which represent the structure of that field.

The preceding discussion of guidelines for the selection of content topics is not a comprehensive review. Yet, it does establish the range of viewpoints available to a teacher and curriculum builder. An analysis of these various positions will lead to the conclusion that representative content topics can be selected from several perspectives and that the basis of selection may influence teaching behaviors.

CHARACTER OF LEARNER

"Conceived in iniquity and born in sin," was the Puritan concept of the nature of a child. The child, a learner in the elementary school, was viewed as a "sinner" from whom the devil must be beaten. To learn what the adult Puritan knew was the only thing that would "save" the child from Satan. The discipline and content topics of these colonial schools were rigid and strict.

Later, the child was viewed as a "little adult," limited in capacities and learning processes. Often, the child was considered a blank tablet (*tabula rasa*) upon which learning experiences might be inscribed: "If the child learns as I learn, then what I know the child can know as I know it." The child was viewed as having the capacities for both good and bad: "The child would become good if I made, guided, and led."

One common belief was that learning preceded development. This position encouraged teacher behavior which implied that if learning can be forced, guided, or stimulated, then development will naturally follow. These beliefs were firmly entrenched until Piaget helped establish the principle that development preceded learning. Is the child good or bad, or neither? Is the child a little adult? Does learning precede development or does development precede learning? All these positions have been and are assumed by teachers, and each influences teaching behaviors.

DEFINITION OF METHOD

The pouring in, the drilling in, and the tricking in of content have all been practiced as methods. The conditioning of, training of, extension of, and reinforcement of have also been practiced as methods. Is method something done *to* a learner, done *with* a learner, or done *for* a learner? Are there social studies methods, reading methods, science methods, math methods, and other methods of teaching content? Are the methods of discipline, motivation, and evaluation tailored to produce the behavior desired? Are methods merely tricks, games, and simulations? Is there a method that characterizes the natural behavior of a child when learning?

Answers to such questions are found in the literature and can be observed in the behaviors of practicing teachers. Each teacher assumes, adopts, adapts, and develops something called "method."

Method or methodology is a descriptive term used to label the teacher's procedures, manipulations, and facilitations of content, control, and learning. The fragmentation of methods into the separate compartments of social studies methods, science methods, language arts methods, and so forth seems to be lessening. The method or methodology of good teaching is now being viewed as a concomitant element of a good learning environment rather than as the functional means of transmitting content. For example, evaluation procedures are similar whether the context of the evaluation is in reading, arithmetic, or behavior.

Thus, the traditional source of methods, the subject being transmitted, is being replaced or supplemented through an analysis of a supportive learning environment.

ESTABLISHING A LEARNING ENVIRONMENT

What constitutes a learning environment? We find many variations in classroom arrangements and practices:

Desks bolted to the floor to form straight lines

Open spaces, listening centers, science centers, reading areas, tables, movable furniture

Children sitting, listening, reciting, answering questions, completing worksheets

Children moving, talking, handling objects and equipment, asking questions, planning, demonstrating

Teachers talking, telling, questioning, assigning, testing, correcting

Teachers listening, answering, facilitating, planning, organizing, reinforcing

Are any of these basic to a learning environment? Descriptions of an environment supportive of learning have changed considerably. We now describe a supportive environment as one in which the learners are actively participating in the definition and manipulation of what is to be learned. Active participation includes the behaviors of the cognitive, affective, and psychomotor domains. Participation means that the teaching role is shared so that each participant is both teacher and learner. Each participant asks and answers, explains and hypothesizes, cooperates and directs, assigns and corrects, rewards and punishes.

SITUATION 5.1   Take a few minutes to write your concept of the learning environment:

What does it look like?

What is the interaction between teacher and learner?

What are the teacher's responsibilities to the learner? Make a list.

CHOOSING OBJECTIVES

For purposes of this discussion, objectives are defined as the intended outcomes resulting from instruction. Objectives are those behaviors which are rewarded. The range of behaviors that is valued, and therefore rewarded, has been consistently expanding. Beginning with the low-energy cognitive behaviors of recalling and recognizing, we now stress the high-energy cognitive behaviors of analyzing, synthesizing, and developing evaluative criteria. Beginning with the low-energy affective behaviors of passively attending and responding of children when called upon, we now stress the high-energy affective behaviors of choosing, prizing, and acting from self-directive systems of values. Formerly, pupils were conditioned to comply when observed by established officers of authority. Today, the modern elementary school strives to support the development of self-disciplined, self-actualizing individuals, with or without the presence of authority figures. From emphasis upon objectives which were global in nature, the modern elementary school now focuses on those objectives which identify observable behaviors, and it seeks to make such objectives public. From viewing pupils as not having constitutional rights, the modern elementary school now honors, welcomes, teaches, practices, and protects the constitutional rights of pupils.

These examples represent the potential range of movement available in the modern elementary school. Distributed all along the continuum will be found schools and teachers exemplifying assumptions concerning objectives—global or observable, low energy or high energy. At each point on the continuum the behaviors of those conducting learning activities will be influenced by and be representative of the assumptions maintained. And each assumption concerning objectives, whether global or observable, low energy or high energy, will influence the behaviors of those conducting learning activities.

CHOOSING GOALS

Chapter 2 provided a selected sampling of influential goals and purpose statements. A careful study of these samplings will suggest that goals are usually more global than objectives and that the differences among the various statements are more of degree than of kind. Statements of goals identify in broad, sweeping, directional terms the generalized characteristic of the school and its planned impact upon learners. Statements of objectives define the specifics of institutional and individual behaviors which are appropriate to the accomplishment of a goal. For example: Being in Chicago would be analogous to a goal, whereas traveling route 77 from St. Louis to Chicago would be analogous to an objective.

DEVELOPING A THEORY OF INSTRUCTION

The use of the terms "theory" and "theories" in relation to the process of education is not new. Titles such as *Theory and Practice of Teaching* and *Theories of Learning* have been used freely in educational literature for many decades. Activity in the area of theory building has, however, been increasing in recent years, particularly in educational administration, curriculum, and instruction.

Writers use the terms "general principles," "guidelines," "frame of reference," "postulates," and "assumptions" to explain what they mean by a theory. For example: "The term 'theory' is often used to mean general principles which seem to predict or account for events with an accuracy so much better than chance that we may say that the principles are 'true.' "[1] Bruner contended that a theory of learning is not a theory of instruction; that the former is descriptive, while the latter is prescriptive. He says, in discussing a theory of instruction:

> It is not a description of what has happened when learning has taken place—
> it is something which is normative, which gives you something to shoot at and

[1] Arthur P. Coladarchi and Jacob W. Getzels, *The Uses of Theory in Educational Administration.* (Stanford, Calif.: Stanford University Press, 1955).

which, in the end, must state something about what you do when you put instruction together in the form of courses.[2]

One of the difficulties in theory development in any area is the tendency of school people to think of theory and practice as separate entities—to think of theorizing as an impractical activity engaged in by persons who are far removed from practical situations. Those who are concerned with developing a theory of instruction and with making it operational in classroom situations, therefore, point out that theory and practice are interrelated aspects of the teacher's behavior and that without guiding principles teaching can be only accidentally successful. Teachers, like all human beings, are constantly making decisions. Moreover, they make these decisions within a frame of reference. When their frames of reference are explicit and examinable, they are said to be using "intelligent method." When teachers act in conformity with guiding principles, they are testing their theories; the theories are formulated, tested in practice, and more powerful theories are formulated.

Bruner has stated that, in developing a theory of instruction, "Unfortunately, we shall have to start pretty nearly at the beginning, for there is very little literature to guide us in this subtle enterprise."[3] He believed that a valid theory of instruction must concern itself with the factors which predispose a child to learn effectively, with the optimal structuring of knowledge, with the optimal sequence required for learning, and with the nature and pacing of rewards and punishments.

A theory of instruction would serve a teacher in several ways. First, it would elevate to consciousness, and thereby help legitimatize, the assumptions which tend to generate and guide teaching behaviors. Second, it would provide a frame of reference for the establishment of a dynamic feedback system—a feedback system that supplies data related to the consistency of teaching behaviors with valid assumptions and to the determination of success in the accomplishment of objectives and thereby goals.

BENCHMARKS FOR A STRATEGY OF INSTRUCTION

A theory of instruction may be premature, but the author feels that sufficient alternatives are now available so that a strategy of instruction can be systematized to direct teaching behaviors. A theory explains and predicts; a strategy is a plan for action. A strategy is a predisposition to act, based upon the selection and organization of prior commitments.

This section presents a strategy of instruction predicated upon the selection of certain commitments within the issues of curriculum. The issue areas discussed in previous sections of this chapter provide the sources for the identification of

[2] Jerome S. Bruner, "Needed: A Theory of Instruction," *Educational Leadership* (May 1963), pp. 523–527.
[3] Bruner, p. 524.

the elements of this normative strategy. These issues consist of perspectives concerning content, learners, method, learning environment, objectives, and goals.

The strategies of instruction that do exist may be overt, covert, incomplete, or even inadequate. Yet, in the literature, and most importantly within each teacher, strategy is evident. These strategies consist of perspectives and assumptions utilized by the practitioner to control and direct their behavior during the processes of instruction. Since strategies exist, then we must consciously synthesize their common aspects into a criterion statement, even if the latter itself seems somewhat incomplete.

The power of a proposed strategy partially depends upon the potency of the questions which generate the system. The fundamental questions for this strategy of instruction are:

What content do we teach?
What is the learner we teach?
What is (are) the method(s) of teaching?
What is the communication environment of teaching?
What are the observable behaviors of learning?
What are the global statements of goals of teaching?

SITUATION 5.2   Interview a college professor in education and an elementary teacher concerning their personal strategies of instruction. What provisions are allowed by the professor and the teacher to accommodate the area of

a. content?
b. learners?
c. method(s)?
d. learning environment?
e. objectives and/or goals?

In your personal opinion are their strategies aimed at the central purpose of education; that is, to develop the ability to think?

Selecting Content To Be Taught

Boundaries, vocabulary, tools, literature, and tradition—each contributes to defining subject matter; each contributes to determining what information and how information fits into or outside the confines of a discipline.

We should identify those information clusters within a discipline (field of study) which best represent it. This selection is necessary because we must sample rather than broadly describe. To cover all aspects of an already sizable discipline which is consistently changing and expanding seems impossible. However, a sampling is possible if a discipline is viewed as an organized system of coordinated information clusters.

The phrase "information clusters" is used to describe the grouping or re-grouping of what is known in order to clarify what is unknown. This act of grouping and regrouping of what is known affirms the existence of information clusters. The pain and the joy of this approach lies in the plastic nature of single items of data as well as in the nature of information clusters themselves. An individual item of data can be nested within and regenerated by various clusters. The points here are that clusters exist and others can be created; the creation and use of clusters are fundamental acts in producing new data. Information clusters are useful for conveying data, but they can also function in the generation of new data.

The phrase "organized system" is used to describe the behaviors of re-searchers as they provide a plastic or permanent unity for the grouping and regrouping of data into clusters. Within the discipline axioms, premises of principles apparently exist which provide for the logical grouping and regrouping of information.

To sample a discipline is not to be thought of in terms of a random sampling; the sampling must consist of those clusters which represent the power within the field of study to clarify and/or predict existing phenomena. Further, the sampling must serve to identify those clusters which are most plastic in the grouping and regeneration of information. This idea of sampling can be thought of as analogous to the sampling involved during the construction of an achievement test. A reading achievement test, for example, does not contain items measuring all possible behaviors involved in reading. Fifty or a hundred reading behaviors are tested, and then a performance score for all reading behaviors is predicted. A test to obtain a driver's license is another example of sampling. A few selected incidences involved in driving are selected and the examinee's performance of these is observed. Upon successful completion of these selected incidences, a license is issued, enabling the examinee to experience all behaviors involved in driving.

The primary difference between sampling for the selection of information clusters and the sampling for reading or driving achievement lies in the degree of expertise assumed. Within the former, sampling for the selection of information clusters, the existence of competent behaviors in some aspects does not automatically imply competence in all other aspects within the discipline. The implication is made, however, that if the learner experiences one information cluster within the discipline in processes identical to those holding expertise within the particular field of study, the learner has learned how to learn other clusters within that field.

Jerome Bruner made a powerful formation for the selection of content. Bruner utilized a concept he termed "structure" to describe those aspects within a discipline that should be taught. Structure denoted those aspects of a discipline that simplified, clustered, and generated. Bruner seemed to perceive some kind of a unifying whole which operated within and throughout a field of study. His contribution—structure—had tremendous and significant impact upon the organization of curriculum during the 1960s, especially upon math and the sciences. During the early 1970s, however, the concept of structure within a discipline seemed to be falling out of favor, perhaps even of Bruner's. This falling from favor might partially be explained by the possibility that some items identified as structure did not serve well. In addition, the sequencing of these "structures" into the graded system resulted in what appeared to be the teaching of algebra, for example, to first graders. Whether from misunderstanding, mis-application, or some inadequacy in the concept of structure, Bruner did call attention to the need to reconsider how content is selected.

Some basis within a discipline itself for the selection of areas of content is a necessity for the development of a strategy of instruction. To be representative of the discipline of biology, sound biological information clusters are needed. To best represent the discipline of mathematics, samples of sound mathematical information clusters are needed. A discipline is best represented by its own information clusters. Other criteria are needed to further refine the selection of content, but the initial selection must originate within the discipline itself. Some refinement of Bruner's concept of structure is appropriate and even necessary, but the essence of his concept still seems the most functional and powerful means for the selection of representative content topics from fields of study.

Additional Criteria

After representative information clusters that have integrity within a discipline are selected, then the following criteria could be applied to further refine the selection: relevancy, humaneness, classical and/or practical. Each of these was discussed in the first portion of this chapter, so only examples of their applications will be given here. A brief reminder, though, that the source of each of these as a criterion lies outside a field of study, and therefore must be applied after representative content has been selected.

Relevancy is the criterion that selects content because of its anticipated functionality, both for the present and the future. Although an element of prophecy is involved in applying the criterion of relevancy, it is a viable means to help include or exclude content topics. For example, a popular topic in math textbooks of the 1950s was the reading of electric, gas, and water meters. This topic did enable the teacher to deal with the representative mathematical concept of place value, but the relevancy to the common practice of reading meters is doubtful in today's and tomorrow's world. So, the criterion of relevancy would suggest that a new topic be used to carry the mathematical concept of place value. The significance of relevancy as a criterion is that it encourages the selection of content topics that are present in the real world of the learner.

Humaneness is the criterion used to select content topics because they depict the nature of man. This criterion is of philosophical and even sociological origin at times. Sexism is, for example, a criterion of humaneness which deals with the elimination of topics which impose a limited stereotyped role upon an individual because of gender. One issue pertinent to this criterion is the depiction of a woman in many basal readers as being only a mother and wife. Humaneness suggests that each person should not be culturally conditioned to fit a predetermined role.

Humaneness also calls attention to the careless and limiting characterizations sometimes portrayed of members from ethnic minorities. Humaneness asks that real people in real situations be depicted by each topic of content. Humaneness reminds us that real people sweat, strive, cry, and care, and that these are essential human attributes. Humaneness values topics in which options and decision-making activities are available, and in which the natural consequences of these choices and decisions are expressed. The ultimate value of humaneness as a criterion for the selection of content topics is in its offering of possibilities to a human-learner to relate to oneself through the vehicle of content.

The classical criterion guides in the selection of content topics which are recognized by the prevailing society as being in the possession of an educated person. The strength of this criterion lies in the potentially positive reinforcement by the society to the learner. If the prevailing society values rapid and accurate mathematical computations, then a learner with these abilities is apt to be more valued within the society. The problem inherent in this criterion is that awareness within the prevailing society may lag significantly behind the developments within a discipline.

The practical criterion guides in the selection of content topics which are related to the initial employment of the learner. The validity of the criterion rests in the fact that most learners enter the world of work and that all learners are influenced by it. Career education is an example of a development fostered through application of this criterion. The criterion of practicality requires the sorting of content topics in terms of their potential applicability for the learner as a potential producer of goods or services.

Selection and Sorting

The first step in the selection of content topics is the utilization of a criterion integral to the nature of a discipline. This provides a sample of sound information clusters. Bruner's concept of structure is a powerful tool for this step. The sample resulting from this first selection is now re-sorted through the application of the criteria: relevancy, humaneness, classical, and/or practical. The end product should be a representative sample of sound content topics that are relevant, humane, classical, and practical.

If this procedure within a strategy for instruction seems involved, then review the inadequacies which result whenever content is selected from a single criterion. Also, notice the range of resources brought to the selection of content topics: the content expert, the philosopher, the sociologist, the educator, the employer, the public, and others. If a learner is asked to devote energy and heartbeats to the vehicle of content, then the professional educator must devote even more energy and heartbeats to the definition of the vehicle (see Fig. 5.1).

The preceding discussion of content selection should illustrate a potential element of a strategy of instruction and how this element might both operate and be derived.

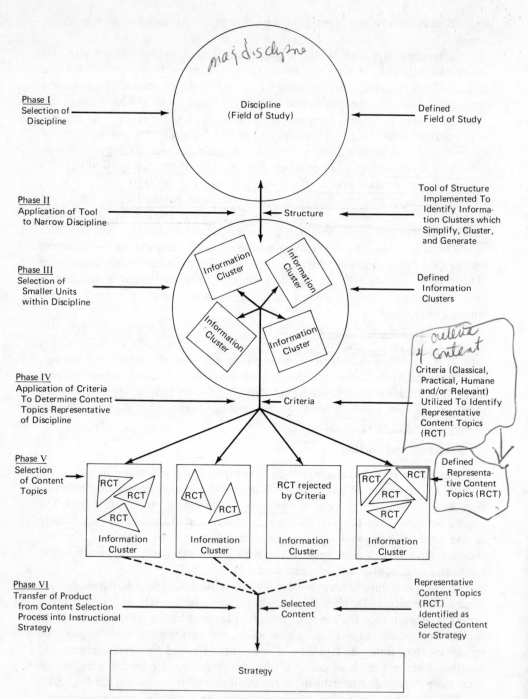

Figure 5.1   Selection of content. For strategy, see paradigm, Fig. 5.6, p. 187.

teaching environment is observed that can be primarily characterized by drill, one reasonable explanation might be the inappropriateness of the activities for the developmental levels of the learners involved. When learners are not approached at their developmental levels, they can be conditioned to the right answer, but they cannot cognitively process the event conveying the right answer.

A strategy of instruction might then assume, with Piaget, that development precedes learning and that the developmental levels of learners can be characterized by the cognitive processes available to them. This element of a strategy would enable curriculum builders, responsible for the modern elementary school to select content, events, and situations in which the cognitive perception and processes required are appropriate to the developmental levels of the learners.

The Method(s) of Teaching

Method, or methodology, is a descriptive term used to label those procedures, techniques, manipulations, and facilitations of content and the learning environment which are performed by teachers. A strategy of instruction must include an element providing for the creation, selection, and evaluation of methodology.

Traditionally, methods have been derived from those content and control-oriented behaviors which we choose to reinforce. Consequently, methods of reading, mathematics, science, social studies, and so forth were developed along with presentation procedures (for example, lecture, discussion, demonstration, read-recite-test, drill). To facilitate the reinforcing of behaviors, methods of rewarding, punishing, restricting, and controlling were developed.

Where and what are the sources of methodology? Is it the content and its topics? Is it information transmission and packaging? Or is it the psychology of behavior modification? A strategy of instruction must accommodate the source or sources for the development of methodology.

The strategy proposed here will present "inquiry" as the source of methodology. Inquiry is defined as the processes of exploration, invention, and discovery. These processes—exploration, invention, and discovery—describe the learner's interactions within a learning environment. The strategy will refer only to inquiry as method. The other performances by teachers upon the learning environment will be referred to as procedures, techniques, manipulations, and facilitations.

The selection of inquiry as the method of the strategy is not done to devalue the supportive procedures, techniques, manipulations, and facilitations employed by the teacher, but rather to provide a framework from which those teacher performances may be created, selected, or adapted. Inquiry provides a normative description of the processes of interaction employed by learners. Teacher performances are then deployed to fit and further stimulate the inquiry processes of exploration, invention, and discovery.

Exploration

The initial phase of inquiry is the process of exploration. When confronted with an environment, a potential learner begins to sort, identify, and label those properties and characteristics of the environment that are familiar. This is not necessarily a random process because the recognition of what is familiar serves as the catalyst for the organization of the learner's behaviors. Learners must do this for themselves. They cannot be told what is familar to them. Although the environment can be equipped to facilitate the learner's identification of what is familiar, familiarity is ultimately a function of the learner's developmental level and previous experiences.

An understanding of Piaget helps in equipping the learning environments with objects, events, actions, and data which are appropriate to the developmental level of a learner. The appropriate equipping of the environment maximizes opportunities for the learner during exploration to interact with the familiar, thus increasing the likelihood of that particular learning environment's being perceived and processed by the learner. This is crucial, as successful exploration is a prerequisite to a successful learning cycle. Teacher performances (procedures, techniques, manipulations, and facilitations) can then be selected, designed, and adapted to further promote exploration.

The techniques of demonstration, for example, can be employed as a powerful means for furthering exploratory behaviors. When employed during the exploration phase of inquiry, demonstration would be planned around an equipped environment appropriate to the learner's developmental level. The demonstration would display the properties and characteristics of the objects and actions involved in the learning activity, and discussion during the demonstration would identify them. The discussion during the demonstration would emphasize the observation of the "what's" and "how's" rather than the "why's" of the event or situation. The other information presentation procedures (for example, lecture discussion, reading assignments, media) would be adapted in similar ways during the exploration phase of inquiry. The manipulations and facilitations of individuals into groups, committees, field trips, or other units would also be adapted during exploration to emphasize the observations and interactions of the learner with the equipped environment.

Invention

The second phase of inquiry is the process of invention. Invention occurs as a result of the learner's explorations. Whatever intake the learner has experienced during exploration is now reorganized. During invention, the learner clusters and groups the inputs of explorations into a description, an explanation, a classification, or a hypothesis. The power of the invention as a stage for additional learning is dependent upon the exploration phase of inquiry. If the stimuli avaliable and the procedures employed during exploration have been appropriate to the learner's developmental level, then the learner's invention(s) will be self-actualizing.

The performances employed by the teacher during the process of invention are designed to emphasize the learner's choosing, displaying, and prizing of personally derived inventions. These performances may also be utilized to clarify the learner's use of inputs from personal exploration. However, teaching procedures of telling and drilling seem inappropriate during invention because learners are processing the classifications, descriptions, explanations, and hypotheses which are fundamental to their present and future learnings. Therefore, the manipulations and facilitations of discussing, questioning, displaying, and acting seem more appropriate. Although the technique of lecturing, for example, can be employed to present the teacher's inventions for the learner's exploration, the learner's inventions must be displayed individually; no one else processes them. The teacher performances during invention stress the learner's output behaviors of speaking and writing, rather than the input behaviors of listening and reading.

The potential for future self-directed behaviors of the learner will nest within the inventions. Learners who are not self-directive have probably been blocked from the development of inventions, for exploration behaviors tend to leave the learner with only what is presently familiar. Inventions guide and direct behaviors in both familiar and new environments. The teacher within the modern elementary school provides time, gentleness, and patience to the learner, and facilitates an environment to honor the learner's inventions.

Discovery

The third phase of inquiry is discovery. Discovery occurs as a result of the learner's inventions, and this process begins when the learner's behaviors are directed toward them. Discovery is the testing of an invention's adequacy. Does it work? Will it account for new objects, actions, events, or situations? Discovery serves to strengthen, establish, modify, or destroy inventions, and even if the discovery systems displaces them, they serve powerful and useful functions. For example, the behaviors based upon the testing of an incompleted invention foster modification of invention behaviors, which then become more adequate or comprehensive.

Teacher performances employed during discovery are designed to guide the learners to "find out" the strength, logic, and integrity of their inventions. These teaching behaviors act as a catalyst which supplies the learner with the means for verifying an invention. Within the modern elementary school, the teacher serves as a "means for verification," not as an "external verifier" (for example, "That's right," "That's wrong"). As with exploration, teacher performances may be employed to support both the input and output behaviors of listening, speaking, reading, and writing. The information-presenting techniques are now modified to provide means, examples, and illustrations to test and find out about an invention. Just as with exploration and invention, the behaviors of discovery must be appropriate for the developmental level of the learner. For example, a preoperational learner who cannot mentally reverse an action cannot use reversal as a means for discovery.

Some incomplete inventions will eventually be confirmed through discovery as a function of a learner's developmental level and experiences. When changes occur in either the developmental level or experiences of the learner, each invention contains the seeds of its own modification. Therefore, the comprehensiveness and adequacy of a discovery system and its impact upon an invention should be perceived as a continuum. A concrete operational learner will abandon the invention and discovery systems of the preoperational learner. Be patient! Each successful inquiry cycle increases the readiness for changes in both the developmental level and experiences of the learner.

SITUATION 5.3   Review books or articles on inquiry. Describe the observable behavior of the learner during each phase of the inquiry cycle: exploration, invention, discovery. Describe the teacher's role during each of these phases.

Coordinating Elements of Inquiry

Successful inquiry will usually include several cycles through the processes of exploration, invention, and discovery. If affective blocks do not occur when a discovery system displaces an invention, the learner will return to exploration, recreate an invention, and reapply a discovery system. Piaget used the term "disequilibrium" for this recycling of an unsupported invention. He further stated that each equilibrium (an affirmed invention) contains the potential seeds for future disequilibrium. In order for recycling and its companion "disequilibrium" to occur, the manipulations and facilitations must be very supportive of the need for affective reinforcement. A more comprehensive discussion of Piaget was given in Chapter 3.

A potential source, then, for the reward and punishment procedures of classroom control is the inquiry cycle. As learners are directed through inquiry, the intrinsic energy available for interacting with the learning environment is magnified, thereby reducing somewhat both the energy available and the learner's need to engage in other behaviors. According to the proposed strategy, the reward and punishment systems of a classroom would be judged in terms of its reinforcement of the learners as they experience inquiry (see Fig. 5.3).

Inquiry as an element within the strategy provides a meeting ground for what is presently identified as methods of reading, arithmetic, social studies, and other subjects. The content topics of all these areas of study can be appropriate to inquiry when selected by structure, the first element of the strategy. Therefore, inquiry can be the method which unites the behaviors of learning with the vehicles of content drawn from reading, arithmetic, social studies, and so on. More specific examples of this uniting function of inquiry will be provided in Part III.

Inquiry as an element of the strategy also provides a foundation for the selection of teacher performances. This foundation enables a teacher to answer, for example, the question: "Is the procedure of drill good or bad?" Without a foundation—in this case, inquiry—the author suggests the question has no answer. With the foundation of inquiry, drill can be evaluated as a technique useful for establishing at a high efficiency level those inventions affirmed through

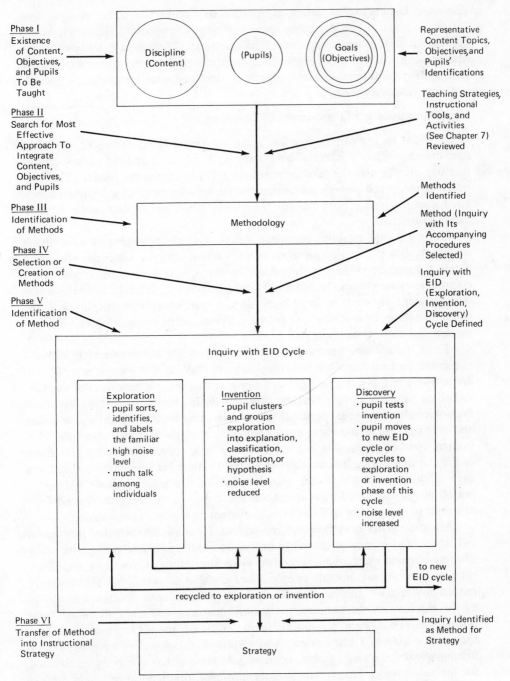

Figure 5.3   The inquiry cycle. For discipline (content), see Fig. 5.1, p. 164; for goals (objectives), see Fig. 5.5, pp. 184–185; for strategy, see Fig. 5.6, p. 187.

discovery. Drill is useless during exploration or discovery. Another nonquestion, "Is media good or bad?", has no answer without a foundation (inquiry). Media can be adopted to serve exploration or discovery. The objects, actions, events, and situations of the media are to be appropriate to the behaviors of exploration or discovery. Without additional adaptions, media adapted for exploration would not serve discovery well.

The Communication Environment of Teaching

A proposed strategy of instruction must account for the nature of the communications within a learning environment. A prime ingredient of a learning-teaching situation is the establishment of a communications system. The proposed strategy will provide guidelines for the development of a communication environment which is both consistent with objectives and facilitates the achievement of objectives.

To teach is to establish communications. To reflect learning is to establish communications. The development of interaction analysis systems and instruments is based upon these assumptions. Interaction analysis is the study of the communication networks within a learning environment. Interaction analysis systems attempt to describe and then display for interpretation purposes the communications of teaching and learning. As we learn to describe and display, we can then learn to evaluate.

From the author's perspective, efforts to study the communication within a classroom evolved from the recurring study of, "What is a good teacher?" The first answers to this question were still being written into the contracts of teachers as late as the early 1900s. Teacher contracts during this period prescribed their dress; church attendance; personal habits related to smoking, drinking, courting and shaving. Some contracts even contained a clause for the dismissal of a woman upon marriage. These attributes may have served well those protectors of the children during this period, but by the 1920s it became obvious that these were inadequate answers to the question, "What is a good teacher?" Although not all people discarded these questions and answers, the majority shifted their attention to personality traits as keys to evaluating teacher competence.

A good teacher is extravertive, masculine, feminine, charismatic, intelligent, tall, short, and otherwise desirably descriptive. Although interesting, the study of these personality traits has failed to yield any stable, consistently significant relationships. Again, not all people ignored these answers, but the majority moved on to answer the question of capability in terms of the content knowledge of the teacher, on the assumption that the learners will learn the most from those teachers who know the most content. Truly, the more I know of discipline, the more questions I can answer. The results of these studies have been conflicting. Again, a strong, stable, positive relationship has not been established for this assumption. This is not to imply, however, that ignorance makes a good teacher, but rather that, after some point, additional content knowledge of the teacher is not necessarily reflected in increased learning of content by pupils. The majority of people are probably still operating upon and testing this last assumption.

The study of classroom communications, called "interaction analysis," was furthered by the observation that pupils taught by teachers who vary widely in their knowledge of content may achieve similar amounts of growth in achievement. If this is true, then perhaps some commonness other than knowledge of content exists among teachers who typically have classes characterized by high growth in achievement. The purpose for the study of interaction analysis is to investigate and verify that communication patterns may be one commonality among such teachers.

The studies related to common communication patterns among teachers who typically obtain high achievement do not consistently show a high, strong, positive relationship. The studies do show, however, that a positive relationship exists which cannot be explained by chance, and that it is possible to describe and display the communication patterns of a teacher. It seems reasonable to predict that other relationships do exist, and as the study matures these relationships will become more sharply displayed. It is with this faith that the strategy includes interaction analysis as an element to research and display the aspects of the communications networks within a learning environment.

One area of study within interaction analysis has been the use of questions. Questions are a form of communication frequently used by teachers. Questions can be characterized by form, content load, and their anticipated impact upon the learning environment. The form of a question is dependent upon the way a question is presented by the teacher. The content load of the question is estimated by placement of the question according to the domain and classification levels given in Bloom's Taxonomy of Educational Objectives.

The manner in which a question is presented may affect the nature of the communication. For example, "John, what is the name of this book?" does not produce the same behavior as, "What is the name of the book?" (pause) "John?" When the respondent is identified before the question is presented, the teacher is saying that this communication is between only two people; the other students are released from attending to the communication. When the question is presented first, and then a pupil is identified to respond, the teacher is saying that the communication is for all.

Ben Harris has identified five question forms: solitary, controlled, uncontrolled, spontaneous, and mass.

1. Solitary: *The teacher identifies the respondent; the question is presented; the teacher responds.*
2. Controlled: *The question is presented; the teacher identifies the respondent; the pupil responds; the teacher responds.*
3. Uncontrolled: *The question is presented; a pause occurs, during which pupils signal through raised hands, eye contact, or other means, whether or not they wish to respond; the teacher identifies the respondent; the pupil responds; the teacher responds.*

4. Spontaneous: *The question is presented; a pause occurs until a pupil self-selects himself and responds to the question; another pupil responds to either the question or the first pupil's response; another pupil . . . etc.; teacher possibly intervenes for clarification, review, summary, etc. . . .*

5. Mass: *The question is presented for the total group to respond simultaneously; the teacher responds.*[5]

Apparently teachers develop habitual patterns in the use of one or more of these forms. The majority of teachers with whom the author has had contact use the solitary and controlled question forms almost exclusively. A question should be presented in a form to support the intent. For example, if group discussion is to occur, the communication must move to the spontaneous form. If a pupil seems inattentive, the use of the pupil's name first, as exemplified in the solitary form, seems most appropriate. Further, it is the author's opinion that the use of the controlled form for an inattentive pupil seems most cruel. A person's name is the communication most apt to be heard; to use what the pupil's behavior has already demonstrated (that is, the pupil is inattentive) in an effort to get attention does not seem wise.

When a teacher uses the solitary or controlled forms, the teacher is the total center of communication. The teacher becomes the only mediator of what is significant communication; of who should communicate; and of who should not communicate. When using the uncontrolled or spontaneous form, the teacher becomes only one of the potential centers of communication and is sharing the mediation of what is significant, and who should or should not communicate. The opportunity to help pupils learn group processes seems to require the use of uncontrolled and spontaneous question forms.

Questions can also be described in terms of their content load. What is the nature of the cognitive or affective content of the question? Sanders[6] and others have attempted to describe the content load of questions through the use of the *Taxonomy of Educational Objectives.* It seems reasonable that the success of teachers might be related to their skills in posing questions in which the content load represents all classification levels and domains. A teacher, for example, whose practice is to ask only low-energy cognitive questions (recall, recognition) would seem to be offering limited opportunities to pupils.

Brophy's book, *Looking in Classrooms,* cites studies which suggest that teachers are the primary actors in 84 percent of classroom communication; two-thirds of the questions asked by teachers require only recall or recognition cognitive behaviors; and the number of questions and the existence of praise for a correct answer varies according to the teacher's perceptions of the pupil as a high or low achiever.[7]

Other studies suggest that in most classrooms there is an action zone, a

[5] Ben M. Harris, *Supervisory Behavior in Education.* (Englewood Cliffs, N.J.: Prentice-Hall, Inc., 1963), p. 165.

[6] Norris M. Sanders, *Classroom Questions: What Kinds?* (New York: Harper & Row, Publishers, 1966).

[7] Thomas L. Good and Jere E. Brophy, *Looking in Classrooms.* (New York: Harper & Row, Publishers, 1973).

test (1st)

territory from which most of the communication is directed and originated. Guilford characterizes questions as either "divergent" or "convergent."[8] Convergent questions tend to have a single answer or are designed to sort toward a single answer. Divergent questions are designed to generate a range of numerous alternative answers and possibilities.

Several interaction analysis instruments have been developed to guide the observation of the communication networks within a classroom. Amidon and Hunter's instrument, Verbal Interaction Category System (VICS) is an example.[9] The VICS provides four codes to account for the performance of teachers in initiative communication: providing information, giving directions, asking narrow questions, and asking broad questions. It also has several codes for pupil talk: short, factual, predictable answers; longer, less predictable responses; initiated responses to other pupils; initiated responses to the teacher. The VICS also codes the teacher responses back to pupil communication as being either the acceptance or rejection of ideas, behaviors, or feelings.

Interaction analysis instruments enable an observer to quickly and reliably code, display, and interpret the emphasis, distribution, and relationship of the transactions within a communications environment. Consider the communication network illustrated in Pattern A. The display for Pattern A provides evidence concerning:

PATTERN A

INSTRUCTIONAL SEQUENCES	DESCRIPTION OF ENVIRONMENT	COMMUNICATION ANALYSIS
I	Teacher reminds class of poor work habits demonstrated yesterday.	Teacher rejects behavior.
	Teacher informs students that the next chapter is concerned with life on a ranch in the Old West.	Teacher orients, presents content.
	Teacher: "Now, turn to page 26 and read to page 45. Answer the questions on page 45."	Teacher gives directions.
II	There occur sounds of pupils opening books; reaching in desks; taking out books, pencils, and paper.	Silence—activities related to assigned task.
	Several loud exchanges occur between pupils, not related to the directions of the teacher.	Confusion—activities unrelated to assigned task.
	Teacher reminds group that they missed having recess yesterday because they did not settle down.	Teacher rejects behavior.
	Teacher: "Be quiet, open your books and start immediately to work."	Teacher gives direction.

[8] J. P. Guilford, "Structures of Intellect," *Psychology Bulletin, LIII* (1956), pp. 267–293.
[9] Edmund Amidon and Elizabeth Hunter, *Improving Teaching.* (New York: Holt, Rinehart and Winston, 1966), pp. 209–221.

INSTRUCTIONAL SEQUENCES	DESCRIPTION OF ENVIRONMENT	COMMUNICATION ANALYSIS
	Pupils begin to settle into a busy noise as they read, write, turn papers, etc.	Silence—activities related to assigned task.
	Teacher moves around room to insure pupils are working. Teacher stops at Johnny's desk and says, "Put that away and get to work."	Teacher rejects behavior.
	Teacher returns to desk. Upon noticing interaction between two students, teacher directs comment to them: "Do your own work."	
	When the majority of students appear to be halfway through the question exercise, the teacher says, "You have five more minutes to finish the assignment."	Teacher gives directions.
III	Teacher recaps what students have read and explains to the students that they were reading to discover the nature of life in the Old West.	Teacher presents information students have read and states objective.
IV	Teacher instructs students: "Turn to page 45 and let's answer the questions. Danny, read question number one."	Teacher gives directions.
	Danny reads: "What kind of food did the pioneers eat?"	Student responds to teacher.
	Teacher: "Who knows the answer to question one?"	Teacher asks narrow question.
	Students raise hands and teacher selects Billy.	Teacher gives directions.
	Billy: "They grew some foods like corn on the ranch."	Student responds to teacher.
	Teacher: "Good."	Teacher accepts idea.
	Teacher: What else did the book say the pioneers ate, Susie?"	Teacher asks narrow question.
	Susie: "Sometimes they killed deer to eat."	Student responds to teacher.
	Teacher: "Okay, good."	Teacher accepts idea.
	Teacher: "What else did the book say?"	Teacher repeats narrow question.
	Teacher: "Johnny, go put that gum in the trash right now."	Teacher rejects behavior.
	Students giggle or talk among themselves as they wait for Johnny to throw his gum away.	Confusion—activities unrelated to assigned task.
	Teacher: "Sally, read question number two."	Teacher gives directions.
	Sally reads: "Who did most of the chores on the ranch?"	Student responds to teacher.
	Teacher: "What's the answer to the question Sally read, Johnny?"	Teacher asks narrow question.

1. *Dominance*: All pupil responses were short, factual responses to a teacher-initiated question and usually were followed by another teacher question.
2. *Acceptance*: When acceptance did follow pupil responses, it was applied only to ideas.
3. *Rejection*: Frequent and sharp remarks were directed at behavior not perceived as immediately productive to assigned tasks.
4. *Initiative*: No pupil-initiated communications directed to either the teacher or to other pupils were related to the lesson.
5. *Cognitive Analysis*: No broad, divergent questions were asked or any paraphrasing of what had been read.

Now consider the communication network in Pattern B. For Pattern B the display provides evidence concerning:

PATTERN B

INSTRUCTIONAL SEQUENCE	DESCRIPTION OF ENVIRONMENT	COMMUNICATION ANALYSIS
I	Teacher reinforces recent student behaviors regarding work habits.	Teacher accepts behavior.
	Teacher states that students will be discovering what life was like on a ranch in the Old West as they read the next chapter.	Teacher orients and presents content.
	At this point teacher asks questions designed to reveal student experiences related to ranches or to relatives who were frontier pioneers, etc.	Teacher asks questions to trigger student interaction with content.
	Teacher reinforces the behaviors of students in which they share experiences.	Teacher accepts behavior.
	Teacher informs students they will be reading pages 26 through 45 for information related to questions presented on page 45.	Teacher presents objective.
	Teacher instructs pupils: "Turn to page 26 and read to page 45. Answer the questions on page 45."	Teacher gives directions.
II	Students begin making sounds related to opening books, getting pencils, and paper.	Silence—activities related to assigned task.
	Teacher moves among students and acknowledges the study behavior of one student who has turned to the questions on page 45 before beginning to read.	Teacher accepts behaviors desired.
	Other students pattern, adapt, or adjust their behaviors to resemble those reinforced and acknowledged by the teacher as they complete assigned task.	Silence—activities related to assigned task.
	Teacher instructs students to finish present work and prepare to share information gained.	Teacher gives directions.

INSTRUCTIONAL SEQUENCE	DESCRIPTION OF ENVIRONMENT	COMMUNICATION ANALYSIS
III	Teacher opens with broad affective-type questions: "What would have been your fears as a pioneer?" or "What would you have liked about pioneer life?"	Teacher asks broad questions.
	Students provide responses in which they project and share feelings.	
	John: "I would like to live off the land and hunt big game."	Students respond to teacher.
	Billy: "Yea, me too, like bears and elk."	Students respond to student.
	Phil: "Not me, I'd be afraid. Bears can be mean."	Student responds to student.
	Teacher: "Yes. I would suppose the pioneers were both afraid and intrigued by the adventures of living in the Old west."	Teacher accepts behaviors and feelings.
	Jill: "The children of pioneer families had to work hard and do lots of chores. Didn't they ever go to school or have any fun?"	Student initiates comment to teacher.
	Teacher at this point gives factual information related to the schooling of children in the Old West.	Teacher provides information.
	Teacher shares dominance through questions: "Do any of you know about games pioneer children played?" or "What did the pioneers do for entertainment?"	Teacher asks broad question related to student's question.
	Nancy: Well, lots of the time the family did things together because other children or families didn't live close by like in the cities."	Student responds to teacher.
	Tanya: "And another reason the family did things together was because the entertainment and fun had to be at night after the chores were done."	Student responds to student.
	Joe: "My grandfather told me that on winter nights he would sit around the fire and listen to ghost stories while he whittled."	Student responds to student.
	Teacher: "That's right, the frontier families did often do fun activities together."	Teacher accepts ideas.
	Teacher: Joe used the word "whittle." Who besides Joe can show us what it means?"	Teacher asks question.

1. *Dominance*: Teacher questions were usually followed by several responses from different pupils, and contributions were provided by most participants. The amount of teacher communication decreased.
2. *Acceptance*: The ideas, feelings, and behaviors of pupils were accepted by both the teacher and other pupils.
3. *Rejections*: Rejection was infrequent and apparently privately given to behaviors not perceived as potentially productive to the discussion.
4. *Initiative*: Frequent examples occurred of pupil-initiated responses and questions both to other pupils and the teacher.
5. *Cognitive Analysis*: Many broad, divergent questions which generated inventions and discovery systems.

Communication patterns often become habitual. The displays and interpretations made possible through the interaction analysis instruments will enable a teacher to better perceive the flexibiilty or lack of flexibility that characterizes patterns:

Studies by Good and Brophy,[10] utilizing interactions analysis procedures, suggest the following as characteristic patterns:

1. Emmer reported in 1967 that teachers grossly underestimated the amount of time they talked in classrooms.

2. In 1970 Ehman reported that the ratings teachers gave to their own selected classroom behaviors differed sharply from those ratings given to their behaviors by pupils and observers. The ratings of the pupils and observers, however, were very similar.

3. In 1970 Adams and Biddle reported that 84 percent of the time teachers were the actors in classroom communication situations. They also reported that feelings and personal relationships made up less than one-half of 1 percent of classroom communication.

4. In 1970 Borg et al. summarized the many studies done since 1912 of the content load of teacher questions. Their summary suggested that content load of teacher questions had not significantly changed.

5. In 1969 Hudgins and Ahlbrand stated: "The chief properties of formal pupil communication in the classroom are its brevity and inequality of its distributions."

6. Good and Brophy have an excellent, concise summary of many studies in their 1973 publication, *Looking in Classrooms*.[11]

The above comments on interaction analysis as a developing field of study are not intended as a comprehensive review. Perhaps, though, sufficient examples have been cited to establish for the reader that it is both possible and profitable to describe, display, and interpret the communication transactions within the classroom. Much is yet to be done in this area. The author predicts that the keys to answering, "What is teaching?" and maybe even, "What is a

---

[10] Good and Brophy, pp. 22–38.
[11] Good and Brophy, pp. 22–38.

good teacher?" nest in the study of the communication networks within class-rooms (see Fig. 5.4).

The Observable Behaviors of Learning

Those behaviors of pupils which, when observed by the teacher, are rewarded or punished represent the objectives of that teacher. A proposed strategy of in-struction must incorporate a frame of reference for the identification and classi-fication of the behaviors of learning. The author views the *Taxonomy of Edu-cational Objectives*[12] as the most effective tool available at this time.

Other tools are available, and should be studied and considered by the reader. The primary objective of this section, therefore, is to establish the need for and the value of a tool to perform these functions. A somewhat secondary objective is to present the *Taxonomy of Educational Objectives* as the tool.

Chapter 2 discussed the movement to make objectives both public and visible for purposes of accountability. The primary public is the pupil in a class-room. It is to the pupil that the modern elementary teacher is first accountable. The pupil has the right to know openly and directly what the objectives are and which behavior represents the achievement of these objectives.

In becoming accountable to the pupils, teachers must also become account-able to themselves. A consciously developed and applied framework for objec-tives will reinforce the patience, distance, and consistencies necessary for con-ducting a class. When objectives are both overt and visible within a strategy, the teacher has a means of viewing the consistencies and inconsistencies of pupil or teacher behaviors with the accomplishment of objectives. The modern ele-mentary teacher has moved from, "Oh, this class is never interested," or "You can never depend upon this class and must watch them every moment", to "My behaviors and pupils' behaviors are intimately related," or "Where are my behaviors part of the problem rather than the solution?" When objectives are not openly available to the learner, it is equally likely that the teacher is also only vaguely aware of the objectives.

The *Taxonomy of Educational Objectives* was developed by Bloom and his associates as a hierarchical classification system of the behaviors of learners which teachers value. These behaviors were grouped into three domains and then into a hierarchical classification within each domain. The *Taxonomy of Educational Objectives* itself does not present a value system concerning the interrelationships among domains and classification levels, but it can be used as a display for the behaviors valued by the selector. The *Taxonomy of Educational Objectives*, like any other tool, should be viewed as such. A tool derives value from its application rather than from its existence, and as a tool it is most func-tional when its application is consistent with its design. For example, a hammer is neither valuable nor functional for cutting lumber. Likewise, the *Taxonomy*

---

[12] Benjamin Bloom (Ed.), *Taxonomy of Educational Objectives, Handbook I: Cognitive Do-main.* (London: Longmans, Green & Co., Ltd., 1956); Benjamin Bloom (Ed.), *Taxonomy of Educational Objectives, Handbook II: Affective Domain.* (New York: David McKay Company, Inc., 1964).

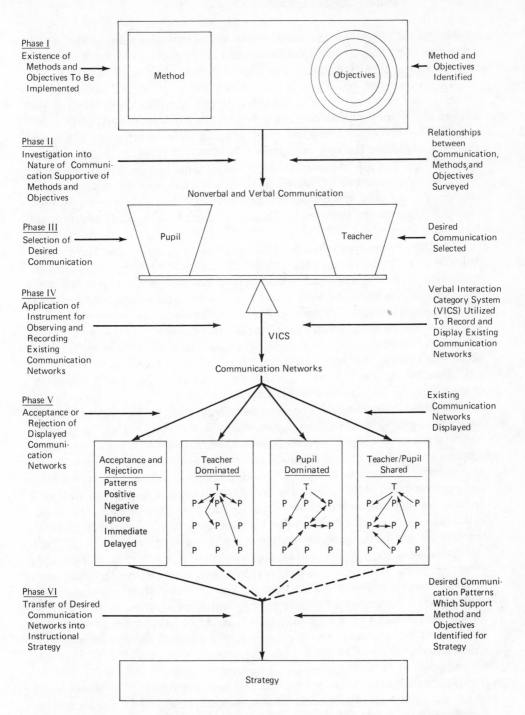

Phase I
Existence of Methods and Objectives To Be Implemented

Method

Objectives

Method and Objectives Identified

Phase II
Investigation into Nature of Communication Supportive of Methods and Objectives

Relationships between Communication, Methods, and Objectives Surveyed

Nonverbal and Verbal Communication

Phase III
Selection of Desired Communication

Pupil

Teacher

Desired Communication Selected

Phase IV
Application of Instrument for Observing and Recording Existing Communication Networks

VICS

Verbal Interaction Category System (VICS) Utilized To Record and Display Existing Communication Networks

Communication Networks

Phase V
Acceptance or Rejection of Displayed Communication Networks

Existing Communication Networks Displayed

Acceptance and Rejection
Patterns
Positive
Negative
Ignore
Immediate
Delayed

Teacher Dominated

Pupil Dominated

Teacher/Pupil Shared

Phase VI
Transfer of Desired Communication Networks into Instructional Strategy

Desired Communication Patterns Which Support Method and Objectives Identified for Strategy

Strategy

Figure 5.4 The communications network. For method, see Fig. 5.2, p. 166; for objectives, see Fig. 5.5, pp. 184–185; for acceptance and rejection patterns, see pp. 175–178; for strategy, see Fig. 5.6, p. 187.

of Educational Objectives as a value system would be inappropriate. The use of a hammer to hit people would not be valued, and neither should the *Taxonomy of Educational Objectives* be used to impose qualifications upon all behaviors.

The domains of the *Taxonomy of Educational Objectives* are cognitive, affective, and psychomotor. The cognitive domain classifies those learning behaviors which are primarily expressed through the exercise of intellectual skills and abilities. The affective domain classifies those learning behaviors which are primarily expressed through emotions as feelings, attitudes, awarenesses, and appreciations. The psychomotor domain classifies those learning behaviors which are primarily expressed through the intaking and outputting processing of sensory perceptions. The authors of the *Taxonomy of Educational Objectives* provide definitions of the domains which are sufficient to adequately identify behaviors by domain.

The behaviors within a domain are arranged in an accumulative, hierarchical order of classification levels. The classification levels are accumulative in that each succeeding level includes the behaviors of previous levels as prerequisites. The classification levels are hierarchical in that each succeeding level represents an increasingly complex, comprehensive set of behaviors requiring increasing degrees of energy from within the learner. In this context, "energy from within the learner" means what other contexts sometimes refer to as "intrinsic motivation." The concept of energy seems more appropriate here because of the internalization aspects, the increasing complexity of the behaviors, and the strength of the acts as a determiner of future behaviors.

The classifications within the cognitive domain are in hierarchical order: knowledge, comprehension, application, analysis, synthesis, evaluation. Knowledge behaviors are those lowest-energy intellectual skills of recall and recognition, while the classification level of evaluation behaviors are those highest-energy intellectual skills of criterion development, criterion, justification, and criterion-based performance. The classification levels of knowledge, comprehension, and application are referred to as low-energy levels; analysis, synthesis, and evaluation are classified as the high-energy levels. Each level is both required for and included within the behaviors of the succeeding level.

The classification levels within the affective domain are in hierarchical order: receiving, responding, valuing, organization, characterization. Receiving behaviors are those lowest energy feelings and attitudes of merely attending, while the classification level of characterizing behaviors are those highest energy feelings and attitudes of self-identification. The classification levels of receiving and responding are referred to as low-energy levels; valuing, organizing, and characterizing are classified as the high-energy levels. Each level is both required for and included within the behaviors of the succeeding level.

The classification levels within the psychomotor domain, in hierarchical order, are reflex, basic-fundamental, perceptual, physical, skilled, nondiscursive communication. Reflex behaviors are those lowest-energy neuromuscular skills of stretching and positive adjustments, while the classification level of nondiscursive communication behaviors are those highest-energy neuromuscular acts of choreographed body language. The classification levels of reflex, basic-fundamental, and perceptual are referred to as the low-energy levels; physical, skilled, and nondiscursive communication classification levels are classified as the high-energy levels. Each level is both required for and included within the behaviors of the succeeding level.

SITUATION 5.4   Write a low-level and a high-level cognitive behavioral objective. Write a low-level and a high-level affective behavioral objective. Write a low-level and a high-level psychomotor behavioral objective.

The definitions of the classification levels within the *Taxonomy of Educational Objectives* are sufficiently logical and precise to facilitate the valid and reliable classification of behaviors. The *Taxonomy of Educational Objectives* potentially provides a system for the definition and location of behaviors represented in objectives. The modern elementary teacher may utilize the taxonomy to display the range of behaviors within objectives. Are only cognitive behaviors present? Low energy? High energy? Affective and psychomotor? If educational goals provide the intended directions, then the *Taxonomy of Educational Objectives* provides the map guiding all learning behaviors in goal direction.

Research data from studies of both interaction analysis and objectives suggest that a significantly disproportionate number of objectives are within the low-energy cognitive levels, with few high-energy behaviors in any domain. As an element of the proposed strategy, the *Taxonomy of Educational Objectives* would provide an opportunity to identify and interact with these imbalances.

The Global Statements of Teaching Goals

Granted the sources of goals for the modern elementary school are varied and diverse. This diversity of sources results in a diversity of goals. A proposed strategy of instruction must provide a central goal which would serve as a sorter and translator of all other goals. The author proposes that the NEA essay, "Central Purposes of American Education," provided a master goal statement. The central purpose of the modern elementary school is "the development of the ability to think."[13]

This essay was thoroughly presented in Chapter 2. A persuasive commitment to the central goal (learning to learn, developing the rational powers, developing the ability to think) would serve to sort and translate other goals into forms with unity. A central goal would unite and integrate all goal-directed activities within the modern elementary school.

FORMULATING STRATEGY OF INSTRUCTION

The elements of the proposed strategy of instruction are structure, developmental levels, inquiry, interaction analysis, *Taxonomy of Educational Objectives*,

---

[13] Education Policies Commission, "The Central Purposes of American Education." (Washington, D.C.: National Education Association, 1962), p. 12.

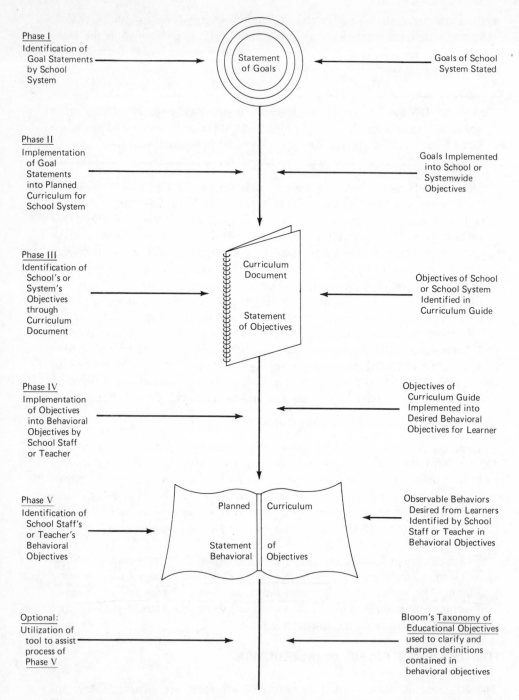

Figure 5.5 Formulating a strategy of instruction. For strategy, see Fig. 5.6, p. 187.

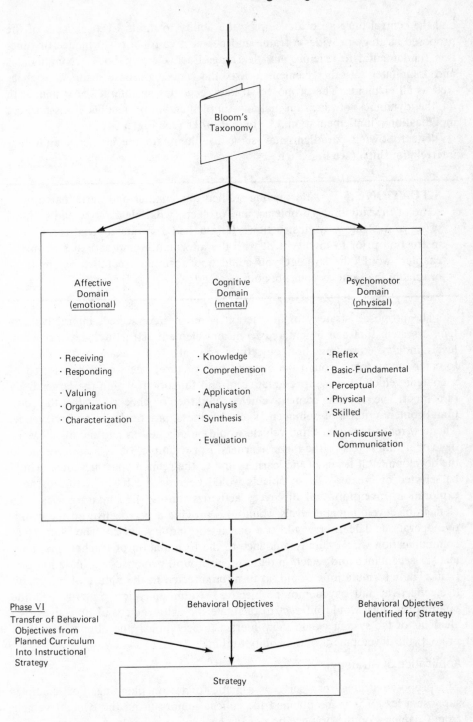

Bloom's
Taxonomy

Affective
Domain
(emotional)

· Receiving
· Responding

· Valuing
· Organization
· Characterization

Cognitive
Domain
(mental)

· Knowledge
· Comprehension

· Application
· Analysis
· Synthesis

· Evaluation

Psychomotor
Domain
(physical)

· Reflex
· Basic-Fundamental
· Perceptual
· Physical
· Skilled

· Non-discursive
  Communication

Phase VI
Transfer of Behavioral
Objectives from
Planned Curriculum
Into Instructional
Strategy

Behavioral Objectives

Behavioral Objectives
Identified for Strategy

Strategy

and the central purpose of developing the ability to think. Each element of the proposed strategy provides a frame and perspective for a performance or function fundamental to teaching and learning. Each element both accommodates and assimilates all other elements. Also, the central purpose mediates each as well as all elements. The proposed strategy becomes an interactive system with all the dynamics of decision-making→implementation→feedback→assessment modification→implementation . . . , in that order (see Fig. 5.5).

The following paradigm may serve to illuminate the elements and their interrelationships (see Fig. 5.6).

SITUATION 5.5   After having studied this chapter and participated in some of the situations, problems, and projects, what elements would comprise your strategy of instruction? If you had formulated a strategy of instruction prior to involvement with the information and activities of this chapter, would the strategy you could now formulate conflict, resemble, or remain the same as your previous strategy?

The proposed strategy of instruction is an interconnected, interactive system, a system that can be entered from any element: structure, developmental levels, inquiry, communication, objectives, or goals. If, for example, one chooses to enter the system through the element of structure, one would be assured of a content vehicle that is representative of and functional within the larger body of content. The resulting content vehicle would then be checked against the additional content criteria of humaneness, classicalness, practicalness, and relevancy. The now refined content topic vehicle would be adapted to and modified by the developmental levels of the target learners. For example, objects appropriate to the developmental levels of the learners and to the refined content vehicle would be selected or created. These objects would become the basis of the learner's exploration, invention, and discovery activities during the inquiry cycles. The element of developmental levels would also provide a perspective on the cognitive operations a learner would use during the inquiry cycles. The element of communication would supply guidance to the formulation of teacher questions, teacher acceptance and rejection patterns, and pupil response and initiation patterns. These formulations would, in turn, be directed to the nature of the cognitive, affective, and psychomotor objectives. Communication patterns and the phases of inquiry would interact to facilitate the achievement of objectives. All elements of the system would then interact to accomplish the ultimate outcome or goal: the development of the ability to think.

Application of Strategy

The proposed strategy can serve as a guide for lesson planning. For example, suppose a lesson is to be planned for college juniors using the content vehicle from Chapter 4 on the organization of the elementary schools. A skeleton lesson plan might resemble the following:

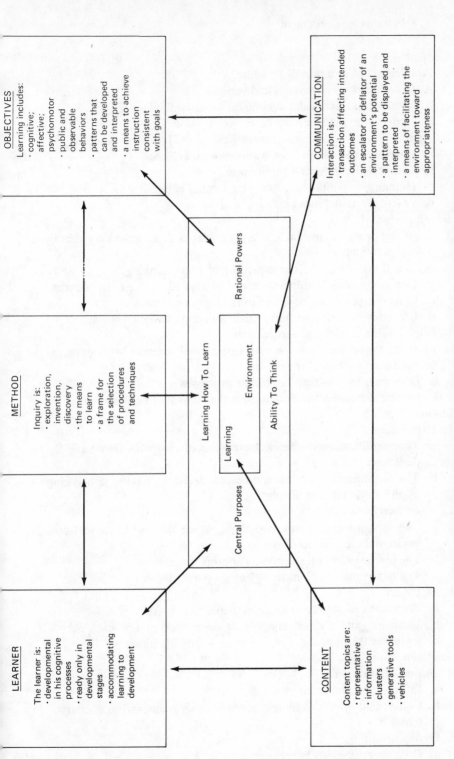

Figure 5.6 The elements involved in formulating a strategy of instruction and their interrelationships.

A. Content
  1. Application of criterion of structure
     a. Simplification: horizontal and vertical axis
     b. Clustering: relationship among organizational plans
     c. Generating: development of an organization
  2. Application of criteria of relevant, classical, humane, practical
     a. Relevant: derivation from reality and experiences
     b. Classical: definitions from literature
     c. Humane: assumptions concerning human variability
     d. Practical: model for explaining what is
B. Developmental Levels
  1. Cognitive processes available (Assumption: college juniors are usually post-concrete operational)
     a. Can think about the consequences of their thinking
     b. Can cognitively manipulate a model related to their experiences
     c. Can control two or more variables in an experiment
     d. Can conserve, reverse, and explain an action based on social factors.
  2. Model of horizontal and vertical axis
     a. Is an object for post-concrete operational learners who have experienced aspects of the model
     b. Does require "if—then" cognitive processes
     c. Can be experimented with through the control of variables
C. Inquiry
  1. Exploration
     a. The identification of the characteristics of the plans they have experienced
     b. The identification of the sources of decision making concerning pupil entry, exit, and movement.
  2. Invention
     a. The separation of plans into those which deal with vertical and horizontal movements of pupils.
     b. The placement of plans upon an appropriate axis
     c. The description of plans to logically separate them
  3. Discovery
     a. The testing of the placement of a plan upon an axis
     b. The testing of the discreteness of the description of a plan
     c. Applying the model to a plan not previously identified
D. Communications
  1. During exploration
     a. Information presented by teacher
     b. Convergent questions by teacher to identify plans and item characteristics
  2. During invention
     a. Divergent questions by teacher
     b. Pupil-to-pupil responses and initiation

  c. Descriptive statements from pupils to explain their plan and/or its placement

 3. During discovery

  a. Divergent questions by teacher

  b. Teacher presentations of alternative ways to test or apply inventions

  c. Pupil-to-pupil presentations of their testing procedures and corresponding interpretations

E. Objectives

 1. Cognitive

  a. Recall and recognition of the plans and their characteristics

  b. Application of the model to place the plans

  c. Analysis and synthesis of the model to the possible combination of plans

  d. Evaluation of the strengths and weaknesses of the model and the various combinations of plans

 2. Affective

  a. Receiving and responding to the development of the plans and models

  b. Valuing by defending their choice of a plan, its description and placement

  c. Organizing a combination of plans that fits their concept of human variability

D. Goal

 1. Development of rational powers

  a. Classifying: placement of plans

  b. Comparing: characterizing plans

  c. Imagining: developing mentally a utopian plan

 2. Development of the ability to think

  a. Objectives concerned with full range of cognitive and affective behaviors

  b. Data appropriate to developmental levels

  c. Communication networks to support objectives

  d. Model utilized to explain events not taught

SUMMARY

 1. The fundamental issues within organizing instruction are content, learner, method, communications, objectives, and goals.

 2. The selection of content topics begins with the identification of "structure." The resulting topics are modified by the criteria of relevancy, humaneness, classicalness, and practicality.

 3. Elementary pupils are preoperational or concrete operational in their cog-

nitive processes. With development preceding learning, the interactions with the environment must be appropriate to the developmental level of the pupil.

4. Traditionally, methods have been derived from those content and classroom control-oriented behaviors to be reinforced. Inquiry, as a method, provides a framework for the selection, creation, and adaption of other procedures—a framework which is independent of specific content topics or control techniques.

5. The phases of inquiry are: exploration, invention, and discovery. A completed interaction with an environment will involve one or more cycles through all three phases of inquiry.

6. Changes in a learner's developmental level or experiences will result in the modification of previous inventions.

7. Interaction analysis techniques identify and display the data significant to the communication networks within a learning situation.

8. Teaching includes the management and facilitation of communication networks consistent with the objectives.

9. The *Taxonomy of Educational Objectives* is a hierarchical classification of pupil behaviors in three domains: cognitive, affective, and psychomotor.

10. The utilization of the taxonomy enables one to gather, display, and interpret the range of learning behaviors involved in an environment.

11. The central purpose of education is the development of the ability to think.

12. The elements of the proposed strategy are structure, developmental levels, inquiry, interaction analysis, *Taxonomy of Educational Objectives*, and the goals of developing the ability to think.

Problems and Projects

1. Read *The Process of Education* by Jerome Bruner. What current practices within the modern elementary school could be associated with Bruner's theories of learning and instruction?

2. Examine Bloom's *The Taxonomy of Educational Objectives: (I) Cognitive Domain* and *(II) The Taxonomy of Educational Objectives: Affective Domain.* Pay particular attention to the sections which provide sample objectives and question types from each classification level within the domain. For each classification level within the cognitive domain, construct a question designed to elicit (from the learner) specific behaviors related to cognition (that is, those behaviors which characterize knowledge, comprehension, application, analysis, synthesis, evaluation). Write an objective in behavioral form for each classification level within the affective domain.

3. Observe a lesson in the elementary school. Analyze the lesson in terms of inquiry cycles (exploration, invention, discovery). How many cycles occurred? Which phases were characterized by high cognitive activities?

4. Observe a learning environment (college or elementary or other) for 15 minutes. Analyze the communication patterns and networks: question types; percentage and nature of teacher talk to teacher; percentage and nature of student talk to students.

5. After obtaining the written goals for an elementary school within a public school system, refer to "The Central Purposes of American Education" provided in Chapter 2 of this text. List those goals which are in conflict with or related to "The Central Purposes of American Education." Briefly narrate "why" to support your decisions.

Selected Readings

Bruner, Jerome, *The Process of Education*. New York: Random House, Inc. (Vantage Books), 1960.

Bruner, Jerome, *Toward a Theory of Instruction*. Cambridge, Mass.: Harvard University Press, 1966.

Phenix, Phillip H., *Realms of Meaning*. New York: McGraw-Hill, Inc., 1964. A discussion of what is a discipline and its organizations.

Phillips, John, Jr., *The Origins of Intellect: Piaget's Theory*. San Francisco: W. H. Freeman and Company, 1969.

Rosenshire, Barak, and Norma Furst, "The Use of Direct Observation to Study Teaching," in *Second Handbook of Research on Teaching*. Skokie, Ill.: Rand McNally & Company, 1973, pp. 122–183.

Schaefer, Robert J., *The School as a Center of Inquiry*. New York: Harper & Row, Publishers, 1967. A discussion of inquiry and its applications to curriculum.

chapter 6

Organizing
ENVIRONMENTS

A curriculum that systematizes, edits, and simplifies experiences from a perspective of adult life patterns that do not and will not exist is without relevancy. A curriculum that doesn't relate to and implement the purposes of the school is without relevancy.

John W. Renner, Gene D. Shepherd, and Robert F. Bibens, *Guiding Learning in the Elementary School* (New York: Harper & Row, Publishers, 1973), p. 170.

This chapter is concerned with curriculum of the modern elementary school. The author defines "curriculum" as that which includes all experiences of children for which the school accepts responsibility. This definition encompasses the course offerings; the documents which express the curriculum; the instructional processes which transmit, transpose, and translate the documents of curriculum; and especially the interactions and experiences of individuals.[1]

The first section of this chapter emphasizes the nature and functioning of the curriculum documents (guides). The second section illustrates the programs, tools, and activities employed during the transmission, transposition, and translation processes. The previous chapter (Chapter 5) focused upon the instructional processes which transmit, transpose, and translate the curriculum.

PLANNED CURRICULUM

In the literature of curriculum the patterns and premises of existing curricula are classified. Do curriculum builders select a premise and pattern, and then construct a curriculum? Or, does a pattern evolve and then a later analysis classify it as having been derived from certain patterns and premises? Do curriculum patterns evolve from the apparent weaknesses of previous patterns? Were curriculum patterns developed through a rational process or a trial-and-error process, or through the classical stereotype descriptions of the educated person?

---

[1] See preface of this book.

These questions, although perhaps rhetorical, should exist in the mind of every writer, reader, and developer of curriculum.

Curriculum guides—the documents in which the transcription of curriculum occurs—record the decisions made by individuals and groups, generalists and specialists, lay people and professionals. The decisions are expressed through the content selected, the scope and sequence provided, and the experiences judged as appropriate for the achievement of objectives and goals.

The primary function of a curriculum guide is to provide a valid, generalized framework for the guidance of teachers, individually and collectively. In contrast, this framework serves pupils collectively, but not individually; for example, it anticipates what the six-year-old child or a first-grader is ready to experience about reading, based on the best information available about reading, learning, development, and the findings among large numbers of six-year-olds or first-graders. Therefore, the guide must include the negotiation procedures through which the generalized framework is modified for the transmissions, transpositions, and translations, consistent with a specific set of individual differences —one child. The negotiation procedures should always favor the specific individual differences of a child over the normative, generalized differences transcribed in the guides. The power of the generalized framework (curriculum guide) is dependent upon the quality of the generalized knowledges utilized concerning the growth, learning, and development of children; the selection, sequencing, spiraling, and scoping of content vehicles; the relevancy of the included experiences to both the child's and the school's objectives; the input-output feedback mechanisms for evaluation; and the integrity of the negotiation system to diagnose individual differences and adapt the generalized framework.

The generalized framework also presents a special environment that has been systematized, edited, and simplified in ways that are appropriate to the child, the content vehicles, and the school. The curriculum is not as broad as life itself, but must select and organize life experiences that are relevant to the child and the school.

The generalized framework (curriculum guide) provides a basis for communication between and among professionals. It can be communicated because it is derived from information and knowledge available to all. Because the curriculum documents can be communicated, preparation programs for teachers and curriculum committees are dependent upon these generalized frameworks of curriculum. In contrast, however, the dynamic curriculum—that curriculum which results from the adaption of the generalized framework to a specific set of individual differences—can be communicated only to those who have equal access to a particular child and that child's set of individual differences.

Curriculum Documents

The written document called a "guide" is regarded by some as the curriculum.[2] The author and others regard these written documents as only the transcription

---

[2] George A. Beauchamp, *Curriculum Theory*, 2d ed.   (Wilmette, Ill.: The Kagg Press, 1968), p. 83.

phase of curriculum. In either case, both definitions would include similar components within a guide. The guide can serve a very useful purpose when (1) it is based on sound information about children, the school, and society; (2) it is presented as a resource to be used by teachers rather than as a set of rigid requirements to be met or content to be covered; (3) teachers understand it, accept it, and use it; (4) teachers are encouraged to make adaptations in terms of individual differences in pupils; and (5) teachers and pupils are free to initiate learning experiences that are not mentioned in the document. Those experiences, which arise from events which no planning committee could predict, are frequently as valuable as any that are planned in advance.

Components of a Curriculum Guide

Although curriculum guides differ widely in content, length, and format, certain features are present in most of them.

1. Curriculum guides generally contain at least a brief statement of the general philosophy of the school. Releasing human potential, improving conditions of living, supporting social ideals, and developing the rational powers are some goals that are frequently mentioned. The statement which follows is perhaps typical: "We as teachers subscribe to the central purpose of education as being the development of the rational powers with inquiry as the process, content as the vehicle, and self-actualization as the goal."[3]

2. Curriculum guides generally present a chart or other device which indicates the scope of the curriculum in terms of subject matter to be taught, concepts to be developed, mental processes to be used, or a combination of all three of these bases. The older curriculum guides (generally called "courses of study") emphasized subject matter to be taught as the basis for organizing learning experiences. Until recently, the scope of an elementary school science program was generally listed somewhat as follows: the earth, beyond the earth, living things, physical and chemical changes, conditions necessary to life, and man's attempts to control his environment. Listed under each of these major divisions were many specific topics to be studied. With the advent of the new curricula in science, the emphasis has been placed on the processes used in scientific inquiry. The scope of the science program is now more likely to be listed as observation, measurement, experimentation, interpretation of data, prediction, and the like. A statewide curriculum committee concerned with the improvement of science instruction in grades K through 6 stated the rationale for this approach as follows:

Science is a natural vehicle with which to develop a child's ability to think objectively. In order to accomplish this goal, however, the emphasis in science teaching must shift from the teaching of "facts" to the development of a child's ability to observe carefully, collect information, and draw logical inferences.[4]

[3] Norman Public Schools, Norman, Oklahoma, "Statement of Philosophy," 1975.
[4] State Science Committee of the Oklahoma Curriculum Improvement Commission, *The Improvement of Science Instruction in Oklahoma—Grades K–6.* (Oklahoma City: Oklahoma State Department of Education, 1974), p. 1.

3. Curriculum guides generally suggest an arrangement or sequence of learning experiences for the period of time that the child spends in the elementary school. A scope and sequence chart may be included to indicate both the scope of the program and the sequence of learning experiences. Because it is desirable to provide for continuity in the learning experiences of children, curriculum planning groups are interested in the sequence of learning. Providing for continuity means essentially that what pupils are expected to study today depends to some extent upon what has already been learned and what is learned today will determine to some extent what can be learned tomorrow. Studies of the mental development of children and experimentation with the placement of content have altered the thinking of many school people regarding what children can learn at various age levels. When are children ready to study geometry, physics, or economics? According to the "ladder" system of grade placement, geometry was a tenth-grade subject; physics was taught in the twelfth grade; and economics was generally reserved for the college years. The "spiral" system of determining the sequence of learning experiences introduces children to certain aspects of these subjects as soon as they enter the elementary school and makes provision for "revisiting" them in more complex forms every year. No document can make certain that there will be continuity in the learning experiences of each child—each teacher must be concerned with this problem. However, the curriculum guide or framework can provide a favorable setting for achieving this objective.

4. Curriculum guides generally contain a statement of objectives. This is another area in which curriculum planning has experienced a shift in emphasis in recent years. Objectives are now stated in behavioral terms, meaning that the terminal behaviors, conditions under which the behavior occurs, and a minimum level of acceptable performance are specified.[5]

5. Curriculum guides generally suggest appropriate educational media for use in the instructional program. The classroom teacher or teaching team cannot be expected to keep up with the increasing volume of teaching resources. Specialists in instructional media can examine, test, and suggest effective new media, and these can be listed in the curriculum guide.

6. Curriculum guides generally suggest instruments and procedures for evaluating pupil progress and program effectiveness. This is another area of research and experimentation which is changing rapidly. Modern curriculum guides provide specific aid to diagnostic teaching. Diagnostic teaching includes preassessment activities to determine the readiness of the learner, a planning of alternative routes appropriate to the evidence gained from the diagnosis, a series of formative diagnoses to assess the ongoing instructional progress, and a summative assessment as part of the culminating activities.

Purposes of a Curriculum Guide

1. The primary purpose of a curriculum guide is to provide a generalized framework to assure each teacher and learner a minimum foundation of quality

5 Robert M. Gagné, "Behavioral Objectives? Yes!" in Glen Hass, *Curriculum Planning*. (Boston: Allyn & Bacon, Inc., 1974), pp. 221–224.

guide to identify subject matter,

experiences. This generalized framework exists for teachers, individually and collectively. It exists for pupils as a group, collectively, but not individually. For example, the curriculum guide anticipates from the best knowledge available what an eleven-year-old pupil is developmentally ready to experience. It *readiness* also includes the means to diagnose the readiness of any specific group or individual who may be entering the activities. The teacher then negotiates the differences between the generalized knowledge contained in the curriculum guide *individual* and the knowledge of a specific set of eleven-year-olds to be instructed. Nego- *difference* tiations should always place priority upon the specific set of individual differ- *priority* ences and not upon the generalities of the curriculum guide.

Concrete terms
2. The curriculum guide is a guideline for the development of a special *framework* environment that has been systematized, edited, and simplified in ways that are appropriate to pupils and the purposes of the school. A modern guide will present sound representative content that has been tested for relevancy and humaneness. (See Chapter 5.) The content will have been adjusted to be functional in light of the developmental levels of the intended populations. (See Chapter 3.) A guide that does not relate to or does not implement the purposes of the school is without relevancy.

information
3. The curriculum guide provides a basis for communication between and *source for* among teachers as well as between teachers and the community. The curriculum *community +* guide is created from generalized knowledge and can be communicated because *school* it is predicated upon knowledge available to all.

into
4. The curriculum guide provides the framework for the establishment of *system* an evaluation and feedback system. The objectives of the guide establish intended inputs that can be compared to the outputs of the instructional program. Feedback of the relationships that are discovered between the intended inputs and the outputs serve as the dynamics of a continuing revision of the guide.

SITUATION 6.1   Examine several curriculum guides produced by state or local curriculum committees. Cite evidence of the trend toward process-oriented programs; the uses of concepts as centers for organizing content and activities; emphasis on developing inquiry skills.

How should Curriculum organized –

Principles of Curriculum Organization

Curriculum organization should be regarded as the means to help achieve the objectives of the school. There is no advantage in introducing an innovation in curriculum organization unless the school faculty sees clearly that the existing organization is out of harmony with the accepted objectives of the school. Since educational objectives are always in the process of modification and expansion, the overall design of the curriculum must likewise be subject to continuous study and modification; it cannot be completed at any given time. The following principles of curriculum organization should serve as useful guides for teachers engaged in such study.

1. *Curriculum organization should help to coordinate the efforts of teachers.* The program must be arranged so that the various staff members who work with the same group of children will supplement rather than duplicate one another's efforts. What one teacher does for the child must be determined to some extent by what other teachers have done for him and by what future teachers are expected to do.

2. *Curriculum organization should provide a well-balanced day of living for boys and girls.* Opportunities for the systematic study of subject-matter areas as well as for work on units that cut across subject-matter lines should be provided. Experiences that develop understanding and insight as well as provision for systematic drill when it is needed should also be provided. Period of strenuous activity should be balanced by periods for rest and relaxation, opportunities for self-expression and initiative should be balanced by experiences in conforming to group standards, and provision should be made for children to work on individual as well as group projects.

3. *Curriculum organization should provide for continuity in the development of the child.* The study of child development (see Chapter 3) has furnished many guiding principles for curriculum organization. Among these principles are: (1) development is the result of both growth and learning rather than of the mere accumulation of knowledge, skills, or an increase in amount; (2) development is continuous and sequential; (3) individuals differ in the rate of development through the stages, levels, tasks, and other experiences; (4) development requires experiencing.

The sequence of experiences found in many elementary schools violates these principles. The ladder system of grade placement—which dictates that long division be completed in one grade and fractions in another; that reading should be taught only in the elementary school, that all children who enter school at the same time will be ready to begin reading at a given time, and that economics is so complex and difficult a subject that it should not be taught until the student is in college—presents a direct contradiction of the principle of development as continuous. Minimum grade standards, annual promotions, and the class-as-a-whole method of teaching are other examples of the failure to observe generally accepted principles of development. These examples show that a curriculum organization which achieves continuity in the subjects to be taught will frequently result in no continuity at all for the learner.

The elimination of school subjects and the substitution of experiences based on immediately felt needs of pupils do not solve the problem of continuity. Curriculum experiences need to be planned in such a way that children master increasingly more complex materials and experiences increasingly more mature developmental sequences. They need to move gradually from what is familiar and concrete to what is remote and abstract. For example, the development of social concepts such as interdependence, tolerance, and democracy begins with the immediate social group, the family, and moves gradually to more complex situations involving larger groups. Such concepts cannot be mastered once and for all at any grade level: they must recur again and again in different and increasingly more mature social contexts.

4. *Curriculum organization should provide for unified learning.* Many critics of education have pointed to the failure to develop individuals who can bring anything but a specialized orientation to problems and issues. Other critics have been concerned about the failure, as they see it, to focus attention effectively on specific content, problems, and skills. Thus, teachers and principals face a perennial conflict between those who urge specialization and those who see the need for integration.

The point of view has already been expressed in this book that provision should be made for both the direct teaching of subjects and for broad, meaningful experiences for children—experiences that cut across subject lines. Because experience has shown that learning in the subject areas is more effective as well as more meaningful when provision is made for seeing the interrelationship between various subjects, many elementary schools provide for both the teaching of subjects at regularly scheduled periods and for long, uninterrupted periods for planning and working on problems or units.

5. *Curriculum organization must assimilate the best information from all sources.* For example, the concept of structure from the logical source is modified by the information from the psychological source when Bruner states, "The task of teaching a subject to a child at any particular age is one of representing the structure of the subject in terms of the child's way of viewing things."[6]

6. *Curriculum organization must take into account the principles of quality, equality, relevancy, and personalization.* Quality is the development of a curriculum which promotes pupil growth in the areas of intellectual, psychological, physical, and social development. Equality is the inclusion of quality experiences for the full range of pupil variations in these same areas. Personalization is the assignment and allocation of the programs to the specific set of individual differences to be instructed. Relevancy is the presenting of a special environment appropriate to the pupil, the society, and the purposes of the school.

Organizational Patterns of Curriculum Guides

The development of the general design of the curriculum has been given much attention for several decades in educational literature and at educational conferences. Many terms have been used to designate developments in curriculum organization. Correlation, fusion, broad fields, the core curriculum, persistent life situations, and the experience curriculum have all had staunch defenders and relentless critics. Actually, it is seldom, if ever, possible to find any one of these types operating in pure form in a curriculum guide. Frequently a curriculum guide is given one of these labels with no counterpart found in actual practice.

The important thing is whether [this] structure permits instruction and activities needed to serve the objectives of the school, and not how it can be classified. Since the nature of the general organization of the curriculum determines

---

[6] Jerome Bruner, *The Process of Education.* (New York: Random House, Inc.: Vantage Books, 1960), p. 33.

what can be done in the classroom, the dominant organization of the program should be flexible enough to permit a variety of specific approaches to curriculum and teaching. This cannot be done by an obstinate loyalty to a given form, no matter what its merits are.[7]

Nevertheless, in order to have some basis for making practical decisions, the elementary school teacher needs to know the general characteristics of the principal types of organization of curriculum guides.

Each pattern of curriculum organization adopts a certain idea of scope because it adopts certain centers of organization. Each also tends to adopt certain special criteria for sequence, continuity, and integration and therefore provides for these characteristics in a different manner.[8]

The organization of curriculum guides seems to center upon the logic of the subject matter, the nature and needs of children, or the demands of society. Each of these—logical, psychological, and social—has served as a basis for organizing learning experiences.

Organization by Subject Matter

Subject matter was the first basis for curriculum organization. Curriculum guides were organized to express a viewpoint oriented toward the logic of the discipline, the subject matter.

A discipline is an organized body of knowledge about a unique domain of things and events (the facts, data, observations, sensations, perceptions, and sensibilities that constitute the basic elements of knowledge or from which knowledge is derived), for which basic rules or definitions are formulated for determining what falls within or without the domain; and a recognized structure exists for organizing the body of the knowledge into the discipline, and for undertaking the discovery of knowledge essential to the extension, refinement, and validation of the discipline. Moreover, a discipline has a history and a tradition that give it status as a field of scholarly investigation and research as a body of knowledge that continues to contribute to man's increasing control over his universe.[9]

From the logical source, several organizational patterns for guides appeared. These evolved in both a chronological order and as the motivating force for a succeeding pattern. There is no reason to think that this evolutionary process has stopped.

SEPARATE-SUBJECTS ORGANIZATION

This type of organization views each school subject, each discipline, as being totally independent of other disciplines. Each has its own scope and

[7] Hilda Taba, "General Techniques of Curriculum Planning," in Forty-fourth Yearbook, Part I, National Society for the Study of Education, *Curriculum Reconstruction.* (Chicago: University of Chicago Press, 1945), p. 108.

[8] Hilda Taba, *Curriculum Development, Theory and Practice.* (New York: Harcourt Brace Jovanovich, Inc., 1962), p. 382.

[9] J. Galen Saylor and William M. Alexander, *Curriculum Planning for Modern Schools.* (New York: Holt, Rinehart and Winston, Inc., 1966), p. 164.

3 R's

sequence of content, skills, knowledges, and appreciations. The original disciplines were the 3 Rs: reading, writing, and arithmetic. Later, many new disciplines were added and given independence. Although some of these subjects were not scheduled every day, pupils took separate courses in spelling, grammar, literature, history, geography, government, physiology, hygiene, nature study, art, agriculture, domestic science, and manual training. Eventually the separate-subjects pattern expanded to include, with independence, some fifteen or more subjects.

The commitment of the separate-subjects organizational pattern to the independence of the disciplines became the focus for its critics. The artificial separation of subjects and the resulting fragmentation of the curriculum was criticized as being inconsistent with the fullest integration of disciplines as well as with the intellectual, psychological, and social development of pupils.

2 CORRELATED-SUBJECTS PATTERN

The first effort to achieve more integration in the learning experiences of pupils was to present similar topics in two or more subjects. Smith, Stanley, and Shores said, "The correlated curriculum is a subject curriculum in which two or more subjects are articulated and relationships between and among them are made part of the instruction without destroying the subject boundaries."[10]

The correlated pattern of organizing curriculum guides maintained the independence of subjects, especially with regard to skills, but did select similar content from the subject areas. For example, the colonial period in history and the New England states in geography would be taught during the same six-week period. Music and art are correlated in a similar fashion.

The critics of the correlated-subject pattern said that the minimal adjustment of the scope and sequence of a curriculum to achieve further integration was a significant but very short and inadequate step toward the achievement of a unified curriculum. The correlated pattern was also the first pattern to recognize the importance of transfer of learning and pupil motivation as factors to be considered when organizing curriculum. However, according to its critics, the correlated pattern did not accomplish this to a satisfactory degree.

FUSION OR BROAD FIELDS PATTERN

The curriculum areas of language arts and social studies were developed within this organizational pattern, and they characterize this type. The broad fields or fusion pattern accepted the subjects of the correlated pattern, but adjusted the scope and sequence to achieve a greater integration of learning experiences. The classroom schedule had longer periods of time; transfer of learning was encouraged and rewarded within these longer blocks of study; and the method called "unit teaching" was developed. The units were subject-

---

[10] B. Othanel Smith, William O. Stanley, and J. Harlan Shores, *Fundamentals of Curriculum Development*, rev. ed.   (New York: Harcourt Brace Jovanovich, Inc., 1957), p. 252.

centered, but were planned to related skills, knowledges, and appreciations within these larger areas of study. This pattern also added emphasis to the importance of pupil involvement, interest, and motivation as a positive factor in pupil achievement and curriculum planning.

An excellent example of the broad-fields type of organization is found in the unified language arts program. Instead of scheduling reading, writing, spelling, listening, and other separate subjects for approximately 10 minutes each, a longer (perhaps 50 minutes) is scheduled for language arts. Another example is found in the social studies. Instead of scheduling history, geography, economics, and other separate subjects for a brief period each, a longer period is set aside for a unified social studies program. This type of organization is explained in greater detail in Part III.

Critics of the broad-fields or fusion pattern for organizing curriculum guides suggested that it was still too subject-centered and therefore did not provide for a fully integrated and interrelated learning experience. According to its critics, if this much adjustment in scope and sequence is good, why maintain a subject-centered organization at all?

MULTI- AND INTERDISCIPLINARY

A more recent approach is to utilize one discipline or a view of several disciplines as a center for organizing curriculum. For example, the structure of the economics discipline, might form the skeleton. Concepts from the other social sciences would be utilized to flesh out the skeleton and to enrich both the study of social sciences and also the study of economics. This is an interdisciplinary center in which one discipline serves as the principal organizer, with related disciplines serving as vital adjuncts, yet supplemental to the principal organizer.

A multidisciplinary approach occurs when structures or concepts are selected from various disciplines, to create a new field of study. This new field results from intermingling the abstracted concepts and is independent of the separate discipline from which it was formed. This approach seems particularly valuable whenever the "tions" are studied rather than the "ics." The study of pollution, communication, transportation, and population requires the use of mathematics, physics, economics, politics, genetics, and other "ics."

The interdisciplinary approach seems to be prevailing, probably because student teachers study the "ics" rather than the "tions." Therefore, an interdisciplinary curriculum can be found whose center organizer is an "ic" that a teacher has studied.

SITUATION 6.2   Give specific examples from social studies units of how art can be related with geography; literature with history; mathematics with economics; and music with various areas of the social studies. Explain how health can be related with science; with physical education.

Organization by Psychological Integration

The organization of curriculum guides to achieve an integration of the individual both within himself and with his environment is the center of curriculum organizations developed from the psychological source. The "integrative curriculum" eliminates subjects as the basis for organizing the scope and sequence of curriculum, for it is individuals, not subjects, which are to be integrated. The two examples to be given are the child-centered and the experience patterns. These patterns differ slightly in terms of the basis selected for organizing the daily program and in the extent to which the curriculum is planned in advance.

THE CHILD-CENTERED PATTERN

The program that John Dewey established in his school at the University of Chicago in 1896 organized learning experiences around four human impulses: the social impulse, the constructive impulse, the impulse to investigate and experiment, and the expressive or artistic impulse. Meriam's school, established at the University of Missouri in 1904, used the normal activities of children as the basis for organizing learning experiences. He regarded observation, play, stories, and handwork as normal child activities. Collings introduced the child-centered curriculum into the public schools of McDonald County, Missouri, in 1917. He used play projects, excursion projects, and story projects as the centers about which learning activities were organized. Although these experimental schools did much to direct attention to the child as an important factor in curriculum planning, this type of organization has never been very widely used in public schools.[11]

THE EXPERIENCE-CURRICULUM PATTERN

This type resembles the child-centered pattern in that it uses the concerns of children as the basis for organizing the work of the school. It differs from the child-centered programs in its view that the interests and needs of children cannot be anticipated and that therefore no preplanned curriculum framework can be agreed upon. The child-centered programs, on the other hand, set up in advance certain areas of normal child activity and to that extent planned the framework of the curriculum beforehand. It should be pointed out that even these child-centered programs emphasized the value of curriculum planning "on the spot" by each teacher and the group of children, but this planning of details of projects and procedures existed within a curriculum framework set up in advance.

With the experience pattern, the interests and felt needs of children determine the curriculum. Growth and learning are completely dependent upon the active participation of children in activities that are in line with their felt needs.

[11] See John Dewey, *School and Society.* (Chicago: University of Chicago Press, 1915); Junius L. Meriam, *Child Life and the Curriculum.* (New York: Harcourt Brace Jovanovich, Inc., 1920); and Ellsworth Collings. *An Experiment with a Project Curriculum.* (New York: Crowell Collier and Macmillan, Inc., 1923).

Subjects fields represent resources that may be drawn upon as they assist children in a solution of problems of their choosing.

Organization by Sociological Integration

The organization of curriculum guides around the major functions of social life is the basis of curriculum organization developed from the sociological source. The sociological source of curriculum allows the learner to work on the solution of problems which are recurring life situations. These basic life functions are significant in a societal aspect because they are related to the basic life activities of all people.

SOCIAL-FUNCTION PATTERN

The Virginia Course of Study for Elementary Schools, published in 1934, was organized around areas of living, such as protection, conservation, production, consumption, communication, transportation, recreation, expression of aesthetic and religious impulses. Centers of interest were listed for each grade, such as home and school life for the first grade and community life for the second grade. Although a plan similar to this is frequently used for organizing the social studies program, this scheme was for organizing the entire program of the elementary school.

The social functions curriculum organization probably provides opportunity for the greatest amount of integration of learnings. Under such a plan, traditional subject-matter lines disappear, and teacher and children draw upon whatever discipline can contribute to the solution of problems that are being studied. For example, a fifth-grade class might study a unit on how the early pioneers moved westward. Such a unit would draw heavily upon traditional subjects like geography, history, economics, and sociology, but there are many science learnings that would also be included. Questions relating to weather and climate, animal life, vegetation, desert regions, and the like might be answered by drawing freely upon both the physical and biological sciences. Children would also learn and practice many reading study skills as they searched for information about early methods of transportation and prepared reports. The children might spend the large block of time set aside for work on the unit on any one or more of these kinds of experiences. On some days, learning activities might draw more heavily upon geography or history as we know them traditionally, but at other times the emphasis might be on science, the language arts, or the fine arts.

PERSISTENT-LIFE SITUATIONS PATTERN

Florence B. Stratemeyer and her associates, in the book *Developing a Curriculum for Modern Living*, proposed a curriculum organization from the sociological source that is organized around "those situations that recur in the life of an individual in many different ways as he grows from infancy to maturity."[12] The situations of everyday living that provide the scope, sequence, and

12 Florence B. Stratemeyer, Hamden L. Forkner, Margaret G. McKim, and A. Harry Passow, *Developing a Curriculum for Modern Living.* (New York: Teachers College Press, 1957), p. 115.

continuity for the persistent life situations curriculum are "living in the home, as a member of a family; in the community, as a participant in civic and social activities; in work, as a member of an occupational group; in leisure time; and in spiritual activities, whether or not connected with an organized religious group."[13] These situations are grouped into three divisions: growth in individual capacities, in social participation, and in ability to deal with environmental factors and forces. Stratemeyer and co-authors, when presenting the concept of the persistent life situations curriculum, stated:

> *This is a concept of curriculum organization in which . . .*
>
> *the basic problems and situations which are central in life itself are central in education*
>
> *the content and organization of learning experiences are determined by the experiences of the learners as they deal with their everyday concerns and the persistent life situations which are part of them (these situations of everyday living take the place of "subjects" and the varied other ways of focusing the curriculum)*
>
> *the scope lies in the range of persistent life situations with which, to some extent, every individual deals*
>
> *the sequence and continuity are determined by the changing aspects of persistent life situations as the learner moves from childhood into the full responsibilities of adulthood. . . .*[14]

SITUATION 6.3   After having read the descriptions of organizational patterns of curriculum guides (organized by subject matter, psychological integration, sociological integration), to what organizational pattern do you presently hold the strongest commitment? Why? How does the pattern relate to other educational philosophies you are presently formalizing or evaluating?

A Continuing Concern

Developing the design of the curriculum can never be regarded as a completed task. The goal is not a planless or a rigidly planned curriculum; it is continuous planning of the curriculum. No other choice is available in the dynamic era in which we are living. No one can say exactly what type of curriculum organization will emerge in elementary schools by 1980, what name it will bear, or what terminology will be used to designate its significant components. Indeed, the individual who has been out of contact with elementary education for ten years and decides to take "refresher" courses may need a little time to comprehend what is meant by "modes of inquiry," "conceptual framework," and "organizing centers." We can expect, however, that curriculum organization will be

---

[13] Stratemeyer et al., p. 148.
[14] Stratemeyer et al., pp. 116–117.

increasingly responsive to certain movements which we can already see developing:

1. Fuller utilization of instructional technology will demand a more flexible curriculum organization, modular scheduling, and the listing of newer media in curriculum guides for various areas rather than in separate bulletins.

2. The systems approach will provide more rational control over planning and designing programs of instruction by single-unit structuring of goals, media, personnel, and evaluation.[15] Becker pointed out that the systems approach to instructional design is not yet a well-defined science. As more educators use this approach and learn to use it effectively, better organization and improved instruction should result.[16]

3. Emphasis on helping children develop their rational powers and acquire the skills involved in inquiry is already beginning to influence the contents of curriculum guides. Goodlad, for example, suggested that "organizing centers" should be specified, which would provide the means for developing concepts, generalizations, and modes of inquiry.[17] Thus, curriculum guides in the next few decades can be expected to be process-oriented as well as content-oriented.

4. There is increasing concern about forces which threaten to dehumanize education. It is to be expected that curriculum organization will be determined to some extent at least by the desire to nurture humaneness in education.[18]

5. There is increasing interest in revising present objectives or creating objectives which are concerned with the
  - quality of immediate experiences rather than preparation for the future and its resulting emphasis upon delayed gratification.
  - exploitation of the consumer, overconsumption, and the pollution of the environment.
  - congruency that may exist between the expected behaviors of the school and the actual behaviors of the society.
  - valuing of the new, the unfamiliar, and the development of a participating democracy.
  - freedom for "every man" and his emancipation from the fixed authorities of institutions, and from social and political pressure.

DYNAMIC CURRICULUM

The dynamic curriculum, that curriculum which a learner experiences, results from the instructional processes which transpose, transmit, and translate the

15 Ralph A. Dusseldorp, "The Systems Approach," *NEA Journal*, 56:24, (February 1967).

16 James M. Becker, "Organizing the Social Studies Program," in Dorothy McClure Fraser (Ed.), *Social Studies Curriculum Development: Prospects and Problems*. (Washington, D.C.: National Council for the Social Studies, 1969), p. 77.

17 John I. Goodlad, "Toward Improved Curriculum Organizations," in Edmund C. Short and George D. Marconnit (Eds.), *Contemporary Thought on Public School Curriculum: Readings*. (Dubuque, Iowa: William C. Brown Company, Publishers, 1968), p. 315.

18 R. O. Nystrand and L. L. Cunningham, "Organizing Schools to Develop Humane Capabilities," in *To Nurture Humaneness*. (Washington, D.C.: Association for Supervision and Curriculum Development, 1970), chap. 14.

documents of curriculum into alternatives appropriate to a specific set of individual differences. The opportunity to learn to use increasingly more complex modes of inquiry, for example, may be either enhanced or diminished by the instructional processes used. Developing the rational powers, involving pupils in their own education, forging intellectual tools for use during a lifetime of learning, all these remain mere expressions of hope until teaching strategies put them into operation. New curriculum guides can accomplish nothing until learning environments give them vitality. It is the purpose of this section to examine some of the programs, activities, and tools employed during the transmission, transposition, and translation processes.

Programs

Curriculum programs are those systems which subsume the activities and tools of the transmission, transposition, and translation processes. Activities supplement and enrich programs, but they function most effectively within a program system. Tools implement and extend either activities or programs by accruing value only in the context of an activity or program.

Unit Teaching

The unit of work is regarded by many teachers as a useful device for achieving many of the broader objectives of the elementary school. When this method is used, learning takes place through a great variety of activities; activities are unified around a central theme, problem, or purpose; pupils participate in planning and executing the activities involved in the unit; and the teacher serves as a leader rather than as a taskmaster.

TYPES OF UNITS

References can be found in educational publications to resource units, curriculum records, teaching units, learning units, subject-matter units, experience units, commercial units, activity units, core units, functional subject-matter units, and survey units. In general, however, two principal types of units are recognized: subject-matter units and experience units. It is obvious that any unit uses both experience and subject matter. The difference is primarily one of emphasis. In one type, experience receives the primary emphasis, whereas in the other, subject matter is given more emphasis. A learning experience in which the central concern is the acquisition of information, in which the experiences involved are few and formal, is referred to as a subject-matter unit. A learning experience in which the central concern is with the development of desirable traits of behavior, in which numerous and varied learning experiences are involved, in which subject matter functions as a means to an end is referred to as an experience unit.

Although it is useful to understand the meaning of such terms as "subject-matter unit" and "experience unit," it should be realized that in actual practice the terminology used is not the most important consideration. The teacher in actual classroom situations is concerned with providing rich and varied experiences for children, with providing opportunities for pupils to participate in planning, executing, and evaluating experiences, and with selecting and organizing experiences in relation to worthwhile purposes that are significant to children.

PROBLEMS INVOLVED IN DEVELOPING UNITS

Outlines of the principal steps, stages, or problems involved in developing units of work are available from many sources. These outlines should not be followed rigidly in any school; instead, each school should develop an outline of its own which expresses clearly what the teachers are trying to accomplish in that particular school. Certainly, the various steps in unit development should not be considered as separate and distinct. Evaluation, for example, is not something that is undertaken after the other steps have been completed; it is something that goes on continuously throughout the time spent on the unit. The following discussion is intended merely to emphasize the problems teachers must be prepared to meet as they work with children in planning and developing units of work.

FORMAT FOR DEVELOPING UNITS

Orientation or Approach. Even in classical schools where teaching has been organized on the basis of the recitation, good teachers have never been satisfied merely to assign lessons without first arousing the interest of pupils and otherwise preparing them for understanding the significance of the lesson. The success of the unit of work depends in large measure upon the ability of the teacher to (1) create an interest in the unit, (2) help the pupils to see the significance of the unit, (3) relate the unit to past experiences of the pupils, (4) utilize the sources of the local community in orienting the children to the problem, and (5) provide a classroom environment that stimulates interest in the unit.

During the orientation period the teacher must be alert to discover the interest, needs, and capacities of individuals; to look for leads to worthwhile activities for individuals and groups; and to develop a feeling of group unity and enthusiasm. Observation of a master teacher during the orientation period of a unit of work leads to the impression that a great deal of time is being wasted in getting the unit under way, unless the observer understands the crucial importance of enlisting the enthusiastic participation of every pupil in the enterprise.

Through skillful planning of class discussions during the orientation period, it is possible for the teacher to help pupils see themselves in relation to the new unit so that a high degree of involvement occurs from the outset. Such was the case in one study of community health problems in which the teacher began with a discussion of health problems the students themselves had faced. It was discovered that more than half of the class had had malaria. The students wondered whether they were representative of the total population of the city. They found that local health authorities had no reliable data, and so the students proposed to find answers to their questions by a direct survey. Interest was high by this time, and the work was planned carefully and executed well. The time had been well spent in orienting the pupils to the undertaking.

The sources available from which the approach to the unit may be developed differ from one situation to another. Some common sources are: (1) discussions in the classroom or elsewhere, (2) materials brought from the homes of pupils, (3) exhibits and displays, (4) an important event reported in the papers, (5) the presence of an outstanding visitor, (6) a motion picture being shown locally, (7) a vacation trip taken by the teacher or a pupil, (8) an excursion, (9) a book, magazine, or poem, (10) an educational film, (11) an experience from a previous unit.

2. *Teacher-Pupil Planning*. The pupils, under the guidance of the teacher, should have a large share in planning the activities to be included in the unit. Plans must be made concerning (1) the objectives of the unit, (2) what activities are necessary, (3) what committees will be needed, (4) what responsibilities each committee will have, (5) what activities each pupil should undertake, and (6) how the unit is to be evaluated. It is through participation in planning that pupils are given opportunities for democratic living in the classroom. As the children suggest objectives, activities, or procedures, the teacher writes them on the chalkboard. It is the teacher's responsibility to suggest others that the children may overlook. After the suggestions have been listed, the children and the teacher evaluate them to discover relationships, eliminate duplications, and organize problems in sequential order and thematic groups.

3. *The Working Period*. The activities that constitute the working period of a modern unit are lifelike, adjusted to the maturity levels of pupils, varied, and socially significant. During the working period the children, under the guidance of the teacher, put into effect the plans previously made. The activities during this period will vary from day to day. There will be periods for working individually at gathering information, reading, or writing for materials, and other periods when the children work in groups, planning reports or excursions, or working on exhibits.

A question frequently raised by teachers who have not had experience with directing the varied activities involved in a modern unit of work is: How can the teacher maintain order with so many different activities going on at the same time? A certain amount of noise is to be expected if a group of children is enthusiastically engaged in various enterprises. This does not imply that rudeness and near-bedlam are to be condoned. Many classrooms can be found in which children work on meaningful activities without an undue amount of noise or confusion. It must be admitted, too, that a teacher with an organized mind and organizing ability, with knowledge of the psychology of learning, with knowledge of the principles of leadership, and with possession of some executive talent is necessary to the orderly management of the working period.

4. *The Culminating Activity*. The culminating activity may take the form of a play, an exhibit of work, an assembly program, or a party. It is important that

this activity be carefully planned so that the children will have a feeling of accomplishment and a greater sense of solidarity. Details of the culminating activity are usually planned during the progress of the unit so that this activity serves as a summary of the important achievements of the unit.

5. *Evaluation Activities.* Evaluation is an important phase of unit development. It is used for determining the extent to which the objectives of the unit are being realized, for helping each child determine his own progress, and for conferences with parents. The following principles of evaluation apply to unit teaching as well as to other phases of the instructional program:

1. *Evaluation should be comprehensive.* Evidence should be collected concerning all phases of a child's development and not merely the mental development or mastery of specific knowledges and skills. Evaluation cannot be accomplished through the use of paper-and-pencil tests alone. These must be supplemented by teacher observation, anecdotal records, samples of the work of the pupil, case studies, sociometric tests, and teachers' ratings for responsibility, initiative, cooperation, work habits, and other habits and attitudes.

2. *Evaluation must be continuous.* In a unit of work, evaluation cannot be accomplished at a specific time. It is a continuous process that goes on during the orientation period, the planning period, the working period, and the culminating activity.

3. *Evaluation must be cooperative.* Opportunities must be provided for each child to check individual progress and to participate in the group evaluation of the work of the unit. Qualities of initiative, self-direction, and responsibility cannot be developed if pupils must always look to the teacher for evaluation of their progress.

ADVANTAGES OF UNIT TEACHING

The unit of work is not an educational panacea. Although the unit of work may form a large part of the curriculum in the elementary school, it does not constitute the whole curriculum. Children will read many books not specifically related to any unit; there is music that is valuable for its own sake as well as music related to a unit of work; and some skills will need practice for mastery which does not come from the unit of work. However, a number of values can be derived from units of work if each unit is carefully planned, if the teacher has a considerable amount of skill in managing group work, and if the class schedule is so arranged that a considerable block of time can be allotted to work on a unit. Some of these values are:

1. A unit can provide admirably for individual differences because of the wide variety of activities involved; each child can find an activity in which successful participation and recognition are gained.

2. The unit can be adapted readily to the characteristics, needs and resources of the community.

3. Materials can be drawn from many subject-matter fields.

4. The work lends itself to the use of many concrete materials.

5. The unit provides opportunities for the development of initiative, self-direction, and responsibility.

6. The students gain opportunities for the acquistion of useful information and skills through their applications to meaningful situations.

Learning Centers

The movement to establish open classrooms and schools has been a catalyst for the development of learning centers. Learning centers are integral ingredients for the successful operation of any school, but especially an open school.

A learning center enlarges the learning environment, contributes to the development of a self-actualizing learner, and provides for a greater range of learning rates, styles, and developmental levels. The center is a place for remediation, practice, and review. Pupils in a center may work independently or cooperatively. The learning center is truly a resource of learning, central and sensitive to the needs and interests of its clientele.

For a more elaborate discussion of learning centers—their operation, establishment, and value—the reader should see Zilpha Billings, *The Self-Selection Classroom*[19] and Ralph Voight, *Invitation to Learning*.[20]

One of the most important factors influencing the quality of living and learning in elementary schools is the availability and use of resources for learning. One of the most significant differences between the elementary school of 1900 and that of today is the vast expansion that has taken place in learning resources. Indeed, the term "revolution in the schools," when it is used by the mass media, generally means the revolution in learning resources. Those who attended elementary school during the first two decades of this century depended upon a single textbook for learning in any one curriculum area. Today, the learning resources include other books; maps, globes, and charts; laboratory supplies; audiovisual materials; community resources; television and programmed materials. The following materials can generally be found in the *resource center* of an elementary school:

Books	Periodicals
Pamphlets	Disc recordings
Charts	Tape recordings
Flat pictures	35-mm slides
Filmstrips	Newspapers
Maps	Programmed materials
Globes	Sound filmstrips
Models	Realia
8-mm motion picture loops	Viewmaster reels
Transparencies	Show-and-tell recordings

[19] Zilpha W. Billings, *The Self-Selection Classroom*. (Washington, D.C.: American Association of Elementary-Kindergarten-Nursery Educators, 1970).

[20] Ralph Claude Voight, *Invitation to Learning: Center Teaching with Instructional Depth*, Vol. II. (Washington D.C.: Acropolis Books Ltd., 1974).

Equipment needed to use these materials is available in the resource center. It includes:

Opaque projector	Record players
Overhead projectors	AM/FM radio
2 × 2 slide projectors	Television receiver
Filmstrip projectors	Sight-and-sound projector
16-mm projector	Viewmasters
8-mm projector	Reading pacer
Tape recorders	Controlled reader
Show-and-tell-machine	Earphones and listening stations
VTR equipment	Art production supplies
Construction tools	Visual production supplies

Activities

Activities are those aspects of the transmission, transposition, and translation processes utilized within a program framework to supplement and enrich the instructional processes.

Simulated Environments

Simulation games may be called an educational innovation. Using games in classrooms is, of course, not new; the technique of simulation, however, is. No one who observes a group of students who are using one of the many simulation games that are available can fail to be impressed by the potential of this technique. There is evidence that when this technique is used, students become highly motivated; they learn more; they learn the need for cooperation; they get a more realistic understanding of how things are done in life outside the school; and they gain an appreciation of the complexity of real-life situations.[21]

Conventional methods of teaching may not give students much preparation for making decisions in adult life. Simulation games place students in situations which require them to make decisions. They can then view these decisions in retrospect without the fear of having to suffer the consequences that would be involved in real life.

Simulation games tend to focus the attention of students on the task at hand more effectively than do other devices; discipline arises from the task itself; and the games shift responsibility for judging success away from the teacher—the players know whether they have won or lost, without being told.

In her article "The Game Doesn't End with Winning," Judith A. Gillespie discussed the debriefing session.[22] This is a way of evaluating what is learned in a simulation game. She discussed three major aspects of a good debriefing session: (1) It needs to be carefully developed around a set of questions which

21 S. Boocock and James S. Coleman, "Games with Simulated Environments in Learning," *Sociology of Education* (Summer 1966), pp. 215–237.
22 Judith A. Gillespie, "The Game Doesn't End with Winning," *Viewpoints* (November 1973), pp. 21–28.

will draw out students' experiences so they can be studied and evaluated; (2) it must also include some vehicle through which students can transfer their knowledge to new and related situations; (3) there needs to be a link "between the gaming experience and future learning." The debriefing session seems to be an evaluation, not only for the teacher but for the student as well.

THE GAME OF DEMOCRACY

Each player assumes the role of a legislator; success—being reelected at the end of the game—is determined by the players success in getting passed or defeated those measures constituents want passed or defeated. (Source: National 4-H Center, 7100 Connecticut Avenue, Washington, D.C.).

INNER-CITY SIMULATION LABORATORY AND TEACHING PROBLEMS LABORATORY

Fictitious, but lifelike, classrooms are created. The participants assume the role of the teacher in one of the imaginary situations. They are presented with the problems in teaching and classroom management identified as frequent and severe by teachers across the country. The participants solve these problems by making decisions based on the information available. (Source: *Two Simulated Teaching Programs,* Science Research Associates, 259 East Erie Street, Chicago, Ill. 60611.)

Volume 49 of the 1973 issue of *Viewpoints* is devoted to articles on simulation, the identification of simulation materials, and discussion of the strengths and weaknesses of this as a procedure.

Group Processes

The quality of group living makes all the difference between an excellent teaching-learning situation and a poor one when evaluated in the light of democratic values. The teacher who understands the meaning of group dynamics and who uses the techniques of group leadership intelligently has solved many of the problems relating to the broader concept of method. This does not imply that these techniques are new or that there is any particular virtue in the term "group dynamics" as such. Many teachers have been using group processes successfully for years without knowing that the term existed. Other teachers have wondered why they have so much difficulty with groups, why their pupils seem to learn slowly, and why they have so many discipline problems. Teachers have always known that a child's behavior is different when that child is a member of a group, that a group is something more than just an aggregation of individuals, and that there are good groups and groups that are difficult to manage. The term "group dynamics" seems to be a convenient expression for those principles and procedures that provide greater insight into and greater skill in the solution of problems of group management. As teaching becomes more highly professional, it is to be expected that new and more technical terms will be applied to various aspects of the teacher's work. Teachers, therefore, are making a greater effort than ever before to understand the implications of such terms as "group dynamics" and to help parents and other interested citizens see more clearly what such terms mean in relation to the effort to provide better educational opportunities for children.

THE MEANING OF GROUP DYNAMICS

Group dynamics refers to the study of what happens when human beings work in groups. It is concerned with discovering the extent to which human beings behave differently when they are members of a group than when they are alone; the factors that promote group productivity; and the techniques that are effective in group discussion, planning, and evaluating. It is concerned with helping individuals understand what is happening in the group, assume their responsibilities as group members, and learn the techniques of group leadership.

The study of the nature of groups, group processes, and group leadership is receiving increasing attention in books for school administrators and supervisors. It is recognized that the faculty of a school must represent more than a mere aggregation of individuals if the objectives of the modern elementary school are to be realized; the faculty must be bound into a closely knit social organization with common purposes, intense loyalties, and effective ways of working together. The administrator or supervisor must know a great deal about human relationships, group processes, and leadership techniques if the staff is to be directed toward the accomplishment of the goals of education. Some of the techniques used for this purpose were discussed in Chapter 4.

The study of group dynamics has also had a profound influence on the methods of teaching used in modern elementary schools. Teachers have learned to use sociometric tests to determine the structure of human relationships within a given group of children and the degree of acceptance or rejection of each child by the group. They are learning the techniques for studying the group behavior of boys and girls, and for fostering group discussion, planning and evaluation.

VALUES DERIVED FROM PARTICIPATION IN GROUP PROCESSES

Cooperative group work is essential to democratic living. A group of children around a conference table setting up goals, making plans, assuming responsibilities, or evaluating achievements represents an essential prelude to intelligent, responsible citizenship. Children learn from one another through sharing ideas; group action is more effective when several individuals have shared in the planning; individuals find a place in group projects for making contribution in line with special talents; and morale is higher when children work together cooperatively on group projects. This is not meant to imply that there is no place in the modern classroom for individual effort; there should be a time for both individual and group activity. However, effective group work is the phase that is usually neglected because the techniques for directing this part of the program are more difficult to master than the techniques for working with individual pupils.

Although it is generally agreed that learning to work with others is an essential prelude to responsible, intelligent citizenship, teachers have not always selected the kinds of group activities that have been effective in achieving this goal. Curriculum content and activities are not selected solely on the basis of providing opportunities for pupils to work in groups; rather, learning to work with others is a by-product that is attained as pupils work on many types of content and at many types of activities.

Some teachers use voting as a technique for training in democracy; they have pupils settle issues themselves by a majority decision. Some teachers may go so far as to set up a voting booth in the classroom because they feel that knowledge of voting procedures promotes democratic citizenship. Although such activities may be useful on occasion, they can hardly be depended upon to give pupils a clear understanding of the rights of self and others in a democracy. Pupils need also to learn about the historical evolution of human rights and responsibilities, and then to have opportunities to practice democratic living in the classroom.

Pupils in modern elementary schools have many opportunities to work in groups in connection with practically every curriculum area. One example comes from a sixth-grade class that plans and publishes a newspaper. Standards for narrative and expository writing are developed in the language-arts class; a writing clinic is held once a week, devoted to the improvement of written expression; and time is also set aside for planning the details of production and the allocation of responsibilities. Omar Khayyam Moore has used the example of a first-grade class that published a newspaper as an example of what he calls the "responsive environment for learning." These pupils learned word construction, reading, writing, and other skills in an enterprise that they regarded as their own.[23]

Teacher Knowledge of Organization

When the primary purpose of the elementary school is regarded as the mastery of the knowledge and skills relating to the three Rs, and when the aristocratic philosophy of selection and elimination prevails, classroom organization is a relatively simple matter. Knowledge and skills considered important by experts in the various fields are selected and divided into quotas, with a certain quota assigned to each grade. The classroom teacher has only to organize the materials assigned to his grade in an orderly sequence and proceed to cover a certain amount of the content each week.

On the other hand, when learning is regarded as the modification of behavior, and when the democratic philosophy of educating each child to the fullest extent prevails, organizing the class for living and learning becomes one of the most difficult and at the same time one of the most crucial tasks confronting the teacher.

The effective teacher in the elementary school must, therefore, be somewhat of an expert in human relations, must be a good administrator, must know how to keep several groups working harmoniously and profitably, must have an inti-

[23] Omar Khayyam Moore, "Autotelic Responsive Environments for Learning," in Ronald Gross and Judith Murphy, *The Revolution in the Schools.* (New York: Harcourt Brace Jovanovich, Inc., 1964), pp. 184–219.

mate knowledge of each pupil's needs and abilities, must have a wide acquaintance with various types of resources for learning, and must have the ability to
capitalize upon pupils' capacities for leadership and to enlist their wholehearted
cooperation.

The teacher's time and effort spent in establishing rapport during the first
few days pay large dividends later. One purpose of this effort is to establish a
friendly relationship in which each child regards the teacher as a helpful and
trusted member of the group who is really interested in each child as a person.
Another purpose is to provide opportunities for pupils to know one another and
to build a framework of mutual understanding and trust, without which effective group work is impossible. Good teachers go about the job of establishing
rapport in many ways. Studying individual records before meeting the group
for the first time, talking with individual pupils or small groups informally as
time permits, observing children on the way to school or on the playground,
recognizing individual interests and talents, encouraging children to talk freely
about out-of-school interests and experiences, choosing wisely the words used,
and being able to call each pupil's name without hesitation are some of the
ways in which the teacher can help to create an environment for cooperative
learning in the classroom.

Children need help from the teacher in setting up group goals. Although the
goals will have more meaning if children express them in their own words, it is
necessary for the teacher to help them decide what they are going to do and
how they are to begin. The group will need assistance in finding ways to integrate individual aims with those of the group. Usually, a way can be found to
help the individual realize personal goals while contributing to the realization
of the goals of the group.

Once individual and group goals are clear to members of the group, the
teacher must help the group organize in ways to attain these goals. The class
is usually divided into several committees for working on various aspects of the
problem selected. Some teachers find it difficult to give the various committees
enough freedom to work out their problems in their own way; others fail to give
them enough guidance, and the result is chaos. The teacher should be sure that
necessary materials are available and that the children know where and how to
obtain them. Certain members of the group may take responsibility for distribution of materials and for keeping a record of materials used. In any case it is
well to remember that children learn to plan only through planning and that
experiences in cooperative planning can yield valuable learnings.

One important factor in the success of a group is leadership. The members
of the group need help in choosing the group leader wisely. The leader needs
help in understanding the functions of the leader. The film, *Broader Concept of
Method*, illustrates how the teacher can help a pupil understand what a leader
is expected to do.[24]

---

[24] "Broader Concept of Method, Part II, Teacher and Pupils Planning and Working Together"
is a 22-minute film by McGraw-Hill illustrating how pupils learn to work together in functional groups. Further information may be obtained by writing: McGraw-Hill, Inc., Text-Film
Dept., 330 W. 42nd St., New York, N.Y. 10036.

Group processes are, of course, used by teachers in the U.S.S.R., but for different purposes. There, they are used to produce standardized behavior to serve the interests of a collective society. A democracy prizes the worth of the individual, and pupils are expected to make their own unique contributions to group enterprises. In this framework, the growth of the individual rather than standardized behavior is the end sought.

Values-Clarification Strategies

Simon, Howe, and Kirschenbaum have advocated a systematic approach to values clarification.[25] They recommend that the traditional approaches of (1) moralizing, (2) laissez-faire, and (3) modeling of the adult to guide the young in making value choices be supplemented to include a values-clarification strategy. They have created and adapted a number of strategies to implement the theoretical approach of Raths.[26]

Raths' approach is not concerned with the content of values but with the process of valuing. He identifies seven subprocesses of the process of valuing. The values-clarification approach is a series of strategies incorporating the subprocesses. As pupils interact with a strategy, they experience both the subprocesses and the process of valuing. Raths' seven subprocesses are:

A. Prizing one's beliefs and behaviors
   1. Prizing and cherishing
   2. Publicly affirming, when appropriate
B. Choosing one's beliefs and behaviors
   3. Choosing from alternatives
   4. Choosing after consideration of consequences
   5. Choosing freely
C. Acting on one's beliefs
   6. Acting
   7. Acting with a pattern, consistency, and repetition.[27]

The values-clarification strategies can be utilized in three ways. A specific amount of time can be allocated each day or week, 5 minutes up to an hour or more. Elective courses and mini-courses can be offered. Also, values-clarification strategies can be incorporated into the existing content of the curriculum. If added to existing content, the following levels of pupil experiencing would be available: fact, concept, and values. Simon said:

> The small amount of empirical research . . . and the large amount of practical experience by thousands of teachers indicate that students who have been exposed to this approach are less apathetic, less flighty, less conforming, less over-dissenting . . . more zestful and energetic, more critical in their thinking,

[25] Sidney B. Simon, Leland W. Howe, and Howard Kirschenbaum, *Values Clarification: A Handbook of Practical Strategies for Teachers and Students.* (New York: Hart Publishing Company, Inc., 1972), pp. 13–22.
[26] Louis Raths, Harmin Merrell, and Sidney Simon, *Values Teaching.* (Columbus, Ohio: Charles E. Merrill Publishing Co., 1966).
[27] Simon et al., p. 19.

more likely to follow through on their decisions . . . and in the case of under-achievers, values-clarification has led to better success in school.[28]

Values-clarification approaches are receiving considerable attention. A thoughtful reader may construct a parallel between inquiry as discussed in Chapter 5 and the values-clarification approaches presented here. Values-clarification approaches attempt to reduce the imposition of values and to provide the individual with a system of inquiry into the development of a values organization. The individual's behaviors of choosing, prizing, and acting and how they become the emprical data base of a feedback system provided through the processes of values-clarification strategies to curriculum areas will be discussed in Part III.

SITUATION 6.4   Examine three simulation games or activities. List the conditions under which the simulation would be advantageous to the learner. Briefly discuss your personal evaluations of the simulation games or activities examined. Relate the values-clarification activities recommended by Simon to the simulation games or activities you examined.

MAGIC CIRCLE

Another activity emphasizing the affective domain is called "Magic Circle."[29] These activities are designed as a presentative, developmental approach to self-awareness, self-confidence, and social understanding. The three main areas are (1) awareness—knowing what your thoughts, feelings, and actions really are; (2) mastery—knowing what your abilities are and how to use them; and (3) social interaction—knowing other people.

The basic procedures involve forming a circle, with the teacher presenting cues to stimulate discussion. The rules are: Everyone may have a turn to share if desired; everyone listens when someone else is talking; and no evaluative labels applied to the speaker may be used by teacher or pupils. (Textbooks are available from preschool through sixth grade.)

Career Education

Almost all children presently in classes within the elementary school will spend a considerable part of their lives as producers in the world of work. Approximately 25 percent will enter their vocational world before high school graduation. Some will enter after high school graduation; others will enter after trade, vocational, or technical training, and still others after graduation from a college or university.

The stability and variety of positions within the vocational world has been drastically affected by technology; so drastically, that our society and the indi-

---

[28] Simon et al., p. 20.
[29] Harold Besell and Uvaldo Palomares, *Methods in Human Development: Theory Manual.* (El Cajon, Calif: Human Development Training Institute, 1970).

vidual may no longer depend upon apprenticeships and incidental contacts with potential vocational models. A reasonable speculation is that most of the positions that today's child in elementary school will fill are not yet in existence.

Career education activities are designed to help individuals inventory their aptitudes and interests, and to develop awarenesses of the possibilities and alternatives available as vocational choices. During the elementary school years the child begins investigating the behaviors, qualifications, and functions of the major categories of employment. These investigations are much more comprehensive than casual field trips to the post office or fire station. The child learns to interview persons, use the basic references of the occupational world, research magazines and newspapers, and generally to conduct an inquiry into a position or field within the vocational world.

Career education activities integrate academic and career preparation, emphasize career exploration, expand career options and choices, provide an in-depth study of how the economic system operates and prepares pupils for the continuing education required to enter the careers of their choices.[30] Part III of this text will illustrate the implications and applications of career education activities to the various areas.

Tools

Tools are those elements of the transmission, transposition, and translation processes utilized within a program or activity frame to implement and extend the curriculum. The value of a tool can be best judged in relationship to its effectiveness and efficiency with regard to an activity or program. For example, instructional technology is in and of itself neutral, neither good or bad. Yet its contributions to the achievement of a program's or activity's objectives can be evaluated.

The Textbook

Because the single textbook determined the scope of the curriculum in elementary schools of the past, it does not follow that textbooks have no place in modern elementary classrooms. A good series of textbooks represents the best efforts of competent specialists in elementary education and the services of the editorial staff of the publishers. These books incorporate the findings of the most recent research in the various phases of the elementary school program, and certainly have much to offer when they are used wisely. It is not unusual to find at the end of a chapter or unit in a modern textbook some excellent suggestions for projects and activities which pupils can use to make the contents of the chapter more meaningful, some suggested readings, and some suggestions for audiovisual resources and field trips to be used in connection with the chapter or unit. The teachers' manual, which accompanies a series of textbooks, offers many suggestions concerning the teaching of concepts and skills.

---

[30] Richard A. Gibboney et al., *The Career Intern Program: Preliminary Results of an Experiment in Career Education,* Vol. I. (Washington, D.C.: National Institute of Education, 1975), p. 13.

Many and varied materials are necessary to support the modern elementary school.

Critics of textbooks fail to differentiate between possible faults in the textbook and the misapplication of the textbook. This is somewhat like the position of critics who find fault with a hammer because it does not cut wood effectively. Not that many of available textbooks do not have faults. For example, some of the older books reflect stereotyping but these are being corrected, and the profession must constantly communicate and coordinate with the makers of textbooks to eradicate these intrusions. But the publisher should not be blamed when his materials are misapplied. A text, for example, does not dictate rate, only sequence. If a teacher insists that a book be used when the learner is not ready, this is a serious fault of the instructor, not the tool. The more modern texts provide definitions of scope, sequence, diagnostic activities, provision for individual differences, and enrichment and remedial activities.

Teachers in most school systems now serve on committees which select the textbooks to be used in the local school system, choosing from lists prepared by state textbook commissions. Whether the teacher is serving on such a committee or selecting the textbooks for an individual classroom, the teacher should be familiar with accepted criteria for textbook selection. Such items as the following should be given consideration: *authorship*—recognition in the field, use of appropriate technical vocabulary, use of pertinent research findings, appropriate style of writing; *mechanical features*—size of type, quality of paper, appropriate illustrations, and cost; *contents*—balance in terms of social significance, sufficient detail to make concepts meaningful, application to life situations, organization in terms of principles of learning; *helps for teacher and pupils*

—teacher's manual, study helps for pupils, adequate summaries and previews, table of contents, index, glossary, emphasis on problem solving.[31]

Instructional Technology

Instructional technology is a term used to designate communication media such as television, motion pictures, and textbooks. It is also used to designate the process through which research findings of the behavioral sciences are applied to problems of instruction. The rapid growth of instructional technology in recent years has caused a great deal of confusion and has aroused many abnormal fears among educators. The most common fear is that instructional television, programmed material, and other forms of communication media will dehumanize the curriculum.

David Engler presented convincing arguments that the supposed conflict between the humanist curriculum and instructional technology is based on false assumptions. He pointed out that

1. *Instructional technology is essentially a tool which can be used to implement any curriculum decision.*
2. *There can be no curriculum without an instructional technology—conventional methods and materials represent an instructional technology.*
3. *The current problem is how to devise an instructional technology which will further humanize the curriculum.*
4. *Our present strategies and instruments of instruction are not adequate to accomplish what is expected of our schools.*[32]

INSTRUCTIONAL TELEVISION

An increasing number of school systems own television facilities, employ television teachers for various curriculum areas, and schedule viewing periods regularly in all classrooms. In view of the knowledge explosion, many believe that conventional methods and devices cannot be expected to provide children with the information they need in a rapidly changing society. Television and other communication media are therefore regarded by many as real breakthroughs in the information-giving aspect of education.[33] The Project on Instruction of the National Education Association made the following recommendation in 1963:

The use of educational television (ETV) and radio to broaden and deepen learning should be encouraged. Such use should be accompanied by a vigorous program of research and experimentation.[34]

A child usually averages more hours spent in front of a television set than

[31] A checklist for evaluating textbooks can be found in John U. Michaelis, *Social Studies for Children in a Democracy,* 4th ed.   (Englewood Cliffs, N.J.: Prentice-Hall, Inc., 1968), p. 318.
[32] David Engler, "Instructional Technology and the Curriculum," *Phi Delta Kappan* (March 1970), pp. 379–381.
[33] George B. Leonard, *Education and Ecstasy.* (New York: Dell Publishing Company, Delacorte Press, 1968), pp. 15–16.
[34] Project on Instruction, NEA, *Schools for the Sixties.* (New York: McGraw-Hill, Inc., 1963), p. 99.

Modern technology can enrich and extend the learning and experiencing of children.

in a classroom. An estimated 35 percent of school children watch "Electric Company" during school hours, while nine million watch "Sesame Street" during the hours they are not in school. A critic of educational television described "Sesame Street" as, "at best a program of limited skill-oriented objectives offering traditional pedagogy." Granted, children do seem to learn early skills from these programs, but this learning is not a substitute for the activities and experiences involved in the parent-child relationship.[35]

COMPUTER-BASED INSTRUCTION

There can be little doubt that computer-based instruction can speed up learning, provide opportunities for the student to assume more responsibility, help tailor instruction to individual needs and capabilities, and free teachers for more creative aspects of teaching. Most computer-based instruction programs employ the same basic methods:

1. The learner is presented with a stimulus which gives him information, requires a response, or does both.

2. There is a continual necessity for the learner to utilize this information in making some response or decision.

3. After responding, the learner is presented with feedback information

[35] Carol Hastie, "Sesame Street: The Establishment Easy Street," in Harold Sobel and Arthur Solz (Eds.), *The Radical Papers: Readings in Education.* (New York: Harper & Row, Publishers, 1972).

which enables him to ascertain the appropriateness of his response. The immediate feedback gives the student motivation for continuing with the process.

Suppes made the following evaluation of computer-based instruction:

The speed of computer-based instruction will not lead to a reduction of teachers but to a substantial increase in the quality of education. Teachers will learn to use computer-based terminals the way in which they now use textbooks.[36]

MEDIA

The organized information forms used for purposes of instruction are called "media." Information is displayed in four primary forms: print, pictorial, oral, and realia. Media are created through the organization of one or more combinations of these primary information forms to be used in instruction.

The printed form for information display in media includes textbooks, trade books, programmed materials, kits, and so on. The pictorial form of media includes pictures, charts, films, slides, transparencies, and television. The oral form includes tapes, cassettes, records, and radio. The realia form of media information includes specimens, models, objects, laboratory tools, and similar equipment.

No single form of information display or media has a clearly established superiority for all phases of instruction. The tendency is for a specific media form to enjoy popularity and then decline; for example: radio, to television, to teaching machines, to computer-assisted instruction. Eventually, each form of media finds its level of functioning and becomes one of the alternatives available to facilitate activities and programs.

Media and Methodology. The teacher is, as usual, responsible for the selection of the media form which best fits the objectives of the curriculum. The following lists illustrate the requirements that a methodology (inquiry) places upon media selection. Inquiry as a methodology consists of three phases: exploration, invention, and discovery (see Chapter 5). A particular media form may support one or more of these phases of inquiry. For it to support exploration (the first phase of inquiry), it must

1. Be within the experience background of the learner-user.
2. Involve the learner-user in such intrinsic activities as observing, classifying, manipulating, clustering, reordering, comparing, and contrasting.
3. Be flexible so that the learner-user may elect exploraton activities. For example, one learner may classify by color, another by size, another by shape, and so on.
4. Contain no explanation of the events, situations, or objects depicted. It should not say, "This what you saw, and this is what it means." Predigested conclusions from any source restrict the exploration of the learner-user.
5. Include the object-action-operation and concrete-vicarious-abstract rela-

[36] Patrick Suppes, in Maurie Hillson, *Elementary Education: Current Issues and Research.* (New York: The Free Press, 1967), p. 217.

A superior alternative—serving to
facilitate learning.

tionships appropriate to the developmental level of the learner-user (see Chapter 3).

2. For a media form to support invention (the second phase of inquiry), it must

1. Be divergent in any explanation of the events, actions, situations, or objects depicted. It could, for example, illustrate how one hypothesis accounts for certain observations, but not others, and invite the learner-user to modify the hypothesis.
2. Contain a surprise or discriminating ingredient that seems to conflict with the first predictions of the learner-user.
3. Stimulate the learner-user to both physical and rational involvement.

3. For a media form to support discovery (the third phase of inquiry), it must

1. Suggest means of testing its hypothesis or other hypotheses.
2. Provide ways to gather and display data collected during exploration, and tell how this can be interpreted.
3. Suggest alternative applications to similar and different situations.
4. Provide additional data to enable the learner-user to verify or modify hypotheses.

Media in the various existing forms can be useful in inquiry. However, existing media seem inadequate when evaluated by these standards. The author anticipates a significant increase in the organization of media forms to serve inquiry.

Behavioral-Instructional Objectives

Objectives are statements designed to communicate the intent of the curriculum, and its programs and activities. A statement to communicate the intended outcomes of a learning experience is an objective. The intended outcomes of a learning experience are changes in behaviors. Learning is evidenced by and inferred from changes in behaviors as a result of interactions with one's environment. These statements shape one of the premises of the tool called "behavioral objectives."

The second premise of those who advocate behavioral objectives is the ambiguity of the objectives stated in other than behavioral terms. This ambiguity and the resulting confusion in communication forces a learner to identify the intended outcomes of instruction through a trial-and-error, guessing, and hidden agenda process. This leads to fragmentation of the learner's energies and inefficiency in accomplishing whatever was intended. The advocates of behavioral objectives argues that an "up front" statement of intended outcomes focuses energies and supports an efficient accomplishment of them.

A third premise is that an evaluation system derived from ambiguous objectives will itself be ambiguous. A precise statement of outcomes is a prerequisite for the development of effective evaluation activities. An effective evaluation

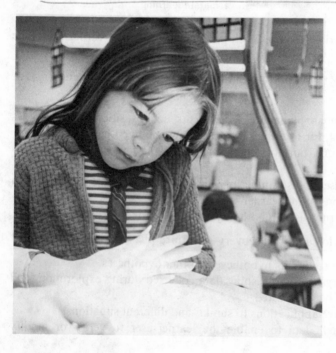

Inquiring with media.

activity is one which provides relevant data to the learner, establishing a specific relationship between behaviors and intended outcomes.

Behavioral objectives, then, comprise a form of objectives predicated upon the intended outcomes of instruction; the focusing of learner and teacher energies for efficient and effective accomplishment; and the specific basis for evaluation activities. Gagné said, "It is reasonable to suppose that a student who knows what the objective is will be able to approach the task of learning with an advantage over one who does not."[37]

The general form for writing objectives in behavioral form incorporates

1. The specific identification of the type and class of behavior expected at the conclusion of the experience.
2. A description of the conditions in which the intended outcome behavior is to occur.
3. The minimum level of performance efficiency, accuracy, or frequency of the behavior that will be evaluated as being successful.

R. F. Mager is usually credited with spelling out the form for writing behavioral objectives.[38] This movement has been a fundamental aspect of such tools as criterion-referenced instruction, accountability systems, computer-assisted instruction, competency-based instruction, and many of the individualized programs.

The critics of the behavioral form of objectives usually argue that such a tool has a mechanistic S-R association learning theory as its base; that behaviors cannot be specified by the desired intended outcomes; that a staggering number of objectives would be required for one course and one student; and that those behaviors which can be specified are apt to be the trivia of instruction.[39]

COMPETENCY MOVEMENTS

Competency-based instructions, criteria-referenced instruction, prescriptive teaching, and similar innovations are systems based upon behavioral objectives. The distinctions among these developments are not always discrete; yet, each has its own models and advocates. A common commitment among these systems is the sequence advocated for program planning. The sequence is the writing of objectives in performance, instructional, or behavioral terms; a preassessment of the learners' behaviors with regard to both prerequisite behaviors and outcome behaviors; alternative paths and channels selected as a result of the preassessment; a post-assessment derived from the level of performances stated in the objectives; and a recycling of those learners who have not achieved the intended behaviors and levels of performance. Further information on these significant systems may be found in Chapter 2 and Chapter 13, in addition to the Selected Readings section located at the end of this chapter.

37 Robert M. Gagné, "Behavioral Objectives? Yes!" in Hass, p. 224.
38 R. F. Mager, *Preparing Instructional Objectives.* (Belmont, Calif.: Fearon Publishers, 1962).
39 George F. Kneller, "Behavioral Objectives? No!" in Hass, *Curriculum Planning*, pp. 225–228.

SITUATION 6.5   Read three journal articles related to competency-based instruction. How does this concept relate to elementary school learners? Further, how can competency-based instruction be most effectively utilized within the modern elementary school?

SUMMARY

1. *Curriculum* means all the experiences of children for which the school accepts responsibility.
2. Curriculum guides are the documents in which the decisions concerning the content, the scope and sequence, and the experiences of learners are recorded.
3. Curriculum guides provide a generalized framework for teachers; include the best insights available; present a systematized, edited, and simplified environment; and form a basis for communication.
4. General types of curriculum organization include those designed from the logic of the discipline (logical), the nature and needs of the learner (psychological), and the demands of society (sociological).
5. That which a learner experiences is called the "dynamic" curriculum and results from the instructional processes, which transpose, translate, and transmit the documents of the planned curriculum into experiences.
6. Curriculum programs are those systems which subsume the activities and tools of the transmission, transposition, and translation processes.
7. Curriculum activities include simulations, group processes, values-clarification strategies, and career education.
8. Curriculum tools include textbooks, instructional technology (media such as television and computer-assisted instruction), behavioral objectives, and their related competency movements.

Problems and Projects

1. Examine the curriculum guides for a particular curriculum area in which you have interest. Be concerned with questions such as the following:
   a. By whom were the guides written?
   b. Do the purposes stated within the guide indicate an emphasis upon content or process?
   c. Are objectives stated in behavioral terms? Upon what criteria did you base your decision?
   d. What are the common procedures recommended for pupil evaluation?
   e. What is the organizational format (content, psychological, sociological)?
2. Prepare an outline for an "experience" unit at a specific level within an elementary school. Indicate the age of the learners. Provide at least two specific exam-

ples of activities under the following sections: teacher-pupil planning; working period; evaluation.

3. Graduating or beginning teachers often feel inadequately prepared in the areas of knowledge of materials available; actual manipulation of interest or learning centers; and experience with and utilization of curriculum guides. Into what phases of the teacher preparation programs should training, activities, and experiences be instituted in order to help relieve some of the inadequacy felt by graduating teachers who are supposedly prepared to teach? List a sampling of the types of training, activities, or experiences which would be beneficial.

Selected Readings

Bruner, Jerome S., *The Process of Education*. Cambridge, Mass.: Harvard University Press, 1962. "Readiness for Learning," chap. 3, explains the relationship between child development and curriculum organization.

Doll, Ronald C., *Curriculum Improvement: Decision-Making and Process*. Boston: Allyn & Bacon, Inc., 1964. Chapter 11 deals with the problem of organizing learning experiences.

Gwynn, J. Minor, and John B. Chase, Jr., *Curriculum Principles and Social Trends*. New York: Crowell Collier and Macmillan, Inc., 1969. Part 3 contains descriptions of curriculum developments, experimentation, and change in the elementary school.

Hyman, Ronald T., *Approaches in Curriculum*. Englewood Cliffs, N.J.: Prentice-Hall, Inc., 1973. A collection of the writings of curriculum theorists, including Dewey, Kilpatric, Stratemeyer, Bellack, and others.

Kapfer, Marian B. (Ed.), *Behavioral Objectives in Curriculum Development*. Englewood Cliffs, N.J.: Educational Technology Publications, 1971. A collection of readings on behavioral objectives and curriculum planning.

Krug, Mark M., *What Will Be Taught the Next Decade?* Itasca, Ill.: F. E. Peacock Publishers, Inc., 1972. A collection of writings assessing the current scene and predicting future trends in many curriculum areas.

Mager, R. F., *Goal Analysis*. Belmont, Calif.: Fearon Publishers, 1972. Suggests steps through which intangible goals can be "tangiblitated."

Phenix, Phillip H., *Realms of Meaning: A Philosophy of the Curriculum for General Education*. New York: McGraw-Hill, Inc., 1964. Chapter 2 presents the thesis that the proper aim of education is to promote the growth of meaning; presents a logical classification of meanings as a basis for the curriculum in general education.

Ragan, William B., and George Henderson, *Foundations of American Education*. New York: Harper & Row, Publishers, 1970. Chapter 8 is concerned with a review of curriculum reform projects in various curriculum areas.

Saylor, J. Galen, and William M. Alexander, *Curriculum Planning for Modern Schools*. New York: Holt, Rinehart and Winston, 1966. Parts 3 and 4 are concerned with the bases and organizations of curriculum and instruction.

Taba, Hilda, *Curriculum Development: Theory and Practice*. New York: Harcourt Brace Jovanovich, Inc., 1962. Chapter 21 examines current patterns of curriculum organization.

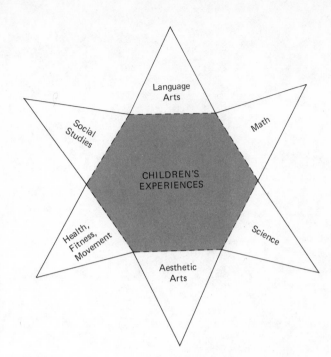

Language Arts

Social Studies

Math

CHILDREN'S EXPERIENCES

Health, Fitness, Movement

Science

Aesthetic Arts

Part **3**

PROGRAMS for CURRICULUM

The individual curriculum areas provide both discrete and unifying contributions to the curriculum of the modern elementary school. Part 3 explores each of these areas.

chapter 7

Inquiring
LANGUAGE ARTS

The abstractness of language is the source of its power to express an infinite variety of experiences and to represent the real word in all its depth and complexity. By this miracle of language the boundless world is open to shared understanding.

Philip H. Phenix, *Realms of Meaning*. (New York: McGraw-Hill, Inc., 1964), p. 70.

The most personal and personalized area of the curriculum is language arts; nothing is so characteristic of people as their language. Language gives evidence of values, cultural influences, geographic beginnings, capacities, prejudices, and other facets of an individual's background. To openly share language with someone in communication is to reveal this background. To understand the communications of a person's language is to understand that person. To accept someone's communications through language is to accept that person. To reject communication is to reject the individual.

To help children express thoughts and feelings through language is to develop the art of communication. It is in this context that the teacher in the modern elementary school approaches instruction in the language arts. Genuineness, empathy, and outgoing warmth are the affective prerequisites in helping young children to communicate.

Language has no inherent content. Rather it is the vehicle used to encode and decode content derived from the experiences of feeling, thinking, sensing, and other faculties. Composition, for example, is a tool used to transmit the content of living, knowing, being, science, and mathematics, among other sensory and learning experiences. Spelling is a tool for encoding the symbols of a content to be communicated. Reading is a tool for decoding the printed symbols of communication.

Thus, the curriculum area of language arts consists of the skills and tools of communicating, and their application to bodies of content. To study only the language arts would be to study only skills and tools outside their functioning environment. Language arts is a *dependent* curriculum area, one which must be supplemented by other areas for meaningfulness.

This chapter deals with some of the major features of a modern language arts program, the findings of some of the more important studies that have been made in the language arts field, and problems and issues relating to teaching of the language arts. It contains a brief summary of purposes, programs, and trends in reading, listening, handwriting, spelling, oral and written expression, and children's literature in elementary schools.

MAJOR FEATURES OF A LANGUAGE ARTS PROGRAM

Modern elementary schools do not leave the development of language abilities to chance; the program is carefully planned so that each child becomes as efficient as possible in the use of language. This program provides for both the incidental learning of language in connection with the everyday activities in which children normally engage and for the systematic teaching of language during periods set aside specifically for that purpose.

Educational research and the experience of successful teachers have provided many guidelines for the development of a functional program of language arts instruction. An analysis of some of the major features of a modern program of language arts instruction is essential if teachers are to see clearly the goals and objectives toward which they want to work.

Objectives

SITUATION 7.1   Before reading further, list the skills and communication tools which fall under the curriculum area of language arts.

There is general agreement among teachers and parents that children should be taught to read well, listen attentively, speak clearly, write legibly, and spell accurately. However, teachers and parents do not always understand what is involved in reading well or spelling accurately. Reading, for example, requires much more than mere word calling. It serves a wide range of functional purposes, among which are: ability to comprehend what is read, independence in word recognition, ability to use an index and table of contents, ability to skim through material rapidly, development of attitudes favorable to reading, ability to get information needed from reliable sources, and so on.

There is a great difference, also, between learning to spell the words in the daily spelling lesson and habitually using correct spelling in all written work done at school and elsewhere. The teacher who understands the broader objectives of spelling provides many opportunities for children to learn to spell in connection with units of work and other curriculum areas.

A program of language arts instruction must recognize the functioning of language in the development of a child, in the maintenance of a culture, and in the continuity of the development of generations. Through language the child becomes acculturated and socialized. The language patterns of the family and peer groups are first imitated and then adopted by the child. This imitation and adoption enables the child to become an accepted social being. The values, mores, and traditions of an ethnic group are both encoded and perpetuated by the patterns of syntax, grammar, and vocabulary. The child adopts these ethnic patterns as a fundamental means of gaining acceptance and recognition as a member of a group. Language also serves to provide continuity in the experiencing of succeeding generations. The learnings of each previous generation are preserved and transmitted through their encoding into symbols and patterns for language communication.

The language arts curriculum in a modern elementary school is concerned with all forms and functions of language. It provides meaningful situations for both the learning and application of the tools of language arts.

Development through Experience

Just as the language of a child is developed through experiencing, so is the language arts program. The symbols and patterns of language are abstractions applied to the realities of the objects, events, and values experienced by a culture and an individual. Without these applications, the mastery of the skills and tools of language is somewhat like practicing a violin in a vacuum; even if a skill is mastered in abstract, it is inert and valueless until it is activated in a social experience. For example, the skill of diagramming a sentence (for the elementary child) does not conduct into significant changes in the oral or even written language patterns of the child. On the other hand, learning to perceive differences in sounds and patterns does seem to significantly influence the child's oral and written language. Listening and voicing imitations are concrete experiences; diagramming is an abstract experience.

Instruction in language arts must therefore begin with the social maturation and experiences which are already encoded by the learner. From this beginning, additional social maturation and experiencing must be provided as the foundation for the new symbols and patterns to be learned.

The language arts activities in many elementary schools grow out of the everyday experiences of children, such as trips, pets, toys, vacations, and current happenings. A fifth-grade boy who had attended a Cub Scout day camp was eager to tell the class about his experiences, although he had previously been timid about participating in oral language activities. A first-grade teacher, upon showing the class a film about the passenger train, discovered that few of the children had ever taken a train ride. The parents cooperated, arranging to take the children on a train ride to the nearest town, about 15 miles away. The next day the children were eager to talk about their experiences, and an experience chart was developed. It consisted of such sentences as the following:

We took a ride on the train.
We walked to the station.

We bought our tickets at the station.
We gave our tickets to the conductor.
We looked out the train windows.
We saw some cows in the pasture.

Educational research supports the practice of helping children develop knowledge of words and skill in expression by providing contacts with the real world around them. Bloom and his associates reported that, on the average, children from culturally deprived homes fall behind grade norms in reading by as much as three years. Further, they indicated that the absence of objects in the home, the lack of interest in learning on the part of parents, and the limited conversation and encouragement the child gets in the home are significant in the failure of these children to progress at the normal rate in language.[1]

The Unified Language Arts Program

The unified language arts program includes reading, spelling, composition, grammar, literature, and the dramatic arts. All skill and tool areas functioning to facilitate listening, speaking, reading, and writing are aspects of the broad field of the language arts curriculum.

The child's development in one aspect of language does not take place independently of development in other aspects. Children listen before they talk, talk before they read, and read before they write, although no one of these skills in the sequence is completed before the other is started. Each of the language regions—listening, speaking, reading, and writing—contributes to and reinforces the other. None can be taught well in isolation from the others.

Listening is the region of language through which children gain most understanding and perceive the most meanings. Figuratively, for children, the listening region is where they have the most power, simply because it is at that level where they can hear and perceive the most meanings. Thus, the area of listening can then be thought of as the largest segment of the language arts.

Speaking is the next largest and most powerful language area for children. Children can usually say more than they can read or write. Yet, their speech may not include all the meanings apparently available to them through listening. However, what meanings they do speak are those they have first heard.

Reading is the third largest and most powerful language region for children. What meanings children read best are those meanings they have experienced through listening and speaking. For children to read meanings they cannot hear or speak reduces their reading skill to word calling, which is a very poor form of reading, if it can be called that at all.

Writing is the fourth largest and most powerful language region for children. What meanings children tend to write best are those that they have heard, spoken, and recognized in reading form (see Fig. 7.1).

[1] Benjamin S. Bloom, Allison Davis, and Robert Hess, *Compensatory Education for Cultural Deprivation.* (New York: Holt, Rinehart and Winston, Inc., 1965), pp. 69–75.

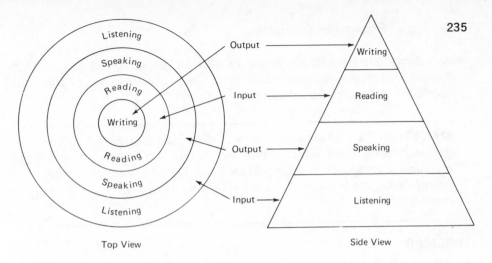

Top View   Side View

Figure 7.1 Listening, speaking, reading, and writing develop in sequence as interrelated parts of the language arts curriculum.

To summarize, then, in simplistic but relatively accurate terms, the listening region provides the foundation of meanings, which then become available in a speaking, reading, and writing sequence. The importance of this for a unified language arts program is that all initial teaching acts should begin with the input language region of listening, while all initial displays of learning should be through the output language region of speaking. When listening and speaking precede reading and writing, the learner is enabled by the power and capacity of more meanings. The teacher who begins by saying, "Open your book to page 302," is asking the children to attempt learning when part of their capacities for learning is restricted.

The unified language arts program, with its longer periods for uninterrupted work, is in harmony with modern principles of learning. Organizing activities around large centers of interest capitalizes on the natural interrelatedness of the language arts, develops skills as they are needed in meaningful situations, contributes to individual pupil needs, and develops independence in study.

Educational research and teaching experience indicate that skills are learned more efficiently when they are put to some real use—learning to spell words used in an invitation or announcement, reading to get information needed in a unit, or speaking clearly and distinctly in reporting an actual experience to the class. After a visit to the zoo, a group of children can have many desirable learning experiences such as writing stories, dramatizing events, and sharing ideas. Separate periods for drill may be scheduled when needed.

The unified program makes it possible to adjust activities to a wide range of abilities and interests. The slow-learning pupil as well as the extremely talented one can make individual contributions to the activity without having to be rated in terms of the accomplishments of others. Since the unit involves a variety of activities, each child can work at a task which is recognizable by the group as a unique contribution. When textbooks prove too difficult for some pupils, as they frequently are, the opportunity to work with many types of material from many sources offers a solution to the problem of individual differences. The additional interest shown by children in the unit type of program leads to greater effort and more independent habits of work.

SITUATION 7.2   Talk with a primary elementary teacher and an intermediate teacher about activities they incorporate into their language arts programs to expand the four language regions: listening, speaking, reading, writing. What are some of the more effective activities they have experienced with learners?

LISTENING

Listening, the fundamental communication region, is in some respects a more difficult process to master than reading. Children have no control over the rate at which they must listen; they do not have the page before them so that they can go back and reexamine ideas; and the language to which they listen is not always as well organized as that which they read. Nevertheless, the listening skills are vitally important—research has shown that children in the elementary grades spend more than one-half of the school day engaged in listening activities.

Teachers have always given a great deal of attention to teaching the child to read, but they are just beginning to realize that a carefully planned program for helping the child learn to listen effectively is also essential. There has been very little research concerning the teaching of listening and the skills of listening. In 1953, the first standardized test of listening was published; in 1957, the first book. For example, within a twelve-page listing of instructional materials and products released since January 1974, only four items mention listening in the statements describing their use and purpose.[2] In school, as well as in life outside the school, listening is one of the principal avenues for learning. When children enter school, they have already had a considerable amount of experience in listening, but they must be taught to listen purposefully, accurately, and responsively. The situations in which children need to listen effectively begin with kindergarten, and increase in number and intensity as they proceed through the elementary school.

Listening is an integral part of the modern language arts program. The kindergarten child learns to listen to directions given by the teacher, to stories that are read or told, and to music. Speech development requires careful listening if the child is to learn to pronounce words correctly. Development in reading and spelling depends upon the ability to listen carefully and to identify sounds with words. Children must be good listeners to enjoy poetry fully, to participate in conversations, debates, panels, and forums, and to evaluate ideas presented by speakers.

[2] Hilda Stauffer, "New Materials on the Market," *The Reading Teacher*, Vol. XXIX, No. 5 (February 1976), pp. 474–485.

The skills of listening are not well defined. It appears that those who write about these skills apply them as they would the selected skills of reading—that is, recall; comprehension; sequence; inference; critical and creative listening; and similar aspects. There are basic parallels between listening and reading; both are receptive skills and both are dependent upon experience to determine the quality and quantity of meanings. Some of the basic differences between listening and reading are (1) listening skills are developed before reading skills; (2) listening skills are utilized to develop models which are reproduced and imitated in a different language form—speech; (3) the preliminary measurements of listening levels of elementary children show them to be significantly higher than reading levels; (4) listening does not receive the teaching emphasis that reading does; (5) authorities recommend that reading and listening are important, yet have provided only reading curricula. A fundamental inconsistency seems to exist between the words of the experts of language arts and their actions. They stress listening as a prerequisite area to successful reading, but have studied reading to draw implications about listening.

Listening functions not only in the school, but in family life, social life, and business as well. Life situations that require the ability to listen include attending church, the movies, lectures and concerts, listening to the radio or television, using the telephone, and engaging in conversation. What the individual derives from these and many other activities depends largely upon the ability to listen well, to evaluate, and to use what has been learned.

Several factors influence the effectiveness of listening. Hearing is as important for listening as seeing is for reading. If the hearing of the child is impaired, the teacher must see that school and community health services are utilized to remedy the defects, if that is possible, and alter classroom seating arrangements to place the child in the best position for hearing. Physical factors in the classroom environment—such as temperature, noises from the street, or persons moving about in the room—may hinder listening. The teacher should make every effort to provide a classroom environment that is conducive to effective listening.

Even if the child does not have hearing defects and the classroom is conducive to listening, a carefully planned program of instruction is necessary if the child is to learn to listen effectively. Listening is not a separate subject to be added to the curriculum—it is a skill to be developed in relation to many aspects of the elementary school program. The school assembly programs, radio and television programs, oral reports, dramatizations, recordings and transcriptions, musical programs, sound films, announcements, and discussion groups provide opportunities for developing good listening.

The following suggestions for developing more effective listening in elementary schools may be useful:

1. Make listening an integral part of the curriculum in the language arts, social studies, science, music, and other areas.

2. The primary source of noise in the classroom is the floor. Carpet may be far more important for a good listening environment than acoustical ceilings.

3. Provide a classroom environment that is conducive to good listening by attending to temperature, seating, and the reduction of noises as well as by making certain that children are prepared to listen before anything is presented orally.

4. Develop listening readiness by relating the material to previous experiences of pupils, teaching the meaning of new words needed, and stimulating questions.

5. Help pupils develop a purpose for listening, such as listening for enjoyment, finding answers to questions, or finding flaws in an argument.

6. Suit the material to the maturity level, attention span, and previous experiences of children.

7. Provide guidance for pupils in reproducing, summarizing, and explaining what they have heard.

8. Help pupils evaluate the programs to which they listen, to detect malicious propaganda, half-truths, and false claims.

9. Teach pupils the importance of courteous listening for effective group relationships.

10. Make radio, television, and tape listening a valuable part of the curriculum by selecting programs carefully, using programs to motivate regularly scheduled lessons, and planning follow-up activities.

11. Use commercially prepared materials and equipment which are designed to promote purposeful listening, such as the listening stations and Russell's *Listening Aids through the Grades*.[3]

12. Develop an awareness and tolerance for the assumption: "It is reasonable that I be misunderstood."

13. Provide experiences with the following language activities:
    a. The listener must paraphrase the meaning of the speaker to the speaker's satisfaction before adding to the communication.
    b. The teacher should make a tape of a group's discussion and then transcribe the tape. Separate the transcription into contributions by speakers, scramble them, and then invite group members to reconstruct the discussion in the order of the original contributions.
    c. Have the participants take time to unravel the miscommunications that are often the basis for disagreements.
    d. The teacher should be a model of good listening habits. The teacher should listen, to audit the pupil's frame of references; look at the speaker; use the differences between the speed of thinking and listening to think about the speaker; recognize the listening skills that are depressed when strong emotions are aroused; and try harder.

---

[3] David H. and Elizabeth F. Russell, *Listening Aids through the Grades.* (New York: Teachers College Press, 1959).

Until more is known about listening, the teacher must work to establish good listening-habit patterns and develop listening behaviors like those of reading: recalling, sequencing, interpreting, comprehending, and so on. But most importantly, the listening area must be regarded as the area in which the largest number and greatest shadings of meaning are available to the learner. These meanings provide the foundation for the skills that will become available to the learner in the areas of speaking, reading, and writing.

Some additional guidelines for utilizing and relating listening behaviors to other areas of language are found in the answers to the following questions:

1. Can the pupils listen for and recognize the inappropriate words, sounds, constructions, and meanings being reproduced in their speaking area? Until a speaking difficulty is audited through listening by the speaker, the odds are that the difficulty will continue.

2. Can pupils listen to their own reading? Do the listening skills serve as a check and balance of the words and meanings being received through reading? A pupil who miscalls a word while reading, and recognizes the error through listening, is apt to correct the error.

3. Can pupils use their listening areas to recognize the appropriate usages for written language? Through auditing a situation, the learner adjusts personal language constructions and vocabulary so that they are appropriate to the situation. Until errors in oral usage are heard, the drilling of correct usage in the written form of language is nonproductive.

These three guidelines are predicated upon the premise that listening is the first language area, and that speech is derived from the models existing in that area. Therefore, listening should serve as the primary guiding and modeling system in language.

SITUATION 7.3   The importance of listening skills has been recognized by educators, and instruction in these skills should constitute a significant portion of the curriculum in the modern elementary school. What are the outcomes to be realized through the development of adequate listening skills?

SPEAKING

Speech and speaking is the first productive and second language system to occur. Speech is apparently rooted in and generated from the meanings and experiences decoded by the receptive language form of listening. Children speak the language in which they are immersed.

In learning to speak, a child reproduces the grammar of the listening environment. The child also, ". . . formulates the semantic relationships with the real world, the internal and conceptual linguistic relations of an abstract world, the syntactic patterns of grammar, and the phonological rules by which meaning is communicated through speech."[4] This miraculous development occurs without formal instruction!

What may appear to the adult as errors in the child's speech may be accurate reproductions of what has been received through listening in a particular environment, or by global generalizations that have not yet been refined by the child. The refinement occurs as the child learns to speak by talking with others and making adjustments in the grammatical system guided by the feedback of the interaction. This is truly a "learning to do by doing" procedure. Perhaps that is why formal teaching in these early stages is not needed. What is needed are people in the environment who act and interact with the "doings" (talking) of the learner. The importance of the spoken word in influencing the social behavior of people, in improving human relations, and in living and working together is recognized more clearly than ever before. Modern world leaders have proved how powerful the spoken word may be in influencing the minds of men and in improving group action. The voices of the President of the United States and other leaders can be heard by millions of people; their speeches and interviews appear throughout the world. The spoken word can be a tool of power and grace, if the idea is vital and it is presented attractively.

Oral language is important also from the standpoint of the development of the child. Language plays an important part in helping children understand the world around them, work and play effectively with others, and gain satisfaction through self-expression.

Much progress has been made in recent years in developing programs in oral language in terms of what is known about children. From the evidence available, it is clear that the key to language development is enriched experience; that language is a part of the child's general pattern of development; and that we should not ask children to speak about things they do not understand. It is clear also that a child's speaking is an indication of personal adjustment, and that improvement in speaking may depend more upon finding and removing the causes of frustration and conflict than upon extra drill.

Children of elementary school age are normally keenly interested in language; the proof of this is found in the eagerness with which they pick up slang and other colorful expressions. They are interested in developing new skills which will give them status in the group and help them become persons in their own right. Developing skills and understanding in oral language can therefore be a joyous adventure for both the teacher and the pupils if the natural desire for learning is not inhibited by formal processes.

Purposes of the Oral Language Program

The first step in improving the program in oral language is a clear understanding of the purposes of the program. The following purposes are mentioned frequently in courses of study and curriculum guides:

---

[4] Kenneth Hoskison and Bernadette Krohm, "Reading by Immersion: Assisted Reading," in Iris M. Tiedt (Ed.), *What's New in Reading*. (Urbana, Ill.: National Council for Teachers of English, 1974), p. 24.

1. To provide an atmosphere that will encourage the child to speak freely about experiences in daily living
2. To provide opportunities for cooperative group undertakings, personality development, and satisfaction in school work
3. To encourage originality and variety of expression
4. To develop the desire for a rich vocabulary to meet individual, vocational, and social needs
5. To develop the habit of accurate observation, to make the child conscious of the richness of his experience, and to encourage him to express his ideas and emotions

Suggestions for Improving Oral Language Instruction

Modern courses of study and curriculum guides for elementary schools contain many suggestions for enriching the oral language experiences of children. The following suggestions are among those commonly listed:

1. Growth in language is fostered by a classroom environment that permits face-to-face relationships, provides stimulating materials, and maintains a relaxed, informal atmosphere.

2. Rows of seats screwed to the floor, rigid time schedules, and artificial learning activities centering around drill are detrimental to language development.

3. The teacher who has faith in the children's capabilities and knows how to enlist their cooperation can do a great deal to improve the learning environment in any type of classroom.

4. In the primary grades the amount of time to oral expression should be greater than that given to written expression.

5. The personality of the child, the influence of the language in the home, and the child's need for security and satisfaction are taken into account in the oral language program.

6. Conversation, choral speaking, dramatization, and creative expression are emphasized along with the more formal procedures for developing language skills.

7. The time needed for drill on mechanics is lessened by providing frequent opportunities for use in meaningful situations. What drill is needed is provided in close connection with significant speaking situations.

8. Remedial work in usage is based upon a record of the child's own usage errors.

9. Opportunities are provided for individual and group evaluation of progress under the guidance of the teacher. Instead of coming after a unit has been completed, evaluation of progress goes on continuously as an integral part of the teaching-learning process.

Recommended Forms of Oral Expression

An examination of curriculum guides for elementary schools indicates that the following forms of oral expression are emphasized:

1. Informal conversation
2. Purposeful discussion
3. Messages, announcements, and reports
4. Dramatic play
5. Choral speech
6. Observance of social amenities
7. Storytelling, jokes, and riddles
8. Giving and following directions
9. Club meetings
10. Using the telephone

The importance of oral expression cannot be overemphasized. It has been estimated that the average person talks at least a hundred times for every time the individual reads or writes. Moreover, when the teacher helps the child build acceptable speech patterns, the teacher is helping to increase the child's power to read and write.

In classrooms where there is a rich program of learning activities, it is rarely necessary for the teacher to set up artificial situations to encourage oral language expression. As children study about their social and physical world, they learn things they can share with another class, with the whole school in a school assembly, or with their parents at a parents' program. To prepare for the program, they must read to gather information and write reports; they must engage in class discussions to plan the program; there are invitations to write and permissions to secure. Finally, there is the program itself, and the presentation of reports or stories to the audience. Activities such as these are in contrast to the language class where children are assigned to write a composition on how electricity travels or about life in a feudal community.

Among the artificial situations set up to promote oral language development, many primary teachers include time in their daily schedule for "show and tell." Children are encouraged to bring in an interesting object from home, to show it to the class, and to tell about it. When children have something worthwhile to show and tell, they should indeed be encouraged to do so. Children who find a cocoon, an interesting shell, or a picture relating to what is being studied should share their find with the class. But it is questionable whether such a period should be regularly scheduled in the daily program. As a part of every school day, "show and tell" too often degenerates into a period when children will display objects of no interest to anyone, including themselves, just for the sake of having a turn. Meanwhile, the captive audience is enjoined by the teacher to sit still and listen politely.

A more real and functional situation to promote oral language development is a teacher-pupil planning session. During these sessions, the teacher and pupils plan, schedule, and record the sequencing and options of the day's activities. At the end of the day, a review and evaluation session could begin with "How well did our schedule work?"; and later, "What did we learn today?"

Language arts activities rarely need to be especially planned to give children practice in speaking. Later, activities such as creative writing and dramatics will foster more creative expression as well as language practice. At this stage, announcements, directions, and class discussions fill a practical value by communicating needed information. When the school day is full of significant learning activities, language is needed to carry them out, and oral language serves a legitimate purpose recognized by the class, and children are more easily motivated to improve their language expression.

This is not to say that all children's needs in oral expression can be taken care of in connection with other subjects. Separate periods are needed for remedial work; for vocabuary building; for direct instruction on how to express oneself more clearly, forcefully, correctly, and creatively. But in the modern language program such instruction is related to and grows out of the child's language needs in other areas; oral skills are not taught as ends in themselves.

Procedures for Relating Speaking, Reading, and Writing

The movement of the learner from effective oral communication to effective reading and written communication can be facilitated by the following procedures:

A. Aural-Oral Language Chart
   1. The learner has had concrete experiences with an object, event, or situation.
   2. The teacher transcribes the phrases and vocabularies of the learner's discussion. The transcription is done in a scramble system on the chalkboard, large-tablet chart paper, or "butcher" paper.
   3. The teacher transcribes because the teacher's writing skills more nearly match the oral skills of the learners; the learners' writing skills do not yet match their oral skills and therefore are not sufficient for the meanings to be transcribed.
   4. The learners see in written form the key phrases and vocabulary of their oral communication.
   5. By incorporating the scramble system (the scattering of the learners' phrases and words), the learners recognize that only parts of their oral communication is recorded; later, the teacher and learners can combine, classify, and compare different parts of the recorded words and phrases to sharpen and expand the written message.

B. Experience Chart
   1. An experience chart is a written description of a concrete experience around some organized theme: sequence, functions, people, objects, and so on.
   2. The experience chart is best derived from the phrases and vocabularies of an aural-oral language chart.
   3. The teacher then transcribes the sentences orally constructed by the learners, expressing the organizing theme. (See A-5).
   4. Many experience charts may be developed from one aural-oral language chart.

C. Reading Chart

　　1. A reading chart is constructed by the teacher from the experience charts. Each reading chart is organized to reinforce the practicing of a specific reading skill.

　　2. Many reading charts can be teacher-constructed from a single experience chart.

　　3. The sentence length and vocabulary is appropriate to the instructional reading level of the learners.

　　4. The reading chart is likely to be very short as compared to an experience chart.

Dramatic Activities

Dramatic activities that have valuable contributions to make to the language arts program include sociodramas, work with puppets, pageants, pantomimes, and tableaux.

Sociodrama centers around social experiences; children identify themselves completely with the characters they portray. They do not act parts as in dramatization; rather, they are the persons or things they represent. Before they reach school age, this is a favorite activity of children when they engage in playing house, playing school, or playing train. After they start school, they gradually gain a wider range of experiences and learn to carry on their sociodramas with a larger group of children under the direction of a teacher who knows how to use techniques that make the activity profitable and enjoyable. This activity is useful for pure enjoyment, for helping pupils develop emotionally, for revealing alternatives, for developing good conversation, and for providing an opportunity for learning related to the natural and social environment. If the teacher really understands young children, sociodramas will never be used for putting on a show, but simply to provide an opportunity for the children to do something that is interesting and worthwhile for themselves. As they begin to feel themselves a part of the school, children may want to perform for another class or grade.

In general, sociodrama is most suitable for children and increases in effectiveness as children grow older, especially as more mature social experiences are used as the theme. Certain types of equipment are essential for making the most effective use of sociodrama. Dolls, toy trains, toy airplanes, blocks of various sizes, and materials for improvising costumes are useful in providing experiences relating to familiar phases of everyday life.

Dramatization of familiar stories and poems begin in the primary grades, but it is particularly useful at the nine-year-old level and beyond. It is not imposed upon children by the teacher; rather, stories are dramatized because children like them. The teacher provides guidance for the children in planning and evaluating, but does not dominate the situation. The pupils are free to interpret the spirit of the story as they understand it, and are not forced to reproduce the exact language of the story.

A great deal of planning and organization takes place before the actual dramatization of a story. The teacher sees to it that all children participate and not just a few. The steps involved in dramatizing a story include reading and discussing the story, deciding whether the story lends itself to dramatization, listing characters, selecting equipment, selecting pupils to play the various parts, discussing the personalities of the characters in the story, preparing to dramatize the story by getting better acquainted with the action and conversation of the characters, dramatizing the story, making individual and group evaluations, and replaying the story.

Puppet and show plays provide an effective release for tensions of the inhibited child and enable the timid child to express feelings more freely because of the separation from the audience by a screen. Hand puppets made from clothespins, wooden jump figures manipulated by strings, shadow puppets made from cardboard mounted on sticks, stuffed puppets, and marionettes controlled by strings are types that can be used successfully by elementary school children.

Pageants, pantomimes, and tableaux are other types of dramatics that are adapted to use in elementary schools. They provide enjoyable experiences for children, foster creative expression, and develop facility in the enrichment of the oral language.

Role playing is also an excellent dramatic activity within a modern elementary classroom. This procedure enables a pupil to act out his perceptions and stereotypes of events and people while being protected through the role of an "actor." Alternative solutions can be played out as well as the different perceptions of the pupils.

Second Language Programs

The introduction of instruction in a second language into the curriculum of the modern elementary school was one of the most rapidly developing movements of the early 1960s. The movement has now experienced a severe depression, as most schools have now dropped a second language from the curriculum. But, as Richards, an educational consultant in California, said in 1975, ". . . many schools have begun to establish programs to teach a second language."[5]

During the late 1950s and early 1960s when the movement was at its zenith, the following reasons for offering a second language in the elementary school were given:

1. Promotes appreciation and understanding of other cultures and broadening world understanding
2. Serves as a challenge for gifted children
3. "Language puberty" occurs after the age of 12, making the learning of a second language more difficult and artificial[6]
4. Ensures greater proficiency in foreign languages in high school
5. Improves pupil's command of English

[5] Regina G. Richards, "Singing: A Fun Route to a Second Language," *The Reading Teacher,* Vol. XXIX, No. 3 (December 1975), p. 283.
[6] Richards, p. 283.

6. Prepares for travel, work, and living outside the United States
7. Is consistent with the trends of the times
8. Creates more interest in other languages.[7]

The second-language programs in some elementary schools used certified language teachers, some used native speakers but not certified teachers, but most programs utilized television, radio, tapes, listening centers, pictures, and printed materials to support the regular classroom teacher. The evidence was that the elementary child could, with some ease, learn a second language. The general methodology was to use an aural-oral approach to immerse the learner in a second language. The goal was speaking, not reading or writing. The elementary child was to become a truly bilingual speaker: a coordinate bilingual who can think and speak in the second language rather than a compound bilingual who translates into a native language for thinking and speaking. The aural-oral approach was, and is, patterned after the ways in which the first language is learned: listening to speaking.

Bilingual Programs

The U.S. Office of Education estimated that in the early 1970s there were at least five million children in schools who needed special language programs because English was not spoken in their homes. In Illinois, 141 different languages have been identified, while the 1974 annual student racial survey in Chicago indicated that the non-English speaking population in Chicago has been increasing 15 percent a year for the past four years.[8].

In 1970 the U.S. Supreme Court ruled that under Title VI of the Civil Rights Act of 1964, ". . . all school districts are compelled to provide children who speak little or no English with special language programs to give them an equal opportunity to an education."[9] Mandatory legislation requiring bilingual programs have been introduced in several states and passed by four: Massachusetts, Texas, Illinois, and New Jersey. The Department of Health, Education and Welfare provides funds to districts with a hundred or more Vietnamese children or where Vietnamese constitute 1 percent or more of the enrollment. Several organizations are sources of materials and information for bilingual bicultural programs: Center for Applied Linguistics, Washington, D.C.; School of Language and Linguistics, Georgetown University; National Council of Teachers of English, Urbana, Illinois; National Association for Bilingual Education, San Antonio, Texas.

In a typical bilingual, bicultural program, children are taught to read and write in their native language. Usually the non-English speaking children are assigned with English speaking children to such classes as art, music, and physical education. When the non-English speaking children have built an English speaking vocabulary through these and other associations, they begin

---

[7] Elizabeth Henson, "What About Teaching a Second Language to Elementary School Children?" *Childhood Education* (April 1958), pp. 367– 370.

[8] Laura S. Johnson, "Bilingual Bicultural Education: A Two-Way Street," *The Reading Teacher,* Vol. XXIX, No. 3 (December 1975), p. 234.

[9] Johnson, p. 234.

to receive instruction in English as a second language. The teaching of English as a second language follows the aural-oral approach. This approach was discussed in a previous section. When the non-English speaking children have an extensive English vocabulary and can read in their first language, they are first introduced to the reading and then the writing of English. In general, these bilingual bicultural programs are marvelously consistent with the oral language or language experience approaches recommended for the teaching of reading and writing to English speaking children.

Dialect Programs

Children with dialects (non-standard English forms of oral language) fail to learn to read with alarming frequency. Some of the more common dialects spoken are Black, Appalachian, Chicano, Puerto Rican, American Indian, Eskimo, and Hawaiian. The differences between the "in-school" language (standard English) and the "out-of-school" language (dialect) are apparently related to the high frequency of failure of children with dialects.

A common element of the programs planned for children with dialects is the provision of an experience in a language-enriched environment. Many objects, events, field trips, films, tapes, people, and other unfamiliar cultural accoutrements are brought into the school environment to immerse these children in both the new language (standard English) and experiences. Some programs continue this teaching of the dominant language until the child can be taught to read in standard English. Other programs introduce reading, but the children read the traditional reading materials in their own dialect. For example, a Black dialect speaker might read the standard English sentence, "Gene pointed to John" in dialect as "Gene point to John." The assumption is that this is a surface translation: for the reader-speakers to translate they must have comprehended (read) the standard English version. Studies indicate that when readers read orally in their own dialect, they understand the written version of the message and then translate the meaning into dialectal expression.[10] In a few cases, programs have been planned to utilize the materials written in the dialect of the pupils. William A. Stewart wrote:

> It's the night before Christmas and here in our house,
> It ain't nothing moving, not even no mouse.
> There go we-all stockings, hanging high up off the floor
> So Santa Claus can fill them up if he walk in through our door.[11]

The assumptions of these programs utilizing dialect-specific materials is that the dialect reader would have greater predictability for reading and that reading would "sound like" oral language.

Research studies do not yet provide strong data supporting that any one of

---

[10] Yetta Goodman and Rudine Sims, "Whose Dialect for Beginning Readers?" in Iris M. Tiedt (Ed.), *What's New in Reading*, p. 30.
[11] Nila Benton Smith, "Cultural Dialects: Current Problems and Solutions," *The Reading Teacher*, Vol. XXIX, No. 2 (November 1975), p. 140.

these three program approaches possesses a significant advantage. The common element, the language experience approach, and the recommendation of authorities seem to imply that an experience in a language-enriched environment is the fundamental ingredient. The second fundamental element seems to be teacher attitudes toward dialect-speaking learners. If the attitude of the teacher is not supportive to a developing a positive self-concept, then the dialect-speaker-learner has "bought it!"

SITUATION 7.4   List five activities which would expand the experiences of children from language-deficient backgrounds or language environments inconsistent with "in school" language instruction.

READING

When Voltaire posed for himself the question of who is to lead mankind, he remarked, "Those who know how to read and write." In one of his letters, Thomas Jefferson once wrote, "People who can read can be free because reading banishes ignorance and superstition." World leaders consider the ability to read of extreme importance, because they realize that the nations which really lead are those where the literacy level is high. James E. Allen, Jr., when U.S. Commissioner of Education, stated, ". . . we should immediately set for ourselves the goal of assuring that by the end of the 1970s the right to read shall be a reality for all—that no one shall be leaving our schools without the skill and the desire necessary to read to the full limits of his capability."[12]

Teaching children to read has always been one of the most important responsibilities of the elementary school. Every child needs to become fully competent in reading in order to succeed in school and to discharge responsibilities as a citizen of a democratic society. A citizen who reads has the capacity to actively participate in the continuity of learning.

Reading is the foundation of much of the enjoyment the individual gets out of life, and is closely related to vocational efficiency. Reading is intimately related to the success of the democratic way of life. Citizens need to understand the meaning of democracy and to keep well enough informed to act wisely in its behalf. They need the abilities to detect pernicious propaganda, to weigh the opinions of others, to talk intelligently, and to work effectively with others.

Since the child needs considerable ability in reading in order to succeed in school, since the adult in our society needs to do a great deal of reading both as a leisure activity and in order to keep abreast vocationally, and since the success of our democratic way of life depends to a great extent upon the ability of citizens to read, it is understandable that much attention has been devoted to the improvement of reading instruction.

---

[12] James E. Allen, Jr., "The Right to Read—Target for the 70's," *Journal of Reading* (November 1969), pp. 95–101.

The language arts of reading and writing have served the human race as the great time-binders. Through these language arts, the human race has the tools to transmit to each succeeding generation. Before these arts of reading and writing became generally available, information could be learned only from those people and experiences present within a particular time and place; listening and speaking were the time-binders, and both required proximity. Through reading, time can be spanned between the reader and persons in whatever time, place, or culture learnings were gained. Figuratively, reading allows one to listen to the wisdom and people of the ages. This is the overreaching goal of the teacher of reading—to enable each person to be a time-binder.

Objectives

The objectives of a modern reading program include extending and enriching the experience of the child; broadening interests and tastes in reading; fostering the personal social adjustment of the child; providing worthwhile recreational interests and skills; encouraging critical analysis of ideas; developing resourcefulness in locating information; promoting self-direction; and achieving satisfactory progress in such basic reading skills as word recognition, vocabulary development, comprehension, and speed. If these objectives are to be realized, the sequence of the reading program must be extended beyond the elementary school into high school and college, and attention must be given to reading in every phase of the school program rather than merely at specified periods.

Approaches to the Teaching of Reading

It is difficult for adults to realize how complicated a task it is for a child to learn to walk, to learn to talk, or to learn to read. Learning to read is not a simple process. After learning to talk, perhaps learning to read is the most diffi-

Reading, like language, is very personal and private; yet, at times, it must be shared.

cult and complex task the child encounters in the process of growing up. It is not surprising, therefore, to find that many children have difficulty in learning to read, that high school and college youth are frequently handicapped by low reading abilities, and that many adults do very little reading.

Historical Approaches

The evolution of methods of teaching beginning reading constitutes an interesting study. This problem has received such extensive treatment elsewhere that detailed discussion here would be needless repetition.[13] It should be useful, however, to briefly review earlier methods of teaching reading, as a background for understanding current methods. Also, a look at the practices used in the past which have proved to be undesirable and ineffective may encourage educators to avoid further excesses, to have respect for practices which have been of lasting value, and to reject the revival of practices which have proved fallacious. Schreiner and Tanner discussed in more detail the history of reading teaching.[14]

ALPHABET METHOD

For many centuries, the first step in learning to read was memorization of the letters of the alphabet. The importance attached to learning the letters of the alphabet is demonstrated in the account of a Greek who purchased twenty-five slaves for his son, giving each slave the name of a letter of the alphabet; Quintilian, the Roman philosopher, urged that children be given ivory alphabet blocks in order to learn the letters. It has been said that the Hebrew child centuries ago was given edible letters covered with honey to discover "how sweet the process of learning could be."

During colonial times, the content of the first books children were supposed to read was far removed from the experiences and concepts. of children. The *New England Primer* was used during this period, and the content was based on the religious and moral goals of the times, while the method continued to emphasize the learning of the alphabet. This *primer* contained such sentences as, "In Adam's fall we sinned all," and "Peter denied his Lord, and cryed." Around 1776 another emphasis became apparent in the teaching of reading: The influence of the patriot orators resulted in much emphasis on oral reading in an eloquent manner with accompanying gestures. In Webster's *American Spelling Book,* published about 1800, reading was to be taught as spelling. First the letters were learned separately; then they were put together to form syllables; syllables were combined to form words; words were combined to form sentences; and, finally, sentences were combined to form a short story. The student

---

[13] See Nila Banton Smith, *American Reading Instruction.* (Newark, Del.: International Reading Association, Inc., 1965); Lillian Gray, *Teaching Children to Read,* 3d ed. (New York: The Ronald Press Company, 1963), chap. 3; Gertrude Hildreth, *Learning the Three R's,* 2d ed. (New York: Educational Publishers, 1947), chap. 8; and William S. Gray, *On Their Own in Reading.* (Glenview, Ill.: Scott, Foresman and Company, 1948), chap. 1.

[14] Robert Schreiner and Linda R. Tanner, "What History Says about Teaching Reading," *The Reading Teacher,* Vol. XXIX, No. 5 (February 1976), pp. 468–473.

had to learn the spelling and pronunciation of long lists of words before given the opportunity of reading sentences. The sentences which occasionally accompanied the lists of words were usually unrelated to each other. Only after many months and possibly years of instruction could the student encounter reading material in story form. Around 1840, the *McGuffey Eclectic Readers* were published. These were of particular significance in that they were the first set of graded readers for children, and the stories were more interesting and appropriate to the children. However, the instructional method used continued to be that of the alphabet–spelling method.

WORD METHOD

The first serious threat to the alphabet–spelling method was promoted by Horace Mann about 1840. After traveling abroad to examine various educational systems, Mann began a crusade for teaching reading by the word method. He contended that letters conveyed no meaning to the child and that emphasis should be placed on the word as a unit which was meaningful. Obviously, there are faults in the word method because the reader has no means for analyzing words which are not recognized by sight. However, Mann's contribution was great in that for the first time attention was focused on gaining meaning from the printed symbols.

SYNTHETIC PHONIC METHOD

Both the alphabet–spelling method and the word method of teaching beginning reading were replaced by the phonetic method. Instead of learning the letters or entire words first, children were introduced to the sounds that occur in many words; words with similar sounds were arranged in vertical columns, and most of the reading program was consumed by formal practice on sounds. These sessions were sometimes referred to as "hiss and spit" or "huff and puff" sessions. During this period (1870–1917) the material read consisted primarily of the classics. The purpose was to develop our culture through an emphasis on appreciation of literature. Also, all reading was done orally, as had been a custom from the time our country was settled.

Reaction against Traditional Methods

With the advent of World War I, many young men were examined for induction into the armed services. The *Army Alpha* tests were administered, and the results indicated that numbers of young men had inferior silent-reading skills. A reaction against phonics, oral reading, and literary materials began in the 1920s and reached fanatic extremes in the early 1930s. It was claimed that no systematic teaching of reading by any method was necessary if the child was interested in learning to read, and that "the best way to teach reading was not to teach it at all."

By 1940 the failure of unplanned, haphazard procedures for teaching beginning reading became apparent, and parents as well as teachers began to insist that greater attention be given to the development of basic reading programs for the purpose of giving the child more independence in attacking new words.

Developmental reading programs today include a systematic presentation of skills for mastering new words. The modern reading program includes not only a variety of skills for identifying words—sight, visual context clues, verbal context clues, phonetic and structural analysis—but is also designed to teach the student to apply the skill which provides the most rapid means for identifying a word. At the preprimer level of reading, the teacher directs the pupil's attention to structural elements of a word—its root, suffixes, and word parts in a compound word. Children learn to read words ending in -s, -ed, and -ing when the root word is known. They also learn to read words like "something" and "firehouse" which are made up of familiar words.

At the primer level, when the child has built a small sight vocabulary the teacher begins instruction on certain sound elements. Consonants such as b, d, l, s, and p, which do not vary in sound when they begin a word, are taught first. These are taught as children encounter difficulty; obviously if they know the sound a letter represents (and many bright children make this association for themselves), they do not need instruction on the sound. Instruction at the primer level also includes consonant blends (bl, fr, for example) and double consonants that represent a single consonant sound (ch, sh, th). Structural analysis is continued along with this type of phonetic analysis.

Beyond the primer level, various types of vowel elements are introduced. These include single-vowel letters (a as in "hat"), two-vowel letters (oo as in "good"), and diphthongs (ou as in "house"). At this introductory stage, only one-syllable words are analyzed.

At higher levels of word analysis, the pupil learns to identify a syllable, the syllable or syllables receiving stress, and to apply to each syllable in a word the phonetic skills learned at preceding levels. Additional phonetic skills are also taught—the variant pronunciations of vowels and how to determine the sound to be associated with a vowel or vowel combination.

From this brief overview of word-analysis skills, the reader can see that in order to attack a new word, the pupils must have more skills in their possession than mere knowledge of the sound to be associated with a particular letter. This fact is not always understood by critics, who urge the schools to return to an alphabet approach to teaching reading. These critics would have the teacher first teach one of the sounds associated with the letter a, then the letter b, and so on through the rest of the alphabet.

Learning to read by the alphabet system is very difficult, and when it was in vogue many children failed to learn to read. Consider the first letter to be taught, the letter a. It may have one of five different sounds: a, ā, ä, à, ə. Eventually, children should be able to associate the correct sounds with these letters as they meet them in such varied spellings as hat, āte, fäther, dàw, and banana (bənanə). However, the modern program of word analysis teaches the simplest, least variable sounds first, regardless of their alphabetical order, and proceeds step by careful step to more difficult levels. Such a program is psychological more valid than one that introduces sound elements with no regard for their complexity and regularity.

Current Approaches to Teaching Reading

There is a multitude of approaches to beginning instruction in reading. Seven approaches which are currently used in school systems have been selected for brief treatment here. These include the basal reader approach, the experience chart approach, the individualized reading approach, the language-experience approach, the linguistics approach, the phonics approach, and the regularized code-alphabet approach.

BASAL READER APPROACH

Although the emphasis varies from one series of basal readers to another, every series is intended to help build a reading vocabulary, develop an interest in books, increase skills in word recognition, grasp the meaning of what is read, acquire study skills, and develop oral and silent reading skills. The beginning readers contain many pictures of children engaged in a variety of activities. The content is centered around the conversations of children. Pupils look at the pictures, discuss them, and develop a basic sight vocabulary. This approach generally known as the "look-say" approach. New words are introduced gradually and repeated frequently to encourage mastery at sight. As the

One of the many paths toward learning to read.

children develop a better understanding of time and space, the range of topics is broadened to include stories of events in distant places and in the past. Pupils are taught to recognize the sounds associated with letters, combinations of letters, and whole words, but instruction is not limited to these devices. As Gates has stated, "The aim is to give the pupil a kit of many tools, not just one, with which to deal with all types of word recognition problems that he will encounter."[15] Austin and Morrison identified the role of basal readers as follows:

When properly used, the basal readers serve as a springboard from a skills-development program to reading books in the classroom, school, or public library for pleasure and information.[16]

Sheldon[17] identified some of the possible advantages and disadvantages of their use.

Advantages
1. The manuals prepared for most basal series provide the teacher with remarkable aids to instruction.
2. A value of the basal series is the carefully prepared practice materals.
3. The basal books are carefully prepared in terms of an increase in difficulty related to aspects of learning to read.

Disadvantages
1. Basal readers are not universally applicable to children of the grade level for which they are designed.
2. The basal readers of the 1940s and 1950s seemed to have been designed for the children of an essentially middle-class suburban society.
3. In the past, the concept and vocabulary load of the first and second grades was too light for able children.
4. Basal readers are virtually uni-dialect (standard English).
5. Basal reader stories usually concern noncontroversial topics.

EXPERIENCE CHART APPROACH

The use of experience charts is founded on the principle that children's first reading experiences should be based on their actual experiences. Before books are introduced, pupils are encouraged to relate interesting experiences which they have had (preferably an outgrowth of a common experience in which all have shared, such as a class field trip), the teacher records the "stories" on the chalkboard or a chart, and pupils read the stories to recognize words, phrases, and sentences. Later, the stories are transferred from the chalkboard or chart to a booklet that is kept on the library table in the classroom. These experi-

---

15 Arthur I. Gates, "The Teaching of Reading—Objective Evidence versus Opinion," *Phi Delta Kappan* (February 1962), p. 200.

16 Mary C. Austin and Coleman Morrison, *The First R: The Harvard Report on Reading in the Elementary Schools.* (New York: Crowell Collier and Macmillan, Inc., 1963), p. 22.

17 William D. Sheldon, "Basal Reading Programs: How Do They Stand Today?" in Nila Banton Smith (Ed.), *Current Issues in Reading*, Proceedings of the International Reading Association, Vol. 13, Part 2, 1969, pp. 295–299.

ence stories may be planned so that they contain the basic sight words that are found in the preprimers.

Some possible advantages and disadvantages of the use of experience charts are as follows:

Advantages
1. The experiences which the children have had can be made more meaningful by preparing charts for reading and discussion.
2. The stories are more interesting to the children because they are about their experiences.
3. Understanding is present because the vocabulary is that of the children.
4. Children have the opportunity to acquire a broader reading vocabulary in that the vocabulary is not controlled.
5. The relationships between the expressive (speaking and writing) language skills and the receptive (reading and listening) language skills become evident as the children participate in the preparation of the experience story.
6. There are no restrictions on the content which may be used as a basis for the story.

Disadvantages
1. Vocabulary is not controlled, and the children may not learn any of the words when too many are introduced.
2. The relationships between the receptive and expressive language skills can become evident without writing stories.
3. The better students will usually control the content of the story and may suggest vocabulary which is not meaningful to many of the children.
4. The teacher must spend much time helping the students develop an experience story and may be derelict in other areas of the curriculum.
5. The experience stories are not as interesting to children as other well-written stories with different content.
6. A lack of carefully controlled practice materials, aids to instruction, and a planned sequence for increases in difficulty may nullify the value of experience charts.[18]

Although there are numerous objections to the use of experience charts as the primary or sole method for teaching reading, there is unquestionable merit in their use in conjunction with other materials and instructional methodologies. The reader may wish to relate this approach to part B of the list previously given in the section "Procedures for Relating Speaking, Reading, and Writing."

INDIVIDUALIZED READING APPROACH

This approach has sometimes been called the "self-selection" approach. However, it is based on three developmental characteristics of children: seeking, self-selection, and pacing. Children "seek" those experiences from their

---

[18] Sheldon, pp. 295–299.

environments which are appropriate to their maturity and needs, "select" for themselves those activities or books which are of interest and in which they can experience success, and "pace" or progress at their own rates. More specifically, pupils select from a wide variety of books available in the classroom the ones they want to read. The available books should include a variety of topics and a range of reading levels. The teacher has an individual conference with each pupil, during which a check is made on word recognition, vocabulary development, comprehension, and other phases of learning to read. Records are kept of the difficulties of each pupil, and the teacher may provide individual instruction or may group children with common difficulties for instructional purposes. A sharing time is arranged during which pupils interchange with other members of the class interesting items from the books they have read. Effective use of this approach requires teachers who are particularly competent in the fields of child development, children's literature, and evaluation of pupil learnings in reading.[19]

The following list of advantages and disadvantages of the individualized approach to reading instruction is based on longer lists developed by Sartain.[20]

Advantages
1. The reading material can be the best of children's literature rather than being limited to a set of textbooks.
2. It is possible to capitalize on each child's special interests and unique background of experiences.
3. The child can progress at an individual rate.
4. The child's available learning time can be utilized instead of sitting and listening while different children struggle with oral reading of some of the selections.
5. The individual conference is personalized rather than mechanical—it provides an opportunity for the development of human traits and values which are unique in the individual and which are fostered by personal interaction.
6. The individual conference has special appeal for the children.
7. Children seem to develop more favorable attitudes toward reading, so they usually read more books.

Disadvantages
1. Children may have difficulty selecting a book of the appropriate level to stimulate progress.
2. There are few opportunities to develop readiness for reading a new selection—motivation, background information, and techniques for attacking new vocabulary.

[19] See Jeannette Veatch, *Individualizing Your Reading Program*. (New York: G. P. Putnam's Sons, 1959); and Walter S. Barbe, *Educator's Guide to Personalized Reading Instruction*. (Englewood Cliffs, N.J.: Prentice-Hall, Inc., 1961).
[20] Harry W. Sartain, "What Are the Advantages and Disadvantages of Individualized Instruction?" in Nila Banton Smith (Ed.), *Current Issues in Reading*, Proceedings of the International Reading Association, Vol. 13, Part 2 (1969), pp. 328–343.

3. There is no systematic procedure for gradual introduction or repetition of the vocabulary and concepts that are being learned.
4. The conscientious teacher feels a great deal of time pressure in trying to complete profitably as many conferences as necessary in a day.
5. There is some doubt about the adequacy and permanence of skill learnings that are developed in brief, infrequent conferences.
6. There is a danger that children will not read enough different types of books to broaden their literary interests.
7. There is little opportunity for group interaction of the type needed to develop critical thinking and to refine literary tastes.

LANGUAGE EXPERIENCE APPROACH

This approach puts into practice what has been emphasized earlier in the text, the interrelationships among the various communication skills.[21] Recognizing that success in reading is influenced by spoken vocabulary, the teacher encourages the pupils to express their thoughts orally, to paint, and to use other means of expression. Emphasis is placed on pupil-prepared reading materials.

Some possible advantages and disadvantages of this approach are:

Advantages
1. It develops a high interest in learning to read and encourages the integration of the communication skills.
2. It fosters creative expression.
3. It helps develop independence in making choices.
4. Representing speech sounds with the printed symbols places phonics in a natural and appropriate role in language development.
5. Children can begin to read with the vocabulary they have developed in the home and community.
6. The reading vocabulary is much greater than that found in basal reader series.

Disadvantages
1. There is no evidence that children can easily make the transition into reading materials prepared by others.
2. Teachers may not be fully aware of the reading skills that are important to develop at any given stage of learning to read.
3. Memorization of words may be mistaken for reading.
4. Teachers may fail to correct errors of spelling, punctuation, and language, which may later result in habits difficult to eliminate.

[21] See Elaine C. Vilscek (Ed.), *A Decade of Innovations: Approaches to Beginning Reading*, Proceedings of the International Reading Association, Vol. 12, Part 3, 1968; R. V. Allen, "The Language-Experience Approach," in Joe L. Frost (Ed.), *Issues and Innovations in the Teaching of Reading*. (Glenview, Ill.: Scott, Foresman and Company, 1967), pp. 171–180; and Doris M. Lee and R. V. Allen, *Learning to Read through Experience*, 2d ed. (New York: Appleton-Century-Crofts, 1963).

LINGUISTICS APPROACH

In recent years, linguists have become interested in applying the knowledge gained from studying the English language to the teaching of reading. Two schools of linguistic scientists have focused their attention on the improvement of reading instruction: structuralists, those who emphasize word order, word function, word groups that modify, expand, or change expressions, and intonation; and phonologists, those who recommend that reading be taught as a process of translating basic sounds into words.[22] Materials for reading instruction have been designed after either of these schools of linguists. Most, if not all, of these materials are arranged into a graded set of materials in the same format as the basal reader series. The principal differences are in the content and methods for developing the reading skills. At the present time, there is not sufficient evidence concerning the usefulness of the linguistic approach to evaluate future benefits which may accrue through improvement and experimentation. Materials designed by phonologists will provide for developing word-attack skills, but may sacrifice comprehension; whereas materials designed by structuralists will place emphasis on the development of meaning and the understanding of the material read.

Advantages
1. A description of language is an essential basis for understanding reading processes.
2. An intonational basis for teaching comprehension and word-recognition skills is provided.
3. An expanded basis for the utility of context clues; semantic and linguistic structures are built into this approach.

Disadvantages
1. A description of language is not an all-inclusive basis for understanding reading.
2. Reading is more than a process of decoding print into speech.
3. There exists disagreement among the linguists as to what basics of language are significant for understanding reading.

PHONICS APPROACH

Many varieties of the phonics approach are in use in modern schools. Indeed, Heilman stated that "there are no nonphonetic methods in use in America today."[23] A comparison of the phonics program presented in the basal readers with that presented by one of the leading publishers of materials to be used in the separate phonics approach revealed that the principal differences

---

[22] See Leonard Bloomfield and C. L. Barnhart, *Let's Read.* (Detroit: Wayne State University Press, 1961); Charles C. Fries, *Linguistics and Reading.* (New York: Holt, Rinehart and Winston, 1963); and Carl A. Lefevre, *Linguistics and the Teaching of Reading.* (New York: McGraw Hill, Inc., 1964).

[23] Arthur W. Heilman, *Principles and Practices of Teaching Reading.* (Columbus, Ohio: Charles E. Merrill Books, Inc., 1961), p. 241.

lay in the timing of systematic instruction in phonics, the amount of time devoted to it in the first grade, and the sequence in which the phonic skills are introduced. The separate phonics program presents to children the sounds of letters and the rules that apply to reading before they learn words by sight; the basal reader approach delays the study of these items until the latter part of the first grade or the beginning of the second grade. Austin and Morrison reported that one school system used a separate phonics approach which called for the introduction of all twenty-six letters of the alphabet on the first day. The program in phonics included seventy phonograms, thirteen phonic rules, and twenty-six spelling rules—most of which were to be taught in the first grade.[24]

A detailed analysis of the content of the program using the separate phonics approach is beyond the scope of this chapter. Several of the readings listed at the close of this chapter supply this information. (See Chall and Dallman.)

Some of the possible advantages and disadvantages of this approach are:

Advantages
1. Children can learn more in the area of phonics in the first grade than has been included in most of the basal reader series.
2. Learning the elements and generalizations of phonics gives children a tool which is useful in many reading situations.
3. Becoming independent in word recognition earlier eliminates the necessity for the rigidly controlled vocabulary and constant repetition found in many basal reader series.

Disadvantages
1. The approach incorporates a large amount of drill in the early stages. Many children reject this type of program.
2. Lack of attention to meaning and the emphasis on drill is dominant. Comprehension is not well-developed because of the emphasis on drill.
3. The children have little interest in reading because of the drill emphasis.
4. The approach may develop slow, laborious readers.
5. Numerous sounds must be taught for some codes.

REGULARIZED CODE–ALPHABET APPROACH

This approach originated from the complex and potentially confusing sound–symbol relationships of the traditional alphabet. Traditional orthography has twenty-six letters (symbols) to represent forty-four phonemes (sounds). The Initial Teaching Alphabet (ITA) approach uses a letter symbol for each sound, but ITA is a design of print for children's books and readers, and in fact is not necessarily a method of instruction. Instruction simply utilizes the ITA as a reading medium.

The Bullock report of 1975, published in Britain by the Department of Education and Science stated:

[24] Austin and Morrison, pp. 24–25.

There is no evidence whatsoever for the belief that the best way to learn to read in traditional orthography is to learn to read in traditional orthography. It would appear that the best way to learn to read in traditional orthography is to learn to read in the Initial Teaching Alphabet.[25]

The report also mentioned a consistently higher quality of writing by children in ITA as compared with that of children instructed in traditional orthography.

Advantages
1. The new letters (symbols) regularize the sound-symbol relationships of reading and writing.
2. Phonetic generalizations are consistent.
3. Children write with a higher quality.

Disadvantages
1. The transition to traditional orthography may be difficult.
2. Adults may be unable to read ITA.
3. Traditional orthography is traditional.

Forms of Reading

The seven approaches described in the preceding section are applicable to forms of reading commonly identified as silent reading, oral reading, work-study reading, and recreational reading. The generalizations governing the effectiveness of these forms are stable and vary little among the approaches.

Silent Reading

Silent reading for instructional purposes must satisfy the following guidelines:

1. Silent reading should be preceded by an oral discussion in which the new meanings and words are spoken and heard by the pupils.
2. The written form of the word(s) should be presented during the discussion.
3. Objectives for silent reading should be set: comprehension; prediction; sequence; agreement or disagreement; comparison; and similar purposes.

Oral Reading

Oral reading for instructional purposes must satisfy the following guidelines:

1. Oral reading should be preceded by silent reading. Pupils should not read material orally until they have first read it silently.
2. Listeners are paying attention.
3. If narration is being read, then it is read to prove a point, establish an agreement, verify a prediction, or to serve some other purpose.
4. If prose or poetry is being read, then it is read to entertain, or to share a feeling, an experience, or a happening.

[25] John Downing, "The Bullock Commission's Judgment of I.T.A.," *The Reading Teacher,* XXIX, No. 4 (January 1976), p. 380.

5. The oral reading is done with vocal tone, stress, dynamics, rhythm, and pitch appropriate to the narration, prose, or poetry.

Work–Study Reading

Work–study reading for instructional purposes includes (1) developing the ability to read in connection with various school subjects; (2) reading for problem solving; (3) developing the ability to use maps, charts, graphs, tables, indexes, tables of contents, dictionaries, and card files; and (4) developing the ability to take notes, to outline, to summarize, to skim, and to organize data.

The following guidelines must be satisfied in the teaching of work–study reading:

1. Opportunities should be provided for practicing the needed skills in meaningful situations rather than in isolated exercises.
2. A wide variety of reading materials should be available.
3. The improvement of reading should be stressed not only during periods set aside for that purpose but also in connection with the social studies, science, health, and other curriculum areas.
4. Pupils should learn when to master specific details and when to retain only the main ideas.
5. Pupils should learn to make notes, to give a report, to tell a story, and to follow directions.
6. The difficulty of material should be adjusted to individual differences in interests and abilities.
7. Pupils should learn to adjust reading speed to the material being read.

Recreational Reading

The purposes of recreational reading are to help the child acquire a continuing interests in reading as a leisure activity, to stimulate a desire to read widely, and to encourage the enjoyment of reading materials of increasingly better quality.

The following suggestions may be useful in improving the teaching of recreational reading:

1. A wide range of materials from the standpoints of difficulty, content, and type should be provided.
2. An informal classroom atmosphere should be maintained so that children can select materials within their own areas of interest.
3. Children should have the opportunity individually to share with the group a particularly enjoyable selection.
4. A part of a story should be read and children should be encouraged to complete it.
5. Children should be allowed to browse through books and magazines.
6. Children should be asked to recommend books to the class by means of a talk, poster, or some other medium.

Literature for Children

Books written especially for children are available in greater quantity and better quality than ever before. Many public libraries are well stocked with books appropriate for children of elementary school age; many elementary schools have central libraries and classroom libraries containing children's books selected from approved lists; and teachers are working with parents in the selection of appropriate books for home reading.[26] There is evidence, however, that teachers and parents frequently fail to take full advantage of these resources for helping children acquire a love for reading.

Good books make many contributions to the enrichment of living. They cannot serve as substitutes for direct firsthand experience, but they can add greatly to the richness of living for both children and adults. Well-written books for children provide a means of gaining information, of extending experience, and of relieving tensions. They can help the child see personal problems in true perspective, develop sensitivity to the life-styles of people of other lands, and enrich leisure living. Reading, as a means of developing better socioemotional adjustment, is receiving an increasing amount of attention.[27]

Bibliotherapy is the use of selected reading materials to aid in the modification of attitudes and behaviors of pupils.[28] The assumption is that they will be affected by what is read, since the reading materials are selected to relate to the needs of the readers and to influence the way they resolve problems, issues, or needs.

Teachers generally recognize the importance of meeting the emotional needs of children, and books of the right kind do much to develop stable, well-adjusted individuals. The feelings of security, of achievement, and of being accepted by the group are fostered when children enter vicariously into the experiences of their book friends. Books help children develop an appreciation for moral and spiritual values, satisfy the desire for beauty, and provide an avenue of escape from time to time from the monotony and routine of daily living. Teachers must be alert, however, to discover children who have a tendency to spend too much time in a dream world and lose their sense of reality.

If teachers are to make full use of the rich legacy that exists in the form of good books for children, they must know hundreds of books in many fields, their strengths and weaknesses; they must also know a great deal about the interests and needs of the children for whom the books are intended. A book that the teacher or parent regards as a classic may not be a good book for par-

---

[26] See Nancy Larrick, *A Parent's Guide to Children's Reading*, 3d ed. (New York: Doubleday & Company, Inc., 1969); and, Mildred Dawson (Ed.), *Children, Books and Reading*, Perspectives in Reading No. 3 (Newark, Del.: International Reading Association, Inc., 1964).

[27] See Hilda Taba, *Reading Ladders for Human Relations*. (Washington, D.C.: American Council on Education, 1947); and Association for Childhood Education, *Helping Children Solve Their Problems*. (Washington, D.C.: The Association, 1950).

[28] Corinne W. Riggs, *Bibliotherapy, An Annotated Bibliography*. (Newark, Del.: International Reading Association, Inc., 1971), Foreword.

ticular children unless they can read and enjoy it. Scores of incidents illustrating the wide gap that exists between the teacher's appreciation of a book and what the child thinks of it can be drawn from actual classroom situations. One of the best illustrations is provided by the child who told the teacher, "This book tells more about penguins than I want to know."

The world of books can be made fascinating for children by the teacher who reads aloud to the group, displays pictures related to the material read, relates interesting facts about the author, and encourages children to read similar interesting books. The teacher begins at the level where the pupils select books related to their backgrounds of experience, and works gradually toward improvement of tastes in reading. The program in children's literature should be conducted in an informal manner so that children look forward to it as a pleasant experience.

The procedures used in teaching children to read determine to a great extent the enjoyment they derive from books. There can be little doubt that some teachers, in their ardor for teaching the skills of reading, overlook the effect of the process on the child's desire to read interesting books.[29] On the other hand, the teacher who is concerned with the effect the reading program has on children's enjoyment of books looks for answers to the following questions: Do they turn naturally to books in their spare time? Are they eager to discuss the books they have read? Do they suggest that others read some of the books they have read? Do they express positive likes and dislikes for characters in books? Have they acquired new interests through reading? Do they like to read and do they complete reading of books rather than tend to lose interest and set them aside?

Parents and teachers need help in evaluating books for children, for these, like books for adults, vary widely in quality. Informational books should contain significant and reliable content, have illustrations of high artistic quality, and be suitable for the age of the children who will use them. Story books should be ethically sound, well written, and full of action. Suggestions for evaluating books for children are available from many sources. One of the best sources, May Hill Arbuthnot's *Children and Books*, contains an excellent analysis of the basic needs of children which can be supplied through reading good books. It also points out the values to be derived from such types of literature as Mother Goose, ballads and story–poems, verse choirs, folk tales, fables and myths, historical fiction, animal stories, biography, and informational books.[30]

Experts in the various field have carefully prepared lists of books for children. These lists are found in publications as the *Horn Book* magazine, *Wilson Library Bulletin*, the *Booklist*, *Children's Catalogue*, and Snow's *Basic Book Collection for Elementary Grades*. Courses of study and curriculum guides for

---

29 See Lois Lenski, "What Are Books For, Anyway?" in Department of Elementary School Principals, *Elementary School Libraries Today, Thirtieth Yearbook.* (Washington, D.C.: National Education Association, 1951), p. 271.

30 May Hill Arbuthnot, *Children and Books,* 4th ed. (Glenview, Ill.: Scott, Foresman and Company, 1972).

elementary schools usually contain suggestions for the selection of books for various purposes, and the Association for Children Education International publishes lists of the best inexpensive books for children.

WRITING

Writing is the smallest, and the last language area to be developed for the elementary school child. What children choose to write has two roots. The first root is in the experiences and the meanings learned from those experiences. The second root is the application of those meanings in the prerequisite language areas of listening, speaking, and reading. A six-year-old child comes to school with a listening vocabulary of approximately 500 to 25,000 words and a speaking vocabulary of approximately 2,500 to 3,500 words.[31] These are the words that the six-year-old is most ready to meet in printed form through reading, and to reproduce through writing.

Writing includes the skills of handwriting, spelling, expository writing, and creative writing. A modern elementary school's curriculum will provide experiences, skills, and opportunities for writing and communication in all these areas.

Writing in the modern elementary school is not an end in itself, but a tool for communication and self-expression. It meets the need that pupils have for recording ideas, writing messages, signing their names, writing letters, and labeling objects. The school has the responsibility for helping children meet the ordinary demands of modern living by learning to write easily, legibly, accurately, and with sufficient speed to suit their purposes. A great deal of time has been wasted in the past in trying to bring all children up to a common standard of ornate penmanship by the use of daily drill on isolated elements. Most authorities now agree that more can be accomplished by developing a desire to write legibly and accurately as a matter of simple courtesy, using real situations for the purpose of teaching writing, and emphasizing good writing in all written work.

In teaching writing, as in other curriculum areas, most schools use practical, middle-ground approaches. It is generally agreed that writing should grow out of the child's normal classroom activities, such as writing invitations, making labels, and preparing material for the class newsletter. This functional learning, however, may have to be supplemented with regular practice periods until sufficient progress has been made in developing skill in writing. Such periods should be brief and should be organized so that each child can work on individual writing difficulties.

Handwriting

The curriculum of the modern elementary school provides instruction in handwriting throughout the program, with special emphasis given to the introduction of manuscript style and the transition from manuscript to cursive style.

[31] Dorothy Rubin, *Teaching Elementary Language Arts.* (New York: Holt, Rinehart and Winston, 1975), p. 276.

Manuscript is the first written form introduced to children. It is utilized for labeling in kindergarten, appears in picture books when print is used, and is used in printed primary reading materials. Cursive writing is introduced after children have developed some skills in both reading and manuscript writing. The transition from manuscript to cursive takes place typically during the last part of the second grade or the first part of the third grade. Cursive writing is the form used by adults. In the modern elementary school, the transition from manuscript to cursive writing forms is intended to provide the learner with two forms of writing. The initial skills of the learner in manuscript are maintained and extended throughout the curriculum.

Manuscript writing was introduced into the United States during the early 1920s by Marjorie Wise from England. Its advantages as the initial form of writing include: the simple strokes (straight lines and circles) are more appropriate to the small muscle coordination abilities of young children; the simplicity of the letter forms enables the learner to perceive the shapes and relationships; the letter forms are like those printed letter forms in beginning readers. The latter may be arguable, for this author sometimes wonders which came first, the educational rationale for manuscript or the limitation of technology on the mechanical printing presses used for mass production in the 1920s.

The transition from manuscript to cursive writing is supported by the following assumptions: The learners are motivated to use letter forms similar to those used by the significant adults in their environments; it is claimed that cursive writing is easier and quicker than manuscript; and an individual's style is better expressed through cursive. Research has yet to establish a significant difference between manuscript and cursive with regard to speed and style. Some evidence suggests that manuscript maintains a better legibility. Research does establish that most adults use the form of cursive. The research basis for supporting manuscript or cursive or the transition between manuscript and cursive is inconclusive.

Spelling

Spelling, like handwriting, is a tool used in communicating with others and as a means of self-expression. The ease and freedom with which children engage in various forms of written expression of ideas depends upon their ability to spell. Correct spelling is important for the adult as a matter of common courtesy, as a social asset, and as a vocational tool. Instead of placing less emphasis on this skill, as is sometimes supposed, modern schools provide many opportunities for learning to spell correctly, not only in spelling class but throughout the day. Efforts are made to develop a consciousness of the need for spelling correctly, to promote self-direction on the part of the child, to provide situations in which children need to learn how to spell certain words, to teach the words children use most frequently in their written work, and to individualize instruction.

A large proportion of the words an adult knows how to spell were learned through use in meaningful situations. Children learn in many situations other than the formal spelling lesson. They learn from seeing words in the books they read at home and at school, in stores and motion pictures, on signboards and in newspapers. The modern school, therefore, provides for both the systematic teaching of spelling and for giving attention to it in connection with the whole school program.

Modern practices in the teaching of spelling reflect the influence of the newer psychology of learning, research dealing with words that children use in writing, and the trend toward unified teaching.

Applied Principles of Learning

The concept of learning that emphasizes the modification of behavior rather than merely the acquisition of knowledge and skills is illustrated in the modern spelling program. How children spell from day to day in various types of written work, rather than the score made on a list of spelling words, constitutes the proof of learning. Learning through use in meaningful situations rather than through abstract drill is also emphasized.

In teaching children to spell, the normal steps of learning are observed. Their firsthand experience with an object in the environment, such as a ball. They hear the word "ball" used to refer to the object; they learn to say "ball"; they play with the "ball"; they learn to read the word in a sentence; they learn to write it from a copy; and finally they learn to spell the word from memory. The more meaning the word has for children, the more easily they learn to spell it. All modern systems of teaching spelling utilize the senses of seeing and hearing, and the kinesthetic sense. Some children learn more readily by seeing the word in its context, some by hearing the word, and others by writing it, but all children learn best when spelling is associated with meaningful situations.

Children learn more readily when spelling is related to purposes that are real to them. By creating situations in which children need to spell in order to write something, by developing a consciousness of the need for correct spelling, and by helping pupils develop initiative and independence in learning how to spell new words, the teacher utilizes the powerful force of pupil purposes in the task of learning to spell.

No single list of words presented to the entire class without regard for individual interests and capability can meet the spelling needs of all members of the class. Teachers who understand the nature and extent of individual differences realize that graded lists of words represent directional goals rather than uniform grade standards. Some children may already know how to spell most of the words in the list for a certain grade, whereas others may not be able to spell all of them by the end of the year. To expect a higher level of achievement than one for which children are ready results in discouragement and dislike for spelling; failing to challenge them to work at their full capacities is equally harmful. Children need help in setting up their own goals in spelling and in evaluating progress toward these goals. A proper regard for the needs of individual children will lead to individual instruction in spelling, which allows individuals and small groups within the class to progress as slowly or as rapidly as their abilities and efforts will permit.

In the modern school, the spelling program takes into account the level of maturity of the child. It is a waste of time and effort to teach children to spell words before they will use them in writing. Words needed in adult life are best learned at a later time. If children are required to learn such words purely through drill, they will have forgotten how to spell most of them and will have to learn them over again when they are needed.

Research in Spelling

Research in spelling during the past half-century has indicated that learning this skill is largely an individual matter—few children conform to any one method of learning to spell words. Research also indicates that teachers should (1) select spelling lists from words commonly used, (2) give careful attention to individual learning problems, (3) create in the pupils an interest in and an appreciation for correct spelling, (4) give attention to spelling in all areas of the curriculum, and (5) use visual, auditory, and kinesthetic avenues to learning to spell.

Spelling lists are typically derived from one or a combination of two sources. One source consists of the words appearing most frequently in adult writing. For example, the three hundred highest frequency words in adult writing account for almost 75 percent of all words utilized by adults. Therefore, some researchers argue that these words have a high utilitarian value which justifies their teaching and learning. Note that this is an example of the classical and practical criteria (see Chapter 5) being applied to the selection of content vehicles.

A second source for spelling lists consists of the words appearing in children's writings. In 1945, Rinsland at the University of Oklahoma compiled a list of approximately a hundred thousand words appearing in the spontaneous writings of children.[32] Note that this is an example of the relevancy criteria (see Chapter 5) applied to the selection of content vehicles. Rinsland's list has contributed to the vocabularies in spellers, readers, and texts prepared for elementary school children.

The frequency of use of words may be a factor in determining which words should be taught. How these words are grouped into graded and weekly lists also varies among texts. Most graded weekly lists reflect the frequency of appearance of these words in readers and in children's or adults' writings. Other graded, weekly lists group the high-frequency words that illustrate a phonetic or word analysis generalization. A study by Davis suggested that the maintenance and sequences of phonetic and/or word analysis generalizations in these texts were inconsistent.[33] Generalizations were introduced and then not maintained or reviewed until several grades later.

One study identified the 17,000 words most common in the writings of

---

[32] Henry D. Rinsland, *A Basic Vocabulary to Elementary School Children.* (New York: Crowell Collier and Macmillan, 1945).

[33] Lillie Smith Davis, "The Applicability of Phonic Generalizations to Selected Spelling Programs." (Norman, Okla.: University of Oklahoma, unpublished doctoral dissertation, 1969).

United States citizens.[34] Almost half of these words could be spelled correctly through the use of approximately three hundred specialized rules. With tongue in cheek, the author speculates that if the child learns almost three hundred specialized rules and correctly applies them to this list of 17,000 words, almost half could be spelled correctly. Yet the child would be failed on Friday's spelling test, because 70 percent is passing.

Although the evidence from research is not precise, the "general practice" and most authorities agree that spelling should be taught continuously, incidentally, and from lists. Teaching from lists should be done in frequent, short 15-minute intervals. Continuous teaching is done as writing occurs in all school subjects, and incidental teaching occurs as the child requires a word to communicate a special meaning.

SITUATION 7.5   Select one grade or level within the elementary school and write three activities which utilize spelling and handwriting as communication tools (means to an end, not ends in themselves).

Forms of Writing

Expository Writing

Expository writing is the narrative style used in reporting, summarizing, comparing, clarifying, classifying, and other factual exercises. Creative acts may be involved, but the purpose of the communication is to transmit meanings without the use of aesthetic, literary illusions.

The forms and generalizations of expository writing must be taught to and experienced by pupils in the modern elementary school. The bases of this kind of writing are the concrete experiences of the writer. When children's expository writings appear to have been copied from encyclopedias, it may be that the experience is an abstraction of an object or event (that is, a description in the encyclopedia). The modern elementary school program provides concrete, manipulatory, and exploratory experiences as the subjects of expository writing.

Creative Writing

Creative writing is the use of figurative language and literary techniques to transmit an aesthetic message. Both expository and creative writings are unique communications, but the latter usually follow affective experiencing, whereas expository writings are based on cognitive experiencing.

The literary forms and techniques need first to be experienced by children through their listening and speaking language. From this and a strong affective motivation, children can and will generate beautifully creative communications. The evaluation of their work must be in terms of the effectiveness of the affective message transmitted, not the grading of the mechanics of spelling and

[34] Paul R. Hanna et al., *Phonemegrapheme Correspondence as Cues to Spelling Improvement*, U.S. Project No. 1991. (Washington, D.C.: Department of Health, Education and Welfare, 1966).

grammatical constructions. Creativity is an inherent art, more fostered than taught and mastered.

READINESS

A flagrant and recurring error in the literature on instruction in language arts is to limit the concepts of readiness to reading. Readiness is a functioning aspect of all language arts areas—listening, speaking, reading, and writing. Each of the language arts areas is so dependent on each other that difficulties in one area may be the result of unreadiness in a preceding area, or even a lack of coordination between the preceding one and the one being studied. Readiness is an aspect for diagnosis, evaluation, and instruction within all the language arts areas.

Readiness begins in the psychomotor domain, the domain identified in the *Taxonomy of Educational Objectives*, which classifies the behaviors of sensory perceiving, processing, and outputting.[35] Static in these sensory behaviors can originate from the physical tasks of hearing and seeing, or apparently from the act of processing the data, called "dyslexia." Research in and programs for what is labeled "learning disabilities" has provided sophisticated tools for diagnosis of these readinesses. Unfortunately, these tools and diagnostic procedures are often limited to remedial rather than developmental use.

This section briefly presents the aspects of readiness relevant to each language arts area. The reader is cautioned to keep in mind that readiness is a continuous phenomenon occurring in each language art and interacting across all language learning areas. The reader must not make the error that many reading specialists do; that is, isolating readiness in one language arts area rather than treating it within each *and* across all areas.

Listening

The physical aspects of listening readiness can be assessed through the use of an audiometer. An audiometer measures auditory sensitivity and will detect the frequencies and intensities of sound available to an individual. The modern elementary school screens kindergarten, first grade, and transfer students. With instruction, a teacher may learn to operate an audiometer. Pupils' abilities to audit differences and similarities between phonemes should also be assessed. (The Wepman Auditory Discrimination Test from Language Research Associates is an example of an instrument to perform this screening.) If a learner cannot audit differences in phonemes, then of what value are phonic generalizations?

The range of diagnostic instruments available to assess the pupil's functioning and readinesses in listening is limited but increasing. Mavrogenes and her associates list several tests in the January 1976 issue of *The Reading Teacher*.[36]

---

[35] See Chapter 5 for a further discussion of the *Taxonomy of Educational Objectives* and the psychomotor domain, or see Anita J. Harrow's book, *Taxonomy of the Psychomotor Domain: A Guide to Developing Behavioral Objectives*. (New York: David McKay and Co.), 1972.

[36] Nancy A. Mavrogenes, Earl F. Hanson, and Carol K. Winkley, "A Guide to Tests of Factors that Inhibit Learning To Read," *The Reading Teacher*, Vol. XXIX, No. 4 (January 1976), p. 343.

The listening experiences and environments in which they occur are a basic determiner of a child's readiness. If children have experienced language as a short, declarative, command medium, then they are probably not ready for the use of language to persuade, negotiate, and discuss. If children have heard only a nonstandard-English dialect, then they are probably not ready to distinguish and discriminate among the phonemes of standard English. If children have not heard English as a native language, then they will probably have extreme difficulty receiving instruction in a nonnative language. The reader is referred to the earlier section in this chapter on "Bilingual Program" for a discussion of these problems.

For listening, as with all the areas of language arts, childrens' fundamental readiness depends on the meanings of the experiences they have had. If children have not had the opportunities to decode a wide range of experience-related meanings, then they are severely handicapped when these meanings are encoded by others.

Speaking

The physical aspects of readiness for speaking must be assessed by a speech pathologist, physician, and dentist. The pupil's ability to reproduce the phonemes and sounds of English can be assessed through instruments such as the Goldman-Fristoe Test of Articulation or the Templin-Darby Tests of Articulation.[37] The instruments to diagnose speech performances and readiness are limited and generally must be used by a specialist. Fortunately, the administrative time for these instruments is short (5 to 15 minutes); therefore, a modern elementary school can provide a preliminary screening of all five-and six-year-old children.

As with listening, the children's experiences and environments are primary factors in their readinesses to achieve in school. Children encode (speak) what has first been decoded (heard).

Reading

Research in child development has shown that readiness to do such things as walking and talking appears at rather definite periods. Of course the age limits for beginning these activities vary with individual children, but it has been found that forcing a child to begin a specific activity before developmental readiness causes strain, develops negativistic attitudes, and accomplishes little. A child cannot be expected to make much progress in reading until ready for it. Research indicates that children who have had only an enriched school program and no formal introduction to reading in books in the first grade were more successful in learning to read than a comparable group which received formal instruction of a conventional nature. Studies of retardation in reading indicate that children who have been introduced prematurely to the mechanics

---

[37] Mavrogenes, pp. 352–353.

of reading have built up antagonisms to it, have lost confidence in themselves, and have come to expect failure rather than success. When a child is ready for reading, rapid progress can be made when taught by any one of a wide variety of methods. Numerous studies indicate that the teacher is a more significant factor in determining the success or failure of a child to learn to read than are the instructional materials.[38] A child may be ready for reading anywhere between the chronological ages of four and eight. Girls tend to be more mature in language development than boys of the same age, and they learn to read earlier. Of the children referred to remedial reading clinics for special treatment, from 75 to 90 percent are boys.[39]

There is little to be gained from rushing into a program of reading from books before there is evidence that the child is ready for it. Most children who enter the first grade need time to continue to grow, to adjust to group living, and to experience success in small undertakings adjusted to their level of maturity. They need to develop a growing interest in the environment, to develop concepts, to use oral language more effectively, to follow directions, and to develop a desire for learning to read.

There are many factors that influence readiness for reading. The teacher cannot assume that a child who does not make satisfactory progress in the initial stages of reading is either stupid or lazy; instead, the teacher should, in advance of formal instruction, determine whether the child is unready for reading in some respect, find out in what respects handicaps exist, and plan a program for correcting the defects. Principals and teachers in the elementary school have no more important responsibility than that of understanding the factors which influence reading readiness and of planning a program of activities for developing abilities needed in beginning reading. The following paragraphs call attention to some of the important factors to be considered.

Visual Factors

Vision plays an important role in learning to read. Since reading involves receiving and interpreting visual stimuli, it is necessary for children to have normal vision before they can read comfortably and with enjoyment. A child without minimally adequate visual acuity or with binocular difficulties will either have trouble in seeing words or will experience sufficient discomfort to avoid any activities requiring near-point vision. Even though children may possess normal vision, it is essential that they acquire adequate visual discrimination ability. For reading purposes, the child must have learned to distinguish between likenesses and differences in letters and words. This is a learned skill, and the teacher must be certain that it is developed in advance

---

[38] Russell G. Stauffer (Ed.), *The First Grade Reading Studies*. (Newark, Del.: International Reading Association, Inc., 1967).
[39] Nita M. Wyatt, "The Reading Achievement of First Grade Boys Versus First Grade Girls," in Russell G. Stauffer (Ed.), *The First Grade Reading Studies*. (Newark, Del.: International Reading Association, Inc., 1967), pp. 161–165.

of formal instruction in books. The research concerning the effect of visual defects on success in reading is inconclusive; nevertheless, the good teacher, because of concern for the whole child, will continue to look for indications of visual defects. The child who must hold materials too close or too far away, the child who has to walk up to the board to see what is written, the child who always misses the ball during games, the child whose penmanship is not in alignment, will be noted by the teacher and, when the evidence exists, will refer the child to a specialist for testing and correction of the difficulty.

The Ortho-Rather or the Telebinocular instruments can be used by teachers, after some training, to assess the visual readiness of pupils. Tests such as Marianne Frostig's Developmental Test of Visual Perception can be used by a clinician to assess the perceptual readiness of children.[40]

Auditory Factors

Auditory acuity is a factor of vital importance to reading readiness. It has been estimated that three million school children have impaired hearing. Defective hearing may retard speech development when it prevents the child from auditorily discriminating among sounds. The inability to hear likenesses and differences among sounds is closely associated with failure to learn to read. The student who possesses normal hearing may or may not be able to make auditory discriminations. The teacher must evaluate the strengths and weaknesses of each student to hear differences in sounds and must design an instructional program for developing this skill in students with deficiencies before formal instruction in reading. The most realiable instrument for determining hearing defects is the audiometer. (See the section "Listening.")

Mental Maturity

Very few children do not have sufficient mental maturity to profit from a formal program of reading instruction. Memory span, vocabulary of spoken words, knowledge of spatial relationships, ability to see likenesses and differences in objects and words, and attention span are closely associated with mental maturity. If children are deficient in any of these abilities, conscious effort must be made to help develop them to full capacity before a formal program of reading instruction is introduced. Research evidence concerning the minimum mental age at which formal instruction in reading should begin is inconclusive; however, some of the research indicates that a child should have a mental age of at least six and one-half years.

Cognitive Maturity

The cognitive operations available to a learner are a determinant of both readiness and initial approaches to the formal teaching of reading. For example, the figure-ground perceptions, cognitive reversals, and conservations required within a separate phonics approach are not available to a preoperational learner. The reader is referred to Chapter 3 section "Intellectual Development."

[40] Mavrogenes, p. 346.

Social and Emotional Factors

Some children are not well enough adjusted socially and emotionally to succeed in reading. The child who is unhappy, who has difficulty in learning to live with the group, and who lacks confidence has a difficult time learning to read. These children must be identified and helped to make a happy adjustment to school living before satisfactory progress can be made in reading.

Background of Experience

Some children have traveled widely and have been taught to observe closely, whereas others have never been out of their own neighborhood; some six-year-olds have attended kindergarten, whereas others have not; some come from homes that have children's books and magazines in abundance, whereas others come from homes in which there is very little reading material. The material in even the preprimers may be entirely foreign to the experience of some children. Some recent research indicates that there is no single factor related to reading which has a greater effect on the ability of the student to comprehend than a background of experience. It is the responsibility of the teacher to identify those children who have had a limited background of experience, and to provide experiences that will make reading meaningful to them.

SITUATION 7.6 Watch a children's educational program for one-half hour (for example, "Sesame Street," "Mister Rogers," "Electric Company"). List the language readiness experiences or activities you observed.

Language Facility

It is essential that the child develop facility in the use of oral language. Language and speech development are fundamental to success in learning to read because reading involves the arousing of concepts and meanings for the printed symbols from the experiences which the child has had previously. Children with inadequate language development—inability to communicate, limited vocabularies, and poor articulation—will experience difficulty in learning to read; those children with advanced language development will experience success in learning to read. The teacher must evaluate the language development of each child and provide opportunities for those with limited facility in language to acquire the necessary skills before introducing them to formal instruction in reading.

Tests for Readiness

The teacher can determine when children are physically, mentally, emotionally, and socially mature enough for beginning reading by using intelligence tests, reading readiness tests, and systematic observation. Some reading readiness tests that are widely used for this purpose are:

American School Reading Readiness Test and Lee-Clark Reading Readiness
Test (California Test Bureau)
Gates-MacGinitie Readiness Skills Test (Teachers College Press)
Harrison-Stroud Reading Readiness Profiles (Houghton Mifflin Company)
Metropolitan Readiness Test and Murphy-Durrell Reading Readiness
Analysis (Harcourt Brace Jovanovich, Inc.)
Readiness tests that accompany basal reading series

Although teachers will want to use one of these tests to check their own
judgments, it should be pointed out that readiness tests cannot and should not
take the place of careful observation by the teacher. Many children do not do
well on readiness tests because of factors in the test situation, not in their reading ability. One six-year-old who was reading second-grade material with ease
before entrance almost failed the readiness test because of a confusion in following directions. Another able reader did poorly as a result of his clumsy
physical coordination.

Use of Checklists

Many schools prepare checklists to be used by kindergarten, preprimary,
and first-grade teachers in making systematic observations relating to various
factors in reading readiness. An example of this type of instrument follows.

SITUATION 7.7   Examine a reading readiness program. What are the
objectives? What skills are emphasized?

Writing

Readiness for writing includes the growth factors of small-muscle coordination
and the developmental factors of experiencing. One of the justifications claimed
for starting with manuscript is the accommodation to the readinesses of muscular coordination. Cursive writing is delayed until additional growth in coordination occurs.

The readiness to write is also dependent upon the meaning-experiences
included within the listening, speaking, and reading language arts areas. A rich
input through listening and reading, plus an output through speaking, prepares
the learner for writing. When learners' writings appear to have been copied from
encyclopedias and textbooks, the odds are that the developmental readinesses
for writing have not been satisfied.

MEDIA AND MATERIALS

Instruction in the language arts once consisted primarily of teaching children
the contents of the basic texts in reading, spelling, and grammar. The single text
has been supplanted in modern elementary schools by multiple texts, library

CHECKLIST FOR READING READINESS

FACTORS	HIGH	AVERAGE	LOW

Physiological Factors
1. Is there evidence of good organic condition, good nutrition, and good health habits?
2. Is there evidence of normal vision?
3. Does the child have good general coordination when engaging in games?
4. Does the child have a normal amount of energy?
5. Does the child's hearing seem to be normal?
6. Does the child respond quickly when spoken to?

Psychological Factors
1. Does the child have a wide speaking vocabulary?
2. Can the child relate a personal experience in logical sequence?
3. Can the child repeat from memory a rhyme or verse?
4. Can the child listen attentively to a story?
5. Does the child listen to directions and execute them accurately?
6. Does the child notice likenesses and differences in objects, forms, colors?
7. Can likenesses and differences in sounds of words be heard?
8. Does the child have a normal span of attention?
9. Does the child have curiosity about books, things, and places?
10. Does the child want to learn to read?

Social and Emotional Factors
1. Does the child enter into group activities?
2. Does the child form friendships easily?
3. Does the child assume responsibilities well?
4. Is the child free from nervousness, worry, and excessive fears?
5. Can the child work independently without too much help from the teacher?
6. Does the child stay with a task until it is finished?
7. Can disappointments be accepted without undue display of emotions?

Background of Experience
1. Has the child visited parks, zoos, or airports?
2. Has the child had many of the experiences which will be read about?
3. Does the home have children's books and magazines?
4. Has the child attended kindergarten?
5. Do the parents encourage initiative and independence?
6. Has the child had experience with automobiles, trains, airplanes, and buses?
7. Has the child seen many movies?
8. Does the home have a radio or television set?

books,[41] magazines, newspapers, mimeographed materials, workbooks, and children's encyclopedias. Media have contributed many superior resources for the language arts. Cassette tapes, filmstrips and viewers, sound and silent films, still and motion picture cameras, including television, have all become viable resources. The new type of language arts program, with its emphasis on unified learning, calls for the use of every type of medium the school and community can furnish to serve the language needs of children.

Instructional materials are selected cooperatively by teachers, principals, children, and parents. If the material is not available, then schools use their learning-resource centers to prepare their own. Children often prepare materials for language arts when a committee develops a newspaper or mural.

Learning Centers

The learning center, discussed in Chapter 6, is fundamental to the unified language arts curriculum in the modern elementary school. Listening stations; speaking, role playing, and dramatization areas; reference and trade books; construction and art materials; picture taking and projecting equipment—all these and others are essential for a rich curriculum. The February 1976 issue of *The Reading Teacher* lists the materials and equipment released since 1974.[42]

Basal Readers and Manuals

The problem of providing a better quality of books, particularly basal textbook series, still deserves attention even though the publishers have recently updated most of the basal reader series. It is reasonable to expect that publishers will continue to modify these books as research provides evidence supporting a need for modification. The basal textbook series of the future will, no doubt, exhibit a less rigidly controlled vocabulary, involve less repetition, present a more realistic picture of life in this century, and reflect less social class bias than do those currently used in most of our schools. Several basal reader series have been published recently which reflect less bias than those of several years ago.

A basal reading series usually includes a teacher's manual, pupil activity book (workbook), and pre- and postassessment materials. The teacher's manual deserves special mention and attention, since it contains the core of the program. Those materials provided for pupil use are expressions and applications of the objectives, skills, sequence, and scope presented in the manual. Also included are many additional diagnostics—enrichment and reinforcing listening, speaking, reading, and writing language activities. Individualization of instruction as well as continuity of instruction begins with the diligent and

---

[41] For information on the types and sources of children's books, see Charlotte S. Huck, *Children's Literature in the Elementary School*, 3d ed. (New York: Holt, Rinehart and Winston, Inc., 1976); Winifred C. Ladley (Ed.), *Sources of Good Books and Magazines for Children.* (Newark, Del.: International Reading Association, Inc., 1965); and George D. Spache, *Sources of Good Books for Poor Readers.* (Newark, Del.: International Reading Association, Inc., 1966).
[42] Stauffer, pp. 474–485.

responsible utilization of the manual. An inappropriate practice is to overutilize the pupil pages and to underutilize the teacher pages.

Reading Workbooks

The workbooks accompanying a basal reader series are an integral element of a comprehensive basal reader program. Like textbooks, they may be used either as valuable resources for learning or as substitutes for good teaching. If workbooks are used merely to enable a teacher to keep a large group of children busy and quiet, their use should be discouraged. If, on the other hand, they are a means to individualize instruction, to help pupils learn to follow directions, to provide reinforcement of skills, and to help pupils develop self-direction and independence, their use should be encouraged.

Workbooks are not intended to be homework for the teacher. Class, group, and individual time should be provided for teaching from the activities contained within a workbook as well as the assessment of pupil performances on these activities. Some teachers creatively utilize pages from different workbooks by tearing them from the workbooks and filing them by skill objectives. The file can then be adapted to include pages for preassessment, practice, and postassessment of the various skills. The workbook for a basal reader series will identify which pages are appropriate for a particular objective.

ISSUES

No aspect of the elementary school program has been the subject of more controversy in recent years than has the reading program. The controversy is understandable in view of the increasing recognition that learning to read is the fundamental activity on which the rest of the child's education depends. The controversy traditionally revolves around three continuing issues: which approach; phonics versus word method; and the nature of language. Two issues, literacy and stereotyping, have recently begun to receive attention. The following subsections briefly present the nature of the controversy in each of these areas.

Which Approach?

Seven approaches were described in the section of this chapter entitled "Current Approaches to Teaching Reading." Combinations of these seven approaches yield a potential of over 5,000 possible variations. Although all 5,000 combinations are probably not in operation, it is also improbable that a pure form of teaching reading can be found. Methods of teaching tend to be eclectic and global, utilizing aspects of several approaches while stressing one. Yet, more research studies of reading have been done than of any other curriculum area, with many of these studies attempting to compare two or more approaches to instruction. These studies generally have yielded inconclusive and inconsistent results. Russell Stauffer, when introducing *The First Grade Reading Studies,* said, "And where does all this leave us? No single approach in these twenty-seven studies has overcome individual differences or eliminated reading disabilities at the first grade level."[43]

Perhaps, the paucity of criteria is a function of the crudeness of research tools, or of the eclectic nature of existing programs, or of the lack of a superior program, but whatever the reason, no approach can clearly demonstrate a research basis for its claimed superiority. MacGinitie has suggested that in spite of the critics who discourage "method studies" that ". . . researchers could learn from the mistakes of the past and design method studies that would avoid many of the problems for which such studies have been criticized."[44]

Literacy

Literacy—the ability to read and write one's name; to score third grade or above or a standardized test; to score eighth grade or above on a standardized test; to functionally apply language and arithmetic skills in everyday life. All of these have served as the definitions of literacy at some time. The definition that seems dominant in the mid-1970s is that of functional competency, or functional literacy. According to a two-year research project sponsored by the National Institute of Education:

> a substantial portion of the U.S. population does read well enough to function in society. Some 12 million people 14 years of age and older cannot read as well as the average fourth grader, yet seventh grade reading ability is required to perform such skilled or semiskilled jobs as machinist or cook. An estimated 18 million adults cannot read well enough to file applications for Medicaid, Social Security, bank loans or driver's licenses. They have difficulty reading voting literature, telephone directories, employment brochures, product labels and other consumer information.[45]

Many newspapers have headlined the results of a four-year research project sponsored by the U.S. Office of Education. An example is:

> U.S. Illiteracy Rate Is Called "Shocking"—The United States Office of Education today released results of a four year study which indicated that 23 million U.S. adults are functionally illiterate, meaning they are unable to do such things as read help wanted ads or make the most economical purchases . . . one of five Americans is incompetent or functions with difficulty.[46]

This type of information plus the falling scores of students on college entrance examinations, complemented by a tendency to look back to other times for solutions, has contributed to another cry to go "back to the basics." If returning to the basics could include a previous definition of literacy—third-grade reading—

[43] Russell G. Stauffer (Ed.), The First Grade Reading Studies: Findings of Individual Investigations. (Newark, Del.: International Reading Association, 1967), p. vii.
[44] Walter H. MacGinitie, "Research Suggestions from the 'Literature Search,'" The Reading Research Quarterly, Vol. XI, No. 1 (1975–1976), p. 24.
[45] Deborah L. Eaton, "NIE Attacks the Reading and Language Skills Problem," American Education (May 1974), p. 35.
[46] Associated Press dispatch, The Oklahoma City (Oklahoma) Times, October 29, 1975.

and a less demanding technological society, it might work. The real issue is that the nature of society has redefined literacy while the schools continue to use practices adapted to earlier circumstances. The modern elementary school will not satisfy the new requirements for literacy by reinstating past practices.

Phonics

Much of the controversy has centered around the relative merits of the "look–say" approach used in some of the basal reader series and around the phonics approach to beginning reading. More specifically, the components of the controversy include: (1) different interpretations of the meaning of reading—word calling versus broader objectives; (2) the use of one method versus the use of a combination of methods; (3) highly structured procedures versus more flexible ones; (4) when formal instruction in phonics should begin; (5) the strengths and weaknesses of the leading basal reader series; and (6) the extent to which textbooks should constitute the reading program of pupils.

Gibson has made a contribution to the understanding of the sources of the controversy.

True, most children do learn to read. But some learn to read badly, so that school systems must provide remedial clinics; and a small proportion (but still a large number of future citizens) remain functional illiterates. The fashions which have led to classroom experiments, such as the "whole word" method, emphasis on context and pictures for "meaning," the "flash" method, "speed reading," revised alphabets, the "return" to "phonics," and so on, have done little to change the situation.[47]

Goodman added to the controversy when he said, "The preoccupation with phoneme-grapheme correspondence or sound correspondence or phonics in any form in reading instruction is at best a peripheral concern."[48] Curry and Mercer have helped to clarify the controversy through their research and writings concerning the usefulness of phonic generalizations.[49] In their article, "A Summary of Studies on the Usefulness of Phonic Generalizations," they summarized seven studies dealing with the usefulness of forty-five phonic generalizations as applied to textbooks in a variety of content areas: reading, spelling, mathematics, science, and social studies. To be considered useful, a phonic generalization must have been applicable to at least twenty words in a series and 75 percent of the words must have been consistent with the phonic generalization. Twelve of the forty-five generalizations were shown to be useful in all seven studies; thirteen were found to be useful in most of the seven studies. Seventeen of the phonic generalizations failed to be useful in any of the seven studies; three of them were useful in some of the seven studies. One popular phonic generalization is: When there are two vowels side by side, the long sound of the first vowel is

[47] Eleanor J. Gibson, "Learning To Read," *Science* (May 21, 1965), p. 1066.
[48] Kenneth S. Goodman, "Miscue Reading," *The Reading Teacher*, Vol. XXVIII, No. 8 (April 1975), p. 627.
[49] Robert L. Curry and Lynna Geis Mercer, "A Summary of Studies on the Usefulness of Phonic Generalizations." (Norman, Okla.: College of Education, University of Oklahoma, 1976).

heard and the second vowel is usually silent. In the seven studies, there were 14,104 words with double vowels, and the generalization was applicable for only 35 percent of the words. Curry and Mercer concluded that only twenty-five of the forty-five most commonly taught phonic generalizations were useful.

Perhaps, the issue of phonics can never be settled. First, the present alphabet (orthography) is phonetically irregular. Second, all reading programs do, and must, include the study of phonics; therefore, the issue is one of order and emphasis rather than phonics or no phonics.

Changes in Language

Changes in the elementary school curriculum during the past few years have been influenced to a large extent by an increasing emphasis on the structure and contributions of disciplines such as English, mathematics, science, geography, and economics. Scholars in these and other academic disciplines have become more active in developing programs for elementary schools. They have become concerned about teaching better content with a different approach.[50]

The language arts program in modern elementary schools is becoming more effective as principles derived from the study of linguistics are utilized. One of these principles is that language is in a condition of constant growth and change; another is that the actual changing usage of people constitutes the basis of all the "correctness" there can be in language. Fries provided some interesting illustrations of these principles in connection with the new view of language represented by the *Oxford English Dictionary*.[51] The editors of that dictionary had in hand more than six million dated quotations as a basis for their conclusions; the final part came to press seventy years after the collection of data started. The word "nice" appeared in this work as signifying general approval, and it has appeared in our literature with that meaning ever since that time. Before that, it had been used to mean stupid, hard to please, and carefully accurate.

Another principle advanced by many linguists is that the printed materials which children read should reflect the vocabulary of children, and that the sentence structure should consist of the same patterns as the structure of the oral language which children use. The contention is that many printed materials used for instructional purposes have sentence patterning which is quite unlike children's spoken language, and that these differences create a most difficult situation when children are learning to read.[52]

Linguistics includes the study of levels of language usage. The natures of both the communication and the environment in which the communication is to occur apparently influence the level of usage utilized. The nature of the syntax, stress, vocabulary, and grammar seems to change to fit the various environments

---

[50] Association for Supervision and Curriculum Development, *Using Current Curriculum Developments*. (Washington, D.C.: The Association for Supervision and Curriculum Development, 1963).

[51] Charles C. Fries, *Linguistics and Reading*. (New York: Holt, Rinehart and Winston, Inc., 1963), chap. 2.

[52] Carl A. Lefevre, *Linguistics and the Teaching of Reading*. (New York: McGraw-Hill, Inc., 1964).

in which communication occurs. Individuals "shooting the bull" with friends do not use the same patterns when presenting themselves to a potential employer.

One of the major learnings concerning language is the ability to adapt language practices to the environment. "Incorrect" usage results when the language pattern is inappropriate to the situation. A *formal level* of usage is appropriate when the environment is formal (for example, in dissertations, legal documents, research papers). A more *standard level* is appropriate in environments such as textbooks, term papers, letters of introduction, beginning conversations with status individuals. A more *colloquial level* of usage is appropriate in environments such as family dinner tables, dates, letters to friends, group discussions with friends. Another level of usage—more emotional because it draws upon God, mother, and bodily functions as prime sources for its vocabulary and meanings—may be appropriate within some economic classes, with intimate friends, and when expressing strong feelings.

Each of these levels of usage has its own pattern of grammar. For example, the pattern presented in the older English textbooks was that of latinized, formal usage. A level of usage which is appropriately concerned with split infinitives, gerunds, "ain't", and ending sentences with a preposition is not where it's at! The unified teaching of language, described previously in this chapter, would provide an individual with the opportunities to learn and communicate effectively at all levels of usage.

Language Differences

There is much to be said about the special problems of children who come from the various backgrounds of our pluralistic culture. Whipple stated, "Children without come from families without. Such families crowd the inner sections of large cities, but they also are found in suburban and rural areas."[53] These children represent no single race or national group. Nevertheless, they have many common characteristics which contribute to the inability to learn as efficiently as children from a more adequate background. The children without are often seriously retarded in language development. Many come from homes in which a special dialect is spoken; often the homes are bilingual. The sentences spoken in school and encountered in printed materials are confusing to the child because they are unlike those heard in the home. The child therefore has difficulty in understanding explanations and directions given by the teacher as well as difficulty in understanding the printed symbols. These children's vocabularies are often restricted to certain levels of usage, which results in an inability to express themselves and comprehend oral or written language in other levels of usage.

There is a serious mismatch of the "out of school" language of these children and the "in school" language used for instruction. In fact, for some of

[53] Gertrude Whipple, "The Special Needs of Children Without," in Ira E. Aaron (Ed.), *Reading for Children Without—Our Disadvantaged Youth*. (Newark, Del.: International Reading Association, Inc., 1966), p. 1.

these children, using language to resolve personal disagreements is considered a sign of weakness by their socioeconomic or language peers.

In school, however, to use language as a means to resolve personal disagreements is considered a sign of strength. These children may have, from necessity, learned to not listen. The sounds and noise decibels of their environment are not always pleasant or conducive to privacy; therefore, learning to not listen becomes another way of dealing with these situations.

Because of the deprivation in their backgrounds, many language-disadvantaged children are subjected to unfair competition from the day they enter school; they often fail to achieve as much as their abilities would permit, and never seem able to enter fully into the life of the group. Assignments that are reasonable for children with adequate language backgrounds are almost impossible tasks for these children. If the language arts program is to have meaning for them, it must take into account the circumstances in which they live. Many programs have been initiated and materials have been written to compensate for the deficiencies in language backgrounds; however, there obviously is much more improvement to be made in the future.

Stereotyping

All elementary materials, especially reading, have been criticized for a stereotyped representation of ethnic groups and sex roles. The criticisms of the late 1960s may no longer be appropriate for two reasons. First, publishers and authors have revised the materials in question or have discontinued the more objectionable materials. Secondly, until the revisions are used and studied, it is too early to praise or criticize the changes.[54]

Teachers still, however, need to be alert to the range of alternatives which instructional materials present for ethnic groups and sex roles. Sometimes sexism and racism appear in such subtle ways that the impact on young, developing learners is underestimated or overlooked by the adult.

Research

A review of the available research relevant to the language arts areas is beyond the scope of this text. This section identifies the sources where the research has been gathered, classified, and summarized, and in addition, calls to attention the areas where further research is needed.

Compilations of research appear in:
1. *Journal of Educational Research*, Vol. LXVII, No. 9 (May–June 1974), pp. 387–420.
2. *Reading Research Quarterly*, Vol. X, No. 3 (1974–1975), pp. 267–543.
3. *Reading Research Quarterly*, Vol. XI, No. 1 (1975–1975), pp. 7–35.
4. *Language Arts*, Vol. LIII, No. 1 (January 1976), pp. 85–110.

[54] Anne Stevens Fishman, "A Criticism of Sexism in Elementary Readers," *The Reading Teacher*, Vol. XXIX, No. 5 (February 1976), pp. 443–446.

Areas in which existing research seems inadequate and additional studies are needed include:

1. The effectiveness of one language procedure as compared to others. Perhaps an approach might be to study a particular procedure for a particular child for a particular element of instruction.
2. The cognitive operations that a learner must perform in learning to read, as well as the cognitive operations needed to comprehend the teaching instructions for reading.
3. The relationship between spoken and written language forms.
4. The knowledge and use of language by the teacher as an aspect of language instruction.
5. How meaning is conveyed in language.
6. How the writing system influences and is related to language, especially reading.
7. The issues of cultural dialects and language differences related to learning standard English.
8. When, where, and how the S-R association and/or field theories operate to further the learning of language.
9. How to operationalize present and future findings from language research.

This is not an exhaustive list of the research needs. It does reflect the author's analysis of the needs. Item 9 above may be the most significant of all.

Wish I'd Said That!

Nancy Whitelaw of Buffalo, New York, has expressed in poetic form some fundamental issues of reading instruction.[55]

Some Negative and Positive Thoughts on Reading in School
Having a reading program based on just diagnosis and prescription is like making a cake and not tasting it—
　　　　Like notes of music on paper—
　　　　Like a library with closed doors—
　　　　Like a marriage by contract.

Reading without sharing is like watching a circus without saying anything—
　　　　Like a commercial without a TV program—
　　　　Like a frame without a picture—
　　　　Like describing a spiral staircase without using your hands.

Explaining the rule for determining whether g is "hard" or "soft" is like outlining how to play jazz—
　　　　Like instructing how to kiss—
　　　　Like using a compass without a map—
　　　　Like explaining a bad joke.

Measuring .3 year's growth in reading is like measuring a sunrise—
　　　　Like measuring a laugh—

55 Nancy Whitelaw, "Some Negative and Positive Thoughts on Reading in School," *The Reading Teacher*, Vol. XXIX, No. 2 (November 1975), p. 145.

Like measuring an idea—
Like weighing happiness.

Reading is not a Forty-five Minute Period of Instruction with Behavioral Objectives and Predictable Outcomes.

Reading is enjoying, learning, feeling, becoming, sensing, laughing, crying, hating, deciding, loving, growing, sympathizing, listening.
Reading is All Day—
Being and Becoming—
Growing and Growing.

INTERDISCIPLINARY APPROACHES

The theme of this section will also appear in each of the subsequent chapters on the various curriculum areas. The discussion will present those special programs which interrelate curriculum areas. When special programs within an area deserve mentioning, they, too, will appear under this section title. The purpose is to remind the reader that all instruction is enhanced when the relationships between and among areas are recognized. Three special programs have been selected to illustrate the potential of a multidisciplinary approach: values-clarification strategies; career awareness activities; and the "Right to Read" program. Because Chapter 6 presented the fundamental premises, objectives, and approaches of these programs, only their applications will be described.

Values-Clarification Strategies

Several of the values-clarification strategies involve interviewing; public interview, interview chain, and group interview are examples. The questions of the interviewer may be prepared in advance (written) or be spontaneous (spoken). The interview may be on a topic for which the participants have prepared (reading) as a getting-acquainted type of interview. Other strategies suggest that the pupil keep a diary, autobiography, list of frustrations, or other personal record. A student may voluntarily share these personal writings or keep them private.

Literature provides an excellent opportunity to apply values-clarification strategies. For example, perhaps, the plot of a particular story involves a dilemma. Strategies may be to develop alternatives and their consequences, to rank the characters of the literature, or to complete a passage in literature if the reading of the literature is stopped before the resolution is presented.

Role playing and dramatization are fundamental to values-clarification strategies. These may be based on incidents from school and classroom behaviors, from textbooks and source books, or from the literature. A rule for role playing is that the actor always be called by the name of the character being played. Simon and others provided a listing of values-clarification strategies.[56]

---

[56] Sidney B. Simon, Leland W. Howe, and Howard Kirschenbaum, *Values Clarification: A Handbook of Practical Strategies for Teachers and Students.* (New York: Hart Publishing Company, Inc., 1972).

Career Awareness Activities

The tools of language—listening, speaking, reading, and writing—are utilized in all vocations. Therefore, almost any vocation can be investigated to determine the form, content, and level of proficiency required for application of these tools. Letters can be written to inquire about the nature of a particular vocation. Vocational sources can be read, reported, or summarized as language arts and career awareness activities. The occupations of the characters in literature can be identified and related to the plot of the story. Literature portraying various ethnic groups, and both men and women, can be read and discussed. Application forms can be gathered, completed, and prepared. Resumés can be prepared; manuals and policy books can be read; the possibilities are unlimited.

"Right To Read"

"Right to Read" is a national program with the goal of increasing functional literacy. By 1980, the aim of the "Right to Read" program is to have 99 percent of people under sixteen years of age and 90 percent of those over that age possess reading competencies sufficient to function effectively as adults. The program, started in 1971 under Commissioner of Education James Allen, is designed to focus national attention on reading, to identify changes needed to reduce reading problems, to identify resources, to initiate innovative and effective reading programs in all types of agencies and institutions, and to demonstrate effective reading techniques and programs.

By 1975, over 1,500 programs had been established as part of the "Right to Read" project. Of these, 222 programs have been selected as having strong promise, 27 have been identified by the American Institute for Research as having exhibited positive reading gains over several years, and 12 were selected by the "Right to Read" project as models for in-service programs.[57]

Through the coordination and stimulation activities of the "Right to Read" effort, many varied and flexible programs have been created by public and private groups. The results of evaluation are still inconclusive. Many of the programs report significant gains, but the research designs are not always firm. The project has established that varied approaches do accomplish reading gains, but it has not yet identified which approaches specifically and significantly relate to those gains.

Language Arts and the Curriculum

The language arts curriculum is the prime agent to interrelate all curricula. Other than literature, there is little content in language arts—only skills and tools. These skills and tools must be applied to content generated from other sources: affective needs; social studies; science; mathematics; and so on. The language arts curriculum focuses on the organization of tools and skills of communication, which must be specifically taught and learned. However, the test of

[57] "National Right To Read Effort," *Effective Reading Programs: Summaries of 222 Selected Programs.* (Washington, D.C.: U.S. Office of Education, 1975), pp. v–viii.

this teaching and learning is in the quality of communication generated—not in the neatness of the handwriting, the accuracy of the spelling, the answers to questions about comprehension, or other characteristics.

SITUATION 7.8   Select one grade or level within the elementary school and list ten reading-enrichment activities suitable to that grade or level.

STRATEGY OF INSTRUCTION

This section briefly discusses the application of the strategy to the language arts curriculum introduced in Chapter 5.

Selection of Content

The selection of representative content for the language arts curriculum needs much research. Presently, the external criteria of classicalness and practicalness seems to be dominating the selection of language arts content topics. Efforts are being made to select topics that are more relevant and humane (values-clarification and bibliotherapy). The internal criteria for selection of content, structure, is a controversial issue. Two approaches (phonics and language experience) to linguistics are examples of efforts to identify structure, but neither is generally accepted, and the research on their impact is inconsistent. Those authorities committed to phonics argue that this approach is the simplifying, clustering, and generating elements of reading, if not language itself. Yet, there is evidence that the English language is not a phonetically stable and predictable language. The language experience approach implies that the interactions and relationships among the listening, speaking, reading, and writing language arts areas represent structure. As an idea, this seems functional, but the research data are again inconsistent.

From the premise that no approach can presently provide a data base that establishes its superiority, the author concludes that the organizing concepts and structure(s) of the language arts curriculum have not yet been identified.

Learning and Development

The S-R (stimulus-response) association theories are expressed in the approaches oriented toward phonics. The field theories are expressed in the aural-oral language experience approaches. In terms of current practice and the "innovative" new programs, the author concludes that the S-R association theories are influencing language arts curriculum more than the field theories of learning.

The implications of the developmentalists—Piaget, Maslow, Kohlberg, and Erikson—seem to have not yet penetrated the planning of the language arts curriculum. For example, Piaget's description of the preoperational learners implies that their cognitive processes are not sufficient to perceive the figure-ground relationships and reversibilities necessary to apply phonic generalizations. Possibly, bibliotherapy and the selection of literature follow (or at least could be adapted to) the developmentalists' theories.

Methodology

When a language approach is characterized by commitments to grammar, phonics, and an S-R theory, then the teaching procedures tend to be those of review, repetition, and drill. When a language approach is characterized by commitments to listening, speaking, reading, and writing relationships, and to a language experience approach, the teaching procedures become those of inquiry: exploration, invention, and discovery. When the content of a curriculum is not appropriate to the developmental levels of the learners, the teaching procedures again become those of review, repetition, and drill. The procedures presently utilized to transmit, translate, and transpose the language arts curriculum seem to be based primarily upon an S-R association theory or are eclectic, with no consistent pattern for selection other than "use what works."

Communication

Communication patterns used to translate the language arts curriculum are characterized by convergent questions. This seems especially true when the emphasis is upon the skills of reading and writing. The tendency seems to be to use the same patterns when translating the tools of the language arts curriculum. There is evidence that the "in school" language communication pattern (standard English) introduces a static character into the learning environment for nonstandard-English speaking learners. Bilingual education is an effort to reduce this static quality and thereby to increase the achievement of nonstandard-English speaking learners.

Objectives

As with all curricula, the language arts curriculum should emphasize objectives in each domain of learner behaviors—cognitive, affective, and psychomotor. The new programs for children with learning disabilities stress the psychomotor domain. Recently developed behavioral tests in the psychomotor domain evaluate perceptual and sensory-motor skills. Perhaps these two movements will influence the inclusion of these behaviors into all language curriculums. As a matter of fact, much is being written to stress the affective domain. Adjustments in the literature selected, the characters and plots of instructional reading materials, and the topics of student writings suggest that progress is being made. The range of student behaviors emphasized in the cognitive domain is still suspect, especially when the skills of language are being presented within an S-R association learning theory frame.

Goals

The goals of language curriculum tend to be expressed in terms of skill competencies or global language proficiencies, but more attention to the role of language as the vehicle for rational thought is needed.

SUMMARY

1. Language arts is the most personal and intimate curriculum area.

2. It is by means of language that children can avail themselves of their cultural heritage, and prepare for the intellectual and social cooperation involved in democratic living.

3. The primary purpose of the language arts is to promote the wholesome growth of the child by helping to meet as effectively as possible those life situations involving the use of language.

4. Instruction in the language arts begins with the social maturation and experiences encoded by the learner.

5. All the skills and tools areas functioning to facilitate listening, speaking, reading, and writing are ingredients of the unified language arts curriculum.

6. The language areas—in order of development, size, and power—are listening, speaking, reading, and writing.

7. The activities and programs for developing listening as a fundamental aspect of the language arts curriculum need strengthening.

8. The speaking area of the language arts curriculum includes the support for reading and writing, and for recent innovations in bilingual and dialect programs.

9. The overriding goal of reading instruction is to enable each learner to be a time-binder.

10. The seven approaches to reading instruction have certain characteristics which include advantages and disadvantages.

11. Presently, research cannot clearly establish the superiority of any one approach to reading instruction.

12. Writing as an ingredient of the unified language arts curriculum includes handwriting, spelling, and the composition forms of exposition and creative writing.

13. Readiness is a functioning aspect of all language arts areas: listening, speaking, reading, and writing.

14. Tests to assess, diagnose, and evaluate readiness in reading are more numerous than those for listening, speaking, and writing.

15. The learning center, with its wide range of materials and media, is an important part of the unified language arts curriculum.

16. The unified language arts curriculum is a prime vehicle to interrelate all curriculum areas.

17. The application of the strategy of instruction (Chapter 5) to the language arts curriculum illustrates that much needs to be done in selecting content vehicles, accommodating developmental levels, incorporating inquiry methods, and establishing objectives.

Problems and Projects

1. From the parents, employers, critics, and society: "Johnny can't read." "The schools are not teaching our youth to read." From middle-school, mid-high, and

senior high administrators and teachers: "We are receiving students who are vertically promoted from the elementary schools but are unable to read well enough to
successfully complete assignments in other curriculum areas." The blame seems
repeatedly to fall upon the shoulders of the primary teacher. Gather information
which reports research data regarding the reading development of children. What is
Piaget's position? Granted, "The child will read when ready," but has this expression become a "cop-out" for teachers to wait until that magic moment, that "teachable" moment when the child is "ready?" What are the responsibilities of the teacher
to a learner who will be ready to read later than the majority of his or her peers?
If possible, interview kindergarten, first-grade, and second-grade teachers concerning
their strategies of instruction for late-developing readers.

2. Discuss with a language arts supervisor, or an elementary teacher having at
least ten years experience, the evolution and innovations within language arts during
the past ten years. What changes in society have caused these adjustments in the
curriculum? What educational research findings may have influenced the alterations
in language art programs?

3. Examine three basal reading series. Compare and contrast the characteristics
of the three series. If you were asked to select one of the three series you examined,
what series would you select? What factors determined your decision?

4. Review reading journals for publications about diagnosing reading difficulties.
What alternatives are available to a teacher? What are the indicators to a trained
observer that a child may be having reading problems?

5. The present cry of "back to the basics" and the evidence concerning the functional illiteracy of 20 percent of the adult population are being related as a justification for "back to the basics." What relationships do you perceive?

Selected Readings

Burron, Arnold, and Amo L. Claybaugh, *Using Reading To Teach Subject Matter.*
Columbus, Ohio: Charles E. Merrill Publishing Company, 1974. Ideas for the
teaching of reading in various subject fields.

Chall, Jeanne, *Learning To Read: The Great Debate.* New York: McGraw-Hill,
1967. Critical analysis of research in reading.

Cullinan, Bernice E. (Ed.), *Black Dialects and Reading.* Urbana, Ill.: National
Council of Teachers of English, 1974. Dialect problems in the teaching of oral
language and reading.

Curry, Robert L., and Lynna Geis Mercer, *Guide to Concepts and Skills in Reading.*
Dubuque, Iowa: Kendall/Hunt Publishing Co., 1976.

Dallman, Martha, R. L. Rouch, L. Y. C. Chang, and John DeBoer, *The Teaching of
Reading.* New York: Holt, Rinehart and Winston, 1974. Textbook for the teaching of reading.

Harrow, Anita J., *Taxonomy of the Psychomotor Domain: A Guide for Developing
Behavioral Objectives.* New York: David McKay Co., Inc., 1972.

Huck, Charlotte S., *Children's Literature in the Elementary School* (3rd ed.). New
York: Holt, Rinehart and Winston, 1975.

King, Martha L., Robert Emans, and Patricia J. Cianciolo (Eds.), *The Language
Arts in the Elementary School: A Forum for Focus.* Urbana, Ill.: National Coun-
cil of Teachers of English, 1973. Readings on language arts, including one on
Piaget.

Krug, Mark M., *What Will Be Taught the Next Decade?* Itasca, Ill.: F. E. Peacock

Publishers, Inc., 1972. Evaluates the direction of several subjects, including English.

Marckwardt, Albert H. (Ed.), *Linguistics in School Programs*. 69th Yearbook, Part II. Chicago: National Society for the Study of Education, 1970. Discusses languages and dialects.

Rubin, Dorothy, *Teaching Elementary Language Arts*. New York: Holt, Rinehart and Winston, 1975. Textbook on the teaching of language arts.

Ruddell, Robert B., *Reading-Language Instruction: Innovative Practices*. Englewood Cliffs, N.J.: Prentice-Hall, Inc., 1974. Integrates reading and language arts instruction.

Shane, Harold G., James Walden, and Ronald Green (Eds.), *Interpreting Language Arts Research for the Teacher*. Washington, D.C.: Association for Supervision and Curriculum Development, 1971. Summary of research in the language arts areas.

Smith, E. Brooks, Kenneth S. Goodman, and Robert Meredith, *Language and Thinking in the Elementary School*. New York: Holt, Rinehart and Winston, 1970. Chapter on Piaget and Vygotsky.

Stahl, Dona K., and Patricia Anzalone, *Individualized Teaching in Elementary Schools*. West Nyack, N.Y.: Parker Publishing Company, 1970. Guidelines for individualizing the teaching of reading.

chapter 8

Inquiring
SOCIAL STUDIES

*The American people have always expected the schools to contribute
directly to the development of loyalty to the democratic ideal, good citizenship, civic responsibility, and human relationships. These represent the
broader goals of all education, but the social studies have historically assumed a special responsibility toward the attainment of those goals.*

John Jarolimek, *Social Studies in Elementary Education*, 3rd ed.
(New York: Crowell Collier and Macmillan, Inc., 1967), p. 2.

Man is a social being. At each place in time, people have gathered into
groups, and a societal system has evolved, a social system with its accommodations for pecking order, the assignment and regulation of power, barter, tradition, ethics, religion. With time, these systems became increasingly complex and
potentially oppressive, deprecating the worth of the individual members of the
system. Representative democracy is another attempt to create a social system
in which political and economic mechanisms do not oppress the individual.
Presently, the United States has developed its tool-building sciences to a high
degree of efficiency and sophistication, resulting in the most affluent society and
the highest standard of living known to date. Yet, the very products of science
may now be the greatest threat to human existence and dignity. There exists a
threatening imbalance between the power and sophistication of our natural sciences and our social sciences. A great need exists for a knowledge explosion
within the human sciences to match and balance the explosions which have
occurred within the natural sciences.

The idea is frequently expressed that the future of civilization revolves
around the question of whether humans can learn to live with each other. There
is abundant evidence that the future of this nation depends not only upon our
achievements in science, but also upon our knowledge and skill in the realm of
human relations. A high degree of social competence is required in diplomacy,
foreign trade, labor-management relations, intercultural relations, conservation
and effective use of natural and human resources, reduction of crime and de-
linquency, administration of public enterprises, and education.

Although no one expects children in the elementary school to provide solutions for complex national and international problems, almost everyone agrees that the elementary school has a responsibility for aiding the child to interpret society and its problems, because these problems are almost blatantly presented in so many questionable sources—television, movies, printed materials, and so forth. How far to go in the process, how to organize the program, and what methods and materials to use are central problems in curriculum planning.

The social studies program in the modern elementary school cannot take sole responsibility for the social education of children, but it can play an important part in their social growth and provide them with insight into the patterns and processes through which people live, work, and play together. It can help them understand our economic system, our form of government, the history of our nation, the differences and similarities of peoples around the world, the contributions that citizens make to the welfare of the community, and the rights and duties of citizens in a democracy. The content of the modern social studies program is drawn from a wide variety of sources, essentially the social science disciplines. The organization and methods harmonize with what we know about learners and the learning process. Without losing sight of the value of possessing useful information, the program helps children grow continuously in their abilities to learn on their own and to shape attitudes, beliefs, and values that complement life in a free society. Ultimately, the learner must become a competent participant in a democratic social order.

SITUATION 8.1   Before studying the remainder of this chapter, write a few brief statements which reflect your concept of social studies in the elementary school. What would be the "central purpose" of social studies within the elementary school?

THE MEANING OF SOCIAL STUDIES

The term "social studies" came into general use within the first half of this century. The National Education Association gave it official sanction in 1916, and the teachers of social subjects selected the name *National Council for the Social Studies* for their new organization in 1921. The term is now generally used to designate that phase of the curriculum in elementary and high schools that deals with the relations of human beings to one another and to their environment.

Lee said, "Social studies deals with mankind's social, economic and political behavior, at any place where people live or have lived, now or in the past."[1]

Both the social studies and the social sciences deal with human relationships, the former at the level of childhood and adolescence, and the latter at the

[1] John R. Lee, *Teaching Social Studies in the Elementary School.* (New York: The Free Press, 1974), p. 7.

level of the adult. The social scientist is concerned primarily with expanding the boundaries of knowledge and with developing highly specialized scholars in such fields as history, geography, political science, economics, sociology, anthropology, and often social psychology, philosophy, and religion. The social studies are concerned with the wide dissemination of information, the development of social and inquiry skills, and the improvement of social attitudes and behavior. The social studies program draws materials from the various social sciences, but it also uses materials from the local community, current affairs, and world problems that require an inter- or multidisciplinary approach. The social studies program of the modern elementary school does not place major emphasis upon the child's becoming a historian, geographer, economist, or other specialist. It emphasizes the functional use of subject matter from many sources to increase social consciousness, and to develop the socially desirable behaviors that evolve from sound attitudes and appreciations about our country and others. The sources of social studies content include the social science disciplines; the lives of the children; and the lives of people in the immediate, surrounding, and world communities.

The concern of the social studies with the improvement of social behavior has been misinterpreted by some critics of education. They define social behavior rather narrowly in terms of social amenities—the courtesies of "please" and "thank you," sharing equipment, taking turns in a group discussion, and in general learning to act toward others in civilized fashion—and ridicule the school for making these part of the curriculum. But the social amenities are only a small part of socially desirable behavior as defined by educators. Socially desirable behavior in a democracy includes many things, such as exercising one's right to vote; seeing that constitutional rights as defined by the courts are accorded to all regardless of race, creed, or sex; working for community improvement; working for better schools; jealously guarding our freedoms under the Bill of Rights; recognizing one's national responsibilities toward other nations; recognizing that the future of the United States is inextricably bound to that of other parts of the world. In its social studies program, the modern school attempts to teach the tools, concepts, and processes of the social sciences in an environment in which the learner will experience behaviors consistent with acting wisely in a democratic society.

In order to help children develop such desirable social behaviors, the teacher does not necessarily plan a unit or a special activity. But these behaviors are goals the teacher continually has in mind when teaching. Whether the study is centered on South America, medieval Europe, a current-events problem or a playground squabble, concepts stemming from our democratic ideals are introduced, and generalizations that will guide children toward democratic behaviors are taught and experienced.

The term "social education" is frequently found in educational writing. The term is not used as a substitute for the social studies but as a general term to include all phases of the environment that influence the development of social maturity in children. It includes not only the social studies program of the school but also the work of other educative agencies such as the home, the community, the press, radio, motion pictures, and television, which influence the social insight and behavior of children.

"Social living," sometimes used to designate those phases of the school program in which the child participates in group activities, includes not only the organized social studies program, but also such activities as the core program, experience units, assembly programs, and school clubs.

THE OBJECTIVES OF SOCIAL STUDIES

The ultimate objective of the social studies program is the improvement of conditions, not merely in the classroom, but in the community, the nation, and the world; it is designed to develop intelligent, responsible, self-directive citizens. The school, therefore, not only provides opportunities for children to acquire useful information; it also provides a laboratory for social living in which they have opportunities to develop their own potentialities and to contribute their maximum efforts to the improvement of group living. The ultimate objective of social studies can be illustrated by the story of the wise-acting, self-directing women of Weinsburg, Germany. In 1140, the commander of the enemy forces told the women of the conquered town that they could leave, carrying on their backs their most prized possessions. The women left, carrying on their backs their fathers, brothers, or husbands. In the social studies curriculum of the modern elementary school, the pupils experience how to act wisely in choosing their most precious possessions. "The basic justification for teaching social studies is the contribution it makes to an individual's potential for acting wisely in human efforts."[2]

One of the primary reasons for the learning of social studies is the "acquisition of knowledge, the refinement of standards, and the development of reasoned thought."[3] Each of these results from the utilization of the rational powers (see Chapter 2) with experiencing. A paraphrase of Lee's statement based upon Chapter 5 might be: The experiencing of the representative structure of a discipline through the inquiry process which involves the full range of cognitive, affective, and psychomotor behaviors.

Joyce said that the goals of social studies were:

1. *Humanistic education to help the child understand his social life*
2. *Citizenship education, to develop his citizenship behavior*
3. *Intellectual education, to make the tactics of the social scientists available to every citizen*[4]

Joyce justified social studies on the bases of making the best tools (tactics of the social scientists) available to help the individual comprehend life and one's problems.

[2] Lee, p. 8.
[3] Lee, p. 8
[4] Bruce R. Joyce, *Strategies for Elementary Social Science Education.* (Chicago: Science Research Associates, 1965), p. 12.

facts about me...

Social studies can contribute to the comprehension, awareness, and understanding of oneself.

Intellectual Development

The social studies curriculum is designed to provide the pupils with the experiencing of:

1. *Anthropologists*—to learn the activities of people, the ideas they share and hold, and the things produced, especially culture. These anthropological concepts are especially important: culture; society; values; beliefs; traditions; customs; social organizations; processes of social change; families; communities; and the characteristics of civilization.

2. *Economists*—to learn the activities of production, exchange, and consumption of goods and services within the conflict of unlimited wants and limited resources. These economic concepts are especially important: wants and needs; production; consumption; exchange; free enterprise; scarcity; division of labor; specialization; interdependence; goods and services; credit; income; and the involvement of government.

3. Geographers—to learn the activities of human culture in interaction with natural environmental factors. These geographic concepts are especially important: the earth's surface; earth–space relationships; relative location and position; major land and water forms; natural resources; climate; population distribution; settlement patterns; urban and rural regions; conservation; and the symbolism in maps and globes.

4. Historians—to learn the activities of identifying and describing the events of the past. These concepts of history are especially important: sequence;

movements; events; people; cycles; and the evolution of events, people, and ideas.

5. Political scientists—to learn the regulations and assignments of power through legal government. These political science concepts are especially important: authority; decision-making processes; agencies; laws; policies; rules; services; forms and bases of legal power; and formal and informal institutions.

6. Sociologists—to learn the activities of people in groups within a society, culture, and formal and informal institutions. These sociological concepts are especially important: peer group; influences; pecking order; norms; sanctions; values; roles; modeling; and group membership.

7. Philosophers and social psychologists—to learn the activities of shaping basic beliefs and the dynamics of group interactions. These philosophical and social psychological concepts are especially important: logic; origins of beliefs; changes of beliefs; theory; needs; drives; conventions; mobs; public riot; protests; and revolution.

Standards Development

The social studies curriculum of the modern elementary school is designed to provide the pupils with the experiencing of application and the evaluation of their abilities to:

1. utilize inquiry (see Chapter 5). These behaviors are crucial in experiencing inquiry: making systematic observations; developing alternatives; designing testing procedures; relating behavior and consequences; gathering, displaying, and interpreting data.

2. evaluate sources of information. These behaviors are crucial: locating primary and secondary sources to interrelate validity and reliability of sources; detecting and analyzing propaganda; differentiating among reporting, interpreting, and editorializing.

3. use all forms of language: listening; speaking; reading; and writing. These behaviors are crucial: auditing one's own speaking and writing; using paraphrasing to assure understanding of messages; accepting the possibility of being misunderstood; selecting speaking and writing behaviors appropriate for the topic, event, and situation; and becoming a logical critic.

4. work dependently, interdependently, and independently. These behaviors are crucial: being a follower; being a group member; being a leader; following directions; developing directions cooperatively; giving directions; performing an assigned task; participating in defining a task; and assigning a task.

5. operate efficiently and effectively. These behaviors are crucial: negotiating task versus people orientations; differentiating between efficiently and effectively; conserving time, materials, and energy; anticipating the consequences of production.

Rational Power Development

The social studies curriculum of the modern elementary school is designed to provide pupils with the experiencing of human potential to:

1. think about feelings and feel about thinking. These behaviors are crucial: tolerating the changing or reordering of value organizations and characterizations; committing to an ideal that directs behaviors; respecting one's capacities to sustain, subsume, and subscribe; and honoring of oneself and others.
2. believe. These behaviors are crucial: valuing the worth of the individual; providing equality of opportunity; honoring freedom of speech, religion, and to learn; and respecting self and others.
3. generate energies for causes. These behaviors are crucial: searching for new perspectives; expressing new creative relationships among media and people; dealing creatively with old questions and new solutions; and adjusting to the disequilibriums inherent in change.
4. be different and unique. These behaviors are crucial: knowing one's own uniquenesses; honoring and facilitating the uniquenesses of others; cooperating without co-opting; and competing without defeating.

SITUATION 8.2   Construct two social studies activities which would necessitate the inquiry approach for one grade or level within an elementary school.

It is the responsibility of the staff of a local school system to formulate the objectives of the social studies program. The staff will find it useful to review statements of goals of the American way of life, the general purposes of education in American democracy, principles of child growth and development, and statements of social studies objectives developed by national professional organizations and by other school systems. However, no ready-made statement of objectives should be accepted by the staff without revisions, additions, and adaptations to local conditions. The statements that preceded illustrate the intellectual standards and rational power developmental objectives listed in many curriculum guides as objectives of the social studies program. The examples which follow each objective are, of course, not inclusive; they will be expanded and made more explicit as professional educators and subject-matter specialists identify the activities of social studies that are significant in the education of children for wise-acting, self-actualizing citizenship.

TRENDS IN APPROACHES

This section describes the history and trends in curriculum organization and curriculum practice in social studies.

Curriculum Organization

In the organization of any curriculum, two of the fundamental problems are scope and sequence. Sequence is the establishment of a hierarchical order for the curriculum. Scope is the selection, range, and depth of the content vehicles included in the curriculum. The next two sections discuss the evolving scope and sequence of the social studies curriculum.

Scope

As with most curriculum areas, the first curriculum designs for social studies were developed from logical, established sources, and were organized as separate subjects (see Chapter 6). More specifically, the curriculum designs were based on history and geography rather than social data. Within the separate subject patterns, there was no distinct "social studies" area. Gradually, political science became a third, but weak, sister area. Other social science disciplines were not included because they did not develop academic respectability until much later. The prevailing psychology of the mid-1800s viewed the mind as a muscle which required exercise to grow. Therefore, content vehicles were detailed, abstract, and complicated so as to exercise the memory function of the mind.

Early in the twentieth century, a debate arose concerning whether a separate subjects or a "unified" subject approach to designing the social studies curriculum was better. A unified approach during this period of debate meant that history and geography would be combined into one textbook. A separate subject approach meant that history would be taught one semester and geography would be taught the next. During 1951, during his second year of teaching, the author was privileged to serve on a social studies textbook selection committee; the major issue was separate subjects versus "unified" subject. Some issues die hard!

In the 1940s, the curriculum leaders were recommending a unified history and geography social studies curriculum. By the mid-1950s, unified textbooks dominated the market. Political science soon became a full partner in the social studies curriculum. Economic education was being encouraged as a separate subject by such groups as the National Family Finance Council and the Council on Economic Education. The social science disciplines of sociology and anthropology were not yet recognized as part of social studies.

Not until the 1960s did the issue of defining social studies to include anthropology, economics, geography, history, political science, sociology, philosophy, and social psychology become important. Conflict on this issue centered around three positions: no (flat rejection of some of the social sciences); multidisciplinary curriculum; and interdisciplinary coordination. Bruner's bold premise that ". . . any subject can be taught effectively in some intellectually honest form to any child at any stage of development" helped to repress those maintaining the "no" position.[5] It should be noted that Bruner used the term "development" in a Piagetian frame.

---

[5] Jerome Bruner, *Process of Education.* (Cambridge, Mass.: Harvard University Press, 1960), p. 33.

The multidisciplinary approach held that all social sciences should be interwoven into a curriculum so that each discipline was discrete while still related to all other disciplines. This approach seemed to be a minority one. Muessig made an effort to provide a basis for the multidisciplinary approach in *The Social Science Seminar Series.*[6]

The interdisciplinary approach presently seems to be in the majority position. This approach identifies one of the social science disciplines as its core and interrelates the other disciplines to expand and enrich the organizing concepts of the selected core discipline. Several examples of this approach are operational: Senesh, *Our Working World*[7] (economics), and Bruner, *Man A Course of Study*[8] (anthropology). These programs will be mentioned again in this chapter. (See Fig. 8.1.)

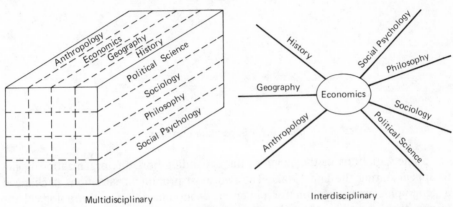

Multidisciplinary   Interdisciplinary

Figure 8.1   Social studies content.

All three positions (no, multidisciplinary, and interdisciplinary) assume that the social studies curriculum is to be developed from the logical source and is organized as a broad field. A rapidly developing position, generally resolved among authorities but not totally among practitioners, is the idea of affective and humane education. These programs will be discussed later. The position itself is translated into terms of curriculum development: Should the curriculum be developed from the sociological source (see Chapter 6) and should it be organized in a thematic pattern?

Sequence

Beginning in 1918 with the report of the National Commission on Secondary Education, the sequence of the social studies curriculum was governed by the "expanding horizons" concept.

The expanding horizons concept, later called "widening horizons" or "ex-

[6] Raymond Muessig, *The Social Science Seminar Series.* (Columbus, Ohio: Charles E. Merrill Publishing Company, 1965).

[7] Lawrence Senesh, *Our Working World: Families at Work.* (Chicago, Ill.: Science Research Associates, Inc., 1963).

[8] Jerome Bruner, *Man, A Course of Study.* (Washington, D.C.: Curriculum Development Associates, Inc., 1970).

panding environments," assumed that each individual built a world of experiences, with the experiencer at the center position. It also assumed that as experiencing expanded, so did the horizons of the experiencer's world. The latter assumption was that learning occurred most efficiently and effectively when it had an experience base.

A geographic application was then overlaid upon these assumptions of the expanding horizons concepts. Therefore, the sequence and scope of social studies became: home and family; school and immediate neighborhood; surrounding community; state; the United States; the Western Hemisphere; and the Eastern Hemisphere. When this sequence and scope was imposed upon the graded plan from the vertical axis, the result was the social studies curriculum. (See Fig. 8.2.)

Figure 8.2   Expanding horizons.

Some variations of the scope of the expanding-horizons organization began to appear during the late 1960s. The two most prominent variations exchanged a geographic interpretation for either an economic or an anthropological interpretation of scope (Senesh: *Our Working World*; and Bruner: *Man, A Course of Study*). For example, Bruner's work utilizes an anthropological interpretation. The child's first experiencing is within the family unit; therefore, the scope of the initial curriculum experiences should be with the various family units of the world. A later section of this chapter will discuss *Man, A Course of Study* further.

The expanding-horizons concept seems sound. Perhaps, a strict geographic interpretation of it is inadequate in light of the mobility of populations and the instant communications of the mass media. If not geography, then will it become anthropology, economics, a child's awareness, or something else?

SITUATION 8.3   Talk with a social studies supervisor and a college social studies methods instructor about organizing concepts or structures within the social studies discipline. Ask what they would like to see incorporated in the classroom instruction.

Three contrasting plans for organizing the social studies curriculum were submitted by Joyce:[9] person-centered, citizen-centered, and social science-

[9] Bruce Joyce, "What Curriculum Approach for Social Studies?" in *Social Studies Extension Program*. (Chicago: Science Research Associates, Inc., 1966), p. 28.

centered. The person-centered plan cites self-understanding, one's purposes and values, others' relationships, and behavior in society as the major objectives. Pupils involved in the citizen-centered plan would be guided to understand societal processes and the development of skills of democratic action in solving social problems. Both plans would include topics selected through teacher-pupil cooperation.

The objectives stated for the social science-centered plan place emphasis on developing understandings of the tools and organizations of the various social science disciplines in the analysis of societal issues. In all three plans, depth studies replace a more superficial coverage of broad topics. The consistent elements in these plans that assure continuity are: (1) the analysis of group dynamics and group inquiry processes; (2) the analysis of democratic institutions; (3) the use of analytic tools from all the social sciences; and (4) the emphasis on values and controversial issues. Another interesting aspect of Joyce's plans is the demand placed upon the teacher to supply fresh content and ideas each year while the fundamental ideas, skills, and values are being developed.

Essential to any organizational plan for the presentation of social studies content is a carefully planned sequence of experiences for learners. A scope-and-sequence chart is designed to prevent undue duplication, to provide proper balance in the program, and to assist in the selection of materials. Efforts are made to relate learning experiences to the maturity of children at various developmental levels, to capitalize on conditions and resources of the community, and to promote the development of democratic behavior. An apparent strength evidenced in the new social studies curriculum packages is the attention given to sequencing materials and experiences to allow for individual differences. Programs prepared for implementation on a K through 12 basis emphasize flexibility and encourage cooperative planning by local school staff members to assure the most effective use of the materials.

Curriculum Guides

Modern curriculum guides have three aspects in common: inquiry and process; experience units; and either an inter- or multidisciplinary approach. The traditional functions of a guide are also continued: objectives, scope, sequence, spiraling, assessment, and provisions for individual differences. Modern guides seem to group themselves to three forms.

Some of the modern guides modify the geographic interpretation of the expanding-horizons concept. The basic sequence is still home, school, neighborhood, community, state, and nation, but the scope has been modified to include homes, neighborhoods, communities, and local groups from other cultures. This expansion of the scope is an accommodation to the increased mobility of our population and the impact of communication media. These guides have further recognized the value of content from the social science disciplines other than history, geography, and political science. Most of the commercially published programs have maintained the expanding-horizons concept while enlarging the contributions from all social science disciplines.

Another set of these more recent guides has emphasized the selection of representative generalizations from one of the social science disciplines (for example, economics, geography, or anthropology); others have built an interdisciplinary approach through the selection of generalizations from all the social sciences, without emphasis on any particular one. Senesh[10] and Bruner[11] have developed model programs stressing one social science discipline as the core while incorporating the others to enrich the core. Muessig in *The Social Science Seminar Series* has developed models stressing the spiraling of generalizations from each of the disciplines.

A smaller set of the more recent guides has attempted to redefine the expanding-horizons concept. These guides typically define the sequencing of social studies in terms of the continuing activities of man; the assumption is made that man has been faced with similar problems at each period of time and in each place and culture (see Chapter 6). The problems of governance, religion, education, communication, tool development, and other areas have been resolved and re-resolved by each succeeding generation. A social studies curriculum should therefore be organized around the upward spiral of these continuing activities of man, with the scope being adjusted to match the increasing maturity of the learners. In "Basic Activities of Man" the Oklahoma City Public Schools have provided a model of this organization.[12]

Principal Practices

Formulating objectives, developing an overall framework or organization, and planning the sequence of learning experiences are some of the means by which the staff of an elementary school can provide a favorable situation for teaching the social studies. The quality of the program is determined in the final analysis by the procedures used to make the social studies functional and meaningful for children.

The social studies curriculum offers many opportunities for rich and meaningful experiences. The extent to which these opportunities are utilized depends to some extent upon the size of the classroom, the type of furniture in the room, the amount and kind of instructional materials available, and the type of curriculum organization used in the school. It depends to a much greater extent upon the teacher's vision, understanding of the characteristics and needs of children, and resourcefulness in adapting methods and materials to the needs of individuals.

Curriculum planning in the social studies no longer consists merely of the selection of content to be covered. A unit on Latin American neighbors, for example, should suggest content to be studied—such as deserts, mountains, rivers, lakes, groups of people, modes of transportation, education, occupations, and products—but it should contain a great deal more than an outline of con-

[10] Lawrence Senesh, *Our Working World: Families at Work.*
[11] Jerome Bruner, *Man, A Course of Study.*
[12] Oklahoma City Public Schools, "Basic Activities of Man," Manual. (Oklahoma City, Okla.: 1972).

tent to be covered. Various approaches for stimulating interest in the unit should be described; activities should be cooperatively planned by pupils and teacher to involve the social sciences with the language arts, science, art, music, physical education, and health. Pupils should be involved in the selection of evaluative techniques for measuring pupil progress, and lists of available media should be provided.

If elementary school children regard the social studies as dull and uninteresting, the cause can usually be found in one or more of the following conditions:

1. There are no opportunities for wise acting, experiencing, and inquiring.
2. The objects and materials of the environment are inappropriate to the developmental levels and the experiences of the learners.
3. The range of cognitive and affective behaviors is being thwarted.
4. Teaching and learning are considered as the same acts.
5. Information, conclusions, and values are being imposed.

There is no simple formula for effective teaching of the social studies in elementary schools. The teacher who understands the principles of child growth and development, the realities and ideals of contemporary American life, and the broader objectives of the elementary school has the foundation upon which to develop teaching procedures adapted to the teaching situations. These bases of good teaching were discussed in Chapters 1, 3, and 5. Though by no means inclusive, the following topics will call attention to some of the major characteristics of effective procedures in the area of the social studies.

Participation

Reading the textbook and reciting the contents to the teacher and an uninterested group of pupils once constituted virtually the only experience the learner had in the social studies program. In recent years, however, the number and variety of learning activities have increased greatly. It is assumed that if children are to become more effective in meeting social situations, they must have experiences in many meaningful and useful activities that involve human relationships. Merely reading about issues being resolved either by debate or the ballot is not enough; rational discussion, creation of alternatives, and the testing of alternatives must become functional in the lives of children if they are to become informed, participating citizens. Democratic citizenship develops in a classroom in which children practice living as citizens of a democracy.

It is recognized, of course, that an activity program can be carried to undesirable extremes. Activities are not ends in themselves; they are means to learning, just as subject matter is a means to learning. It should not be assumed that just any activity has educational value. Teachers spend a great deal of time in selecting and guiding activities so that they will contribute to the development of useful concepts, attitudes, behaviors, and skills. Unless this is done, the activity program has no more value than a program based on a single textbook. In fact, one of the pitfalls that the modern teacher must avoid is activity for activity's sake. Teachers have sponsored activities of little or no real educational value and have justified them "because the children are so interested" or "because they provide such wonderful opportunities for working in groups."

Here are samples of activities carried on at different grade levels in elementary schools:

First Grade. The children put on a health play for their parents, taken from a magazine for teachers. They memorize their lines, make little costumes out of brown wrapping paper, and learn a song entitled, "Making Our Teeth White and Strong." The hero of the play is Mr. Toothbrush, who finally drives old Mr. Cavity right off the stage in a hilarious climax.

Second Grade. Children build a little post office for the distribution of valentines. They bring in boxes to form a counter and build a stamp window. They cover the boxes with brown paper, paint background, and even erect a roof. They plan and carry out the whole activity in committees. Each child has a box in the post office marked with his name. The children take turns playing clerk and putting the valentines in the proper place.

Third Grade. The community health officer comes to school by invitation to talk to the class about the various ways in which the health office safeguards the health of the community. The class plans for the visit, writes a letter of invitation and a thank-you letter. No posters are made; no art work is involved.

Fourth Grade. Children model an Eskimo village on the sand table. They make pipestem figures dressed as Eskimos, build igloos, and arrange dog sleds and other equipment.

Sixth Grade. Children who have been studying our basic freedoms stage an original play, "The Trial of Peter Zenger." They write the script after studying various records of the trial, plan the scenery and the costumes, and plan other aspects of the production.

An analysis of these activities, utilizing the strategy of instruction presented in Chapter 5, will illustrate the application of the strategy for purposes of evaluation. The public relations impact of putting on a play for parents is likely to be good. The approach to the content of the play emphasizes the cognitive behaviors. The use of moralizing as a substitute for values-clarification strategies in the affective domain implies a significant void in the range of behaviors available to the learner. Six-year-old children are usually preoperational. This means that they do not have the cognitive operations necessary to transfer from a model. Literally, six-year-olds learn how to keep a model tooth from developing cavities. For preoperational children, the model and the object must be the same. The selection of content vehicles which are not representative of the field is apparent. Cavities are not brushed away—plaque is. Finally, the opportunities for inquiry (exploration, invention, and discovery) are nil. As described, the first-grade play is worse than no activity at all. Its only grace is in the "P-R" (public relations) contribution.

The post office activity for second graders also involves using a model to represent reality. Again, preoperational learners do not have the cognitive operations to make this transfer. The selected content topics have little real value in that they do not represent the activities of the postal service. The opportunities for inquiry are limited to the activities of construction. The pupils can explore, invent, and discover with the construction materials and design. Whatever educational value can be generated from the project as described is quite limited.

The community health officer's visit to the third-grade group could generate significant involvements. However, the description of the activities limits the potential involvement to writing letters of invitation and thanks, and to listening to a presentation. The educational return from this level of involvement is nil. Now, if the group had, through an inquiry process, generated a set of information clusters from which questions could be investigated through the resource of a community health officer, the educational possibilities could have been increased tremendously. The inquiry process would have assured that the learners would be working with data and operations appropriate to their developmental levels. A complete inquiry process would have also provided the opportunities for the involvement of behaviors at all levels of the cognitive and affective domains.

The Eskimo activity has little, if any, educational value. The children are carrying on an activity based upon factual information that is out of date: the modern Eskimo no longer lives the kind of primitive life the children are picturing. Furthermore, since the pupils do not have actual materials available, the makeshift igloos, sleds, and costumes bear little relationship to reality, and may actually create erroneous concepts in the children's minds. Activities that truly reproduce the experience of another time or place (such as candle making in a pioneer unit) will help the child better understand other ways of living, but imitations of reality—and too often imitations based upon erroneous information—are a waste of teacher and pupil time.

The original play of the sixth graders provides for a wide range of desirable learning outcomes. The inquiries necessary to capture representative information about Zenger, the organizing necessary for a communication through role playing, scenery, costumes, and the wise acting behavior needed to successfully complete the project, are all potent learning experiences.

The unprofitable use of some of the activities discussed above do not alter the fact that pupils in the modern social studies program learn from many varied activities rather than merely from reading the textbook; the described activities merely emphasize the fact that unit teaching, in which multiple activities are used, requires intelligent planning. Effective use of unit teaching (see Chapter 6) requires intelligent formulation of objectives in terms of selecting representative content topics, adaptations to developmental levels of the learners, opportunities for inquiry, and behaviors of all classification levels of the three domains of the *Taxonomy of Educational Objectives* discussed in Chapter 5. Beauchamp described the "dynamic cycle of education" as: establishing goals, selecting means to achieve the goals, and evaluation.[13] Careful listing of objectives, selecting procedures, and precise planning for evaluation are, of course, futile unless activities are also carefully selected and executed.

SITUATION 8.4   Talk with three to five elementary-school-age children. Ask them to tell you about a social studies lesson in their class. Relate their perceptions of social studies to current trends in the modern elementary school social studies programs.

Materials

The emphasis in modern social studies program should be on instructional materials which include people, humanistic education, citizenship education, intellectual development, wise-acting behavior, objects, and events as well as books and other verbal materials. Experiences with the actual social processes that make up group life in the total culture are to be found in the modern classroom, but the media for learning are not confined entirely to those available in the school. In contrast to the limited opportunity for learning provided by a single textbook, the child learns from many interesting books; from maps, charts, globes, and models; from using tools and art media; from visiting places in the local environment; and from audiovisual resources such as motion pictures, film strips, radio, and television.

Books, nevertheless, constitute an important source of learning in the social studies. Modern textbooks encourage the development of meaningful concepts by providing a less crowded page; by using larger, more colorful, and better pictures; and by gearing the content and illustrations to the maturity of the child. One caution though—of all elementary textbooks, the social studies textbook is likely to have the highest level of reading difficulty. In addition to textbooks, many interesting supplemental books, pamphlets, and periodicals of various levels of difficulty play a part in the social studies program.

The unit procedures used in most elementary schools require learning centers supplied with a wide variety of materials that pupils may use to investigate and attack their individual and group problems. A children's encyclopedia, several different social studies readers in sets of six or eight, children's books presenting pertinent factual materials, sets of materials that can be purchased at low cost (newspapers, news magazines, special-interest magazines) exemplify instructional materials needed in the modern social studies program.[14] Pictures, charts, maps, pamphlets, and samples of products can be obtained from many large commercial organizations if state laws and local school regulations per-

---

[13] George A. Beauchamp, *Basic Dimensions of Elementary Methods,* 2d ed. (Boston: Allyn & Bacon, Inc., 1965), p. 30–31.

[14] Social studies readers are published as a part of the *Curriculum Foundation Program* by Scott, Foresman and Company, Glenview, Ill.

mit the use of such materials.[15] In many school systems, curriculum materials are prepared by local teachers. It is becoming a fairly common practice for teachers to be given release time from classroom duties to write resource units and organize supplemental materials for basic units of study.

In most communities, many valuable instructional materials and resources are available at little or no cost. An excellent project for any school staff would be to compile a community resource file of both materials and people available to contribute to the social studies curriculum. A survey of the community, involving the pupils of the school, would surely reveal a number of potentially rewarding resources that could enhance the social studies program. Ideally, the modern teacher taps a wide variety of interesting resources for each unit and takes advantage of every opportunity to involve the pupils in the implementation of these resources.

Responsibility

The need for children to learn to assume responsibility as rapidly as possible has been recognized for many years. The work of the classroom, as well as the problems of group living that children face daily in the school, provides many opportunities for children to plan, assume responsibility, and work together. Among the numerous opportunities for worthwhile socializing experiences are the following:

1. Cooperatively developing objectives of a unit of work
2. Selecting committees for various phases of the unit
3. Planning activities, such as trips and work periods
4. Suggesting and developing procedures for effective group work
5. Caring for equipment—tools, paint brushes, and playground equipment
6. Making the classroom or school grounds more attractive
7. Serving as a class helper; for example, librarian
8. Participating in a community activity and sharing the experience with the class
9. Planning and arranging bulletin boards
10. Making plans for improving the school lunchroom
11. Planning and conducting assembly programs
12. Caring for plants and animals in the classroom
13. Assuming Safety Patrol duties
14. Developing and evaluating a class behavior code

Units of work, especially in social studies, provide many opportunities for individuals and groups to assume responsibilities and develop leadership abilities. The pupils should have a part in deciding what they will learn and become involved in planning their work. They should have a wide variety of lifelike

---

[15] See J. G. Fowlkes, *Elementary Teacher's Guide to Free Curriculum Materials.* (Randolph, Wis.: Educators Progress Service), published annually.

experiences, many outlets for self-expression, and direct participation in the evaluation of progress toward the objectives they have set up.

Evaluation

For effective direction of the social studies program, for accomplishing the goals of the program, and for discharging the responsibilities of the school to the pupils and the community, an adequate program of evaluation is necessary. Evaluation of pupil progress consists in determining what is happening to boys and girls as a result of social studies experiences and how this relates to the objectives.

Unfortunately, many teachers have reduced the evaluation process to a collection of written examinations, and a learner's progress is measured only from this point of view. While these examinations can be useful for measuring the amount of information pupils have acquired and for revealing low energy, cognitive behaviors of pupils, the social studies program is designed to encourage learning in many other areas. As a result of social studies experiences, the learner is expected to show an understanding of the content studied by accurately using concepts and generalizations to suggest solutions for personal and social problems. A pupil should behave in a manner that reflects a satisfactory internalization of attitudes, appreciations, feelings, and values that are acceptable in a democratic setting, and should practice the skills required for investigation, communication, use of resources, and human interaction or group participation. The program of evaluation is inadequate if it does not provide evidence of pupil progress in each of these aspects of growth. Some of the means by which this can be done are discussed in Chapter 13.

An adequate program of evaluation is carried on as both a formative and summative process, rather than being limited to specific periods just before report cards are given out. Evaluation is an integral part of the teaching–learning process rather than something that takes place after teaching has been completed.

Since there can be no evaluation until the objectives have been clearly defined, the first prerequisite in developing a program of continuous evaluation of pupil progress is a clear understanding of the major objectives of the social studies. For example, if both the teacher and learner understand clearly that one of the major objectives is the development of responsibility, they are in a position to look for such specific evidence as the following questions demand:

1. Is the pupil an active participant in the selection of problems?
2. Does the pupil stay with a task until it is finished?
3. Does the pupil work well with others? Independently?
4. Can the pupil assume the follower role in group activities, following group plans and decisions?
5. Is the pupil helpful and considerate to others?
6. Will the pupil ask for advice and help when needed?
7. Is the pupil resourceful in finding and organizing information?

8. Is the pupil dependable and accepting of responsibility, including activities not particularly enjoyed?
9. Can the pupil complete one or more cycles of inquiry?
10. Is there evidence of the pupil's use of the intellectual operations of comparing, contrasting, classifying, and criteria development?

An adequate program of evaluation is carried on as a cooperative enterprise. Parents, teachers, and pupils are all concerned with the development of objectives, the planning of activities, and the selection of appropriate instruments and procedures for evaluating progress. Parents need to understand clearly what the program is intended to do for children; teachers need to provide leadership, and expert knowledge and skill; and pupils need to participate actively in the program in order to become intelligent, self-directing citizens. In an effort to remove the surprise element that seems to exist at report card time, and to assure a more complete understanding of what a mark represents, continuous and cooperative involvement of pupils, teacher, and parents must occur, from the setting of objectives to the selection of evaluative techniques.

SITUATION 8.5   List five evaluative procedures which you as an elementary teacher would incorporate in determining pupil progress in the curriculum area of social studies.

PROGRAM AREAS

Most of the recent and not so recent developments within the social studies curriculum have been of an additive nature. These developments have not changed the scope, sequence, and/or organization of the social studies curriculum, but have been designed to be included within and added to the existing scope of study. This is not to imply that these additive innovations are not of good quality. In fact, the selection of representative content vehicles by these programs tends to be excellent.

Ecological Education

First appearing as an additive study called "conservation," this program has changed its scope to become ecological education. It has remained as an additive program transmitted by including units of study, modifying existing units, and creating outdoor educational activities.

Some of the new units are concerned with inquiry activities directed toward one or more ecological cycles: pollution, recycling, ecological chains, and so on. Existing units in the home, family, community, and other groups have been modified to include an ecological phase. Outdoor education activities seem to have the greatest potential and are being increasingly implemented.

Outdoor education involves taking a group of learners, teachers, and resource people on a week or longer field trip to a camping or lodge area. Teachers representing several different curriculum areas (for example, social studies, science, mathematics, music, art) attend the camp and come prepared with a plan of a thematic, multidisciplinary curriculum designed for an inquiry approach to one or more ecological problems. For example, a litter census might be the theme and the ecological content. Pupils would select a territory in or near the camp area and develop an inquiry system based upon the litter anticipated, found, and classified within that area. Two territories could be selected, and an inquiry process utilized both within and between the territories. Other social studies activities that might be included are: consumer economics, through the buying of supplies and budgeting; map skills, through use of hiking, plotting, charting, and route orienting; geography and geology, through the study of terrains and formations; and history, through the study of realia (for example, cemeteries). The opportunities for the involvement of other curriculum areas are numerous and seem obvious.[16]

Economic Education

Interest in teaching elementary school children the concepts of economics extends beyond professional education circles. *Readers Digest* for December 1964 carried an article, "How Children Can Learn the Economic Facts of Life," which described the pilot program in the Elkhart, Indiana, schools and other programs throughout the country. *Look* magazine for January 28, 1964 (p. 85), carried an article by Secretary of Commerce Luther H. Hodges, in which he maintained that the main bout in the current world struggle will be staged in the economic arena. "Since Sputnik," he said, "we have made a massive effort to step up science education; now it is high time we took similar steps to increase our economic understanding, and the place to start is in our grade schools."

The need for economic understanding as a prerequisite to effective citizenship has been stressed for several years. The *Purposes of Education in American Democracy* spelled out in considerable detail the behavior of the educated consumer and producer; about one-fourth of this well-known document is devoted to the objectives of economic efficiency.[17] The National Task Force on Economic Education and the National Committee for Education in Family Finance have provided leadership in recent years in identifying the minimum economic understandings essential for good citizenship. Until 1970, the latter has sponsored workshops in a great number of colleges and universities, with impressive attendance by teachers and administrators. These workshops brought together professional educators, economists, bankers, insurance representatives, and other specialists. They have produced curriculum guides and other materials for elementary and secondary schools.

A very useful set of instructional materials, called *Our Working World*, was prepared by Lawrence Senesh, based on his work with the Elkhart, Indiana,

[16] Michael Jacobson and Stuart Palonsky, "School Camping and Elementary Social Studies," *Social Education*, Vol. XL, No. 1 (January 1976), pp. 44–45.
[17] Educational Policies Commission, *The Purposes of Education in American Democracy.* (Washington, D.C.: National Education Association, 1938), pp. 50–108.

schools.[18] The materials available for the first grade consist of a text for each pupil, an activity book or workbook for each pupil, fourteen records, a resource unit for the teacher, and two filmstrips. Materials for subsequent grades are now being developed.

State curriculum commissions and local school systems frequently produce curriculum guides for economic education or include sections on the topic in social studies curriculum guides.[19] These guides usually identify the concepts to be developed in relation to various topics, suggest teaching materials and methods, and indicate the relationship of economic education to other phases of the social studies program.

SITUATION 8.6   List two learning activities for primary students which involve the "processes" taught and developed in economic education.

Family Life Education

The first school was the home, and the first teacher was the mother. As the state has assumed more responsibility for the education of children, the gap between the home and the school has widened. In recent years such movements as parent-teacher associations and child-study programs have caused educators to plan school activities with the values and needs of home life in mind, and have led teachers and parents to become partners in curriculum making. Educators and laymen alike are realizing that strengthening family life will help solve many economic and social problems, and provide a better basis for national defense against unsound ideologies.

Education for worthy home membership begins in the kindergarten or first grade. To see how this purpose of education is translated into action, we can turn to some generalizations that grow out of a study of the home.[20]

Basic social science concepts can be developed by drawing on some of the experiences the child has in the home. By noting how the work is divided in the home, an important economic concept (the division of labor) can be introduced. The geographic concept dealing with earth materials can be exposed by taking a field trip to see the construction of a new house. By discussing who in a family works at an outside job, the teacher can point out how provision is made for basic needs, a concept from anthropology and sociology. Suggestions for the development of a few concepts and generalizations are presented below, accompanied by a definition of the content that would be introduced, some skills that could be stressed, and activities that are relevant for effecting the instruction.

---

18 Lawrence Senesh, *Our Working World: Families at Work.*
19 See Illinois Curriculum Program, *Teaching the Social Studies.* (Springfield, Ill.: Superintendent of Public Instruction, 1962); and Department of Instruction, *Economics for the Primary School.* (Oklahoma City, Okla.: Oklahoma City Public Schools, 1964).
20 The basic generalizations developed here are presented in a sample unit that was prepared by the Department of Instruction of the State of Wisconsin. Used by permission.

Generalization I. The family is the basic social group. It provides for our basic needs and desires—food, clothing, shelter, and security (including love). This generalization comes from the social science disciplines of anthropology and sociology. The content would speak to the question, "Why do we need a house?" Several activities the pupils and teacher might choose include: discussing and drawing a picture of why we live in a house; discussing and drawing or painting a picture of a home and family living; making a scrapbook to point out types of houses and possible family members; singing songs about home and the family; or dramatizing family activities and what we use a house for. Some of the skills that could be developed are: locating appropriate information, telling main ideas, listening, and identifying difficulties and problems.

Generalization II. Earth materials have been used to build our homes and schools. Different materials may be used to build new homes or schools. A geography generalization, this idea is developed by using content that would satisfy the question, "Of what are houses made?" Children can make a collection of building materials and display them in the room or discuss new houses in the neighborhood and the construction of homes. They could also read and sing songs about what houses are made of. Skill development might include analyzing and evaluating information, engaging in fair play, taking turns, increasing vocabulary, and listening.

Generalization III. People make rules in their home, school, and community for their safety and health. Punishment follows when rules are broken. These organized ideas come from political science and can be expected to evolve from content directed to the question, "How do we help in caring for our families and homes?" Some suggested activities are: role-playing a family situation; dramatizing a family scene of a child being punished; discussing a picture showing health or safety hazards. Learners can gain skills in seeing how to disagree, giving constructive criticism, and following rules and laws.

These three generalizations are but a sample of the total number of organized ideas that are found in this one unit at the kindergarten level. Other concepts and generalizations which are taken from the rest of the social sciences are developed in like fashion: the pupils are presented with content that speaks to a theme question, and activities are planned to assure that they will acquire important social studies skills. The learners arrive at the generalizations inductively through these experiences.

Global Education

Elementary schools have for many years been teaching children about other lands, other cultures, and other people; this has been regarded as an essential phase of a basic liberal education. Since World War II, however, a more compelling motive for teaching world understanding has emerged. Our country has assumed a new role in world affairs, science and technology have reduced distances in terms of travel time, the community in which we live has become global in scope. The teaching of world understanding is now regarded as an instrument for building a stable world order. The late President John F. Kennedy said, "Civilization, it was once said, is a race between education and catastrophe—we intend to win the race for civilization." Brameld maintained that the overriding purpose of schools and colleges, the purpose to which all others are of subordinate importance, is "the creation of a world civilization—a world civilization capable both of preventing destruction and of providing the peace and abundance that men everywhere crave."[21] He quoted, in support of this position, the recommendation of Committee E, which was appointed by the United States Commissioner of Education in 1962 to consider pressing problems confronting American schools in the years ahead.

The National Council for the Social Studies devoted its twenty-fifth yearbook (1954) to suggestions for teaching, at all levels, an understanding of world affairs. Again, in 1964, it published a bulletin, *Improving the Teaching of World Affairs: The Glens Falls Story*, which suggested activities and instruments of evaluation for use in teaching this important area.[22] The bulletin also listed[23] organizations that provide free materials, publications lists, and other useful information, including the Division of International Education of the United States Office of Education, the World Confederation of Organizations of the Teaching Profession, and the American Council on Education. Once again, the Council devoted the entire yearbook (1968) to this important topic, concentrating especially on closing the conceptual lag that seems to persist in efforts to explain the world and the place of human beings in it. A special issue of the publication of the National Council for the Social Studies, *Social Education*, was devoted to global education.[24]

Introducing children to a study of world affairs does not necessarily mean that the disciplines of history, geography, and political science will be neglected; it means that basic generalizations from these and other social science disciplines will be deepened and broadened as the pupil proceeds from grade 1 through grade 12. The bulletin of the National Council for the Social Studies[25] lists generalizations that are essentially geographic in nature, generalizations that are essentially economic in nature, generalizations that are essentially social in nature, and generalizations that are essentially political in nature, with appropriate activities through which pupils develop an understanding of these generalizations. Lee provided the following guidelines for global education:

1. *Let's start admitting that all humans are human and stop believing that some of us are more human than others.*
2. *Let's all admit that we have our ethnocentric biases and that these biases*

---

[21] Theodore Brameld, "World Civilization, the Galvanizing Purpose of Public Education," in Stanley Elam (Ed.), *New Dimensions for Educational Progress*. (Bloomington, Ind.: Phi Delta Kappa, Inc., 1962), pp. 3–4.

[22] Harold M. Long and Robert N. King, *Improving the Teaching of World Affairs: The Glens Falls Story*. (Washington, D.C.: National Council for the Social Studies, National Educational Association, 1964).

[23] Long and King, pp. 90–92.

[24] Jayne Millar Wood (Ed.), "Special Issue," *Social Education*, Vol. XXXVIII, No. 7 (November–December 1974).

[25] Long and King, *Improving the Teaching of World Affairs*.

influence perceptions and ideas. Then let's attempt to transcend ethnocentrism to the extent that we will be able to view events from a global perspective.

3. *Let's admit that we already possess multiple loyalties (to our family, our city, our state, our region, our nation) without being unpatriotic, and consider extending our loyalties to some transnational organizations and associations (for example, Catholics owe a loyalty to Rome, but that loyalty does not diminish their loyalty to the United States).*

4. *Let's begin to judge the institutions of others by the criterion that institutions are created to serve human needs, and thus are satisfactory to the extent they do serve needs.*

5. *Let's admit that change and diversity are inevitable features of human life and strive to enjoy life while surrounded by variety.*

6. *Let's admit that major value differences exist in the world about forms of political power and systems of production, and learn to live constructively with the inevitable conflict, distrust, and hostility existing within a loosely structured, emerging society.*[26]

Intercultural Education

The Constitution of the United States guarantees the "equal protection of the laws" for all persons; full respect for the worth of all individuals—regardless of sex, race, or religious belief—is a basic tenet of our democratic tradition. It is generally accepted, therefore, that government, education, communication media, the home, and the church should do everything possible to remove prejudices against minority groups that divide us as a nation and prevent many individuals from full participation in the life of the community and the nation.

Intercultural education is the term used to designate a broadly based program designed to promote the full acceptance of all individuals on the basis of personal merit. The school, as society's chief formal agency for the education of the young, is expected to assume a share of this responsibility. The social studies program, as that phase of the curriculum which deals most directly with human relationships, is expected to make a major contribution to this enterprise, although it is understood that the entire life and program of the school is involved in intercultural education.

Although much has been written about intercultural education, very little has been done about developing systematic programs in this field for elementary schools. One program of this nature has been developed by the Wichita, Kansas, school system.[27] A rather complete, 166-page supplemental guide was prepared by a committee made up of teachers, curriculum personnel, and university consultants. Recognizing that most social studies texts have omitted information concerning various ethnic groups of United States citizens, the supplemental writers prepared material to give teachers and students historical facts and information as well as current knowledge. Important characteristics of this supplemental program are abstracted below.

[26] Lee, p. 151.
[27] Department of Elementary Curriculum, "Social Studies—Human Relations, A Supplemental Guide." (Wichita, Kan.: Unified School District 259, 1967).

Procedures and Experiences

The materials must be presented properly or they will not meet the objectives set by the committee. Complete acceptance by the learners or the teacher of the materials is not requisite, but an intellectually honest presentation of the materials is demanded. By submitting to an objective self-examination, the teacher should recognize individual fears and prejudices to begin with. Then it can be possible for the teacher to eliminate unnecessary personal judgments and lead the class into reflecting, questioning, and value-clarifying experiences. The teacher simply raises questions and presents problems the learner must deal with.

These value-clarifying experiences should

1. develop meaningful and useful skills in daily living.
2. cultivate desirable attitudes and understandings about human relations.
3. enhance the self-concept of all minority-group children.
4. build attitudes of appreciation and understandings of contributions made by minority groups.

Concepts and Understandings Appropriate to Human Relations as They Pertain to Social Studies

1. *All people have basic similarities and needs.* Understand that (a) all people have a need for identification, acceptance, and self-expression; (b) biologically all human beings are similar and have certain basic needs.

2. *There are many different kinds of people.* Understand that (a) the individual is unique, differing in physical characteristics, abilities, skills, and contributions; (b) more differences exist between individuals than between groups.

3. *All people have the potential for contributions to society.* Understand that (a) such contributions have been made by people in the past; (b) contributions to the present will affect the future; (c) greater contributions can be made when individuals can control and direct their own behaviors; (d) all social structures require cooperation if progress is to occur.

4. *Individuals and groups are influenced by factors beyond their control.* Understand that (a) people have physical characteristics they cannot or need not change; (b) the cultures under which individuals mature help shape their behaviors throughout life; (c) the influence of physical, cultural, economic, and social environment determines, to a large degree, the action of a group.

5. *Citizens in a democracy have the same basic rights and responsibilities.* Understand that: (a) all individuals have strengths and weaknesses, but retain the right to be respected as human beings; (b) all people have the right to make positive use of their talents, abilities, and intellect; (c) laws and rules cannot change human attitudes, and change can occur only within the individual; (d) rules and standards are necessary for group performance.

Goals of Human Relations and Multi-Ethnic Education

The supplement dignifies the worth of each person, recognizing and personifying each individual's potential for contributing to society. Good human relations in the classroom should lead to similar behavior in the community and the rest of society. Cited as the desirable outcomes in human relations learnings are that the individual

1. respect oneself and have self-confidence.
2. respect others and be courteous to them.
3. defend the rights of self and others.
4. assume responsibility.
5. have an inquiring mind concerning social problems.
6. identify with and project personal effort into situations.
7. show growth in ability to solve problems.
8. make decisions after considering available information.
9. acquire a meaningful human relations vocabulary.
10. show growth in understanding basic human relations concepts.
11. understand that problems are best solved through the use of intelligence and pertinent information.
12. practice self-evaluation.

The supplement contains units of study in human relations for every grade level. These are presented in a manner to complement the basic social studies text. Each unit includes a set of objectives, content, learning experiences, and a complete resources section.

The teacher who wants to do something constructive about intercultural education can obtain useful suggestions from many sources. One other such source explains how schools can assist children in developing the feeling of identification with others.[28] Fortunately, most of the newer elementary social studies texts consider intercultural education an integral part of the total social studies curriculum, and have woven it neatly into all relevant aspects of the program.

The Immediate Task

The need to drop the deadwood from the social studies curriculum and to revitalize it with representative, relevant, humane, and practical content vehicles is tremendous. Much activity is occurring to accomplish this, more than can be discussed in this section. Perhaps, by closing with an idea from John Lee, the shape of the task will be illustrated. Lee identified four significant topics as the bases, those aspects of the social studies curriculum dealing with the United States: population, ecology, violence, and minorities.[29]

ISSUES

This section briefly presents and describes the parameters of some of the selected issues related to the development of a social studies curriculum. These issues were selected either because of their "currentness" or their longevity.

---

[28] ASCD, *Perceiving–Behaving–Becoming*. (Washington, D.C.: The Association for Supervision and Curriculum Development, 1962), chap. 11.
[29] Lee, p. 135.

Objectives

The issue is to define which objectives characterize the social studies curriculum. The problem is that the objectives of social studies tend to be like or even identical to those of the modern elementary school. For example, Lee provided three primary reasons: the acquisition of knowledge, the refinement of standards, and the development of the reasoned thought.[30] Joyce provided the following three: humanistic education, citizenship education, and intellectual development.[31] Would not these two statements serve equally well as objectives for the elementary school? The author suggests that no curriculum area, other than social studies, claims objectives that parallel those of the total school. The aims of other curriculum areas are supplemental and contributory to the larger goals of the schools. In addition, social studies tend to be so global that its contributions toward the achievement of these larger goals cannot be determined. For example, citizenship is surely a goal of the school and all curriculum areas. If the achievement of citizenship can be determined, can the contribution of social studies be separated from all curriculum areas?

Perhaps social studies is the master curriculum area, and all other areas contribute to the achievement of its objectives; the global statements of the authorities imply this relationship. Yet, the major resource of time assigned to the social studies curriculum does not support this relationship.

None of these statements is intended to devalue the potential contribution of the social studies curriculum. All are intended to call attention to the need for a more consistent and clearly defined definition of the objectives and the role of the social studies curriculum in the modern elementary school.

SITUATION 8.7   Review two critics' statements in journal articles related to the elementary social studies program. What are their strongest objections? What alternatives do they propose?

Sponsored Curriculum Projects

Federal, state, and private monies have been utilized to support the development of curriculum models since Sputnik. The development of curricula in the sciences and mathematics, which were supported by government monies, gained national attention and impact during the mid- and late 1950s.

Although these two models were, and are, severely criticized as being ineffective, too difficult, or lacking in sufficient emphasis on the "basics," neither (science or mathematics) has met with such violent reaction as that received by the social studies curriculum model entitled *Man, A Course of Study* (MACOS).

MACOS was developed with the support of funds from the National Sci-

---

[30] Lee, p. 8.
[31] Joyce, p. 12.

ence Foundation, with Jerome S. Bruner as the senior director of the project. It is an interdisciplinary approach using anthropology as the core discipline. The fundamental methodology is that of inquiry. A major content vehicle is the culture of a nomadic tribe of Alaskan Indians. The norms, sanctions, ethics, sex roles, mores, customs, and rituals of the culture are presented for the inquiry of the students. Opposition to this program arises because these aspects of the tribal culture differ in significant ways from the patterns of our dominant society and culture.

Congressman Conlan's reactions were: ". . . being experimental on thousands of children . . who are . . . set adrift morally after MACOS instruction . . . facing moral and spiritual guidance as the result of MACOS teaching.[32] Notice the difference in the nature of the criticism of the social studies model versus the criticism of other models (see Chapters 9 and 10). The content vehicles of the social studies curriculum are much more vulnerable to criticism than are the vehicles of other disciplines. If, indeed, the social studies curriculum is to present experiences for "wise acting" in social matters, it must select viable, perhaps even controversial, content vehicles. At present the future of MACOS or any proposed curriculum model requesting the support of government monies for development is in doubt.

Readability of Materials

Chapin and Gross stated that there is a ". . . crisis in reading in the social studies."[33] Social studies is ". . . particularly dependent upon the medium of print and the process of reading."[34] The paucity of research on methods of teaching reading as an integral part of the social studies is almost appalling."[35]

These three statements communicate the fundamental aspects of the issue of reading in the social studies. The abilities to obtain meaning from the medium of print is a requisite behavior for the objectives of the social studies: acquisition of knowledge, the refinement of standards, and the development of reasoned thought. Yet, the control and utilization of the reading tool is inadequately understood. For example, the variation in the control of readability within most social studies texts is greater than the variations between texts.[36] Hash applied two readability formulas (Dale-Chall and Fry) to social studies text materials and found a range of six years within some materials.[37] Johnson and Vardian applied four readability formulas to sixty-eight social studies texts and found a range within some intermediate texts of up to twelve years.[38] Vocabulary loading—the

---

[32] John B. Conlan, "MACOS: The Push for a Uniform National Curriculum," *Social Education,* Vol. XXXIX, No. 6 (October 1975), p. 392.

[33] June R. Chapin and Richard Gross, *Teaching Social Studies Skills.* (Boston: Little, Brown and Company, 1973), p. 20.

[34] John P. Linstrum, "Reading in the Social Studies: A Preliminary Analysis of Recent Research," *Social Education,* Vol. XL, No. 1 (January 1976), p. 11.

[35] Linstrum, p. 10.

[36] Linstrum, p. 12.

[37] Linstrum, p. 12.

[38] Linstrum, p. 4.

presentation of an unfamiliar word or familiar words in a complex, unfamiliar set-ting—is also a major reading problem in social studies materials. The concept load and number of generalizations of texts is also high.

Evidently the reading of social studies materials is the most difficult read-ing task in the elementary schools. "It would appear from this analysis of research that it is not possible to provide a clear assessment of the extent and nature of the reading disabilities which impair learning in the social studies.[39] One approach to the resolution of these deficiencies is better control of the readibility, vocabulary, and concept loading of social studies materials. Another approach would be to reduce the present dependence of teaching and learning social studies upon the tool of reading. A modern elementary school would do both.

Content Vehicles

The selection of representative information clusters from the social sciences for the social studies is an issue. Are such clusters selected from one social science discipline, from two, or from all? The reader may wish to refer to an earlier discussion in this chapter concerning inter- or multidisciplinary approaches. Efforts to define the structure of the social sciences (see Chapter 5) have not been particularly successful. So, figuratively—and perhaps literally—the organ-ization of the massive, voluminous bodies of information of the social sciences for the social studies is ill defined, fragmented, and diffused. The criteria for the present content vehicles seem to be relevant, classical, human, or practical; these are used independently rather than as a system. Considerable attention is needed for the selection of repersentative content vehicles and for their organ-ization into a scope and sequence adequate for the social studies curriculum of the modern elementary school.

Another issue is the selection of topics which provide for wise acting, refine-ment of standards, and intellectual development. For these purposes a selected topic must provide opportunities for the identification of alternatives, the test-ing of alternatives, the classification and comparison of models, and similar criteria. Many times these opportunities are found in topics that are considered controversial by a dominant society. In an effort to maintain its dominance, a society may wish to transmit only its present, existing, and traditional practices. The investigation of other alternatives may be threatening to some members of the dominant society. For example, consider the range of dramatic and even traumatic responses to some to these topics: sex education, value-clarification strategies, racism, communism, sexism, death as a phenomenon, the changing family structure. It should be noted that many criticisms of these topics include a reference to the dire effects on American ideals. The leap of logic from the study of a controversial topic by a twelve-year-old to the destruction of the American ideal is a long one.

This is not meant to provide unqualified support for the inclusion of these

---

[39] Linstrum, p. 16.

topics. The curriculum builder and translator must carefully and thoughtfully consider the influence of the social system as topics are selected. The criterion of "the influence of the social system" operates more powerfully and directly upon the topics of social studies than any other curriculum area. A curriculum builder and translator can choose to fight a battle (the selection of a content topic) and lose the war (the support of the dominant society).

INTERDISCIPLINARY APPROACHES

This section briefly presents those special programs and activities which inter-relate social studies with all curriculum areas. These programs and activities have been selected to illustrate the potential and actuality of a multidisciplinary approach: values-clarification strategies, career awareness activities, and law-focused programs.

Values-Clarification Strategies

The social studies curriculum is directed toward the development of human values, but the methods utilized to reach this objective have changed. One method, a direct-telling method, stressed presenting to pupils the merits of honesty, patriotism, cleanliness, and other personal attitudes. A second method, indirect replication, stressed the modeling behaviors of influential adults. Teachers were the models of honesty, cleanliness, good citizenship, and similar attributes. The classroom routinized desirable behavior such as punctuality, orderliness, and obedience. The anticipated impact was that the pupils would internalize these models and routines through their need to be socialized. The third method, the application of reasoned thought, has recently become the most stressed approach.

One aspect of this more recent approach is to confront the learner with a wise-acting dilemma, an event in which several alternative courses of action are available, and in which the various resolutions can be acted out as part of the testing system. A well-constructed, wise-acting dilemma will generate alternatives that distribute themselves along Kohlberg's or Piaget's hierarchy of moral growth as a function of the development of the participants (see Chapter 3).

The general procedures followed in these wise-acting dilemmas are (1) the participant states a position and selects a course of action; (2) the reasoned thought behind the selected position and course of action is explored; (3) and a reflective nonthreatening discussion with others becomes a feedback system.[40] This sequence parallels the choosing, acting, and prizing activities presented in Chapter 6. It is also an implementation of the inquiry process (see Chapter 5) to the values-clarification process.

Simon and his associates provided many examples of strategies such as rank

---

[40] Ronald E. Galbraith and Thomas M. Jones, "Teaching Strategies for Moral Development: An Application of Kohlberg's Theory of Moral Development to the Social Studies Classroom," *Social Education*, Vol. XXXIX (January 1975), p. 19.

ordering, forced choice, voting, continuum, consequences, search, unfinished sentences, and others.[41] The Carnegie-Mellon University groups also developed dilemma-generating situations in *Shaping of Western Society*, a one-semester course published by Holt, Rinehart and Winston.[42]

Career Awareness Activities

Hansen and Tenneyson described career education activities on a continuum related to location of the major emphasis—from job, to work, to self, to life.[43] Within the job-focused career education activity, the emphasis is upon matching and preparing the individual for a specific job. A work-focused emphasis focuses upon the "education for work" concept, with a heavy input of knowledge, experiences, and people representing a wide range of possible vocational choices. A self-focused emphasis redefines work as both compensated (paid) and non-compensated activities and stresses those aspects which support the development of a purposeful life pattern through work. A life-focused emphasis focuses on all life roles that an individual might assume in work, leisure, family, community and institutions, and similar situations.

Career awareness activities in the modern elementary school and within the social studies curriculum, then would focus on the career education activities of self and life. The activities of the primary years would stress: awareness of self, acquisition of a sense of control over one's life, identification with work and workers, acquisition of interpersonal skills, and the abilities to present oneself objectively. The activities of the intermediate years would stress: the development of a positive self-concept, the acquisition of a discipline for work and identification with work as a valued role, and knowledge of work and workers.[44]

The University of Minnesota has constructed a career development curriculum influenced by the theories of Piaget, Erikson, Havighurst, and others (see Chapter 3).[45] The career development curriculum is designed to be developmental with regard to both the learner and the content vehicle—career education.

Some of the titles of their learning packages are: "Life Styles and Work," "Self-Concept Exploration," "Women and the World of Work," "Values Identification," and "The Social Contribution of Work."

> *Career development education accommodates those goals of social studies that have to do with information-processing skills . . . psychological and social problems of individuals, environmental understanding, and concepts of human dignity and acceptance of others.*[46]

[41] Sidney B. Simon, Leland W. Howe, and Howard Kirschenbaum, *Values Clarification: A Handbook of Practical Strategies for Teachers and Students.* (New York: Hart Publishing Company, Inc., 1972), pp. 3–8.
[42] Galbraith, p. 18.
[43] Lorraine Sundal Hansen and W. Wesley Tenneyson, "Career Development as Self-Development," *Social Education*, Vol. XXXIX, No. 5 (May 1975), p. 305.
[44] Hansen and Tenneyson, p. 309.
[45] Hansen and Tenneyson, p. 306.
[46] Hansen and Tenneyson, p. 309.

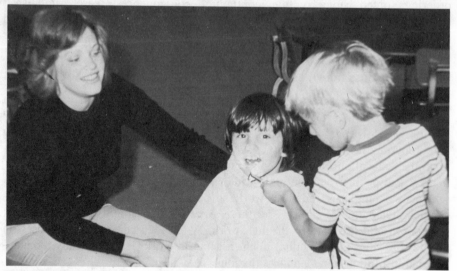

Through career awareness, children experience and identify the world of work and service.

SITUATION 8.8   Inquire into the nature of career education programs present within some large elementary school systems. What might teachers in a small system do to provide similar activities for their students?

Law-Focused Curriculum

"The role of law in our society is a highly proper subject of study for elementary age youngsters."[47] A society governed by law, not men, the United States is a country whose laws are so dynamic that even an elected president must ultimately bow down to them; and yet, every citizen is assured of due process, freedom from search and seizure, and freedom of speech. To be concerned with citizenship, humaneness, refinement of standards, and reasoned thought is to recognize law as a potent content vehicle.

Laws develop slowly, and grow out of civil, social, moral, and criminal conflict. Law promotes peaceful resolutions of conflict and change. The opportunities for wise acting, reasoned thought, and intellectual development abound through the study of law.

Case study is a fundamental procedure in the teaching and learning of law. Consider the opportunities for inquiry in this brief:

> *Gene lives on an acre lot in an area zoned for residential housing. He buys a horse for his children and pastures it on his lot. The neighbors complain of the sight, smell, and potential danger from such a large animal to their small chil-*

[47] Lee, p. 160.

dren. Gene claims that the animal is tame, that the lot is his, and that the horse is not much larger, and certainly no more dangerous, than the large watchdogs of his neighborhood.

The opportunities for the pupils to identify facts, classify facts, reason, and determine relevant sources are numerous in the case study approach.

A mock trial is a useful procedure. It involves preparation, simulation, and evaluation.[48] The usual steps in this procedure are (1) a case study is selected; (2) the participants are specified; (3) the roles are assigned; (4) the trial is conducted; (5) a debriefing and evaluation session are held. Again the opportunities for wise acting, refinement of standards, and reasoned thought abound in this procedures.

Many organizations and institutions have prepared materials to both inform the students of relevant laws and involve the students in the studying of law. Among these groups are The Consultant Center, University of Oklahoma; The American Civil Liberties Union; and The American Bar Association. Most of these groups will supply limited free samples or descriptions of their materials.

STRATEGY OF INSTRUCTION

Chapter 5 presented a strategy of instruction. This section briefly discusses and illustrates the application of the strategy to the social studies curriculum.

Selection of Content

The selection of representative content vehicles for the social studies curriculum needs considerable attention. In the past, the content vehicles seem to have been selected from the external criterion of classicalness (for example, the knowledge of states and capitals, order of presidents, dates of events, influential names). Recently, the criteria of relevancy and humaneness are operating with considerable influence over the selection of content vehicles (for example, values-clarification strategies, ecology, economics, law-focused curriculum).

The internal criteria for the selection of content vehicles for the social studies is operating primarily within the interdisciplinary approaches (for example, economics, Senesh; and anthropology, Bruner). The selection of content vehicles which maximize the opportunities for student involvement still entails the risks of controversy and lack of closure. Apparently the risks of controversy are too high, for although the use of these topics is increasing, they still seem to represent a minor approach. Stereotyping is significantly less, but content vehicles of races, sexes, and nationalities need continued attention. For example, of the social studies textbooks released by six major publishing houses, a study done in 1972 found that only males were pictured in 72 of the 73 "highly paid or prestigious occupations."[49] With some exceptions, it appears to the author

---

[48] Lee, p. 305.

[49] Richard W. O'Donnell, "Sex Bias in Primary Social Studies Textbooks," *Educational Leadership*, Vol. XXXI, No. 2 (November 1973), pp. 137–141.

that the criteria for the selection of content vehicles for the social studies is either too global or too piecemeal. Some of the newer programs discussed in this chapter show promise and the alternatives available are increasing, yet much research is to be done.

Learning and Development

The professional literature in the field of social studies seems to express a commitment to a field theory of learning (that is, whole to part, acting based upon perceptions, and involvement of pupils in the process of inquiry). The developmentalists have quickly become the most influential advocates. The evidence suggests to this author that significant changes are occurring, and will occur more rapidly in the theories of learning and development which govern the transmission, translation, and transposition of the social studies curriculum.

The abstract generalization and concept load of previous (perhaps, even current) social studies programs presents a difficult problem for a concrete operational learner, and is almost an impossible problem for the preoperational learner. According to Piaget, the preoperational learner cannot perform cognitive operations utilizing abstract stimuli. The object must be present and manipulated in ways which parallel the required cognitive operations. The concrete operational learners will learn the "model," rather than what the model represents, if the modeled event or object is not experienced. Concrete operational learners do not think about the consequences of their thinking. An example provided by Lee—"There are three boys; Jack is taller than Bill; Jack is shorter than Tom. Who is the tallest boy?"[50]—will be difficult for the concrete operational learner. With the boys (objects) present, the answer will be easy.

Methodology

When the content vehicles can be characterized as names, dates, places, and events, the characteristic teaching procedures are those of tell, assign, recite, review, and test. As the content vehicles change (display the characteristics of identifying relevant data; create alternatives; and establish testing procedures for the alternatives, that is, inquiry), the teaching procedures become those of demonstration, experimentation, and investigation. There now seem to be several dichotomies concerning methodology within the social studies: new programs versus older programs, recommended practice versus "common" practice, inquiry versus conditioning to American ideals. Perhaps, these dichotomies are unreal, and further evidence will dismiss them or provide resolutions.

Communication

The author assumes that one impact of the newer trends in social studies has been to increase the divergent questioning patterns of teachers. This could be a requisite behavior for the implementation of the inquiry process being generally recommended. A research study of the questioning behaviors of social studies

[50] Lee, p. 127.

teachers reported that during 13 hours of instruction, the 16 teachers involved in the research asked 1,211 cognitive questions. More than 94 percent (1,142) of these questions were classified as encouraging knowledge or comprehension behaviors within the cognitive domain. Only a little more than 5% of these questions encouraged the cognitive behaviors of application, analysis, synthesis, or evaluation.[51] Beyond the behaviors of memory and paraphrasing, these results would not support the social studies goals of refinement of standards, reasoned thought, and intellectual development. Another assumption is that a reduction has occurred in the moralizing and value-impositioning behaviors included within the social studies curriculum. Neither assumption can yet be supported by research. The author defends them and advances them through an interpolation of the nature and impact of the newer trends, programs, and activities recommended for the social studies curriculum.

Objectives

Concern with the establishment and achievement of affective objectives seems to be presently emphasized. The general trend toward humaneness, affective education, and values-clarification strategies are presented as evidence of this conclusion. The recommendation for the use of an inquiry methodology would seem to further both the cognitive and affective ranges of objectives recognized and stressed.

Goals

A previous discussion within this chapter questioned the all-inclusive, global, total, curriculum-like tendency inherent in the goals claimed for the social studies. Attention is needed for those contributions which are specific to the social studies curriculum; for example, the development of the rational powers.

SUMMARY

1. Social studies is defined in many ways. Lee's definition seems sound and representative: "Social Studies deals with mankind's social, economic, and political behavior, at any place where people live or have lived, now or in the past.[52]

2. Among the many reasons for the learning of social studies are those provided by Joyce: to help the child develop a social life, to help the child develop a citizenship behavior, and to make the tactics of the social scientist available to every citizen.[53]

3. The social sciences from which either a multi- or interdisciplinary organization can be developed are: anthropology, economics, geography, history, political science, sociology, and philosophy.

[51] John Vaver Godbold, "Oral Questioning Practices of Teachers in Social Studies Classes," *Educational Leadership*, Vol. XXVIII, No. 1 (October 1970), pp. 61–67.
[52] Lee, p. 7.
[53] Joyce, p. 12.

4. The learning of social studies provides opportunities for the pupils to utilize inquiry processes, evaluate their behaviors and use all forms of language to work independently and dependently, and to demonstrate wise-acting abilities efficiently and effectively.

5. While learning within the social studies, the pupil should experience the human potential to think about feelings and feel about thinking, believe, generate energy for causes, and to be different and unique.

6. Some variations of the expanding-horizons pattern governs the sequence and scope of the present social studies curriculum.

7. Newer emphasis in the social studies program include: teaching of organized ideas from the social disciplines; increasing the utilization of affective education; inclusion of family life education, ecological education, economic education, global education, law focus education, and intercultural education.

8. Some of the issues within the social studies include the inclusiveness of the objectives, sponsored curriculum projects, reading and readability, the inclusion or exclusion of potentially controversial topics.

Problems and Projects

1. Research the nature of social studies in the U.S.S.R. or another country. What are the similarities between the programs for elementary age students? Who and/or what agencies are responsible for the guideline structuring of the curriculum areas in that country?

2. Investigate the development of social studies programs for schools in your community. Who, what group of individuals, or what agencies are responsible for its format, structure, scope, and sequence? Examine a social studies curriculum guide for an elementary school in your area. Is it process-oriented? What criteria influenced your decision?

3. Review five social studies programs for the elementary school. Classify them as to logical source, psychological source, or sociological source.

4. A movement presently occupying one of the educational stages is "values-clarification." Investigate the nature of value education or values-clarification programs. What are the potential risks to the learner? What are the responsibilities and role of the teacher?

Selected Readings

Banks, James A., and Ambrose A. Clegg, Jr., *Teaching Strategies for the Social Studies.* Reading, Mass.: Addison-Wesley Publishing Company, Inc., 1973. An overview of social studies methodologies.

Chapin, June R., and Richard E. Gross, *Teaching Social Studies Skills.* Boston: Little, Brown and Company, 1973. Contains a chapter on readability and the teaching of reading skills through the social studies.

Flanagan, John C., Robert F. Mager, and William M. Shanner, *Behavioral Objectives: Social Studies.* Palo Alto, Calif.: Westinghouse Learning Press, 1971. A listing of behavioral objectives for the social studies.

Gorman, Richard M., *Discovering Piaget*. Columbus, Ohio: Charles E. Merrill Publishing Co., 1972. An introduction to Piaget.

Jarolimek, John, and Huber M. Walsh (Eds.), *Reading for Social Studies in Elementary Education*. New York: Crowell Collier and Macmillan, Inc., 1974. Articles on all aspects of social studies.

Joyce, Bruce R., *New Strategies for Social Education*. Chicago: Science Research Associates, Inc., 1972. Presents strategies for instruction in the social studies.

Lee, John R., *Teaching Social Studies in the Elementary School*. New York: The Free Press, 1974. Contains a practical and thoughtful description of elementary social studies.

Michaelis, John U., *Social Studies for Children in a Democracy*. Englewood Cliffs, N.J.: Prentice-Hall, Inc., 1972. A comprehensive description of social studies instruction.

Muessig, Raymond, *The Social Science Seminar Series*. Columbus, Ohio: Charles E. Merrill Publishing Co., 1965. Muessig and a specialist from one of the social sciences write concerning the contributions of that social science. (Books on history, geology, sociology, economics, political science, and anthropology.)

Piaget, Jean, *The Child's Concept of Time*. New York: Basic Books, Inc., Publishers, 1969. Contains strong implications for the social studies.

Piaget, Jean, and Barbel Inhelder, *The Child's Concept of Space*. London: Routledge & Kegan Paul, Ltd., 1963. Contains strong implications for the social studies.

Smith, James A., *Creative Teaching of the Social Studies in the Elementary School*. Boston: Allyn and Bacon, Inc., 1967. Provides suggestions for enhancing creativity in the elementary social studies curriculum.

Wernick, Walter., *Teaching for Career Development in the Elementary School*. Worthington, Ohio: Charles A. Jones Publishing Company, 1973. Presents career education activities for various subjects and grades.

chapter 9

Inquiring
MATHEMATICS

The three sources of the elementary school mathematics curriculum may be referred to as the nature of the learner, the nature of his or her adult society, and the nature of the cognitive area—mathematics.

Leroy G. Callahan and Vincent J. Glennon, *Elementary School Mathematics,* 4th ed. (Washington, D.C.: Association for Supervision and Curriculum Development, 1975), p. 1.

DEFINITION

Mathematics is a communication system, a communication system that deals with quantity, greater than, less than, equal to, ratio, grouping, regrouping, and other symbolic values or operations. As a communication system, it has its "alphabet and figurative symbols": numerals, serial and cardinal order, equation signs, exponents, and operational signs. As a communication system it has its "latinized" grammar: the algorithms of addition, subtraction, multiplication, and division. As a communication system, it has its own "linguistics": the properties of commutative, associative, distributive, and identity.

As a communication system, it is dependent upon the learner's acquiring meaning–experience relationships to "concrete" the abstractness of the system (for example, the numeral 3 becomes the number 3 through meaning–experience). As a communication system, it is to be read, heard, spoken, or written for transmitting meanings. Without comprehensions, the language of mathematics communication becomes nonsense syllables.

OBJECTIVES

The acquisition of knowledge and skills, the refinement of standards and performances, the exercise of reasoned thought, and wise acting could be the global goals of mathematics. The planners of the mathematics curriculum do not tend to state global goals for mathematics, as was done by the planners of the social studies curriculum. The objectives for mathematics tend to be stated

Quantitative communication involves children and their energies.

in terms of intent to deal with the logical relationships of mathematics (pure subject matter), the application of mathematics to the physical world, and the development of efficient and effective computation.

A typical listing of objectives would account in some manner for the following:

Mathematical Ideals: the concepts of number, operation, relation, set, function and proof

Problem Solving: the abilities to associate a physical event with the appropriate mathematical statement, use computation to solve the statement, and then apply the resolution to the originating physical event

Computation Techniques: the skills to compute effectively and efficiently the sums, differences, products, and quotients of whole and fractional numbers

Language: the meanings and experiences to use the communication system of mathematics to explore, invent, and discover (that is, to *think* mathematics).

In a survey of over 20,000 people conducted in Maryland, the objective of gaining knowledge of mathematical concepts was ranked considerably higher than the objective of mastering computational skills.[1] Apparently the group, which included over 8,400 students and 4,500 parents, valued both conceptual and skill developments. Some discussions of objectives imply a dichotomy: skills *or* concepts. This is an exercise in nonsense, for both skills and concepts must be acquired and mastered. Without skills, concepts are nonfunctional; without concepts, skills are randomized.

CURRICULUM APPROACHES

The logical source (see Chapter 6) has governed the construction of the mathematics curriculum. For example, the curriculum sequence among the content vehicles is controlled by the logic of the mathematical relationships. The scope of the curriculum for mathematics has been influenced, with varying degrees of success at different times, by the sociological source. For example, the mathematical content vehicles are applied to the practical and physical events that a skilled citizen performs. Developmentalists, such as Piaget, are having increasing influence on both the scope and the sequence of the curriculum (the psychological source).

Pedagogy

The word "pedagogy" may be defined as *systematized* instruction relating to principles and methods of teaching. It is used here instead of more common expressions such as "teaching procedures" and "instructional practices" to emphasize the notion that effective teaching in the area of elementary school mathematics requires systematized preparation on the part of the teacher.

Our society, as Chapter 2 indicated, is committed to the goal of fostering the maximum development of the rational powers of the individual. The school is the chief formal agency for achieving this objective. Hence, the school curriculum, including the mathematics program, must be designed to help pupils achieve this objective. A mathematics curriculum consisting of sound and meaningful mathematical concepts is not sufficient; pupils must learn to use these concepts in problem-solving situations and to compute effectively and efficiently.

History

Mathematics has been a part of civilization for centuries. As early 400 B.C., counting was taught as a subject in Greece. In Plato's academy, philosophy was taught through mathematical concepts, and during the period A.D. 100–400, the educated Roman studied arithmetic and geometry. The content of mathematics changed very little from that time until the 1600s, when the scientific revolution led by Copernicus, Galileo, Kepler, Harvey, and Newton reinforced the necessity of a "new" mathematics.

During the sixteenth century, mathematics was taught through the mem-

---

[1] Martin Hershkowitz, Mohannad A. A. Shami, and Thomas E. Rowas, "Mathematics Goals: What Does the Public Want?" *School Science and Mathematics,* Vol. LXXV, No. 8 (December 1975), pp. 723–728.

orization and application of rules. Some rules were expressed in verse; Solomon Lowe even went so far as to express his rules of arithmetic alphabetically and in English verse hexameter.

With the advent of printing in England, two types of mathematics schools began to evolve. In one school, mathematics instruction was algorithmic, based on rules of computation and commercial arithmetic. In the other, mathematics was abacus-oriented and dealt with the properties of numbers and ratios.

During the seventeenth century, mathematics increasingly became a collection of rules and began to deal more specifically with commercial arithmetic. Textbooks were written in the form of questions relating primarily to "how" and seldom to "why." Even into the eighteenth century, arithmetic was not taught as a subject in schools like Eton. During this time the textbooks began to include puzzles (some of which were resurrected from the fifteenth century), and demonstrations began to appear in the newer books. These were included at the foot of the page and took the form of abstract proofs, with little or no object teaching. In addition, an increased proportion of space in textbooks was devoted to teaching the values of monetary exchange.

At the beginning of the nineteenth century, a revolution in mathematics instruction began. The English started incorporating math into their public school instruction and much emphasis was placed upon math as a mental discipline.

Pestalozzi, the Swiss educational reformer, emphasized object teaching, maintaining that learning experiences of children must begin at the concrete level to develop powers of observation and reasoning before proceeding to the abstract level. He placed little emphasis on the uses of arithmetic in commercial life. In 1821, Warren Colburn, an American educator, published his book, *First Lessons in Arithmetic, on the Plan of Pestalozzi,* but it was never widely accepted. Although during this same period other texts were being published in the United States based on Pestalozzi's ideas, teaching continued with little object teaching and much abstract reasoning, or with little object teaching and much drill. The state legislature of Massachusetts sought to change the nature of mathematics in the schools and required the school to provide arithmetic that was "useful in the market place."

During the early 1900s, emphasis was placed on "useful" arithmetic and the solving of problems related to everyday life. Drill was the predominant procedure by which things were taught. In the 1930s and 1940s, attention was given to the gestalt theory, which encouraged the recognition of number facts and computation as a part of the whole, logical system of arithmetic, thereby removing the pressure for memorizing and mechanical figuring. Emphasis was placed on concepts, understandings, and the relationships between numbers.

The late 1950s and the early 1960s are generally referred to as the era of the "new math." This expression took on various meanings for many. To some it meant that, for some unknown reason, mathematical knowledge of the past was being replaced by some strange new kind of mathematics. To others it meant that changes were occurring not only in what but in how mathematics was being taught in our schools. The latter was the direction that the reform movement of the 1960s took in the school mathematics program.

Significant changes first occurred at the secondary level; action toward effecting reform at the elementary level came later. There was a lag of two to three years before any appreciable effort was exerted in changing the elementary school mathematics curriculum. To begin curriculum reform at the secondary level and work down through the elementary level seemed to some to be a questionable procedure. Historically, however, the main concern for reform had been directed toward the secondary program, with little attention given to the elementary school mathematics program. Committees appointed as early as 1890 were charged to make recommendations for the improvement of mathematics at the secondary level. Probably the most significant factor which caused reform at the secondary level to precede that at the elementary level was the readiness of private foundations and government agencies to give financial support to groups interested in renovating the current secondary mathematics program. Later, these same foundations and agencies became interested in providing financial assistance to groups concerned with updating the elementary school mathematics program so that it could keep pace with that of the secondary schools.

The first major effort to bring attention to the need for reform at the elementary school level occurred in 1959 when the School Mathematics Study Group sponsored a conference in Chicago on elementary school mathematics. It was the first time that a large group consisting of secondary, elementary, and college teachers of mathematics, as well as administrators, psychologists, and others interested in mathematics education, had been assembled for the purpose of considering the status of the elementary school mathematics program. As expected, a significant outcome of this conference was the agreement that the success of a secondary program depended on the strength of the elementary school program which preceded it, and that immediate action should be taken to make the program in the elementary school compatible with that being advocated for the secondary.

SITUATION 9.1   Compare Morris Kline's criticisms of the "new math" programs with the criticisms of the writers in the 1960s. (See selected Readings section of this chapter for reference to Kline.)

Changing Emphasis

A critical examination of the programs in mathematics revealed that these programs went far beyond the selection of new content. Several publications dealing with the "new math" called attention to the error involved in regarding these programs as merely the selection of new content. One of these publications stated the problem as follows:

Those who view mathematics for young children in these terms have missed the spirit and intent of the new programs. They view content and terminology as being synonymous with modern mathematics programs when in actuality these are but vehicles enabling young children to enter into experimentation, discovery and creativity.[2]

Another publication stated:

Enthusiasm and knowledge on the part of mathematicians have been important in the development of new programs. However, this same enthusiasm can be a weakness if it is not tempered and directed by persons with knowledge and experience in teaching pupils.[3]

Evidence from psychological studies of how children learn and the views which mathematicians had of mathematics produced a change in the way in which the curriculum was derived. Studies by psychologists indicated that if children understand a concept or a process, they are able to function more effectively than if the learning has been acquired strictly through rote. The emphasis on understanding might be thought of as having its origin in the "meaning" theories of the 1930s. There was a marked difference, however. In the 1930s, an attempt was made to make a concept or process meaningful by showing how it applied to "life situations." In these programs understanding was through an axiomatic approach which was in harmony with the way that the mathematician looked at mathematics. What did the axiomatic approach imply? All mathematics was viewed as a structured system containing a set of elements, operations, and accepted rules (axioms) which governed the elements under the operations. In elementary school mathematics, generally speaking, the elements were numbers, the operations were addition, subtraction, multiplication, and division, and the axioms were properties. These properties provided a freedom as well as established limitations as to what could be done with the numbers involved in the operations. The applications of the properties gave the student an answer to the question "Why?". Given this basis for understanding, the mathematics curriculum attempted to become meaningful to the student.

The real number system is basic to modern elementary school mathematics. The properties of this system which makes sense out of computation for a child are the commutative, the associative, the distributive, and the identity elements. By using the commutative property and the identity elements for addition and multiplication, the student is able to cluster the number of basic "facts" that are learned. For example, the commutative property tells him that 2×3 is the same as 3×2. The associative property may be used to find a sum that the student does not know. Suppose that a child is having difficulty in finding a standard name for $8 + 7$. Instead of asking that the answer be given, the child learns to be resourceful. The child discovers that the ability to find the answer rests on personal knowledge and appreciation of the power of the properties. The child proceeds to rename 8 as $5 + 3$. Then, using the associative property for addition,

---

[2] Ronald C. Welch, "New Mathematics in the Primary Grades," in Evelyn Weber and Sylvia Sunderlin (Eds.), *Primary Education: Changing Dimensions.* (Washington, D.C.: Association for Childhood Education International, 1965), p. 44.

[3] John L. Marks, C. Richard Purdy, and Lucien B. Kinney, *Teaching Elementary School Mathematics for Understanding,* 2d ed. (New York: McGraw-Hill, Inc., 1965), p. 11.

$(5+3)+7$ becomes $5+(3+7)$; the student successfully completes the problem, knowing that what was done to get the answer was "legal."

Using the distributive property to justify the algorithm for finding the product of 57 multiplied by 4, the student can view the process used as a meaningful operation. By decimal numeration, 57 is renamed $50+7$. By the distributive property, $(50+7)\times4$ becomes $(50\times4)+(7\times4)$. As the student progresses toward the algorithm, it is seen why 7 and 50 should each be multiplied by 4 and that the sum of these partial products will give the answer. In other words, questions students ask concerning why it was done this way may be answered by relying on the axiomatic approach.

Formerly, mathematics tended to be presented as a segmented series of topics. Students were told how to perform an algorithm, with little accompanying explanation. Through the axiomatic approach, the elementary school mathematics program attempted to become both more meaningful, intellectually challenging and "legal."

Organization

Another change which should be noted is in the organizational pattern of the subject matter. By the very nature of mathematics, a definite logical order is dictated. However, the practice of presenting unconnected segments and expecting "mastery" before moving on to the next self-contained segment is being phased out. The organization used today is referred to as "spiral." This simply means that a mathematical concept is presented as early as deemed feasible, with opportunity provided for it to grow toward increased maturity by the process of repeated experiences throughout the elementary school program. In other words, a mathematical concept is first introduced at a very informal and intuitive level. With each recurrence, it is enriched and presented in greater depth until the expected maturity level is reached.

Concept Learning

One of the most striking features of the modern approach to teaching mathematics in elementary schools is the increasing emphasis on concept development. This emphasis is evidenced through an examination of recent textbooks on the teaching of elementary mathematics, the publications of the National Council of Teachers of Mathematics, and other recent literature dealing with the subject. This trend is not confined to the area of mathematics; it is evident also in science, social studies, and other areas. It is not difficult to discover the rationale for the recent emphasis on concept development. One obvious reason lies in the explosion of knowledge in almost every field; knowledge in the field of mathematics is said to have doubled since the beginning of the twentieth century. Since it is not possible for pupils to acquire all information available in the field of mathematics, the role of the teacher has become increasingly one of helping pupils develop the skills, understandings, and concepts that will enable them to become more and more self-propelled during a lifetime of learning.

The twenty-fourth yearbook of the National Council of Teachers of Mathematics made an interesting effort to identify basic mathematical concepts and to illustrate how pupils can be helped grow continuously in their understanding and use of these concepts from kindergarten through grade 12. The chapter in the yearbook that presents a *flow chart* to illustrate this notion is titled "Promoting the Continuous Growth of Mathematical Concepts." The authors stated thirty-two mathematical ideas which they regarded as synonymous with *concepts*, and illustrated how pupils deal with these concepts at each of four educational levels: kindergarten through grade 3, grades 4 through 6, grades 7 through 9, and grades 10 through 12. The authors explained, "Although the examples are grouped under four educational levels, there is no distinct line of demarcation among them. An example given for grades 7–9 might even be more appropriate for the superior child in grade 6."[4]

There can be no question about the importance of identifying the basic concepts that provide the common structure of the field of mathematics. This, however, is only the first step; the next step is to learn as much as possible about the process through which the concepts of mature mathematicians become the concepts of children—how children come to own concepts. Cognitive theorists have been giving increasing attention to this problem. Jerome S. Bruner, one of the most quoted of this group, said "What is most important for teaching basic concepts is that the child be helped to pass progressively from concrete thinking to the utilization of more conceptually adequate modes of thought."[5]

Jean Piaget conducted extensive experiments on how children form mathematical concepts. He said, for example,

At age seven, on the average, a child can build a straight fence consistently in any direction across the table, and he will check the straightness of the line by shutting one eye and sighting along it, as a gardener lines up bean poles. Here we have the essence of the projective concept; the line is still a topological line, but the child has grasped that the projective relationship depends on the angle of vision, or point of view.[6]

Piaget's descriptions of the developments of the cognitive process of conservation are particularly valuable. The development of conservation of number and of liquid, the concept of quantity, and spatial relationships, all are illuminated through Piaget's descriptions of developmental levels (see Chapter 3). Interestingly, when discussing spatial relationships, Piaget's said that the psychological order of this development is much closer to "modern" order than the traditional order of geometric concepts. For an excellent and expanded

4 Kenneth E. Brown et al., "Promoting the Continuous Growth of Mathematical Concepts," in *The Growth of Mathematical Ideas: Grades K–12,* Twenty-fourth Yearbook. (Washington, D.C.: National Council of Teachers of Mathematics, 1959), p. 480.

5 Jerome S. Bruner, *The Process of Education.* (Cambridge, Mass.: Harvard University Press, 1962), p. 38.

6 Jean Piaget, "How Children Form Mathematical Concepts," in Richard C. Anderson and David P. Ausubel, *Readings in the Psychology of Cognition.* (New York: Holt, Rinehart and Winston, 1965), p. 409.

discussion by Piaget of the development of mathematical concepts, see "How Children Form Mathematical Concepts."[7]

There is evidence from research on concept formation that most children follow a somewhat similar pattern of sequential development in concept formation. Bruner, for example, identified three stages.[8] During the first stage (inactive), ending at age five or six, the child is concerned with manipulating objects on an intuitive level by trial and error rather than by thoughtful action. The second stage, which occurs after the child has entered school, is called the iconic stage (getting data about the real world and organizing them so that they can be used selectively in the solution of problems). The third stage is called the symbolic stage, in which the child acquires the ability to operate on hypothetical propositions rather than being limited to what has been experienced or what is immediately present.

Although research indicates that most children follow a similar sequence in concept formation, it must be remembered that there is a wide range of difference in the rates at which individuals progress through this sequence. The following suggestion directed to intermediate-grade teachers applies as well to other levels of the school program:

Expectations of every child learning the same thing at the same time must be modified. Flexible classroom organization and differentiated instruction and assignments must become part of the intermediate-grade teacher's thoughts and planning.[9]

SITUATION 9.2   Observe an elementary school math lesson. Identify the concept being taught and compare the approach observed to the approach you experienced as an elementary student.

STRUCTURE

Another significant feature of the instructional approach in elementary school mathematics is the increasing amount of attention given to the structure (organizing concepts) of the discipline. (See Chapter 5.) When pupils learn the structure of mathematics, they learn how its various phases are related and they begin to see that the study of any given information cluster is related to the discipline of mathematics. The importance of mathematical structure is emphasized in the following statement:

It is easier to memorize words than nonsense syllables. It is easier to memorize

---

[7] Jean Piaget, "How Children Form Mathematical Concepts," in Nicholas J. Vigilante (Ed.), *Mathematics in Elementary Education.* (Toronto, Canada: Collier-Macmillan Canada, 1969), pp. 135–141.

[8] Robert G. Underhill, *Teaching Elementary School Mathematics.* (Columbus, Ohio: Charles Merrill Publishing Co., 1972), p. 11.

[9] Ronald C. Welch, "Developing Rational Powers in Intermediate-Grade Mathematics," in Evelyn Weber and Sylvia Sunderlin (Eds.), *Intermediate Education: Changing Dimensions.* (Washington, D.C.: Association for Childhood Education International, 1965), p. 55.

*numbers expressed with digits in a systematic pattern than in a random se-
quence. In like manner, learning in mathematics is accomplished most economically and effectively when the emphasis is on structure and on relationships
and organization in what is learned.*[10]

Attention has been called in previous chapters of this text to the absurdity
of certain notions about readiness for learning, such as (1) the child is ready
to read at six years of age; (2) the child is not ready for economics until high
school or college; and (3) the study of fractions should be postponed until the
fifth grade. Developments in learning theory add a new dimension to the study
of readiness for learning—the structure of the subject. Gagné called attention
to this dimension as follows:

*The planning that precedes effective design for learning is a matter of specify-
ing with some care what may be called the learning structure of any subject to
be acquired. In order to determine what comes before what, the subject must
be analyzed in terms of the types of learning in it.*[11]

Experimental programs dealing with elementary school mathematics have
caused a revision of notions about the inherent difficulty of topics and subjects;
some children have been able to handle much more difficult material than had
previously been supposed, when these materials were presented in a systematic
and challenging manner. Bruner called attention to the futility of trying to
assign specific content to certain age levels as follows:

*Precisely what kinds of materials should be used at what age with what effects
is a subject for research—research of many kinds. . . . Nor need we wait for all
the research findings to be in before proceeding, for a skilled teacher can also
experiment by attempting to teach what seems to be intuitively right for children of different ages, correcting as needed.*[12]

Bruner further stated:

*The basic ideas that lie at the heart of all science and mathematics and the
basic themes that give form to life and literature are as simple as they are powerful. . . . It is only when such basic ideas are put in formalized terms as
equations or elaborated verbal concepts that they are out of reach of the young
child, if he has not first understood them intuitively and had a chance to try
them out on his own.*[13]

Inhelder, who worked with Piaget, reinforced and clarified Bruner's position
when she stated:

*It seems highly arbitrary and very likely incorrect to delay the teaching, for
example, of Euclidean or metric geometry until the end of the primary grades.
. . . Basic notions in these fields are perfectly accessible to children of seven*

[10] Marks, Purdy, and Kinney, p. 50.
[11] Robert M. Gagné, *The Conditions of Learning.* (New York: Holt, Rinehart and Winston,
Inc., 1970), p. 26.
[12] Bruner, p. 53.
[13] Underhill, pp. 11–12.

to ten years of age, provided that they are divorced from their mathematical expression and studied through materials that the child can handle himself.[14]

INQUIRY

Another characteristic of the mathematics programs is the emphasis on inquiry. Referring to the work of the new curriculum projects which have grown up in the United States during recent years, Bruner stated:

For whether one speaks to mathematicians or physicists or historians, one encounters repeatedly an expression of faith in the powerful effects that come from permitting the student to put things toegther for himself, to be his own discoverer.[15]

When pupils are encouraged to discover principles and ideas for themselves, they appear to remember them longer, to relate them to other principles and ideas more readily, and to enjoy learning activities more.

It should not be assumed, however, that inquiry has entirely replaced exposition. When the teaching style consists primarily of exposition, the teacher is manipulating the content, making decisions as to what comes next, and presenting the pupils with ready-made solutions to problems. The pupil is a listener, with no active part in deciding how to put things together to arrive at a solution of a problem. A familiar criticism of this style of teaching is found in the statement: "Telling is not teaching." On the other hand, when inquiry is used, the teacher and the pupil are in a cooperative position; the pupil is not a passive listener, but an active participant in manipulating content, in deciding what steps to take next, and in inventing solutions to problems. It is true that pupils profit from both styles of teaching, but it is equally true that more opportunities need to be provided for pupils to learn by inquiry.

The value of inquiry has been recognized for many years by competent teachers and by specialists in learning theory and development. One reason for the wide recognition which inquiry is receiving today is the fact that our technological age requires the application of knowledge and skills to unsolved problems in industry, in government, and in family living. Although space is not available here for a detailed description of inquiry in mathematics, a few examples will serve to illustrate what it means.

Measurement. The kindergarten room contained several growing plants. Someone suggested that it would be interesting to find out (measure) how much these plants grow over a period of months. Instead of telling the pupils that they should use a ruler and record the height at different intervals, the teacher asked them to suggest how they could go about finding out what they wanted to know. One pupil suggested that a string could be used, another pupil suggested using a piece of paper, and finally one pupil suggested that a ruler be used. This example shows that there is a vast difference between being told

---

[14] Underhill, p. 12.

[15] Jerome S. Bruner, "The Act of Discovery," in Richard C. Anderson and David P. Ausubel, *Readings in the Psychology of Cognition.* (New York: Holt, Rinehart and Winston, Inc., 1965), p. 607.

how to solve a problem in measurement and being allowed to invent the solution.

Addition. The teacher of a fourth-year class in mathematics wanted to use inquiry in teaching addition. The problem in the text was, "If 8 + 8 = 16, then 8 + 9 = ☐. The author of the text was aware that doubles are easier to learn and recall than other combinations, and was attempting to get pupils to use this more easily acquired fact in obtaining a more difficult fact. With this in mind, the teacher asked Tim to relate the order of his thinking in arriving at the sum of 17. Tim's response was, "Well, I thought 8 + 9 = 8 +(2 + 7) = 10 + 7 = 17." Tim missed the mark completely according to the author's intent, but his answer was correct and his reasoning was sound. What did the teacher, using inquiry, do? He asked Tim, "Would it be possible to use 8 + 8 = 16 to help you arrive at the sum of 8 + 9?" Then he reinforced this by providing similar examples.

Multiplication. During preceding sessions the class had been engaged in activities designed to teach the meaning of multiplication with whole numbers. The purpose of this session was to invent the properties of multiplication. The device used was the construction of a chart, using the reversed order of the elements.

×	9	8	7	6	5	4	3	2	1	0
9	81									
8	72	64								
7	63	56	49							
6	54	48	42	36						
5	45	40	35	30	25					
4	36	32	28	24	20	16				
3	27	24	21	18	15	12	9			
2	18	16	14	12	10	8	6	4		
1									1	
1										0

The diagonal was completed first, beginning with 9 × 9 and ending with 2 × 2. This was followed by computing the products below the diagonal through the 2 row. By this time most members of the class were becoming more confident because the task of finding products was becoming progressively easier. One pupil remarked, "Everyone knows that one 9 is 9." However, the teacher went step by step from 1 × 9 to 1 × 1, and then asked the pupils to compare these products (in row 1) with the elements represented on the top of the grid. This they did without noticeable enthusiasm until Gary exclaimed, "Hey! One acts just like zero does in addition." Ann responded, "Yeah." Dick said, hesitatingly, "It does, doesn't it?" This was the essence of pupil inquiry; Gary had not only made an inquiry, he had led others along with him. Inquiry helps pupils develop a sense of satisfaction in achievement and a fascination for the study of mathematics; it gives them experience with a way of working, a way of thinking, and an approach to problem solving.

Motivation

"Motivation," in terms of the teaching-learning process, has at least two meanings: It may refer to the nature of the *motivated state* or it may refer to what the teacher does to motivate pupils.[16] An examination of recent publications in the field of learning theory reveals a tendency to view motivation in a less deterministic fashion than the classic view of S-R association psychologists. There is considerable evidence that children do not merely respond automatically to stimuli from the environment; that their concepts of self, emotions, and particularly their goals play an important part in motivation.[17]

Teachers have understood for many years that pupils will put forth more effort, organize their activities into more definite channels, and persist in their efforts longer when the activity is related to goals that they have set for themselves. The term "instruction" is used to denote control of the external events in the learning situation. Gagné stated, "These are the events that are manipulated by the teacher, the textbook writer, the designer of films or television lessons, the developer of self-instruction programs."[18] The modern program in mathematics is designed to assist teachers in manipulating the external events in the learning situation in such a fashion as to lead pupils to regard achievement in mathematics as something worthwhile for its own sake rather than as something to do to avoid punishment, to receive rewards, or to conform to the expectations of the teacher. This approach involves intrinsic rather than extrinsic motivation. Intrinsic motivation is inherent whenever a complete cycling of inquiry is experienced by the learner. Pupils approach the task as something to do rather than as something to learn about; they approach their learning activities with the attitude that the reward is in the doing itself and not in something external to the learning.

Detailed suggestions concerning instructional practices that encourage pupils to work for real achievement in mathematics rather than for external rewards are found in recent textbooks on the teaching of mathematics in elementary schools, in teachers' manuals that accompany series of textbooks for pupils, and in recent publications dealing with the psychology of classroom teaching. Some principles that are generally emphasized are:

1. Each new mathematical concept or process is introduced in a way that causes it to be significant and interesting to the pupils.

2. Knowledge of progress is generally recognized as effective in motivating pupils. A test score or a program chart may be useful in this respect.

3. Pupils may be motivated to study abstract concepts by showing the application of these concepts to activities in daily life.

4. Pupils are generally motivated to study mathematical concepts when they have an opportunity to explore, invent, and discover.

5. The need for recognition by their classmates may serve as motivation

---

[16] See John M. Stephens, *The Psychology of Classroom Teaching.* (New York: Holt, Rinehart and Winston, Inc., 1965), chap. 4.

[17] See Daniel A. Prescott, *The Child in the Educative Process.* (New York: McGraw-Hill Book Company, Inc., 1957), p. 392; and Rudolf Dreikers, "Do Teachers Understand Children?" *School and Society* (Feb. 28, 1959), pp. 88–90.

[18] Gagné, p. 283.

for some pupils; oral reports and the opportunity to display their work may provide the occasion for such recognition.

6. The order of concept formation is generally from concrete objects, to semiconcrete representation, to abstract ideas; taking objects apart and putting them together, using the number line, using the abacus, and using geometric models are useful in helping pupils understand mathematical structure.

7. The teacher may start with a situation with which pupils are already familiar and in which they are interested, and extend this interest to mathematical processes; the topic of *percent* may be introduced by using their interest in seasonal athletics.

8. A wise use of encouragement or praise may be effective in motivating most pupils. People generally work better when it is known that someone has at least noticed their achievements. There is some research that indicates that positive reinforcement is more effective than negative reinforcement for encouraging intrinsic motivation.

Efficiency in Computation

The development of skills has always held a high priority among tasks involved in teaching mathematics. The recent emphasis on concept development and inquiry was not meant to lessen the attention given to the development of efficient computation. The aims of the modern mathematics program have been stated as follows: development of concepts; development of mathematical understandings; development of computational skills; development of the ability to solve problems; and development of appreciations and favorable attitudes.[19]

Research dealing with the learning process and experimentation in classrooms have, however, brought about changes in the prevailing concept of the nature of a skill and in methods of teaching skills. The mathematics program can become more effective when teachers understand certain principles that have emerged from research and experimentation:

1. A skill is more than an automatic response; it is an organization of specific responses into patterns of behavior that are appropriate to a given situation. A skillful football player is not merely one who has mastered certain mechanical responses: such a player is one who can analyze each situation and decide what response is appropriate to that situation. Skill in mathematics involves more than knowing how to add, subtract, multiply, and divide; it involves knowledge of how and when to use these processes in the solution of problems.

2. Understanding should come before practice. When pupils have explored a process, when they understand when and why it is used, they see the importance of practice, and the practice is regarded as a means of achieving a purpose.

[19] Marks, Purdy, and Kinney, pp. 33–37.

3. Pupils need guidance as they practice skills. If left entirely to themselves, they may merely reinforce wasteful or incorrect habits. The old adage that "practice makes perfect" applies only when pupils are practicing correct and economical methods of learning skills.

4. Practice should be based on diagnosis of individual status in the mastery of skills. It is wasteful to have the whole class practice on facts that all but a few have already learned. It is a relatively simple matter for the teacher to construct a chart, listing the facts to be learned across the top and the names of the pupils from top to bottom of a piece of paper. This will show at a glance what pupils have yet to learn what facts. Then practice can have the virtue of being diagnostic and individualized.

5. The systematic teaching of mathematical skills is essential. The notion that skills are learned most economically through use in meaningful situations should not be taken to mean that it is not necessary to set aside specific periods for practice on skills. Research has indicated that it is not feasible to teach mathematics effectively through an activity program alone.[20] Hence, teachers take time for direct and systematic practice on skills.

6. The development of mathematical skills is a continuous process; the degree of proficiency attained at one maturity level will not suffice for a later stage of development. Children differ so widely in rates of learning and development that teachers at all levels must be prepared to provide individual guidance in the continuing maintenance and learning of skills.

Enumeration—an area for exploration.

[20] Paul R. Hanna, *Opportunities for the Use of Arithmetic in an Activity Program.* (Washington, D.C.: National Council of Teachers of Mathematics, 1965), pp. 85–120.

7. The use of a variety of resources is essential to maintaining interest in practice; textbooks, workbooks, duplicated materials, games, and puzzles are among the resources frequently used.

Objects

The importance of concrete objects to provide manipulative experiences for the learning of mathematics has been one of the persistent recommendations made for the improvement of schools. Pestalozzi emphasized "object teaching," and in 1821 Warren Colburn published *First Lessons in Arithmetic, on the Plan of Pestalozzi*. In 1826, Fröbel in "The Education of M" again emphasized the importance of play and manipulation on learning.

More recent recommendations have made by Bruner,[21] Piaget,[22] and Cuisenaire.[23] Bruner stressed the need of students to manipulate objects in order to form images which can be related to symbols. Cuisenaire went even further and developed materials, Cuisenaire rods, by which mathematical concepts can be manipulated. Piaget's experiments illustrate that mental development begins with motor activity.

An outgrowth of these recommendations is the mathematics laboratory. The purpose of the math lab is the same sense as that of a science laboratory— a place where investigations can be conducted and hypotheses verified through manipulation.

Mathematics laboratories seem to be as many and varied as the persons who operate them, but running through all are a few common characteristics. Each has different stations set up for different types of activities; is rich in materials; has a child-centered program rather than teacher-centered; provides open-ended activities; is flexible; uses a multimedia–multisensory approach; and uses written materials as references. Some math labs are set up for remedial work only; some are set up for advanced students only; some are set up as an enrichment program, which is only a fraction of the total mathematics approach in those particular schools. What remains to be done is to establish a math lab plan which encompasses the widest possible range of activities and abilities and which has a simple underlying structure easily incorporated into any classroom or school situation.

SITUATION 9.3   Read "How Children Form Mathematical Concepts" by Jean Piaget. What current practices in elementary school mathematics programs support Piaget's theories?

---

21 Bruner, "The Act of Discovery," p. 607.

22 Anthony J. Picard, "Piaget's Theory of Development with Implications for Teaching Elementary School Mathematics," *School Science and Mathematics* (January 1972), pp. 48–55.

23 C. Gattegno, *A Teacher's Introduction to the Cuisenaire-Gattegno Method of Teaching Arithmetic*. (Reading, England: Gattegno-Pollock Educational Co., Ltd., 1960).

Evaluating and Reporting

The central purpose of evaluation is to determine the extent to which pupils are achieving the objectives of the mathematics program. Other purposes include providing a basis for planning learning activities, for the selection of instructional materials, for determining the effectiveness of the curriculum, for grouping pupils for instruction, and for reporting to parents. These purposes are achieved through the use of teacher observation, teacher-made tests, standardized tests, and other instruments and procedures. Reporting to parents on the progress of pupils in various subject-matter areas, although not required by law in any state, is almost universally practiced in elementary and secondary schools. The practice has one major objective: to promote more effective home–school cooperation in the interest of giving the child the best possible opportunities for learning.

A detailed treatment of purposes, procedures, and trends in evaluating and reporting pupil progress at this point would duplicate much of the content of Chapter 13. However, since more drastic changes have taken place in the mathematics program than in other areas of the elementary school curriculum, special problems relating specifically to this area must be mentioned. Among these problems are:

1. Because subject-matter readiness must be given serious consideration in the introduction of new topics and processes, the teacher needs to be familiar with the structure of mathematics in order to find out what activities are to be introduced next in promoting pupil progress.

2. The interests of pupils play an important role in motivational readiness,

Involving children is the first and fundamental activity in a system to report pupil progress.

and therefore the teacher must observe pupils closely to determine each pupil's degree of interest and attention, and to decide upon those procedures which help to motivate each.

3. Because psychologists have thrown new light on the stages in concept development that children at various stages of maturity normally pursue, the teacher needs to be familiar with research in this area in order to be proficient in the evaluation of pupil progress in concept development.

4. The modern elementary school mathematics program is designed to encourage thinking on the part of the individual pupil. For this reason the teacher must be concerned with constructing test items and other evaluation procedures with this objective in mind, rather than being content with tests that merely reveal simple recall of information.

5. A special problem in relation to the use of standardized tests has aroused considerable concern on the part of teachers and administrators—namely, the extent to which available standardized tests are in harmony with the content and objectives of the modern elementary school mathematics program. More precisely, concern has been expressed with regard to the "content validity" of available standardized tests in the field of elementary school mathematics. Smith made a study of this problem by investigating the contents of state-adopted mathematics texts for the fourth, fifth, and sixth grades in Oklahoma and Texas, and comparing his findings with items contained in five achievement test batteries most commonly used in these states. His study indicated that the overall differences between the contents of the mathematics textbooks and mathematics achievement tests used in these two states were not substantial, but that there were certain areas in which they differed sufficiently to hinder their most effective use with the same pupils. These areas included geometry, the concepts of set theory, and number systems with bases other than 10.[24]

6. Reporting to parents takes on additional importance in schools using the new content and procedures. Parents need a clear explanation of how the new program differs from the arithmetic they learned in elementary school. This requires more in the area of home–school communication than merely sending out report cards periodically. It requires frequent meetings with groups of parents, clearly written pamphlets or bulletins explaining the program, and lists of books and articles written expressly for nonmathematical readers.

Content

The mathematics found in elementary school programs across the nation consists of some traditional topics and some new ones. The four "basic operations"—addition, subtraction, multiplication, and division of whole numbers and the nonnegative rationals—continue to make up a major portion of the curriculum. The introduction and availability of inexpensive minicalculators has influenced the goals, objectives, and content of the modern mathematics

---

[24] Lee A. Smith, "A Comparison of the Contents of State Adopted Arithmetic Textbooks with Contents of the Arithmetic Sections of Selected Standardized Achievement Batteries." (Norman, Okla.: University of Oklahoma, unpublished doctoral dissertation, 1965).

program. In the past, the primary objective was to train children to be highly skilled in computation. Today's children are still expected to achieve the computational skill necessary for them to function competently in their society. The difference is that, in the past, this goal was paramount to all others, while today it is placed in proper perspective with other skills considered equally important in this changing society. For instance, it is impossible to envision the problems which today's children will be expected to solve tomorrow. Therefore, their abilities to think rationally about problems must be developed so that they will be able to select the proper tools to solve these problems. They must learn "when to add" as well as "how to add." In other words, one of the goals of the modern program is to make mathematics meaningful so that the child understands computation. Some of the newer topics are discussed below.

Sets. The topic which most people associate with the "new math" is sets. A common definition is that a set is a group of things. Although set theory dates back to its creation by Georg Cantor in the 1880s, it is a new concept for the elementary school program. Prior to 1950 it was taught at the graduate level; later, it was discovered that the language and some of the simpler aspects of sets could be most helpful in introducing mathematical concepts to very young children. Research has pointed out that children learn more effectively when concrete materials are used in the early stages of learning a concept. The use of sets serves this purpose.

The opportunity for children to sort, arrange, and compare the members (elements) of a set provides a physical setting for the future development of an abstract mathematical concept. A few of the concepts usually developed by means of some of the simpler properties of sets are cardinal number, order, addition, subtraction, multiplication, and division. For instance, the cardinality of a set is established when a child pairs the members of one set with those of another. After setting up a one-to-one correspondence between sets in this manner, the child sees that there are just as many members in one set as in the other. Thus, a common property has been observed between equivalent sets. This "alikeness" property is identified as "number," which is assigned to all sets of this "family."

The addition operation on numbers is developed from the union operation on sets. Joining a set of two to a set of three and seeing a set of five becomes an interesting and meaningful activity for children. As they are able to dissociate the things (elements) of the set, they begin to abstract the concept, $3 + 2 = 5$.

Two schools of thought concerning the development of multiplication appear in textbooks today. One is that multiplication should be regarded as an operation in its own right; the other is that multiplication should be thought of as repeated addition. The former view is supported by mathematicians, who believe that even at this level it is important to begin building toward the field properties of the real numbers. In either event, sets are applicable. The first approach makes use of a version of the Cartesian product in which a set of three cowboy hats is matched with a set of four boys. The problem is to find how many different boy—hat combinations are possible. The multiplication 3 × 4 = 12 is abstracted following the dissociation of the things. The repeated addition method draws on the union of three equivalent sets of four elements each.

The removal of a subset from an existing set is the usual direction taken in beginning ideas about subtraction. Most classroom teachers agree that this approach to subtraction is more natural for children to comprehend. One danger, however, is that children are apt to confuse the operation on sets with that on numbers. An attempt is made to teach children that they may "take away" a subset, but that they must subtract numbers.

Many other examples of the use of sets might be given to illustrate the ways they may be used to clarify and unify notions about mathematics. The language of sets also provides a precise way of talking about mathematics.

Numeration. The decimal numeration system has been an integral part of the mathematics program since the beginning of formal education. Although our place–value system had been taught and used for years by students, there was continued evidence of very little understanding of its structure and its use in recording number concepts. The introduction of numeration systems using bases other than 10 (those using digits other than the familiar Hindu-Arabic figures), and those without place–value is expected to assist students in understanding a place–value system such as ours. Some educators also believe that such a study will develop an appreciation for the long struggle involved in the development of the Hindu-Arabic system which we use today.

Expanded Notation. With the introduction of the open mathematical sentence, such as $5 + \square = 9$, the informal study of algebra is begun. Here students begin to acquire the concept of a variable by making replacements for the frame to seek a true sentence. Through this, the pupils learn about true, false, and open mathematical sentences. They also discover the role and strength of a counterexample in proof. Not only the "equals" relation is used in open mathematical sentences, but other relations as well, such as $<, >, \leq, \geq$. Students find the solution set of simple mathematical sentences, and also those using the connectives "and" and "or." They learn to graph the solution set of each on the number line. The use of the mathematical sentence to express a problem situation has been found to be most helpful to students in problem solving.

Geometry. The innovative programs agree that the study of geometry should include more than an ability to recognize shapes and to compute their perimeters and areas. Consequently, simple concepts of nonmetric geometry have an important place in today's elementary school mathematics curriculum. The geometric concepts "line," "plane," and "space" are introduced as sets of "points." Children are led to understand these concepts by the use of models drawn from the world in which they live. For example, a string or wire with both ends joined may serve as a model for a simple closed curve. Very young children may understand the notion by joining hands to form a "circle."

Through activities involving the model, the children discover that the inside, the outside, and the curve are different sets of points. Such words as interior, exterior, and region enrich their vocabulary. They learn to think of a region as the interior and its boundary. Later, they describe a region in more precise language as the union of the set of points in the curve and the set of points in its interior.

Metric System. In 1790, the French Academy in Paris devised a system of weights and measures which was invariable. They adopted these principles:

1. The standard of length should be based upon some absolute, unchanging standard found in the physical universe.
2. The basic units of length, volume, and weight should be directly related to each other.
3. The specifically named multiples and subdivisions of the standard units should be decimally related.[25]

The standard unit of length (metre[26]) was designed to be one ten-millionth of an arc representing the distance between the North Pole and the equator.[27] A kilogram was designed to be the weight in a vacuum of 1 cubic decimeter of distilled water at the freezing point. In 1960, the meter was defined as "1,650,763.73 wavelengths of the orange-red line produced by an atom of Krypton 86.[28]

In 1837, France converted to the metric system. By 1975, Britain will be completely metric. Canada intends to be converted by 1980.

Public law 93-380, passed in August of 1974, noted that the increased use of the metric system in the United States is inevitable and that the metric system will become the dominant system. The law also noted that a program to teach the children the use of the metric system is necessary. With most of the major countries of the world utilizing the metric system, and with the likelihood that it will become the dominant system in the United States, many modern elementary schools are now including this system as a content vehicle.[29]

SITUATION 9.4   Examine some elementary school mathematics programs. If you were to analyze the program in terms of influence by the major projects developed in the 1960s, which projects seem to have contributed most to the programs you examined?

---

[25] Arthur E. Hallerber, "The Metric System: Past Present, Future?" *The Arithmetic Teacher* (April 1973), p. 249.

[26] *Note*: The official spelling in the International System (SI) of metric measurement is "metre," but this is likely to be "Americanized" to "meter" when the system is adopted by the United States. Hallerber, p. 249.

[27] Ralph D. Connelly and Brenda Smith, "Measurement: A Look at History and the Metric System," *School Science and Mathematics,* Vol. LXXV, No. 6 (October 1975), p. 488.

[28] Connelly and Smith, p. 488.

[29] K. A. Grzesiak, "America and the Metric System: Present Perspectives," *Elementary School Journal* (January 1976), pp. 195–200.

Another definition of the content vehicles for the mathematics curriculum was supplied by Guy M. Wilson. He attempted to answer the question, "What mathematics is important enough in business and life as to be the mastery program in the elementary school?"[30] (The reader should note that this would be an effort at curriculum building derived from the sociological source. See Chapter 6.)

> . . . the drill material for mastery consists of simple addition—100 primary facts, 300 decade facts, carrying and other process difficulties; simple subtraction—100 primary facts, process difficulties; multiplication—100 primary facts, process difficulties; long division—no committed facts, general scheme and process steps; simple fractions in halves, fourths, and thirds, and in special cases, in eights and twelfths, general acquaintance with other simple fractions; decimals—reading knowledge only.[31]

Materials

The quantity and quality of manipulative materials for the teaching of mathematics has mushroomed in the past few years. Perhaps this growth, a revival of several previous periods beginning with Pestalozzi, can be explained by the impact of Piaget and learning psychologists. Reys abstracted the following as the psychological premise for the use of manipulative materials in the learning of mathematics:

1. *Concept formation is the essence of learning mathematics.*
2. *Learning is based on experience.*
3. *Sensory learning is the foundation of all experience and thus the heart of learning.*
4. *Learning is a growth process and is developmental in nature.*
5. *Learning is characterized by distinct, developmental stages.*
6. *Learning is enhanced by motivation.*
7. *Learning proceeds from the concrete to the abstract.*
8. *Learning requires active participation by the learner.*
9. *Formulation of a mathematical abstraction is a long process.*[32]

There are two types of concrete manipulative objects and materials. One type is in the environment of "real" life situations (for example, shopping situations). The second type is the designing of specifically constructed models to depict and model the mathematical concept or system being studied. Surely, both the "real" life and the constructed models should be used. One could facilitate the learning of concepts, and the other could facilitate the application of the concepts. One note of caution: The concrete operational learner will learn only the model if the concept depicted requires formal operational cognitive processes.

The establishment of mathematics laboratories is a spin-off of the increase

---

[30] Leroy G. Callahan and Vincent J. Glennon, *Elementary School Mathematics,* 4th ed. (Washington, D.C.: Association for Supervision and Curriculum Development, 1975), p. 2.

[31] Callahan and Glennon, p. 3.

[32] Callahan and Glennon, p. 118.

in quantity and quality of manipulative materials, the attention to individual differences, and the stressing of the inquiry processes. A mathematics laboratory is a place where the facilities, equipment, and materials are organized and available to involve the pupils in the learning of mathematics. The existence of a mathematics laboratory does not replace, but does supplement, other instruction in mathematics. Although limited, the evidence suggests that achievement gains occur in a laboratory setting, more positive student attitudes toward mathematics appear, and both teachers and students learn to use the laboratory easily.[33]

ISSUES

Being for or against "new math" seems to be the dominant issue of the mid-1970s. The issue is more aptly framed in terms of computational skills and how to achieve them. In their enthusiasm, a number of critics suggest that some math educators are *against* proficiency in computation. Again, a more precise framing of the question is in terms of (1) which proficiencies; (2) when the proficiencies are to be mastered; and (3) what learning environments best accomplish this objective.

SITUATION 9.5   Review the literature during the past fifteen years which report the findings of studies related to the incorporation of new mathematics programs in elementary schools. List the findings.

The first National Assessment of Educational Progress was conducted during the 1972–1973 school year. Carpenter and associates reported in a summary the results of the assessment concerning mathematics:

> Student performance was strong or at the level of reasonable expectation in terms of . . . whole-number computation, knowledge of numeration concepts, analysis of simple (one-step) word problems. . . . Weaknesses . . . were indicated in the areas of percent, development of fraction concepts, complex word problems, measurement tasks, and understanding of geometry topics.[34]

Carpenter and his associates stated that the data show ". . . thirteen-year-olds perform at about the same level as adults," in whole number computations.[35]

Some critics of the "new math" are concerned with the degree of formalism, the pacing, and the abstractness of the "new" programs. Morris Kline's criticisms are concerned with the validity of the "new math."[36] Kline felt that the

---

[33] Callahan and Glennon, p. 93.
[34] Thomas P. Carpenter, Terrence G. Coburn, Robert E. Reys, and James W. Wilson, "Results and Implications of the N.A.E.P. Mathematics Assessment: Elementary Schools," *The Arithmetic Teacher*, Vol. XXII (October 1975), p. 449.
[35] Carpenter et al., p. 450.
[36] Callahan and Glennon, p. 11.

assumption of "new math" (what was logically sound mathematics was sound pedagogy) was inadequate. He felt that the psychological and sociological bases of curriculum development were inadequately represented, and that the deductive reasoning required was beyond the development of the pupils. Furthermore, from his perspective, the language (terminology and symbolism) served no useful purpose. He also questioned the inclusion of the new content vehicles such as set, nondecimal numeration, and congruence as being empty and abstract, and wasted teaching time. Hard evidence to substantiate the advantages or to discount the disadvantages of "new math" programs is limited. The School Mathematics Study Group (SMSG) sponsored a National Longitudinal Study of Mathematics Abilities (NLSMA), and Begle and Wilson commented on the results of that study:

> The difference between the SMSG textbook group and most conventional textbook groups at any grade level is largely a contrast of computational-level scales on the one hand and understanding of mathematical ideas as indicated by comprehension-, application-, and analysis-level scales on the other. There are exceptions to this of course.[37]

Wilson and Begle also said:

> But not all modern textbooks produced the kind of results that were expected for them. Some of them in fact did rather poorly on all levels—from computation to analysis. Those textbooks which did not do very well were for the most part considerably more formal and more rigorous than the SMSG books. . . . This remark on the greater formalism is conjectural; it is an opinion as to a possible explanation of the poor showing of some textbooks.[38]

Callahan and Glennon summarized the research comparing students in "new" and "traditional" programs:

> In summary, the research comparing student performance in "new" and "traditional" programs seems to confirm a common sense prediction. Students in textbook programs that emphasize conceptual aspects of school mathematics tended to demonstrate higher performance on tests composed of conceptual tasks; those in programs that emphasized the less conceptual aspects demonstrated higher performance on the less conceptual skill tasks. Some qualifying trends appear from the data, however. The advantage in performance of students in "new" programs over "tradition" on more conceptually oriented test tasks seemed to be primarily true for higher ability students. Also, there is evidence of classes in "new" programs that do very well on less conceptual as well as conceptual tasks, and classes in "traditional" programs that do very well on conceptual tasks.[39]

Another recent issue is the use of minicalculators in the teaching and learning of mathematics. In 1974, the Board of Directors of the National Council of Teachers of Mathematics adopted the following position statement:

[37] Callahan and Glennon, p. 14.
[38] Callahan and Glennon, p. 14.
[39] Callahan and Glennon, pp. 15–16.

With the decrease in cost of the mini-calculator, its accessibility to students at all levels is increasing rapidly. Mathematics teachers should recognize the potential contribution of this as a valuable instructional aid. In the classroom, the mini-calculator should be used in imaginative ways to reinforce learning and to motivate the learner as he becomes proficient in mathematics.[40]

At the present time, other potential issues (objects and concrete manipulatory experiences, the importance of the sociological source, and the need for a developmental theory) have been subsumed within and by the "new math" issue. The new programs of the 1960s did make an impact. The criticisms of the resulting changes will make an impact. The modern mathematics curriculum will not be that of the 1950s nor of the 1960s.

INTERDISCIPLINARY APPROACHES

This section, common to each curriculum chapter, briefly discusses those programs and activities which further the interrelationship among curriculum areas. Values-clarification strategies, career awareness activities, and the Unified Science and Mathematics for Elementary Schools Project have been selected for inclusion.

Values-Clarification Strategies

A quick review of the table of contents of eighteen issues of two professional publications in mathematics provided three articles with titles that implied concern with affective education; two were at the college level. To the degree that these publications represent the concern of the members of the profession, and provided their readers accept the limited survey of the author, it would appear that values-clarification strategies are of slight concern in the mathematics curriculum.

A review of the table of contents of Simon's (and associates) book on strategies identified many that utilized mathematics as a data-gathering system for the choosing, acting, prizing sequence.[41] For example, several values-clarification strategies are concerned with the individual's use of time as a direct reflection of a value system. Percentages, bar and line graphs, and other display systems are used to provide feedback to the individual.

Career Awareness Activities

A review of the same eighteen journals mentioned in the preceding section failed to locate an article with a reference to career education in its title. The implication is that the two professional organizations that represent teachers of mathematics are only slightly interested, if at all, in the movement, that is,

---

[40] Callahan and Glennon, p. 125.

[41] Sidney B. Simon, Leland W. Hawes, and Howard Kirschenbaum, *Values Clarification: A Handbook of Practical Strategies for Teachers and Students.* (New York: Hart Publishing Company, Inc., 1972), pp. 3–8.

career education. The author is prepared to be challenged and hopes that he is wrong!

Certainly, individual teachers and the listing of the commonly accepted goals for mathematics education indicate a commitment to career-awareness activities. The opportunities to utilize mathematics as a language system to display the requirements for entry, salaries, location, and similar data for various occupations are numerous. The activities of identifying the mathematical skills operating within various occupations seems challenging. The opportunities are there!

Unified Science and Mathematics for Elementary Schools Project (USMES)

Funded in 1970 by the National Science Foundation, the purpose of USMES is to "develop a curriculum for the elementary schools in which subject areas would be integrated through the work by students on real and practical problems."[42] A real problem, as defined by USMES, is one which is a practical impediment to good, safe, or pleasurable living. This project has developed several resource units or modules as guides to real and practical problem solving within an interdisciplinary approach. A general sequence in the project's approach is (1) discussion of the challenge; (2) determining possible investigations; (3) setting priorities; (4) data collection; (5) data representation; (6) data analysis; (7) construction; and (8) actions resulting from investigations.[43]

STRATEGY OF INSTRUCTION

The strategy of instruction presented in Chapter 5 will be utilized to generalize about the mathematics curriculum. The reader is encouraged to use Chapter 5 as a reference for further clarification of the remainder of this section.

Selection of Content

The programs of the 1960s were intensely concerned with the structures of mathematics. Several topics not common to the mathematics curriculum of earlier years were introduced as aspects of the structure of mathematics (see previous section of this chapter titled "Content"). The critics of the programs of the 1960s are now questioning the selection of certain topics. From their point of view, these topics (that is, sets and nondecimal numeration) either do not represent the structure or are inappropriate for the cognitive development of elementary school pupils. The critics also feel that an overemphasis upon structure has imbalanced the teaching of effective and efficient computational skills. The concern seems to be not with structure as a criterion for the selection of content but with other questions: What are the structures? Can they be

---

[42] Earle L. Lamon, Betty Beck, and Carolyn C. Arbetter, "Real Problem Solving in U.S.M.E.S.: Interdisciplinary Education and Much More," *School Science and Mathematics*, Vol. LXXV, No. 1 (January 1975), p. 54.
[43] Lamon et al., pp. 61–64.

presented at an appropriate cognitive developmental level? How does the structure influence the achievement of computational skills?

Learning and Development

The developmentalists, from Pestalozzi to Piaget, have influenced a reduction in the potential abstractness in the teaching of mathematics. The utilization of concrete objects and manipulatory experiences have rapidly increased during the past several years. The critics of the programs of the 1960s have used a developmental stance (usually Piaget) to question the appropriateness of the requisite cognitive operations for the cognitive development of elementary pupils. It seems that the field learning theories and the developmentalists are influencing the structural and conceptual organization of the curriculum of mathematics. The S-R association theories are presently controlling the approaches in the teaching of efficient and effective computation.

Methodology

Inquiry was an integral element of the programs of the 1960s. Although sometimes referred to as "discovery" or "process," the 1960s' program inevitably stressed inquiry. The justification was that the teaching of concepts and the involvement of the cognitive processes of analysis, synthesis, and evaluation were furthered through inquiry. The critics of the programs of the 1960s typically do not challenge inquiry, but question the imbalance in its use. In order to accomplish a high level of mastery in computational skills, practice, after inquiry is needed. Inquiry should precede practice, but practice should follow inquiry whenever computational efficiency is required.

Communication

Callahan and Glennon reported the research on the verbal interaction patterns of teachers, with special attention to the few studies of mathematics teachers.[44] Although these data are insufficient to generalize with confidence, it does appear that the verbal patterns of mathematics teachers are similar to those of teachers in other areas; for example; all do two-thirds of the talking in a classroom, and teachers of high-achieving groups accept five to six times as many pupil ideas as do teachers of low-achieving students.

Perez's study (1973) found more frequent positive sanctioning in language arts classes than in mathematics classes.[45] It also appears that the verbal interaction patterns of teachers are independent of the content vehicles and perhaps of the stated objective. The reader is referred to Chapter 5 for a more extended discussion concerning the communication patterns of teachers.

Objectives

Objectives related to the development of efficient and effective computational skills tend to emphasize the lower-energy cognitive behaviors of recall, rec-

---

[44] Callahan and Glennon, p. 123.
[45] Callahan and Glennon, p. 123.

ognition, paraphrasing, translating, and applying. Objectives related to the establishment of the processes of inquiry tend to emphasize the higher-energy cognitive behaviors of analysis, synthesis, and evaluation. The curriculum builders of the programs of the 1960s recognized an imbalance in the distribution and achievement of objectives in the older programs. Therefore, the programs of the 1960s were designed to emphasize the higher cognitive behaviors. Critics of the "new math" program in the 1970s see an imbalance in other ways: higher cognitive behaviors over lower cognitive behaviors. Both the 1960 and 1970 groups, pro and con, seem to have reached a compromise in proposing a curriculum with a balanced emphasis and achievement of objectives at all classification levels of all domains.

Goals

The goals of programs in the 1960s was for the pupil to experience and think about mathematics in ways familiar to the mathematician. The goal of programs in the 1970s is for the pupil to experience and think about mathematics in ways which the average citizen does when producing, adapting, and functioning. Notice that both sets of programs stress the need for logical reasoning and refined performance standards, developed through patterned mental processes.

SUMMARY

1. The objectives of mathematics tend to relate to (1) the logical relationships of, and within, the discipline; (2) the application of mathematics to the physical world; and (3) the development of effective and efficient computational skills.

2. The logical approach has controlled the building of the curriculum in mathematics, especially the programs of the 1960s.

3. A changing in the emphasis of the mathematics curriculum is occurring in organization, concept, learning, structure, and materials.

4. S-R association learning theories hold significance for the objectives of skill mastery, while field learning theories and the developmentalists (Piaget) hold significance for other objectives.

5. The mathematics laboratory is a place where the organization of facilities, equipment, and materials encourages the conducting of investigations in skill learnings.

6. The criticisms of the "new math" programs of the 1960s relate to two major concerns: the imbalance between skills and inquiry learning, and the validity of the content vehicles selected as structures.

7. The efforts of the interdisciplinary approaches are directed primarily toward the sciences. Career-awareness activities and values-clarification strategies are just beginning to be adopted in the mathematics curriculum.

8. The pedagogy of the new mathematics program places emphasis on concept learning, inquiry, the structure of the discipline, intrinsic motivation, and the systematic teaching of basic skills.

9. Teachers are generally expected to participate in in-service education programs before attempting to teach the "new" mathematics. The mathematics programs of the 1970s will not be like those of either the 1950s or 1960s.

Problems and Projects

1. Select a lesson from an elementary mathematics program or curriculum guide. Discuss and analyze the potential of the lesson for inquiry methodology. What would be the nature of talk and behavior during exploration? What are plausible inventions which the teacher might expect to hear? What discovery systems are anticipated?

2. Read *The Process of Education* by Jerome Bruner and "How Children Form Mathematical Concepts" by Jean Piaget. What parallels may be drawn between the philosophy of these two individuals concerning the teaching of mathematics?

3. Obtain Cuisenaire rods or some similar mathematical-concept teaching objemt. Observe five elementary school children as they manipulate these objects. Record the different mathematical concepts with which the students interacted.

4. Evaluate the standardized mathematic achievement tests used in your school system for consistency with the adopted school mathematical programs.

Selected Readings

Bruner, Jerome S., *The Process of Education*. Cambridge, Mass.: Harvard University Press, 1962. Powerful statement on education.

Callahan, Leroy G., and Vincent J. Glennon, *Elementary School Mathematics: A Guide to Current Research,* 4th ed. Washington, D.C.: Association for Supervision and Curriculum Development, 1975. Summarizes the research in mathematics education.

Cambridge Conference on School Mathematics, *Goals for the Correlation of Elementary Science and Mathematics.* Boston: Houghton Mifflin Company, 1969. Recommends the use and application of mathematics in correlation with science.

Copland, R. W., *How Children Learn Mathematics: Teaching Implications of Piaget's Research,* 2d ed. New York: Crowell Collier and Macmillan, Inc., 1974. Applies Piaget's theories to the teaching and learning of mathematics.

D'Augustine, C. H., *Multiple Methods of Teaching Mathematics in the Elementary School,* 2d ed. New York: Harper & Row, Publishers, 1973. A source book for techniques and procedures.

Johnston, A. Montgomery, and Paul C. Burns, *Research in Elementary School Mathematics.* Boston: Allyn and Bacon, Inc., 1970. Chapter 5 presents Piaget's experimentation with children's concepts of mathematics.

Kline, Morris, *Why Johnny Can't Add.* New York: St. Martin's Press, Inc., 1973. A criticism of the programs of the 1960s.

Lamon, W. A. (Ed.), *Learning and the Nature of Mathematics.* Chicago: Science Research Associates, Inc., 1972. A collection of articles on the learning of mathematics.

May, L. J., *Teaching Mathematics in the Elementary School,* 2d ed. New York:

Crowell Collier and Macmillan, Inc., 1974. Teaching suggestions emphasizing concrete manipulations.

National Assessment of Educational Progress, *Math Fundamentals: Selected Results from the First Mathematics Assessment, Report 04-MA-01*. Washington, D.C.: U.S. Superintendent of Documents, January 1975. Results of the 1973 assessment of 9-, 13-, and 17-year-olds in math fundamentals.

National Society for the Study of Education, *Mathematics Education*. Chicago: University of Chicago Press, 1970. Section II, "Curriculum Content and Pedagogy," is useful.

Piaget, Jean, *The Child's Conception of Number*. New York: Humanities Press, Inc., 1952. Piaget's observations concerning the development of number concepts.

Piaget, Jean, "How Children Form Mathematical Concepts," in Nicholas J. Vigilante, *Mathematics in Elementary Education*. Toronto, Canada: Collier-Macmillan Canada, 1969, pp. 135–141. Classic statement of Piaget.

Underhill, Robert, *Teaching Elementary School Mathematics*. Columbus, Ohio: Charles E. Merrill Publishing Co., 1972. Part I, on the methodological core, develops Piaget, Bruner, and curriculum design.

chapter 10

Inquiring
SCIENCE

The business of education is forming effective habits of discriminating tested beliefs from mere assertions, guesses, and opinions, to develop a lively, sincere and open-minded preference for conclusions that are properly grounded, and to ingrain into individuals' working habits methods of inquiry and reasoning appropriate to the various problems that present themselves.

John Dewey, *How We Think.* (Lexington, Mass.: D.C. Heath & Company, 1910), pp. 27–28.

DEFINITION

The learning of science is directly dependent upon experiencing through

observation, measurement, experimentation, interpretation, cognitive and affective model construction, and the prediction of consequences.

the rational establishment of organizations which regularize the functions of observation, measurement, and other procedures.

the creative explanations, extensions, and applications of the products of organized systems of observation, measurement, and similar activities.

The evidence of learning science is nested within the wise-acting behaviors of an individual when dealing with nature. Whenever direct experiencing is not the fundamental characteristic of a curriculum, then it is certainly not a science curriculum. When the behaviors of the participants do not demonstrate, ". . . a tendency to be suspicious of absolutes, a respect for tentativeness and a kind of working skepticism,"[1] then it certainly is not a science activity.

[1] Educational Policies Commission, *Education and the Spirit of Science.* (Washington, D.C.: National Education Association, 1966), p. 4.

OBJECTIVES

The present age is one of spectacular changes brought about by humans through science and technology. The past twenty years have witnessed more scientific and technological discoveries than had been witnessed in all previous recorded time. The achievement of many of our natural goals, at home and abroad, depends upon a strong and growing science and technology. New insights into the processes of investigation, new knowledge in the various areas of science, new information concerning what pupils at given levels of development can learn, all require a rethinking of the objectives of science in the elementary school. Science is included in the elementary school curriculum for the contributions it can make to the intellectual, social, and emotional development of children, and for the contributions it can make to the achievement of our national goals. It can cause some pupils to want to share the excitement and satisfaction of a career in science; it can help all children to comprehend the kind of world in which they live and to participate effectively in an increasing number of local and national decisions which require an understanding of science.

Curriculum guides for elementary school science and texts dealing with the teaching of science usually list many objectives for the science program. The point of view emphasized in the preceding paragraph suggests that the following goals should be included: an understanding that the achievement of our national goals, at home and abroad, depends upon the use of science and technology; an understanding of the methods of investigation used by scientists; an appreciation of the excitement and satisfaction involved in a career in science; an understanding of the contributions of science to the achievement of optimum physical health; a preparation for effective participation in local and national decision making on issues that involve an understanding of scientific information and principles.

Renner and his associates stated three synthesizing objectives for elementary school science: To develop in the learner

a command of the rational powers.
the ability and confidence to inquire.
an understanding of the changing nature of the environment in terms of matter, life, energy, and their interactions.[2]

SITUATION 10.1   As an elementary teacher, what are the affective attitudes you wish the learners to develop regarding science?

---

[2] John W. Renner, Don G. Stafford, and William B. Ragan, *Teaching Science in the Elementary School.* (New York: Harper & Row, Publishers, 1973), pp. 52–53.

CURRICULUM APPROACHES

Perhaps more than any other curriculum area within the modern elementary school, the changes proposed for all curriculum areas have been incorporated within the science curriculum. Science curriculum models now available may be characterized by

> a careful sampling of the discipline areas for information clusters that are representative, relevant, classical, practical, and humane.
>
> the thoughtful development of materials supportive of concrete manipulations appropriate for both the development and reinforcement of cognitive processes.
>
> a commitment to and internalization of the inquiry process as the means of directly experiencing the learning of science.
>
> a stressing of the teacher's role as a "facilitator" rather than a "teller."
>
> a conscious attempt to develop learner behaviors in all domains: cognitive, affective, and psychomotor.
>
> a prevailing commitment that learning science must be accompanied by learning how to learn science.

The development of "modern" science curriculum models began during the late 1950s, as did the "modern" movements in other curriculum areas. It began first in high school physics and later moved into the elementary schools. The impact of the "modern" science programs has been, to this author, more enduring and penetrating than programs developed during the same period for other curriculum areas. Perhaps the facts that the science disciplines themselves are investigative, and that investigative processes were utilized to develop the new programs, explain the differences in the impact of the "modern" science curricula.

The inference should not be made that all of the original "modern" models were equally successful or that the science curriculum of each elementary school has been equally effective. Yet, the practicing of these science programs and their potential development continue to progress without being harassed by requests to return to predecessor programs or to be modified by elements of those programs. The pendulum phenomenon, which so often characterizes movements in education, has not yet affected the science curriculum movements in the modern elementary school.

History

The historical development of science as an elementary school subject is a fascinating study. It introduces students to the ideas and activities of many famous educators; it helps them understand the importance of some famous educational movements and theories of learning; and it illuminates many facets of modern educational theory by making applications to a single subject. Students will therefore profit from an examination of some excellent historical overviews.[3]

Science books for children were written as early as 1750, but it was not until 1932 that the first complete series of science textbooks for children was published. William T. Harris, former U.S. Commissioner of Education, published a curriculum guide for elementary science in 1871, but most states did not begin providing separate curriculum guides for elementary science until the 1940s. The sequence of movements which culminated in the modern elementary school science program was as follows: children's literature containing science stories, object teaching, nature study, the fact-centered program, and the inquiry approach.

Scope and Sequence

A few decades ago the scope of the elementary school science program was determined by the broad areas of content that pupils were expected to study: living things, earth and universe, matter and energy, and so on. The trend in recent years has been toward the identification of basic generalizations relating to the various branches of science. These generalizations may be stated in a number of ways; the following list is illustrative only:

1. The earth is only one part of the universe; the universe contains other planets, stars, and celestial bodies.
2. All living things depend upon the earth, its atmosphere, and the sun for their existence.
3. All objects are composed of matter; although matter can be changed, it cannot be created or destroyed by ordinary means.
4. All materials and organisms found on earth experience an evolutionary process of change with time.
5. Environmental factors usually determine the distribution and abundance of organisms.
6. Through a growing knowledge of science, methods can be devised to manipulate natural forces for the purpose of promoting health and well-being.

An additional scope and sequence running concurrently with content vehicles seems to exist within the modern science programs. This sequence is concerned with including and ordering the process essential to the experiencing of science. Renner and his associates provided an example of this parallel scope and sequence in their discussions of observation, measurement, experimentation, interpretation, model building, and prediction as the essential experiences of science inquiry.[4]

[3] Gerald S. Craig, "Elementary Science in the Past Century," *Science Teacher* (February 1957), pp. 11–14; Kuslan, Louis I. and A. Harris Stone, *Teaching Children Science: An Inquiry Approach.* (Belmont, Calif.: Wadsworth Publishing Company, Inc., 1968), chap. 3.
[4] John W. Renner, pp. 135–203.

Planning the scope and sequence of science experiences involves an understanding of child growth, learning and development, and of the structure of the various science disciplines so that what pupils are expected to learn at a given time is based upon what they have already learned.[5] A scope-and-sequence chart is not intended to serve as an exact blueprint of what pupils are expected to learn. Most school systems, however, accept the responsibility for continuous study and planning of the overall program, leaving teachers free to make adaptations to accommodate individual differences among pupils.

Planning

The sequence of science experiences need not be either rigidly planned or completely planless. What is needed is continuous, cooperative planning by the local staff to keep the sequence of science experiences in harmony with the developmental needs of children. The sequence cannot be fixed once and for all or at any given time. No school can borrow and use uncritically the sequence of science experiences used in another school. Rather, the leadership in the local school must provide (as the basis for planning the sequence of science experiences) opportunities for the study of the local environment which are appropriate to the characteristics and needs of the children living in that environment.

The national curriculum-building groups and the publishers of school materials are presenting science programs with two different organizations. One is a sequential package system and the other is a modular package system. A sequential package system is a complete program with a predetermined scope and sequence. A modular package system is a program with many units, modules, or components which can be arranged into a variety of scope and sequence organizations by the user.

The strength of the sequential package system is that it has an ordered system of content vehicles, experiences, and objectives in a scope and sequence, but this means that its purposes, objectives, and ordering must be those of the user. The strength of the modular package system is that the user may select modules to construct a program consistent with his objective. The problem is that the user must provide the ordering of content vehicles, experiences, and objectives in a scope-and-sequence system. Both sequential and modular systems seem equally sound in their approaches to the selection of representative content vehicles, methodologies, and accommodations to the developmental levels of the learners.

Continuity

In accordance with the psychological principle that learning represents behaviors and is not the mere accumulation of knowledge and skills, science experiences in the modern elementary school follow the spiral system of grade placement rather than the ladder system. This means that instead of taking up one area (such as "living things") in one grade and completing it before going

[5] See Jerome S. Bruner, *The Process of Education.* (Cambridge, Mass.: Harvard University Press, 1962), chap. 3.

on to another area (such as "the earth") in the next grade, attention is given to each area at all grade levels. These topics cannot be mastered once and for all at any one grade level. Instead, they must be planned so that children move gradually from what is familiar and concrete to what is remote and abstract, from what is simple to what is complex. This is a change from the traditional patterns of "laddering" discrete content topics for curriculum-building purposes. In the newer pattern, topics penetrate all levels of the curriculum. The topics are selected because they represent the structures, organizing concepts, or persistent activities of the scientist or citizen. Therefore, each topic is reentered at each level according to the developmental levels of the of the learners.

SITUATION 10.2   Examine two or three curriculum guides for elementary school science which have been produced in the past few years by state or local school systems. To what extent are broad concepts used as a basis for organizing learning experiences? Cite evidence that the "spiral" rather than the "ladder" system of grade placement is followed. Would you say that the program is "fact centered" or "process centered"?

Readiness

All children do not develop at the same rate in understanding the various aspects of the environment. Because of differences in abilities, interests, attitudes, and the availability of materials in the immediate environment, one child may be far ahead of another in one aspect (such as weather) but far behind in another aspect (such as the stars). Furthermore, children's interests do not reflect any artificial boundaries, such as physical science and biological science. There is no advantage, therefore, in arbitrarily assigning problems relating to the biological sciences to one grade level and materials relating to the physical sciences to another. The interests of children furnish a better clue to grade placement of topics in the science program of the elementary school than does any artificial allocation based on the fields of subject matter.

The developmental levels of learners also govern their readinesses. Preoperational children will not benefit from experiments which require the cognitive operations of conservation, reversibility, and decentering. The concrete operational learners need an object or event upon which to perform the cognitive operations of conservation, reversibility, and decentering.

MAJOR FEATURES

The effectiveness of the science program in an elementary school is determined, in the final analysis, by what the pupils actually experience. Do their day-by-day experiences actually help pupils to grow in the ability to understand and interpret the phenomena that occur in their physical and biological environments? National science projects have received liberal financial support; they have been staffed with competent scientists and professional educators; and they have produced excellent materials and procedures for the science program in elementary schools. State and local school systems have provided curriculum guides, and a specific time has been set aside for science instruction in the school day. These developments represent excellent beginnings. The quality of children's actual science experiences in the public elementary schools of the nation can continue to improve only as school people and parents participate in defining the kind of science program they would like to have, in evaluating the current programs, and in making specific plans for improving the program. The following analysis of an effective science program provides some guides for this procedure.

1. *Children's interests in science are identified and nurtured.* If science in the elementary school is not an exciting adventure for both teacher and pupil, the fault must lie in the approach to teaching, for surely there can be nothing inherently dull or uninteresting about exploring the physical and biological environment. When children come to school, they are interested in many aspects of the environment—in animals and plants, in butterflies and frogs, in the earth and the sky, in clouds and rain, in heat and cold, in light and darkness, in airplanes and rockets, and in countless other things related to the broad field of science. It is left largely to the teacher to determine whether the child's enthusiasm is suppressed by "teaching is telling" procedures or is kindled by inquiry about this fascinating realm of exploration, invention, and discovery. If the teacher brings to the task an understanding of children, a broad understanding of science, and a willingness to let children observe, experiment, and act to find answers to their many questions, the science period can be a joyous quest, not only for the pupils but for the teacher as well. Some of the most fruitful science activities grow out of the questions and problems raised by pupils.

2. *The teacher has a good background in basic science and in approaches to the teaching of science.* One of the weaknesses of science programs in elementary schools can be traced to inadequate preparation of teachers in the basic sciences. The adage "teach the child instead of the subject" does not make absolute sense, for obviously one must teach the child something. The child's opportunities for learning science may be either restricted or enhanced by the teacher's background in the subject. Specialists in science education generally recommend that the prospective elementary school teacher take at least two years of science during the undergraduate college years. If prospective teachers are to learn the new content and procedures developed by the national science projects, they must, of course, be taught the new content and methods of inquiry by professors in liberal arts departments; more than two-thirds of the courses taken by prospective elementary school teachers are taught by liberal arts professors. Perhaps as high school courses in science improve and as college courses in science become more attractive to students, new teachers coming into elementary schools will have better backgrounds in the basic sciences.

Exploration, invention, and discovery—the tools for learning.

Effective teaching in the elementary school, of course, involves a great deal more than having an adequate background in academic disciplines. (See Chapters 5 and 6.) The teacher must be resourceful in developing a variety of approaches to teaching and learning. Jacobson and Tannenbaum stated this point emphatically:

It is not enough to know the basic generalizations of science; the teacher must also provide a variety of ways that children can be helped to learn something about them. Professional courses in teaching elementary school science are designed to help teachers develop this resourcefulness.[6]

Another aspect of teacher preparation is that of retraining teachers already in the school system to handle the new content and procedures in science. Van Til called attention to this problem:

Even the substantial help of the National Defense Education Act, which now amounts to $181,000,000 for the first five years to strengthen instruction in science, mathematics and modern foreign languages, could not provide sufficient summer offerings for all of the present teachers of the many separate subjects.[7]

In view of this discussion, it seems inevitable that for several years science will have to be taught in elementary schools by some teachers who have had inadequate preparation. Rather than deprive their pupils of instruction in science, these teachers can attend workshops and conferences, and take courses

[6] Willard J. Jacobson and Harold E. Tannenbaum, *Modern Elementary School Science.* (New York: Teachers College Press, 1961), p. 20.
[7] William Van Til, "In a Climate of Change," in Association for Supervision and Curriculum Development, *Role of Supervisor and Curriculum Director in a Climate of Change.* (Washington, D.C.: The Association, 1965), p. 24.

dealing with the teaching of science; read articles in educational journals; use the teacher's manuals that go with the series of textbooks used in the schools; get help from a science teacher in the junior or senior high school; do some of the experiments suggested in curriculum guides for teaching science; and in other ways become better qualified.

3. *Direct teaching is supplemented by unified experiences.* Chapter 6 presented the point of view that curriculum organization should provide both for direct teaching of subjects and for unified experiences. The preceding section of this chapter suggested a scope and sequence for the direct-teaching phase of the science program. Many elementary schools provide a definite period in the daily schedule for instruction in science, but these schools may also provide opportunities for pupils to relate science to arithmetic, language arts, the social studies, art, music, and health while working on units that draw materials from many fields.

Aerospace education, for example, deals with significant aspects of the environment in which children have a compelling interest. How important is the air in which we live? What keeps an airplane up in the air? Why is weather so important to the flyer? At what point does outer space begin? Why does a person flying in space become weightless? How does a satellite overcome gravity? What information about the earth can a satellite in orbit give us? The search for answers to these and other questions has enriched the science program in many elementary schools, and has provided opportunities to relate science to other curriculum areas.

4. *Teaching procedures emphasize learning by inquiry.* Helping pupils learn to use the method of inquiry requires a different conception of the role of facts in the educative process. The facts of science are important, but they are tools used in problem solving rather than ends in themselves. John Dewey recognized this years ago when he defined subject matter as anything that helped a child solve a problem. Science teaching in elementary schools has frequently been ineffective because (1) it emphasized "ready made" answers; (2) it placed too much emphasis on the products of science and not enough emphasis on the processes; and (3) it did not provide enough opportunities for pupils to engage in investigative activities.

Renner and his coauthors explained in some detail the method of inquiry that is receiving so much attention in the current curriculum projects.[8] They indicated that in the process of problem solving, teachers will arrive at the conclusion that telling is not teaching and that hearing is not learning. When inquiry is the method, then discussion, questioning, drill, and demonstration procedures become the vehicles to accomplish inquiry. The basic principle of the method is that the child learns in terms of observations and experiences.

[8] John W. Renner, Gene D. Shepherd, and Robert F. Bibens, *Guiding Learning in the Elementary School.* (New York: Harper & Row, Publishers, 1973), pp. 189–219.

Teacher and pupils work together to isolate and define the problems to be solved. Many of these problems may come from a curriculum bulletin that the school has provided; others may come from pupils' suggestions. Pupils are encouraged to state trial answers (inventions) as to what the problem solution might be; the formal term for this step is "formulating a hypothesis." The teacher must, of course, refrain from imposing "ready made" answers. Any invention to a problem must be tested; discovery procedures must be devised through which pupils can make the necessary observations and measurements to prove or disprove their inventions. Pupils must be allowed, and in fact encouraged, to interpret the data according to their perceptions. Without this prerogative the pupils will accept, but not necessarily learn, only that which has been predetermined as what they should learn. The teacher, of course, has the responsibility to see that erroneous ideas are not accepted. This frequently entails having the pupils repeat a given experiment or seek additional data that will lead them to form more comprehensive concepts.

The steps in the method of inquiry, which have been fruitful in the work of outstanding scientists, are (1) identification and exploration of a problem, (2) statement of an hypothesis, (3) experimentation and gathering of data, (4) selection of a tentative solution, and (5) subjection of the tentative solution to the rigors of disproof. But the teacher must remember that no two minds function exactly alike; each pupil will arrive at individualized "steps," and the teacher must not be alarmed if the pupil's "steps" differ from those of others.

Pupils must be encouraged to share their ideas with others; they will learn much from each other, and will frequently identify other problems that they would like to explore. The very nature of inquiry learning is self-perpetuating. The complexity of inquiry learning will vary from one maturity level to another as pupils progress through the elementary school, but inquiry learning is not confined to any maturity level; children have been learning by inquiry since the day they were born. This method is so natural that pupils find it fun, and teachers find it rewarding.

5. *The school provides adequate equipment and materials for teaching science.* The suggestions provided in Chapter 6 relating to resources for teaching and learning apply to the science program as well as to other curriculum areas. A central library and a qualified librarian are as essential for the science program as they are for other curriculum areas. Textbooks, reference books, films, filmstrips, slides, radio and television programs, and programmed learning materials should be available. Some of these materials should be available in classrooms; others may be made available as needed from a science center in the building. The school program should be flexible enough to permit classes to go on field trips to study scientific phenomena. Resource persons—veterinarians, electricians, scientists—should be invited to participate in the instructional program when their information and skills can make a contribution to the problem the pupils are studying.

Many useful materials for teaching science can be obtained free, if the teacher knows where to write for them.[9] Yet, as Renner pointed out, science requires equipment and equipment costs money. There must be a financial commitment to the program if it is to succeed. For the teacher to build the necessary equipment takes time—time that could be more efficiently spent in lesson preparation or in giving individual help to pupils. Mediocre equipment usually produces mediocre results.[10]

6. *Leadership for the improvement of the science program is provided by a science consultant.* The role of instructional leadership in curriculum improvement was treated in Chapter 4. The new content and procedures being developed by national science projects, and the rapid changes taking place as a result of developments in science and technology, create a need for continuous revision of the science program in local school systems. Many school systems have found it desirable to place a science consultant in charge of program planning and in-service education. The science consultant should have extensive preparation in the physical, biological, and earth sciences; in professional education; and in child growth, learning and development. The consultant should be well acquainted with outstanding science programs in other school systems, and with techniques for involving principals and teachers in decision-making processes. Consultants provide leadership in developing a continuous series of science experiences for the school's kindergarten through grade 12 program, in making certain that the program is consistent with the developmental characteristics of children, in procuring and effectively using equipment and materials, in providing instruction through which pupils learn to use some of the broad generalizations of science to interpret phenomena in their environment and within themselves, and in assisting teachers with instructional problems. Through workshops, institutes, and cooperative evaluation, consultants help administrators and teachers keep abreast of developments in elementary school science.

SITUATION 10.3   Review Chapter 3 of this text. Discuss the potential advantages which the science processes bring to the relationships between science content and Piagetian developmental levels.

Elements

Many similarities in the curriculum improvement projects have been established. Some of their common elements are listed below.

---

[9] Mary H. Saterstorm (Ed.), *Educators' Guide to Free Science Materials*, 10th ed. (Randolph, Wis.: Educators' Progress Service, 1969).

[10] John W. Renner, "The Utopia Elementary School Science Program," in *Utopia in the Elementary School.* (Oklahoma City, Okla.: Department of Elementary School Administrators, Oklahoma Education Association, 1964), p. 33.

1. Emphasis is placed on experiments to be performed by children upon objects, events, and/or situations in order to find answers, rather than on "ready made" answers for them to accept.
2. All projects are concerned with the process of science: inquiry.
3. Opportunities are given the child to develop an understanding of the structure of the discipline.
4. All projects are designed to help children broaden their understanding of the environment.
5. School experiences are expected to result in behavioral changes.

CURRICULUM IMPROVEMENT PROJECTS

The increasing emphasis on developing rational powers, on learning how to learn, and on using the processes involved in inquiry is nowhere more obvious than in the new science curricula. The massive effort by scientists and science educators to develop new designs for science instruction has placed teachers at the threshold of an exciting new era in elementary school science. Financial support has become available to develop and try out new curricula which synthesize process and content; teachers have been provided with a veritable treasure of teaching strategies and materials which were unknown in the past. Only a few of these projects can be described here. The Selected Readings at the end of this chapter contain descriptions of others.

SCIS

The Science Curriculum Improvement Study (SCIS) receives financial support from the National Science Foundation. The director is Robert Karplus at the University of California at Berkeley. Twelve units have been developed from the first level to the sixth level by SCIS,[11] as shown in the accompanying table.

LEVEL	UNITS	
First	Physical Science	Life Science
	Material Objects	Organism
Second	Interaction and Systems	Life Sciences
Third	Subsystems and Variables	Populations
Fourth	Relative Position and Motion	Environments
Fifth	Energy Source	Communities
Sixth	Models: Electric and Magnetic Interaction	Ecosystems

The SCIS program is described by Renner and his coauthors as:

Reorganizable as science by practicing scientists

[11] SCIS, Lawrence Hall of Science, University of California, Berkeley; Robert Karplus, Professor of Physics, Director; Material published by Rand McNally & Company, Skokie, Ill.

Reflecting the cumulative nature of science

Achieving the spirit of scientific inquiry[12]

AAAS

The Commission on Science Education of the American Association for the Advancement of Science (AAAS) has developed "Science—A Process Approach."[13] It is a complete elementary school science program (K-6), which is based on the following premises:

1. Science is essentially an intellectual activity.
2. There is joy in the search for knowledge.
3. There is excitement in seeing into the working of the physical and biological worlds.
4. There is intellectual power to be gained in learning the approach which the scientists use in the solution of problems.
5. The central purpose of science education is to awaken in the child a sense of the joy, the excitement, and the intellectual power of science.

The AAAS elementary school science curriculum was organized around the following process skills:

1. Observing
2. Recognizing and using number relations
3. Measuring
4. Recognizing and using space–time relations
5. Classifying
6. Communicating
7. Inferring
8. Predicting
9. Defining operations
10. Formulating hypothesis
11. Interpreting data
12. Controlling variables
13. Experimenting

In the AAAS model, content topics appropriate to the process skills and the intellectual maturity of learners in grades K–6 were constructed. Each of the seven parts, one for each grade in the K–6 range, has its own distribution of content topics and of process skills.

ESS

The Elementary Science Study (ESS) model[14] is nearly a no-model. The ESS units can be used by a school to develop its own curriculum. From the 56 ESS

[12] Renner et al., p. 267.

[13] American Association for the Advancement of Science, Washington, D.C. Materials published by the Xerox Corporation, New York.

[14] Education Development Center, 55 Chapel Street, Newton, Mass.

units available, each school must select and sequence the ESS units to build a curriculum that is consistent with the school's philosophy, goals, objectives, levels of learners, and so forth.

SITUATION 10.4   Write or refer to two science lessons for elementary school children (one at the primary level and one at the intermediate level). Parallel the inquiry process to the various stages of the lesson.

ISSUES

The issues selected to be presented in this section are the need for more research, The National Assessment of Educational Progress (NAEP), the attitudes and preparation of elementary teachers, and integrated science. These are selected as representative issues; their selection is not intended to imply that they are the only, or even the most important, issues.

Research

Research related to the curriculum in elementary school science has been increasing during the past several years. One book published in 1970 reviewed seven studies which have implications for curriculum planning.[15] These studies include investigation of how much understanding of natural phenomena is brought to school by kindergarten children, children's interests in elementary school science, what sources of information children use, grade placement of light concepts, relative merits of reading and activity methods of teaching science, the advantage of using special teachers, and a comprehension test.

Some rather encouraging evidence has emerged from research that has investigated the influence of the SCIS procedures on the achievement of certain objectives of elementary school science. The studies mentioned below illustrate the type of evidence available. The student can, no doubt, find many other studies relating to the new science curricula.

Wilson studied the frequency of pupil involvement in five "essential science experiences" in classes taught by SCIS-educated teachers as compared with the frequency of pupil involvement in classes taught by teachers who were not educated in the project's methods. Essential science experiences included in the study were observation, measurement, experimentation, interpretation of data, and prediction. One of the six conclusions reached by Wilson seems particularly significant: "The SCIS-educated teachers encouraged pupils to become involved in over twice as many of the essential science experiences as did the traditional science teachers."[16]

---

[15] A. Montgomery Johnston and Paul C. Burns (Eds.), *Research in Elementary School Curriculum,* (Boston: Allyn & Bacon, Inc., 1970), chap. 6.

[16] John H. Wilson, "Differences Between the Inquiry-Discovery and the Traditional Approaches to Teaching Science in Elementary Schools." (Norman, Okla.: University of Oklahoma, unpublished doctoral dissertation, 1967), p. 68.

Porterfield studied the influence of preparation in SCIS on the questioning behavior of selected second- and fourth-grade reading teachers. Analysis of the data indicated that SCIS-educated teachers asked a significantly larger proportion of questions requiring a higher level of thinking than did teachers who had not had this kind of preparation.[17]

Schmidt conducted a study of sixteen teachers who taught both elementary school science and social studies. He reported modifications in their behavior after they had attended a workshop dealing with the inquiry approach:

1. Teachers with the workshop experience asked fewer recall and convergent questions than did other teachers.
2. The questions asked by these teachers encouraged pupils to use higher mental processes more frequently than did those asked by other teachers.
3. A greater number of what are regarded as essential science experiences were provided by teachers who attended the workshop.
4. The modifications in teacher behavior listed above appeared in the social studies classes taught by the same teachers, as well as in the science classes.[18]

Commenting on the Schmidt investigation, Renner and Stafford stated:

The teachers Schmidt observed were using inquiry-centered materials in science following their workshop experience, but they were using traditional materials in their social studies classes. These results seem to suggest that the deviation from the traditional mode of teacher education and not the materials is the significant factor in changing the teachers' instructional patterns.[19]

The modern science curriculum projects have committed themselves to inquiry. The evidence from research generally supports this commitment, but much more study needs to be done before empirically defining the parameters of inquiry.

National Assessment of Educational Progress (NAEP)

The results of the 1972–1973 national assessment of science achievement of nine-, thirteen-, and seventeen-year-olds showed a slight decline in knowledge of fundamental scientific facts and principles when compared to the preliminary survey of 1969–1970.[20] An average decline of approximately two percentage points occurred in all age groups tested on the knowledge of fundamental

[17] Denzil Porterfield, "The Influence of Preparation in the Science Curriculum Improvement Study on the Questioning Behavior of Selected Second and Fourth Grade Reading Teachers." (Norman, Okla.: University of Oklahoma, unpublished doctoral dissertation, 1969).

[18] Frederick B. Schmidt, "The Influence of a Summer Institute in Inquiry-Centered Science Education upon the Teaching Strategies of Elementary Teachers in Two Disciplines." (Norman, Okla.: University of Oklahoma, unpublished doctoral dissertation, 1969).

[19] J. W. Renner and D. G. Stafford, "Inquiry, Children and Teachers," *The Science Teacher* (April 1970), p. 1.

[20] *National Assessments of Science*, 1969–1973; A Capsule Description of Changes in Science Achievement, Science Report 04-S-00. (Washington, D.C.: U.S. Government Printing Office, 1975).

scientific facts and principles. The NAEP was given to a sampling of all students, not just those in science classes.

A majority of the items on the assessment were based on the objective of knowledge, and only a few on the objectives of abilities and skills to engage in the processes of science. And, even fewer items were based on the objectives of understanding the investigative nature of science and the attitudes and appreciations toward science; a less general decline was observed across these objectives.[21]

Roy H. Forbes, director of the National Assessment of Educational Programs, wrote a letter to the editor of *The Science Teacher* in response to an editoral introducing the article written by Ahmann and his associates about the NAEP survey:

A growing body of research evidence suggests that societal factors over which teachers have no control probably have the greatest effects on student achievement levels. Yet, the myth that educators can and should "do it all" persists.

Any conclusion that declining NAEP achievement in science means that teacher training, science curriculum, or materials have declined in quality is not justified. Our results provide no evidence of this. Along with the reported declines on standardized tests in several disciplines, these results could very well be indicators of social changes that affect much more than science education alone.[22]

Attitudes and Preparation

The attitudes that a teacher has toward a curriculum area is probably transmitted in some manner to the perspective learner. Thompson said, ". . . the typical science requirements on the college level only enhance attitudes which will interfere with effective science teaching in the elementary school.[23]

Apparently the "modern" science program has been more directly implemented by the modern elementary schools than by the college departments which provide a science content background for prospective teachers. A significant gap seems to exist between the ways student teachers are taught and prepared to teach content, and the content vehicles and methodology of the "modern" science program for the elemetnary school.

SITUATION 10.5   Ask five elementary school children to name ten fun activities they participate in at school. What percentage of the named activities were related to science? What are your conclusions?

---

[21] J. Stanley Ahmann, Robert Crane, Donald Searls, and Robert Larson, "Science Achievement: The Trend Is Down," *The Science Teacher*, Vol. XLII, No. 7 (September 1975), pp. 23–25.

[22] Roy H. Forbes, "Letters—Education Can't Do It All," *The Science Teacher*, Vol. XLII, No. 10 (December 1975), p. 3.

[23] Robert G. Thompson, "Building Attitudes Toward Science for Pre-Service Teachers: An Experiment," *School Science and Mathematics*, Vol. LXXV, No. 3 (March 1975), p. 213.

Integrated Science

The physical and natural sciences are debating the functioning of a particular science (physics, chemistry, biology, etc) in the teaching of science as a general education subject. Does a science lose its specific identity through a topical approach? Does a science, physics for example, dominate the curriculum with the other sciences contributing to the extension and enrichment of the study? NOTE: See Chapter 8 (Social Studies) for a discussion of the same issue (inter- vs. multi-disciplinary approaches) in the social sciences.

Ost[24] provided some definitions which may help clarify the issue:

1. *Interdisciplinary:* The merging of two or more bodies of content for purposes of instructional expediency.
2. *Unified:* The various sciences are applied to the development of a common theme or concept.
3. *Integrated:* A more sophisticated level of interdisciplinary organization usually involving mathematics for the solving of science problems.
4. *Correlated:* An attempt to relate the skills and concepts of one discipline to another with each discipline maintaining its integrity and identity.
5. *Coordinated:* An effort to reduce the redundancies among courses through the establishment of core courses and conceptual schemes.
6. *Comprehensive Problem Solving:* The student defines a comprehensive problem and applies various skills and concepts from the sciences, mathematics and social sciences in an attempt to optimize the solution.

Whether Ost's definitions are discrete or not, the point is that the efforts to determine the relationships among the science disciplines is a serious and difficult task. Probably the traditional separateness of the "ics" of science (for example, physics, genetics, mathematics, statistics) is apt to be changed to the interrelated "tions" (such as pollution, population, urbanization, communication).

UNESCO

The United Nations Educational, Scientific and Cultural Organization (UNESCO), in consultation with the Committee on Science Teaching of the International Council of Scientific Union (ICSU), has published a series of reports concerning integrated science teaching. One report deals with the need for an integrated science teaching approach. The report begins:

1. *... science must be an element in the general education of all children. ... Clearly science needs to be introduced as an element in primary education and such science would of necessity be an integrated type.*
2. *... if science is to be an element of general education, at least in the lower cycle of secondary education, some form of integrated science teaching is*

[24] David H. Ost, "Changing Curriculum Patterns in Science, Mathematics and Social Studies," *School Science and Mathematics,* Vol. LXXV, No. 1 (January 1975), pp. 48–52.

likely to be more appropriate than courses in the separate disciplines of physics, chemistry, and biology.

3. *Integrated science teaching at the primary and secondary levels provides a sound basis for continuing science education, either in specialist subjects or further integrated science.*[25]

Abraham Blum's rationale, which appears in the UNESCO report for integrated science teaching, provides a psychological and pedagogical perspective for integrating science. A paraphrase of that rationale follows:

1. There is no concensus among learning psychologists (Bruner, Gagné, and Ausubel) concerning the transfer of learinng. Does the narrowness of the learning situation restrict transfer? An integrated science teaching approach, by giving the student more occasions to use concepts and skills from one discipline to another, might enhance transfer.
2. The operations of acquiring, assimilating, and retaining knowledge are the same whether learning biology, chemistry, or physics.
3. A child does not learn in the same logical order as that in which a discipline is organized.
4. The training of a critical mind for work and leisure time requires integrated topics to demonstrate how science and scientific thought influence our lives.

Most of the modern science programs for the elementary schools are integrated—if not in content vehicles and science processes, then at least in the science processes of observation, measurement, experimentation, interpretation, model construction, and prediction. The issue for the elementary schools is to gain support from their receiving institutions, the secondary schools, and for the elementary schools to gain support from their training institutions, the colleges.

INTERDISCIPLINARY APPROACHES

This section briefly presents those activities and programs which have potential for the interrelating of science with other curriculum areas and societal goals. Values-clarification strategies, career awareness activities, and environmental programs have been selected.

Values-Clarification Strategies

Two elements of the values-clarification strategies (facts, to concepts, to values; and choosing, acting, and prizing behaviors) closely parallel the processes of inquiry within the modern science programs. For example, the behaviors of choosing are similar to the behaviors of the first phase of inquiry, exploration (see Chapter 5). During choosing and exploration behaviors, the learners

25 P. E. Richmond (Ed.), *New Trends in Integrated Science Teaching*, Volume II. (Paris: UNESCO, 1973), p. 5.

identify those properties, characteristics, and patterns within their experiences; in other words, whatever is familiar to them. During acting and invention, the learners' behaviors are directed by a commitment to their hypotheses and exploration behaviors. During the behaviors of prizing and discovery, the learners affirm an act or invention through a testing system which results in a deepening, extension, or enrichment of the invention or valued act. Because of parallels between inquiry and values-clarification strategies, the accommodation of values-clarification strategies in the science program would require adjustments primarily in the nature and selection of content vehicles.

SITUATION 10.6   Some communities still oppose public instruction related to sex education. There are, however, within the curriculum area of science some experiences and activities which could quite possibly teach to elementary children some of the same concepts typical of formal sex education program. List five such activities.

Career Awareness Activities

Sidney P. Marland, Jr., U.S. Commissioner of Education in 1972, said:

Basically, my office sees career education as the companion to academic preparation at every grade level. . . . not solely a matter of equipping students for jobs. The heart of the learning process involves science. It is the way a man's mind works, and not just what he can do with his hands, that gives quality and purpose to life.[26]

Marland also said that, ". . . the neglect of career development has done damage to the total educational needs of the individual and the nation."[27] The objectives of science, a command of the rational powers, confidence to inquire, and an understanding of the changing nature of the environment lend themselves easily to the ". . . way a man's mind works." On these premises, career awareness activities can become an integral element in the science curriculum of the modern elementary school.

One aspect of career awareness activities in science would be the general education necessary for an individual to function adequately in most vocations within our technological society. Another aspect would be the development of a free mind for a free society.

Environmental Programs

"Environment, as a matter of educational concern, is at least as much a problem of ethnics and morals, of politics and administration as it is of understanding with the aid of the natural sciences."[28] The 1974 National Education

[26] Sidney P. Marland, Jr., "Education for More Than One Career," *Annual Editions: Readings in Education, '73–'74.* (Guilford, Conn.: Dushkin Publishing Group, 1973), p. 198.
[27] Marland, Jr., p. 199.
[28] Calvin W. Stellman, "Reflections on Environmental Education," in *Annual Editions: Readings in Education, '73–'74.* (Guilford, Conn.: Dushkin Publishing Group, 1973), p. 20.

Association Representative Assembly passed the following continuing resolution:

C-14—Environmental Education
The National Education Association believes that the nation's priorities must include the protection of our environment. It urges the development and improvement of federal legislation, programs and appropriations that provide education: (a) for use, stewardship, and preservation of a viable environment; (b) to eliminate pollution; (c) to promote an understanding of the effects of population change; and (d) to promote establishment of federal wilderness areas. The Association urges its affiliates to support appropriate programs in school systems for grades K through adult.[29]

With the support of concerned citizen groups, large professional organizations, the federal government, and many teachers, environmental education programs are rapidly becoming operational. One project, Center for Urban Research in Environmental Education (CURE), in Miami, Florida, emphasizes the use of field trips in an attempt to demonstrate to and involve students in knowing that humans can control, use, and perceive the environment.[30]

Another program is in Shawnee Mission High School, a suburb of Kansas City, Kansas.[31] Here, a large plot of vacant land has become an outdoor laboratory for studying the many interrelated aspects of the environment.

Seminole, Oklahoma, has established a four-week activity for third, sixth, and ninth graders. The first two weeks are alloted to presite preparatory experiences incorporating mathematics, science, social studies, language arts, aesthetic arts, health, and physical education. The one week on-site experience is held at a nearby youth camp. Third-week work includes classes, field trips, investigations, recreation, and similar activities. A final postsite experience of one week takes place at the school to culminate the four weeks of activities.[32]

Each of these programs has funding support from the federal government. They are being supported to establish models of what other districts might consider. The curriculum for these experiences is a multidisciplinary approach, emphasizing inquiry and involvement.

STRATEGY OF INSTRUCTION

The strategy of instruction presented in Chapter 5 is used here as a basis for analyzing the science education curriculum, activities, and trends. This is done both to summarize and to demonstrate the potential viability of such a strategy.

---

[29] A Federal Environmental Education Act has been passed and funded.
[30] Georgia Slack, "Toward Understanding the Faucet," *American Education*, Vol. X, No. 3 (April 1974), pp. 17–23.
[31] Jerry P. Murry and Dean Jernigan, "Establishing a K–12 Environmental Science Program in a Large Suburban School District," *The Science Teacher*, Vol. XL, No. 5 (May 1973), pp. 52–56.
[32] Vernon Harmon, "Environmental Education in the Seminole City Schools." (Unpublished paper presented for Education 5573, University of Oklahoma, 1975).

Selection of Content

The newer science programs have made a significant effort to organize curricula based upon the logic of the disciplines. A three-pronged approach has been used: one toward the tools and processes of the disciplines; a second toward the selection of representative and generative content vehicles; and a third toward the unification and integration of the sciences. The three approaches represent efforts to define the structures (organizing concepts, information clusters) of the sciences. The builders of science curricula have directly faced the fact that all sciences cannot be taught or learned. Therefore, rational selection and elimination procedures must be used in organizing the disciplines for curriculum building purposes.

Learning and Development

The commitment of the newer science curriculum to direct experiencing through observation, measurement, prediction, and other self-actuated activity, and to direct experiencing through a process of rational inquiry, places the field theories of learning in a dominant position in science curriculum design (see Chapter 3, "Intellectual Development"). The learning theorists most often referenced are Bruner, Gagné, Ausubel, and Piaget.

Because of the concern with direct experiencing which involves concrete manipulations, the impact of Piaget as a cognitive developmentalist on the newer science programs has been considerable. In planning these programs, attention is given to the selection of manipulations that are appropriate to the cognitive development of the learner. This is not meant to imply that Piaget is the only developmentalist valued by the builders of science curricula, but that there seems (in this author's judgment) to be more evidence of attention to him than to other authorities.

SITUATION 10.7   Examine an elementary science program and list the "built-in" characteristics of the program which account for differences between preoperational and concrete operational learners.

Methodology

The commitment of the newer science programs to the processes of inquiry seems quite clear. The terms and definitions used in these programs may vary, but the intent, an inquiry approach, seems constant and stable.

Communication

The newer science programs support the learner as the prime communicator and the teacher as the facilitator of communication. A common thread running throughout the programs is that "teaching is not just telling, and learning is not just hearing."

Objectives

The recurring themes in the newer programs are the development of the rational powers, the development of the ability to think, and the development of the ability to learn on one's own. To be consistent with these themes, the range and distribution of objectives includes behaviors at all classification levels of each domain of Bloom's *Taxonomy of Educational Objectives* (see Chapter 5).

Goals

The goals of science seem to be as equally directed toward the builders and teachers of curriculum as they are toward the learner. The goals of "confidence in inquiry" and "development of the rational powers" place each participant in the roles of both "teacher" and "learner."

SUMMARY

1. Learning science is directly dependent upon experiencing the processes of science applied to representative content vehicles.

2. The study of science serves the child by providing a means of developing rational powers, of understanding the world and of finding answers to many questions; it provides a basis for the technology needed to solve many of the problems confronting society.

3. The science programs of the modern elementary school may be characterized by a careful sampling of the discipline areas, materials supportive of concrete manipulations appropriate to the developmental levels of the learner, the inquiry process, the teacher as a facilitator, and an attempt to develop a wide range of learner behaviors.

4. Science is taught most effectively in elementary schools when (1) children's interests in science are identified and nurtured; (2) the teacher has adequate preparation in science and in procedures for teaching it; (3) pupils are taught to use the processes of science in solving problems; (4) teaching strategies emphasize inquiry; (5) the school provides adequate equipment and materials for teaching science; and (6) leadership is provided by a science consultant.

5. The scope and sequence of science programs for the modern elementary school includes two elements: the ordering of representative content vehicles, and the ordering of the processes essential to the experiencing of science.

6. Curriculum improvement projects in science generally emphasize (1) experimentation by pupils themselves; (2) the development of the ability to think; (3) an understanding of the structure of the discipline; (4) an understanding of th environment; and (5) changes in pupil behavior.

7. The three phases of the inquiry process are exploration, invention, and discovery.

8. The movement to further integrate the sciences, as well as the sciences with other disciplines, is continuing on a national and international scale.

9. Career-awareness activities, values-clarification strategies, and environ-

mental education programs hold great potential for integrating the sciences, for unifying the related sciences to all curriculum areas, and for contributing to the achievement of the school's total goals.

Problems and Projects

1. Select an elementary grade or level in which you have interest. What are the science processes you will be evaluating and observing? Will these processes be different from those evaluated and observed in other grades or levels? What observable behaviors from the learner will serve as evidence that the science processes are present?

2. Examine some of the SCIS units. Research has shown that teachers exposed to the SCIS units and inquiry tend to ask higher-level cognitive questions. What are your own personal evaluations? What characteristics of the program increase the likelihood of higher-energy questions?

3. Most learners in the elementary school are preoperational or concrete operational. Select three concepts related to science and design experiences (at least one experience for each concept) which are appropriate to preoperational learners. Using the same concepts, modify and rewrite the science experiences written for the preoperational learners so that they are more appropriate for concrete operational learners. What differentiation occurred between the criteria for preoperational learners and the criteria for concrete operational learners?

Selected Readings

Blough, G. O., and J. Schwartz, *Elementary School Science*, 5th ed. New York: Holt, Rinehart and Winston, 1974. A textbook and reference for elementary science programs.

Bruner, Jerome S., *The Process of Education*. Cambridge, Mass: Harvard University Press, 1962. Presents the rationale for process and structure.

Friedl, Alfred E., *Teaching Science to Children: The Inquiry Approach Applied*. New York: Random House, Inc., 1972. Textbook for an inquiry-oriented science program.

Goldberg, Lazer, *Children and Science*. New York: Charles Scribner's Sons, 1970. Chapters 2 and 3 present plays and games useful in science teaching.

Howes, Virgil M., *Individualizing Instruction in Science and Mathematics*. New York: Crowell Collier and Macmillan, Inc., 1970. Ideas for individualizing instruction and relating sciences and mathematics.

Johnston, A. Montgomery, and Paul C. Burns (Eds.), *Research in Elementary School Curriculum*. Boston: Allyn and Bacon, Inc., 1970. Chapter 6 reports studies done in science and science teaching.

Piaget, Jean, *The Construction of Reality in the Child*. New York: Basic Books, Inc., Publishers, 1954. Piaget's formulations concerning a child's perceptions and cognitive development concerning reality.

Renner, John W., Don G. Stafford, and William B. Ragan, *Teaching Science in the Elementary School*, 2d ed. New York: Harper & Row, Publishers, 1973. Textbook based on Piaget's formulation and inquiry.

Renner, John W., Gene D. Shepherd, and Robert F. Bibens, *Guiding Learning in the Elementary School*. New York: Harper & Row, Publishers, 1973. Chapters 3, 4, and 5 on inquiry, learner characteristics, and selecting content expand the descriptions of this chapter.

Richmond, P. E. (Ed.), *New Trends in Integrating Science Teaching*, Vol. II. New York: United Nations (Publishing Service), 1973. A series of manuscripts commissioned by UNESCO to further the integration of science teaching.

UNESCO, *New Trends in the Utilization of Educational Technology for Science Education*. New York: United Nations (Publishing Service), 1974. A series of UNESCO-commissioned manuscripts.

chapter 11

Inquiring
HEALTH, FITNESS,
AND MOVEMENT

Learning has two aspects: (1) acquiring new information, and (2) discovering the personal meaning of that information. Information itself is useless. Only when individuals find the link between specific information and their own lives are they able to put it to use.

John Becker, Seigfred Fagerberg, Harold Lerch, and Bryan Smith,
"Childhood Education Program," *Journal of Health, Physical
Education and Recreation*, Vol. XLV, No. 6 (June 1974), p. 20.

The curriculum areas of health and physical education are included within this chapter because of the potential interactions between them. A healthy fit body and a healthy fit mind have equal importance in both areas. Concern with the healthfulness and fitness of the total school environment and with provisions of remedial and developmental services to support the well-being of the learner are requisites to productive instruction. Health and physical education are partners, each with its respective discreteness; yet, they interact with one another to maximize the contributions of each.

DEFINITIONS

The following definitions pertain to the parameters and components of the physical education and health programs. They attempt to characterize these curriculum areas rather than provide dictionary-type definitions.

Physical Education

Dauer and Pangrazi offered the following definition:

Physical education, then, is the education of, by, and through human movement. It is that phase of general education which contributes to the total growth and development of the child primarily through selected movement experiences and physical activities.[1]

This definition establishes physical education as a basic part of the educational program, contributing to the total education of the individual, and including (but not exclusively) recess, physical fitness, athletics, and intramural sports. A balanced physical education program includes the acquisition of skills, the attainment of fitness, the experiences involved in learning to move and moving to learn, and the enhancement of perceptual-motor competencies.[2]

The recommended activities for physical education are body mechanics, movement, rhythms, gymnastics, low-organized games, high-organized games, exercises, classroom discussions, and experiments.

SITUATION 11.1   What federal programs and/or funds were made available to schools during the 1960s and 1970s to increase the quality and relevancy of physical fitness programs?

Health

Good health is a state of physical, mental, and social well-being. It is more than merely the absence of disease or infirmity; it is the capacity for joyous, zestful living. The child with good health is happier, better adjusted socially, and able to do better work in school than the child whose health is poor. Thus, health is not primarily an end in itself, but a means to more effective living and learning.

Mental and physical health are in reality only two aspects of the same thing. The child who has good health is the one who has an abundance of energy, whose body organs are functioning efficiently, who is mentally alert and emotionally stable, and who is able to bring all physical and mental resources to bear upon problems encountered. Educators, therefore, cannot avoid being concerned about the child's health and about the factors that are influencing it if the school is to competently educate the whole child. A satisfactory school health program includes a healthful environment, adequate health services, and a functional program of health education. The development of a unified health program, involving all three phases, requires a great deal of study and planning on the part of the school staff, local physicians, social workers, community health agencies, parents, and other interested citizens.

The organization, personnel, and administration of the school health program vary from one school system to another. However, certain features are common to most well-organized and well-administered programs:

1. The health program is closely geared to the health problems and resources of the community.

---

[1] Victor P. Dauer and Robert P. Pangrazi, *Dynamic Physical Education for Elementary School Children*, 5th ed. (Minneapolis, Minn.: Burgess Publishing Company, 1975), p. 2.
[2] Dauer and Pangrazi, p. vi.

2. The school staff has a clear concept of the relationship between health and the educative process.
3. Health instruction is not left to chance. A definition period is set aside for health instruction in class schedules, and health is integrated with other school subjects.
4. The physical plant of the school is planned, constructed, and maintained to foster healthful living.
5. There is proper coordination of the several phases of the health program. For example, immunization and physical examinations are utilized as educative experiences.
6. Adequate facilities and materials are provided for health programs.
7. School health policies are definitely established and made available to the school staff and to parents.
8. There is effective coordination of school and community health programs.
9. Qualified medical advisers, nurses, health educators, school psychologists, and other specialized health personnel are provided either by the school system or in cooperation with city, county, or state agencies.
10. The school environment is free from accident and fire hazards, is sanitary, and is adaptable to pupil use.
11. The lunchroom is used not only as a laboratory for nutrition education, but also as a place for dispensing food.
12. There are definite provisions for fostering the physical and mental health of employed personnel.
13. Teamwork between the school and community personnel facilitates the health program.
14. Specialized health personnel are selected with due consideration for the adequacy of their training and other qualifications for the work.

The focus of health education is upon behavior—the reinforcing, changing, and practicing of behaviors which influence the well-being of pupils. Although heredity and environment are certainly prime factors in determining one's state of health, one's behaviors can be the most crucial outcome of three criteria: heredity, environment, and behavior.[3]

SITUATION 11.2   Within the past eight years, what programs have been initiated and/or funded by the federal or state governments to increase the health of elementary school children?

OBJECTIVES

Physical and health education programs hold in common with the school the global goal of developing self-actualizing individuals who acquire knowledge, refine standards, and exercise reasoned thought.

[3] Walter D. Sorochan and Stephen J. Bender, *Teaching Elementary Health Science.* (Reading, Mass.: Addison-Wesley Publishing Company, 1975), p. 24.

Physical Education

A variety of statements of objectives, goals, and purposes exists for the physical education program. In various words, each list or statement deals with the ideas of a fully developed healthy individual, the maintenance of physical fitness, competency in fundamental skills, the teaching of social and ethical generalizations, the practice of safety habits, and the importance and pleasure of recreation.

The physical education curriculum is expanding its focus to include objectives related to exploration; creativity; problem-solving processes; concept learning; self-concept, confidence, and image.[4] The objectives of a physical education program in a modern elementary school include and emphasize behaviors from the cognitive, affective, and psychomotor domains. These objectives are to be appropriately distributed across the four areas of physical education: skills, fitness, basic movement, and perceptual-motor competencies.

Health

School health programs are concerned with the general problem of conservation of human resources. It has long been recognized that good health is the principal source of individual happiness and national strength. The general objective of the health program in an elementary school is to help children become increasingly capable of making intelligent decisions about their own health problems and those of the community, state, and nation. Because every aspect of the school program influences the health of children, it is essential that every member of the staff understand the objectives of the school health program and assume some responsibility for contributing to the achievement of these objectives.

Studying ourselves— an important area for intelligent decision-making.

4 Dauer and Pangrazi, *Dynamic Physical Education,* p. 2.

The specific objectives of the health program will vary from one school to another, but the following list illustrates the types of objectives generally accepted:

1. To provide children with basic information that will help them conserve and improve their own health
2. To help children in school to develop habits of healthful living which will enable them to maintain in later life that abundant vigor and vitality necessary for happiness and service in personal, family, and community relationships
3. To help children learn how to protect themselves and others from communicable diseases
4. To help children develop the ability to recognize quackery and nostrums in the field of health services, to refrain from purchasing drugs or cures of unknown value, and to use dependable resources for medical care
5. To teach the common rules for prevention of accidents and how to administer first aid when necessary
6. To encourage children to take increasing responsibility for planning and eating meals that are adequate in every respect
7. To teach how to plan a well-balanced daily schedule of work, play, rest, relaxation, and social activity
8. To create a desire to participate in school and community efforts for health improvement
9. To help children read selectively and understandingly in the field of health
10. To help children accept their own limitations and capitalize on their strong points
11. To help children understand the importance of correct posture, suitable clothing, and personal hygiene

CURRICULUM APPROACHES

This section will briefly present and describe the major elements, trends, and history of the physical education and health curricula. Both areas are experiencing exciting growth of the content vehicles included, of the psychological bases of their activities, and of the alternatives available to accomplish their objectives.

Physical Education

Physical education is another one of the curriculum areas of the modern elementary school which has undergone tremendous changes in the past decade. Modern technology, increased leisure time, current educational innovations, and recent research evidence on growth, development, motor learning, and related areas are but a few of the pressures that have resulted in many significant changes in the philosophy, content, and teaching strategies of elementary school physical education.

In addition to the selection of content, a well-planned physical education program will have established policy guidelines to support the program. Guidelines are necessary for determining the frequency and amount of time to be given to physical education, the need for medical examinations, and the selection of those children to be excused from participation. The responsibility for, and provision of, first aid as well as protection for teacher liability must be directed by guidelines. Guidelines are also needed to determine the availability, maintenance, and inspection of supplies and equipment. These statements should be cooperatively worked out among teachers, physical education specialists, and administrators. The guidelines should be written, used frequently during in-service meetings, and periodically reviewed and revised.

History

The Greeks saw physical activity as a means of developing the whole person. They strove for physical prowess, grace and beauty of movement, and the concept of a sportsman as a moral person. The Romans introduced professionalism and brutal competition, which nullified some of the Greek ideals (for example, the sportsman as a moral person). Until World War I, few physical programs existed within the United States, although such programs, primarily gymnastics and calisthenics, were operating in the schools of Germany and Sweden. In 1916, California passed the first state law requiring physical education. The first state director of physical education was appointed in New York in 1916.

In 1926 the United States provost marshal for the armed services reported that three million draftees had been found physically unfit for service. At that time there were fourteen states with physical training directors. This information precipitated a public demand and fitness and exercise programs were soon started, supported by new state laws. Because the prevailing premise was that physical and mental capabilities were separate functions, these programs stressed only the development of the body.

John Dewey stressed the promotion of health and the worthy use of leisure time as curriculum responsibilities. This helped reduce the previous dualism (separation of body and mind), and strong programs of sports and games subsequently appeared as physical education curricula. With the exception of the Great Depression in the 1929-1939 period, when economic necessity caused a cutback, physical education programs continued to emphasize simple games and sports throughout World War II and into the mid-1950s.

In 1954 Dr. Hans Kaus published the results of a study comparing selected measures of strength and flexibility among American and central European children. In 1956 President Dwight Eisenhower established the President's Council on Youth Fitness. During this same period, the U.S. Office of Education reported that less than 50 percent of the secondary students were active in physical education, that 91 percent of the elementary schools had no gymnasiums, and that 90 percent of elementary schools had less than 5 acres of playing space. The new emphasis upon fitness resulted in the allotment of more time for physical education, better facilities and equipment, more specialized teachers and consultant services, and a series of fitness tests and standards for elementary pupils. The physical education program moved from games and sports to fitness activities.

Movement education from England, based upon the space-force-time-flow concepts of Rudolph Laban, began to challenge the dominance of physical education by fitness activities during the early 1960s.[5] During this period the debate over movement education versus fitness activities was reduced to specifics: training (fitness) versus teaching (movement), and natural approach (movement) versus an unnatural one (fitness). Eventually the dichotomous positions were consolidated, and physical education began to include both fitness activities and movement education.

Also during the 1960s, the perceptual-motor theories originating from Piaget and Montessori were recognized as having significant relation to physical education programs.[6] As a result, Kephart formulated a series of perceptual-motor developments that seemed to enhance academic achievement.[7] Evidence is strong that a certain stage of neuromuscular development is necessary for optimal academic achievement.[8] The perceptual-motor developmental movement did relate physical development and cognitive development as bases for the physical education program.

This brief review of history has traced the beginnings of the four elements of a modern physical education program: acquisition of skills, fitness activities, movement education, and perceptual-motor competencies. A modern program would emphasize each in a balanced manner according to the school's objectives.[9]

Organizing the Program

The establishment of a modern physical education instructional program depends on several factors. In this section, attention is given to the important topics of time allotment, the staffing for physical education, and the availability of adequate facilities and equipment.

TIME ALLOTMENT

The curriculum of the elementary school is not well-rounded unless it provides for regularly scheduled classes in physical education for all pupils. In a position paper prepared for the American Association for Health, Physical Education, and Recreation, a national affiliate of the National Education Association, it was recommended that pupils in elementary schools should participate in an

---

[5] Dauer and Pangrazi, p. 4.

[6] Dauer and Pangrazi, p. 4.

[7] Newell C. Kephart, The Slow-Learner in the Classroom. (Columbus, Ohio: Charles E. Merrill Publishing Co., 1960).

[8] Dauer and Pangrazi, p. 5.

[9] The author is indebted to the reviews of the history of physical education which usually appear in the November, December, or January issues of the Journal of Health, Physical Education and Recreation, and to the review appearing in the text by Dauer and Pangrazi, Dynamic Physical Education.

instructional program of physical education for at least 150 minutes per week. Additional time should be allotted for free and/or supervised play.[10] The plan adopted by New York State in 1974 required 120 minutes per week.[11]

STAFFING THE PROGRAM

In order to conduct a meaningful instructional program in physical education, qualified personnel are needed. In some school districts the classroom teacher, with the help of a supervisor with special preparation, has the responsibility of teaching physical education. An increasingly popular plan is that in which the classroom teacher and the specialist share the responsibility of teaching physical education. The move toward elementary school physical education specialists is an evident national trend.

Recommended minimum preparation for the classroom teacher should include an understanding of the relationship of physical and motor development to the total learning experience of the child. Course work should include the study of movement skills, methods, and content of elementary school physical education. Laboratory experiences in working with young children in physical education are considered essential.

The professional education background for the elementary school physical education specialist should include the minimal experiences in the following studies:

1. Child growth and development with emphasis on motor development and learning
2. Nature and function of human movement
3. Learning processes and factors that facilitate learning, and teaching strategies as they relate to learning outcomes
4. Development of the curriculum to include movement experiences appropriate for all elementary school children
5. Early childhood and elementary school curricula as a phrase of continuing education
6. Directed laboratory experiences focusing on learning to observe critically the movement of children in an elementary school[12]

The organizational patterns for providing staff for the physical education program vary from district to district; however, the following six patterns seem to include most of the existing staff arrangements. The most common pattern commits the self-contained classroom teacher to total responsibility, with no supervisory or consultant help. The second pattern provides consultant help to

10 *Essentials of a Quality Elementary School Physical Education Program.* (Washington, D.C.: American Association for Health, Physical Education and Recreation, 1970).
11 George H. Grover, "New York State's New Regulations Governing Physical Education," *Journal of Health, Physical Education and Recreation,* Vol. XLVI, No. 7 (September 1975), p. 29.
12 *Professional Preparation of the Elementary School Physical Education Teacher.* (Washington, D.C.: American Association for Health, Physical Education and Recreation, 1969).

the classroom teacher who is still fully responsible for physical education. A third pattern provides a specialist to do some part-time teaching which supports the classroom teacher, who still has the major responsibility. A fourth plan provides a full-time, special physical education teacher, supported by the classroom teacher; the special teacher now has the major if not full responsibility. A fifth plan includes a special physical education teacher within one of the administrative organizational patterns of departmentalization, platoon, or team. Finally, a sixth plan permits teachers to arrange, either formally or informally, trading or combining classes.

FACILITIES AND EQUIPMENT

The modern elementary school includes both indoor and outdoor learning laboratories for physical education instructional programs. The outdoor area of an elementary school, included in the recommendations of the National Council on Schoolhouse Construction,[13] should provide a 10-acre site, with an additional acre for every hundred students, for play space. The playground should have both hard-surfaced areas and grassy fields, and it should be equipped with a variety of creative climbing, hanging, and balancing apparatus that invites children's exploratory and imaginative skill development.

Another important feature of the modern elementary school is the indoor play space. Recommended gymnasium size is 50 feet by 75 feet with a 20-foot ceiling. In many situations it is necessary to use an all-purpose room, which may also serve as cafeteria, auditorium, or meeting room. An effective instructional program can be conducted in this type of multi-use facility if carefully scheduled and if priority is given to physical education classes.

The well-equipped gymnasium should include such apparatus as climbing ropes and structures, vaulting boxes and benches, and folding mats. The creative and interested teacher, however, can provide children with a meaningful instructional program in physical education by adapting or constructing improvised equipment at minimum expense.

An ample amount of small manipulative equipment is a necessary part of the movement education approach. An adequate supply of balls, beanbags, ropes, and hoops—one for each child—is recommended.

Developing the Program

Dauer and Pangrazi identified "basic urges" of children that should form the foundation for the building of a physical education program.

1. *The urge for movement*
2. *The urge for success and approval*
3. *The urge to contest*
4. *The urge for physical fitness and attractiveness*
5. *The urge for social competence*
6. *The urge for adventure*

[13] Anon., *Guide for Planning School Plants.* (East Lansing, Mich.: National Council on Schoolhouse Construction, Michigan State University, 1964).

7. *The urge for creative satisfaction*
8. *The urge for rhythmic expression*
9. *The urge to know*[14]

Each of the four fundamental elements of a modern physical education program should contribute to the satisfaction and reinforcement of these nine "urges."

SKILL ACTIVITIES

The basic skills are locomotion (walking, running, jumping), nonlocomotion (bending, pushing, pulling, twisting), and manipulation (throwing, catching, controlling an object). These skills are emphasized in both activities and and movement education aspects of physical education. The special skills of loosely and highly organized games are especially stressed in this activities element of a physical education program. The game and sport activities recommended for the elementary school are rhythmic activities, stunts, tumbling, simple gymnastics, relays, track and field events, swimming, basketball, soccer, and softball.

FITNESS ACTIVITIES

"Every child has the right to become strong, sturdy, quick and agile."[15] This philosophical approach toward a physical education program encourages children to be both knowledgeable and responsible for their own fitness. Such concepts as the relationships among fitness, health, weight, work capacity, and increased efficiency of movement are taught. The components of physical fitness are strength, power, endurance, agility, flexibility, and speed.

A comprehensive fitness program would include activities which develop the force of the large muscles (strength), which require a short all-out effort to apply strength to create movement (power), and which require the application of strength in a controlled fashion over increasing periods of time (endurance). These are the three fundamental components of physical fitness, and should be taught to all elementary children at their appropriate maturation levels. A comprehensive fitness program would also include activities which require a sudden and swift change in the direction of the movements (agility), which require stretching, bending, pushing, and pulling (flexibility), and which require a maximum effort to move quickly and rapidly (speed). All activities of a fitness program must be conducted under carefully controlled and supervised conditions (for example, a prerequisite for participation is a physical examination). Children should not necessarily be excused from these activities, but the activities should be at a pace and level appropriate to the general health of each child.

A self-testing program and records of each student's status and progress should be established. Special programs for the low-fitness child who is otherwise healthy, the handicapped child, and the child with learning disabilities

---

[14] Dauer and Pangrazi, *Dynamic Physical Education*, pp. 10–11.
[15] Dauer and Pangrazi, p. 86.

should also be arranged. The school playground and recess time should be used to enrich and extend the activities of the fitness program.

Movement Education

In an attempt to meet children's needs and interests, a logical result is the necessity of providing a child-centered program rather than an activity-centered program of physical education. With increased emphasis on providing learning environments which permit children to take an active part in their own learning, today's physical education program for elementary school children is movement education. This modern approach focuses on the total development of each child to move and to live effectively in this complex and ever-changing modern world.

The importance of movement education in the elementary school can be assessed only in terms of what happens to each child. The values derived from movement education in the curricular structure are discussed briefly below.

VALUES OF MOVEMENT EDUCATION

Study has shown that movement education

1. *individualizes instruction.* Considering the great variations present in children's neuromuscular development, even at the same chronological age, it is vital that they have the opportunity to learn at their own level of readiness. When encouraged to select movement tasks appropriate to their level of development, children can experience success. As self-confidence and ability increase, the child is challenged to solve movement problems in more varied and complex ways. The teacher soon learns to anticipate as many different "solutions" to movement problems as there are children in the group.
2. *enhances creativity and independent thinking.* In the skill-and-fitness centered elements of physical education, children were told exactly what to do; traditional development of skills included precise explanations and demonstrations by the teacher, followed by the children's attempt to imitate the prescribed skill or activity. Movement education, on the other hand, is structured to enhance the inventiveness, initiative, and imagination of the child. Through free and guided exploration the child is encouraged and stimulated to discover new and more efficient ways of moving. Children are allowed the freedom to interpret or answer the movement task or problem in their own individual and varied ways.
3. *stresses individual responsibility and self-discipline.* As children learn to think about what they are doing, they are also learning to assume responsibility for their own physical actions. A visitor to any well-conducted movement education class is quickly cognizant of the abilities of elementary school children to move freely in space with no collisions; to use equipment and space cooperatively; and to exhibit interest in, enthusiasm for, and concentration on the learning task. Each child is a purposeful

and self-directed learner who is totally involved in understand and controlling the many ways his body can move.

4. *supports perceptual-motor development.* The importance of sensory-motor experiences in child development and learning is no longer a matter for speculation. Many psychologists, medical specialists, and educators have increasingly stressed the importance of the body as the frame of reference from which perceptual judgments develop. With its emphasis on developing children's awarenesses and control of their bodies, movement education has the important role of providing experiences which will enhance children's sensory capacities and increase their perceptions of their bodies.

MOVEMENT EDUCATION CONCEPT

From the earliest age, an individual engages in purposeful movement. The baby moves to explore and thereby learn about the environment, just as the young child must move in order to learn about size, shape, direction, and other perceptual judgments. An individual's movement behavior is clearly recognized as a means of expression and communication.

The elementary school child needs many opportunities during these important formative years to engage in meaningful activities which will benefit total development. As an important avenue of learning, movement education must be a vital part of every child's daily experience and must be included in any consideration of the modern elementary school curriculum.

Rather than focusing on specific games, sports, rhythmic activities, and gymnastic skills, movement education is concerned with helping children learn about their unique movement behaviors. With emphasis on what the body does, and where and how it moves, the movement education approach provides opportunities for the child to develop a movement foundation which is basic to all motor activities in work or in play. As stated previously, the content of movement education is centered in children as they concentrate on their individual body management, which includes both awareness and control of the body in all situations. Specific sports, gymnastics, or rhythmic skills are, then, the meaningful applications or culminating activities of the movement foundation.

ANALYSIS OF PHYSICAL MOVEMENT

A brief look at any movement behavior reveals that all movement, from crossing a busy street to a highly skilled athletic performance, can be basically analyzed by observing the variations in what way the body is moving, in where the body is moving, and in how the body is moving. Since all movement can be analyzed in this way, a closer look at these three elements is necessary.

What way the body can move involves an awareness of the body and its parts, and the locomotor, nonlocomotor, and manipulative skills used for moving. With control and increased ability as their aim, children discover that they can use various combinations of body parts with which to move in some way or on which to support their bodies. The child's action may range from the simple to a much more complex and sophisticated combination or sequential pattern of movements.

Where the body moves is dependent on the use of various aspects of personal and general space. Personal space is all the space a child can reach out to (using nonlocomotor movements) from a stationary base such as standing or sitting on the floor. General space is the space through which children move when their actions take them away from a fixed base, such as in using the locomotor skills of walking or running through all the available space. Within these two aspects of space, a child learns to move in various directions, such as forward, backward, sideways, or diagonally, and also learns to keep various body parts at a high, medium, or low level.

How the body moves relates the elements of time, space, force, and flow. The child learns to move quickly or slowly, with direct or flexible use of space and with varying degrees of strength or force from strong to soft, and to link one movement to another in a controlled sequence.

Effort-shape, a system derived from Rudolf Laban's works, is a set of principles for analyzing the qualitative aspects of movement in dance, therapy, acting, research in psychology, and physical education.[16] Effort qualities are tension flow, weight, time, and space. Each of these qualities is further defined: tension flow is from bound to free; weight is from light to strong; time is from sustained to quick; and space is from indirect to direct. Shape qualities are: shape flow, directional movement, and shaping. Shape qualities characterize the ways in which body parts move in relation to each other and surrounding space.[17]

While initial movement experiences may concentrate on only one of the qualities mentioned, it can be readily seen that they overlap. Individual competence in dealing with the many possible combinations of movement elements provides the base for all physical education programs.

TEACHING STRATEGIES OF MOVEMENT EDUCATION

An important element of the movement education approach is the learning environment established by the teacher. To meet the criteria of active involvement by children in their own learning and of individualized instruction, the teacher's role is to stimulate and to encourage the process of inquiry. Through open-ended questioning and problem solving, children are actively involved in "exploring, inventing solutions to problems, testing alternatives, practicing to refine selected patterns, and developing kinesthetic awareness and understanding."[18]

---

[16] Willis J. Knight, "The Effort-Shape Workshop," *Journal of Health, Physical Education and Recreation*, Vol. XLV, No. 7 (September 1974), pp. 24–25.
[17] Knight, p. 25.
[18] Lorena Porter, *Movement Education for Children*. (Washington, D.C.: American Association of Elementary-Kindergarten-Nursery Educators, 1969), p. 6.

In planning a laboratory for meaningful movement experiences, several teaching methods may be used. The teacher may be direct, by asking children to "run through all the space in the room without touching anyone or anything," or to "lay a skip rope on the floor and practice jumping your rope with both feet together." In a second method, limitation, the teacher limits the choice of activity or movement by some factor. Examples of the limitation method are as follows: "staying in your own space, practice any bouncing movement with your ball," or "move about the room any way you wish and try to change your level each time you cross a yellow line."

The third teaching method employed is the indirect method, in which the choice of activity is left entirely to the child. The teacher utilizing this method may set for children such problems as "take a skip rope and practice any activity of your own choice," or "practice any activity or movement you wish without any apparatus."

In practical terms, the method of presentation used is determined by the amount of choice allowed to the children. When no choice of movement or of equipment is available to the child, the direct method is being employed. The indirect method leaves the choice of activity entirely to the child. The limitation method, a combination of the direct and indirect methods, is employed when the choice of activity or movement is limited in some way by the teacher. All three methods are acceptable and should be used in order to accomplish the objectives of the lesson. With experience, each teacher learns to balance the movement education lesson by varying the method according to the needs of the children as they became involved in the process of discovery.

Creating an environment with movement.

SITUATION 11.3   Investigate the movement education program in your area. Are individual teachers within the elementary school responsible for the planning and directing of movement education activities, or are specialized personnel employed either to aid teachers or to conduct instruction? How congruent is the current program with the new inquiry approach to movement education and research findings?

Following is an incomplete lesson plan[19] for grades 3 and 4 in movement education, which illustrates the relationships between behavioral concepts, requests, and application.

Introduction: *We are going to work on the effect force has on moving an outside object and how our bodies determine what the object will do in space which we share with other people.*

Equipment Needed: 1 *cageball*
10 *table tennis balls*
3 *medicine balls*
5 *weather balloons*
30 *playground balls*
10 *balloons*

WHY (Behavioral Concepts)	WHAT (Requests)	HOW (Application)
Affective 1. Sharing space means awareness of other people and their needs. 2. Accepting of self and other people's abilities. *Psycho-Motor* 3. The more contributing levers used, the more force obtainable. *Cognitive* 4. The application of knowledge of levers improves decisions as to correct amount of necessary force.	1. Drop the ball and count how many times it bounces. 2. Bounce the ball and count how many times it bounces. 3. What produces the difference? 4. See how many times you can make it bounce. 5. Throw it up as high as you can.	1. Get into groups of four with the playground ball. Can you keep it in the air without catching it?

Perceptual-Motor

This is the newest of the four elements of a modern physical education program. Although still somewhat controversial, it has been quickly adopted as part of a comprehensive program. The support for this element comes from the positive relationship which research has established between children of average

---

[19] Bess Leaf, "Happenings," *Journal of Health, Physical Education and Recreation*, Vol. XLIV, No. 3 (March 1973), pp. 40–41.

or above intelligence who have difficulties in reading and speaking, and also have a deficit in certain perceptual-motor competencies. The controversy arises from the lack of evidence to support the assumption that correction of perceptual-motor incompetencies will positively effect achievement in reading and speaking.[20]

SITUATION 11.4   Design two perceptual-motor education activities for learners at a particular level or grade within the elementary school. What physical skills must be prerequisites for involvement in the tasks? Write at least one psychomotor behavioral objective for each task you designed.

Another unclear aspect is the identification of the factors which comprise perceptual-motor competency. The following are generally agreed upon: general coordination; spatial orientation; balance; body image; hand–eye and foot–eye coordination; hearing discrimination; form; perception; tactile discrimination; and the fitness elements of strength, flexibility, and agility.[21]

SITUATION 11.5   Compare two elementary physical education curriculum guides. If you were given the responsibility of selecting one of the guides for adoption by a school system, which one would you select? In outline form, record the criteria on which you based your selection. What, specifically, were the advantageous factors of the program you selected?

Health Education

A comprehensive health curriculum in the modern elementary school includes a healthful school and learning environment, health services, and instruction in health.

A Healthful School Environment

Education is a process of interaction involving the learner and the environment. The environment and the way the child responds to it from day to day determine the direction growth will take. Because children are required by law to attend school, it should be a place designed to serve their legitimate needs. If the school environment is drab, unattractive, and unsanitary, the child's physical, social, and intellectual growth will be limited. The school cannot, of course, control all the environmental factors that affect the child, but it should make this portion of the child's universe as safe, sanitary, comfortable, attractive, and functional as possible.

[20] Anne F. Millan, "Perceptual-Motor Development: Panacea or Palaver," *Journal of Health, Physical Education and Recreation*, Vol. XLIV, No. 1 (January 1973), p. 27.
[21] Dauer and Pangrazi, *Dynamic Physical Education*, p. 150.

The relationship between the physical plant of the school and the mental and physical health of its occupants is widely recognized. The American Association of School Administrators said, "Educational growth of children to the fullest potential cannot be achieved unless every aspect of the physical environment is so controlled that it contributes to the comfort and health of the pupils and professional staff."[22]

SITUATION 11.6   List twenty physical factors within the school plant which will contribute to the maintenance of good health and optimum functioning of its citizens. Indicate those items on the list with which a teacher may have direct involvement.

PHYSICAL ENVIRONMENT

The architecture of the modern elementary school reflects the principle that the total environment is part of the educative process. Instead of huge edifices to "house" children, the schools of today are built to accommodate children's expanding needs and interests. Flexibility of space appears to be one of the major criteria, and therefore school construction focuses on adaptability of areas to various learning laboratories. The "schools without walls" have been popular innovations of the past decade.

While it is not within the purposes of this text to include all the specifics of school building construction, such features should not be overlooked. Many lists of standards have been published which deal with the latest information on such factors as construction materials, lighting, heat and ventilation, acoustics, sanitation, fire protection, and safety of the building and grounds. Several popular sources of information on school construction are:

Athletic Institute, *Planning Areas and Facilities for Health, Physical Education, and Recreation.* Washington, D.C.: American Association for Health, Physical Education, and Recreation, 1965.

Healthful School Environment. Washington, D.C.: National Education Association, 1969.

Guide for Planning School Plants. East Lansing, Mich.: National Council on Schoolhouse Construction, Michigan State University, 1964.

While teachers cannot control all physical aspects of the school, they are under obligation to report conditions that are not conducive to health. Cooperation among the total school staff can often lead to improvements in lighting, drinking fountains, toilet conditions, and seating facilities.

The teacher and pupils can do much to keep the classroom neat and attractive. Habits of using the wastebasket, of placing wraps and rubbers in the proper places, of eliminating many dust-collecting materials, of washing the

---

[22] American Association of School Administrators, *Health in Schools.* (Washington, D.C.: National Education Association, 1951), p. 89.

hands before lunch, of maintaining proper room temperature, of keeping chalk-boards clean and window shades adjusted properly—all are important aspects of the healthful environment. Pupils with impaired hearing or eyesight should be placed as favorably as possible in the room; seats should be arranged so that pupils get the best possible light; and artificial light should be used with care and intelligence. Pupils should be taught how to use drinking fountains safely, to keep everything in its place, and to clear their desks at the close of the school day.

EMOTIONAL ENVIRONMENT

Of perhaps more importance than the physical environment is the necessity of adapting the emotional tone and environment of a school to children's varied and changing needs. Consideration must be given to such matters as adapting the curriculum to individual differences; the health implications of examina-tions, homework assignments, and standards for pupil progress; organizing the school day to avoid fatigue; discipline practices; and interpersonal relationships.

Since all school staff—including custodians, cafeteria personnel, office staff, school nurse, teachers, and administrators—set the emotional tone of the school, all must share in the responsibility for making the school a good place to learn. The staff must continually evaluate the total climate of the school, and they must be constantly alert for ways to improve the environment.

School Health Services

School health services are provided through the cooperative efforts of the school, the local health department, parents, physicians, nurses, dentists, civic clubs, and other citizens of the community. These services are provided for the purpose of taking care of emergencies, preventing the spread of communi-cable diseases, discovering and correcting physical defects, and giving pupils and their parents the guidance they need in solving their own health problems.

Health services may be used as educative experiences for increasing the knowledge, improving the attitudes, and influencing the behavior of children in relation to health problems. For example, the immunization program may motivate pupils to study how immunization helps the body build defenses against disease; the heightened interest manifest during epidemics or accidents can stimulate student discussion and study of these events.

TYPES OF SERVICES

The modern elementary school provides many types of health services. Some of the more important ones are discussed in the next several paragraphs.

Care of Emergencies. It is the responsibility of the elementary school prin-cipal to see that the school has clearly defined programs relating to the care of emergencies, that teachers and children understand these programs, and that the programs are made effective when emergencies arise. In every school some accidents will happen and some children will have sudden illness. Teach-ers should know what procedures they are authorized to use in such cases. The children should also know these procedures so that their attempts to be helpful at times of accident or sudden illness will not make matters worse and cause needless suffering.

SITUATION 11.7   Teachers in elementary schools may be confronted with one or more emergencies during a school year. What is your viewpoint concerning the completion of a proficiency course in first aid fundamental procedures as a degree or certification requirement for graduating teachers?

The following policies are generally recognized as sound by competent educational and medical authorities:

1. The school staff, in cooperation with medical advisors, should prepare a written statement of procedures to be followed in cases of accidents or sudden illness.
2. At least one staff member who is well trained in first aid should be present at all times.
3. The school should have an adequate supply of first-aid materials and first-aid manuals containing directions for their use.
4. Members of the school staff should not diagnose a condition and should not administer medications unless they have been prescribed by a physician.
5. Sick or injured children should not be sent home alone. Parents should be notified immediately and asked to which physician, hospital, or home address the child should be taken.
6. If neither parent can be reached, the pupil's own family physician should be called. The pupil's permanent health record should contain the name, address, and telephone number of the family physician.
7. Members of the school staff should know what treatment facilities are available in the community, and should be prepared to help parents who are new in the community, or who have no family physician, to find these facilities. A list of local physicians and hospitals should be posted in the principal's office, giving names, addresses, and telephone numbers.
8. If school physicians or nurses are available, they will be expected to take charge of emergencies, but their responsibility should be limited strictly to emergency care and should end when the parents place the child in the care of the family physician.

Prevention and Control of Communicable Diseases. The school shares with the home and the community the responsibility for prevention and control of communicable diseases. Because children are required by law to attend school, because the incidence of communicable diseases is quite high among school-age children, and because many cases of such diseases are discovered while children are at school, it is obvious that the school has considerable, though by no means sole, responsibility for the prevention and control of such diseases. The principal responsibilities of the school in the control of communicable diseases consist of encouraging parents to make full use of immunizations' and other preventive measures, conducting daily observations for symptoms of communicable diseases, seeing that children who are ill are not allowed to attend school, notifying parents when communicable diseases have occurred among the child's classmates, and protecting children against exposure to communicable diseases by providing sanitary buildings and adequate washroom facilities.

The policy of awarding certificates for perfect attendance—a policy encouraged by the distribution of state school funds on the basis of average daily attendance—sometimes hinders the efforts of the school to control the spread of communicable diseases. There are methods of motivating regular attendance which are less harmful to the health of the child and his classmates. Furthermore, experience has proved that the exclusion from school of children who show symptoms of the beginnings of communicable diseases or who are suffering from severe colds does less damage to attendance records in the long run than the spread of colds or diseases, which results in prolonged absences of more children.[23]

SITUATION 11.8   What immunizations are required before a child may enter school? Is the requirement a state or local law, or is it simply the policy of the local school system? What immunizations are provided within the school year as a part of community health services?

Health Guidance. The health guidance program is concerned with discovering the health needs and problems of children and with helping them and their parents find ways of meeting these needs. It is a means of promoting better cooperation among the home, the school, and the community for the purpose of protecting and improving the health of each child. Discovering the health needs of children involves such activities as the preschool roundup, developing a health history for each child, daily health observations by the teacher, dental and physical examinations, and conferences with parents.

The preschool roundup program, which is usually conducted during the summer before the child enters school for the first time, has done much to make parents aware of the health needs of children. Where such programs are conducted, the child who enters school for the first time has had a medical examination and a dental examination, and has been given the necessary vaccinations and immunizations. If the youngster has any physical defects such as impaired vision or hearing, the school is informed and can be prepared to alter the child's program to take care of these handicaps.

A dependable health history for each child provides invaluable information

---

[23] American Association of School Administration, p. 329.

for the health guidance program. It will reveal whether or not the child is examined regularly by a family physician and dentist; what contagious diseases have occurred; the dates of immunizations and vaccinations; environmental and hereditary health data; and habits relating to rest, play, sleep, and nutrition.

Daily observation by the teacher for the purpose of detecting signs of abnormality is an important source of information concerning the health needs of children. For example, a teacher discovered during the physical education period that one girl had symptoms of curvature of the spinal column. The teacher reported this observation to the parents, who then had the child examined by a bone specialist; it was found that the child needed regular and prolonged treatment to prevent her from becoming hopelessly deformed.

There has been a trend in recent years to deemphasize the annual school health examination. This has resulted from the facts that medical, dental, and nursing personnel often do not have time for more than a hasty examination and that the records of the examination have frequently been filed but not followed up. Although the best school examination cannot replace examinations made by the family physician or dentist in a properly equipped office or clinic, some children do not have the services of either a family physician or dentist. It is therefore necessary that the schools provide for periodic examinations of these children, either by school physicians or by public health personnel. Following the school health examination, the staff of the school should maintain contact with the parents to see that further diagnosis, correction, and treatment are carried out by private physicians or by community health agencies.

SITUATION 11.9   A child who is not physically well will not be capable of operating at his or her potential mental capacity. If you, as a modern elementary school teacher, observed a student who displayed physically unhealthy symptoms which could be reflective of home environmental conditions (for example, malnutrition, insomnia), what recourse would you elect? As a teacher, do you have responsibilities to the child to become involved in physical care of the child outside the classroom?

Health Instruction

The third area of a school health program, health education, is defined as "the process of providing learning experiences which favorably influence understandings, attitudes, and conduct with regard to individual and community health."[24] This definition recognizes that pupils learn from their experiences and that this learning may include pupil knowledge, attitudes, and behavior. Recognizing that health education is a process indicates that it needs to be planned and that it cannot be merely the result of incidental occurrences.

The development of a functional program of health education involves

[24] *Health Education*, 5th ed. (Washington, D.C.: National Educational Association, 1961), p. 7.

cooperation between the school and the community. Even in small communities there are many organized groups, as well as individuals with specialized skills, which may be utilized in planning the program. Alert educational leadership will recognize that health is a cooperative enterprise, and will develop procedures for bringing all valuable resources to bear on the health education program. The community health council provides the means for cooperative planning and action in many communities. These councils usually consist of representatives from the school administration, teachers, custodians, students, physicians, dentists, nurses, public health officials, and representatives from various lay organizations.

THE MODERN CONCEPT

Health education is not just hygiene, nor is it superficial biology or watered-down anatomy or physiology. It is, rather, an important part of the total curriculum which, through organization of health knowledge, is primarily concerned with the well-being of individuals and groups. "The goal of health education is not directed at a high level of health simply for health's sake, but rather to help each individual view health as a way of life that will help to attain individual goals and utilize one's highest potential for the betterment of self, family, and community."[25]

As an applied field of learning, health education relies largely upon the knowledge of the physical, biological, and medical sciences and related fields for its subject matter, and upon the application of behavioral science theory for its methodology. As such, health education is a discipline in which the relevant knowledge and ideas from several fields are combined and synthesized.

The past decade has witnessed a phenomenal increase in knowledge in each of the topical areas which have constituted the subject matter of health education. This fact, along with current interest in behavioral change, has resulted in new curriculum designs. Health education, like many other academic fields, has turned to the concept-oriented approach in curriculum planning and development. Under the concept approach, the child arrives at health concepts through an active thinking process. The concepts become internalized, and hence they are meaningful.[26]

Organizing the Program

Just as there is a need for learning combinations in arithmetic and vocabulary in reading, so there is need for building a factual basis for healthful living. This does not mean, however, that facts must always be learned by abstract drill or by reciting from a textbook during a period set aside for health instruction alone. No single method of incorporating health instruction into the curriculum

[25] School Health Education Study, *Health Education: A Conceptual Approach to Curriculum Design.* (St. Paul, Minn.: 3M Educators Press, 1967), p. 11.
[26] *Health Concepts: Guides for Health Instruction.* (Washington, D.C.: American Association for Health, Physical Education and Recreation, 1967), p. 2.

will suffice; the well-organized program will give proper emphasis to incidental teaching, to correlation with other curriculum areas, and to direct teaching.

INCIDENTAL TEACHING

In the primary grades, health instruction consists largely in helping children live more healthfully each day and in making use of incidents as they arise in connection with school living to improve health practices and understanding. The alert teacher finds many opportunities for relating health instruction to such experiences as dental and medical examinations, immunizations, weighing and measuring, hand washing, playground activities, and the lunch period. Incidental teaching of health can continue to supplement direct teaching in the grades above the primary level.

CORRELATION

Opportunities for developing understanding of health problems and influencing health behavior exist in many curriculum areas. Oral and written composition may well utilize content relating to health; arithmetic provides opportunities for such experiences as constructing height-and-weight charts, and computing the caloric values of foods and the percentages of deaths caused by certain diseases; science provides opportunities for learning the principles of reproduction, growth, and survival; the social studies provide opportunities for studying about food, clothing, shelter, and other problems relating to health and safety in the home and community as well as in other countries; and music, art, dance, and drama may well employ content from the area of health. In a school that is organized on the "self-contained-classroom" basis,[27] the teacher is in a very favorable position for taking advantage of opportunities for health teaching in connection with other school experiences. If the departmental organization is in use, a great deal of cooperative planning on the part of the school staff is necessary in order to avoid duplications and omissions in content and activities relating to health.

DIRECT TEACHING

Since health is recognized as one of the most important objectives of education, it should be given time and attention as in any other curriculum area. The teacher and administrator should see that whatever time is necessary for fostering the health of pupils is available and used. In many schools this problem is solved, in part at least, by setting aside a definite time in the schedule for health instruction.

Structure

Most current health education programs are structured around conceptual statements which contain key concepts and integrate substantive elements. The

---

[27] The "self-contained classroom" is a term used to describe a situation in which one teacher teaches all subjects, in contrast to a departmentalized organization in which one teacher teaches arithmetic, another teaches the language arts, and another, the social studies.

structure of a current health education project, the SHE Study,[28] highlights the logical relationships among three basic elements—three key concepts, ten concepts (generalizations), and subconcepts.

The three key concepts identified by the study are growing and developing, interacting, and decision making. These major concepts characterize the processes underlying health. The second level of the hierarchy includes ten conceptual statements which are viewed as the major organizing elements of the curriculum, or as indicators of the direction of the learning experiences. It is important to note here that concepts, as such, are not taught, but they serve as bases for a framework within which facts, ideas, generalizations, and values are structured and organized.

In the SHE Study the ten concepts and their respective subconcepts are:

1. *Growth and development influence and are influenced by the structuring and functioning of the individual.*
   a. *Heredity prescribes the potential for growth and development.*
   b. *Growth and development may be promoted or hindered by functions, environmental conditions, and the use of certain substances.*
   c. *Various parts of the body perform different functions, but also work together to influence growth [learning] and development.*
2. *Growth [learning] and development follow a predictable sequence, yet are unique for each individual.*
   a. *All individuals grow [learn] and develop in a similar, predictable sequence.*
   b. *Body parts, systems, and functions grow . . . in each individual in a unique way.*
   c. *Unique differences in the rate and the status of growth [learning] and development occur among individuals.*
3. *Protection and promotion of health are individual, community, and international responsibilities.*
   a. *Some health problems can be approached most effectively on a community basis.*
   b. *Community and international health are promoted most effectively through organized group action utilizing all resources.*
4. *The potential for hazards and accidents exists, whatever the environment.*
   a. *Accidents are caused by human and environmental factors and may result in injury, property damage, or death.*
   b. *Safe living involves the development and use of safety precautions while recognizing the inevitability and appeal of risk taking.*
   c. *Natural and [artificial] environmental factors influence health and safety.*
   d. *Some environmental conditions can be modified and controlled.*
5. *There are reciprocal relationships involving [humans], disease, and environment.*
   a. *Some diseases which impair health are caused by microorganisms.*

---

[28] School Health Education Study.

    b. Some diseases indicate a disturbance in the equilibrium between a person and particular microorganisms ranging from subclinical to clinical cases.

    c. There are measures by which some diseases can be prevented and controlled.

    d. Some diseases develop as a result of a specific body dysfunction and cannot be transmitted.

6. *The family serves . . . to fulfill certain health needs.*

    a. The family is the social group in our society in which members can relate most intimately to each other and in which children are raised from infancy to adulthood.

    b. The selection of a . . . partner is a highly personalized process, fundamental to the nature of . . . life.

    c. The sex drive, a basic and powerful force, is related to pleasure, the desire to belong, and reproduction, and requires understanding, acceptance, and management.

    d. Each family grows and develops in its own unique way.

7. *Personal health practices are affected by a complexity of forces, often conflicting.*

    a. Individually balanced programs of rest, sleep, relaxation, and activity influence well-being.

    b. Care of the teeth and supporting structures of the mouth are aspects of personal health behavior.

    c. The well-being of the individual is affected by the choices . . . [made] in personal health care.

8. *Utilization of health information, products, and services is guided by values and perceptions.*

    a. Appraisal, selection, and use of health information, products, and services are influenced by one's past experiences and the environment.

    b. Sources and evaluation of health information, products, and services influence their selection and use.

9. *Use of substances that modify mood and behavior arises from a variety of motivations.*

    a. Substances that modify mood and behavior range from mild to strong, have multiple uses, and produce many and varied effects in individuals who use them.

    b. Use of substances that modify mood and behavior may result in health and safety problems.

    c. Many factors and forces influence the use of substances that modify mood and behavior.

10. *Food selection and eating patterns are determined by physical, social, mental, economic, and cultural factors.*

    a. Choice of foods determines nutritional balance.

    b. A balanced diet affects well-being and the desire for well-being affects food choices.

    c. Food selection and eating patterns serve social and psychological purposes as well as filling physiological needs.

In addition to providing the conceptual structure of health education, the SHE Study suggests progressions and sequences for teaching–learning experiences stated in behavioral terms. Two levels, one for primary and one for intermediate grades, are used rather than the traditional grade groupings; this plan allows for individual differences, variations in administrative and organization patterns, revolutionary methods and instructional approaches, and other factors that require increasing flexibility in the educational process.

SITUATION 11.10   Design an activity for primary children which would allow experiences with good nutrition.

Materials

Modern textbooks for use in the health education program are available in increasing variety and improved quality. There can be little question that an elementary school should have available for use one or more of the excellent series of textbooks now on the market. They provide ideal reading material for children, suggestions for teachers relating to suitable content, and useful data relating to health problems. The textbook does not, however, constitute the only source of instructional material. Instructional materials should include printed materials, such as books, magazines, newspapers, and pamphlets; audiovisual resources, such as motion pictures, slides, graphs, models, posters, and charts; and environmental materials found in the home, school, and community.

The following criteria should be observed in the selection of materials for health education:

1. Materials should be scientifically sound.
2. Materials selected should provide for individual differences and needs.
3. Materials selected should provide for progression in activities and present opportunities for growth.
4. Materials selected should be closely related to experiences of children so that they will be meaningful.
5. Materials selected should have important content and not merely entertainment appeal.

ISSUES

The issues in health and physical education tend to center around either the inclusion or exclusion of topic of instruction versus imbalances between program areas. This section has selected four topics for discussion (dance, death, drug abuse, human sexuality) which are often accompanied by controversy and three potential imbalances between program areas (inter- versus intra-; staff versus staff; advocates of fitness versus advocates of movement and perceptual-motor education).

Controversial Topics

Whenever health and physical education programs include the topics of dance, death, drugs, or human sexuality, the potential for controversy is present. In many communities the dominant society rejects the inclusion of one or more of these topics. The reasons given for the rejection of these as appropriate topics are: religious; moral; the topics are the responsibility of the home; and the topics are not suitable to the maturity of the children. The school may well be in a position of fighting a battle (to include an issue) and losing a war (the support of the community). Artful, yet forceful, leadership is needed under these conditions.

Dance

The case for the inclusion of dance starts with: "dance is one of the lifetime sports."[29] The individual may, through dance, increase the flexibility, agility, strength, endurance, spatial perception, and rhythm of the body. In modern dance, each individual competes with personal past behaviors and personally desired goals and objectives, using the physical, mental, and emotional responses that exist within the individual. Modern dance is a dance for physical fitness. The body must be controlled in dance as in any sport. "Each student has the right to experience the pleasure that rhythmic, physical movement can bring."[30]

The case for dance in physical education can be built from each of the four areas of physical education: skills, fitness, movement, and perceptual-motor competencies. In addition, the possibilities of relating social studies and physical education, for example, are tremendous. Laban suggested: ". . . while 'doing' is purposeful and preserves life, 'dancing' is necessary to recover from the strain of 'doing' and is the primary means of expression from which the arts originate."[31]

Death

The case for the inclusion of death as a topic of health education could start with the old adage: "Nothing is certain but death and taxes." Death is relevant to life, just as life is relevant to death. A child will, through maturation, experience the "trauma" induced by death of pets, friends, or family. The teaching of the life cycle, one of the unifying concepts of science and health, necessarily includes death as one phase.

Bauer, in summarizing the research conducted on the fears of children, concluded:

> The fears children have about their performance in competitive academic settings are secondary to their real concerns. Such fears are diverse and confront professionals with fundamental questions about the meaning of life and death in an urban technological society.[32]

[29]Mary Cowden Snyder, "Dance as a Lifetime Sport," *Journal of Health, Physical Education and Recreation*, Vol. XLVI, No. 6 (June 1975), p. 36.
[30] Snyder, p. 37.
[31] Joan Russell, *Creative Dance in the Primary School*. (London: MacDonald and Evans, Ltd., 1965), p. 11.
[32] David H. Bauer, "Children's Fears: Reflections on Research," *Educational Leadership*, Vol. XXXI, No. 6 (March 1974), pp. 555–560.

Death is a phenomenon that characterizes all forms of life. It is from this perspective that sound instruction can be planned.

Drug Abuse

Several states (Oklahoma, for example) have passed legislation requiring instruction in drug abuse in elementary schools. Although several models for drug education programs are available, no one model has yet established itself as the most effective. The existing programs have shifted from the "scare" tactics of the earlier programs to an emphasis upon values-clarification strategies, self-awareness, self-esteem, and self-concept.

Bernard Bard[33] quotes Annette Abrams, staff member of the foundation-funded Drug Abuse Council of Washington, D.C., who says of the schools' massive drug prevention campaigns:

> *Vast expenditures of time, money, and effort succeeded only in producing a generation of sophisticated junior pharmacologists who, to our disillusionment, continued to use and experiment with drugs despite the wealth of facts available to them.*

Sorochan and Bender provided the following as the underlying principles basic to effective drug education:

1. *Only sound, scientific and up-to-date information has a place in drug education.*
2. *Scare tactics have little long-lasting value.*
3. *Drug education includes instruction about all mood-modifying substances; alcohol and tobacco are no exception.*
4. *When expression of biases and/or moralizing become overly apparent, the objectivity of drug education suffers and instruction loses its impact.*
5. *Instruction relative to drug use and abuse should be handled only by a well-informed, empathetic, and competent teacher.*
6. *Drug education is on-going and comprehensive in nature. "One shot" endeavors are of little value.*
7. *Drug education encompasses far more than mere cognitive information. By its very nature, drug education deals with behavior and this implies that the affective and action [psychomotor] domains are explored.*[34]

For information or guidance in planning a drug abuse program, write to Information Services, National Clearinghouse for Drug Abuse Information, WT 240, 5454 Wisconsin Avenue, Chevy Chase, Maryland 20015.

Human Sexuality

Human sexuality does not begin or climax with the physical characteristics which distinguish male and female. Sexual intercourse is but one of many aspects in a comprehensive human sexuality program. The fact that instruction con-

---

[33] Bernard Bard, "The Failure of Our School Drug Abuse Programs," *Phi Delta Kappan*, Vol. LVII, No. 4 (December 1975), p. 255.
[34] Sorochan and Bender, p. 292.

cerning sexual intercourse is typically not included in the elementary school program does not lessen the need for instruction and learning concerning healthy sexuality. The program of the elementary school in human sexuality emphasizes sexual roles (sister, brother, boy, girl, father, mother); relationships with the individuals of the same and opposite sex (friends, classmates); awarenesses of reproduction, birth, and the dependence period of the young as part of the pattern in nature for all living things. Achieving the potential of human sexuality includes conscious awarenesses of the stereotypes, the alternative roles available to the individual, and processes for becoming comfortable with one's role and conscious choices. The theme articles in the November 1973 issue of *Educational Leadership* provided a range of information and alternatives available to the school concerning the sterotyping for sex roles.[35]

Human sexuality includes the capacities for loving, for personal commitment, for sharing but not conquering, for receiving but not possessing, and for being one together but distinctly individual parts of the whole.

Children experience the tensions of these issues and bring to these learnings the same curiosities and "urges" to know as to any other relevant learnings. Some guidelines for this were provided by McClurg,[36] and the Sex Information and Education Council of the United States (SIECUS).

Human sexuality programs in schools have been supported by the National Education Association, The American Medical Association, The National Congress of Parents and Teachers, The National Council of Churches, The American Public Health Association, The American College of Obstetricians and Gynecologists, and others, but these endorsements apparently do not counterbalance the active and even violent resistance persisting in many communities. For example, a superintendent of a district involved in such a dispute said:

> *The results of all this go far beyond sex education. You don't turn off hatred just like that. It spreads and spreads. People in the community have stopped talking to each other. People come to school board meetings now and question our textbooks on other subjects. Where will it all stop?*[37]

SITUATION 11.11 List potential problems for students attending a school system in which sex education instruction is prohibited by the community.

Program Imbalances

The area of physical education is prone to imbalances among program areas as are all curriculum areas. Accusations of "imbalance" are often louder in this area because of the public visibility and potential acclaim accruing to

---

[35] *Educational Leadership*, Vol. XXI, No. 2 (November 1973), pp. 99–135.

[36] Janet F. McClurg, "To Teach Loving," *Educational Leadership*, Vol. XXXI, No. 1 (October 1973), pp. 14–17.

[37] "Sex in School: The Birds, The Bees and the Birchers," *Look* Magazine (Sept. 9, 1969).

aspects of the program: for example, athletics. Other imbalances may occur as newer programs arrive and departmental heads attempt to find a place for them by displacing something else. The potential imbalances discussed here are interschool varsity competition vesus intramural competition; staff versus staff; and advocates of fitness versus advocates of movement and perceptual-motor education.

Inter- versus Intra-

Both interschool and intramural programs are supplements and extensions of, but not replacements for, a basic physical education program. The first potential imbalance often occurs here when the existence of an inter- or intra-program is at the expense of the staffing and equipping of the basic physical education program. A second imbalance is the existence of an interschool program in absence of an intramural program. The modern elementary school provides sports competition, both team and individual, for all children. A comprehensive modern physical education program will provide a basic physical education program which includes: skills, fitness, movement, and perceptual-motor experiences for all children; an intramural program for most, if not all; and a program for especially talented children. If and when funds to support a comprehensive program become limited, then priority (for the author) would be first given to the support of the most broadly based program involving the greatest number of participants, and then in descending order on that basis to other programs.

Staff versus Staff

All members of a faculty are "staff." Some serve the school's clientele in different ways. An imbalance ocurs when some staff members are valued because of their public visibility rather than for their behaviors as teachers. Staff members who "coach" intramural or interschool teams in the elementary school must be teachers first, and not necessarily experts in preparing teams for competition in one or more sports events. Another imbalance occurs when the assumption is made that an expert in preparing teams for competition is automatically a teacher of physical education. The speciality of "coaching" does not necessarily encompass the speciality of "physical education teacher."

Advocates of Fitness versus Advocates of Movement and Perceptual-Motor Education

Except for the content vehicles forming the issues, the building of a comprehensive physical education program has experienced conflict among advocates similar to that in all curriculum areas. The advocate areas within the physical education remain skills versus fitness, fitness versus movement education, movement education versus fitness and skills, and perceptual-motor versus movement education. Each of the four fundamental areas of what is now a modern physical education program initially claimed that it could do it all (see the section "History" in this chapter). Therefore, a series of artificial "either-or" choices were created. Neither time nor research has established that any one of the four areas can stand alone and do it all. More research is needed to identify the discrete contributions of each area. Until then, a comprehensive program must be built from the broadest perspectives of a growing, learning, and developing human being. In physical education, as in many other areas, research evidence does not confirm superiority of one method for the accomplishment of multiple goals. Therefore, the areas of the physical education program should include the goal-related areas of skill acquisition, fitness achievement, movement awareness, and perceptual-motor competencies.

INTERDISCIPLINARY APPROACHES

This section briefly presents those special activities and programs which interrelate the health and physical education curriculum with the other curriculum areas and the goals of the modern elementary school. The following have been selected as illustrations: values-clarification strategies, career awareness activities, controversial topics, and "Every Child a Winner."

Values-Clarification Strategies

The importance and application of values-clarification strategies to the study of such topics as drug abuse, death, dance, and sexuality nests in the premise that behavior is caused. One of the causes of behavior is the strength—or, in some cases, the weakness—within the individual's values organizations. Knowledge of what is the most positive behavior is not necessarily followed by the doing of the most positive behavior. The connection between "knowledge of" and "the doing of" seems to be dependent upon the strength of the value system which relates knowledge to doing. Therefore, drug abuse programs, for example, have moved from merely informing the participants to involving the participants in choosing, acting, and prizing behaviors based upon the transmitted information. Values-clarification strategies are designed to encourage the participant to move from facts to concepts to value organizations. Such strategies as "consequences search" or "alternatives search" are especially useful with the topics of drug abuse, death, dance, and sexuality.[38]

In physical education the potential importance of values-clarification strategies depends upon "outcomes broader than just winning or acquiring skills."[39] The utilization of values-clarification strategies helps accomplish the physical education objectives of self-esteem, self-realization, self-understanding, and positive interpersonal relationships.[40]

The Teacher Education Center for Elementary School Physical Education at the University of North Carolina has experimented with a humanistic ap-

[38] Sidney B. Simon, Leland W. Howe, and Howard Kirschenbaum, *Values Clarification: A Handbook of Practical Strategies for Teachers and Students.* (New York: Hart Publishing Company, Inc., 1972).

[39] Marian E. Knees, "How Human Are You? Exercises in Awareness," *Journal of Health, Physical Education and Recreation*, Vol. XLV, No. 6 (June 1974), p. 32.

[40] Knees, p. 32.

proach to games. This demonstration center feels that selecting one game, thereby assuming that all children can cope equally well with the demands of that game, or that selecting games in which the larger, stronger, quicker or more verbal dominate, are inadequate humanistic approaches. The center believes that a more comprehensive definition of skills and a different approach to teaching game skills are warranted. Of the possible game forms—predetermined (conventional games) or original (created)—the center is experimenting with original game forms which are pupil-designed or teacher-designed to fit a particular set of pupils and a situation. The staff is optimistic about the potential contributions of the use of the original game form to further humanistic objectives.[41]

Career Awareness Activities

The California Department of Transportation commissioned a study from the University of Southern California for the purpose of identifying trends in work prospectives. Among the predictions of the study were: the work week will shrink to 35 hours by 1985, then to 30 hours by the year 2000; vacation periods will increase to five weeks by 1995, and to six weeks by 2005. By 1985 the average American will retire at age 60, by 2005 the retirement age will be 59, and there will be a 50 percent increase in free time by 2000. The biggest problem facing people by 2000 will be how to learn to live with one's leisure when there's so much of it.[42]

The vocational and avocational implications of these predictions provide an overwhelming legitimation for the inclusion and emphasis of career awareness activities within the health and physical education programs. With the potential problem of living with so much leisure time, the career awareness activities that emphasize work as both compensated and uncompensated activities seem especially important.

Controversial Topics

In previous sections, of this chapter the topics of dance, death, drug abuse, and human sexuality were discussed as controversial topics within the health and physical education curriculum. If all curriculum areas were participating in and contributing to the learning experiences provided to pupils through these topics, then perhaps some of the controversy would abate, or at least be diffused.

Every Child a Winner

A principal said, ". . . our discipline has improved tremendously, and I give much of the credit to our physical education program." A teacher said, "The difference this physical education program has made in the children is unbelievable. They're more attentive, better behaved in the classroom." Another

---

[41] Marie Riley, "Games and Humanism," *Journal of Health, Physical Education and Recreation*, Vol. XLVI, No. 2 (February 1975), pp. 46–49.
[42] John L. Bullaro, "Career Potential in Commercial Recreation," *Journal of Health, Physical Education and Recreation*, Vol. XLVI, No. 9 (November–December 1975), p. 36.

principal said, "This physical education program benefits every child—not just a select group with special problems or special abilities." These comments were made in reference to the demonstration center and training site for elementary education in Irwin County, Georgia.[43] The three mains goals of the Georgia program are to improve measurably the fitness levels and motor skills of every child in the program, to enhance self-concept and adjustment, and to plan and implement school health services. The program had been changed from the traditional emphasis on competitive games and sports which foster the "I'm a loser" attitude to a movement education methodology which has provided daily success (winning) experiences for every child. What greater interrelationship could exist between the purposes of the school and all curriculum areas than this?

STRATEGY OF INSTRUCTION

The strategy of instruction presented in Chapter 5 will be utilized in this section to analyze the health and physical education curriculum. This is done to demonstrate the need for such a strategy, the applicability of the proposed strategy, and to present a form of summary.

Selection of Content

As the physical education curriculum has progressed from acquisition of skills and proficiency in games to include movement education activities and perceptual-motor competencies, the possibilities of selecting representative content vehicles have increased. The interaction among the four elements results in a much greater gestalt of human maturation from which to select vehicles that are representative, relevant, classical, humane, and practical.

The scope and sequence of content vehicles for the health education curriculum is not yet clear. For example, Sorochan and Bender cite recommended lists of content vehicles ranging from ten to twenty items.[44] These variances can be partially explained by the fact that some authorities combine topics, even though the range of included topics does vary. This implies that bases for selection of content vehicles have not yet been agreed upon.

In a publication entitled, "Framework for Health Instruction in California," the California Department of Education recommended the following content vehicle areas:

1. *Consumer health*
2. *Mental-emotional health*
3. *Drug use and misuse*
4. *Family health*
5. *Oral health, vision and health*
6. *Nutrition*

---

[43] Syd Blackmarr, "Every Child a Winner," *Journal of Health, Physical Education and Recreation*, Vol. XLV, No. 8 (October 1974), pp. 14–15.
[44] Sorochan and Bender, p. 147.

7. *Exercise*
8. *Rest and posture*
9. *Disease and disorders*
10. *Environmental health hazards*
11. *Community health resources*[45]

Authorities do seem to agree that a comprehensive modern health curriculum should include the physical, social, and emotional aspects of the total school environment; the provisions of health services and guidance; and instruction derived from the health sciences.

Learning and Development

When movement and perceptual-motor education programs became elements of a comprehensive physical education program, the first significant adjustments for developmental levels began to occur. The skills and fitness elements of a more traditional program considered only growth and maturity. Inherent in the movement and perceptual-motor programs is an accommodation for the developmental levels of children.

Sorochan and Bender, when introducing a theory of learning as it relates to health instruction, said, "Maturation must precede learning. Teaching becomes successful when it coincides with the maturational processes of the child. Developmental arrest of one or more developmental processes upsets the functional harmony of the whole class. . . ."[46] (See Piaget, Chapter 3).

Methodology

The inquiry processes, learning by doing, and discovery experiences are becoming the fundamental methodology of physical education and health instruction. Drill, demonstration, lecture, and other teaching procedures are utilized when appropriate. The inquiry process is an integral part of the movement and perceptual-motor programs. In health, "the learner should be an active, rather than a passive, listener or viewer. Learning experiences should be organized so that the child discovers concepts, or the 'big ideas' for himself.[47]

Communication

As the methodology of health and physical education has adjusted to include inquiry, the communication patterns have changed. At one time the communications patterns between teachers and pupils occurred in situations of calisthenics (fitness) or in refereeing organized games (skills). Now the teacher and the pupils plan original games, discuss the effort–space requirements of a movement, and negotiate the perceptual-motor competencies appropriate to the developmental level of a child.

---

[45] "Framework for Health Instruction in California Public Schools." (Sacramento: California State Department of Education, 1970).
[46] Sorochan and Bender, *Teaching Elementary Health Science*, p. 128.
[47] Sorochan and Bender, p. 129.

Objectives

Through movement and perceptual-motor activities, the full range of cognitive, affective, and psychomotor behaviors are stressed. The dualism, formally inherent in fitness, is now replaced by a unified concept of mind and body. The emphasis upon behavior as the primary evidence of learning has supported the extension of the health and physical curriculum into all aspects of human growth, learning, and development.

Goals

The goals of both health and physical education are consistent with the development of a free mind and a free body—a body free of unnecessary handicaps, and a mind free to make rational, informed decisions about maintaining or improving its state of fitness and health.

SUMMARY

1. The four elements of a comprehensive physical education program are achievement of fitness, acquisition of skills, movement awareness, and perceptual-motor competencies.

2. The three aspects of a comprehensive health education program are the physical, social, and emotional environment of the school; health services and guidance; and health instruction.

3. The focus of health and physical education is upon behavior: the reinforcing, changing, and practicing of behaviors which influence the well-being of pupils.

4. The three aspects of a comprehensive physical education program are basic instruction in physical education, intramural programs, and interschool programs.

5. Movement education involves an awareness of the body motions of locomotion, nonlocomotion, and manipulation. Effort-shape is a system for analyzing movement.

6. Lack of perceptual-motor competencies seems to be a common characteristic of children with learning disabilities.

7. The inclusion of certain topics within the health and physical education curriculum generates problems (that is, the support of the community) as well as challenge (the building of a curriculum and the preparation of personnel).

Problems and Projects

1. Investigate the nature and scope of health services available to elementary school children within a large public school system. Compare the services with

those of a smaller community. What responsibilities are shared by teachers employed in either system?

2. From time to time we are reminded that other very vulnerable human beings have become objects of abuse. At some point during our involvement with schools, we—as teachers, supervisors, or administrators—may very well be confronted with one of the most sobering realities of all: child abuse. What are the normal procedures for child abuse cases within your community? Examine some of the literature related to child abuse to acquaint yourself with the following:

    a. Scope of abuse within elementary school children
    b. Parental reactions:
       (1) to the act itself
       (2) the discovery of their (parents) behavior by someone else
       (3) to the child
    c. Alternatives for the child
    d. Usual precedents established by legal procedures

We, as teachers, have a responsibility to our students to teach them about the integrity of their bodies, the respect of their bodies, the care of their bodies, and the rights to legal protection of their bodies. Consider, then, that the young child will most likely return to the environment in which the abuse was received, and will return to those individuals the child loves, but who also inflicted the abuse. What are the possible ramifications for the child's affective characterization constructs as we teach those basic structures of health education regarding the integrity, respect, care, and rights of an individual's body? For the teacher who is concerned with both the affective and cognitive development of the child, there might possibly arise a conflicting situation if the teacher is confronted with children who have been victims of child abuse. At one end of the scale are the responsibilities of the teacher to teach the fundamental health education structures to the child. At the other end of the scale is the potential impact upon the child as interrelationships are reconciled between the restructuring of characterizations within the affective domain (brought about through cognitive data pocessing) and the child's continuing existence within and dependence upon an environment in which there exists the possibility of future, repeated abuse. As a teacher involved in the previously described conflict, what would be your primary concerns? Based upon your personal concepts concerning teacher responsibilities, does a conflict exist?

3. Talk with drug abuse authorities within your community to determine:

    a. the type of drug experimentation within elementary-school-age children.
    b. the participation rate among elementary-school-age children.
    c. observable characteristics, symptoms, or behaviors which might indicate that a child is involved in drug abuse.

Based upon the interviews, design two inquiry activities (one for primary students and one for intermediate students) related to drug abuse and drug respect. What other curriculum area(s) might be particularly suited to the investigation and completion of such activities?

4. Interview ten people from various occupations concerning their opinions of incorporation of the following topics into an elementary school health program:

    a. Dance
    b. Death

    c. Drugs

    d. Human sexuality

What are the dominant opinions for each topic? Do relationships exist between occupations and between supportive or nonsupportive positions? Based upon the
information the four topics into a health program? What modifications would need
to be made?

    5. With the election of President John F. Kennedy in 1960 and the appointment
of Bud Wilkinson as director of the physical fitness program, schools across the
nation became more accountable for the physical development of children—the
nation's future citizens. Review the literature for research related to the results of
innovative physical fitness programs within the past twelve years. How do the findings of recent studies related to the physical fitness of our youth compare to findings
of similar studies conducted in the early 1960s?

    6. What federal and state standards must be met by physical education pro-
grams within your area? How are those standards made known to the individual
directly involved in pupil instruction?

    7. Talk with a curriculum director, a physical education supervisor, or a phys-
ical education instructor who has been serving a school system in that capacity for
ten to fifteen years. Discuss the changes related to the nature of equipment, programs, and instruction since 1960.

    8. If authorized to submit a requisition for the purchase of ten items of indoor
and/or outdoor learning equipment which would encourage both creative and individualized physical education instruction, what items would be included on your
requisition? Beside each item, write a brief statement indicating its potential educational value to the learner.

Selected Readings

Bucher, Charles A., and Evelyn M. Reade, *Physical Education and Health in the
    Elementary Schools.* New York: Crowell Collier and Macmillan, Inc., 1971. One
    of the textbooks relating health and physical education.

Dauer, Victor P., *Essential Movement Experiences for Preschool and Primary Chil-
    dren.* Minneapolis, Minn.: Burgess Publishing Company, 1972. Practiced ideas
    for movement education activities.

Dauer, Victor P., and Robert P. Pangrazi, *Dynamic Physical Education for Ele-
    mentary School Children,* 5th ed. Minneapolis, Minn.: Burgess Publishing Com-
    pany, 1975. A comprehensive textbook for elementary physical education.

Dutton, Marion, *Movement Education.* New York: E. P. Dutton & Co., Inc., 1973.
    General textbook for movement education.

Essentials of a Quality Elementary School Physical Education Program. Washington,
    D.C.: The American Association for Health, Physical Education and Recreation,
    1970. Descriptions of a comprehensive elementary school program.

Every Child a Winner: With Improved Physical Education Equipment. Atlanta, Ga.:
    Georgia Department of Education, 1973. Description of a demonstration program
    and recommended equipment.

Frostig, Marianna, and Phillis Maslow, *Move-Grow-Learn.* Chicago: Follett Pub-
    lishing Company, 1969. Resource book on movement and perceptual-motor edu-
    cation.

Humphrey, James H., *Child Learning Through Elementary School Physical Educa-

tion. Dubuque, Iowa: William C. Brown Company, Publishers, 1974. Relates physical and intellectual development.

Kirchner, Glenn, *Physical Education for Elementary School Children,* 3d ed. Dubuque, Iowa: William C. Brown Company, Publishers, 1974. Textbook for a comprehensive program.

Knowledges and Understandings in Physical Education. Washington, D.C.: The American Association for Health, Physical Education and Recreation, 1973. Establishes a cognitive base for physical education.

MacLean, J., *Leisure Time and the Year 2000—Recreation in a Modern Society.* Boston: Holbrook Press, Inc., 1972. Relates the potential problem of increased leisure time to the physical education program.

Miller, Dean F., *School Health Programs: Their Basis in Law.* Cranberry, N.J.: A. S. Barnes & Company, Inc., 1972. Identifies the significant laws and court rulings which are important for health programs.

Sorochan, Walter D., and Stephen J. Bender, *Teaching Elementary Health Science.* Reading, Mass.: Addison-Wesley Publishing Company, Inc., 1975. A textbook for a comprehensive health education program.

Trends in Elementary School Physical Education. Washington, D.C.: The American Association for Health, Physical Education and Recreation, 1972. Reports the promising practices.

Vanner, Maryhelen, *Teaching Health in Elementary Schools.* Philadelphia: Lea & Febiger, 1974. Comprehensive textbook in health education.

Willgoose, Carl E., *Health Education in the Elementary School.* Philadelphia: W. B. Saunders Company, 1974. Health science textbook stressing instruction.

chapter 12

Inquiring
AESTHETIC ARTS

The adventurous creative life is lived in that no-man's-land between instinct and thought, between feelings and concepts, between emotions and ideas, between shadow and light, between reverie and reason. As the poet Carl Sandburg asked: When does this "borderland of dream and logic, fantasy and reason, where the roots and tentacles of mind and personality float and drift" suddenly crystalize in the shape of "a scheme, a form, a design, an invention, a machine, an image, a song, a symphony, a drama, a poem?"

William Fleming, *Arts and Ideas,* 3d ed. (New York: Holt, Rinehart and Winston, Inc., 1968), p. viii.

When the inner drive toward that which is beautiful, pleasing, and comfortable is combined with the equally powerful drive for exploring, discovering, and performing, a powerful humanizing sum is obtained—the visual and performing arts. These arts permeate every aspect of life, from the most primitive to the most advanced society. The challenge to educators is to use these drives to contribute to the maximum development of children—to their learning power, to their aesthetic sense, to their humanism, to their awareness, to their confidence, and to their understanding of their environment.

Today, few people seriously challenge the idea that the aesthetic arts belong in the elementary school curriculum. Music and art are no longer looked upon as peripheral subjects designed for a few pupils with exceptional talents or for those who expect to become professional musicians or artists; they are regarded as general education subjects—subjects which are important for every citizen in our society.

AESTHETIC EDUCATION

In 1965 the United States Congress created "The National Endowment for the Arts" as part of the "National Foundation on the Arts and the Humanities." This endowment allocated private as well as government funds, matching grants-in-aid, to the fifty states, the District of Columbia, the Virgin Islands,

420

Guam, and Puerto Rico to develop programs, facilities, and services at the community level. This legislation was the result of public demand and a recognized need for developing a society possessing artistic awareness. One of the six precepts in the design is to "Encourage imaginative art programs in the field of education." The Commission on the Humanities stated in its document submitted to Congress, "The United States is not a materialistic nation, but many men believe it to be. They find it hard to fathom the motives of a country which will spend billions on its outward defenses and at the same time do little to maintain the creative and imaginative abilities of its own people. The arts have an unparalled capability for crossing the national barriers imposed by language and contrasting customs."[1]

Specific to public education, Title III of the Elementary and Secondary Education Act likewise opened the door for greater effort on the part of educators to provide cultural experiences for children in the classroom and out of the classroom. These actions resulting from government awareness of a need for strengthening aesthetic attitudes have in turn expanded a social awareness of the need. Educators in the visual and performing arts have made strides in introducing experiences in the general curriculum which will provide children, all children, with greater sensitivity for that which is aesthetic in quality, and with the ability to perform, relate, and produce with better understanding and skill.

The case for the visual and performing arts in the elementary curriculum is founded on commitment to the principles of perception and exploration—to the recognition that greater learning takes place as more senses are involved in the process. Sensory emphasis, basic to the arts, helps children become alert, aware, inquisitive, responsible, and able to interact with others.

> When we speak of perception, we usually mean those physical and mental processes through which we come to know "what is." Using this knowledge, we can learn to interact with other people, and with the objects and events of our environment. We can also say that if input is relevant to output, then as our ability to perceive is improved, so might our ability to interact be improved.[2]

Objectives

Teaching for learning in the arts becomes a matter of teaching for child awareness. It means introducing vitality into teaching and bringing about a vital response in the learning process. The experiences provided in the curriculum should be designed to insure "aesthetic awareness," "creative awareness," "human awareness," "communication awareness," and "selection awareness."

Aesthetic Awareness

Aesthetic awareness has become almost a matter of survival as aesthetic values are associated with the behaviors of humans. Appreciation for both the

---

1 Commission on the Humanities, "Federal Funds and Services for the Arts." (Washington, D.C.: Superintendent of Documents, Cata. No. Fs 5.250:50050, U.S. Government Printing Office, 1967), Introduction.
2 Roy Behrens, "Perception in the Visual Arts," Art Education (March 1969), p. 12.

beliefs and products of humans are tied so closely to individual participation and understanding that to discontinue efforts to educate for cultural sensitivity is risky. The schools are the only institutions universally compulsory and available which can set the patterns for an aesthetically enlightened society. Schools need to clearly define expectations, and to provide the environment and opportunity for independent thinking. They need to be consistent, realistic, and current in expectations. They need to utilize the services of the community, the music, art, dance and drama centers, and the architecture and sculpture. They need to utilize all types of media, printed and nonprinted, as a vast wealth of inspiration to culturally reinforce classroom experiences.

Creative Awareness

Rightfully, creativity is no longer associated only with the arts. The creative mind applied to any human enterprise flourishes in performance; it is the desirable end result of the procedures used in the teaching–learning process. The task is to approach the teaching of the arts in such a way that freedom of expression is the inevitable outcome. The opportunities for a variety of experiences, and of materials and facilities, must be provided. Teachers must become learners as well as teachers in the exploration of media and principles. The environment must be conducive to exploration and discovery. Kids must be turned on, not off. Creative guidance begets creativity. The art processes and media are ideal tools for providing creative experiences in the curriculum.

Human Awareness

The most personal function of the human organism is the expression of oneself. All children have the capacity to express themselves in one way or other, but it is not a capacity that flourishes in a humanistically unaware environment. The visual and performing arts are vehicles for developing self-identity, and are outlets for humanism, for social awareness, ". . . we ought not to compete with the computers or make computers out of students. What is needed is to stress the qualities that make us unique, our humanity."[3]

To paint, print, or sculpt the environment and the beings in it without understanding them is impossible. To write, compose, sing, dance, or instrumentalize successfully without sensory awareness, without great human sensitivity, is impossible. There are many skills of expression to be acquired, all of which are specific to the particular art form, but all forms of expression must seek the people, the creatures, the world around, the times, events, and relationships. Because the arts can function only as an expression of and about all life, they become in education one of our greatest contributions to the growth, learning, and development of children, to the human understanding that might very well be the factor that perpetuates our society and directs its ultimate ordering.

---

[3] Arthur W. Combs, *Humanizing Education: The Person in the Process.* (Washington, D.C.: Association for Supervision and Curriculum Development, 1967), p. 75.

Communication Awareness

More than ever before due to the advance of visual media, people are feeling the impact of the arts and are communicating with each other through the arts. The visual has become almost a necessary adjunct to the audio. Producing and performing artists, their works, their ideas, their personalities, their skills, attributes, and idiosyncrasies are real members of the fireside family. Education is utilizing this phenomenon in the use of teaching media, but educators must do much more to guide children in understanding what they see, hear, and express, in addition to the resulting relationships. A balanced curriculum should include the entire spectrum of communication experiences, painting, sculpting, printing, weaving, embroidering, constructing, singing, photographing, instrumentalizing, dancing, writing, reading, speaking, role-playing, and perhaps other forms waiting for innovation.

Each art form of communication is distinct in that certain unique functions are necessary to the child's performance of it. However, all forms proceed from perception through understanding, performance, and judgment to the children's own expressions of themselves, their environment, and all their experiences. To withhold these opportunities for self-expression is to withhold education.

The aesthetic arts are the means of recapitulating the expressions of the human race in any social era. "Because Art is a means of communication from one generation to another, it establishes a continuity in the culture. It is a form of security as one recognizes the familiar forms of his environment."[4]

Selection Awareness

Not all children will become dramatists, writers, musicians, dancers, sculptors, or painters, but all children will take their places in a material-oriented society with an increasing amount of leisure. Because of the influence of our mass media, a generation of people could very well be indoctrinated into a common acceptance of that which they see and hear the most, or that which makes the most vivid first impression. It would be a risky business for education to step back and permit the molding of a social image that would encourage the disappearance of selectivity and original expression from the culture. The arts might prove to be the catalyst necessary to influence material production of universally pleasing and acceptable forms.

The arts have always been important in the lives of people, in every culture and time, but never before have they been so accessible to the masses. Because of this factor alone they become a curriculum responsibility. Howard Conant and Arne Randall said pertinently, "Art would have no significant place in education, unless it had a place in the lives of everyone."[5]

[4] Mary M. Packwood (Ed.), *Art Education in the Elementary School*. (Washington, D.C.: National Art Education Association, Department of NEA, 1967), p. 8.
[5] Howard Conant and Arne Randall, *Art in Education*. (Peoria, Ill.: Chas. A. Bennett Co., Inc., 1959), p. 5.

If it is believed that art is everywhere, the school becomes responsible for the awesome task of educating for knowledge of the arts, understanding the arts, producing the arts, and perhaps most important—educating for ability to make selections and choices which, when multiplied a thousand-fold and perpetuated, will live in grace and dignity. To select is a normal function for even the very young, if we provide the opportunities. "An individual develops his taste as he is exposed to art experiences—both as an observer and as one who makes works of art. Gradually he becomes more critical in his like-dislike behavior. . . . Because taste is developed from many sources, it will reflect one's background of experience. . . . The schools can be a center for raising the level of public taste, understanding, and appreciation of the arts."[6]

Every individual ultimately is called upon to select a home, furnishings, decor, and automobile. Individuals are called upon to make social decisions which may be necessary to the cultural welfare of a society, but which infringe on their own desires. Commitments are part of the selective process. Few subject areas have greater potential for offering a myriad of choices.

Experience Awareness

Through the visual and performing arts, children should have vicarious and direct experiences in

1. sharpening sensory perceptions. (See movement and perceptual-motor sections in Chapter 11.)
2. fostering spontaneity of expression. (See dramatics section in Chapter 7.)
3. being individualized in the allowance of simple or complex behaviors. (See inquiry section in Chapter 5.)
4. allowing for an increase in the range of media. (See materials section in Chapter 6.)
5. involving all behaviors of the psychomotor, affective, and cognitive domains. (See objectives section in Chapter 5.)

SITUATION 12.1 List ten aesthetic education concepts students should have formulated before entering middle-schools or its equivalent.

CURRICULUM APPROACHES

This section describes the approaches involved in organizing the school, the environment, and the curriculum in the two broad areas of aesthetic education: visual and performing arts.

Visual Arts

Probably the most significant advance in the visual arts in the past decade is the widespread acceptance that learning does not take place by using patterns

[6] Packwood, *Art Education*, p. 13.

or making something with exclusive emphasis on the end product. Art is a subject, a process, a skill development. It has its own unique understandings, and art educators recognize that when properly taught, it is for all children an adventure into perception and awareness. Even when using art media and techniques to reinforce learnings in what is termed "content experiences," these experiences are strengthened by applying visual concepts of order and arrangement. The art of making an experience visual can become the criterion for judging the degree of understanding gained through the experience.

Teacher

Who is to teach art in the elementary school is a decision subject to the organizational structure of the school. The organization of a school or school system is determined by the educational philosophy to which the school is committed. Many schools strongly believe that integrated experiences in a homelike environment with a quality teacher can do a better job of individualizing, providing guidance, and achieving total development. This means that most elementary teachers are responsible for the art experiences their children receive.

As in all subjects basic to the general education of children, the elementary teacher needs to acquire the understandings and skills necessary for the subject. This is no simple task, but neither is it an impossible one. Understanding the content is paramount; with this understanding, subject correlations and relationships are a natural outcome. Various devices are used by schools and school systems to assist teachers to gain security in all areas of education, including the visual arts. Workshops are held, usually with no cost to teachers. Televised lessons are broadcast. Colleges and universities offer special teaching courses in the summer and in-service opportunities during the school terms. Helping teachers are provided. Curriculum guidelines are made available. All manner of good films and audiovisual aids are within the grasp of the quality teacher. There is a constant upgrading of art books, pamphlet texts, and work sheets. Publishers now are using the discovery approach in the visual arts, as in other curriculum areas.

The greatest problem the elementary school special art teacher has is to achieve a specialized art education. At the same time the teacher must have sufficient depth in elementary school preparation to enable art instruction to function on the levels of development appropriate and natural to children, while effectively achieving learning correlation. The demand for the special elementary art teacher has not been too great. Team teaching is a possible solution —the depth specialist working with the generalist.

Environment

Modern elementary school classroom designs include running water, sink, and storage areas, ideal for maintaining an art center in the classroom. In some buildings the materials center provides the equipment and materials for art activities and checks out these supplies to the classroom teachers. Some have art carts available to the teachers. In buildings that were constructed prior to these innovations, teachers find that plastic buckets for water are easy to carry and store; many art activities do not require water.

An art corner in any style of classroom can be an inspiration to children. In such an area reproductions of masterpieces, published articles, artifacts, and children's work may be kept on display. Varied materials should be available. Boxes should be provided to hold scraps of fabric, yarn, string, burlap, and felt. Another container should provide wood, plastic, wire, screen, and tile. All leftover scraps of decorative papers should be saved for display and construction purposes. The color sections of magazines are effective for collage. The ad sections of the newspapers are fine for painting. The teacher needs to have paints, brushes, paste, glue, scissors, tapestry needles, crayons, colored chalk, masking tape, brayers (ink rollers), inks, and many other media accessible to children. The visual arts are concerned with the feel of things as well as the sound and sight of things. The trend in the visual arts is toward three-dimensional presentation. Children, as do adults, enjoy the shapes of things free standing, in relief, and in mobiles. The emphasis is upon many media and mixed media.

Appreciation Studies

Great strides have been made in the area of art appreciation since the days of picture study exclusively concentrated on the old masters and their works. There has been a change from the chronological, historical approach to art that parallels this same change in social studies to contemporary problem solving with emphasis upon the activities of man, past and present. Artists in the community and at community institutions for the visual arts are offering many opportunities for classroom teachers to utilize their services. Film publishers are creating appropriate, accurate, and beautiful media for use by elementary teachers. A number of artists series published in book form are suitable for elementary school children. Reading and maturity levels in the choice of subjects are being given consideration. Publishers are providing a wealth of beautifully printed art reproductions in individual study and classroom sizes at minimal costs.

"Art doing" lessons should be taught in such a way that related artifacts and reproductions of master artists' and artisans' work are included. Relating the child's efforts to works of art, past and present, helps bring about the recognition of relationships, spreads the cultural base, and develops sensitive awareness to that which is beautiful in the environment.

Instructional Programs

The best art instruction is centered around valid experiences and activities in which children are involved, and want to express visually. When the teacher selects the outcome prior to setting the stage for the lesson development, the results will be copies, less real, and without total learning. When the children are permitted to explore potential production in light of the idea they have achieved, desirable art understandings and skills become important and worthy of exploration. The teacher's task is to guide the youngsters, and provide the opportunity, environment, and facilities to help them learn to

perceive.
use and understand art language.
recognize the names of artists and their art creations.
judge and select.
use tools and materials.
produce art objects.
experience behaviors like those of artists.

SITUATION 12.2   If you, as an intermediate elementary teacher, could select only ten tactile art media with which to provide students experiences (for example, paint, clay), list those you would choose. Then eliminate five of those you chose. Write brief criteria statements which justify the removal of each of the five media you eliminated from the list.

Every lesson requires (1) preparation specific to the particular lesson, and (2) an organizational plan for distribution of the materials necessary to the production. There must be an adequate number of tools, which are appropriate to the physical maturity of the children, so that thought and selection will not be interrupted in the search for needed tools.

Lessons should be designed to emphasize and realize certain encompassing conceptual understandings: surface, form and shape, arrangement, and variety. Color permeates all of these. Whether color is used to change a surface, define a shape, indicate a form, help in an arrangement, or offer variety in media and impact is a matter of choice. All these concepts may also be developed without color. However, it is important that every child have the opportunity to produce art pieces with an awareness of the part played by these conceptual areas. Gradually, with lesson following lesson and each building on previous understandings, the child gains in judgment and aesthetic appreciation, and understands why one process or medium is superior to another.

Evaluation

The most meaningful evaluation in the art program is that which the teacher provides along with the child during art production, and that which class groups perform in discussion and enjoyment of each other's work under the teacher's guidance. If a warning is necessary in the consideration of children's art work, it is not to inflict adult judgment on the children as they express themselves.

Teachers need to observe well and acquire a sensitive realization of the quality of painting, constructing, cutting, pasting, tearing, molding, and sewing children can attain at certain levels of intellectual and manipulative ability. If a principle is involved, it should be applied during and after the expression, and not in isolation or as a criticism. For example, contrasts can be observed by children as they notice the little girl in the light blue sweater standing next to the little girl in the dark red dress. Evaluation is part of the teaching–learning process.

Teachers should never encourage copying pictures that adults have achieved in the works of art and illustrations available to children in such great numbers today, nor should they apply criteria appropriate to adult production. Such practices gradually diminish confidences, self-expression, and creativity.

If the giving of grades is necessary, the system chosen should measure only those characteristics the teacher has actually presented. This system might include categories such as manipulative skills, controlling media, completing projects, working well with others, taking care of equipment and materials, art language, and making better choices.

As in any other learning of content, it is most important that teachers determine what art experiences children should have in order to accomplish the goals desired. Evaluation decisions must be directly related to the program of experiences provided.

SITUATION 12.3   What are the art competencies you believe students should possess before attending middle-school or its equivalent?

Performing Arts

Dance, drama, and music comprise the performing arts included within the curriculum of the modern elementary school. The performing arts are taught in elementary schools because of the contributions they make to those learnings considered essential to the general education of everyone. Burmeister identified three phases of general education to which the performing arts can make contributions: aesthetic growth, productive use of leisure time, and emotional development. He said, "In the plainest language possible, we like music because it makes us feel good."[7] If music, dance, and drama can make children feel good about their school, if the fun associated with the performing arts is not thwarted, they contribute to wholesome emotional development.

Children respond to the performing arts by their behaviors in three domains: affective, cognitive, and psychomotor. At the same time, however, these programs contribute a truly unique quality to the curriculum in that they create areas of aesthetic experience. To acquire the skills necessary to become more than superficially competent in music, dance, or drama—and thus become aesthetically involved—requires the formal training which the school can provide. The performing arts are therefore instrumental in the acquisition of individual, creative fulfillment.

No one who observes a normal child can fail to recognize that the performing arts have a strong appeal. Infants respond readily and happily to their

[7] C. A. Burmeister, "The Role of Music in General Education," in National Society for the Study of Education, *Basic Concepts in Music Education.* (Chicago: University of Chicago Press, 1958), p. 221.

mother's songs and lullabies; later, children express feelings in dance rhythm, play-acting and chants and melodies. If given guidance from adults who understand not only these activities, but children as well, the performing arts will continue to be a means of expressing feeling and enjoying what is beautiful in the world. Those who plan curriculum guides for elementary schools use what is known about various aspects of child development and the structure of the discipline which is called "the performing arts."

Child Development

Many concepts relating to child development and education were presented in Chapter 3. These concepts provide direction for those who plan the curriculum in the performing arts. The work of Piaget, Bruner, Skinner, Rogers, Kohlberg, Maslow, Erikson, and others has influenced the aesthetic education program. Certainly, there is much to be *learned* if the child is to gain proficiency in these areas. The curriculum planner needs to be well informed about the intellectual development of children. Since there is more to education than gaining information, the curriculum planner needs also to be well informed about the emotional and social development of children. Stated in different terminology, the curriculum in music, for example, should reflect the best that is known about cognitive and affective behavior. Aronoff commented on this idea as follows:

> It cannot be overemphasized that education is a dual process; its concern is for *affective together with cognitive growth. Ideas are not normally isolated from emotional context by the young child unless or until the child has been taught, directly or indirectly, to ignore or subdue his emotions as he concentrates on the accumulation of knowledge and concepts. He relates his cognitive and affective behaviors in musical expression, especially as he involves his whole body and his personal feelings of previous and current experiences. . . . Music experiences for young children can be planned on a cognitive basis and at the same time easily provide affective benefits; the child's involvement in his own movement and imagery will necessarily cause affective response.*[8]

More and more emphasis is being placed on discovery and creativity in the elementary performing arts program. Children are to take the concepts at their own levels and do something with them; right or wrong, they are to interact. Today's music programs are emphasizing the consideration of the physical and psychological aspects of children.

Social Development

The performing arts can also meet the needs of the individual's sense of self-worth, and completeness can be experienced through some mode of music, dance, or drama. As children discover their own responses to the performing arts and then learn to be creative, the resulting self-knowledge and self-expressions may lead to their personal fulfillment. These feelings of self-worth and

[8] Frances Webber Aronoff, *Music for the Young Child.* (New York: Holt, Rinehart and Winston, Inc., 1969), pp. 8–9.

acceptance can then lead to creative accomplishments which earn the respect of their peers.

One of the most urgent social needs of school children is the need for recognition and acceptance by the teacher and by classmates. The performing arts organization can provide a laboratory for social interaction and social development. For example, music can be used to help teachers work with children who have behavioral problems. The following incident could be duplicated in many elementary schools:

Music helped Matt to grow socially. He was a very aggressive five-year-old, eager for attention regardless of how it was gained. He swaggered up to Miss S. who was standing near the piano. "I'll bet you don't know 'Ten Little Indians,'" he boasted. The teacher smiled, sat down, and played the song. "Is that the song you mean?" Matt nodded. She replied, "Sing it with me." Together they sang several songs. Matt not only enjoyed singing but found in singing an acceptable form of recognition. Opportunities for music expression leave children with less need to release feelings in less acceptable ways.[9]

Teacher

Special teachers are often available in both vocal and instrumental music. Yet, the existence of these special teachers should not serve to segregate these performing arts from the classroom and the school. Although providing performances for audiences of peers and parents constitute one phase of music and the other performing arts, it is not until they extend, complement, and are complemented by the other curriculum areas that a comprehensive program exists. The number of instruments taught or the variety of vocal groups within a program do not alone comprise a comprehensive program.

If special teachers are not always available for the dance and drama areas of the performing arts curriculum, help may often be found among school personnel. A physical education teacher with background and experience in movement education can easily team with a classroom teacher to provide a simple but sound program in dance. Many times, private dance teachers will volunteer their services to help the physical education and/or classroom teacher with the various dance forms. Help in drama can be found in resource personnel outside the school. Yet, within the school staff there usually are teachers who are proficient in the use of dramatization or of sociodrama in the language arts (see Chapter 7). With some support and positive reinforcement, classroom teachers can build an adequate program in drama.

Environment

Other than the practice rooms appropriate for aspects of the vocal and instrumental programs, special facilities are not required for the performing arts. In fact, the performing arts can contribute in significant ways to the

[9] Sarah Lou Hammond, Ruth J. Dale, Dora S. Skipper, and Ralph L. Witherspoon, *Good Schools for Young Children.* (New York: Crowell Collier and Macmillan, Inc., 1963), pp. 282–283.

lightening, brightening, and creative utilization of existing spaces. For example, a stage does not make a dramatization, but a dramatization makes a stage. Existing spaces, classrooms, physical education areas, outdoors, and indoors, corridors, and similar areas are all adaptable to the space needs of dance.

Specially designed facilities for musical groups, dramatic activities, and dance movements are valuable, and do contribute to the enhancement of a performing arts curriculum. Yet, the existence of any one of these programs is not dependent upon special facilities. The availability of equipment however, is a crucial problem. The performing arts require a wide and varied range of equipment (for example, pianos, lumber, tumbling mats, rhythm instruments, paint, exercise bars, dressing rooms, costumes, scraps of material, wigs).

Regardless of its physical aspects, the essential requirement of the environment is one of attitude—an attitude of awareness, sensitivity to products and their creators, and creativeness on the part of the instructional staff. All provide the foundation for a comprehensive performing arts program which will serve to model the desired behaviors.

Instructional Programs

In vocal and instrumental music, the five elements of music (pitch, texture, timbre, dynamics, and duration) should form the foci of instruction. These parameters, or elements, of music should be experienced through the combination of the three media of music: instrument, performer, and composition. An instrument functions as a medium which provides a tool for the conveyance of organized sound. The instruments typically associated with the elementary school music program are: autoharp, tonettes, voice, rhythm sticks, drums, bells, tone blocks, instrumental bands, and oatmeal box tom-toms. The modern elementary school should also provide learners with experience involving tape recordings of orchestra, bassoon, viola, harmonica, and guitar as part of the general education program for all students. Either these recordings or "live" performances are used to demonstrate that the performer functions as a medium which controls the instrument and the interpretation of the composition, and that the composition functions as a medium which provides a language system to guide the performer. The composition can be in a recorded form, a written notation form, a creative form guided by a set of instructions to the performer, or an improvised form guided by a unique, sound image in the mind of the performer.

The primary activity of dance is to explore movement as a self-expressive, creative activity which is both dependent on and independent of music. The social forms of dancing are ballroom, rock or popular, and folk. These dances are created by the culture to celebrate events, including the celebration of life and being. A study of these dances and the situations in which they occur will often provide powerful insights into the nature of a society (its concerns, its mores, its role definitions, and other characteristics). The involvement in and study of ballet, a more formal dance form, and contemporary (modern) dance allows not only creative, self-expressive experiences for the participant, but also develops insights into the more formal aesthetic activities of a society. It further provides opportunities for the participant to operate at the highest levels within the psychomotor domain. The contemporary (modern) dance form is a form often independent of music. If music accompanies the dance, it is designed to follow rather than direct the movement, as it is used in ballet or ballroom dancing. Modern dance follows whatever rhythms and emotions the participant feels and translates into movement. All dancing forms employ the psychomotor domain to express, release, and transmit the behaviors of both cognitive and affective domains.

Children's drama, whether formal theater or informal creative dramatics, comprise: characterization, plot, theme, action, dialogue, emotional conflict, and/or crisis, style, and form. The elements of the story of the play are characterization, plot, and theme, which are displayed and presented through action and dialogue. What the characters do or say is governed by the emotional conflict or crisis. The unique manner in which a play reveals its character, plot, theme, and emotional conflict or crisis is the style or form of the play. Creative dramatics refers to creative role playing developed around an idea, incident, event, or person. It emphasizes the elements of characterization, action, and dialogue while unfolding in a spontaneous manner—sometimes fragmented, but fun.

SITUATION 12.4   What are the drama competencies you believe students should possess before attending middle-school or its equivalent? What are the dance competencies you believe students should possess before attending middle-school or its equivalent?

Evaluation

As with the visual arts, evaluation should focus on the process behaviors of the participants rather than the product. It should stress only those elements of the performing arts that have been specifically taught and previously experienced by the doer, performer, or learner. The product is a shared activity, with the intents and values of the performance shaping the major focus of the evaluation.

The program itself should be evaluated from two perspectives. First, is it an adequate representation of the elements or parameters of music, dance, and dramatization? Secondly, is it truly a general education program? The performing arts are to be experienced by all children, not just the especially talented children who choose to participate in performing groups such as the band or orchestra. Such statements are not intended to deemphasize the value of performing groups, but to remind the reader that, as in physical education, performing arts must first generate a broadly based, general education program with every child a winning participant.

SITUATION 12.5   Visual and performing arts are the intimate fibers which bond together the dreams, visions, perceptions, imagination, senses, and in some instances the ultimate expression and communication from an individual. How can the evaluative processes of students' interactions with the visual and performing arts respect and honor the fragility and privacy of creativity?

PROGRAMS

The choices available to the modern elementary school for the selection of innovative program models for the aesthetic arts have increased considerably in the past few years. The author predicts that the range of the model programs in the aesthetic arts will increase at an increasingly rapid pace during the next few years. Some of the model activities are supported by local funds, others by monies from private foundations, and a few are federally supported. The following sections will briefly discuss some of the innovative models.

CEMEREL, Inc.

The Central Midwestern Regional Educational Laboratory of St. Louis, Missouri, has designed a comprehensive aesthetic education program[10] (CEMEREL) to present the aesthetic qualities of all the arts and to focus upon the impact of these qualities in daily life. The programs are packaged in classroom kits designed to be used by teachers as well as art specialists. Each kit contains materials for thirty children, including all audiovisual aids and equipment.

The CEMEREL program is divided into four major areas:

I. *Introduction to Aesthetic Phenomena.* This area includes work involving the basic physical elements of the arts, that is, light, sound, motion, time, and shape.

II. *Elements in the Art Disciplines and the Environment.* Kits in this area provide for interaction with elements within the arts, including texture in music, shape in visual art, and patterns of conflict in drama.

III. *Process of Transformation.* Included in this area are kits designed to lead the student through the creative process of synthesizing aesthetic and physical elements into a work of art.

IV. *People in the Arts.* This series of kits is designed to help students understand who artists are, what they do, and the processes they use.

Although the kits are graded by the publisher, the grade levels are extremely flexible. Those identified as being for primary grades have been used successfully with children from third grade through junior high. The materials are high in aesthetic qualities, high in interest levels, and adaptable to different situations.

[10] *Aesthetic Education Program.* (St. Louis, Mo.: CEMEREL, Inc., 1971).

They include comprehensive teacher's guides as well as pre- and posttests to help evaluate the progress of the pupils.

SITUATION 12.6   What are the music competencies you believe students should possess before attending middle-school or its equivalent?

IMPACT

Project IMPACT (Interdisciplinary Model Program in the Arts for Children and Teachers) was initiated in 1970 by the U.S. Office of Education in cooperation with four associations concerned with the arts: The Dance Division of the American Association for Health, Physical Education and Recreation; The American Educational Theatre Association; The National Art Association; and The Music Educators National Conference.[11] Five school districts were selected to develop a model school program which was to be art-centered. The chosen sites were located in Alabama, California, Ohio, Oregon, and Pennsylvania.

The broad objectives of Project IMPACT were to

1. reconstruct the educational program and the administrative climate of the schools in an effort to achieve parity between the arts and the other instructional areas, as well as between the affective and cognitive learnings provided in the total school program.
2. develop educational programs of high artistic quality in the visual and performing arts.
3. conduct in-service programs for the training of teachers, administrators, and other school personnel in the implementation of programs into the school curriculum which exemplify high aesthetic and artistic quality.
4. develop ways for infusing the arts into all aspects of the school curriculum for the purpose of enhancing and improving the quality and quantity of aesthetic education offered; and thus, provide a principal means for affective learning experiences within the total school program.
5. utilize a number of outstanding artists, performers, and educators from outside the school system for the purpose of heightening the quality of the art experiences for children.[12]

An evaluation of IMPACT by a general self-reporting survey concluded that

1. students learned the basics at least as well as before, and in some instances better.
2. there was no indication of a direct transfer of skills from learning music notation to learning arithmetic.

[11] Gene C. Wenner, "Project IMPACT," *Music Educators Journal*, Vol. LIX, No. 5 (January 1973), p. 29.

[12] David Boyle and Robert L. Lathrop, "The IMPACT Experience: An Evaluation," *Music Educators Journal*, Vol. LIX, No. 5 (January 1973), pp. 42–47.

3. the climate of the classroom became more open, exciting, and challenging, with many unusual and innovative methods in all curriculum areas.
4. the enhancement of the students' self-concepts was reported as well as a reduction in dropouts and truancy.[13]

MMCP

The Manhattanville Music Curriculum Program (MMCP) has developed a curriculum for the teaching of music in the modern elementary school which identifies the structures of music, spirals the activities in a simple to complex sequence, and emphasizes the use of inquiry.[14] The structures (see Chapter 5) of music have been identified as timbre (tone quality), dynamics (loud–soft), duration (short–long and rhythmic elements), pitch (melody, harmony, and polyphony), and form. At each level of the MMCP, the pupil experiences activities involving each of these structures of music. The complexity of the activities increase as the pupil progresses from level to level (spiraling). The inquiry method (exploration, invention, and discovery) is described as musical discovery, invention, and composition. Musical discovery activities are those of exploration; musical inventions are those of invention; and musical compositions are those discovery activities of directing a behavior based upon previous explorations and inventions (see Methodology, Chapter 5).

The MMCP curriculum for children ages 3 through 8 is "MMCP Interaction: Early Childhood Music Curriculum"; and for children ages 9 and above, "MMCP Synthesis."[15] Both curriculums are similar in design to that described above, and both stress the activities of composing, conducting, performing, and evaluating music. The MMCP curriculum exemplifies the application of the strategy described in Chapter 5 to the building of a music curriculum.

Music should be the discovery of musical sound—what it is like, what produces it, how [one] might respond to it, how it is organized, and how [one] might manipulate it. On [one's] level [one] is a researcher (young musicologist), writer of music (composer), a listener (analyst and critic), and a performer of music.[16]

SITUATION 12.7   Given the five parameters of music—pitch, duration, timbre, texture, and dynamics—find or create one musical experience for elementary students which will increase understanding of and involve direct interaction with each of the five parameters.

---

13 "Overtones," *Music Educators Journal*, Vol. LIX, No. 5 (January 1973), p. 5.
14 Robert E. Nye and Vernice T. Nye, *Essentials of Teaching Elementary School Music.* (Englewood Cliffs, N.J.: Prentice-Hall, Inc., 1974).
15 Manhattanville Music Curriculum Program. (Media Materials, Inc., P.O. Box 533, Bardonia, N.Y.: 10954).
16 Robert E. Nye and Vernice T. Nye, *Music in the Elementary School.* (Englewood Cliffs, N.J.: Prentice-Hall, Inc., 1970), p. 12.

Orff System

Developed in Germany by Carl Orff, the Orff system of music education involves children in singing, movement, and the playing of rhythmic, melodic percussion instruments.[17] Among the instruments used most consistently are the soprano and alto glockenspiel, the soprano and alto metalophone, a six-stringed viola da gamba, and a bordun (bass two-stringed instrument) are also used. The Orff system stresses the active participation of children as they inquire into the correlation of singing, rhythmic activities, and instrumental performances.[18]

Kodály Method

This method developed by Zoltan Kodály in Hungary, where music is a major part of the school program, employs folk and ethnic music from a variety of cultures.[19] The method stresses composition, movement, dance, and improvisation. The recorder and percussion instruments are used most often.[20]

Suzuki Talent Education

The Talent Education Program, developed in Japan by Shinichi Suzuki, is specifically designed for teaching the violin to young children.[21] Movement, very much like that of movement education (see Chapter 11), provides the basis of Suzuki's approach. The three general elements are parent, teacher, and pupil involvement; imitation, exploration, and freedom; and physical movement as a basis of learning.[22]

ISSUES

Although activities such as competency-based instruction, behavioral objectives, and accountability are issues in the aesthetic arts (as with other curriculum areas), the fundamental issues, in the opinion of this author, seem to be (1) performance, and (2) separate versus correlated versus interrelated programs.

Performance

Certainly within a comprehensive aesthetic arts program in the modern elementary school, performance is an unreal issue. It arises when practices do not follow what is known—the existence of performing groups (band, orchestra, chorus) for the especially talented pupils, while others are not provided oppor-

[17] Irving Cheyette and Herbert Cheyette, *Teaching Music Creatively in the Elementary Schools.* (New York: McGraw-Hill Book Company, Inc., 1969), pp. 355–356.
[18] Orff-Schulwerk, *Music for Children Series.* (New York: Associated Music Publishers, 1960).
[19] Mary Helen Richards, *Threshold to Music.* (San Francisco: Fearon Publishers, 1964).
[20] Cheyette and Cheyette, p. 357.
[21] Alfred Garson, "Suzuki and Movement Education," *Music Educators Journal*, Vol. LX, No. 4 (December 1973), pp. 34–37.
[22] John W. Kendall, *Listen and Play.* (Evanston, Ill.: Summy-Birchard Company, 1961).

tunities to experience music. Such a problem is similar to the situation in the physical education program when athletics dominate and sometimes even eliminate intramural activities and a basic physical education program. A comprehensive program involves all pupils in each of the aesthetic arts, regardless of the external judgments of their products and performances.

Separate versus Correlated versus Interrelated Programs

Again, modern programs tend to be either correlated among themselves or interrelated with other curriculum areas. Careless practices are sometimes perpetuated and thereby may separate the components of a naturally correlated aesthetic arts program, and present them in an artificially discrete manner. The failure to interrelate the aesthetic arts with other curriculum areas can occur when either the aesthetic arts are not correlated with each other or the other curriculum areas are not correlated and interrelated. Programs such as IMPACT demonstrate the value and educational profit derived from a correlated and interrelated aesthetic arts program.

SITUATION 12.8   Parallel the processes of beginning reading programs or beginning reading-readiness programs with the processes of each of the following: The development of
1. visual perceptions in art.
2. aural perceptions in music.
3. oral facility in drama.
4. balance and physical coordination in dance.

INTERDISCIPLINARY APPROACHES

This section discusses those programs which possess the potential to interrelate the aesthetic arts curriculum area with other curriculum areas. The strategies of values-clarification and the activities of career awareness are discussed.

Values-Clarification Strategies

The literature of the aesthetic arts states the purposes of the arts in various ways, usually a fundamental reference is made to, say, the valuing of music or the value of music to the self-esteem, confidence, and expression of the individual. Yet, a review of the same literature did not, for this author, provide evidence of an awareness of the contribution of Kohlberg, Maslow, Piaget, and others who have provided generalizations useful for values-clarification.

The importance of self-expression and creativeness to the individual's development is unquestionably related to the freedom and knowledge potentially available from the aesthetic arts. Could not the aesthetic arts capitalize upon those strengths which seem inherent within their areas, and at the same time utilize, in a more overt manner, the values-clarification strategies? For example, music as therapy is commonly used at a very sophisticated level.[23] A leading theorist in music therapy, E. Thayer Gaston, believed creative expression is possible for all:

> ... *man cannot escape the formation of esthetic constructs. The great potential of his nervous system takes him beyond bare animal adaptation. Furthermore esthetic experience may be one of the best devices to help him adjust and adapt to his environment.*[24]

Career-Awareness Activities

The opportunities for career-awareness activities within the aesthetic arts curriculum are numerous. The most obvious is the preparation of an individual for a vocational career. Equally obvious is the preparation of. an individual as an aesthetically aware consumer—one who values beauty in design, form, function, color, and so forth. Equally important, but not always so obvious, is the avocational use of the aesthetic arts as an individual uses leisure time in productive, creative, and self-expressive ways. One primary aspect of a fully developed career-awareness program is self-awareness, including the knowledge and acceptance of the uniqueness of oneself. The aesthetic arts make a functional and primary input into these activities of a career-awareness program.

STRATEGY OF INSTRUCTION

This section illustrates the applicability of the strategy of instruction (presented in Chapter 5) to the aesthetic arts.

Selection of Content

The newer curriculum programs within the aesthetic arts have made significant efforts to identify the organizing concepts and structures of a particular art area. Potentially, the ideas of movement may serve to increase the unity of the arts, among themselves and with the other curriculum areas. For example, recall the functioning of movement in dance, drama, and now in the Suzuki method for teaching violin. Also recall the importance of movement education to a comprehensive physical education program. Although great progress has been made in the aesthetic arts program, much is yet to be done in areas such as: interrelating the arts; selecting works of art to transmit cultural heritage; and providing for the experiences which serve the individual as a consumer, and as a avocational user and producer of art.

Learning and Development

The relationships between Piaget's stages of intellectual development and the stages of representation within a child's art works were discussed by Lowen-

---

[23] William W. Sears, "Processes in Music Therapy," in E. Thayer Gaston (Ed.), *Music in Therapy.* (New York: Crowell Collier and Macmillan, Inc., 1968), p. 15.
[24] Sears, p. 15.

feld and Brittain.[25] They concluded, "Although Piaget's stages are for intellectual development, it isn't surprising to find the same stages in art."[26]

The application of Piaget's stages of development to other areas of the aesthetic arts is just beginning. Presently, each of the arts has a description of the general progress which children make as they interact with the area in a simple-to-complex sequence.

Other than the practice for individuals and performing groups, the dominant theory of learning appears to have been derived from the field theories (see Chapter 3). The forming and shaping of perceptions, followed by conscious directing of behaviors guided by these perceptions, is the focus of the field theory learning in the aesthetic arts.

Methodology

The processes identified as inquiry in Chapter 5 seem to characterize the methodological approaches of the newer curriculum models in the aesthetic arts, (for example, see the preceding discussion of the methodology of the MMCP). Inquiry in dance and drama occurs as the individual is guided to experience future experiences.

Communication

The newer programs stress the behaviors of doing, modeling, analyzing, and discussing. All these behaviors or procedures would serve to increase the amount of communication from pupils to other pupils and from pupils to teachers, thus decreasing the amount of teacher communication. It should be noted that the newer programs advise the teacher to serve as a facilitator, who asks about other possibilities, inquires about "why," and questions about intent, rather than serves as one who "tells" the learners.

Objectives

The drive to strengthen both cognitive and affective impacts of the aesthetic arts seems common to the newer programs. Also, there is a growing awareness of the importance of the psychomotor domain, as evidenced by the emphasis on movement as the basis for learning.

Goals

The development of a self-actualizing person who interacts with competency and demonstrates pleasure with life through the aesthetic arts seems to be a goal statement that adequately summarizes the various statements of goals which are presented for the aesthetic arts.

[25] Viktor Lowenfeld and W. Lambert Brittain, *Creative and Mental Growth*, 6th ed. (New York: Crowell Collier and Macmillan, Inc., 1975), pp. 50–55.
[26] Lowenfeld and Brittain, p. 52.

SUMMARY

1. Teaching in the area of the aesthetic arts has become a matter of teaching for child awareness, aesthetic awareness, creative awareness, human awareness, communication awareness, selection awareness, and experience awareness.

2. The aesthetic arts are processes, skill developments, and adventures into perceptions and awareness. They are for all children.

3. The schools have the responsibility of educating for knowledge of the arts, understanding the arts, producing the arts, and developing the ability to make selections and choices.

4. Important tasks involved in education in the aesthetic arts includes developing teachers who have the needed understandings and skills; providing instructional space, materials, and supplies; developing effective teaching strategies; and providing for systematic evaluation of the program.

5. The instructional program in the aesthetic arts provides opportunities to learn to perceive; learn to use and understand the languages characteristic of the aesthetic arts; learn to recognize the names of artists and their art creations; learn to judge and select; learn to use tools and media; learn to produce art objects; and learn to experience in each of the three domains (cognitive, affective, and psychomotor) the behaviors common among artists.

6. Dance, drama, and music comprise the performing arts.

7. The organizing concepts of the performing arts include music (pitch, texture, timbre, dynamics, and duration), dance (movement, space-effort, and the correlation of the behaviors of the psychomotor, affective, and cognitive domains), and drama (character, plot, theme, action, dialogue, conflict or crisis, style, and form).

8. The aesthetic arts are beginning to interrelate among themselves and with other curriculum areas.

Problems and Projects

---

1. Beginning with the assumption that learning in aesthetic education is a process, select one elementary grade or level and write one high-energy cognitive objective and one high-energy affective objective which you consider to be of paramount importance in the teaching of aesthetic education. Accepting the assumption that there does exist interrelationships between cognitive, affective, and psychomotor domains, design for the grade or level in that grade two (one high-energy and one low-energy) psychomotor activities for each of the following content areas within the visual and performing arts: art, drama, and dance. Examine the psychomotor activities you designed and write a brief statement analyzing the interrelations between each activity, and the cognitive and/or affective objective written at the beginning of this problem and project.

2. A few years ago, a movement started in California to discontinue instruction in some of the aesthetic arts curriculum areas within the elementary public schools. Examine some recent statistics which compare university enrollments in fine arts

colleges to other colleges (for example, education, business, engineering). What are the implications of the statistics for aesthetic education within the elementary school?

3. Aesthetic education has been repeatedly delegated the responsibility of sophisticating the discriminating processes of the senses. We, as human creations, may choose to interact with the visual or performing arts as a participant and/or observer. For each aesthetic education curriculum area of music, art, drama, and dance, indicate those senses utilized by an observer and those senses utilized by a participant. In the comparison of the sensory/participant list and the sensory/observer list, are there implications for general educational instruction? Why or why not?

4. "Tone deaf," "monotone," "color blind," "uncoordinated"—all are labels which are assigned periodically to individuals lacking the possession or development of particular sensory perceptions. After investigating the definitions of the labels above, design two activities involving

    a. color for the child who is "color blind"; choose one for primary students and one for intermediate students.

    b. sound discrimination for the child who is "tone deaf."

    c. pitch variations for the child who is "monotone."

    d. balance and body manipulations for the child who is "uncoordinated."

What are the potential effects upon the child participating in the activities you designed? Evaluate the relevancy of these activities, and write objectives for each. What are your conclusions?

5. CEMEREL, Inc., provides a comprehensive aesthetic education program. Examine other curriculum packages on the market or other innovative aesthetic education pilot programs.

6. Examine basal readers and trade books for stories of children engaged in visual or performing arts experiences or activities. What percent of the stories depict a child taking part in the visual or performing arts? Ask five boys and five girls of elementary school age what careers they would like to follow. What percent of those asked were interested in a career in the visual or performing arts areas? Talk with ten university or college students (include five elementary education majors) who are not majoring in the fine arts. Ask each of these ten individuals to provide a brief characterization of a

    a. male music major.

    b. female music major.

    c. male art major.

    d. female art major.

    e. male dance major.

    f. female dance major.

    g. male drama major.

    h. female drama major.

Based upon the investigations suggested above, plus your own attitudes, what inventions can you develop? What can an elementary school do to support individuals who choose to embark upon a visual or performing arts career?

Selected Readings

Arnheim, Rudolf, *Art and Visual Perception*. Berkeley: University of California Press, 1974. Presents the stages of differentiation in visual perceptions.

Aronoff, Frances Webber, *Music and Young Children*. New York: Holt, Rinehart and Winston, 1969. Explains cognitive and affective development of children, the structure of music, the processes of musical growth; presents examples of music experiences and suggests procedures for evaluating pupil growth in music.

Cheyette, Irving, and Herbert Cheyette, *Teaching Music Creatively in the Elementary School*. New York: McGraw-Hill, Inc., 1969. Chapter 1 presents the developing of musical literacy in a sequence of ear to voice to eye.

Chocksy, Lois, *The Kodaly Method*. Englewood Cliffs, N.J.: Prentice-Hall, Inc., 1974. Provides a description of the Kodaly method.

Croft, Doreen J., and Robert D. Hess, *An Activities Handbook for Teachers of Young Children*. Boston: Houghton Mifflin Company, 1972.

Dewey, John, *Art as Experience*. New York: G. P. Putnam's Sons (Minton, Balch & Co.), 1934. Contains Dewey's statement on the value of aesthetic education.

Dimondstein, Geraldine, *Exploring the Arts with Children*. New York: Crowell Collier and Macmillan, Inc., 1974. Provides activities in painting, sculpturing, and dancing.

Eisner, Elliot W., *Educating Artist Vision*. New York: Crowell Collier and Macmillan, Inc., 1972. Chapter 5 presents the empirical studies of artistic learning.

Fleming, William, *Arts and Ideas: New and Brief Edition*. New York: Holt, Rinehart and Winston, Inc., 1974. Presents a history of art, music, literature, and ideas from the fifth century to the 1970s.

Gaitskell, Charles D., and Al Hurwitz, *Children and Their Art: Methods for the Elementary School*, 3d ed. New York: Harcourt Brace Jovanovich, Inc., 1975. Chapter 2 presents descriptions of sound and faulty teaching practices in art.

Greenberg, Marvin, and Beatrix MacGregor, *Music Handbook for the Elementary School*. Englewood Cliffs, N.J.: Parker Publishing Company, Inc. (Prentice-Hall, Inc.). Part I describes the elements of music.

Hurwitz, Al (Ed.), *Programs of Promise, Art in the Schools*. New York: Harcourt Brace Jovanovich, Inc., 1972. Readings exploring the various directions of art education.

Klotman, Robert R., *The School Music Administrator and Supervisor: Catalyst for Change in Music Education*. Englewood Cliffs, N.J.: Prentice-Hall, Inc., 1973. Handbook for the principal or supervisor of aesthetic education programs.

Lowenfeld, Viktor, and W. Lambert Brittain, *Creative and Mental Growth*, 6th ed. New York: Crowell Collier and Macmillan, Inc., 1975. Discusses the stages of maturation of children in regards to aesthetic education.

Nye, Robert E., and Vernice T. Nye, *Essentials of Teaching Elementary School Music*. Englewood Cliffs, N.J.: Prentice-Hall, Inc., 1974. Chapter 3 introduces strategies for the teaching of music.

Ritson, John E., and James A. Smith, *Creative Teaching of Art in the Elementary School*. Boston: Allyn and Bacon, Inc., 1975. Chapter 1 describes the nature of creative teaching.

Sheehy, Emma D., *Children Discover Music and Dance*. New York: Holt, Rinehart and Winston, 1959. Relates the teaching of dance and music.

Siks, Geraldine Brain, *Creative Dramatics: An Art for Children*. New York: Harper & Row, Publishers, 1958. Chapter 3 presents a discussion of the art elements of drama.

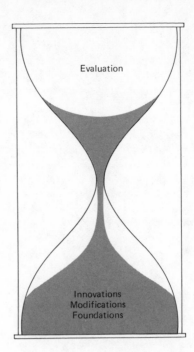

Evaluation

Innovations
Modifications
Foundations

Part 4

PERSPECTIVES for CURRICULUM

The preparation for the decisions which modify or maintain curriculum begin with a comprehensive evaluation activity. Part 4 explores the various aspects of evaluation.

chapter 13

Perceiving
EDUCATIONAL
EVALUATION

*If education is to serve youth and society under these new and very
fluid conditions, it is evident that schools and teachers must learn to work
in new ways . . . it is clear that both evaluation and teaching must undergo
marked transformation if they are to be adequate to the new demands
placed on them.*

Benjamin S. Bloom, J. Thomas Hastings, and George F. Madaus,
*Handbook on Formative and Summative Evaluation of Student
Learning.* (New York: McGraw-Hill, Inc., 1971), p. 6.

The innovations in curriculum and organization of the modern elementary
school are developing along lines quite different from those of the past. These
new approaches must understandably be paralleled by new approaches in the
processes of evaluation. New questions demand both a pruning and an expansion of the data that define, display, and interpret activities incorporated
within an evaluation system. Therefore, educational evaluation may be regarded
as a *system* of defining, gathering, displaying, and interpreting data relevant to
the objectives of instruction and/or education.

An evaluation system yields both a product and a process. The product of
the evaluation system is the fundamental and functional data utilized in the
decision-making activities concerning the accomplishment of objectives. The
process of the evaluation system is the involvement of personnel in the cycle
of selecting goals; identifying objectives; defining data; gathering data; displaying data; interpreting data; and decision making related to goals, objectives,
and the evaluation system. "Evaluation is quality control of the processes and
outcomes of an educational program."[1]

---

[1] John M. Gottman and Robert E. Clasen, *Evaluation in Education, A Practitioner's Guide.*
(Itasca, Ill.: F. E. Peacock Publishers, Inc., 1972), p. 16.

CHARACTERISTICS OF THE EVALUATION SYSTEM

The planning of a curriculum slightly precedes the planning of an evaluation system. Comprehensive curriculum planning includes the selection of goals based upon the needs of the learners, the society, and the institution; the identification of objectives that accommodate and accomplish the needs expressed in goal form; the selection of approaches, procedures, activities, materials, and other facilities to implement the objectives; and a continuous decision-making process for modifying, eliminating, or perpetuating the proposed curriculum. Therefore, to have adequately planned a curriculum is to have done all but the data gathering, displaying, and interpreting activities of an evaluation system.

This is not to imply that an evaluation system is of secondary importance. Rather, curriculum planning processes which do not inherently provide for and include evaluation are likely to be incomplete. Evaluation is a tool of curriculum planning.

Dependency

An evaluation system is dependent upon the adequacy of the planning which resulted in the selected or created curriculum programs, activities, procedures, materials, and other elements to be evaluated. At times, the evaluation processes can reassess the facts, return to the original curriculum planning proposals, and provide the needs, goals, and objective descriptions necessary. This, however, is a patchwork approach and often results in a disorganized system of defining, gathering, displaying, and interpreting data.

Evaluation systems are also dependent upon the utility and integrity of the specific data to be gathered, displayed, and interpreted. The process of selecting which and what items of information are relevant to an objective is a process of logical judgment. Given clearly stated objectives, this judgmental process is apt to function with integrity. Inevitably, a sampling process is used for the identification of data because identifying all possible items of data would be a too massive, unnecessary, redundant, impossible, or expensive procedure. Therefore, the criteria of availability, economy, and convenience are employed to screen the multiple possibilities down to a selection of manageable, representative data items. For example, the number of behaviors involved in reading are tremendous; yet, with confidence, a sampling of approximately a hundred of these behaviors will support a conclusion concerning the level of performance for the behaviors involved in reading. Or, a test for a driver's license rates approximately twenty-five major behaviors, and from these the implication is drawn that the person is or is not qualified to be a licensed driver. The defining of data items is a problem of their validity within the context of the subject evaluated.

The evaluation system is also dependent upon the reliability of the data gathering instruments and processes. When will data be gathered? How often? Under what conditions? Are repeated measurements to be used? How many times must the behavior to be evaluated be exhibited before assumptions related to its strength and direction can be made? Again the criteria of availability, economy, and convenience are employed to screen down the multiple possibilities to a manageable data-gathering system.

Sometimes the steps of defining, gathering, displaying, and interpreting data are performed by the selection of tests. If so, the validity and reliability of each instrument must be analyzed and judged as adequate for the tasks. An instrument with published information concerning its validity and reliability is not automatically the most appropriate one for any particular task. Date defining, gathering, displaying, and interpreting instruments have an inherent error factor; the problem is to select the errors that minimize the potential loss.

Continuity

The evaluation system begins with curriculum decisions which result in the identification of the first goal. It continues throughout the planning process into the implementation activities and cycles back to the planning process, from which point the cycle begins again. The terms "formative" and "summative" are used to describe the functions of evaluation. Summative evaluation refers to those evaluation activities done at the end of an activity, program, school term, or other period. Formative evaluation refers to those evaluation activities done during the ongoing program which provide immediate feedback into the activity, thus resulting in a modification, the selection of an alternative; and/or a continuous adjustment of the activity to accommodate conditions existing at that moment. Bloom and his coauthors have provided a definitive discussion of formative and summative evaluation procedures.[2]

Cooperativeness

An adequate evaluation system involves at least two levels of cooperation. The first concerns the integrity of the relationships established among the planning, implementing, and evaluation phases of curriculum building. The second concerns the comprehensive involvement of all parties which have legitimate input into or from the program's activities and/or its evaluation systems. A "needs" assessment evaluation activity without the involvement of pupils, for example, would not have been done cooperatively, nor would the selection of goals, without the involvement of the community. Data defining, gathering, displaying, and interpreting are all acts which require cooperation. The determination of what constitutes success or failure requires the cooperative involvement of those who plan and implement, and are affected by the program.

FOCUS OF EVALUATION

Evaluation systems are usually directed toward the planning processes of the institution or program, the implementation and transmission phases of the insti-

[2] Benjamin S. Bloom, et al. *Handbook on Formative and Summative Evaluation of Student Learning.*

Children can provide formative evaluation to one another.

tution or program, and the accomplishments of the institution or program which are related to the achievements of pupils or the management of resources. Evaluation systems can be directed across two of these objectives or even all. For purposes of discussion, the subsequent sections will discuss evaluation systems that are directed toward pupils, teachers, and the curriculum.

Pupil Systems

This section discusses the characteristics, factors, and practices of an evaluation system directed toward pupils. The program for evaluating pupil progress will vary from one school to another in terms of local conditions and resources. However, the following general principles and characteristics may be useful guides for the development of the program.

Objectives and Activities of the Curriculum

First, a comprehensive list of objectives is compiled by the teacher and pupils for the unit or assignment undertaken. These must be in harmony with the goals and objectives accepted by the school. Next, the activities through which the objectives are to be achieved are selected. The evaluation procedures used will be determined by the nature of the objectives and the activities. Thus, objectives, activities, and evaluation are dynamic, continuous, and integral parts of the educative process.

To the greater extent that objectives, activities, or evaluation are treated separately, they become formal subjects unrelated to the total teaching–learning situation. Failure to realize the relationships among them has resulted in a program of teacher education in which the prospective teacher studies philosophy of education (goals) in one course, methods of teaching in another, and evaluation in another. In public school practice a similar approach has resulted in having one group formulate objectives and another group doing the actual evaluation. Consequently, tests frequently given to pupils assess behaviors which pupils have not experienced. Pupil progress should be evaluated by the persons immediately concerned with the education process—the teacher, the pupils, the parents, and the local school staff.

A Comprehensive Evaluation Program

As indicated earlier, the objectives of the traditional elementary school were narrow and restricted primarily to the mastery of the low-energy cognitive activities of recall, recognition, paraphrasing, and translating. The evaluation procedures used were correspondingly narrow, consisting primarily of paper-and-pencil tests. Much progress has been made in developing a greater variety of learning experiences at all energy levels of the cognitive, affective, and psychomotor domains, but progress in developing and using evaluation procedures to match the increased breadth and depth of these newer learning experiences has been slow.

The evaluation of academic achievement is extremely important, but evidence concerning personal-social adjustment, physical growth, habits of work, interests and attitudes, special aptitudes, growth in creative ability, and home and community background must also be available if the school is to do the best job possible in fostering the wholesome growth of children and preparing them for effective citizenship in a democratic society.

Modern evaluation procedures attempt to obtain as complete a picture as possible of the individual. Although it is necessary to sample different aspects of behavior at different times by using a variety of instruments and procedures, interpretations of behavior relating to specific objectives must be made in terms of the total personality. For this reason it is important not only to find instruments and procedures that yield accurate information concerning the various aspects of child development, but also to interpret these various indexes of behavior against the whole educational background of the child.

SITUATION 13.1   Take a few moments to list the evaluative procedures which were used to evaluate your behavior or progress as an elementary student. Beside each listing, denote if the evaluative procedure was process- or product-oriented.

CONTINUOUS EVALUATION

Evaluation is not something that is done after teaching has been completed; it takes place simultaneously with teaching and learning. This is the kind of evaluation found everywhere in life except in certain classrooms. Compare the evaluation of a new employee in a hardware store with the kind practiced in many schools. If the owner of the store used the procedure common in classrooms, the new employee would be put to work for four and one half months while the employer would pay little attention to his or her productivity. Then, at the end of the period, an entire week would be set aside for evaluating the progress of the new employee. The doors of the store would be locked and no selling would go on until the employer decided whether or not the employee could answer 70 percent of the questions asked. Anyone who has worked in a business knows that this procedure is useless. Yet, everyone who has attended a school will recall experiences with evaluation procedures corresponding roughly to that practice.

The evaluation process should be continuous during the time that the teacher can observe the pupil, and not merely at stated intervals when tests are given or report cards are sent to parents. Not only results of paper-and-pencil tests but also every detail of behavior that the teacher can observe should be material for the evaluation process. It is during the elementary school period that the process of evaluation reveals differences in aptitudes, abilities, achievements, interests, and environmental backgrounds that determine to a large degree the educational needs of high school and college youth.

The evaluation of pupil learnings involves preassessment, diagnosis, and postassessment. Preassessment evaluation activities determine the readiness prerequisites needed by the pupil. When the readiness prerequisites are not present, diagnostic evaluation activities identify the underlying causes and provide a basis for remediation programs. Postassessment activities evaluate the relative degree of accomplishment of the intended outcomes. All three phases—preassessment, diagnosis, and postassessment—are equally concerned with behaviors in the cognitive, affective, and psychomotor domain.

Preassessment evaluation is designed to define, gather, display, and interpret readiness prerequisites needed by the pupil to achieve the intended outcomes of the learning activities. These prerequisites may be in the areas of skills, developmental levels, and experience background. This preassessment provides data which establish the learner's relative position with regard to intended terminal behaviors as well as readiness to begin proposed learning activities.

If the results of the preassessment phase suggest that a particular learner or group is not ready to enter a proposed learning activity, then diagnostic procedures are utilized. The diagnostic phase probes into the lack of readiness within the learner or group in an effort to identify a course of action. For example, what skills are missing or operating inefficiently so as to contribute to the lack of readiness? When a lack of readiness is shown, the results of the preassessment phase should redirect the learner to the proposed activities. The diagnostic phase should specify the developmental or remedial activities appropriate to redirect, and thereby increase, the readiness of the learner.

Formative assessment activities are designed to provide immediate feedback to both the teacher and the learner relative to the progress or problems occurring during the activity. The outcomes of a formative assessment may, for example, increase or decrease the pacing of the activity, modify or eliminate an activity, demonstrate the need for an alternative activity or a temporary re-cycling, and provide reinforcement for the continued expenditure of energies.

The postassessment activities yield results related to the learner's attain-ment of the intended behaviors of the learning activities. The results of the postassessment could result in some learners proceeding to different learning activities while other learners are recycled into additional activities related to the intended behaviors of the original learning activities. The revision of learn-ing activities is also partially based upon the results of the postassessment.

The principal purpose of these procedures is to enable the teacher to better provide the educational experience most appropriate to the needs, readiness, and developmental levels of children through the tool of a continuous evalua-tion system.

COOPERATIVE EVALUATION

Pupils should be encouraged to engage in self-evaluation. This represents an important phase of the child's education. Failure to develop in children both the desire to and the ability to evaluate their own progress, or at least to participate under the guidance of the teacher, in the process has resulted in many types of educational weaknesses. It has produced high school and college youth who must always wait for the verdict of the instructor concerning their progress—even graduate students who constantly ask instructors, "Is this the way you wanted it done?" It is responsible for much of the cheating on exam-inations for the purpose of deceiving the instructor and getting a higher mark. Furthermore, an authoritarian system of evaluation is hardly conducive to the development of a nation of adults capable of assuming responsibility for their own behaviors and habituated to evaluating their own efforts—characteristics essential in a society that gives allegiance to the democratic ideal.

FACTORS

The final criterion by which school practices must be evaluated consists of what is happening to the child. It is the function of evaluation, therefore, to reveal the potentialities of each child, the factors that are promoting and retarding progress, and a factual basis upon which the teacher can best deter-mine educational experiences. In the following ten sections, major factors in pupil growth are examined. An effort is made to give at least a partial answer to three questions regarding each factor: (1) *Why* is it important to evaluate this factor in pupil growth? (2) *What* specific items relating to this factor need to be evaluated? (3) *How* can the teacher evaluate the growth of pupils in terms of this factor?[3] It should be understood, of course, that these factors of pupil growth are interrelated and that the teacher has the responsibility for interpreting and synthesizing the information obtained into a composite picture of the child against the background of the total learning environment.

---

[3] O. Buros, *Mental Measurements Yearbook.* (Highland Park, N.J.: Gryphon Press, published annually). This is an invaluable source of help in selecting tests.

Mental Abilities or Academic Aptitudes

Few problems in education have aroused more controversy than the nature of intelligence, the relative influence of nature and nurture on intelligence, and the quality that is actually measured by intelligence tests. It is easy to become so involved in a theoretical discussion of these problems that the more immediate problem of what use to make of information relating to the abilities of children is entirely overlooked. This is not to say that the problems discussed above are unimportant. In addition to gaining a clear understanding of these problems, however, the teacher in the modern elementary school has the obligation to use information relating to the abilities of children in such a manner as to foster the optimum growth of each toward the realization of those personal and social values for which the elementary school in democratic society accepts responsibility. What the teacher needs is not merely a single index of the general mental abilities of children, but information concerning the various types of abilities they may possess. Very little progress can be made toward individualizing instruction in the several curriculum areas until the various aptitudes of the children are known. Pupils need to be evaluated to determine the educational directions and distances they are best equipped to travel. Instead of a single grade standard for reading, for example, the teacher needs information concerning the reading achievement that can be predicted for each child. Evaluation of the abilities of children in the modern elementary school is for the purpose of guidance rather than selection.

The function of evaluation in the modern elementary school is to determine as objectively as possible the kind of educational opportunities from which the individual can profit most. The oldest and best known instruments in this area yield a single index of mental ability—the intelligence quotient. The Terman-Merrill revision of the Stanford-Binet Scale is regarded as a good single measure of intelligence. Since this is an individually administered test and requires the services of an expert, most schools can use it only for special cases, if at all. The Otis Quick-Scoring Mental Ability Test, the Kuhlmann-Anderson Tests, and the Pinter General Ability Tests are widely used for group testing of general mental ability.

Many schools prefer tests that provide information concerning both language and nonlanguage factors of scholastic aptitude. The California Test of Mental Maturity and the Cornell-Coxe Perfomance Ability Scale are examples of this type.

Care must be taken in interpreting the results of intelligence tests. A test cannot measure intellectual capacity; it can test only the functioning of the intellect upon the experiences of an individual. The measurement of intelligence is inferential; for example, if two individuals have had similar experiences with a grapefruit, then the individual who can display the greatest range of behaviors with the grapefruit is inferred to have the greater intellectual capacity. But what if one of the individuals had not previously experienced the object or event from which inference of intellectual capacity is made? Many children from impoverished environments, denied the advantages of those experiences in early childhood which would provide them with the percepts and concepts that contribute to the growth of intelligence, do not perform well on tests of intelligence. Yet, phenomenal gains have sometimes been reported after such children have been exposed to an enriched environment for a year or more.

While we do not have reliable evidence as yet on changes in American intelligence, two interesting trends have been noted. One is the drop in the mean intelligence quotients reported in large cities as upper- and middle-class families move out to the suburbs or place their children in private schools. The public schools in cities like New York and Los Angeles are now enrolling a majority of lower economic class children, many of whom come to school not knowing the English language, or come from homes where opportunities for "book learning" and a drive to do well in school are lacking. Because these children score low on intelligence tests, it should not be assumed that they are stupid and cannot learn. It does mean, however, that schools enrolling such pupils have a heavy responsibility to provide a rich learning environment to help compensate for their impoverished backgrounds.

Evaluation of Achievement in the Various Curriculum Areas

Since the program of the elementary school has been extended and enriched, the need has been increasingly recognized for evaluation procedures that measure more than the memorization of facts and the repetition of mechanical skills. Techniques for measuring factual knowledge and fundamental skills have been worked out and used fairly well in classrooms, but teachers have assumed too frequently that after they have measured factual knowledge and skills, there is nothing left to measure. In traditional testing procedures, very little emphasis is given to the measurement of the full range of cognitive, affective, and psychomotor behaviors. There is no question about the importance of measuring progress in the fundamental skills in phases of the conventional school subjects, but all behaviors are important. Unless pupil progress in understanding, in seeing relationships, and in making practical applications of facts and skills learned to the solution of problems in living are evaluated, these important aspects of the education of the child will continue to be neglected. Some of the procedures used in evaluating achievement will be discussed.

STANDARDIZED ACHIEVEMENT TESTS

When used wisely, standardized achievement tests furnish a basis for the assessment of progress and the diagnosis of learning difficulties, and focus attention on weaknesses in the curriculum and in teaching procedures. Certain limitations of these tests must be kept in mind, however. First, the norms are prepared on the basis of the median scores of many pupils in many school systems. These may be suitable standards of attainment for the average pupil, but too high for slow pupils and too low for pupils who are above average in mental ability. Second, it is difficult to find a standardized test that parallels the objectives and the scope and sequence of the curriculum in a local school.

Third, if the teacher is to be rated on the basis of the scores made by pupils on standardized tests, the teacher is likely to teach for the tests—that is, limit teaching to drill on the textbook materials emphasized by the tests. This misuse of standardized achievement tests has tended to crystallize outmoded methods of teaching, has prevented teachers from taking advantage of opportunities to relate learning to living, and has retarded efforts to make adequate provisions for individual differences among pupils. Fourth, unjustified comparisons of one child with another have been made on the basis of single test scores without regard to differences in backgrounds and potentialities for learning. Unwholesome competition of individual against individual and school against school, and even teacher against teacher, has been fostered by this misuse of standardized tests.

The need for achievement tests that reveal more than the ability to recall information has long been recognized; the pupil who can recall information frequently is incapable of paraphrasing it or of using it in novel situations. The 1946 yearbook of the National Society for the Study of Education represented a pioneer effort to develop tests that included items designed to reveal understanding as well as those that involved merely simple recall. The yearbook contained illustrative test items designed to evaluate understanding in all the major curriculum areas.[4] Since that time, college texts in the field of measurement and evaluation have frequently contained a chapter on evaluating pupil understandings.[5]

In 1956 and 1964, a significant contribution was made by Benjamin Bloom and his associates when they developed and published a classification system for educational objectives in first the cognitive domain[6] and then the affective domain.[7] The classification system was presented in the form of a taxonomy of the intellectual behaviors (cognitive domain), and a taxonomy of the attitudes, awarenesses, and appreciations (affective domain). Each domain presented a hierarchical ordering and a logically precise definition of the behaviors within that domain. The intellectual skills and behaviors within the cognitive domain are knowledge, comprehension, application, analysis, synthesis, and evaluation. The behaviors within the affective domain are receiving, responding, valuing, organizing, and characterizing. Bloom and his associates stated: "Curriculum builders should find the taxonomy helps them to specify objectives so that it becomes easier to plan learning experiences and prepare evaluation devices."[8] Many of the breakthroughs in testing are in some way related to the contributions resulting from the building of the *Taxonomy of Educational Objectives.*

---

[4] National Society for the Study of Education, *The Measurement of Understanding.* (Chicago: University of Chicago Press, 1946).

[5] J. Stanley Ahmann et al., *Evaluating Elementary School Pupils.* (Boston: Allyn & Bacon, Inc., 1960), chap. 7.

[6] Benjamin S. Bloom (Ed.), *Taxonomy of Educational Objectives, Handbook I: Cognitive Domain.* (New York: David McKay Co., Inc., 1956), pp. 201–207.

[7] Dr. R. Krathwohl, B. S. Bloom, and B. B. Masia, *Taxonomy of Educational Objectives, Handbook II: Affective Domain.* (New York: David McKay Co., Inc., 1964), pp. 176–185.

[8] Bloom, *Taxonomy of Educational Objectives, Handbook I*, Preface.

SITUATION 13.2   Review three to five studies which investigated the relationships between standardized achievement scores and actual pupil achievement. List the studies and provide a brief abstract of your findings.

Considerable progress has been made in minimizing the traditional, and perhaps inherent, weaknesses in the standardized test. For example, the groups upon which test norms are developed have been expanded by most developers and publishers of tests to include a wider range of ethnic and culturally different individuals. Some publishers even provide norms for selected ethnic groups. In addition, some tests are organized as criterion-referenced tests. A criterion-referenced test is one in which an objective is stated in behavioral terms and then the test items related to that objective are indexed back to it. Therefore, a modern elementary school could literally construct its own test by selecting those objectives and indexed items which matched the objectives of that school. Also, many tests of achievement have attempted to test a wider range of behaviors, especially in the cognitive domain. In fact, it can be said that in some respects one can now match the quality of teaching with an appropriate quality of testing.

If the limitations of standardized achievement tests are kept in mind, they can be used profitably in those subjects in which grade placement and instructional objectives vary least from classroom to classroom. Even in these subjects, such tests should be used for guidance purposes and not for passing or failing, for rating teachers, or for regimenting pupils to a single standard of achievement. Some widely used standardized achievement tests are Sequential Tests of Educational Progress, Stanford Achievement Tests, Progressive Achievement Tests, Metropolitan Achievement Tests, and Iowa Every-Pupil Tests of Basic Skills.

TEACHER-MADE TESTS

A comprehensive treatment of the problem of test construction is beyond the scope of this chapter.[9] Although teacher-made tests usually lack the technical refinement of standardized achievement tests, they should probably be used more widely than they are, for several reasons. Teacher-made tests can fit the instructional objectives for a specific group better than standardized tests. The constructing of tests may benefit the professional growth of the teacher. The cost of standardized tests limits their use in many schools. Standardized tests are available only for whole subjects or large units of subject matter, and can usually be adapted for evaluation of achievement only at the beginning and the end of a semester or year. Teacher-made tests can, on the other hand, be revised and used for continuous evaluation.

---

[9] Information is available for this purpose in many excellent books written by specialists in the field of evaluation and measurement. See, for example. Benjamin S. Bloom, et al., *Handbook on Formative and Summative Evaluation of Learning*, Part I.

Personal-Social Adjustment

Teaching children the basic subjects is a firmly established objective of the elementary school, but other objectives may well be supplemental. Should the school be concerned with the kind of person the child is becoming? Should the school help children think well of themselves? Should it help them build effective relationships with others? Should the school, in brief, be concerned about the personal-social adjustments of pupils? Current educational theory and practice support an affirmative answer to these questions.

Many competent individuals and groups have recently expressed concern about limiting the responsibility of the school, but it cannot always be assumed that they are not concerned about personal-social adjustment. The Educational Policies Commission, for example, published a bulletin in 1961 which stated that the central purpose of American education should be the cultivation of the rational powers of the individual. The bulletin, however, stated emphatically that the rational powers are not all of life; stated that the individual must be intelligently aware of the role of emotions in life; and recognized the validity of other obligations that the school has traditionally accepted. "The basic American value, respect for the individual, has led to one of the major charges which the American people have placed on their schools: to foster that development of individual capacities which will enable human beings to become the best people they are capable of becoming."[10]

Hansen defined the primary objective of formal education as education in the basic subjects, but he suggested that the hostile child is not receptive to learning and recommended that the schools employ auxiliary services needed to improve the educability of children.[11] The 1962 yearbook of the Association for Supervision and Curriculum Development proposed a new focus for education. It stated, "The fullest possible flowering of human potential is the business of education."[12] This publication, which was mentioned in a previous chapter, provides strong support for the idea that the school should be concerned with the kind of person the child is becoming.

Since helping the individual to develop a positive image of self and to develop effective relationships with others are important objectives of education, techniques for evaluating personal-social adjustment are needed. A great variety of instruments and procedures are available for this purpose: informal observation by the teacher, formal instruments for use by clinicians, anecdotal records, sociograms, and inventories. These instruments and procedures are generally not as reliable and valid as standardized aptitude and achievement tests, and therefore, as with all instruments and procedures, it is essential that their limitations as well as their contributions be understood.

[10] Educational Policies Commission, *The Central Purpose of American Education.* (Washington, D.C.: National Education Association, 1961), p. 1.
[11] Carl F. Hansen, *The Amidon Elementary School: A Successful Demonstration in Basic Education.* (Englewood Cliffs, N.J.: Prentice-Hall, Inc., 1962), pp. 32–35.
[12] Anon., *Perceiving, Behaving, Becoming.* (Washington, D.C.: Association for Supervision and Curriculum Development, 1962), p. 2.

TEACHER OBSERVATION

Teachers have many opportunities to observe pupils in the classroom, on the playground, in the cafeteria, and in the auditorium. Observation over a period of time in these situations may provide information not revealed in an artificial test situation. For example, pupils may answer yes to a test item, "Do you prefer to work with others rather than by yourself?", when careful observation of their behavior may reveal that they seldom participate in the activities of a group. Observation also provides an opportunity to report actual behavior. The pupils who are asked to report on their own behaviors in a formal test situation are likely to give what they believe to be the expected answer. The report of direct observation is likely, in this instance, to be more reliable than test results. The teacher may also learn a great deal about the personal-social development of children by observing their creative activities. Do the pupils enjoy the activity for its own sake, or do they work primarily for good marks? Do they express their own feelings in their drawings and paintings, or do they prefer to copy the ideas of others?

Scales have been developed to guide the teacher's observations. Sometimes, these scales ask teachers to check their own powers of observation by asking them at the end of a school day to select high, middle, and low achieving pupils and describe their behaviors throughout the day.

PERSONALITY TESTS AND RATING SCALES

Personality tests may be used to encourage pupils to examine carefully their own characteristics, to locate pupils who are experiencing adjustment difficulties, and to provide information that will serve as a starting point for conferences among teachers, counselors and individual pupils. A wise teacher or counselor, however, will not accept the results of a personality test as conclusive evidence of poor adjustment unless these results are verified by careful observation and well-planned interviews. Personality tests are based on the reaction of the individual to a series of questions or situations. *Rating scales*, on the other hand, are executed by counselors, teachers, parents, or others. Rating scales have the advantage that they can be used with children who are too young to read questionnaires or evaluate their own reactions to situations. Another advantage is that persons are less likely to be biased in their judgments of others than they are in estimates of themselves. The reliability of rating scales can be increased by having several persons rate the same individual and then combine the ratings. A publication of the Association for Supervision and Curriculum Development has listed more than twenty personality tests and rating scales, with brief descriptions and addresses of distributors.[13]

SOCIOGRAMS

A sociogram is a chart of the interrelationships within a group. Its purpose is to discover the relation of any one pupil to the class as a whole. Sociograms

---

[13] Anon., *Improving Educational Assessment and an Inventory of Affective Behavior.* (Washington, D.C.: Association for Supervision and Curriculum Development, 1969), pp. 129–140.

have been widely used in elementary schools for helping individual pupils improve their social relationships, for reshaping administrative practices, for grouping for committee work, and for grouping for play activities. Some teachers are more alert than others in detecting the status of individual pupils in the group, but all teachers need the help of some systematic device for supplementing personal observation.

Although the sociogram may be very useful in revealing interpersonal relationships among the pupils that the teacher did not detect through observation, it should not be regarded as the final answer. A sociogram may serve as an effective starting point for the study of social dynamics in the classroom, but it should be followed by careful study of the group dynamics from time to time. The teacher should not assume that one sociogram will reveal the class structure over a period of time or that the grouping for play will be the same as that for class work. The sociogram is a professional instrument to be used only by those who understand its uses and limitations. It will not be worth much unless it is supplemented by other techniques of evaluation, and unless definite action is taken to make use of the information in helping individual pupils gain status in the group.

Sociograms may be used for a variety of purposes, such as selecting committees to work on a social studies unit, dividing children into groups for play activities, and planning a school party or program. The first step is to ask the children, "With whom would you like to work on a committee?" Children are asked to write their own names at the top of a 3- by 5-inch card and then to write the names of their first choice, second choice, and third choice. The choices may then be tabulated in the form shown in the illustration (see Fig. 13.1).

The tabulation form of the collected cards provides a great deal of information about the twelve children and constitutes the basic data used in drawing the sociogram. The tabulation and the sociogram together show the isolates, such as Pat, Rose, and Walter; the stars, such as Jane and John; and the mutual choices, such as John and Robert, Jane and Karen, and David and Robert.

After the tabulation form has been completed, the teacher may construct a sociogram (see Fig. 13.2), using circles for boys and triangles for girls. If the class is large, it may be advisable to use a cardboard approximately 30 by 30 inches for the drawing. The general procedure is to locate the "stars" near the center and the "isolates" on the periphery to minimize the number of long lines and the number of intersecting lines.

The teacher can use the information revealed by the sociogram for the purpose of locating pupils who have not achieved status in the group, and for helping them overcome handicaps that prevent them from gaining acceptance by their peers.

The Physical Status of Pupils

Teachers are concerned with evaluating the physical status of pupils because it determines the amount of energy available for school work and other

Chooser \ Chosen	David	Jane	John	Karen	Martha	Pat	Robert	Rose	Stephen	Stewart	Susan	Walter
David			1				2			3		
Jane			3	1	2							
John	2						1			3		
Karen		1			2						3	
Martha		1								2	3	
Pat		3	1						2			
Robert	2		1						3			
Rose		1		3							2	
Stephen	2		1				3					
Stewart	2	3	1									
Susan		1	3	2								
Walter			3						2	1		
Chosen as:												
1st choice	0	4	5	1	0	0	1	0	0	1	0	0
2d choice	4	0	0	1	2	0	1	0	2	1	1	0
3d choice	0	2	3	1	0	0	1	0	1	2	2	0
Total	4	6	8	3	2	0	3	0	3	4	3	0

Figure 13.1   Tabulation form showing the choices of seven boys and five girls. Adapted from Helen Hall Jennings, *Sociometry in Group Relations*. (Washington, D.C.: American Council on Education, 1948), p. 18.

activities, it is related to the social and emotional adjustment of the pupil, and it accounts to a large extent for the pupil's success in every part of the school program. If every child could be examined by a physician every day of the school year, it would be unnecessary for teachers to be concerned with this type of evaluation. Since this is obviously impossible, teachers must accept the responsibility for the detection of physical disorders that interfere with normal growth and educational progress, as well as for fostering a positive approach to healthful living.

It does not require a great deal of preparation or special equipment for teachers to be able to detect the symptoms of common physical disorders and

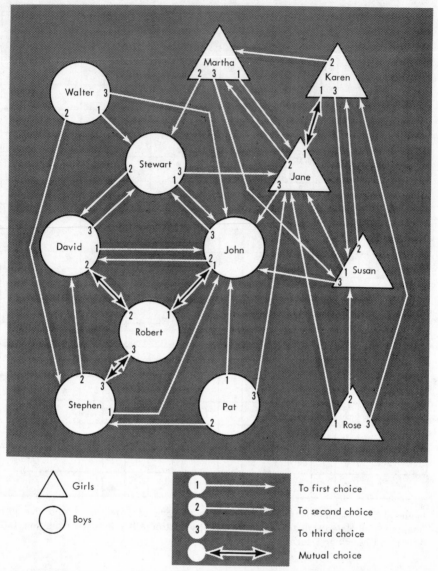

Figure 13.2   A sociogram based on the data presented in Figure 13.1.

to call attention to the need for an examination by a physician. Teachers need to know how to check on general health; height and weight; posture; symptoms of nervous disorders; cleanliness and suitability of clothing; and the condition of eyes, ears, nose, throat, chest, arms, legs, neck, face, lips, hair, scalp, teeth, back, and feet.

Procedures and instruments used for evaluating the physical status of pupils include a complete physical examination by a physician, daily observations by the teacher, adequate health records, the clinical thermometer, the audiometer, the whispered speech test, the watch-tick test, the Snellen Chart, the Eames Eye Test, and the Betts Telebinocular.

Evaluating Growth in Interests

Since learning is more rapid and more lasting, and has more valuable concomitants when it is based on pupil interest, and since teachers have a responsibility for helping pupils develop more worthwhile interests, it follows that teachers need to be concerned with procedures for evaluating the interests of pupils.

Children's interests in people, in books, in the natural environment, in games, and in various kinds of activities need to be evaluated. The dimensions of children's interests also need to be evaluated. These include a range of preferences or variety of interests, range of participation or variety of activities, and intensity or depth of interest in any specific activity.

Procedures for evaluating growth in interests include analysis of books borrowed; questionnaires or inventories in which children are asked to list the books they have read, the activities in which they have engaged, and their preferences among them; and teacher observations of the activities in which the children have engaged, the games they have played, and their favorite topics of conversation.

SITUATION 13.3   Construct five activities for a particular elementary grade or level which would aid a teacher or pupil in evaluating areas of particular interest.

Evaluating Growth in Attitudes

The school cannot escape concern with the attitudes that children develop both in and out of school. The children's attitudes toward their playmates, teachers, and parents, and toward social customs and institutions, are all related to their mental health. Behavior does not result from the intellect alone; it is influenced by the individual's background of attitude patterns and experiences. The child's attitudes affect what is learned, what is remembered, what is thought about, and what is done. Hence, evaluation of children's attitudes—their feelings for and against things—assumes a fundamental role in guiding their development.

Formal instruments for evaluating attitudes are limited primarily to the high school and adult levels. However, attitude scales and questionnaires can be adapted for use in the elementary school. These may be supplemented by evidence recorded informally by teachers from observations of pupils' actions, conversations, discussions, and written work.

SITUATION 13.4   Since increasing emphasis is being placed on affective and value education, review the research to determine what instruments are now being made available for evaluating processes within the affective domain.

Evaluating Growth in Work–Study Skills

The development of effective skills for learning is coming to be regarded as one of the most important functions of the elementary school. These skills, rather than the amount of information stored for future use, will determine to a large extent the child's future success, both as a student and as an adult worker. The development of these skills is especially important in the upper grades of the elementary school. Work–study skills include the ability to read maps, charts, graphs, and tables; to use the table of contents and index of a book; to locate books in the library by use of the card index; and to outline, organize, and tabulate data.

Some of these skills are included in achievement tests in reading. Others may be evaluated by means of such tests as the Iowa Every-Pupil Test of Basic Study Skills and the Pirtle Library Test 6B. Informal methods of evaluating growth in work–study skills include observation of pupils in committee work, problem solving, and group discussions, observing samples of written work of pupils, and checking on pupils' skill in the use of the library.

SITUATION 13.5   Creativity: How do we as teachers measure this aspect of the child? Should the area of creativity be measured at all? Are the natures of the creative tasks themselves evaluative? Construct two evaluative creative tasks for elementary students: write one task for primary students and one task for intermediate students.

Evaluating Growth in Creative Self-Expression

Elementary school teachers and principals are becoming increasingly aware of the responsibility for fostering creative self-expression in pupils. They realize that adjusting effectively to our complex society and contributing to social progress require individuals who are creative in their approach to people, situations, problems, and materials. The development of creative abilities represents one of the most important contributions of the school to the building of a better social order and to fostering the mental health of children.

The development of creative abilities is an objective of many, if not all, parts of the curriculum. It may consist of the ability to express original ideas through art or music, to plan and perform unique experiments in science, or to plan and carry out an enterprise in group living. Evaluation of growth in creative self-expression is therefore an aspect of evaluation in all areas of the curriculum. Since creative ability is seen in terms of the child's own standards, it is particularly difficult to evaluate by means of formal instruments and procedures. Teachers need to develop criteria for evaluating creative efforts, such as the originality of ideas used in written work or art; variety of ideas expressed; and richness, ease, and fluency of expression. Evaluation of growth in creative expression consists largely of preserving pupil products in language, art, and science, and of observation of pupil behavior.

Evaluating Growth in Critical Thinking

Most teachers realize that one of their responsibilities is to help children learn how to think for themselves in solving real problems. Some teachers, however, confuse critical thinking with the ability to give the answers expected. Critical thinking requires the ability to collect and interpret data; to refrain from drawing conclusions that surpass the data collected; to apply principles and generalizations to new situations; and to evaluate the arguments, ideas, and conclusions of others.

If instructional practices are to foster the abilities necessary to critical thinking, methods of evaluating these abilities must be found. Several tests applicable to this area are available at the upper elementary school level. One of the best is a Test of Critical Thinking in School Studies (Bureau of Publications, Teachers College, Columbia University). It measures the ability to obtain facts from graphs, maps, references, newspapers, and magazines; the ability to draw reasonable conclusions from facts collected; and the ability to apply generalizations to new situations.

Evaluating the Home and Community Background

Intelligent guidance of the child in school involves an understanding of his or her total learning environment. Not only is it true that the whole child comes to school, but also that the home and community background come with the child.

Information concerning the home background of the pupil, which the school should assemble and use, includes the attitude of the parents toward the school, parent-to-parent relationships, parent-to-child relationships, child-to-child relationships, and socioeconomic status. The data on parents should include amount of schooling, occupation, health, birthplace, citizenship, and language spoken. Information about the community should reflect economic conditions, customs and traditions, facilities for recreation, and community resources that can be used for instructional purposes.

The method of obtaining information concerning home and community background may be interviews, questionnaires for parents to fill out (if children are very young), questionnaires for pupils to fill out, and community surveys.

Teacher Systems

The evaluation of teachers and teaching has been one of the perplexing, continuing problems of education. These evaluations have always been done for purposes of hiring, firing, promoting, and awarding tenure. More recently, in addition to other purposes, the evaluation of teachers and teaching has been used as a basis for improving teaching behaviors.

The premises and assumptions which governed the evaluation of teachers and teaching have changed over the years. The first set of assumptions had an ethical and moralistic orientation. Such traits as the teacher's attendance at Sunday and Wednesday-night church services, a skirt below the ankles, not being shaven in a barber shop, not leaving town with the opposite sex without permission of the president of the school board, not smoking or drinking, and being an unmarried woman were so related to being a good teacher that these personal habits were written into the contracts of teachers. Not until the early 1900s did these clauses disappear from written contracts; today, some may still be important in the minds of a few individuals. The relationship between "unacceptable" traits and the concept of being a "good teacher" began to change as the mores of the dominant society changed. For example, women demonstrated that their marital status was not a factor in their performances as teachers.

The next set of premises used to govern the evaluation of teachers and teaching was oriented toward personality traits. The "good teacher" was extrovertive, heterosexual, of high mental capacity, possessed the traits of leadership, and possessed a positive self-concept. The efforts to establish a research-based relationship between these traits and the "good teacher" generally resulted in studies which reported no significant differences. For example, the achievement of pupils did not seem to be related, except by chance, to the introvertive or extrovertive personality traits of the teacher. Perhaps the lack of significant relationships resulted from the inadequacies of the criteria by which personality traits and pupil growth in achievement were measured. Whatever the reason, a positive relationship between personality traits and pupil achievement has yet to be substantiated by research.

The next set of premises to evolve was centered on the competencies of the teacher with regard to the subject matter being taught. This approach assumed that the more a teacher knew of mathematics, for example, the more pupils would gain in their achievement in mathematics. A number of studies have matched teachers who vary from an adequate knowledge to an extensive knowledge of subject matter, but few have shown significant differences in pupil gain scores. The degree of teacher competency in knowledge of subject matter continues to be a matter of debate. Will a teacher with 24 college hours of mathematics produce higher pupil gain scores than one who has only 18 hours? The evidence is that some teachers with 18 hours produced as much as or less pupil gain as teachers with 24 hours of instruction. At present, pupil gain scores have not been predictably related (except by chance) to the teacher's degree of competency (average to excellent) in a content area.

The current efforts to evaluate teachers and teaching are oriented toward the nature of the communications existing within the learning environment. These efforts are directed more toward evaluation procedures to improve teaching than they are toward hiring, firing, and promotion. It is anticipated that if data which are significantly related to pupil gain in achievement can be displayed for the teacher's interpretation, then the teacher can resume growing as a teacher. The communication network is defined to include the content loads of teacher questions, the forms in which questions are presented, the verbal and nonverbal acceptance and rejection patterns, the frequency and kind of student-initiated or student-response communication, the duration of teacher talk, the use of pauses and silences, and other pertinent data. This field of study is generally labeled "interaction analysis." Again, the research evidence produced within this set of premises is somewhat inconclusive, but in this author's judgment it is holding together (see "Communication" in Chapter 5) as well or better than the bodies of research generated from the other studies.

The efforts through research to identify the moralistic behaviors, personality traits, knowledge (content) competencies, and the communication behavior patterns have not yet led to a statistically defensible answer. Therefore, the answer to the problem of teacher evaluation is often assumed to be found in one of those identities or some combination of them, with teacher preparation and evaluation programs being planned on corresponding assumptions.

Accountability programs include the evaluation of teaching personnel as one aspect of the program. This subject was discussed in Chapter 2 and is expanded in this chapter. This author chooses to discuss them under the later section "Issues" so that the reader will realize that accountability programs are *not* limited to teaching personnel.

SITUATION 13.6   Under what circumstances would you as a teacher use student evaluations of students? Under what circumstances would you as a teacher use student evaluations of teachers?

Curriculum Systems

This section discusses the use of educational specifications, illustrates the development of educational specifications derived from the strategy presented in Chapter 5, presents evaluative criteria, reviews the four types of evaluation, suggests guidelines for evaluating the curriculum, and defines the steps in a cooperative evaluation program.

Educational Specifications

Bloom made many suggestions for developing educational specifications. He is convinced that evaluation instruments and procedures can be developed and used properly only after a set of explicit specifications has been provided.[14] The development of educational specifications is no simple task; it involves coming to grips with many issues in elementary education today.

[14] Benjamin S. Bloom, in National Society for the Study of Education, *Educational Evaluation: New Roles, New Means.* (Chicago: University of Chicago Press, 1969), pp. 33–35.

1. The view that subject matter is an end in itself calls for one type of specification; the view that it is only a means to an end calls for another type.

2. Specifications of two types need to be considered: content and process. Significant content from the various academic disciplines needs to be listed; how the student can organize, integrate, and internalize this content so that it can be used is also important.

3. How detailed should the set of specifications be? It is possible, of course, to list hundreds of objectives to be attained through the study of any school subject or curriculum area. The current emphasis on the identification of major concepts around which specific items of information can be organized cuts down on the number of specifications needed.

4. How much freedom should teachers and pupils have to pursue non-specified objectives? Objectives which emerge after instruction begins are frequently as important as those which are listed in advance. Provision should be made for evaluating these objectives.

5. Teachers generally tend to state objectives in broad, general terms. "To teach the child to appreciate democratic heritage" is an example. Stating educational specifications in precise, behavioral terms requires time, study, and patience. It is, however, a rewarding professional experience—one which provides an effective means of promoting the professional growth of teachers.[15]

6. It is not likely that the educational specifications developed for one school system will be appropriate for use in another. It is for this reason that most authorities favor the "grass roots" approach to school evaluation programs. The staff of the local school system, with the help of competent consultants, develops its own evaluative criteria.

Strategy Specifications

The proposed strategy of instruction was presented in Chapter 5. This strategy will be used to illustrate the development of educational specifications. A comprehensive breakdown is listed below. The reader may wish to refer to Chapter 5 for a review.

I. The Content
  A. The information clusters are recognizable as representative of the discipline.
  B. Furthermore, the information clusters are relevant, humane, classical, and/or practical.
  C. The possession of the information clusters enables the learner to learn aspects of the discipline not taught.
II. The Learning and Development
  A. The developmental level, preoperational and/or concrete operational, of the learner is a fundamental factor influencing all educational decisions.
  B. The objects, events, and situations of the environment are supportive of the learner's developmental level.

[15] See Robert F. Mager, *Preparing Instructional Objectives*. (Palo Alto, Calif.: Fearon Publishers, 1962).

C. The cognitive processes of the learner's developmental level are reinforced through social transmission, accommodation, and assimilation.

D. Field and S-R Association theories are appropriately used to guide and plan learning experiences.

III. The Methodology

A. Each learner experiences exploration, invention, and discovery as phases of an inquiry cycle.

B. Teaching procedures are adjusted to serve the appropriate phase of inquiry: exploration, invention, or discovery.

C. The learner learns to do through the behaviors of doing.

IV. The Communication

A. The communication networks are adjusted to be consistent with and supportive of the range of objectives which comprise a learning experience.

B. Pupil-initiated communications are frequent and spontaneous, with a high degree of pupil-to-pupil interaction.

C. Each participant within the network communicates both as a teacher and as a learner.

V. The Objectives

A. Cognitive, affective, and psychomotor objectives are adequately represented.

B. Classification levels of each domain are included within the intended objectives.

C. The general flow of energy is from low-energy affective to low-energy cognitive, to high-energy cognitive, and then to high-energy affective objectives.

VI. The Goal

A. The central purpose is the development of the learner's abilities to think.

B. The pupil experiences learning how to learn.

C. The diverse goals of the school are united and integrated.

Evaluative Criteria

Criteria for evaluating the elementary school curriculum emerge from a point of view with regard to child development and learning, the role of subject matter in the educative process, a philosophy of education, and the realities and enduring values of contemporary American society. The evaluative criteria listed in the sample evaluation manual found in the Appendix have been gleaned from the chapters of this text. They typify, therefore, the kind of elementary school curriculum envisioned by this author.

Four Types of Evaluation

There are, of course, many types of evaluation. The four types explained below are particularly important from the standpoint of understanding the role of evaluation in curriculum improvement.

Informal evaluation may be regarded as the process of making judgments or decisions explicit without identifying the values, data, experience, theory, and knowledge upon which they are based. The elementary school curriculum will be evaluated whether the professional staff wills it or not. The results of informal evaluations are all too apparent in unwarranted criticisms of the school program, misunderstanding of its purposes and procedures, and failure to do anything constructive about improving it.

Formal evaluation makes judgments and decisions explicit, but it also makes explicit the bases for these judgments and decisions. The elementary school curriculum can generally be improved when administrators, teachers, parents, and qualified consultants engage in formal evaluation for the purposes of locating the strengths and weaknesses of the current program and making specific plans for needed improvements.

Summative evaluation is used at the completion of a curriculum program, project, or activity. It is used to make the judgments about dropping, modifying, or continuing of the program, project, or activity. It does not provide feedback during the operation of the program to improve or redirect its course.

Formative evaluation is used during the operation of a curriculum program, project, or activity. The results of formative evaluations are utilized to modify, extend, and recycle the program, project, or activity during its course of operation. It does provide immediate and frequent feedback during the existence of the program.

Guidelines for Evaluating the Curriculum

Although the details of organization and procedures used in evaluating school programs will vary from one school to another in response to local conditions, there are certain guidelines that deserve serious consideration:

1. Each elementary school should be evaluated in terms of the objectives (specifications) formulated and accepted by administrators, teachers, and representative parents.
2. The evaluation should be comprehensive in scope. It should include an evaluation of objectives, curriculum organization, provision for cooperative planning, teaching strategies, procedures for evaluating and reporting pupil progress, and the program in each of the curriculum areas.
3. Everyone concerned with the work of the school should be involved in one way or another in the evaluation program, although much of the actual work may be carried out by committees and consultants.
4. Evaluation should not be regarded as an end in itself; it is worthwhile only when it results in some type of action to improve the curriculum.

Steps in a Cooperative Program

The first step in the evaluation process (after the approval of the board of education has been obtained) is the organization of study groups for the purpose of defining the kind of curriculum desired; a separate committee may be needed for each area mentioned in item 2 above. This step is sometimes called the "development of evaluative criteria." The various chapters in this text, as well as the selected readings, have provided a background for this task.

The second step in the evaluation process consists of the selection or development of instruments and procedures for evaluating the current program. The checklists contained in the Appendix may be adapted for use along with many other instruments and procedures.

The third step is the actual evaluation of the current program in terms of the criteria established in the first step.

The fourth step in the cooperative evaluation process is the development of specific plans for improving those areas of the curriculum which have been found to be in greatest need of improvement. In some schools there may not be sufficient learning resources; in some, the health program may need improvement; and in others, there may be a need for more cooperative planning by the school staff. Whatever the need, the chances for improving the situation are increased when the professional staff of the school, competent consultants, and selected parents engage in cooperative, formal evaluation of the curriculum. When school systems have carried out formal, cooperative programs for evaluating the elementary school curriculum, school-community relations have been improved, staff morale has been improved, the professional growth of teachers has been promoted, and unjustified criticisms of the schools have been decreased.

Improving Reporting Practices

A comprehensive reporting program serves three masters: the pupil, the parents or guardians, and the institution. This means that an adequate reporting program must anticipate and provide for the varying needs of these three audiences. It seems obvious that a child needs to be communicated with as a child and not as a cumulative folder or parent. The institution needs to maintain in a professional form and manner those items of information which are descriptive and predictive as a basis for future educational guidance decisions. The parent benefits from a mutual sharing of information relative to the behaviors indicative of growth, learning, and development.

Reporting to Pupils

The developmental levels of pupils require that the evaluation and reporting program be frequent, immediate to the task or behavior, positive, and include cooperative participation in both the judgments and the setting of new objectives. For some children, what appears on a nine-week performance card has no perceived relationship with their performances during the third or fourth week of school. In general, formative evaluations and reporting practices are more suitable for children than summative practices.

The pupil benefits from pupil–teacher conferences. At a minimum there should be two pupil–teacher conferences per instructional activity. The first conference should be a part of the preassessment phase, during which the teacher and pupil share perspectives and information concerning the pupil's readiness, and cooperatively establish objectives and activities. The second pupil–teacher conference should be a part of the postassessment phase, during which the pupil and teacher review the pupils' participation in the planned activities, the achievement of objectives, and the pupils' feelings and attitudes about the activities as well as the pupils' self-concepts.

There needs to be some open, legitimate code system understood by the pupil which is regularly used to communicate progress. The code system can be a "happy face," a star, a score, or some such symbol. Whatever the selection, it needs to report the achievements rather than the mistakes of the pupil. This system needs to be open to the extent that the pupil can use it individually. The teacher and the pupil need to organize a file in which either may place items which depict the pupil's progress, intended achievements, and private communications.

The alternatives for reporting to pupils are (1) systems based on the five-category scale (A,B,C,D,F) or modifications of that scale; (2) percentage or numerical ratings, listed, graphed, or charted; (3) check lists of behavioral objectives, character traits, progressive performance steps, or some other evalutive criteria; (4) written evaluations; and (5) conferences.[16]

The forms that report to pupils can assume are also changing. The current forms for the written reports are mastery grading, contract grading, and self-assigned grading. Mastery grading does not consider the length of time involved in achieving a specific performance; it simply reports on the achievement and allows the learner to control the amount of time necessary to achieve. Contract grading is a form in which the teacher and the pupil negotiate an agreement which specifies what the pupil will do and the qualities of performance appropriate for the various grades. Self-assigned grading allows the pupil to specify the criteria for and the assignment of grades to the tasks.

The rewarding and reinforcing of pupil behaviors is a much more comprehensive and inclusive program than that of reporting to pupils. Reporting to pupils is one phase of a total program calculated to reinforce desired behaviors. Although the alternatives are increasing, it remains for future development to resolve which form and approach are best. For example, the January 1975 issue of *Educational Leadership* was devoted to the theme, "Alternatives to Grading."[17]

A comprehensive and successful reporting program begins with the pupils. Given a cooperative and participatory reporting program for pupils, then a successful reporting program for the parent and the institution can be developed.

Reporting to Parents

The improvement of practices in reporting to parents on the progress of the children in school is an integral part of curriculum improvement. These practices influence children's personal-social adjustments, serve as goals toward

---

[16] Donovan R. Walling, "Designing a Report Card that Communicates," *Educational Leadership*, Vol. XXXII, No. 4 (January 1975), p. 258.

[17] Association for Supervision and Curriculum Development, *Educational Leadership*, Vol. XXXII, No. 4 (January 1975).

which people work, and indicate to parents what the school considers to be important in the growth, learning, and development of children. Accurate and diagnostic reports of pupil progress provide a basis for mutual understanding, goodwill, and cooperation between parents and teachers in their efforts to improve the total learning environment of the child. The realization that the report to parents may either build goodwill or destroy it—may either enlist or alienate the cooperation of parents and children—accounts, no doubt, for the increasing amount of attention that is being given by principals, teachers, and parents to the problem of improving reporting practices.

Should S and U grades be used instead of A, B, C, D, E, and F? Should written reports be abolished in favor of parent–teacher conferences? Should there be a different type of reporting system used for the various levels of the school program, such as the primary, intermediate, and upper grades? These questions can be answered satisfactorily only after a thorough study has been made by the principal, teachers, and parents of an individual school. There is no best system of reporting to parents; rather, the system preferred is one that has been developed cooperatively by those concerned, that incorporates the findings of research relating to child growth, learning, and development, and that is clearly understood by teachers, pupils, and parents.

The following suggestions may be helpful to groups interested in improving reporting practices:

1. The purpose of reporting to parents is to enlist their cooperation in providing the best educational opportunities possible for the child.

2. The reporting procedure should include an appraisal of the physical, mental, emotional, and social growth of the child.

3. The reporting procedure should emphasize the child's progress in terms of abilities and past achievements rather than the standing in comparison to other members of the class.

4. The reporting procedure should emphasize guiding the child rather than judging.

5. The reporting procedure should reflect a comprehensive picture of the achievement of the child without requiring too much clerical work on the part of the teacher.

6. Report cards should be supplemented by letters to parents, samples of the child's work, parent-teacher conferences, telephone calls, and home visits.

7. The reporting procedure should be consistent with the philosophy of the school.

8. The reporting practices should report in meaningful terms what the school is teaching.

The Parent-Teacher Conference

The individual conference is regarded by many as the most effective single device for reporting to parents. Many teachers arrange to hold a conference with the parents of every child in the room during the first six weeks of school and as frequently as possible during the remainder of the school year. The value of the conference depends largely upon the preparation the teacher has made for it and the skill used in conducting it. The task of making adequate preparation for an interview with a parent and of using the appropriate techniques in conducting the interview are far from simple. Unless the preservice education of the teacher has included both theory and practice in the art of conducting interviews, the parent-teacher conference is likely to be unsatisfactory to both the teacher and the parent. If the conference is to be successful in establishing better working relationships between the home and the school, certain basic principles must be observed:

1. The teacher must be relaxed and comfortable, and must make the parent feel comfortable also.

2. The teacher should approach the conference with the attitude that the parent can provide much information that can be useful in working with the child.

3. The parent should have an opportunity to ask questions about how the child is getting along in school, why certain procedures are used in the school, and what the parent can do to help the child make the best use of opportunities.

4. The conference should not be regarded as a means of completing a neat plan for working with the child; at best, it can provide only a few new insights.

Reporting to the Institution

The modern elementary school maintains both cumulative and permanent record files of each pupil. The cumulative record folder is for those items of information which are of temporary significance and will be periodically reviewed to either discard or transfer to the permanent record folder. The permanent record folder will contain only those items of information which are of continuing significance to the educational guidance of the pupil. Both files are to be available, upon written request, to parents or guardians.

Staffing Conferences

Periodically, the teachers and those special service personnel who have had involvements with a pupil should meet in a staffing conference. A staffing conference is appropriate whenever educational guidance decisions are to be made about a pupil. Such conferences are crucial for those organizations utilizing team teaching, open schools, or nongradedness. The purpose of this conference is to build as broad a base for decision making as possible.

ISSUES

This section discusses some of the issues related to the use and tools of an evaluation system. The topics selected for discussion are: accountability; behavioral objectives; and standardized testing.

Accountability

The concept, definition, and a general discussion of accountability appears in Chapter 2. It appears here because an accountability system is at issue as an evaluation system. Accountability does encompass both the product and the process aspects of evaluation. Those who support accountability programs will refer to the process aspects of evaluation to assure those who are concerned that they will have significant input into the determination of what is to be evaluated. The advocates then say, why should you worry about the evaluation? Those who are critics of accountability programs will sometimes refer to the lack of control the teachers and schools may have over either the process or the product aspects of evaluation within an accountability system. For example, the National Education Association's Resolution 75-39 on Accountability and Assessment includes these statements:

(1) The National Education Association recognizes that the term "accountability," as applied to public education, is subject to varied interpretations.
(2) The Association believes that classroom teachers can be accountable only to the degree that they share responsibility in educational decision-making and to the degree that other parties who share this responsibility—legislators, other government officials, school boards, administrators, parents, students, and tax-payers—are also held accountable.
(3) The Association believes that there should be no single or statewide accountability system.
(4) The Association believes that specific behavioral objectives should not be used as course objectives, nor as a basis for determining accountability.[18]

As of the fall of 1973, fifteen states had a statewide testing or assessment program; thirteen states required the utilization of a Management Information System (PPBS, for example), and nine states required the evaluation of professional personnel.[19] Michigan has a comprehensive state plan for accountability. The Michigan plan requires the identification of statewide goals, the development of measurable objectives to meet these goals, the assessment of student needs to meet these objectives, analysis of an instructional delivery system, evaluation of that delivery system, and recommendations for changes and improvements. Florida's accountability plan includes the establishment of statewide educational objectives, the establishment of priorities, a time period for the objectives, the establishment of a sound financial support program, the coordination and distribution of funds efficiently, the establishment of minimum standards for achievement and quality control, the assistance of local districts by the state in evaluating the results, and the development of a good information system on the facts and conditions of education.[20] Among

[18] Robert C. Snider, "Should Teachers Say No to MBO?" *Today's Education*, Vol. LXV, No. 2 (March–April, 1976), p. 46.
[19] Richard L. Del Novellis and Arthur J. Lewis, *Schools Become Accountable: A PACT Approach.* (Washington, D.C.: Association for Supervision and Curriculum Development, 1974), p. 9.
[20] Del Novellis and Lewis, p. 9.

the nine states that relate the evaluation of personnel and accountability, California's legislation specifies, "all local teacher evaluation systems must include standards of expected student progress in each area of study, and certificated personnel are to be assessed in relation to the established standards."[21] Kansas legislation simply provides that each board of education shall develop procedures for the evaluation of professional employees within general guidelines.[22]

In President Nixon's 1970 message to Congress on educational reform, he stated:

> *In developing these new measurements, we will want to begin by comparing the actual educational effectiveness of schools in similar economic and geographic circumstances. We will want to be alert to the fact that in our present educational system we will often find our most devoted, most talented, hardest working teachers in those very schools where the general level of achievement is lowest. They are often there because their commitment to their profession sends them where the demands upon their profession are the greatest.*
>
> *From these considerations we derive another new concept,* accountability. *School administrators and school teachers alike are responsible for their performance and it is in their interest as well as the interests of their pupils that they be held accountable.* . . . [23]

The enactment of legislation to establish accountability programs seems to have slowed somewhat. Yet, more than half of the states now have some form of an accountability system required by statute. Del Novellis and Lewis have provided some general guidelines for applying accountability to the schools:

> 1. *The purpose of maintaining an educational accountability program is to improve the quality of education.*
> 2. *Any person or group sharing responsibility for the quality or nature of educational experiences should be accountable to the affected children, parents, community and to the larger society.*
> 3. *Although accountability is related to the products of education, accountability should be measured in terms of the input and process, as well as the products of education.*
> 4. *Schools, teachers and others should be held accountable for objectives in the affective and psychomotor realms as well as the cognitive realm.*[24]

The concept of accountability does receive strong support from the public. Yet, it has led to conflict among teachers, administrators, boards of education, legislators, and the public. Accountability has come to include so many different and differing interpretations that Leon Lessinger, sometimes called the "father" of the accountability movement,[25] said in 1974:

21 Del Novellis and Lewis, p. 10.
22 Del Novellis and Lewis, p. 11.
23 Del Novellis and Lewis, p. 7.
24 Del Novellis and Lewis, pp. 12–17.
25 William S. Dederburg, Kent J. Chabotar, and Larry Lad, "Conflict Over Educational Accountability: The Case of Michigan," *Kappa Delta Phi Record*, Vol. XI, No. 3 (February 1975), p. 74.

I refuse to be held accountable for accountability and all the things that are done in its name. Like all movements, it had to spread and shift until it fits everybody's predilection.[26]

Behavioral Objectives

The prime element of accountability systems, management by objectives systems, or the evaluation of instructional programs is the existence of behavioral objectives. Behavioral objectives emphasize the product of an educational endeavor. The nature of the product is described in such a way that the evidence of accomplishment is observable and therefore measurable. Ralph Tyler, Hilda Taba, B. F. Skinner, and Robert Mager are some of the contributors to the trend toward objectives stated in behavioral terms. For an objective to be in behavioral form, the three general conditions are: the behavior to be developed at the end of the activity is to be described in observable, measurable, and communicable terms; the conditions under which this behavior is to appear, to be displayed, and to occur must be specified; and the frequency, accuracy, and minimum level of competency intended are to be specified.

The arguments about the tool of behavioral objectives can be grouped into three categories: the inflexible mode that behavioral objectives may impose on instruction, and the implied lack of confidence in a teacher to make good quality, extemporaneous teaching decisions[27]; the burden of work required of teachers to establish behavioral objectives for the multiple objectives within an instructional environment and the potential scape-goating of teachers and administrators[28]; and the narrow emphasis of behavioral objectives upon low-energy cognitive activities because they can be measured.[29]

Behavioral objectives comprise a tool that the teachers in the modern elementary school will be utilizing. The range and impact of the application of this tool is not yet fully researched and known. For a more thorough discussion, the reader is referred to Chapter 2.

Standardized Testing

Written tests were not used extensively in American schools before 1845. Horace Mann predicted, in the *Common School Journal* for October 1, 1845, that this "novel" mode of examination would constitute a new era in the history of our schools. He said that the new method—using printed questions and written answers—settled the question of what quality of instruction had been given by the master as definitely as it did the question of what amount of proficiency had been gained by the pupils.[30] His unbounded enthusiasm for written

[26] Leon Lessinger, *Education U.S.A.*, Vol. 16, No. 21 (Jan. 21, 1974), p. 111.

[27] David N. Campbell, "Behavioral Objectives—The Grand Charade," *Today's Education*, Vol. LXV, No. 2 (March–April 1976), p. 43.

[28] Snider, p. 46.

[29] Arthur W. Combs, *Educational Accountability: Beyond Behavioral Objectives*. (Washington, D.C.: Association for Supervision and Curriculum Development, 1972), p. 46.

[30] See Otis W. Caldwell and Stuart A. Curtis, *Then and Now in Education*. (New York: Harcourt Brace Jovanovich, Inc., 1925), pp. 238–244.

examinations provided an interesting prelude to what was to happen later as a consequence of the scientific movement in education and the rapid growth in the use of objective tests.

The date for the beginning of the movement for the scientific study of education has frequently been set at 1831, when Friedrich Herbart, a professor at the University of Koenigsberg, Germany, published *Letters Dealing with the Application of Psychology to the Art of Teaching.* It was not until the last two decades of the nineteenth century, however, that the scientific study of education developed on a significant scale in the United States. With local school systems in this country free to carry on experiments, and with the application of science remaking other forms of organized activity in this country, it was inevitable that schools would seek scientific solutions to educational problems.

J. M. Rice, then editor of the magazine *Forum*, wrote a series of articles in 1897 that served to direct the study of education into new channels. He pointed out that personal judgments could not be relied upon as bases for evaluating teaching and learning, that objective evidence was needed. When he devised objective tests, first in spelling and later for other facets of the instructional program, a distinct step was taken toward more exact measurement of educational results. Leonard P. Ayres wrote, in 1915, "We have awakened to a startling realization that in education, as in other forms of organized activity, applied science may avail to better even those processes that have rested secure in the sanction of generations of acceptance. Since this statement by Ayres, the testing movement has expanded to include tests designed to provide objective evidence with regard to almost every conceivable aspect of teaching and administrating. As early as 1940, the authors of a well-known text in the history of education stated: "The popular confidence in tests is today, if anything, too great."[32] The same authors warned against endowing a given test with prestige and authority "far beyond its true deserts."

Five departments of the National Education Association cooperated in the preparation of a pamphlet, published in 1961, which emphasized the child's right to be different, deplored the trend toward impersonality in school programs, and suggested that any innovation should be evaluated in terms of what it does for the individual pupil. The pamphlet pointed out that at no time in history have schools placed so much faith in tests made by agencies outside the school system. It raised this question: "If the individual pupil counts, is good or evil to be found in a barrage of standardized tests, college board examinations, searches for talent, statewide examinations, and national survey tests?"[33] A professor of mathematics at a university in New York has been

[31] Leonard P. Ayres, *Making Education Definite*, Bulletin No. 11. (Bloomington, Ind.: Indiana University Press, 1915).

[32] D. Russell and C. H. Judd, *The American Educational System.* (Boston: Houghton Mifflin Company, 1940), p. 460.

[33] American Association of School Administrators, Association for Supervision and Curriculum Development, National Association of Secondary School Principals, National Department of Elementary School Principals, and NEA Department of Rural Education, *Labels and Fingerprints.* (Washington, D.C.: National Education Association, 1961), p. 6.

especially critical of standardized achievement tests which have a tendency to penalize the bright and imaginative pupils and to reward the uncreative ones.[34] An article in a bulletin of the Association for Higher Education pointed out that high school seniors spend a disproportionate amount of time taking tests on the basis of which only a few will be selected for scholarships; that so much testing puts undue pressure on students and their parents; that some evidence exists that cheating, suicides, and hypertension in the adolescent population correlates with the pressures of the academic scene; and that ways should be found to test disadvantaged students so that their real potential will be revealed, as contrasted with potential distorted by cultural disadvantages. The author of the article pointed out, however, that most of the responsibility for the malfunctioning of testing lies with the users rather than with the test designers.[35]

One aspect of the testing movement which has aroused much opposition has been the use of personality tests. William H. Whyte was highly critical of the use of these tests by corporations for the purpose of selecting personnel who conform to the image of the *organization man*—the conforming man, who would cause few problems and create few new ideas.[36] Whyte also called attention to the tendency of pupils in school to give the expected answer to test items rather than the answer that expressed their feelings.

More recent issues are related to the use of tests for the classification (tracking) of pupils[37]; the limited norms available for minority and ethnic groups; the relationship between accountability and standardized testing programs; the possible bias constructed into existing intelligence tests, which may unfairly depress the scores of minority groups; and the potential "self-fulfilling prophecy" impact of test results upon the user to the disadvantage of the learner. Yet, many critics of standardized tests are perilously close to criticizing a tool because of the clumsiness of its users.

One aspect of the larger controversy concerning standardized testing is the "intelligence tests," or "IQ tests." Intelligence tests, as do other tests, define the relevant behaviors, sample the possible universe of behaviors, display in a quantitative form the results of the sampling, and provide a normative basis for interpreting the quantitative results. "Intelligence was only vaguely defined by the test makers, but the tests were used to define intelligence."[38] The sampling of behaviors on an intelligence test is not of behaviors which directly reflect the general capacity for learning, but are "direct measures only of achievement in learning."[39] The inference from direct measures of achievement in learning to a

[34] Banesh Hoffman, *The Tyranny of Testing*. (New York: Crowell Collier and Macmillan, Inc., 1962).

[35] Lewis B. Mayhew, "The Testing Controversy," *College and University Bulletin* of the Association for Higher Education, National Education Association (Feb. 15, 1964).

[36] William H. Whyte, *The Organization Man*. (New York: Simon & Schuster, Inc., 1956).

[37] *Smuck* v. *Hobson*, 408 F 2d 175 (D. C. Circuit, 1969) Case No. 86.

[38] Lillian Zack, "The I.Q. Debate," in *Annual Editions, Readings in Education*. (Guilford, Conn.: Dushkin Publishing Co., 1973–1974), p. 73.

[39] Zack, p. 74.

general, native capacity for learning is a long one! Also of concern is that the sampling assumes every child to have had equal exposure to the behaviors selected for sampling, so that differences in behaviors are a reflection of learning rather than experience. The inherent problem in this is apparent, especially when the sampling is related to norming. The assumption that the norming has has been done on a representative, national sample of children can be challenged by "the fact that the national sample is heavily weighted by average white children."[40]

Some of the critics of intelligence testing arrived at the position that if the interpretations of the results were qualified in light of the limitations of the tool, and if the uses were for diagnosis rather than classification, then the intelligence tests were functional. Both Zack and Ornstein commented:

> The intelligence tests, not the I.Q. score, can tell us the level of the child's functioning in a variety of tasks which measure general intelligence and which are intimately correlated with classroom learning.[41]
>
> The remedy is not the elimination of the test or alteration of skills demanded by the school, so that there will be no need for such tests, but the elimination of learning inequalities and social inequalities. One would not declare the tuberculin test unfair or biased because minority and poor children live in an environment that predisposes them, more than middle-class children, to the disease, or because the test measures exposure to a disease which is related to environmental conditions. In terms of function, both the IQ and the tuberculin tests are reflecting a given point of development which should not be ignored.[42]

In November of 1975, appointed representatives of twenty-five national education associations, government agencies, and educational groups met in Washington, D.C., to investigate the educational, social, and legal implications of the increasing use of standardized tests. The following statement was included in the group's recommendations to their governing boards:

> We believe that the public, and especially educators, parents, and children, need fair and effective assessment processes that can be used for diagnosing and prescribing for the needs of individual children. We also believe that the use of fair, effective assessment practices is one way of being held accountable for providing quality education for all students. We have grave reservations, however, about any continued use of so-called IQ tests.[43]

An increasing number of professional groups are becoming concerned and opposed to the standardized testing excesses. Terry Herndon, Director of the National Education Association, said in a speech: "The only real beneficiaries, aside from the test marketers themselves, are insecure managers striving for comfort in their relations with school boards, legislators, and governors."[44]

The Association for Supervision and Curriculum Development (ASCD),

[40] Zack, p. 74.
[41] Zack, p. 74.
[42] Allen Ornstein, "I.Q. Tests and the Culture Issue," *Phi Delta Kappan*, Vol. LVII, No. 6 (February 1976), p. 404.
[43] ASCD, *News Exchange*, Vol. XVII, No. 4 (December 1975), p. 7.
[44] ASCD, *News Exchange*, Vol. XVIII, No. 1 (February 1976), p. 1.

in its 1975 annual conference, passed a resolution calling for an inquest into the "nature, content, utilization, and implications" of standardized test use.[45] The National Association of Elementary School Principals (NAESP) in its July–August 1975 journal (*National Elementary Principal*) called for a national probe of standardized tests. In an April 24, 1975 issue of *News Release*, it was announced that "The *National Elementary Principal* today called on citizens and educators to mount an intensive national inquiry into I.Q. and achievement tests annually administered to over 40 million American youngsters."[46] The *News Release* also quoted Jerrold R. Zacharias, Professor of Physics, Emeritus, at the Massachusetts Institute of Technology:

> *MIT's Zacharias sums up his criticisms of standardized tests with a checklist of pitfalls they pose for students, teachers, and schools. Among the demands tests make on students, he charges, are a "disproportionate facility in reading and writing, the need to understand the tester's language and jargon and to "guess what the tester wants," plus a need for speed and a "toleration of boredom." Test items, Zacharias maintains, are frequently "ambiguous, meaningless, irrelevant to anything the student knows or cares about, trivial and misleading, time wasting, unnecessarily complex, or tricky." As for the class, school, or system, Zacharias says the tests may set false standards for performance or for goals of learning, penalize creative teachers, and damage the morale of everyone concerned, including parents.*
>
> *For these and other reasons, he concludes, the administration of IQ tests as they now exist "should cease and desist," and a major effort should be made to find "some reasonable collection of procedures" to assess a child's general competence.*[47]

The concern over the quality and use of standardized tests is an increasing one, and it is coming at a time when there are more standardized tests available and more testing done than ever before.

National Assessment

In the November 1975 issue of *U.S. News and World Report*, some preliminary results from the recent National Assessment of Educational Progress, a federally funded Denver-based project, were given. The seventeen-year-olds correctly answering a typical science question decreased from 49 percent in 1969–1970 to 46 percent in 1972–1973. The average score on a written essay test decreased on an 8-point scale from 5.12 in 1969 to 4.85 in 1974. The nine-year-olds' average scores on the written essay tests remained much the same between the 1969 and 1974 tests.

The article also made comparisons between the 1963 and 1975 Scholastic Aptitude Test and the College Entrance Examination Board tests. The Verbal Ability average score in 1963 was 478, and in 1975 was 434. The Mathematical Ability average score was 502 in 1963, and 472 in 1975.

---

45 ASCD, *News Exchange*, Vol. XVIII, No. 1 (February 1976), p. 1.
46 NAESP, *News Release* (April 24, 1975).
47 NAESP, *News Release* (April 24, 1975).

The Association for Supervision and Curriculum Development invited professionals to provide their reactions:

> *National scores on the verbal section of the Scholastic Aptitude Test have fallen 44 points since 1963 and 30 on the mathematical sections (on a scale of 200–800). There was a 10 point drop in the verbal and an 8 point drop in the mathematical section scores in just the last year. There was also a 2 point decline in CEEB achievement test scores from 1974 to 1975. To what factors do you attribute this decline, and what are the implications of this for the schools' curriculum?*[48]

Among the respondents was S. P. Marland, President of the College Entrance Examination Board. He wrote:

> *To suggest curricular implications is not possible, for we do not now know the reasons for the score decline. We have, however, appointed an external panel of measurement and other scholars to review the data, study the psychometric integrity of the SAT, and explore the hypotheses advanced to explain the decline.*
>
> *Remember, the SAT is a measure of those verbal and mathematical reasoning abilities—developed over time, in and out of school—that are commonly needed for successful academic performance in college. The SAT was designed to predict such performance and research indicates that its validity remains high.*
>
> *The SAT was not designed to measure school quality and should not be used for that purpose.*[49]

Phillip L. Hosford, the 1975–1976 President of the Association for Supervision and Curriculum Development wrote:

> *The decline in national scores is real. I wish I could join those who shrug off the reports as being a fluke of testing or the result of bad research, but neither is true.*
>
> *We do not know if increased attention in other curriculum areas relates to the drop in scores in the skill areas. We could more easily conjecture that the drop is due to changes in grading procedures, a retreat from comprehensive teacher-made tests, rising truancy, weakened family control, and teacher attitudes.*
>
> *In any case, the implications are clear: we must correct the trend and do so without retreating from gains made in other curriculum areas.*[50]

SUMMARY

1. Educational evaluation is a system of defining, gathering, displaying, and interpreting data relevant to the objectives of instruction and/or education.

[48] ASCD, *News Exchange*, Vol. XVIII, No. 1 (February 1976), pp. 6–7.
[49] ASCD, pp. 6–7.
[50] ASCD, pp. 6–7.

2. Schools use evaluation to reveal to teachers what is happening to pupils, to motivate pupils to put forth more effort, to provide a basis for improving teaching strategies and resources for learning, for course improvement, and for curriculum improvement.

3. An adequate program of evaluation is in harmony with the objectives of the school, comprehensive, continuous, and cooperative.

4. A comprehensive evaluation system is focused on pupils, teachers, curriculum, and reporting.

5. Aspects of pupil growth which are generally evaluated include mental ability, achievement in school subjects, personal-social adjustment, physical status, interests, attitudes, work-study skills, creative self-expression, critical thinking, and home and community background.

6. The evaluation of teachers and teaching has evolved through moralistic behaviors, personality traits, knowledge of content, and interaction patterns.

7. The establishment of educational specifications is a fundamental act in the curriculum evaluation system.

8. A comprehensive reporting program includes activities directed toward the pupils, the parents, and the institution.

9. The current issues in evaluation are the accountability program, the tool of behavioral objectives, the nature and use of standardized tests, and the movement of national assessment.

Problems and Projects

1. Discuss with an elementary school teacher the various evaluation procedures used in his or her school. Classify the teacher's listing by cognitive, affective, and psychomotor domain, and also by high- or low-energy levels within the domain.

2. Many of the "unloving critics" have blasted the evaluation techniques within our schools, and rightfully so when evaluation procedures have been geared solely to low cognitive activities. Now, however, the nature of curriculum has shifted to the teaching of "processes" and has necessitated reform in the evaluation programs. Select a particular area in which you are interested. Review a curriculum guide or package program for that area. Does the guide or program contain evaluation procedures? If so, what domains are to be represented? As a teacher of the package or guide you examined, which ten measurable and observable skills or processes would you select for evaluation? How would you evaluate the ten skills or processes you listed?

3. Select a standardized test which was used twenty-five years ago. Examine a current test and compare it with the older test. What modifications have occurred within the modern test to increase its validity?

4. Provide a criterion upon which you would base an evaluation of textbooks. Sharpen your criterion to focus upon textbooks in college elementary curriculum courses. Based upon the criterion you developed, evaluate this fifth-edition of *Modern Elementary Curriculum*.

5. Observe three individual students during a 15-minute learning period. Record the evaluative techniques which were being used while you observed and those which might have been used to evaluate experience which occurred within the learner

during the 15-minute learning period. Talk with the students you observed. How do they evaluate their experiences?

6. Read three recent articles related to teacher-parent conferences. Do the articles set up any boundaries for particular topics which should not be discussed? What right does the child have to be present at teacher-parent conferences? Develop an outline for a teacher-parent conference, based upon information from this text and the articles reviewed.

7. Review the literature related to the selection of curriculum packages or programs. Develop from your readings and experience the criteria you as an elementary teacher would adopt in selecting a curriculum package or program.

Selected Readings

Anderson, Scarvia, Samuel Ball, Richard T. Murphy, *Encyclopedia of Educational Evaluation*. San Francisco: Jossey-Bass, Inc., Publishers, 1974. A sourcebook on most aspects of evaluation.

Association for Supervision and Curriculum Development, *Improving Educational Assessment and an Inventory of Measures of Affective Behavior*. Washington, D.C.: Association for Supervision and Curriculum Development, 1969. Presents guidelines for assessment of behaviors in the affective domain.

Association for Supervision and Curriculum Development, *Perceiving, Behaving, Becoming*. Washington, D.C.: Association for Supervision and Curriculum Development, 1962. A classical statement on pupil development.

Bloom, Benjamin, J. Thomas Hastings, and George F. Madaus, *Handbook of Formative and Summative Evaluation of Learning*. New York: McGraw-Hill Book Company, Inc., 1971. Relates the *Taxonomy of Educational Objectives* to the formative and summative evaluation of learning through testing.

Bloom, Benjamin S. (Ed.), *Taxonomy of Educational Objectives: Cognitive Domain*. New York: David McKay Co., Inc., 1956. A hierarchical classification of the behaviors of intellectual skills and abilities.

Buros, Oscar K., *The Seventh Mental Measurement Yearbook*. Highland Park, N.J.: The Gryphon Society, 1972. Contains critiques and descriptions of a wide range of published tests.

Combs, Arthur W., *Educational Accountability: Beyond Behavioral Objectives*. Washington, D.C.: Association for Supervision and Curriculum Development, 1972. A humanistic approach to accountability.

Del Novellis, Richard L., and Arthur J. Lewis, *Schools Become Accountable: A PACT Approach*. Washington, D.C.: Association for Supervision and Curriculum Development, 1974. Presents a plan for organizing an accountability system.

Educational Testing Service, *State Educational Assessment Programs*. Englewood Cliffs, N.J.: Prentice-Hall, Inc., 1972. Describes level approaches of various states to accountability.

Harrow, Anita J., *Taxonomy of the Psychomotor Domain: A Guide for Developing Behavioral Objectives*. New York: David McKay Co., Inc., 1972. A classification of movement behaviors.

Gottman, John M., and Robert E. Clasen, *Evaluation in Education, A Practitioner's Guide*. Itasca, Ill.: F. E. Peacock Publishers, Inc., 1972. A practical guide for designing evaluation programs.

Hedges, William D., *Evaluation in Elementary School*. New York: Holt, Rinehart and Winston, 1969. Chapter 4 presents the use of observation as an evaluation device.

Krathwohl, David R., Benjamin S. Bloom, and Bert Masia, *Taxonomy of Educational Objectives: Affective Domain*. New York: David McKay Co., Inc., 1964. A hierarchical classification of the behaviors of feelings, attitudes, and awarenesses.

chapter 14

Perceiving TOMORROW

*Some men see things as
they are and say, "Why?"
I dream things that never were
and say, "Why not?"*

Robert F. Kennedy

UNCERTAINTY AND FUTURISM

During these times when one of the basic certainties is the uncertainty of the future, predictions and prophecies concerning the shape of the future have become popular and appropriate. Prophets and scholars who predict the nature of the "house of tomorrow" are honored by our attention. We honor those who project to tomorrow because we hope to live there.

Futurism, a systematic attempt to project the direction and scope of future developments, has become a recognized field of scholarship. Will the environments of the future be like those of today? Can the future be predicted by looking at yesterday? Are the environments of the future so different that present and past patterns provide no frames of reference?

SITUATION 14.1   Before continuing, take a few minutes to write a brief paragraph describing your visions for the "house of tomorrow" in the field of education.

Unquestionably, the rate of change has accelerated significantly. In fact, the rate has accelerated so rapidly that Toffler's term, "future shock" has become a common expression.[1] "Future shock" means the disorientation of individuals when their past life experiences provide inadequate or ineffective frames of reference for effective decision making in today's living.

[1] Alvin Toffler, *Future Shock*. (New York: Random House, Inc., 1970).

484

An observation commonly expressed by some American Indian tribes is that white people are so aware of where they have been in the "past" and so interested in where they are going in the "future," that they do not know where are in the "present." This expression preceded the label applied to the psychological phenomenon known as "delayed gratification" (that is, if you work hard now, you will be rewarded in the future). The attractiveness of future rewards is lessened when the future is uncertain and when their cost deprecates the rewards of the present.

When technological and cultural changes were slow and were merely linear modifications of existing or past patterns, a thorough understanding of these previous models provided a direction for adapting to present and future life patterns. But, for example, what now provides an orientation into the vocational world when three-fourths of the people employed by the industrial world in 1986 will be producing goods and services not now in existence?[2]

Will the changes of the future continue to be super-rapid? Will scientific breakthroughs continue to provide satisfactory answers to the multiplicity of current problems? Will technology continue to flourish and continue to produce a society characterized by increased convenience and leisure? Or will a more simple life-style, like that of the early 1900s, evolve as a result of the crushing complexities of future patterns?

Professionals and scholars such as Toffler, McLuhan, Postman, Weingartner, Drucker, Pulliam, Diagon, and Dempsey have provided some fascinating and challenging prophecies concerning the shape of the future. The impact of their combined predictions upon teaching and curriculum building is almost overwhelming. Nevertheless, the future is all that is ahead: most individuals—especially children—will go there by choice, while some other individuals will still continue to look back toward the "good old days."

INSTABILITY

The life experiences of the past and present, and those projected for the future, are sources for the experiences to be included in the construction of curriculum. Yet, in the period of "future shock," how can curriculum experiences be selected? The following analysis of the criteria identified in Chapter 5 for the selection of content (classical, relevant, practical, and humane), provides an example of "future shock" in curriculum building. Classicalness as a criterion for the selection of experiences is oriented toward the past. Granted, individuals are partial products of their past, but they live and produce in the present, and consume in the future. Relevancy as a criterion for the selection of experiences focuses upon the anticipated appropriateness and functionality of those selected. Thus, relevancy as a criterion requires reliable prophecies and predictions of the future. Practicalness as a criterion selects experiences which offer relationships to the initial employment of the learner. With futurists predicting that 75

---

[2] Dean C. Corrigan, "The Future: Implications for the Preparation of Educational Personnel," *Journal of Teacher Evaluation*, Vol. 25, No. 2 (Summer 1974), p. 100.

percent of the people employed in 1986 will be producing goods and services not now in existence, how can future experiences be selected?[3] Humaneness as a criterion advocates the selection of experiences which depict the spirit and nature of humans and human societies. If there is to be a future for humans, then humans will exist, but what will be the nature of their spirits and their societies?

When the life experiences of succeeding generations were similar or congruent to contemporary generations, the equating of wisdom with age (length and depth of life experiences) was appropriate. Individuals who had thoughtfully analyzed their previous experiences and transmitted them to succeeding and contemporary generations were honored and valued for their wisdom. But these were times when their knowledge was congruent or similar to what the younger generations would experience. Now, however, this similarity and congruence of knowledge between generations no longer exists, and a great hiatus between the past and the present, as well as between the present and the future, has broken those threads of continuity so that few guidelines remain sufficiently absolute to be useful in predicting life experiences in the future. Still, it is possible to detect trends, and it is upon those that we must depend to attempt formulating curricula.

CHALLENGE

Toffler, in *Learning for Tomorrow*, wrote of his experience with a group of thirty-three high school students.[4] He asked that they record the events which they anticipated would occur in the future. The students quickly generated 193 forecast events. Only six students and sixteen forecasts included a personal reference. Toffler concluded that ". . . while the future was clearly exciting subject matter, it was (perceived as) distinctly impersonal."[5]

This author suggests that the "impersonal future" of the schools includes the potential and potent changes which may occur in the nature of the tools and technology utilized. Computers, chemicals, calculators, systems, simulations, and strategies may become the sophisticated and commonplace tools, programs, and procedures of the future. But to project, predict, or forecast these changes alone would be to miss or ignore the most dynamic impact of the future. The real and most widespread effects will be evident in human terms. The personal, affective, and attitudinal accommodations of individuals to the changes of the future are the most demanding. The performance of a familiar task, ritual, or ceremony with an unfamiliar tool and/or procedure is difficult and stressful. But to have a familiar event or routine become strange because it must be done with unfamiliar tools (and/or procedures) is shocking!

The personal future of teachers is one of attitudinally and affectively accommodating and assimilating the impact of change as professionals. Literally, the

---

[3] Corrigan, p. 100.
[4] Alvin Toffler (Ed.), *Learning for Tomorrow*. (New York: Random House, Inc., 1974), p. 6.
[5] Toffler, p. 9.

individual who functions as a teacher will have two sets of accommodations to make, which may not necessarily be supportive. The first set of accommodations are those which allow the individual to function adequately as a person in the present society. For the individual who also functions as a teacher, the second set of accommodations are those to be made in order for the constraints and limitations of the teacher's personal accommodations not to be imposed upon those who will "live in the house of tomorrow." For example, the odds are that the mathematical knowledge of an individual who is a teacher is adequate for personal needs. Yet, as a teacher, the individual must strive not to impose the limitations of personal knowledge and level of mathematics upon those who will live and function in a time when a greater and different knowledge of mathematics will most likely be demanded.

Rhetorical question: A frequent comment of teachers concerning the "modern" mathematics program of the 1960s was: "It's too hard for the children." Is this a comment of individuals whose level of competency in mathematics is sufficient for them as a functioning individuals, but is insufficient for them as teachers? If so, they must unlearn and relearn mathematics so that they can better serve children who will be required to function at a higher level of competency. The level required of the teacher to function as an individual may be presently satisfactory, but it will decrease in efficiency as time goes on unless competency is upgraded. This illustration is not intended to defend the modern math program of the 1960s, but to illustrate the attitudinal changes must be made to adjust to the "shock" of teaching for tomorrow.

ATTITUDINAL CHANGES

The most dynamic impact of the future may be upon the attitudes necessary and appropriate to accommodate and assimilate the potential changes in goals, roles, and processes. The major attitudinal changes for tomorrow's teacher will most likely be related to the function of an unlearning process and the role of pluralism.

Unlearning

Attitudinally, teachers have come to value learning and the accumulation of correct answers as the characteristic pattern of learning. This attitude was, and is, reinforced by the premise that the past and the future will be highly similar (a linear projection of the past). Given this premise, the accumulation of the correct answers of the past would provide sufficient preparation for similar correct answers of the future, and an answer which was inappropriate in the past would also be inappropriate in the future. Therefore, teaching patterns were perpetuated which tended to devalue and punish inappropriate answers, and overvalue and reward correct answers from the past.

Because a primary function of education is preparation for the future, teaching patterns and the planned curricula are based upon perspectives of the future. Therefore, the concern is not whether the curriculum should prepare pupils for the future, but rather what projections and resulting premises comprise the bases of a curriculum for tomorrow.

An alternative to a linear projection of the past is the projection that the future will not be congruent with the past and perhaps not even similar. Whatever the approach, the odds seem high that the "answers" of the past and present may undergo transformation as rapidly as the accelerated adjustments characterizing other aspects of the future.

If these answers are to be reconsidered, then obviously some or all parts of each are inappropriate. For this reason, an answer in this category may well become extinct. This premise and the resulting pattern (call it pattern A)

> correct answer from the past and present → reconsidered and either affirmed, modified, or denied → pattern repeated

is significantly different from the linear pattern (pattern B)

> the right answer (past) → the right answer (present) → the right answer (future)

which is derived from a linear projection of the past to the future.

Projections (other than linear) to the future propose a changed function for inappropriate answers. Because each answer may at some time become inappropriate, all answers must be presented and experienced as successive approximations which will be refined and adapted as more and more data become available in the future. This does not mean, nor does it imply, that appropriate answers are not to be taught and learned. They are! It does mean, however, that the pattern for arriving at answers has been changed. The old pattern (B) was to reject inappropriate answers in order to obtain the enduring correct answers. The new pattern (A) is a progressive process in that it may modify or reject a seemingly acceptable previous answer in order to find the correct one.

Even though the older pattern is subsumed within the newer pattern, the added phase of unlearning tremendously changes the older pattern. Unlearning is the rejection and modification of previously learned, correct organizations of experiences in order to learn a new organization which is more nearly appropriate to the new environment.

Dewey defined education as "the reconstruction or reorganization of experience which adds to the meaning of the experience, and which increases the ability to direct the course of subsequent experience."[6] Notice the emphasis upon the preparation for the future "to direct the course of subsequent experience." Dewey's definition of education remains a fundamental one. When facing a dynamic future, however, the necessity of a reeducation experience becomes important.

Reeducation is the process of unlearning the old set of perceptions, answers,

---

[6] John Dewey, *Democracy and Education*. (New York: Crowell Collier and Macmillan, Inc., 1916), p. 89.

adjustive mechanisms, and organizations which previously directed habits of conduct, and the process of learning a new set which is appropriate to a changed environment. A comprehensive curriculum in the future may encompass both the educative organizations defined by Dewey and the reeducative organizations defined here.[7]

The primary difference between the patterns A and B lies in the "unlearning" as a fundamental adjustive process for the future. The initial educative experiences provide the first organizations to direct subsequent behaviors, while the reeducative experiences provide the adjustive capabilities to accommodate changes which make the initial educative organizations ineffective and/or socially inappropriate. While continuous learning has been the characteristic sequence for education, the sequence for the future may become learning, unlearning, and learning.

The differences between the learning and unlearning processes nest in the loss of organizations (answers), which previously directed behaviors. During this period of loss, individuals are threatened, anxious, and vulnerable. They relinquish the power and control provided by previous organizations, and then experience a transitional period which is preliminary to the forming of new organizations.

In an initial learning sequence, learners are always moving toward organizations which will provide increased powers, control, and effective behaviors. During the unlearning phase, they initially move away from power, control, and the once effective behaviors in order to start a new learning cycle. Figuratively—and perhaps literally—in an educative sequence, the individual moves from insecurity (uneducated) to security (educated). In a reeducative sequence, the individual moves from security (educated) to insecurity (uneducated) to security (reeducated).

Teaching behaviors during reeducation must be much more supportive than during education. The individual becomes independent through the initial organization of experience, but during reeducation the individual is requested to give up this initial independence for a more effective future independence. Individuals may be very reluctant to do this, and are more likely to accept the dependence (uneducated) for independence (educated) trade-off than the independence (educated) to dependence (uneducated) to independence (reeducated) process involved in reeducation.

SITUATION 14.2   Discuss the teacher's role in providing affective support during the "unlearning-reeducation" process.

Specific programs presently in existence which have importance and application to reeducation are the decision-making activities inherent in inquiry

[7] For further discussion of "reeducation" see George Sharp, *Curriculum as Re-education of the Teacher.* (New York: Teacher's College Press, Columbia University, 1951).

methodology, values-clarification, and affective education. In these activities, the teacher's role becomes that of, "I don't know exactly what you need or ought to know, but I can support and guide you as you experience an inquiry process which will provide a series of tested successive approximations."

The teacher of the future must provide a curriculum in which the experiences of learning, unlearning, and reeducation are included and fundamental.

Personalized Pluralism

The prevailing attitudes toward individualization of instruction in the recent past, and perhaps in the present, have been generated from an industrial society. In an industrial society the attributes of interchangeable parts, mass production, integration toward sameness, planned obsolescence, and accurate predictions are dominant. The same attributes generate parallel attitudes which enhance the virtues of the attributes.

These attributes and their virtue-enhancing attitudes have also found an application in schools. Educational research, for example, is typically focused upon the group (mass production) rather than the individual. Conclusions concerning the group are made applicable to the individuals (interchangeable parts). Brophy and Good said, ". . . little educational research has focused upon the individual student. We believe that it is a major reason why educational research has contributed relatively little knowledge that teachers can apply in the classroom."[8]

The concept of the school as the "melting pot" of society can be interpreted within an industrial society to mean an integration toward sameness. This interpretation would maintain ·that the school functions to reduce the cultural and ethnic differences among peoples and to provide a common American culture. In this frame, the attributes of culture, and to a considerable degree individual uniqueness, may be devalued. An awkward analogy is the discard of a part from an assembly line because its dimensional tolerances cannot be integrated with the tolerances (allowable difference range) of all other parts.

Applications of the integration toward sameness to the curriculum results in an identical sequence of skills and content for all pupils; the focus on mean standardized test scores of groups; the rejection of pupils because of a variation from commonness (for example, economic status, ethnic membership, IQ); the treatment of pupils based upon the label or grade assigned to them (cooperative, troublemaker, special education, accelerated); an emphasis upon group goals and identities; and a span of similar operations.

The theme and major thrust of the Association for Supervision and Curriculum Development (ASCD) during 1975 was "Cultural Pluralism." This theme was adopted as a result of three major considerations:

(a) a broadening concern for educational futures; (b) a realization of the social and cultural changes taking place in our society, and the impact of these

---

[8] Jere E. Brophy and Thomas L. Good, *Teacher-Student Relationships, Causes and Consequences.* (New York: Holt, Rinehart and Winston, 1974), p. 3.

changes on the organization in terms of its constituency and functioning; and (c) the historically evolved nexus of values that had come to distinguish ASCD from other professional organizations.[9]

A panel of futurists—including Toffler, L. Brown, and John Platt—sponsored by ASCD, gathered to consider the possible responses to a dramatically changing future. The panel identified the two most probable responses as (1) a friendly, fascist state, or (2) the development of intentional communities with pluralistic life styles. ASCD opted for "an intentional development of pluralistic life styles," that is, cultural pluralism.

This author projects a future in which the personalization of pluralism will be necessary and appropriate. To substitute the word "personalization" for culture is to indicate a movement from honoring ethnic groups for their tradition and potential to honoring individuals for their uniqueness and potential. This substitution envisions an environment in which the differences and variances among people are maximized and accommodated, where prejudgments do not govern those professionals responsible for creating and managing the environment, and where the inherent capacity of the individual to change is not denied in practice, fact, or myth.

For this environment to emerge, those real attributes of children must be perceived, while some of the present virtue-enhancing attitudes associated with the perception of these attributes must change. Some of the real attributes of children are socioeconomic class, ability, race, gender, achievement level, personalities, physical appearance, penmanship, and dialect. Brophy and Good gathered, displayed, and interpreted the studies which demonstrate that the attitudes of teachers associated with their perceptions of these attributes ". . . affect teacher expectations and attitudes regarding students, and in turn affect the way the teacher deals with the students."[10]

Brophy and Good also identified teachers' reactions to their perceptions of these individual-group attributes. According to them, some teachers react passively and predictably to their perceptions of these attributes and become reactors rather than interactors. Other teachers are less conditioned by their virtue-enhancing attitudes accruing from their perceptions of these attributes and are more effective in changing student behaviors. Still other teachers are over-reactors and treat the children as stereotypes rather than individuals.[11] In a personalized, pluralistic curriculum, teachers in the future would be less conditioned by their perceptions and virtue-enhancing attitudes, and therefore more effective as interactive, intervening agents of change (learning).

Personalized Change

The challenge and threat of the future to teachers does not nest in the sophisticated and complicated technological and mechanical advances which are likely

[9] James B. McDonald, "Cultural Pluralism as A.S.C.D.'s Major Thrust," *Educational Leadership*, Vol. XXXII, No. 3 (December 1974), p. 167.
[10] Brophy and Good, p. 29.
[11] Brophy and Good, p. ix.

to be made. Rather, the challenge and threat will be manifest in the confrontation between the virtue-enhancing attitudes of an industrial society and the virtue-enhancing attitudes of a personalized, pluralistic society.

Perhaps that which is perceived will change, but to a lesser degree than the virtue-enhancing attitudes from which perceptions are interpreted and translated into patterns and habits of conduct. The subsequent sections present those areas of perceptions which should remain stable in the future.

STABILITY

It seems to this author that the predictions related to the continuing stabilities from the past to the present to the future have an importance equal to that of predictions related to the instabilities within society. Are there not some aspects of our past and present which will continue to be in the future? Perhaps the environments surrounding these stable aspects will change, but why not focus on what was, is, and will be? Accepting the same risks as the professional futurist, this author predicts that the following aspects will be in our future: children, learning, teaching, curricula, schooling, humanness, and dreams.

SITUATION 14.3　　Review the paragraph you wrote at the beginning of the chapter. Draw parallels between your visions and the enduring stabilities predicted by the author: children, learning, teaching, curricula, schooling, humanism, dreams.

Children

There will be children! Perhaps fewer in numbers or even more, but children will be, or the future won't be. Quite possibly the baby will be conceived, carried, and delivered in different ways (test tubes and incubators) and born of and into different "marriage-family" units; but there will still be children—children through whom adults and society will strive to attain immortality by perpetuating themselves.

A child will still experience a stage of dependency, a formative period when the child must experience from external sources such as parents or surrogates the feelings of safety, security, warmth, and love; a period during which the responsiveness of a potential adult is shaped; a period when growth, learning, and development are characterized by the capacity for becoming; and a period ruled by eagerness, activity, curiosity, creativity, imagination, risk taking, and the desire to know.

Regardless of the nature of the increased brightness of children—whether chemically induced, selectively bred, or environmentally enriched—the child will still learn as a child with the cognitive and affective modes that characterize children. The child will not be a little adult; the child will be a child!

Learning

Albert Schweitzer said, "As we turn more and more to authority for answers and become skeptical about our powers to develop our own thinking, we are easily led into becoming tools rather than people who use tools!"[12]

There will be learning! The need to adopt, adapt, and create behaviors which are effective and efficient for the individual and society will endure. The human capacity to organize experiences for the guidance and direction of further experiences will prevail. When changing conditions make previous organizations of behaviors inadequate, there will remain the strength or weakness to reorganize, or fail to reorganize, behaviors.

Perhaps the content of the learning will be significantly different, and indeed even the nature of the learning process itself may differ; yet, the need to learn, and the value and power of knowing will prevail. Learning is the means through which the human being gains power and becomes a controller of experiences and the environment. Humans need to know. Learning will continue!

Teaching

Because there are children with the drive, curiosity, and capacity to learn, the teaching function will exist. Perhaps the teaching function will be performed by humans not trained and licensed as now practiced, but the value of foresight and hindsight for the ordering and individualization of the learning will continue.

The functions of guiding, directing, praising, availability to, and caring for the human learner will serve all futures. The dependency of the child-learner needs to be shared, shared with someone, a "teacher" who does not through dependency victimize the sharer; shared with someone, a "teacher" who will facilitate the growth of independence through the participatory dependence. Most probably the environment, content vehicles, tools, rewards, and even punishments will change, but there will be a demand for the functions of teaching.

Curricula

The need to systematize, simplify, and edit information and those learning processes which are relevant, humane, classical, and practical will prevail. Granted that there may be significant differences in *what is* and how it is organized, but the vehicle of curriculum will be moved into the future as a servant. The expertise which brings a flexible ordering rather than a randomness to the inherent trial-and-error process formerly involved in learning will increase. Because there will be children, learning, and teaching, the need to bring order, purpose, and direction to information and learning processes will mandate curricula.

12 Emma D. Sheehy, *Children Discover Music and Dance*. (New York: Holt, Rinehart and Winston, Inc., 1959), p. 275.

Schooling

The requirements of inducting the young, transmitting cultural heritage, and maintaining or changing a social order mandate the functions of schooling. Schooling may not occur in our present institutions or even in systems that resemble our present institutions, but the functions of schooling will be performed. These functions have existed and even endured in forms no longer adequate, but the functions have been and will continue to be. The present institution called "school" is a relatively new creation established to serve a continuing need; schooling will happen!

Humanness

Emerson, in his Phi Beta Kappa address "The American Scholar," said that the greatest danger threatening American life at that time was, "the tendency of man as he takes on a trade or profession to become, for example, a farmer rather than a man who farms."[13]

The ultimate stability is that of our humanness. The manners and expressions of humanness may change, but we remain human. We can never be other than human and, more significantly, never more than human.

Dreams

The capacity to perceive things as they could be, the awareness of the gap between practice and potential, and the courage to dedicate life energies to the achievement of dreams will continue to guide us and those who live in the "schools" of tomorrow. Dreams are among the triggering factors which move humans and their societies. Dreams embed in humankind the courage to reach beyond the known. Dreams will be!

I Dream of Human Learning

Learn to interact in a rational way with the objects, events, and situations characterizing the environment.

Learn to experience the joys and power of knowing and of how to know.

Learn to value the functions of relativeness and change as aspects of growth.

Learn to love and regard oneself.

Learn to regard differences as newnesses rather than as strangenesses.

Learn to start or continue through both success and failure.

Learn to balance collectiveness and individualness.

Learn to follow and to lead, based upon the criterion: "quality of service rendered."

Learn to develop the continuing pleasures of curiosity, investigation, and trying.

Learn to value and honor human sexuality.

Learn to recognize the nature, functioning, and value of institutional safeguards of freedom.

[13] Sheehy, p. 275.

"Your move."

Learn to honor the continuity of knowledge and of mankind.
Learn to identify with a belief that is larger than oneself.

Problems and Projects

1. Review five educational journal articles written during the past three years on the subject of "futurism." Prepare a bibliography for the five articles, noting under each entry the predictions stated by the author.

2. Once during a teaching job interview, an applicant was asked, "Is the world round or flat?" Knowing that the securement of the job depended upon the answer, the applicant replied, "I can teach it either way. Which way do you want it?" Select one presently "believed to be true" (not yet disproved) statement (for example, children will always need to be taught to read). Construct a logical but contradictory explanation for the "believed to be true" statement you selected. Outline two strategies of instruction for teaching:

    a. the "believed to be true" statement

    b. the logical yet contradictory explanation.

3. Given the following situation:

Time: 1997

Setting: An extremely effective teacher and successful professional has been placed in a curriculum supervisor's role.

Problem: Discuss the reeducation of this person (see the section "Attitudinal Changes"). Also, include in the discussion the potential affective ramifications of the reeducative processes.

Selected Readings

Brameld, Theodore, *The Climatic Decades*. New York: Praeger Publishers, Inc., 1970. Presents preliminary corrections for a radically energized conception of education by a reconstructionist.

Brown, Lester R., *World without Borders*. New York: Random House, Inc. (Vintage Books), 1972. Discusses the interactions among peoples and problems which may strike down the political and social borders of nations.

Callahan, Raymond E., *Education and the Cult of Efficiency*. Chicago: University of Chicago Press, 1962. Discusses the strength of the business ideology in American culture and the extreme weakness and vulnerability of school personnel.

Daigon, Arthur, and Richard A. Dempsey, *School, Pass at Your Own Risk*. Englewood Cliffs, N.J.: Prentice-Hall, Inc., 1974. Provides evidence related to "how it is" in schools today.

Drucker, Peter F., *The Age of Discontinuity: Guidelines to Our Changing Society*. New York: Harper & Row, Publishers, 1969. The "discontinuities" which are likely to mold and shape tomorrow are reported.

Fisher, Robert J., and Wilfred R. Smith (Eds.), *Schools in an Age of Crisis*. New York: Van Nostrand Reinhold Company, 1972. Contains articles by members of the profession who are actually involved in controversial, critical thinking.

Goodlad, John I., *The Changing School Curriculum*. New York: Fund for Advancement of Education, 1966. Presents a discussion of the school as the great sorting machine.

Hipple, Theodore (Ed.), *The Future of Education 1975–2000*. Pacific Palisades, Calif.: Goodyear Publishing Co., Inc., 1974. Gives a collection of readings concerning the future of education.

McLuhan, Marshall, *Counterblast*. New York: Harcourt Brace Jovanovich, Inc., 1969. Places a counter-environment as a means of perceiving the dominant one.

McLuhan, Marshall, and Quentin Fiore, *The Medium Is the Message*. New York: Bantam Books, Inc., 1967. Discusses the shaping of societies by the nature of the media of communication rather than the content of the communication.

Postman, Neil, and Charles Weingartner, *Teaching as a Subversive Activity*. New York: Dell Publishing Co., Inc., 1969. Discusses fear, coercion, and rote memory as methods used with obsolete content.

Pulliam, John D., and Jim R. Bowman, *Educational Futurism in Pursuance of Survival*. Norman, Okla.: University of Oklahoma Press, 1974. The authors write from the perspective that "surviving the future appears to depend upon either slowing the rate of change or radically altering the means by which people are educated."

Shane, Harold G., *The Educational Significance of the Future*. Bloomington, Ind.: Phi Delta Kappa, 1973. Presents an interpretation and projection of the implications of the future for education.

Appendix

AN ILLUSTRATIVE EVALUATION SYSTEM FOR THE CURRICULUM OF A MODERN ELEMENTARY SCHOOL

This evaluation system has two scales. The first scale (1,2,3,4) deals with the building unit's data base for its evaluation program, and the existence and frequency of a condition, facility, or behavior. The second scale (A,B,C) deals with the utilization and effectiveness of the building unit's evaluation program. The assumptions behind these scales are that a modern elementary school would be consistently gathering data, constantly interpreting data, and continuously adjusting the curriculum based upon the data.

No ready-made system or potential evaluative instrument should be used in a particular building unit until the staff of the unit has studied and then adapted the instrument. The items of this system are presented as examples of those having potential significance for the decision-making activities of a building unit.

Rating Scale I

1. The condition, facility, or behavior is not observable or measurable, and the existence of the condition, facility, or behavior cannot be inferred.
2. The condition, facility, or behavior is not observable or measurable, but the existence of the condition, facility, or behavior can be inferred from other phenomena.
3. The condition, facility, or behavior is usually observable and measurable in applicable situations and settings.
4. The condition, facility, or behavior is observable and measurable in applicable situations and settings.

Rating Scale II

A. A modification of the condition, facility, or behavior has occurred within the past three years, based upon specific observation and measurement of the condition, facility, or behavior.
B. The condition, facility, or behavior has continued to exist for more than three years with no modification, but with observation and measurement of the condition, facility, or behavior.

C. The condition, facility, or behavior has continued to exist without observation and measurement.

<table>
<tr><td align="center">ITEM</td><td align="center">RATING
SCALES
I   II</td></tr>
</table>

I. GOALS AND OBJECTIVES
   A. Goals
   1. The goals of the school exist in writing and are easily accessible.
   2. The goals of the school reflect a consideration of the professional literature.
   3. The goals of the school reflect a consideration of the community setting.
   4. The goals of the school evolve through the interaction of the community, pupils, and the professional staff.
   5. The goals of the school specify concern for each of the following:
      a. The growth, learning, and development of all pupils
      b. A provided basis for the selection of effective and efficient experiences
      c. The contribution of a comprehensive evaluation system
      d. An accountability program
   6. The goals of the school specify concern for a participatory, constitutionally based democracy in the operation, decision-making process, and evaluation of the school.
   B. Objectives
   1. The objectives are written and readily accessible.
   2. The objectives are cooperatively formulated by pupils, teachers, administrators, and community members.
   3. The objectives are specifically referenced to the statement of goals.
   4. The objectives are stated in observable and/or measurable terms.
   5. The objectives are continuously reviewed concerning their integrity and applicability.
   6. The objectives accommodate the variations of individuals, both staff and pupils.
   7. The objectives specify concern with all aspects of children's growth, learning, and development.
   8. The objectives stress the active participation in representative democratic experiences for both staff and pupils.
   9. The objectives recognize the need for developing a command of the fundamental processes.
   10. The objectives recognize the importance of developing the creative abilities of children.

11. The objectives increase opportunities for developing skill in human and civil relationships.
12. The objectives allow pupils to become increasingly self-actualizing.
13. The objectives are limited to those that the school has a reasonable chance to achieve.

II. ENVIRONMENT
  A. Facilities
    1. The school site is large enough to provide space for
       a. driveways.
       b. parking space.
       c. ecological plots.
       d. differentiated play areas for older and younger children (5 acres plus 1 acre for each 100 pupils).
    2. The school site is maintained in good condition and appearance.
    3. The facilities are utilized to maximize the desired educational program.
    4. The instructional areas are large enough to permit multiple learning activities, with adequate storage space (approximately 1,000 square feet for 25 to 30 pupils).
    5. Instructional areas have adequate heating, lighting, sound control, and ventilation for the health and comfort of pupils.
    6. Teachers, pupils, and custodians cooperate to make areas attractive and usable.
    7. The toilet, lavatory facilities, and drinking fountains provided for pupils and teachers are adequate in number and location.
    8. Spaces for individual and small-group specialized activities are available.
    9. The school has an area large enough to accommodate the larger groups that attend school functions.
    10. The school has an all-purpose area which can be used for many school activities.
    11. Space is flexible, and is creatively and regularly utilized.
  B-1. Personnel in General
    1. The certification of personnel is appropriate for their respective assignments.
    2. The majority of personnel have participated in in-service activities within the past six months.
    3. Personnel move through a probationary period to continuing contract or tenure investure.
    4. The staff represents a diversity in

ITEM

    a. age.
    b. experience.
    c. sex.
    d. race.
    e. geographic origins.
    f. places of preparations.
    g. cultural backgrounds.

5. The informal social system and the formal institutional system are mutually supportive, but independent.

6. The functioning of and procedures for acquiring the services of specialized personnel are known and adequate for the needs of the building unit.

7. Noncertificated support personnel provide services such as secretaries, cooks, custodians, drivers, aides.

B-2. Principal

8. The building unit has the services of a full-time, nonteaching principal plus an assistant principal for each six hundred pupils.

9. The principal initiates staff participation and negotiation in the development and evaluation of school policies.

10. The principal manages the resources of the unit effectively (that is, time, monies, space, personnel, materials).

11. The principal spends significant portions of time related to curriculum in
    a. classrooms.
    b. conferences with teachers concerning classroom experiences.
    c. contact with individuals.
    d. small groups of pupils.

12. The principal maintains regular communication with community groups and individuals.

13. The principal is
    a. knowledgeable concerning the curriculum programs of the unit.
    b. capable of directing the processes of review, evaluation, and selection of educational materials and experiences.

B-3. Supervisor

14. The supervisor spends significant portions of time in
    a. classrooms.
    b. conferences with teachers.
    c. providing in-service opportunities.
    d. performing demonstrations.

15. The supervisor has superior skills in diagnosing and evaluating instructional procedures, experiences, and materials.

16. The supervisor is a skilled observer and interpreter of classroom and group processes.

B-4. Teacher

17. The teacher is a skilled observer and diagnostician of pupil behaviors.

18. The teacher maintains warm, empathetic, and supportive interactions with each pupil.

19. The teacher is thoroughly familiar with
    a. curriculum guides.
    b. available materials.
    c. personal lesson plans.

20. The teacher creatively plans alternatives to the documented curriculum, based upon a diagnosis of both the document and the needs of individuals and groups.

21. The teacher displays a positive, supportive relationship with each child through
    a. voice tone.
    b. vocabulary.
    c. posture.
    d. manner of touching.

22. The teacher's descriptions of children are cast in descriptions of behaviors and potentials, with few judgments and global generalizations.

C. Quality of Living and Learning

1. The communications in the classroom are appropriate to the objectives, activities, and needs of the participants.

2. The human relations in the classroom are comfortable, free from excessive tensions, and conducive to learning.

3. Children are free to make mistakes, ask questions, tell about their own experiences, and reveal their honest feelings.

4. Teachers help pupils establish worthwhile objectives toward which to work.

5. Children are encouraged to make choices, exercise initiative, and assume responsibilities.

6. Pupils enter into all their learning experiences with a high degree of enthusiasm, interest, and purpose.

7. Pupils are encouraged and supported as they extend and challenge their capabilities and capacities.

8. Pupils demonstrate awareness and move efficiently to the locations of materials and spaces appropriate for their tasks.

9. The physical arrangement of the room provides areas for various interest and activity centers (for example, library corner, science center, art center).

10. Children are encouraged to do some things together

just for relaxation or enjoyment, using poetry, music, story telling, rhythms, and conversations.

11. The physical environment of classrooms is healthful, comfortable, and conducive to learning.

12. Classroom activities are varied so that all pupils may participate with interest and success.

13. People, places, and things in the community are utilized in the instructional program.

14. Pupils learn the fundamental skills through use in meaningful situations.

15. Pupils are exposed to a great variety of learning materials, media, and resources.

16. Multiple types of intraclass and interclass groupings are utilized to meet the interests, needs, and abilities of children.

17. Units of work are selected wisely and used effectively.

18. Pupils describe with enthusiasm their learning experiences, options, and objectives.

19. The activities of teachers and pupils are characterized by
    a. observation.
    b. measurement.
    c. experimentation.
    d. interpretation.
    e. model building.
    f. predictions.

20. The interactions of teachers and pupils are characterized by
    a. decision making.
    b. wise-acting.
    c. acquisition of relevant knowledges.

21. The selection of instructional experiences is comprehensive and flexible in approaches, materials, and content vehicles; yet, it provides continuity for individuals and groups.

22. The full range of behaviors in the following domains are emphasized and displayed by pupils and teachers:
    a. cognitive
    b. affective
    c. psychomotor

23. The objects, events, situations, and concepts of the environment are appropriate to the preoperational or concrete operational learner.

III. OPERATION
    A. Administration
        1. Individuals have access to the principal to present their grievances.

2. The practices of the building unit are appropriate
to the statutes of civil rights and the constitutional
conditions of due process, freedom of speech, and
all others set forth.

3. The use of resources are periodically audited, reported,
and evaluated.

4. The extent to which objectives are achieved is regularly
made available to interested parties.

5. The process of conflict resolution is done in an orderly
manner with integrity and without malice or revenge.

6. The policies governing the operations of a building unit
are in writing and are accessible.

B. Supervision
1. The functioning of a supervisor is cooperatively,
professionally, and publicly defined.

2. Any charges of inadequacies or incompetencies are in
writing and made available to the individual.

3. An individual's records and reputation are protected,
honored, and available to that individual.

C. Participation
1. Those with expertise and/or those influenced by the
nature of a policy or decision are involved in the
formulation of that policy or decision.

2. The leadership for a particular task is assumed by those
with the skills and experiences most appropriate
for the task.

3. Although all personnel participate, the degree and
amount of participation can vary according to
circumstances, without undue reward or punishment.

4. The contributions resulting from individuals or groups
are recognized.

D. Resources
1. Resources are distributed according to need.

2. The following are all considered, utilized, and valued
as resources:
a. time
b. space
c. money
d. community
e. pupils

3. Those most affected by the use of resources have a
voice in the policies which determine the distribution
of those resources.

IV. EVALUATION
A. Accountability
1. Both a definition and application of an accountability
system are developed and implemented.

ITEM

      2. The data gathered and displayed plus their
interpretations are available.

      3. Each professional contributes to and benefits from the
the accountability system.

B. Program

      1. The school staff engages in continuous study, planning,
and evaluation of the curriculum.

      2. Study of the conditions, needs, and resources of the
community occurs regularly as a part of the
curriculum planning.

      3. The study of growth, learning, and developmental needs
of children is emphasized in curriculum planning.

      4. Representatives of the community and the pupils
participate systematically in curriculum study,
planning, and evaluation.

      5. Curriculum documents provide for the scope, continuity,
and sequence of learning experiences.

      6. Time is scheduled for purposes of coordination, but is
flexible enough to accommodate the needs of the
learning environment.

      7. Time during the school days is provided for
in-service activities, planning, and committee
activities.

      8. The data gathered and the data gathering procedures
for purposes of evaluation are determined by and
consistent with the statements of objectives.

      9. The curriculum documents are readily accessible.

     10. The impact of the evaluation procedures is evidenced
by the nature of the revisions of previous curriculum
documents.

C. Pupils

      1. The diagnostic phase of the pupil evaluation program
is comprehensive (for example: data collected on
developmental levels, cognitive capabilities,
achievement, personal-social adjustment, physical
status, interests, attitudes, work-study skills, creative
expression, and home-community backgrounds
of pupils).

      2. The diagnosis and evaluation of pupil progress
is continuous.

      3. The areas of diagnosis and evaluation are determined
by and consistent with the objectives.

      4. Instructional activities are derived from the diagnostic
and evaluation procedures.

      5. A comprehensive system of permanent and
cumulative records is maintained.

6. Teachers use a variety of evaluation instruments and procedures, such as systematic observation, interviews, tests, anecdotal records, sociograms, and case studies.
7. Pupils participate, under the guidance of the teacher, in the evaluation of their own progress.
8. Services of a psychologist and or psychiatrist are available for referral of students by parents and teachers.

D. Reporting
1. The system of reporting to parents is developed cooperatively by pupils, parents, teachers, and administrators.
2. Reports to parents include
   a. parent-teacher conferences.
   b. personal letters.
   c. telephone calls.
   d. home visits.
3. Reports to parents are made whenever there is a need for them, rather than merely at stated intervals.
4. Reports to parents meet the following criteria:
   a. accurate
   b. diagnostic
   c. constructive
   d. based upon individual assessments
   e. based upon group assessments
5. Parents and teachers understand the objectives of each curriculum area on which pupil progress is evaluated.

V. CURRICULUM AREAS
A. Language Arts
1. Instruction in the language arts is both specific to each of the language arts areas and unified as a study of language arts.
2. Instruction in the language arts is experienced-based and sequenced through listening, speaking, reading, and writing.
3. The skills, experiences, and meanings derived through listening form a primary aspect of all language arts instruction.
4. The context and content of a pupil's speaking form the bases for the language arts activities involving reading and writing.
5. The skills, experiences, and meanings derived through an oral language approach form a primary aspect of all language arts instruction.
6. Second languages and bilingual programs are operational where appropriate.

7. Special provisions are made for nonstandard English (dialect) speakers.
8. Instruction in reading is specific and unified with all areas of the language arts.
9. Instruction in reading is comprehensive and flexible with regard to approach, materials, and methods, but maintains continuity for individual learners.
10. The selection of approaches, materials, and methods is predicated upon the diagnostic procedures.
11. Instruction in writing is specific and unified with all areas of the language arts.
12. Instruction in writing includes the skills and experiences of
    a. penmanship.
    b. spelling.
    c. expository writing.
    d. creative writing.
13. The accommodation and assessment of an individual's readinesses are fundamental in the planning of experiences related to listening, speaking, reading, and writing.
14. The following influential factors related to readiness are completely diagnosed:
    a. physical
    b. cognitive
    c. affective
    d. social
15. The content of the language arts is based upon
    a. pupil experiences.
    b. needs in other curriculum areas.
    c. needs for human development.
16. The application, enrichment, and extension of language arts skills occur in all areas of the curriculum.
17. The evaluations of the language arts program and of pupils are derived from the statement of objectives.
18. The program is appropriate for preoperational and concrete operational learners.

B. Social Studies
1. The content vehicles, experiences, and instruction in social studies represent each of the social science disciplines.
2. Instruction in social studies is comprehensive and flexible with regard to approach, materials, and methods, yet maintains continuity for the individual learner.

  3. The experiences of pupils during social studies
emphasize opportunities for
    a. inquiry.
    b. decision making.
    c. acquisition of relevant knowledges.
  4. The social studies program is well balanced in terms of
significant aspects of living.
  5. The program is flexible enough to take advantage of
current happenings in community, state, and nation.
  6. The program is appropriate for preoperational and
concrete operational learners.
  7. Teaching procedures utilize units of work and
other forms of group work in which pupils assume
responsibilities, and plan and evaluate activities.
  8. Reading materials are provided on a wide variety of
topics, covering a wide range of reading abilities.
  9. Attention is given to developing work skills such as
    a. note taking.
    b. outlining.
    c. summarizing.
    d. reporting.
10. Learning experiences are sufficiently varied so that
every child can participate with satisfaction and success.
11. The application, enrichment, and extension of the
social studies skills and experiences occur in all other
curriculum areas.
12. The program and the pupils are evaluated in terms
of the objectives.
13. Children use democratic procedures in choosing
leaders, planning and executing activities, and
evaluating outcomes.
14. Children study group life in the community, such as the
local government, civic organizations, business and
industry, and recreation and amusement.

C. Mathematics
  1. The content vehicles are representative of mathematics
and stress
    a. computation.
    b. problem solving.
    c. mathematics as a communication system.
  2. Sensory and manipulatory materials are utilized with
mathematical concepts appropriate to a laboratory,
and to the preoperational and concrete operational
learner.
  3. The approach supports the mathematical inquiry
of the pupil.

4. The nature of the communication system supports the teaching objectives and the affective needs of the pupils.

5. The full range of the following behaviors are involved and displayed:
   a. cognitive
   b. affective
   c. psychomotor

6. Instruction in mathematics is comprehensive and flexible with regard to approach, materials, and methods, but maintains continuity for each learner.

7. Instruction is adapted to abilities, achievements, and needs of individual pupils.

8. The evaluations of the program and of the pupils are based upon the stated objectives.

9. The approaches, materials, and time distribution represent a balance between computational skills and concept building.

10. The application, enrichment, and extension of mathematical skills and concepts occur in all other curriculum areas.

D. Science

   1. The content vehicles, experiences, and instruction of science stress life and physical sciences.

   2. Instruction in science is comprehensive and flexible in approach, materials, and content vehicles, but maintains continuity for each learner.

   4. The experiences of pupils during science emphasize decision making and the acquisition of relevant knowledges.

   5. A variety of learning activities is provided, such as
      a. field trips.
      b. demonstrations.
      c. experiments.
      d. use of resource persons.
      e. reading.

   6. Periodic checks are made on the abilities of pupils to
      a. observe accurately.
      b. locate information.
      c. distinguish between fact and fiction.

   7. A wide range of materials and equipment is available to further and support a laboratory approach.

   8. During science instruction, pupils have experiences which are essential in
      a. measurement.
      b. experimentation.
      c. interpretation.

    d. model building.
    e. prediction.
  9. The evaluations of the program and the pupils are
     based upon the stated objectives.
E. Health, Fitness, and Movement
  1. The health and physical education programs exist
     dependently and independently of each other and the
     other curriculum areas.
  2. The physical education program includes
     a. the acquisition of skills.
     b. the attainment of fitness.
     c. learning to move.
     d. moving to learn.
     e. the enhancement of perceptual-motor competencies.
  3. The health program includes
     a. healthful school environment.
     b. health services.
     c. instruction in mental well-being.
     d. instruction in physical well-being.
     e. instruction in social well-being.
  4. The activities of the physical education programs
     for all children are adapted to their pace, level, and
     general health.
  5. The activities of the health program are for all
     children and are adapted to individual and community
     health needs.
  6. Instruction in health and physical education occurs
     directly and indirectly during these periods and
     in other curriculum areas.
  7. The inclusion of potentially controversial topics
     is neither avoided nor forced. Such inclusion or
     exclusion is a matter for public and professional
     discussion.
  8. The evaluations of the program and of pupils are
     based upon the stated objectives.
  9. An adequate supply of books and other instructional
     materials is provided for health, physical education,
     and safety.
 10. Events in school living such as the following are
     included and utilized for teaching health:
     a. lunch period
     b. physical examinations
     c. immunizations
 11. The curriculum in health is well balanced in terms
     of the following major areas:
     a. nutrition

    b. rest

    c. safety

    d. communicable diseases

    e. clothing

    f. personal hygiene

    g. posture

    h. mental health

12. A safety council or committee coordinates the safety program.

13. Lists of school health policies are available to pupils, teachers, and parents.

14. Teachers observe pupils systematically for symptoms of abnormality.

15. One or more persons on the school staff are competent to administer first aid.

16. Fire drills and other exit drills are held regularly.

17. The building is inspected regularly for fire and safety hazards.

F. Aesthetic Arts

  1. Instruction in the aesthetic arts includes experiences in

    a. aesthetic awarenesses.

    b. creative awarenesses.

    c. human awarenesses.

    d. communication awarenesses.

    e. selection awarenesses.

  2. Vicarious and direct experiences are provided in

    a. sharpened sensory perceptions.

    b. spontaneity of expression.

    c. range of media.

  3. Instruction in the performing and visual arts is an integral aspect of the general education of all pupils and includes enrichment experiences for the talented.

  4. Experiences in dance and drama are incorporated in the aesthetic arts curriculum.

  5. The experiencies of pupils participating in the aesthetic arts are integrated within the arts and among other curriculum areas.

  6. The evaluations of the program and the pupils are based upon the stated objectives.

  7. An adequate supply of materials and equipment is available to encourage experimentation and participation by all children.

  8. Art resources of the community such as museums, exhibits, and local talent are utilized in the school program.

NAME INDEX

The following symbols have been incorporated to facilitate the reader's utilization of the index as a reference/research tool:

    page number only: entry appears in text
    page number followed by "n": entry appears in footnote only
    page number/"n": entry appears in text and footnote
    page number followed by "r": entry appears in selected readings

No page numbers have been included for summaries which appear at the end of each chapter.

SUBJECT INDEX

The following symbols have been incorporated to facilitate the reader's utilization of the index as a reference/research tool:

  page number only: entry appears in text
  page number followed by "n": entry appears in footnote only
  page number/"n": entry appears in text and footnote
  page number followed by "r": entry appears in selected readings

No page numbers have been included for summaries which appear at the end of each chapter.